Our Own Worst Enemy?

The Belfer Center Studies in International Security book series is edited at the Belfer Center for Science and International Affairs at the Harvard Kennedy School and is published by The MIT Press. The series publishes books on contemporary issues in international security policy, as well as their conceptual and historical foundations. Topics of particular interest to the series include the spread of weapons of mass destruction, internal conflict, the international effects of democracy and democratization, and U.S. defense policy. A complete list of Belfer Center Studies appears at the back of this volume.

Our Own Worst Enemy?

Institutional Interests and the Proliferation of Nuclear Weapons Expertise

Sharon K. Weiner

Belfer Center Studies in International Security

The MIT Press
Cambridge, Massachusetts
London, England

Library of Congress Cataloging-in-Publication Data

Weiner, Sharon K., 1963–
Our own worst enemy? : institutional interests and the proliferation of nuclear weapons expertise / Sharon K. Weiner.
  p. cm. — (Belfer Center studies in international security)
Includes bibliographical references and index.
ISBN 978-0-262-01565-3 (hardcover : alk. paper) — ISBN 978-0-262-51588-7 (pbk. : alk. paper)
1. Nuclear nonproliferation. 2. Nuclear nonproliferation—United States. 3. Expertise—Political aspects—United States. I. Title.
JZ5675.W45   2011
327.1'747—dc22

2010047084

10 9 8 7 6 5 4 3 2 1

For Frank and Patricia von Hippel

Contents

Acknowledgments

This book was made possible by the generous support of a host of individuals and organizations. The research and writing that grew into this book started as a project at the Program on Science and Global Security at Princeton University's Woodrow Wilson School of Public and International Affairs. I am especially grateful to Frank von Hippel, Hal Feiveson, and Oleg Bukharin for involving me in the effort to understand and to help foster cooperation on nonproliferation between the United States and Russia after the Cold War. Kenneth Luongo, William E. Hoehn, and Raphael Della Rhatta from the Partnership for Global Security (formerly the Russian-American Nuclear Security Advisory Council) were an important part of this research and policy agenda and I have benefited from their insights.

I am especially grateful to the more than 150 scientists, program managers, policymakers, and others who granted me interviews and provided insights into cooperative nonproliferation efforts in the former Soviet Union. Most of them asked to remain nameless and I thank them here, anonymously, for their contributions. This book would certainly not have been possible without them. I also thank the U.S. Government Accountability Office and the Congressional Research Service, whose work in the public's service results in a wealth of publications, analysis, and information that is crucial for researchers such as myself.

This book benefited from comments by or conversations with David Bernstein, Barry Cohen, Anatoli Diakov, Zia Mian, Eugene Miasnikov, Gennady Pshakin, and several others who asked to remain anonymous. I have also had exceptional research assistance from Yana Lantsberg, Kirsten Jelic, Ahnde Lin, and Jacob Poushter. The comments of Sean Lynn-Jones made my argument stronger, the editorial assistance of Karen Motley and Zachary Rapp helped me convey it in a clearer, more understandable fashion, and the technical assistance of Neal Doyle and Abby Roake ensured that my book appeared in its current form.

This book was made possible in part by a grant from the Carnegie Corporation of New York. Their Carnegie Scholar 2001 award provided me crucial financial support to pursue this research project. Patricia

Rosenfield, the former director of the Carnegie Scholars Program, was an important source of encouragement.

This project travelled with me from Princeton to the School of International Service at American University, in Washington, D.C. I owe a debt to my colleagues and students at American University's School of International Service for their reminders to stay focused and finish the book. Louis Goodman and Tamar Gutner deserve specific thanks for their support, as do Shoon Murray, Philip Brenner, and Betsy Cohn, who protected my time for research and writing. American University also provided two grants to help fill in parts of my research.

From 2005–2006, I was a visiting scholar at the American Academy of Arts and Sciences. I thank them for their financial support, but also for the chance to interact with a community of scholars who took an interest in and encouraged my research. I recall especially the late Carl Kaysen, who was a source of inspiration.

No doubt I will remember other people who deserve acknowledgement but go unmentioned here. For this oversight, I apologize. And although I have appreciated the contributions and support of those mentioned above, the statements made and views expressed in this book are solely my responsibility, as are any errors.

On a personal note, thanks are due to Pavel Podvig and Tatyana Vinichenko, for their friendship and for providing me a home away from home in Moscow, and to Cindy Deckerd and Karen Gibson, who accompanied me across central Russia and Central Asia, respectively. Finally, I thank Zia Mian, for support and encouragement to travel the world, and the reminders to come home soon.

List of Acronyms

AIDCO	American Industrial Development Corporation
BEP	Biosecurity Engagement Program
BII	BioIndustry Initiative
BISNIS	Business Information Service for the Newly Independent States
BTRP	Biological Threat Reduction Program
BW	Biological Weapon
CEES	Center for Energy and Environmental Studies, Princeton University
CISAC	Center for International Security and Cooperation, Stanford University
CNCP	Closed Nuclear Cities Partnership
CRADA	Cooperative Research and Development Agreement
CRDF	Civilian Research and Development Foundation
CTR	Cooperative Threat Reduction
CW	Chemical Weapon
DCAA	Defense Contract Audit Agency
DEF	Defense Enterprise Fund
DNA	Defense Nuclear Agency
DOD	U.S. Department of Defense
DOE	U.S. Department of Energy
DSTO	Database on Nuclear Smuggling, Theft, and Orphan Radiation Sources, Stanford University
DSWA	Defense Special Weapons Agency
DTRA	Defense Threat Reduction Agency

EBRD	European Bank for Reconstruction and Development
EML	Environmental Monitoring Lab
ETRI	Expanded Threat Reduction Initiative
EXBS	Export Control and Border Security
FDI	Foreign Direct Investment
FSA	Freedom Support Act
FSB	Federal Security Service, Russia
FTE	Full Time Equivalent
GAO	U.S. Government Accountability Office (formerly U.S. General Accounting Office)
GIPP	Global Initiatives for Proliferation Prevention
GosNIIAS	State Research Institute for Aviation Systems
GosNIIOKhT	State Union Scientific Research Institute of Organic Chemistry and Technology, Moscow
HEU	Highly-Enriched Uranium
IAEA	International Atomic Energy Agency
IDC	International Development Centers
ILAB	Inter-Laboratory Advisory Board
IMEMO	Institute of World Economy and International Relations
INTAS	International Association for the Promotion of Cooperation with Scientists from the New Independent States of the Former Soviet Union
IPP	Industrial Partnering Program
ISO	International Organization for Standardization
ISTC	International Science and Technology Center
LEU	Low-Enriched Uranium
MOD	Ministry of Defense, Russia
MPC&A	Material Protection, Control, and Accounting
MPTI	Moscow Physical Technical Institute
NADR	Nonproliferation, Anti-Terrorism, Demining and Related issues account, U.S. Department of State
NAS	National Academies of Science
NCI	Nuclear Cities Initiative
NII IS	Institute of Measurement Systems, Nizhny Novgorod
NNSA	National Nuclear Security Administration
NSC	U.S. National Security Council

NTI	Nuclear Threat Initiative
NWMDE	Nonproliferation of Weapons of Mass Destruction Expertise, U.S. Department of State
OPIC	Overseas Private Investment Corporation
PI	Principal Investigator
POO	Purity of Objective factor
RANSAC	Russian-American Nuclear Security Advisory Council
RTI	Russian Transition Initiatives
SABIT	Special American Business Internship Training Program
STCU	Science and Technology Center in Ukraine
TACIS	Technical Aid to the Commonwealth of Independent States
TDA	U.S. Trade and Development Agency
USAID	U.S. Agency for International Development
USIC	United States Industry Coalition
VNIIA	Institute of Automatics, Moscow
VNIIEF	All-Russian Research Institute of Experimental Physics, Sarov
VNII IT	Institute of Impulse Technologies, Moscow
VNIITF	All-Russian Research Institute of Technical Physics, Snezhinsk
WMD	Weapons of Mass Destruction
ZATO	Closed Administrative Territory

Our Own Worst Enemy?

Chapter 1

Controlling the Proliferation of Nuclear Knowledge

An Introduction

In October of 1996, Vladimir Nechai committed suicide. His death was newsworthy, but not because of the means; suicide was not so unusual in Russia, largely due to the widespread financial deprivation in the years following the collapse of the Soviet Union. Nechai's act was reported by the Western news media because of his position as director of one of the Soviet Union's premier nuclear weapons research and design facilities. According to the note he left behind, Nechai took his own life partially out of shame. Much of the research at his institute had been suspended indefinitely for lack of funds, and the people who worked there had not been paid in five months. Even when salaries were delivered, they left people in near-poverty conditions, with the average member of Nechai's nuclear weapons workforce making about $30 a month.[1]

The situation in other parts of the former Soviet nuclear weapons complex was no better. There were strikes in some facilities, with thousands of workers demanding back wages and higher pay. Some nuclear weapons scientists made the journey to Moscow to protest directly to the federal government. In other areas, institute directors reported critical shortages of medical supplies and other necessities.

The Russian government was well aware of the grim conditions across the vast complex of nuclear, biological, and chemical weapons facilities that had been created in the Soviet Union. But it had been struggling with even bigger economic and political problems, and felt powerless to help these scientists.

The U.S. government also knew of the financial problems in the states of the former Soviet Union and was particularly concerned about what was happening in the weapons facilities. Based on the assumption that a financially desperate weapons scientist is a proliferation risk, the U.S. government had engaged the Departments of Defense, Energy, and State in trying to create alternative jobs or provide temporary research contracts to former Soviet experts in weapons of mass destruction (WMD). By the time of Nechai's death in 1996, these efforts were several years old.

---

1. Unless otherwise specified, all figures cited are in U.S. dollars.

Since the breakup of the Soviet Union, the danger of the proliferation of WMD knowledge has been a persistent theme in U.S. policy. Anecdotes have surfaced about former Soviet weapons experts helping Iran, Iraq, and North Korea with their nuclear programs. A Senate staffer claims to have obtained a flyer from China advertising "detailed files of hundreds of former Soviet Union experts in the field of rocket, missile, and nuclear weapons. These weapons experts are willing to work in a country which needs their skills and can offer reasonable pay."[2] Subsequent polls showed that many Russian WMD experts were willing to work on military programs for other countries, including places such as North Korea, Syria, Iran, or Iraq.

On September 11, 2001, the attacks on the United States brought these fears closer to home. Besides concerns about possible terrorist use of nuclear weapons against the United States, the subsequent anthrax-tainted letters extended this anxiety to include biological weapons. In the 2004 presidential election, George W. Bush and John Kerry may have agreed on little else except the danger posed by nuclear proliferation: both candidates claimed it was the primary security threat facing the United States. Four years later, this agreement still held for the 2008 Democratic and Republican presidential hopefuls. Newly elected president Barack Obama declared in April 2009 that nuclear terrorism was "the most immediate and extreme threat to global security," and pledged that the United States would lead the way in securing all vulnerable nuclear materials within four years.[3] Over time, candidates, politicians, and pundits from both parties have also shared one other commonality: a belief that one of the most likely sources of the materials and expertise needed to make WMD is the former Soviet Union.

From the collapse of the Soviet Union in 1991 through 2008, the United States spent over $1.2 billion trying to discourage the proliferation of nuclear, biological, and chemical weapons expertise from Soviet successor states.[4] Some of this money funded short-term research contracts intended to provide scientists with much-needed income while keeping them engaged in interesting work. Other funds went toward a more long-term solution: creating permanent non-weapons jobs or converting entire institutes to civilian occupations. In the process, this effort spawned a dialogue that led to unprecedented cooperation and a level of commitment from some quarters that was and remains nothing short of extraordinary. As the Obama administration assumed office, there was every indication

2. U.S. Congress, Senate, Committee on Governmental Affairs, Permanent Subcommittee on Investigations, *Global Proliferation of Weapons of Mass Destruction*, Part II, 104th Cong., 2nd sess., March 13, 20, 22, 1996, pp. 7, 139.

3. Office of the Press Secretary, White House, "Remarks by President Barack Obama," Prague, April 5, 2009, http://whitehouse.gov/the_press_office/Remarks-By-President-Barack-Obama-In-Prague-As-Delivered/.

4. This includes annual spending through 2008 for the major programs in the Departments of Defense, Energy, and State. In the late 1990s, both State and Defense started additional efforts aimed at biological weapons experts. Collectively, these would add over $300 million more to this total.

that these "knowledge nonproliferation" efforts—that is, programs aimed at fighting the proliferation of weapons expertise—would be sustained and probably expanded.

Given the importance of this agenda and the commitment of those involved, it comes as a surprise that these efforts enjoyed only mixed success. Although temporary salaries were provided for thousands of former Soviet WMD experts, few job creation or conversion efforts succeeded. Moreover, despite continued concerns about proliferation, the pace and political impetus given to this effort lagged after the 1990s, and as the second Bush administration drew to a close, the United States was poised to end its cooperative nonproliferation work with Russia in favor of expanding to other countries beyond the former Soviet states. Yet much work remained undone.

This book chronicles the design, implementation, and evolution of four U.S. programs, each of which was aimed at countering the threat of proliferation of WMD expertise from the former Soviet Union by creating jobs for these weapons workers. These programs are examined from their origins at the end of the Cold War, through three different U.S. presidential administrations, various changes in U.S.-Russian relations, Russia's partial and, as of 2008, likely temporary, economic recovery, up until the advent of the Obama administration. The book also situates each of these programs within three important narratives: one describes the state of the former Soviet WMD complex and how the threat of proliferation changed over time; another illustrates the often-contentious domestic political debate within the United States over how to respond to the collapse of the Soviet Union; and the third juxtaposes the institutional interests and dynamics of three different government departments with the common task they were given.

The result, I argue, supports three broad conclusions. The first, as mentioned above, is that U.S. programs did not succeed at redirecting or converting significant parts of the former Soviet WMD complex. They did not achieve this goal despite general and persistent agreement about its importance, unprecedented cooperation between the United States and Russia, and the tremendous personal and in many cases institutional dedication of parts of the U.S. Departments of Defense, Energy, and State, which were given this assignment. This commitment was duplicated within parts of the Russian WMD complex, where key individuals took a brave stance in favor of such cooperation and then did their best to challenge institutional, political, and cultural obstacles. If importance, hard work, and perseverance were the only criteria, these programs would have succeeded years ago.

The second conclusion is that despite the poor overall results at conversion and job creation, there were two important successes. One is that during critical periods, some former Soviet nuclear, biological, and chemical weapons scientists had an income only or mostly due to U.S. funding. During the early 1990s, when economic conditions were the most dismal, the United States provided WMD experts with salaries through short-term research contracts. For some institutes, this meant the difference between life and death. The other success is that these programs, and the larger Cooperative Threat Reduction (CTR) effort to which they are related, forced the United States to work more closely with the Soviet successor states, and especially Russia, than U.S. political leaders would have chosen to do otherwise. This meant a closer relationship between former Cold War enemies that has been extremely important to U.S. national security, even though by 2002–2003 it had begun to show strong signs of fatigue and wear.

The third conclusion is about why these programs did not accomplish more. Many experts attribute this deficiency to externally imposed constraints, such as insufficient budgets, a lack of high-level coordination within the U.S. government, or uncooperative external actors—usually Russia. Although these impediments are real, I argue that they are insufficient to explain failure. Instead, I place the blame on two enduring features of the U.S. policy process: democracy and bureaucratic institutions.

In the case of WMD expertise from the former Soviet Union, democracy hindered U.S. counterproliferation efforts because the debate over how to respond to the collapse of the Soviet Union was never resolved. In 1990, policymakers argued about whether helping Russia secure, downsize, or destroy its WMD assets was in the national security interest of the United States or more properly considered as charity to a former enemy. Although Congress officially came down on the side of "cooperative security" when it funded the CTR program in 1991, each subsequent reauthorization of program authority or funding was subjected to complaints that such money helped Russia's own weapons effort, was wasted, would be better spent at home, or some combination of all of these. Occasionally, critics succeeded in getting Congress to apply conditions to U.S. spending. Usually, these conditions made it harder for programs to achieve the nonproliferation task they were given. Always, the threat of future conditions or funding restrictions was on the mind of program personnel, and it influenced how they defined goals, implemented programs, and learned from experience. Although this unresolved debate influenced CTR overall, it was especially important to programs aimed at the proliferation of WMD expertise because these were often considered the most peripheral—and therefore expendable—part of the CTR agenda. In particular, my case studies show that two of the four knowledge nonproliferation programs funded by the United States were significantly, and negatively, influenced by this disagreement over whether they were part of U.S. defense spending or, instead, foreign aid.

Part of this narrative about U.S. domestic politics also includes the presidency. With the exception of a few years during Clinton's first term in office, knowledge nonproliferation programs claimed little presidential attention. Under the administration of George W. Bush, they were at times subjected to not-so-benign neglect. Repeated calls for increased attention from the executive, or a designated "czar," went unheeded. The result was ineffective advocacy with Congress and the public, a lack of inter-program coordination, and a dialogue with Russia that lacked the political clout to solve persistent problems.

Although the consequences of this U.S. domestic political context have been important, in the pages that follow, I argue that bureaucratic institutions, and especially their interests and cultures, have been the bigger problem. Even more strongly, I argue that had Russia cooperated fully, Congress significantly increased spending, and the "security versus charity" debate been resolved, the United States would still have lagged behind in its efforts to create alternative jobs for Soviet WMD experts. This is because each of the three bureaucracies that were given this task defined it, implemented solutions, and measured success in ways that satisfied their own needs rather than the requirements for creating jobs for former Soviet WMD experts. For very different reasons, the Departments of Defense, Energy, and State all became victim to the same pathology: they let institutional interests replace U.S. national security needs.

Such substitution should come as no surprise. The literature on national security, the policy process, and most specific policy areas are all replete with illustrations of the power of institutional interest.[5] In this book I do more than provide another example. I directly compare explanations based on the presumption of rational decision-making with those whose explanatory power is rooted in the history, internal politics, and sense of mission of institutions. Further, I show how institutional interests, external constraints, and past legacies in three very different organizations—the Departments of Defense, Energy, and State—all led to similar results, and how the power of institutional interests and needs was reinforced by the domestic political debate within which these programs functioned. Moreover, I argue that these results could have been anticipated and mitigated, although not eliminated. For this reason, I claim that in the U.S. fight to stem the proliferation of WMD knowledge from the former Soviet Union, we were our own worst enemy.

Three Departments, Four Programs, and a Bunch of Acronyms

This book looks at the evolution and success of U.S. efforts to counter knowledge proliferation from the Soviet nuclear weapons complex during the period of 1990–2008. Most succinctly phrased, this involves ISTC, STCU, NCI, and IPP (which together were RTI and then later GIPP), and a defunct set of defense conversion efforts in the Defense Department that initially managed to avoid being known by an acronym but later became DEF. These programs were housed in the Departments of Defense, Energy,

---

5. I use the terms "organization" and "institution" interchangeably. The literature that focuses on organizational interests tends to assume organizations have a stable set of interests that arise from their sense of mission and are pursued through instrumentally rational processes. Institutionalism and new institutionalism, on the other hand, focus on the dynamics of preference development and change in institutions, arguing that interests arise from past history, experience, environment, and the preferences of personnel and that these, in turn, both influence goals and processes and are influenced by them. Although I make use of the dynamics of the new institutionalist approach, I use organization and institution as synonyms for stylistic reasons and because my work seeks to explain the outcome of a particular policy decision rather than expand upon new institutionalism per se.

and State and collectively formed a small part of what is known as CTR, or Cooperative Threat Reduction. Rephrasing this without acronyms requires a bit less brevity.[6]

During the 1990s, the U.S. government created four main programs to deal with the threat of the proliferation of nuclear, biological, and chemical weapons knowledge from the former Soviet Union. The first program, which was located in the U.S. Department of Defense, was an effort to convert WMD-related defense institutes in Russia, Ukraine, Belarus, and Kazakhstan by partnering spin-offs from these institutes with U.S. business partners. This program, which to my knowledge never received a formal title or acronym, will be referred to as the Defense Conversion program.[7] In the mid-1990s, the Defense Conversion program was terminated by Congress, and the Defense Department's efforts to deal with the proliferation of expertise continued as the Defense Enterprise Fund, or DEF.[8] DEF was an investment fund that provided loans and grants to cooperative business ventures between U.S. companies and spin-offs from former Soviet defense enterprises. Because of mismanagement, it was closed in 2003.

The second program comprised the Science Centers, of which there were two: the International Science and Technology Center (ISTC), based in Moscow, and the Science and Technology Center Ukraine (STCU), in Kiev. These centers were multinational clearinghouses for research cooperation among weapons experts in the states of the former Soviet Union and the United States, the European Union, Canada, South Korea, Japan, and Norway. Each center operated on a similar but independent basis, and U.S. participation in both was managed by the State Department. Each center funded collaborative research between Western scientists and former Soviet nuclear, biological, and chemical weapons scientists as well as missile experts. This collaboration took two forms. One involved short-term work with the intent of completing a given research project. The second involved collaboration aimed at validating a technology or demonstrating a concept that might lead to additional cooperation or permanent reemployment away from the weapons complex. As of early 2009, the centers continued to fund both types of projects, and the center in Moscow was poised to expand its services to other countries.

---

6. Cooperative Threat Reduction, or CTR, was also referred to as "Nunn-Lugar" after its congressional sponsors. During the early 1990s, CTR tended to refer to programs managed by the Defense Department. As responsibility for some parts of CTR shifted to other departments, and specially the Department of Energy, CTR came to stand for a variety of efforts. By 2008, however, CTR was again the favored term for programs in the Defense Department, while those at the Departments of Energy and State were considered "threat reduction" or "nonproliferation assistance." See Amy F. Woolf, *Nonproliferation and Threat Reduction Assistance: U.S. Programs in the Former Soviet Union*, Congressional Research Service, February 11, 2009, p. 4.

7. In reports by one analyst, these conversion efforts are referred to as the Industrial Partnering Program, but this title does not seem to have caught on and creates confusion with IPP, which originally also was called the Industrial Partnering Program.

8. Initially, DEF stood for Demilitarization Enterprise Fund.

The third and fourth programs were both found in the Department of Energy, and took their project managers mainly from the U.S. national laboratory complex. Initiatives for Proliferation Prevention (IPP) dates from the early 1990s. IPP projects involved collaborative research between U.S. and former Soviet WMD scientists and a U.S. business partner. The goal was to reemploy the former Soviet scientists by getting a U.S. business interested in either their scientific skills or a technology they had pioneered. IPP-funded research was aimed at taking a technology or idea from conception to the marketplace.

The other DOE program, which began in 1998, was the Nuclear Cities Initiative (NCI). NCI focused on several "closed nuclear cities" in Russia which were the heart of the Soviet nuclear weapons complex. Originally, NCI's mission was to reemploy weapons experts by encouraging business development in these cities, improving living standards and city infrastructure, and helping Russia reduce the size of its nuclear weapons complex by negotiating the conversion of specific facilities.

In 2002, IPP and NCI merged to form Russian Transition Initiatives (RTI), although both programs remained largely independent. In 2006, RTI's name was changed to Global Initiatives for Proliferation Prevention (GIPP) to reflect programmatic activities beyond the states of the former Soviet Union. During this time, support for NCI waned, and as of September 2006, its activities had ended. By early 2009, IPP had become GIPP and expanded to include scientists in Iraq, Libya, and potentially also North Korea.

Other Nonproliferation Efforts

Although the Defense Conversion program, the Science Centers, IPP, and NCI were the main mechanisms the United States employed to counter the proliferation of WMD knowledge, from 1990 to 2008 there were a variety of other efforts aimed at redirecting or converting former Soviet WMD experts. Described below, these activities are not included here as objects for analysis because of their size or scope. Some are excluded because they were much smaller than the programs at Defense, Energy, and State and lacked significant resources to devote to fighting the proliferation of WMD expertise. Other programs are left out because they dealt only tangentially with the proliferation of expertise; their main missions focused elsewhere.

A trio of efforts aimed at biological weapons experts is not so much excluded as it is considered under the rubric of the Science Centers. In 1998, the Defense Department began the Biological Weapons Proliferation Program which was renamed the Biological Threat Reduction Program (BTRP) in 2007. As of 2008, BTRP was really four efforts, only one of which—the Cooperative Biodefense Research Program—was aimed at the proliferation of WMD expertise.[9] Under this program, Defense funded

---

9. The other three parts focused on dismantling facilities that used to produce biological weapons, increasing safety and security at institutes that store and handle pathogens and potentially weapons-relevant materials, and developing surveillance and warning systems

short-term collaborative research between U.S. scientists and former bio-logical weapons workers in Russia, Uzbekistan, Kazakhstan, and Georgia. The goal was to discourage proliferation by reorienting scientists toward non-weapons work, increase transparency with respect to both experts and their work at Russian institutes, and help improve U.S. defenses against biological weapons.[10] By 2008, the program had spent some $62 million on collaborative projects in the former Soviet Union.[11] In 2007, however, the Defense Department announced that it would end the pro-gram's work in Russia because of a combination of problems getting ac-cess to the biological weapons institutes where the research took place and the belief that the Russian government could now afford to sustain these institutes without U.S. assistance.[12]

Under the Biosecurity Engagement Program (BEP), the State Depart-ment also funded two efforts directed at former Soviet weapons experts. The Bio-Chem Redirect Program provided money to the U.S. Department of Health and Human Services, the Department of Agriculture, and the Environmental Protection Agency to collaborate in research projects with Soviet biological and chemical weapons experts. Projects focused on pub-lic health, environmental monitoring and rehabilitation, and livestock and plant issues, as well as defense against biological terrorism. The other program was the BioIndustry Initiative, or BII. Started in response to the September 11, 2001, terrorist attacks and subsequent anthrax-laced letters, through BII the State Department funded efforts by the Departments of Health and Human Services, Agriculture, and the Environmental Protec-tion Agency to engage in collaborative research to develop vaccines for highly infectious diseases. In Russia, both programs were administered through ISTC.

Similar to the Defense Department, in 2007 the State Department an-nounced that it would cut back its collaborative research projects in Rus-sia. Citing the increased capabilities of the Russian government and econ-omy, plus emerging public health concerns and terrorist threats, the State Department planned to redirect BEP toward cooperation with experts in South and Southeast Asia and the Middle East.[13]

---

for storage facilities.

10. Department of Defense, Defense Threat Reduction Agency, "Cooperative Threat Reduction Annual Report to Congress, " fiscal year 2006, Washington, D.C., p. 53.

11. National Research Council, *The Biological Threat Reduction Program of the Department of Defense: From Foreign Assistance to Sustainable Partnerships* (Washington, D.C.: National Academy of Science, 2007), p. 37. For a list of specific projects, see Department of Defense, Defense Threat Reduction Agency, "CTR Annual Report to Congress," fiscal year 2007, Washington, D.C., pp. 35–37. Projects not located in Russia were administered through the U.S. National Academies of Science or the Civilian Research and Development Foundation (CRDF).

12. Yudhijit Bhattacharjee, "Rising Asian Threat Leaves Russia in the Lurch," *Science*, Vol. 317 (August 3, 2007), p. 581

13. Ibid.

Also excluded from my analysis is the Civilian Research and Development Foundation (CRDF).[14] CRDF was created in 1995 by the National Science Foundation at the request of Congress and gets funding from the U.S. government, U.S.-based foundations, and a variety of private companies. Its purpose is to support the maintenance of a scientific infrastructure in post-Soviet countries by providing scientific and technical experts with opportunities for employment at home that uses their skills. CRDF's nonproliferation programs specifically targeted former Soviet WMD experts for conversion to non-weapons work. CRDF funded research collaborations and product validation and development, in addition to conferences, business training and networking, travel, and peer review of research proposals. Some collaboration was among scientists; most involved U.S. industry or government agencies. According to CRDF's 2005 annual report, during its first decade it funded research that involved over 25,000 scientists, of whom 2,500 were former weapons experts from Europe, Asia, the Middle East, and North Africa.[15]

CRDF played an important role in the collaborative research projects sponsored by the Defense and State departments and IPP. Because it had some tax-exempt privileges in former Soviet states, these programs often used CRDF to administer and oversee their cooperative research projects. CRDF managed the importation of any needed equipment and supplies, provided salary payments to former Soviet experts, and could also provide in-country project support and oversight. In return, U.S. government agencies paid a fee of around 10 percent to CRDF.[16] As of 2008, CRDF continued to play a role in both IPP and Science Center projects, but also acted more broadly in funding scientific cooperation.

The Commerce Department had several programs to help U.S. businesses exploit opportunities in the former Soviet Union. Although these were not aimed specifically at WMD experts, a few were involved. The Special American Business Internship Training Program (SABIT) funded U.S.-based short-term internships for former Soviet entrepreneurs and offered courses in business development in Russia. The Business Information Service for the Newly Independent States (BISNIS) provided market and investment information about opportunities in former Soviet states, including some former defense and WMD enterprises. Commerce also maintained a directory of defense enterprises in the former Soviet Union that were interested in collaborative relationships with industry.

With a similar focus, the U.S. Trade and Development Agency (TDA) used U.S. funding to promote development projects in other countries in cooperation with U.S. businesses. As part of its business development efforts, TDA funded studies of defense conversion projects.

---

14. More information on CRDF can be found at www.crdf.org.

15. Civilian Research & Development Foundation, "2005 Annual Report," Arlington, Va., pp. 8, 20.

16. Electronic communication with CRDF, August 22, 2007.

The U.S. government also provided money to a variety of investment funds that helped businesses establish ventures in the former Soviet Union. From the perspective of WMD experts, the two most important ones were USIC and OPIC. The United States Industry Coalition (USIC) is a non-profit association of U.S. companies and universities that was established specifically to help companies exploit commercialization opportunities with former WMD experts. Companies that were involved in IPP projects had to be members of USIC. The Overseas Private Investment Corporation (OPIC) helped reduce the financial risk when U.S. companies invested in business opportunities that also furthered U.S. foreign policy objectives. A small number of OPIC loans went to projects involving former Soviet WMD experts, although this was not OPIC's main mission.

A significant though infrequently acknowledged contributor to the reemployment of former Soviet weapons experts was the HEU Purchase Agreement. In 1993, the United States negotiated an agreement with Russia to buy 500 metric tons of highly-enriched uranium from dismantled nuclear weapons. When Russia dismantles a nuclear weapon, it dilutes the highly-enriched uranium (HEU) until it becomes low-enriched uranium (LEU), which can be used as fuel in nuclear reactors. This LEU is then shipped to the United States where it is sold as fuel to the nuclear power industry. Under this agreement, Russia had turned 14,090 nuclear warheads into nuclear reactor fuel by the end of 2008.[17]

The HEU Purchase Agreement, which was originally intended to cover a span of twenty years, will eventually provide approximately $8 billion to Russia.[18] Some of this money, in turn, was used by the Russian central government to fund consolidation and job-creation efforts in the nuclear weapons complex. The HEU Deal, as it is sometimes called, has also provided thousands of jobs for Russian experts, including dismantling nuclear warheads and turning HEU into LEU.[19] Moreover, up until about 2000, approximately one-third of the money Russia earned through this agreement went to the Ministry of Atomic Energy, where it became a significant source of funding for conversion efforts in the nuclear weapons complex.[20]

Besides the government, several private foundations and organizations provided programs and services that, as of early 2009, continue to impact former Soviet WMD experts. Among these, three figured most prominently.

---

17. United States Enrichment Corporation, U.S.-Russian Megatons to Megawatts Program, "Fact Sheet," http://www.usec.com. The website provides periodic updates of nuclear warhead destruction under the HEU Purchase Agreement.

18. As originally negotiated, the HEU Purchase Agreement would have netted $12 billion for Russia, but changes in the market price of uranium eventually forced the renegotiation of this amount to $8 billion.

19. Oleg Bukharin, Harold Feiveson, Frank von Hippel, Sharon K. Weiner, Matthew Bunn, William Hoehn, and Kenneth Luongo, Helping Russia Downsize its Nuclear Complex: A Focus on the Closed Nuclear Cities (Princeton, N.J.: Center for Energy and Environmental Studies, Princeton University, June 2000), p. 17.

20. Bukharin, et al., Helping Russia Downsize its Nuclear Complex, p. 19.

The National Academies of Science (NAS) provided advice to the U.S. government on scientific collaboration and published important studies about the state of collaboration with former Soviet weapons institutes.[21] NAS also participated in and reviewed collaborative research with former biological weapons experts and was instrumental in encouraging the U.S. government to seek out and engage key biological weapons institutes in Russia. The Soros Foundation helped some WMD-related cities with their communications infrastructure and provided funding to CRDF. Finally, the Nuclear Threat Initiative (NTI) provided funding, information, and advocacy for various nonproliferation efforts, including those focused on WMD expertise. NTI was created by CNN founder Ted Turner and former U.S. Senator Sam Nunn and can be credited with raising public awareness and lobbying for increased government spending for a variety of nonproliferation efforts, some of which were aimed at controlling the spread of weapons knowledge. NTI funded a variety of studies and status reports about the state of security among former Soviet WMD facilities and workers and maintains a website that offers perhaps the most significant, although sometimes dated, collection of information and analysis about past and current efforts to cope with the legacy of the Soviet WMD complex.[22]

Finally, several other countries also started or continue to fund programs aimed at controlling the spread of WMD knowledge. Besides the United States, the Science Centers involve the European Union, Japan, Canada, Norway, and the Republic of Korea; this arrangement is explained in more detail in Chapter 5. In 1991, the European Union launched Technical Aid to the Commonwealth of Independent States (TACIS), a program of financial assistance to former Soviet states that aims to help them with legal, administrative, and economic reform; infrastructure development; environmental protection; and nuclear reactor safety. The International Association for the Promotion of Cooperation with Scientists from the New Independent States of the Former Soviet Union (INTAS), also a creation of the European Union, funds scientific cooperation between states of the European Union and the former Soviet Union. The focus of both TACIS and INTAS is much broader than the proliferation of

---

21. For example, see National Research Council, Office of International Affairs, *An Assessment of the International Science and Technology Center: Redirecting Expertise in Weapons of Mass Destruction in the Former Soviet Union* (Washington, D.C.: National Academy Press, 1996); National Academy of Sciences, Institute of Medicine, and National Research Council, U.S.-Russian Collaborative Program for Research and Monitoring of Pathogens of Global Importance Committee, *Controlling Dangerous Pathogens: A Blueprint for U.S.-Russian Cooperation, A Report to the Cooperative Threat Reduction Program of the U.S. Department of Defense* (Washington, D.C.: National Academy Press, 1997); National Research Council, Office of International Affairs, *Protecting Nuclear Weapons Material in Russia* (Washington, D.C.: National Academy Press, 1999); National Research Council, *Successes and Difficulties of Small Innovative Firms in Russian Nuclear Cities* (Washington, D.C.: National Academy Press, 2002); and National Research Council, *Biological Science and Biotechnology in Russia: Controlling Diseases and Enhancing Security* (Washington, D.C.: National Academy Press, 2005).

22. See http://www.nti.org.

WMD knowledge, but a small number of their grants have involved such experts.

Additionally, the United Kingdom began funding the Closed Nuclear Cities Partnership (CNCP) in 2004. Similar to the U.S. Nuclear Cities Initiative, the goals of CNCP were to create sustainable non-weapons jobs for nuclear experts and to help improve the social and economic environments in these cities. As of 2007, the UK had committed an estimated $17 million to these projects and created some 560 jobs, with an estimated 800 additional jobs to follow.[23] A similar program, the European Nuclear Cities Initiative, failed to get off the ground due to problems getting member-state agreement on identifying specific projects for funding.

Finally, although this book focuses on programs aimed at the proliferation of weapons expertise, there is a broader literature that takes a more comprehensive look at CTR, its history, and its implementation. A good start is *Defense by Other Means: The Politics of US-NIS Threat Reduction and Nuclear Security Cooperation,* by Jason Ellis. Ellis provides a history of CTR through the mid-1990s, focusing specifically on implementation in Russia and Ukraine, as well as the role of Congress and interagency politics in CTR's implementation and progress.[24] In *Dismantling the Cold War,* John M. Shields and William C. Potter bring together authors who look at U.S., Russian, and NIS perspectives on CTR, as well as case studies of several CTR programs.[25] For updates on the status of various CTR programs, as well as an analysis of problems and possible solutions, Matthew Bunn provides yearly updates in the *Securing the Bomb* series.[26]

Leon Sigal's *Hang Separately: Cooperative Security between the United States and Russia, 1984–1994,* takes a broader look at U.S. aid to the Soviet Union and Russia. Sigal argues that as the Soviet Union was breaking apart, the United States was too hesitant to assist and encourage democratic and market-based reforms or help with nuclear security. As a result, the United States missed many important opportunities to increase its own security and encourage the development of future cooperative relations

---

23. Department of Trade and Industry, "United Kingdom-Russia Closed Nuclear Cities Partnership (CNCP)," http://www.pe-international.ru/eng. For more information about CNCP, see http://www.dti.gov.uk/energy/environment/soviet-nuclear-legacy/programme-portfolio/cncp/index.html.

24. Ellis, Jason D., *Defense by Other Means: The Politics of U.S.-NIS Threat Reduction and Nuclear Security Cooperation* (Westport, Conn.: Praeger, 2001).

25. Shields, John M., and William C. Potter, eds., *Dismantling the Cold War: U.S. and NIS Perspectives on the Nunn-Lugar Cooperative Threat Reduction Program* (Cambridge, Mass.: MIT Press, 1997).

26. See, for example, Matthew Bunn and Anthony Wier, *Securing the Bomb: An Agenda for Action* (Cambridge, Mass., and Washington, D.C.: Project on Managing the Atom at Harvard University and Nuclear Threat Initiative, 2004); *Securing the Bomb 2005: The New Global Imperatives* (Cambridge, Mass., and Washington, D.C.: Project on Managing the Atom at Harvard University and Nuclear Threat Initiative, 2005); *Securing the Bomb 2006* (Cambridge, Mass., and Washington, D.C.: Project on Managing the Atom at Harvard University and Nuclear Threat Initiative, 2006); and Matthew Bunn, *Securing the Bomb 2007* (Cambridge, Mass., and Washington, D.C.: Project on Managing the Atom at Harvard University and Nuclear Threat Initiative, 2007).

with Russia.[27] Additionally, *Power and Purpose*, by James M. Goldgeier and Michael McFaul, provides a comparative analysis of U.S. aid to Russia for the promotion of democracy, economic and, specifically, market-oriented reforms, and CTR.[28] In parsing out the worldviews of Presidents George H.W. Bush, Bill Clinton, and George W. Bush, and situating this within the parochial issues that dominate domestic and congressional politics in the United States, the book argues that U.S. policy toward Russia has lacked a grand strategy for building and sustaining the cooperative relationship that would be beneficial to both countries. Instead, with the exception of a few years during the first Clinton administration, policy has been hampered by the pursuit of specific domestic and foreign policy interests and conducted in a manner and language that discounts both Russia's own interests and its status as a major power in the international system.

Methodological Issues

Before providing a roadmap for subsequent chapters and arguments, a few pre-scripts are in order. The focus of this book is WMD expertise and the danger of its proliferation from the former Soviet Union. Because Russia inherited the bulk of the Soviet WMD complexes, Russia will be the central focus of attention. Other states of the former Soviet Union are referenced when they help to explain the fate of the Russian weapons complex or the outcome of U.S. activities there.

Additionally, nuclear weapons expertise is my central concern. Although this book refers to all WMD and discusses biological weapons expertise in some detail, this is done so that activities aimed at nuclear nonproliferation can be better understood and put in appropriate context. For example, as the case studies show, it is not possible to understand the deficit in U.S. activities in Russia's core nuclear weapons facilities without also understanding the concurrent rise in emphasis on biological weapons institutes in both Russia and other parts of the former Soviet Union. Although the expertise required for chemical weapons, weapons delivery systems, and nuclear energy is also discussed, this too is done only to further our understanding of the fate of nuclear weapons experts. I claim no comprehensive analysis of these subjects, and the conclusions offered here apply first and foremost to the proliferation of nuclear weapons knowledge.

All of the programs discussed here evolved over time. Two ended prior to 2008, but the Science Centers and IPP continue. This book, however, covers these programs and their processes and results through 2008.

A brief discussion of terminology is also important. This book will refer frequently to weapons of mass destruction (WMD). By this I mean nuclear, biological, and chemical weapons. Although chemical weapons

---

27. Sigal, Leon V., *Hang Separately: Cooperative Security between the United States and Russia, 1985–1994* (New York: Century Foundation Press, 2000).

28. James M. Goldgeier and Michael McFaul, *Power and Purpose: U.S. Policy Toward Russia After the Cold War* (Washington, D.C.: Brookings Institution Press, 2003).

are often included in the category of WMD, they are not capable of causing the destruction of entire cities or large populations except in very particular circumstances. This is why experts increasingly apply the WMD label only to nuclear and biological weapons.[29] It is also the case that, with respect to the proliferation of expertise, the vast majority of U.S. resources have focused on nuclear and biological weapons specialists. I use WMD to refer to nuclear, biological, and chemical weapons simply for ease of use and because almost all U.S. government programs continue to use "WMD" in this manner.

Finally, a word about sources is necessary. The programs at the Departments of Defense, Energy, and State are the case studies I analyze to understand how the United States attempted to discourage the proliferation of WMD expertise from the former Soviet Union. In addition to the small secondary literature on the proliferation of weapons expertise, my conclusions are drawn primarily from two sources. The first is primary documents, including annual reports and other official publications from each program, internal strategic planning documents, memoranda, communications, and project-specific writings.

The second source is the approximately 150 interviews I conducted in the United States, Europe, Japan, and some states of the former Soviet Union. This includes interviews with current and former congressional staff; project participants in various states of the former Soviet Union, mostly Russia; former and current U.S. and Russian government officials; Western business partners; various other individuals who were in some way involved in these activities; and program managers and personnel in the Departments of Defense, Energy, and State. In almost all cases, these interviews are cited here according to affiliations or broader descriptions as negotiated with each interviewee. The reasons for this anonymity vary. In some cases, the projects or jobs of individuals might have suffered due to their candor. In a few cases, former project participants requested that their names be omitted to protect their relationships with individuals or organizations. Sometimes I offered anonymity to encourage a dialogue; in other cases it was granted because naming one interviewee would have made it possible to identify others. I do not provide the names of former Soviet weapons scientists and some experts in Russia in case doing so harms their chances for future collaborative projects, damages their relationships with their parent institutes, or makes them suspect because of shifting interpretations of Russia's rules and regulations about sensitive information.

The degree to which I rely on anonymous interviews makes my conclusions difficult for others to verify independently. To help mitigate this problem, where possible I cite publicly available information and docu-

---

29. See, for example, U.S. Congress, Office of Technology Assessment, *Proliferation of Weapons of Mass Destruction: Assessing the Risks,* OTA-ISC-559 (Washington, D.C.: Government Printing Office, August 1993), pp. 52–55; and Wolfgang K.H. Panofsky, "A Damaging Designation," *Bulletin of the Atomic Scientists,* Vol. 63, No. 1 (January/February 2007), pp. 37–39.

mentation instead of information from interviews. Except in a few places that are noted in the citations, I offer conclusions based upon interviews only when those conclusions can be supported by more than two interviewees or other material.

A Roadmap

This book is organized into three sections. The first part—Chapters 2 and 3—provides the context within which the battle against the proliferation of WMD expertise has been waged. Chapter 2 focuses on the former Soviet Union. This chapter traces the fate of the Soviet defense complex, with particular emphasis on nuclear weapons institutes and experts. Information about structural and social changes that have an effect on WMD experts, as well as Russia's own conversion efforts, is often less than comprehensive or verifiable. With these caveats in mind, the chapter offers a way to evaluate the threat of the proliferation of expertise and how that threat changed after the collapse of the Soviet Union. In turn, the case studies discuss the degree to which U.S. programs adapted in response to these changes.

Chapter 3 provides additional context, but in this case the focus is domestic politics in the United States. Programs aimed at countering the proliferation of WMD expertise were a small part of the wider CTR agenda, which also included programs focused on helping the Russians transport, dismantle, and destroy nuclear weapons, their delivery systems, stockpiles of chemical weapons, and infrastructure and equipment that were once part of the biological weapons complex. Knowledge nonproliferation efforts were strongly influenced by political debates surrounding CTR; Chapter 3 discusses both the process of attaining and sustaining political support for CTR, as well as the consequences specifically for the Defense Conversion program, the Science Centers, IPP, and NCI. In turn, this provides the background for understanding some of the domestic political constraints within which these programs were implemented and which influenced their evolution.

The second part of this book—Chapters 4 through 7—consists of case studies of programs designed to counter the proliferation of WMD expertise. The programs are grouped together in terms of the agency in charge of their administration; those housed in the Defense Department come first, followed by the State Department's programs in Chapter 5. The Department of Energy's IPP and NCI programs constitute Chapters 6 and 7, respectively.

Each case study follows a parallel route. First I describe the program, including details about job creation and conversion projects and how they are developed and managed from the early 1990s through 2008. The specifics of program decision-making and logistics are important; these details provide evidence that is later used to show whether programs were influenced more by a rational assessment of how to meet goals and work around externally imposed constraints, or whether the imperatives of an institution's history, internal power dynamics, and perceived threats to autonomy were more predominant.

Then, I dissect the relationship between the task each program was given and the goals it came to pursue. More specifically, in each case study I illustrate how a program identified and interpreted the threat from the former Soviet WMD complex, changes in that threat over time, and the resulting adaptations in policy design and implementation. In particular, I focus on performance metrics—that is, the measurements that each program came to use as indicators of its success or failure. The literature on institutions documents the tendency for goal displacement: organizations come to substitute their own measurements for more meaningful indicators of whether they have succeeded at a given task.[30] For example, goals may shift to tasks that are more in sync with an organization's sense of its own mission; outcomes become goals because they can be easily measured; or the focus shifts to documenting things an organization does well, rather than the task it was given. Although goal displacement is well-documented in the literature on public policy and organizations and is often assumed by case studies of national security, there are relatively few works that analyze the process of goal displacement in national security institutions.[31] I help remedy this gap by using part of each case study to discuss the degree to which each program came to focus on something other than the reemployment of WMD experts and why. Moreover, I also clearly establish that originally one of the main tasks assigned to each program was the permanent redirection of WMD expertise through the creation of sustainable non-weapons work outside of the former Soviet WMD complex. In other words, regardless of the tasks that programs came to measure or advertise, one of their core national security missions remained job creation.

Next I turn to the question of results. Here I use two sets of metrics to judge each program. First, I let the programs speak for themselves and assess the degree to which they achieved success as they define it. Unfortunately, in many cases I am able to offer only broad conclusions

---

30. Classic examples include Peter Blau and W. Richard Scott, *Formal Organizations* (San Francisco, Calif.: Chandler, 1962), p. 220; Anthony Downs, *Inside Bureaucracy* (Boston, Mass.: Little Brown, 1967), pp. 146–147; Charles Perrow, *Complex Organizations*, 3rd ed. (New York: McGraw-Hill, 1986), p. 263; and Philip Selznick, *TVA and the Grass Roots: A Study of the Sociology of Formal Organization* (Berkeley, Calif.: University of California Press, 1949), chaps. 1–2.

31. Many works assume or discuss the role of bureaucratic parochialism in defense and national security institutions and policy, but relatively few deal specifically with how goals come to be displaced and for what reasons. Examples of works that discuss goal displacement more specifically include Harvey M. Sapolsky, *The Polaris System Development: Bureaucratic and Programmatic Success in Government* (Cambridge, Mass.: Harvard University Press, 1972); David Alan Rosenberg, "The Origins of Overkill: Nuclear Weapons and American Strategy, 1945–1960," *International Security*, Vol. 7, No. 4 (Spring 1983), pp. 3–71; Scott D. Sagan, "The Perils of Proliferation: Organization Theory, Deterrence Theory, and the Spread of Nuclear Weapons," *International Security*, Vol. 18, No. 4 (Spring 1994), pp. 66–107; and Lynn Eden, *Whole World on Fire: Organizations, Knowledge, and Nuclear Weapons Devastation* (Ithaca, N.Y.: Cornell University Press, 2004).

rather than systematic analysis. More rigor proves problematic because some programs adopted multiple metrics, each of which requires quite precise data that were not consistently reported by the program or for which independent measurement is difficult. In other cases, programs reported outcomes in an inconsistent or less than thorough fashion and, as a consequence, it is impossible to compare results reported in different years. In each case study, I elaborate on the degree to which these problems are applicable and, perhaps more important, discuss the relationship between the construction of multiple metrics and the constraints placed on a program by its environment. Second, I measure the degree to which each program supported U.S. national security by creating jobs for former Soviet WMD experts. Here, too, there are problems that arise from inconsistent definitions of "weapons expertise" and what it means to create a "sustainable" job, as well as difficulties associated with independent verification of the results as reported by each program. Consequently, in most cases I offer only general estimates of the number of jobs created. In all cases, however, there is enough data to judge whether a program created only a few or many jobs. Moreover, these problems and inconsistencies with measuring and defining job creation by themselves attest to the failure of programs to more directly connect their activities to their original goals.

The final part of each case study examines the reasons behind these outcomes. Here I consider three explanations. Two of these explanations focus on the degree to which the rational pursuit of policy goals is influenced by constraints external to the implementing organization. According to this logic, organizations implement policy based upon a reasoned analysis of how best to mitigate a problem within a given set of constraints. This is more than simply asking whether policy implementation successfully took into account external factors. Organizations are not hostage to their environments; rather, they make strategic choices about whether and how to influence those environments and the limitations they pose. Policy failure can therefore be explained by external constraints or the inability to work around those constraints, not a mismatch between goals and implementation. More specifically, with respect to the task of countering the proliferation of WMD expertise from the former Soviet Union, two such constraints predominate: Russia and U.S. domestic politics.

Russia was often assumed to be or accused of being a major impediment to U.S. nonproliferation goals. There are several variations of this argument. One is that Russian WMD experts had little experience with producing services or technology for commercial purposes or in a market economy. Moreover, the Soviet system skewed scientists toward products that embodied interesting science or made use of available resources, regardless of their commercial value. As a result, former Soviet WMD experts were willing to engage in interesting research but less able or inclined to participate in projects that would cause commercial firms to develop an interest in employing them.[32] Another argument is that

32. The overwhelming majority of U.S. project managers or participants that I interviewed

reemploying weapons experts directly conflicted with Russia's ability to maintain a robust WMD complex. Therefore former Soviet institute managers or government officials had incentives to impede U.S. job-creation activities. Third, because of the history of the Cold War and the presumed high value of WMD to national security, the Russian government and in particular its security services were hesitant to cooperate with the United States. In fact, analyses of CTR and related projects, including those aimed at the proliferation of expertise, frequently highlight problems with access to Russian nuclear and biological weapons facilities and experts.[33]

The fourth potential constraint was the state of the Russian economy. After the collapse of the Soviet Union, Russia was saddled with significant foreign debt, inflation, and a ruble that was worth little in terms of hard currency. Moreover, the central government was unable to guarantee intellectual property rights, respect for patents, or protect investors from corruption or arbitrary taxes and fees. It is clear that the Russian economy and government were significant barriers to job creation. However, it is also the case that Westerners, U.S. companies, and local Russians did invest. One crude indicator of interest is Foreign Direct Investment (FDI). Statistics from the United Nations Conference on Trade and Development's *World Investment Report* show that FDI in the early 1990s was indeed quite low in Russia, averaging around $900 million per year.[34] FDI had grown to almost $2 billion by 1995, and to over $15 billion by 2004.[35] By 2002, Russia was considered one of the top twenty-five countries for investment; by 2008, it was considered one of the largest economies in the

---

who were active in U.S.-Russian cooperation during the early 1990s complained about the difficulties convincing former Soviet scientists to focus on research with commercial potential or for which there was market demand.

33. For examples, see Department of Energy, The Secretary of Energy Advisory Board, Howard Baker and Lloyd Cutler, *A Report Card on the Department of Energy's Nonproliferation Programs with Russia* (Washington, D.C.: Department of Energy, January 10, 2001), p. 22; and Robert J. Einhorn and Michele A. Flournoy, eds., *Protecting Against the Spread of Nuclear, Biological and Chemical Weapons: An Action Agenda for Global Leadership, Volume 1: Agenda for Action* (Washington, D.C.: Center for Strategic and International Studies, January 2003), p. 12. A variety of reports by the Government Accountability Office, formerly the General Accounting Office, offer evidence of the persistence of problems with access. For examples, see General Accounting Office, *Weapons of Mass Destruction: Reducing the Threat from the Former Soviet Union: An Update*, Washington, D.C. (June 1995); General Accounting Office, *Weapons of Mass Destruction: Status of the Cooperative Threat Reduction Program*, Washington, D.C. (September 1996); Government Accountability Office, *Biological Weapons: Effort to Reduce Former Soviet Threat Offers Benefits, Poses New Risks*, Washington, D.C. (April 2000); and Government Accountability Office, *Cooperative Threat Reduction: DOD Has Improved Its Management and Internal Controls but Challenges Remain*, Washington, D.C. (June 2005).

34. United Nations Conference on Trade and Development, *World Investment Report 2001* (New York: United Nations, 2001), p. 295.

35. United Nations Conference on Trade and Development, *World Investment Report 1997* (New York: United Nations, 1997), p. 307; and United Nations Conference on Trade and Development, *World Investment Report 2007* (New York: United Nations, 2007), p. 253.

world.[36] Moreover, there is anecdotal evidence that U.S. companies did invest in Russia, including in cities devoted to nuclear weapons work.[37] Finally, many of the barriers to investment that concerned companies were precisely the problems that U.S. government programs could help mitigate. As explained by one program participant, the goal was to lure companies into a relationship with Russia before they could be "horrified by the conditions" there and to hook them on the "goodies" before they got scared about doing business in Russia.[38]

Besides Russia, the other most logical place to look for constraints on the rational pursuit of U.S. nonproliferation goals is in U.S. domestic politics. Here I investigate three possibilities. One is that the president was forced to pursue a goal not of his own making and sought to sabotage these programs by limiting their budgets or placing other restrictions upon their activities. As explained in Chapter 3, George H.W. Bush was hesitant to embrace the CTR agenda, Bill Clinton was initially enthusiastic but later more distracted, and George W. Bush consistently sought to have Russia assume more responsibility. To what extent did presidential support make a difference? A second possibility is that Congress or groups of members within Congress were the source of these constraints. The third option is that the design of these programs was intentionally suboptimal. Even though the creation of a new program would suggest a victory for policy supporters, it is also the case that politicians expect and plan for future struggles over policy. Political scientist Terry Moe argues that programs and policies are often designed with an eye toward the day when supporters are no longer in power.[39] Therefore, Moe explains, Congress often saddles policy implementation with restrictions, reporting requirements or other complicated rules that undermine program efficiency.[40] To what extent did nonproliferation programs suffer such a fate?

In addition to external constraints such as those posed by the president or Congress, a third possible explanation for policy failure can be found within the implementing organization itself. It is no secret that institutions often come to see policy goals in terms of their own interests. An institution's sense of itself and its mission permeates an agency's employees and the policies and processes they design to carry out their assigned tasks. But institutional interest is not static; it influences and is influenced

---

36. A. T. Kearney, Global Business Policy Council, *Foreign Direct Investment Confidence Index*, 1998–2005; Stephen Kotkin, *Armageddon Averted: The Soviet Collapse 1970-2000* (Oxford: Oxford University Press, 2008), p. 203.

37. For example, one of the most successful conversion projects in Sarov was a computer services and programming center started by Intel without any U.S. government funding or cooperation.

38. Interview with Initiatives for Proliferation Prevention staffer 1, July 16, 2003.

39. Terry Moe, "Political Institutions: The Neglected Side of the Story," *Journal of Law, Economics, and Organization*, Vol. 6 (Special Issue, 1990), pp. 213–253. For an application of this idea to national security institutions, see Amy B. Zegart, *Flawed By Design: The Evolution of the CIA, JCS, and NSC* (Stanford, Calif.: Stanford University Press, 1999).

40. Moe, "Political Institutions," p. 228.

by internal power struggles, tasks that are non-routine or unfamiliar, past legacies of embarrassment or success, and a host of other factors. For these reasons, policy comes to be a reflection of the implementing organization, rather than a rational assessment of the best means of pursuing a given goal. Policy failure, therefore, can be traced to variables internal to a specific institution. In terms of the fight to control the proliferation of WMD expertise, this means looking at the influence of institutional interest and dynamics in the Departments of Defense, Energy, and State.

The final part of this book—Chapter 8—offers conclusions. These are drawn from across the case studies and from situating those case studies within the context of U.S. domestic politics and the changing nature of the threat from the former Soviet WMD complex. I argue that institutional interest is the most persuasive explanation for why U.S. nonproliferation programs succeeded at engaging former Soviet WMD experts in collaborative research but failed to create more permanent jobs. In all four case studies, policy was implemented using actors and processes that were chosen because of institutional needs, not the dictates of reason or efficiency. Moreover, in each case, these institution-centered influences were made worse by a domestic political environment that made continued program support uncertain. Perhaps most seriously, there is little evidence to support a connection between the changing nature of the threat of WMD proliferation from Russia and U.S. programs aimed at former weapons experts.

Understanding this situation is important for improving efforts aimed at the proliferation of WMD expertise and U.S. national security policy more generally, as well as the policymaking and implementation processes. But there are additional imperatives. As the conclusion argues, the threat from the former Soviet WMD complex changed significantly between the early 1990s and 2008. The proliferation dangers that remain arise from different circumstances and must be met in a different context. Yet U.S. programs to reemploy WMD experts have done little to reconsider this threat. More problematically, they remain wedded to programmatic processes and policy goals that evolved according to their own rather than U.S. national security interests. Furthermore, the Washington consensus, as of 2008, seemed to favor winding down U.S. financing for these programs and turning their maintenance over to Russia. But many of these proliferation concerns matter more to the United States than to Russia, and thus may not receive the attention the United States thinks they deserve. The effort to shift the burden for parts of CTR to Russia also began at a time when that country was flush with revenue from the sale of oil and natural gas. As of 2008, this was no longer the case. For economic reasons, Russia may well come to neglect or abandon these efforts. Finally, the story of U.S. knowledge nonproliferation efforts is important because the United States is in the process of expanding the Science Centers and IPP to new countries and areas. If this is done uncritically, it promises to duplicate or enlarge the failures imbedded within these programs that have caused them to fall short of their mandate.

Chapter 2

The Proliferation Threat

The ability of U.S. policy to stop or mitigate the proliferation of weapons of mass destruction (WMD) expertise depends, in no small part, on the fit between programmatic response and threat. Obviously, policy cannot succeed if it fails to understand the problem that prompted it, or if it focuses on symptoms while allowing root causes to persist. Equally important, however, is that even with perfect knowledge of a problem, policy will fail if it disregards resource constraints or political commitment. In other words, solutions to policy dilemmas depend upon understanding both the problem and the political context within which that problem is defined and addressed. This chapter provides an assessment of the number and types of WMD experts in the former Soviet Union, their proliferation potential, and how this changed from 1990 to 2008.

The first section of this chapter provides an overview of the Soviet nuclear, biological, and chemical weapons complexes, as well as missile technology–related institutes, with an emphasis on the number of employees and their specialties. This section also chronicles Russian government and institute efforts to downsize and convert after the Cold War, and provides a snapshot of the state of these complexes as of 2007–2008. These weapons groups are not treated equally; in no case is comprehensive data available. Much more is known about the former Soviet nuclear weapons complex and specifically the closed nuclear cities in Russia. There is some information available about the biological weapons complex in Russia, relatively little about the chemical and missile technology complexes, and almost nothing about the fate of weapons experts outside of Russia. Based on anecdotal evidence and inference, however, it is possible to piece together an overall picture about which experts fared better after the Cold War and which remained a concern.

The second section of this chapter looks at the degree to which weapons knowledge spread from the former Soviet WMD complex during this same time. In many ways, this is a short and simple story: there were very few confirmed cases of weapons experts moving to countries other than the United States, Western Europe, or Israel. But considered within the context of other forms of proliferation, most specifically the theft of weapons-relevant materials by insiders and sharing knowledge by means other than emigration, this story becomes more complicated. Combined with shortcomings in the means used to detect such proliferation, it is not at all clear that this apparent lack of confirmed cases so far means there will be little proliferation in the future.

One caveat is in order. The focus here is on knowledge proliferation and not the ability of Russia or other post-Soviet countries to maintain a certain level of military capability. Therefore, the concern is employment opportunities, or lack thereof, for weapons experts and not the ability of Russia, or other countries, to maintain the knowledge base necessary to produce new weapons, keep old weapons in safe working order, or do weapons research and development. Included, however, is the question of whether Russia can sustain defense spending such that people will remain gainfully employed in the complex or will be forced to look elsewhere for jobs.

The Rise, Fall, and Partial Recovery of the Soviet Weapons Complex

During the Cold War, the Soviet Union built and maintained a large nuclear weapons complex that, by the mid-1980s, consisted of 20 major facilities and employed over 1 million people.[1] For comparison, at the end of the Cold War, the U.S. nuclear weapons complex totaled 16 major facilities[2] and employed an estimated 80,000.[3] Although the Soviet Union did produce a nuclear stockpile that eventually reached 45,000 warheads, this does not explain why the complex was so large. The Soviet approach to military production, including nuclear weapons, was to rely on multiple redundant systems and a surge capacity. As a result, the nuclear weapons complex was much larger than needed to produce and maintain the Soviet arsenal. The Soviet Union also investigated and produced a larger variety of warhead types and sizes, and this diversification may have contributed to making the complex bigger. Additionally, and most significantly, the Soviet complex was large because it counted as official employees everyone from scientists and engineers to construction workers and custodians.

Like its U.S. counterpart, the Soviet nuclear weapons complex covered all aspects of nuclear weapons research, development, production, and maintenance. Table 2.1 lists the main facilities that made up this complex in the mid-1980s, their locations and their primary functions.

---

1. Oleg Bukharin, *Downsizing of Russia's Nuclear Warhead Production Infrastructure*, PU/CEES Report No. 323 (Princeton, N.J.: Center for Energy and Environmental Studies, Princeton University, May 2000), p. 5, 24; Oleg Bukharin, *Russia's Nuclear Complex: Surviving the End of the Cold War* (Princeton, N.J.: Program on Science and Global Security, Woodrow Wilson School of Public and International Affairs, Princeton University, May 2004), p. 5.

2. Department of Energy, *The Legacy Story* (Washington, D.C.: Department of Energy, 1997), Chap. 1.

3. This is the number of people employed in fiscal year 1990 and includes those working for the Department of Energy as well as its contractors. See *The Nuclear Weapons Complex: Management for Health, Safety, and the Environment* (Washington, D.C.: National Academy of Sciences, 1989), p. 1.

According to analysis by Oleg Bukharin, in addition to these major facilities and test sites, there were approximately 150 other establishments that did nuclear weapons–related work but whose mandate also included basic nuclear and high-energy physics research, nuclear energy–related efforts, and other non-weapons areas.[4] Some of these facilities were located in Soviet republics other than Russia. For example, Ukraine had several institutes with expertise in metallurgy and materials science, as well as some uranium mining and processing facilities; Kazakhstan was home to the Semipalatinsk nuclear weapons test site, two nuclear research institutes, a facility for making nuclear reactor fuel, and a plutonium-producing reactor; and Uzbekistan had a couple of nuclear research reactors. Russia, however, was the main location for such facilities and was home to about 80 percent of the Soviet Union's nuclear weapons–related facilities, and 850,000 of its workers.[5]

This weapons complex was managed by the Soviet Ministry of Medium Machine Building or Minsredmash, which was also responsible for most aspects of nuclear power research and production. Although Minsredmash was also responsible for conducting nuclear tests, the actual test sites fell under the jurisdiction of the Ministry of Defense.

At the core of this complex were ten secret "nuclear cities." These cities were intentionally scattered throughout the Soviet Union and were developed, and in some cases built from scratch, specifically to house nuclear weapons facilities. In cases where there were already cities or towns, by the early part of the Cold War those cities were no longer printed on Soviet maps and, until 1992, their existence and location was a state secret. Even their names were disguised: the cities were known only by postal codes attached to the names of larger nearby cities.[6] For example, the city of Zheleznogorsk, formerly known as Krasnoyarsk-26, is located approximately 42 miles from Krasnoyarsk. Map 2.1 (see p. 26) below shows the locations of these nuclear cities.

These cities were isolated from the rest of the Soviet Union. Each city was designed to be self-contained; besides the nuclear facility, each city had the social infrastructure needed to support the families associated with the nuclear workforce.[7] Private businesses within the cities were very limited and usually connected to the nuclear facilities in some way. Mail

4. Bukharin, *Russia's Nuclear Complex: Surviving the End of the Cold War.*

5. Ibid., p. 6. According to Viktor Mikhailov, Russian Minister of Atomic Energy from 1992–1998, 7 percent of Minatom's industries were in Ukraine, 4 percent in Kazakhstan, 2 percent in Uzbekistan, 2 percent in Estonia, and 5 percent in other republics. See Viktor Mikhailov, "Conversion of the Nuclear Complex, Nuclear Disarmament and the Safety of Nuclear Tests at Novaya Zemlya," May 4, 1992 speech at FOA Ursvik, as translated in Lars B. Wallin, ed., *Lectures and Contributions to East European Studies at FOA* (Stockholm: Swedish National Defence Establishment, 1996), p. 6.

6. During the Cold War, even these postal codes changed sometimes.

7. Oleg Bukharin, "What Are Russia's Closed Nuclear Cities?" in Oleg Bukharin, Frank N. von Hippel, and Sharon K. Weiner, *Conversion and Job Creation in Russia's Closed Nuclear Cities* (Princeton, N.J.: Program on Nuclear Policy Alternatives, Center for Energy and Environmental Studies, Princeton University, 2000), p. 73.

to and from the cities was monitored, and residents were initially allowed to leave only on official business.[8] The cities were surrounded by fences and armed guards, as were the nuclear institutes within the cities. Authority for access to the cities was dispersed; Minsredmash had authority over the nuclear institutes and personnel, troops from the Ministry of the Internal Affairs guarded the cities, and the Soviet Committee for State Security (KGB) controlled the movement of people into and out of the cities. At their peak in the mid-1980s, these ten secret cities employed 150,000 people[9] as part of the nuclear complex and were home to approximately 700,000 people.[10]

Table 2.1. The Soviet Nuclear Weapons Complex in the Mid-1980s.

Facility	Main Functions
Fissile Material Production	
Mayak Production Association Ozersk (Chelyabinsk-65)	Produced plutonium, tritium Made HEU and plutonium weapons components
Siberian Mining and Chemical Combine Zheleznogorsk (Krasnoyarsk-26)	Produced plutonium
Siberian Chemical Combine Seversk (Tomsk-7)	Produced plutonium, HEU Made HEU and plutonium weapons components
Urals Electro-Chemical Combine Novouralsk (Sverdlovsk-44)	Produced HEU
Electro-Chemical Plant Zelenogorsk (Krasnoyarsk-45)	Produced HEU
Research and Development	
All-Russian Research Institute of Experimental Physics (VNIIEF) Sarov (Arzamas-16)	Warhead design Stockpile maintenance
All-Russian Research Institute of Technical Physics (VNIITF) Snezhinsk (Chelyabinsk-70)	Warhead design Stockpile maintenance
Institute of Automatics (VNIIA) Moscow	Warhead design and engineering Design of non-nuclear components Stockpile maintenance-related work
Institute of Measurement Systems (NII IS) Nizhny Novgorod	Design of non-nuclear components

8. In the mid-1950s, residents of the closed cities were allowed to leave for other reasons, but even this access was tightly controlled. See Bukharin, "What Are Russia's Closed Nuclear Cities?" p. 74.

9. Ministry of Atomic Energy of the Russian Federation, "Primary Objectives and Tasks," p. 3.

10. Mikhailov, "Conversion of the Nuclear Complex, Nuclear Disarmament and the Safety of Nuclear Tests at Novaya Zemlya," p. 7.

Table 2.1. *(continued)*

Production	
Electrokhimpribor Lesnoy (Sverdlovsk-45)	Warhead assembly and disassembly
Avangard Electromechanical Plant Sarov (Arzamas-16)	Warhead assembly and disassembly
Start Production Association Zarechny (Penza-19)	Warhead assembly and disassembly
Device-Building Plant Trekhgorny (Zlatoust-36)	Warhead assembly and disassembly
Sever Production Association Novosibirsk	Made non-nuclear components for weapons
Molniya Production Association Moscow	Made non-nuclear components for weapons
Urals Electromechanical Plant Yekaterinburg	Made non-nuclear components for weapons
Nizhneturinsky Mechanical Plant Nizhnyaya Tura	Made non-nuclear components for weapons and support equipment
Kuznetsk Machine-Building Plant Kuznetsk	Made non-nuclear components for weapons and support equipment
Testing	
Institute of Impulse Technologies (VNII IT) Moscow	Nuclear test diagnostics
Design Bureau of Road Equipment (KB ATO) Mytischy, Moscow Region	Warhead transportation and handling equipment
Central Test Site Novaya Zemlya	Weapons testing
Semipalatinsk Test Site Semipalatinsk, Kazakhstan	Weapons testing

SOURCES: This chart is based upon the work of Oleg Bukharin as found in Oleg Bukharin, "Downsizing Russia's Nuclear Warhead Production Infrastructure," *Nonproliferation Review*, Vol. 8, Issue 1 (Spring 2001), p. 117; and Thomas B. Cochran, Robert S. Norris, and Oleg A. Bukharin, *Making the Russian Bomb From Stalin to Yeltsin* (Boulder, Colo.: Westview, 1995), pp. 46–47.

NOTE: As discussed later in this chapter, the locations of many of these facilities were secret, and the cities were known by a postal code associated with a nearby city. In the early 1990s, the names of these cities were made public for the first time. To avoid confusion, Table 2.1 includes both names for each city.

Map 2.1. Russia's Closed Nuclear Cities.

SOURCE: Sharon K. Weiner, "Nuclear Cities News," Center for Energy and Environmental Studies, Princeton University, and the Russian-American Nuclear Security Advisory Council (RANSAC), Vol. 1 (December 1999).

In the late 1980s, the Soviet Union started the process of downsizing and converting parts of its nuclear weapons complex. The economic stagnation that prompted Gorbachev to try to restructure the Soviet economy also demanded less government spending, particularly in defense production. This coincided with a series of arms control agreements that brought nuclear weapons reductions and limitations and promised more in the future. Also, Soviet defense authorities realized that stockpiles of highly-enriched uranium (HEU) and plutonium were much larger than required for defense purposes and fissile material production was cut back.[11] This process was hastened by the nuclear reactor accident at Chernobyl in 1986, which sharply curtailed plans to expand the nuclear power industry. In 1988, the production of HEU for weapons purposes ended; by 1992, plutonium production was also reduced significantly.

The disintegration of the Soviet state did more than redistribute the Soviet nuclear weapons infrastructure over several successor states. Although Russia got the bulk of those facilities and most of the people that were directly involved in nuclear weapons work, it also inherited a moribund economy and a complex that was oversized even for Russian

11. Oleg Bukharin, "The Future of Russia's Plutonium Cities," *International Security*, Vol. 21, No. 4 (Spring 1997), p. 131.

needs. With the collapse of the Soviet Union, the Russian government re-organized the nuclear weapons complex, and in 1992, it was put under the control of the new Ministry of Atomic Energy or Minatom.[12] This reorganization could do little to shore up the complex, and Russian spending on nuclear weapons and nuclear energy declined dramatically in the early to mid-1990s.

Overall statistics on the decline of the Soviet nuclear weapons complex are virtually non-existent; reliable and comprehensive spending, downsizing, and conversion data have yet to be released by the Russian government.[13] From the available data and anecdotal evidence, however, it is possible to infer the state of the complex. What is clear is that, across the board, Minatom facilities saw a significant drop in government funding; often the amount facilities received was significantly less than what was initially budgeted.[14] Most facilities were unable to pay a large percentage of their workers; forced leave, salary delays, and reduced work weeks were not unusual. Many facilities had problems paying their utility bills. Some went bankrupt. Although data on the precise specifics of this decline are not yet available, it is widely agreed that the collapse of the Soviet Union put the nuclear weapons complex into a financial crisis that deepened until the mid- to late 1990s.

This situation had an impact that rippled beyond just the main nuclear weapons facilities. Places that provided supplies or services to the nuclear complex suffered because of the reduced demand. In some cases where there was demand and ability to pay, institutes found that their suppliers now lived in different countries and it was difficult to ensure access to materials. In facilities that focused on weapons work, those employed extended beyond scientists and engineers. Each facility had an associated infrastructure that often went beyond weapons-related work and included producing supplies or processing raw materials, the design and

---

12. There was one intermediary step: after Chernobyl, the Ministry of Nuclear Power was created, and in 1989 this merged with Minsredmash to become the Ministry of Atomic Power and Industry. In 1992, this became Minatom. Minatom itself was further divided into three areas: nuclear weapons development and testing, nuclear weapons production, and the nuclear fuel cycle. See Bukharin, *Downsizing of Russia's Nuclear Warhead Production Infrastructure*, p. 1.

13. Ivan Safranchuk of the Moscow office of the World Security Institute (formerly the Center for Defense Information) points out that another complicating factor is that the nuclear weapons program falls under budget categories that include spending for non-weapons activities. Moreover, the nuclear weapons program benefits from funding that is not included in the federal budget, including international collaboration, commercial work conducted by the nuclear facilities themselves, tax exemptions allowed to certain closed cities, and revenues from the U.S.-Russian HEU Agreement. According to Safranchuk's estimates, after 1992, funding for the nuclear weapons complex fell from between 37–75 percent until the devaluation of the ruble in 1998, which brought further economic troubles. Government spending on nuclear weapons programs only began to approach and surpass 1992 levels in 2002. Electronic communication with author, March 17, 2006.

14. For example, plutonium-producing reactor facilities received only 70 percent of the promised government funding from 1994–1995. See Bukharin, "The Future of Russia's Plutonium Cities," p. 132.

production of specialized or general equipment, construction, and, in the case of the nuclear cities, a social infrastructure. The chain of facilities associated with plutonium-producing reactors, described by Oleg Bukharin, is illustrative:

> Each of the plutonium combines was equipped with a power plant, research laboratories, facilities to design and produce chemical-processing equipment and instrumentation, mechanical and repair workshops, specialized construction units, and training institutes. Support for the plutonium complex was also provided by many outside institutions.[15]

Therefore, "employees" of the nuclear weapons complex included nuclear physicists and engineers, as well as technicians, construction workers, and a variety of other professions. According to former Minister for Atomic Energy Viktor Mikhailov, in the early 1990s, less than 20 percent of Minatom's workforce was scientific.[16]

Although the situation was desperate across the board, there were some differences. According to Bukharin, weapons institutes in open cities lost up to two-thirds of their staff, but generally fared better because there were opportunities in the commercial sector.[17] Those institutes that did indirect weapons-related work or focused on basic research often lost most of their government funding and essentially were left to fend for themselves. Facilities associated with Minatom's work on nuclear power suffered because of less government spending, but also because planned foreign orders were severely reduced due to a preference for Western equipment in the wake of Chernobyl.[18] In addition, the end of the production of fissile materials and reduced defense orders for nuclear submarines meant that all facilities associated with nuclear fuel production were affected.[19]

In general, salaries and job opportunities declined more the further one got from Moscow.[20] Initially, those outside of Russia were probably in

---

15. Bukharin, "The Future of Russia's Plutonium Cities," p. 131.

16. Mikhailov, "Conversion of the Nuclear Complex, Nuclear Disarmament and the Safety of Nuclear Tests at Novaya Zemlya," p. 4. According to Mikhailov, at the time Minatom's workforce was 47.2 percent industrial, 16.5 percent scientific, 19.4 percent construction, and 16.9 percent other types of work.

17. Oleg Bukharin, *Downsizing Russia's Nuclear Warhead Production Infrastructure*, p. 121.

18. This delay in production also meant that Russian technology fell behind that of the West. See Oleg Bukharin, *Russia's Nuclear Complex: Surviving the End of the Cold War*, p. 7.

19. The one brief exception was in the uranium mining industry. Russia inherited stocks of uranium from the Soviet Union, and many of these were dumped on the market in the early 1990s. Although this depressed the price for uranium, it did provide a much needed influx of hard currency, which helped provide income in the industry for a short time. See Bukharin, *Russia's Nuclear Complex: Surviving the End of the Cold War*, p. 10.

20. One of the few pieces of evidence available comes from the former director of the

the worst predicament. No other Soviet successor state had the money to sustain the weapons institutes it inherited. Moreover, in 1992, Belarus, Kazakhstan, and Ukraine all agreed to be non-nuclear weapons states under the Lisbon Protocol; therefore, the nuclear weapons–related workers they inherited had little future. By 1996, all Soviet nuclear weapons had been moved to Russia. With no state budgets to support them and no future in weapons-related work, many of these facilities and workers were left to fend for themselves. By the turn of the twenty-first century, however, Kazakhstan was in a better position. Thanks to revenues from natural gas and oil exports, its economy, and with it alternative job prospects, were booming.

The closed nuclear cities in Russia were among the hardest-hit areas. There the reduction in government spending was felt more strongly and was compounded by the very structure of the cities themselves.[21] One reason for their plight was that the nuclear cities were almost totally dependent, either directly or indirectly, on the nuclear weapons complex for jobs. The cities of Sarov and Snezhinsk were home to nuclear weapons research and design facilities. Estimates suggest that in Sarov, half of the city's working population was employed at the All-Russian Research Institute of Experimental Physics (VNIIEF) or the Avangard facility and that a similar fraction in Snezhinsk worked at the All-Russian Research Institute of Technical Physics (VNIITF).[22] By early 1992, weapons-related activities accounted for only 60 percent of the work at VNIIEF and half at VNIITF;[23] by the mid-1990s, VNIIEF's budget was one-quarter of what it had been before the Soviet collapse.[24] In Snezhinsk, the situation became so desperate that VNIITF's director Vladimir Nechai committed suicide in October 1996. In mid-July 1998, several thousand workers in Sarov went on strike for three hours, demanding back wages and a pay increase. Later that same year, nuclear workers from several of the nuclear cities went on

---

International Science and Technology Center, Glenn Schweitzer, who estimated that in the mid-1990s, some 2,000 weapons workers in Georgia were paid $2–$5 per month. U.S. Congress, Senate, Permanent Subcommittee on Investigations, Committee on Governmental Affairs, Testimony of Glenn Schweitzer, *Global Proliferation of Weapons of Mass Destruction*, Part II, 104th Cong., 2nd sess., March 13, 20, and 22, 1996, p. 64.

21.   This discussion about the plight of the nuclear cities is based in part on previous work which appeared as Sharon K. Weiner, "Preventing Nuclear Entrepreneurship in Russia's Nuclear Cities," *International Security*, Vol. 27, No. 2 (Fall 2002), pp. 126–158.

22.   These figures are based upon Oleg Bukharin, "Appendix 1. Populations, Employment and Conversion in Russia's Closed Nuclear Cities," in Bukharin, et. al., *Conversion and Job Creation in Russia's Closed Nuclear Cities*, pp. 38–44. Both VNIIEF and VNIITF are nuclear research and design centers. The Avangard facility, also called the Electro-Mechanical Plant "Avangard," had the function of warhead assembly and disassembly.

23.   Federation of American Scientists and Natural Resources Defense Council, "Report of the Fourth International Workshop on Nuclear Warhead Elimination and Nonproliferation," Washington, D.C., February 26–27, 1992, p. 13.

24.   National Research Council, Office of International Affairs, *An Assessment of the International Science and Technology Center: Redirecting Expertise in Weapons of Mass Destruction in the Former Soviet Union* (Washington, D.C.: National Academy Press, 1996), pp. 1–2.

strike; some traveled to Moscow to protest their plight at Minatom head-quarters.

The cities of Lesnoy, Zarechny, and Trekhgorny, which focused on war-head assembly and disassembly, had a combined population of 155,000 at the end of the Cold War, an estimated 27,400 of whom were employed at weapons-related institutes.[25] Assuming only half were of working age, at least one third of the population depended directly on the state for their income. Yet, during the 1990s, the production of warheads declined to the point where it was approximately 8 percent of Cold War levels.[26]

The remaining five cities focused primarily or exclusively on fissile material production. In 1988, production of HEU for weapons stopped, and by the early 1990s, the uranium enrichment complex was working at only half of its capacity.[27] Between 1987 and 1992, ten of thirteen plutoni-um-producing reactors were also shut down; three reactors remained in operation because they were the sole source of heat and energy for two cities. According to Bukharin, at Seversk, Zheleznogorsk, and Ozersk, where plutonium production took place, the nuclear facilities lost up to an estimated 25 percent of their staff, dropping from a combined total of 49,000 to 37,000.[28]

Those who no longer had work at the weapons facilities usually had nowhere else to go. Because the nuclear cities were closed, there were few opportunities to leave to look for other work. As mentioned previously, workers were not free to leave without government permission, and even though this was granted more frequently during the 1990s, permission was still required.[29] And, at least in the early to mid-1990s, few non-government-related businesses were started because of access and invest-ment restrictions in the cities. Moreover, as the Russian economy dis-integrated, concerns about organized crime, drugs, and fraud increased, and the isolation of the cities was seen as a source of safety.[30] Finally, even if workers had been willing and able to leave, they would have faced one additional problem: housing. In the Soviet Union, housing was usually provided by employers. The small residential housing market would have made it very difficult to find rental housing.[31]

---

25. These figures are based upon Bukharin, "Appendix 1. Populations, Employment and Conversion in Russia's Closed Nuclear Cities," in Bukharin, et. al., *Conversion and Job Creation in Russia's Closed Nuclear Cities*, pp. 57–59.

26. Bukharin, *Downsizing Russia's Nuclear Warhead Production Infrastructure*, p. 121.

27. Bukharin, *Russia's Nuclear Complex: Surviving the End of the Cold War*, p. 13.

28. Bukharin, "The Future of Russia's Plutonium Cities," p. 133.

29. Bukharin, "Appendix 3. What are Russia's Closed Nuclear Cities," in Bukharin, et. al., *Conversion and Job Creation in Russia's Closed Nuclear Cities*, pp. 74–75.

30. Ibid., p. 75; Glenn E. Schweitzer, *Swords into Market Shares: Technology, Economics, and Security in the New Russia* (Washington, D.C.: Joseph Henry Press, 2000), p. 186; and Judith Perera, "Opening the Closed Towns," *Nuclear Engineering International*, June 1995, p. 44.

31. Maria Lodahl, "The Housing Market in Russia: Disappointing Results," *Economic Bulletin*, No. 6 (Berlin: German Institute for Economic Research, 2001), p. 1.

The problems at Minatom's institutes had a profound effect on the quality of life in the nuclear cities. Because the cities were dependent on the government and the nuclear facilities for revenue, a reduction in orders also meant less money for municipal operations, social welfare programs, healthcare, pensions, and infrastructure. This situation was made worse by a reduction in federal subsidies. From 1996 through 1998, every nuclear city except one saw a decrease in subsidies from the federal government; these reductions ranged from 4 to 50 percent.[32] As a result, the diversity of consumable goods, and in some cases their supply, declined significantly. Pensions for retired workers decreased or went unpaid. With few funds for infrastructure maintenance, transportation, roads, and buildings deteriorated. In early 1998, the mayor of Zelenogorsk wrote to the region's governor that a social explosion in his city was unavoidable unless urgent action was taken; besides unpaid workers, he mentioned a shortage of medical supplies.[33] Anecdotal evidence suggests that each of the nuclear cities faced a similar situation.

The prestige of nuclear workers, especially the top scientists and engineers, also suffered. Even though these specialists lived in closed communities, their role in protecting national security brought them unusual privileges from the government during Soviet times. They had access to higher quality, and in some cases Western, food and goods. Their children got preferential treatment in terms of education. Their health care services were among the best in the Soviet Union. And their families vacationed at government facilities in resort towns that were off limits to average citizens. These perks disappeared in the early 1990s, and with them the sense of elite status that such workers had enjoyed.

Finally, workers in the nuclear cities suffered because of a decline in wages, as did everyone in Russia. Throughout the country, salaries plummeted after the Soviet collapse and were further eroded by inflation and other price increases. In July 1992, the ruble became a legally convertible currency, and its value dropped from a couple of rubles per dollar to hundreds and then thousands. By mid-1994, rubles were valued at approximately 2,500 per U.S. dollar; this was reduced further after October 11, 1994, when the ruble lost close to 25 percent of its value in one day.[34] During this same period, the average salary in Russia ranged from $120 to $180 and, according to a study by the World Bank, the percentage of the population living in poverty rose from 10 percent to over 40 percent.[35]

32. Gregory Brock, "The ZATO Archipelago Revisited—Is the Federal Government Loosening Its Grip? A Research Note," *Europe-Asia Studies*, Vol. 52, No. 7 (November 2000), p. 1356. The exception was Zheleznogorsk, which saw a slight increase in subsidies.

33. Department of Energy, The Secretary of Energy Advisory Board, Howard Baker and Lloyd Cutler, *A Report Card on the Department of Energy's Nonproliferation Programs with Russia* (Washington, D.C.: The Secretary of Energy Advisory Board, Department of Energy, January 20, 2001), p. vii.

34. All ruble to dollar conversions are done using exchange rates from the CIA's *World Fact Book*, Washington, D.C., Central Intelligence Agency, various years, and Department of State, "Russia Economic Policy and Trade Practices," February 1994.

35. Economic figures for Russia in the early to mid-1990s are less than precise because of

Comprehensive salary figures for the WMD complex are not available, but it is possible to extrapolate from what is known about the key nuclear weapons cities of Sarov and Snezhinsk. During the first half of the 1990s, official salaries for nuclear scientists and engineers in these two cities ranged from $100 to about $250, with the top weapons experts making around $340.[36] Discrete information from other weapons-affiliated cities suggests that their workers fared worse.[37] But salary level alone did not reflect take-home income. During the 1990s, wage arrears were common throughout Russia. In December 1994, the number of working-age people owed back wages was just over 38 percent and had climbed to 64 percent by the end of 1998.[38] Those who still had jobs in the nuclear facilities faced significant wage delays. Because of the economic situation and budget cuts, the Russian government found it difficult to pay its bills on time. As a result, wages were often late throughout the government workforce and the Minatom complex, including the nuclear cities.

Minatom began delaying wages in the early 1990s. Although these delays usually amounted to one to three months, they reached their peak by early 1997, when wages in some nuclear cities were more than seven months behind.[39] Salary delays contributed to a significant reduction in income, and by 1995–1996, the average payment to nuclear experts in Sarov

the volatility of the ruble and because different sources use different definitions for "average wage" and "poverty line," as well as different conversion rates. My estimates are based upon Jeni Klugman and Jeanine Braithwaite, "Poverty in Russia during the Transition: An Overview," *World Bank Research Observer*, Vol. 13, No. 1 (1998), pp. 42, 44; and Department of State, Bureau of Economic and Business Affairs, "Russia: 1994 Country Report on Economic Policy and Trade Practices," Washington, D.C. (1995).

36. This range is based upon salary information found in Department of State, Bureau of Political-Military Affairs, "Nonproliferation through Science Cooperation," briefing slides, October 13, 1994; Thomas de Wall, "Security Falters in Decaying Atomic City," *Moscow Times*, August 25, 1994, p. 1–2; and Analytical Center for Non-Proliferation, "An Overview of VNIIEF-STL Experiences and Projects," Sarov, Russia, 2004, pp. 24–25.

37. For example, according to Judith Perera, during the mid-1990s, workers in Minatom's industrial enterprises were making approximately $240 per month, but scientific researchers were getting only about $150. See Judith Perera, *The Nuclear Industry in the Former Soviet Union: Transition from Crisis to Opportunity*, Vol. 2 (London: Financial Times Energy Publishing, 1997), p. 5. According to N.V. Zubarevich and A.G. Machrova, in Dubna, a science city about two hours outside of Moscow that revolves around a nuclear research institute, the average wage was about 80 percent of the all-Russian average. Obninsk, a city about two hours from Moscow that does work on nuclear science and nuclear engineering, had an average wage that was just under 70 percent of the all-Russian average. See N.V. Zubarevich and A.G. Machrova, "Human Development and Intellectual Potential of Russia's Regions," *Human Development Report, Russian Federation 2004* (Moscow: United Nations Development Programme, 2004), p. 96. The exception appears to be Moscow's Kurchatov Institute, where salaries tended to be on par or slightly higher than in the rest of Russia. Interview with Kurchatov Institute staffer 1, August 1, 2002.

38. T. Mroz, D. Mancini, and B. Popkin, "Monitoring Economic Conditions in the Russian Federation: The Russia Longitudinal Monitoring Survey 1992–98," Carolina Population Center, University of North Carolina at Chapel Hill, March 1999, p. 17–18.

39. Matthew Bunn, Oleg Bukharin, Jill Cetina, Kenneth N. Luongo, and Frank N. von Hippel, "Retooling Russia's Nuclear Cities," *Bulletin of the Atomic Scientists*, Vol. 54 (September/October 1998), p. 44.

and Snezhinsk was $30–$50 per month.[40] This, combined with reductions in subsidies to the nuclear cities, resulted in a significant loss of income for residents that was not mirrored throughout Russia. For example, using personal income-tax data for the nuclear cities, Greg Brock shows that between 1996 and 1998, per-capita income in the nuclear cities fell by three times the national average in Russia.[41]

By 1998, however, it appeared that things would improve. In 1996, the Russian government authorized Minatom to borrow money from commercial banks. Two loans totaling $200 million were taken out to help pay salaries.[42] By the fall of 1999, wages in the nuclear cities were being paid on time, although wage arrears in the rest of Russia were still common. At the start of 1998, when the average monthly income per capita in Russia was just over $100, the average monthly wage at VNIIEF in Sarov was around $150.[43]

But this hopeful trend was not to last. In January 1998, the Russian government attempted to stabilize its currency by redenominating the ruble; overnight, 1,000 old rubles were worth one new one. The ruble continued to lose value, culminating in August 1998, when the currency lost 70 percent of its value against the U.S. dollar. The result was devastating to the average Russian worker who, by 1999, was making only about $62 a month.[44] Although the average monthly salary for Minatom's nuclear weapons scientists plunged to just over $50 during this time, workers in Sarov and Snezhinsk made over $90.[45]

After the initial shock, salaries throughout Russia began to recover, but they increased more in Sarov, Snezhinsk, and select other nuclear cities. The average monthly Russian wage had returned to pre-1998 crisis levels by 2002, increased to $260 by 2005, and had climbed to over $500 by mid-2007.[46] Information on salaries in the nuclear cities is sparse. Thanks

---

40. Sergey Leskov, "Uchenogo-atomshika doveli do svintsovoy tochki," *Izvestiya*, November 1, 1996, p. 1, as quoted on http://www.nti.org (accessed July 24, 2005); and Charles Hecker, "Payment Crisis Hits Elite Nuclear Center," *Moscow Times*, June 16, 1995, p. 4. The highest wages appear to have been at VNIIEF in Sarov.

41. Gregory Brock, "The ZATO Archipelago Revisited," p. 1357.

42. Oleg Bukharin, *Russia's Nuclear Complex: Surviving the End of the Cold War*, pp. 17–18.

43. Analytical Center for Non-Proliferation, "An Overview of VNIIEF-STL Experiences," p. 25; and Federal State Statistics Service, Russia, "Living Standards of the Population, Main Socio-Economic Indicators," http://www.gks.ru (accessed July 24, 2006).

44. This figure was calculated using information from the State Committee of the Russian Federation on Statistics.

45. Based upon Valentin Tikhonov, *Russia's Nuclear and Missile Complex: The Human Factor in Proliferation* (Washington, D.C.: Carnegie Endowment for International Peace, 2001), p. 37; Siegfried S. Hecker, "Thoughts About an Integrated Strategy for Nuclear Cooperation with Russia," *Nonproliferation Review*, Vol. 8, No. 2 (Summer 2001), p. 13; and Analytical Center for Non-Proliferation, "An Overview of VNIIEF-STL Experiences," pp. 24, 25, 41. According to the Tikhonov survey, 60 percent of Minatom's workforce in the nuclear cities was making less than $50 a month. Workers in Minatom's nuclear power sector did the best, bringing home $112 per month, followed by industrial workers at $72.

46. John V. Parachini, David E. Moser, John Baker, Keith Crane, Michael Chase, Michael

to the "Quarterly Information Bulletin" published by the Analytical Center for Non-Proliferation in Sarov, there is more wage information available for that city. Table 2.2 compares average monthly wages throughout the city with those employed in "science and scientific activities," which can reasonably be inferred to be experts employed at VNIIEF and Avanguard. It is clear that wages for weapons experts have increased consistently and significantly since the ruble crisis of 1998.

Table 2.2. Average Wages in Sarov.

	Average monthly wage for all employed persons (current U.S. dollars)	Average monthly wage for those employed in science and scientific activities (current U.S. dollars)
1998	$134.5	$147.3
1999	$70.4	$76.3
2000	$114	$129.6
2001	$163	$209
2002	$200	$275
2003	$263	$314
2004	$304.8	$345
2005	$352	$387[a]

[a]Estimated based on extrapolation from 2002–2004 data.

SOURCE: Based on Analytical Center for Non-Proliferation, "Quarterly Information Bulletins," Issues 1–26 (September 1999–June 2006), Sarov, Russia.

In 2007, the average wage at VNIIEF had risen to approximately $650 per month, and requests from younger workers for an increase to $970–$1,170 fell on sympathetic ears.[47]

But workers in other cities also did better than the national average. For example, in 2002, there were reports that top scientists in Snezhinsk were bringing home salaries as high as $700 per month.[48] Wages for "technical workers" at the Siberian Chemical Combine in Seversk were about

Daugherty, *Diversion of Nuclear, Biological, and Chemical Weapons Expertise from the Former Soviet Union: Understanding an Evolving Problem* (Santa Monica, Calif.: RAND, National Security Research Division, 2005), p. 10; Central Bank of the Russian Federation, Social and Economic Situation in January–February 2005, http://www.cbr.ru/eng/analytics/macro/print.asp?file=macroeconomics_jan-feb_05.htm (accessed Feb. 17, 2006); and Russian Federal State Statistics Service, "Main Socio-economic Indicators of Living Standard of Population," http://www.gks.ru/bgd/regl/b08_12/IssWWW.exe/stg/d01/01-01.htm (accessed on May 5, 2009).

47. Open Source Committee (OSC) Summary, "Summary of Key Developments at Russia's Nuclear Institutes," August 30, 2007; and Russia—Open Source Committee (OSC) Summary, "Summary of Reporting on Russian and FSU Nuclear Issues," January 17, 2008.

48. Interview with Los Alamos National Laboratory staffer 2, May 28, 2002.

$800 in 2007, and rose to $920 in 2008; in 2007, wages at the Zheleznogorsk Mining and Chemical Combine were about $930.[49] Wage delays were also eliminated for nuclear workers, but as of 2006 they persisted for 3.6 percent of the workforce throughout Russia.[50]

Because of the average age of former Soviet weapons experts, a brief word is in order about pensions. Until reforms under Putin in 2005, the average Russian worker had only a small pension, which was usually below the subsistence level. Pensioners, including former nuclear weapons–related employees, had to supplement their pensions to make ends meet. In the late 1990s, the average monthly pension across Russia was about $19[51] and only $20 in the nuclear cities.[52] By 2005, the average pension for a Russian worker had increased to $72 per month, and thus was still significantly below the official subsistence wage of $100 per month.[53] According to the Analytical Center for Non-Proliferation at Sarov, pensions in that city increased from an average of $38 per month in 2001 to $98 per month in 2005.[54] Nonetheless, approximately 20 percent of nuclear weapons–related workers who were past retirement age did not leave the complex because pensions were so low.[55] According to the Russian Federal State Statistics Service, as of the end of 2007, the average pensioner needed about $129 each month for subsistence and, on average, got a pension of about $125.[56] There is no evidence that pensions were more than marginally better for the nuclear weapons workforce.

Although information on wages and pensions is far from comprehensive, some conclusions can be inferred from this summary. First, it is clear that all Russian workers suffered during the 1990s, and many continued to struggle after that. Pensioners were among the worst hit, and retirement remained a poor economic choice for most, regardless of occupation. Second, wage delays, although common across Russia, tended to be longer and more severe in the nuclear weapons complex in the mid-1990s. That said, wage delays also disappeared sooner and more completely for the

49. Russia—Open Source Committee (OSC) Summary, "Summary of Reporting on Russian and FSU Nuclear Issues," January 31, 2008; Russia—OSC Summary, "Summary of Reporting on Russian & FSU Nuclear Issues," September 26, 2008.

50. Central Bank of the Russian Federation, Social and Economic Situation in January–February 2005.

51. "Russia to Increase State Pensions by 14 Percent," *Russia Today* (Internet edition), September 24, 1999.

52. Hecker, "Thoughts About an Integrated Strategy for Nuclear Cooperation with Russia," p. 13.

53. Central Bank of the Russian Federation, Social and Economic Situation in January–February 2005.

54. Analytical Center for Non-Proliferation, "Quarterly Information Bulletins," 2001–2006, Sarov, Russia.

55. Bukharin, *Russia's Nuclear Complex: Surviving the End of the Cold War*, p. 21.

56. Russian Federal State Statistics Service, "Main Socio-Economic Indicators of Living Standard of Population," and "Subsistence Minimum Level," http://www.gks.ru/bgd/regl/b08_12/IssWWW.exe/stg/d01/07-01.htm (accessed on May 5, 2009).

nuclear weapons–related workforce than for the rest of Russia. Third, in terms of salaries, workers in the nuclear weapons–related workforce were not all equal. Paradoxically, the least is known about workers in open cities. Perhaps the only reasonable conclusion is that those workers nearest Moscow fared better than those that were further away. More information is available for the closed nuclear cities. Workers in these places tended to be better off than the rest of Russia until about 1994, when their wages, on average, fell below the national average until the late 1990s. Although wages recovered for certain workers in certain cities, the situation across the board is unclear. What is clear is that the closed nature of the cities contributed to a significant drop in living standards during the mid-1990s that was not necessarily as harsh in other parts of Russia. The most is known about workers in the nuclear research and design centers of Sarov and Snezhinsk. Although they too suffered a decline in living standards and wage delays, wages here generally remained above the national average, with the exception of a short period in the mid-1990s. Since 1998, wages for nuclear weapons workers in Sarov and Snezhinsk, and probably other key nuclear cities, outpaced the Russian average and seem poised to continue to rise more rapidly as of 2008.

MINATOM RESPONDS

The decade of the 1990s resulted in significant changes in the former Soviet nuclear weapons complex. This section provides an overview of how institutes and enterprises coped with major reductions in funding and an uncertain future. Much more is known about the part of the complex that Russia inherited, but the fate of places in other post-Soviet states is addressed where possible.

The Soviet nuclear weapons complex numbered about 1 million workers, including those involved in construction and other activities. Russia inherited about 850,000 of these people. As of mid-2002, Russia's nuclear weapons–related workforce numbered around 75,000.[57] At first glance, a reduction from 1 million to approximately 75,000 suggests that massive conversion has taken place. But the vast majority of those who left the complex were not nuclear weapons workers. Instead, they were engaged in construction, maintenance and support services, and other civilian activities; their jobs were simply reclassified as civilian or transferred to civilian agencies and institutes.

In the closed cities, employees associated with local administration and management were transferred to the city government. They were no longer counted as part of the defense complex. The construction sector is another example. It is estimated that 20 percent of Minatom's employees worked in the construction sector.[58] Some of these workers were laid off, but many became part of spin-off construction companies. The shortage

---

57. Lev Ryabev, "Downsizing of the Nuclear Complex and Defense Conversion Programs," presentation at the Conference on Helping Russia Down-Size its Nuclear Weapons Complex, Princeton N.J., March 14–15, 2000.

58. Bukharin, *Russia's Nuclear Complex: Surviving the End of the Cold War*, p. 7.

of residential housing in Russia suggested that such firms were a good investment and, indeed, many local governments and especially the nuclear cities invested in these companies.[59]

Real conversion among nuclear weapons institutes was much less impressive. At the end of the Cold War, approximately 130,000 employees were engaged in nuclear weapons and nuclear power–related work; this was still considered to be the size of the Russian nuclear complex in 2007.[60] Of these 130,000 people, about 75,000 did weapons-related work; the rest were engaged in nuclear power–related commercial activities, management, or environmental issues.[61] Of the weapons workers, 60,000–67,000 were in the closed nuclear cities and the remainder did weapons-related work at other institutes.[62]

Initially, the response of the nuclear weapons complex was to assume that downsizing and conversion were not necessary; if people and institutes simply waited, weapons work would return once Russia was on its feet. Oleg Bukharin argues that in the meantime, the nuclear complex survived initially by relying on internal reserves that were accumulated during the Cold War.[63] Some places rented out their offices and equipment. Others tried to sell goods that were manufactured using current stocks of materials. These resources, however, were exhausted by the mid-1990s, and the complex found itself in an even deeper crisis.[64] By the middle of the decade it was clear that Russia's economic woes were not going away, and that this "wait and see" strategy was doomed to failure.

Those institutes devoted to nuclear power, and especially nuclear fuel cycle services, were the first part of the complex to find a path to recovery. Minatom's income had always depended heavily on the international sale of nuclear energy–related activities. In the early 1990s, for example, it is estimated that 90 percent of the value of exports from the Minatom complex were products and services in the area of natural and enriched uranium, fuel and equipment for nuclear power plants, and rare earth elements.[65] To take advantage of their ability to make money, in the early 1990s the

---

59. Ibid. Many of these construction companies failed, however, because of quality problems in addition to the inability of consumers to afford their products.

60. Ibid., p. 16; and Oleg Bukharin, "Stewards and Custodians: Tomorrow's Crisis for the Russian Nuclear Weapons Complex?" *Nonproliferation Review*, Vol. 6, Issue 4 (Fall 1999), p. 131. This is also the number cited in U.S. Congress, *Ensuring Implementation of the 9/11 Commission Report Act*, S. 328, 110th Cong., 1st sess., January 2007, Title III, Subtitle C, Sec. 322.

61. Bukharin, "Stewards And Custodians: Tomorrow's Crisis For The Russian Nuclear Weapons Complex?" p. 131; and Lev Ryabev, "Downsizing of the Nuclear Complex and Defense Conversion Programs."

62. Bukharin, "Stewards And Custodians: Tomorrow's Crisis For The Russian Nuclear Weapons Complex?" p. 131.

63. Bukharin, *Russia's Nuclear Complex: Surviving the End of the Cold War*," p. 6.

64. Ibid.

65. Mikhailov, "Conversion of the Nuclear Complex, Nuclear Disarmament and the Safety of Nuclear Tests at Novaya Zemlya," p. 56.

parts of Minatom devoted to the nuclear fuel cycle were made into "unitary companies" which, although state-owned and affiliated, were largely independent of Minatom control.[66] Nuclear fuel–related exports became the main source of income for Minatom, and by the mid-1990s this income was enough to support the entire Minatom complex.[67]

As of 2008, parts of the Minatom complex were making nuclear fuel for naval propulsion systems as well as commercial nuclear reactors, and the complex exported fuel to China, India, and Iran, as well as the United States. It also had a significant share of the world market in uranium enrichment. This commercial success sustained a significant part of the workforce at the closed nuclear cities of Ozersk, Seversk, and Zelenogorsk.[68]

A subset of this success has to be attributed to the U.S.-Russian HEU Agreement. In 1993, the United States and Russia signed an agreement whereby Russia agreed to "downblend" the HEU from nuclear warheads, turning it into low-enriched uranium, which would then be sold to the United States as fuel for nuclear power plants. Over a twenty-year period, the United States agreed to pay $8 billion for 500 megatons of converted HEU. This agreement has been a major source of income and employment in the Minatom complex. Institutes in Zarechny, Lesnoy, and Trekhgorny dismantle the warheads, the HEU is converted into uranium oxide at Seversk, and then this compound is downblended at Novouralsk and Zelenogorsk. According to Bukharin, the HEU agreement has provided income and jobs for 8,000 people.[69] Of the money the United States pays as part of this deal, one third was going to the Russian central government and two-thirds to Minatom in 2005. Minatom, in turn, used approximately 30 percent of its share to pay its facilities to do the work of downblending, and part of the rest was used to fund conversion programs.[70] Beginning in 2005, however, the proceeds all went into the broader Russian federal budget.[71]

---

66. Nikolai Yakovlev, director-general of Central Research Institute of Management, Economics and Information, Minatom, as quoted in "Minatom Rising," Nukem, April 2002, pp. 5–6.

67. Bukharin, *Russia's Nuclear Complex: Surviving the End of the Cold War*, p. 18.

68. Ozersk downblends highly-enriched uranium and makes radioisotopes for medical and industrial applications, Seversk also does downblending as well as uranium enrichment, and Zelenogorsk provides spent fuel management services. See Bukharin, *Russia's Nuclear Complex: Surviving the End of the Cold War*, p. 14; and Pavel Podvig, *Consolidating Fissile Materials in Russia's Nuclear Complex* (Princeton, N.J.: International Panel on Fissile Materials, Princeton University, May 2009), pp. 8–12.

69. Bukharin, *Russia's Nuclear Complex: Surviving the End of the Cold War*, p. 18.

70. Oleg Bukharin, Harold Feiveson, Frank von Hippel, Sharon K. Weiner, Matthew Bunn, William Hoehn, and Kenneth Luongo, *Helping Russia Downsize its Nuclear Complex: A Focus on the Closed Nuclear Cities* (Princeton, N.J.: Center for Energy and Environmental Studies, Princeton University, June 2000), p. 18.

71. Analytical Center for Non-Proliferation, "Quarterly Information Bulletin," Issue 26 (2006), Sarov, Russia, p. 54.

CONVERSION EFFORTS BY MINATOM

In the late 1980s, the Russian government began to fund conversion efforts in the nuclear weapons complex. These early efforts were poorly conceived, and resulted in little conversion and few jobs. Minatom's initial conversion plans were to reduce defense orders and switch to commercial employment where feasible. But underlying these objectives was a belief that the complex could be restructured and revived again in the future, when funding was better. According to Minatom, from 1988 to 1997, its own conversion efforts resulted in 20,500–22,500 jobs.[72] Many of these were "easy" in the sense that they involved the transfer of nuclear power–related jobs to spin-off companies and the transfer of construction, industrial, and social service jobs in the nuclear cities to the city administrations.

The creation of new jobs failed because Minatom's underlying attitude was geared toward maintaining the weapons complex. Rather than concentrate defense spending at a few facilities, Minatom continued it throughout the complex. There was a feeling that things would eventually return to normal and that commercial production was a temporary rather than a permanent activity.

According to Bukharin, the result was insufficient investment on the part of Minatom, secrecy about conversion plans and efforts, high production costs, a lack of business and market skills, and resistant organizations.[73] Also, because of the collapse of the Russian economy, there were fewer domestic customers; those who could afford goods put a premium on imports from the West. During this time, people who did leave the nuclear complex largely did so as a result of their own entrepreneurial efforts.

Minatom's attitude had changed by the late 1990s, as it became clear that the Soviet-era complex would not be resurrected. Minatom and many of its institutes realized that cutbacks were irreversible, and that significant restructuring would have to take place in order to survive. Among Russian experts, the general consensus was that the nuclear complex could survive and do its job with approximately one-third of current personnel.[74]

This change in attitude was assisted by a change in ministers. Victor Mikhailov, who had spent some time working at VNIIEF, emphasized maintaining defense capabilities. In 1998, he was replaced as head of Minatom by Yevgeny Adamov, who came from the nuclear power community. Adamov's belief was that maintaining the defense sector depended on promoting conversion and commercial nuclear power–related exports. Under Adamov, conversion became a more serious pursuit.

---

72. Ministry of Atomic Energy of the Russian Federation, Department for Conversion of Atomic Industry (DCAI), "Major Results of Conversion in Defense Complex Enterprises of Minatom, Russia, in 1998–2001," 2002.

73. Bukharin, *Russia's Nuclear Complex: Surviving the End of the Cold War*, p. 19.

74. Ibid.

In 1998, Minatom undertook a second and more successful conversion effort with the announcement of the plan, "On Restructuring and Conversion of the Nuclear Weapons Complex in 1998–2000."[75] This plan called for spending $500 million on conversion efforts and another $500 million to restructure the complex.[76] In terms of restructuring, the goal was to end warhead assembly and disassembly at Sarov and Zarechny, end weapons work at one of the two plants that processed fissile material, and reduce the number of defense workers from 75,000 to 40,000 by 2005.[77] In the end, nuclear weapons work would be concentrated in five cities: Sarov, Snezhinsk, Lesnoy, Trekhgorny, and Ozersk. To complement this restructuring, Minatom formed the Department for Conversion of the Nuclear Industry in April 1999. The department selected conversion projects based upon a methodology developed by the Russian Ministry of Economy, which involved ranking projects in terms of job creation, job needs at the institute, cost, competitiveness, and other criteria.[78]

For its conversion program, the federal government eventually delivered about $136 million to Minatom, significantly less than promised.[79] Part of the problem was institutional battles at the federal level. In particular, the Ministry of Finance focused on Minatom's commercial potential, not its defense needs. It expected Minatom to use its commercial nuclear power activities to bring revenues into central government coffers.[80] As a result, sometimes the Ministry of Finance underfunded defense activities, because it assumed Minatom could make up the difference through commercial sales.[81]

Minatom tended to concentrate its conversion efforts in a few cities. Most funding went to the closed nuclear cities of Sarov, Snezhinsk, Trekhgorny, Lesnoy, and Zheleznogorsk.[82] Yet, with the exception of Zheleznogorsk, these were the cities slated to remain part of the defense complex; little conversion money went to places where defense work was to be terminated or significantly reduced. This suggests that Minatom was

---

75. This program was subsequently extended an additional year.

76. Bukharin, et. al., *Helping Russia Downsize its Nuclear Complex: A Focus on the Closed Nuclear Cities*, p. 11. This cost did not include replacing the nuclear reactors in Seversk and Zheleznogorsk, which, at the time, were scheduled to be replaced with non-plutonium-producing energy sources like fossil fuel power plants.

77. Bukharin, *Downsizing of Russia's Nuclear Warhead Production Infrastructure*, p. 17–18.

78. Bukharin, et. al., *Conversion and Job Creation in Russia's Closed Nuclear Cities*, p. 16.

79. Lev Ryabev, "Downsizing of the Nuclear Complex and Defense Conversion Programs"; and Anatoli S. Diakov, "Conversion of the Russian Nuclear Weapons Complex," presentation at the Conference on Helping Russia Down-Size its Nuclear Weapons Complex, Princeton N.J., March 14–15, 2000.

80. Igor Khripunov, "Russia's Minatom Struggles for Survival: Implications for U.S.-Russian Relations," *Security Dialogue*, Vol. 31, No. 1 (March 2000), pp. 55–69.

81. Ibid.

82. Yuriy Rumyantsev and Aleksey Kholodov, "Conversion Challenges in Russian Nuclear Cities," *Nonproliferation Review*, Vol. 10, Issue 3 (Fall–Winter 2003), p. 177.

still emphasizing preservation of the defense complex over providing jobs for excess workers.

Although the 1998 plan was more successful than earlier efforts, it fell short of expectations. The first phase was completed by the end of 2001, but the previous year Minatom had estimated that the task would take another 10–12 years and had asked for Western assistance to realize its goals sooner.[83] Moreover, Minatom had hoped to create 15,000 jobs by 2000, but its efforts yielded only an estimated 8,100.[84]

Beginning in 2002, Minatom's budget contained funding for a plan to restructure the complex through 2010. According to budget analysis by Peter Romashkin of the Institute of World Economy and International Relations (IMEMO) at the Russian Academy of Sciences, Minatom spent about $2 million on this effort in 2002, $1.7 million in 2003, $1.6 million in 2004, and $46 million in both 2005 and 2006.[85] Budget line items also suggest, however, that this funding ended in 2006 rather than 2010.

Minatom also provided subsidies and grants from the federal government to the budget of the ten closed administrative territories or "ZATOs" that make up the nuclear cities. Among other things, these monies went to development programs, capital investment, relocating the population, and to compensate for previous privileges that were no longer granted. In 2004, the total received by these ten cities was $187 million; in 2006, it had increased to almost $278 million.[86]

CONVERSION EFFORTS IN THE NUCLEAR CITIES

In addition to activities funded by Minatom, many institutes had their own conversion programs. Partially, the success of city conversion efforts can be explained by the social dynamics in the cities. Cities where there was a poor relationship between the city administration and the defense institute did worse; cities where there was close cooperation between the city administration, defense institute, and regional government authorities did better. It also mattered whether institutes saw weapons work as their future or their past. Conversion assistance from the federal govern-

---

83. With Western assistance, Minatom estimated it could meet its restructuring and conversion goals within five to seven years. Lev Ryabev, "Downsizing of the Nuclear Complex and Defense Conversion Programs"; and Alexander Antonov, "Comments," presentation at the Second International Working Group Meeting of the European Nuclear Cities Initiative, Brussels, Belgium, February 25–26, 2002.

84. Ministry of Atomic Energy of the Russian Federation, Department for Conversion of Atomic Industry (DCAI), "Major Results of Conversion in Defense Complex Enterprises of Minatom, Russia, in 1998-2001"; and Lev Ryabev, "Russia's Down-Sizing and Conversion Programs," presentation at the Sam Nunn/Bank of America Policy Forum, Atlanta, Georgia, March 26–27, 2001.

85. Peter Romashkin, "Analysis of Federal Budgets of the Russian Federation in the National Defense Section of Spending, Subsection of the Nuclear Weapons Complex," Institute of World Economy and International Relations (IMEMO), Moscow, May 25, 2006, p. 3–6.

86. These totals are based on information found in the Analytical Center for Non-Proliferation, "Quarterly Information Bulletin," Nos. 21, 22, 23, 25 and 26 (2004–2005), Sarov, Russia.

ment also played a key role. The cities of Sarov and Snezhinsk, which were more aggressive in their own conversion efforts, illustrate these differences.

Minatom institutes in the nuclear cities had the right to pursue commercial business arrangements with domestic and foreign partners, but they needed Minatom approval before any contracts were signed. This gave them considerable freedom of action. More important, starting in 1992, the Russian federal government gave the closed nuclear cities limited status as tax-free zones. This privilege was provided to all such closed administrative territories (ZATOs). Such cities were allowed to keep the taxes collected from companies doing business within their borders and use this money to support the city administration and social infrastructure. Starting in 1996, business growth was encouraged by giving ZATOs the right to offer limited tax breaks to businesses that relocated part of their operations within city boundaries. Some closed cities used this scheme to create successful investments; others used it to finance city government, infrastructure, or other social improvements. Frequently, however, businesses moved to the cities minimally or in name only and, as a result of this abuse, the scheme was cancelled in 2000. Sarov and Snezhinsk were allowed to share a total of $40 million in tax rebates for two more years, and the federal government allowed the remaining closed nuclear cities to share a one-time allocation of $80 million to make up for the loss in revenues.[87] Under this scheme, the cities created several thousand jobs.[88] But there were also setbacks. In particular, Novouralsk's spin-off construction company eventually had to lay off over 8,000 people, and one of the main projects in Zelenogorsk—a synthetic cotton plant—went bankrupt.[89]

Sarov was the most favored city in terms of conversion assistance from the federal government. Minatom channeled conversion dollars to Sarov and consistently gave it preferential treatment in terms of tax incentives and other benefits. Minatom's plans called for Sarov's weapons workforce to be reduced to 10,000–12,000.[90] As of 2000, there were approximately 16,000 employees, down from 25,000 in the 1980s.[91] In 2009, however, after several years of hiring new scientists, estimates put the number of workers closer to 20,000.[92] In 2000, however, such expansion was not expected; instead, it was estimated that jobs would be needed for 4,000–6,000 ex-

87. Bukharin, et. al., *Conversion and Job Creation in Russia's Closed Nuclear Cities*, p. 18.

88. Bukharin, "Appendix 1. Populations, Employment and Conversion in Russia's Closed Nuclear Cities," in Bukharin, et. al., *Conversion and Job Creation in Russia's Closed Nuclear Cities*, pp. 38–59.

89. Ibid., pp. 53, 55.

90. Presentations at "Downsizing Russia's Weapons Complex by Facilitating Economic Development in the Closed Nuclear Cities: New Opportunities for Nuclear Security Cooperation," Russian-American Nuclear Security Advisory Council (RANSAC), Moscow, April 7–11, 1998.

91. Bukharin, "Appendix 1: Downsizing Projections on a City-by-City Basis," in Bukharin, et. al., *Conversion and Job Creation in Russia's Closed Nuclear Cities*, p. 37.

92. Interview with former Russian program manager 1, July 1, 2009.

cess workers. To fill this need, VNIIEF and the Sarov city administration worked together closely but, in practice, this meant that city administrators took direction from the nuclear institute.[93] The city administration was made up largely of people who at one time worked at VNIIEF or the Avangard facility, and they facilitated close cooperation and good communication.[94] Further, the Nizhny Novgorod region, within which Sarov is located, was known for a more progressive style of leadership that embraced the transition to a market economy, encouraged interaction within the region and with the outside world, and fostered innovative thinking.[95]

In a pattern mirrored in conversion projects selected by Minatom and other closed cities, there were two types of conversion efforts. One effort focused on small businesses supplying consumer goods and services. For example, in Sarov people found jobs selling food and goods, making low-tech consumer goods, and manufacturing standard industrial and agricultural machinery.[96] Such efforts succeeded in creating jobs, although not necessarily for weapons scientists and engineers. The second approach focused on projects that involved interesting and demanding science, but with little regard for commercial potential or market demand. For example, VNIIEF set up for-profit divisions to commercialize technologies for use in the oil and gas industries and diamond production.[97] One enterprising group of scientists tried to market peaceful nuclear explosions in underground caverns as a way to destroy biological and chemical munitions and industrial waste.[98] Although these projects were scientifically interesting, few led to commercial jobs because their products either lacked markets or were not competitive.

One exception, which will be discussed in more detail in a later chapter, was a joint project between VNIIEF and the Intel computer company which had resulted in almost 500 jobs by 2004.[99] In 1992, VNIIEF signed an initial contract with Intel to provide software programming services. Initially, 40–50 people from VNIIEF's math division were involved in this

93. Interview with Nuclear Cities Initiative staffer 1, May 29, 2002.

94. Interview with Los Alamos National Laboratory staffer 1, May 21, 2002.

95. Ibid.; and interview with Sandia National Laboratory staffer 6, May 5, 2003. It is also fair to say that the cooperation between Sarov and the oblast was limited, and at times relations were confrontational. See Ivan Safranchuk, "Nuclear Regionalism in the Volga Federal Okrug; Nizhny Novgorod Oblast and the Closed City of Sarov," unpublished paper prepared for the workshop on "Russian 'Nuclear Regionalism' and Challenges for U.S. Nonproliferation Assistance Programs," sponsored by the Center for Nonproliferation Studies, Monterey Institute of International Studies, Monterey, Calif., April 5, 2002.

96. Analytical Center for Non-Proliferation, "An Overview of VNIIEF-STL Experiences," p. 13.

97. Presentations at "Downsizing Russia's Weapons Complex by Facilitating Economic Development in the Closed Nuclear Cities: New Opportunities for Nuclear Security Cooperation."

98. Analytical Center for Non-Proliferation, "An Overview of VNIIEF-STL Experiences," p. 13.

99. Ibid., p. 29.

pilot project; some of these people were employed for less than full-time so that more could work and thus receive income.[100] Further collaboration followed until 1996, when a disagreement over management issues and the structure of the company resulted in two collaborations: one based in Nizhny Novgorod and another which remains in Sarov.[101]

In 1997, Sarov established its own investment zone, using its tax-free status and ability to offer businesses tax breaks for relocating. This plan brought in much-needed revenues which were used to improve social services but also to create jobs. For example, in 2000, the city administration got an estimated $14 million from the investment zone and used the funds to create an estimated 1,200 jobs from 1998–2000.[102] In conjunction with VNIIEF, the city used some of this money for the Fund for Defense Conversion, which invested in high technology spin-off companies but also in small businesses. The Fund also helped local entrepreneurs get access to capital.[103] In contrast to earlier efforts that focused on technology-driven ideas, the fund allocated money on the basis of market analysis and business planning.[104] As of January 1, 2001, however, the investment zone was moribund because the city was no longer allowed to offer tax privileges.

Snezhinsk is home to VNIITF, which also does research and development for nuclear weapons. In the 1980s, VNIITF employed an estimated 15,000 in weapons work. In 2000, the workforce numbered 9,500; projected future employment was in the neighborhood of 7,000, although such reductions are unlikely to have taken place.[105] In contrast to Sarov, conversion at Snezhinsk started later and was much less successful.

VNIITF tried on numerous occasions to create new civilian jobs. In 1998, the focus was on producing medical tomographs, copy machines, and fiber-optic cable. These first efforts saw little success. According to Boris Vodologa, VNIITF's deputy director for conversion, the resulting products were too expensive for local markets, uncompetitive with goods from the West, and suffered from too little capital investment and market knowledge.[106] In 1999, VNIITF tried again by creating SPEKTR, a VNIITF-

---

100. Ibid., pp. 17–18.

101. Ibid.

102. Bukharin, et. al., *Conversion and Job Creation in Russia's Closed Nuclear Cities*, p. 17; and Bukharin, "Appendix 1: Populations, Employment and Conversion in Russia's Closed Nuclear Cities," in Bukharin, et. al., *Conversion and Job Creation in Russia's Closed Nuclear Cities*, p. 40.

103. Presentations at "Downsizing Russia's Weapons Complex by Facilitating Economic Development in the Closed Nuclear Cities: New Opportunities for Nuclear Security Cooperation."

104. Ibid.

105. Bukharin, "Appendix 2: Downsizing Projections on a City-by-City Basis," in Bukharin, et. al., *Conversion and Job Creation in Russia's Closed Nuclear Cities*, p. 39; and Presentations at "Downsizing Russia's Weapons Complex by Facilitating Economic Development in the Closed Nuclear Cities: New Opportunities for Nuclear Security Cooperation."

106. Presentations at "Downsizing Russia's Weapons Complex by Facilitating Economic Development in the Closed Nuclear Cities: New Opportunities for Nuclear Security

based company that was to commercialize products based on institute technology. Four hundred institute employees were ordered to transfer to SPEKTR, and the city administration provided some financial support. As of 2000, however, a lack of success forced most of SPEKTR's employees to return to VNIITF. A small group of 40–60 stayed, cut its ties to the defense institute, and was more successful on its own.[107] As of 2002, SPEKTR-Conversia had an estimated 80–100 employees and some small contracts in the areas of high-temperature ovens, LED stoplights, gemstone polishing, and explosives for use in the oil industry.[108]

Overall, the job creation experience was much less successful in Snezhinsk. Although part of Sarov's success can be explained by the greater economic activity of its region and a closer proximity to Moscow, there were other, perhaps more important factors. First and foremost, VNIITF never gave up the hope that it would return to its focus on defense work; indeed, it was scheduled for the fewest cutbacks from the federal government. Therefore, there was little incentive to pursue long-term conversion. Then, when defense budgets began to increase in 2000, VNIITF simply abandoned conversion all together. This bias against conversion was compounded by the poor working relationship between VNIITF and the city administration. In contrast to Sarov, where these groups worked together, the Snezhinsk mayor and city administration were more interested in conversion and commercial job creation than was VNIITF. In Snezhinsk, the relationship between the city and the nuclear weapons institute was one of conflict and little cooperation.[109] For example, the city lobbied for Western funding to establish a business training and development center that was actively opposed by VNIITF. The two disagreed on the management of SPEKTR, with the city withholding promised funding until ties were broken with the nuclear institute.[110] Further, the Snezhinsk regional government provided little assistance and tended to focus on business development in other areas.

CONVERSION ELSEWHERE IN THE MINATOM COMPLEX

Minatom institutes outside of the nuclear cities followed one of two paths to adapt to the end of the Cold War. Some institutes and facilities simply

---

Cooperation."

107. "Focus on Spektr-Conversia," *Transitions*, Vol. 1, Issue 2 (Fall 2002), p. 3; and Rumyantsev and Kholodov, "Conversion Challenges in Russian Nuclear Cities," p. 175.

108. "Focus on Spektr-Conversia," *Transitions*, p. 3; Department of Energy, Nuclear Cities Initiative, "Annual Report," fiscal year 2002, Washington, D.C.; Rumyantsev and Kholodov, "Conversion Challenges in Russian Nuclear Cities," p. 175; and interview with Lawrence Livermore National Laboratory staffer 11, April 7, 2003.

109. Interview with former Clinton administration official 2, May 21, 2002; interview with Los Alamos National Laboratory staffer 1, May 21, 2002; interview with Lawrence Livermore National Laboratory staffer 11, April 7, 2003; and interview with Nuclear Cities Initiative staffer 1, May 29, 2002.

110. Rumyantsev and Kholodov, "Conversion Challenges in Russian Nuclear Cities," p. 175.

waited for Minatom or the federal government to bail them out. As of 2008, many were still waiting and, for them, conversion will occur when workers get desperate enough to leave or when they die. Other institutes, especially those that were located outside of Moscow and whose work was less relevant to the nuclear weapons program, recognized that their services were probably no longer required. They valued and sought out cooperation with the West and, in particular, survived through research grants given by the Science Centers. Some workers lived from grant to grant. Other institutes tried to restructure their facilities to create technoparks in the hope of attracting research contracts from private companies or other government entities. In general, these technoparks met with little success. Local businesses had no money to invest, and the remote locations of these facilities made it hard to communicate with and encourage outside business contacts. Stories of corruption and lack of government accountability made Western businesses uneasy, and the state of most post-Soviet economies made substantial investment a bad risk.

Probably the most successful technopark was at the Kurchatov Institute. Aided in large part by its location in Moscow and a concentration of Western government funding, the Kurchatov Technopark got contracts for software development, environmental monitoring technologies, and other projects. It also ran an educational program, funded in part by the United States, that trained former nuclear weapons scientists to become software programmers and then helped find them jobs in the civilian computer industry.[111] Even here, however, the number of commercial-focused permanent jobs created by the park has been minimal.[112]

THE RUSSIAN NUCLEAR WEAPONS COMPLEX IN 2008

Compared to the Cold War period, Russia's nuclear weapons complex is much smaller and contains fewer redundant capabilities than the complex inherited from the Soviet Union. Many workers who were once part of that complex—industrial, construction, managerial—are gone. Outside of a handful of places, little is known about the fate of the numerous institutes and workers that did only tangentially relevant work or basic research. As for the nuclear complex, it is split more decisively into nuclear weapons and nuclear power–related activities, with the latter being a significant source of revenue.[113]

The new Russian nuclear weapons complex is largely concentrated in the cities of Sarov and Snezhinsk, which continue with weapons research, weapons design, and stockpile maintenance as their primary foci. Both

111. Interview with Kurchatov Institute staffer 1, August 1, 2002. In the first class they graduated seventeen people and helped find jobs for them all. Information is not available about other classes.

112. Ibid.

113. According to Khripunov, "Russia's Minatom Struggles for Survival: Implications for U.S.-Russian Relations," Minatom's nuclear power program has always been larger than its nuclear weapons program. For example, in the late 1980s, 25 percent of Minatom's operations were in the defense area and as of 2000 this was down to 10 percent.

facilities have been hiring new weapons scientists since 2006–2007. Ozersk has assumed responsibility for fissile material processing operations and making weapons components; Lesnoy makes warhead components; and Lesnoy and Trekhgorny assemble and disassemble warheads.[114] According to Oleg Bukharin's research, the work of the closed nuclear cities will be supplemented by the Institute of Automatics in Moscow, which will work on warhead design and engineering, non-nuclear components, and weapons maintenance instrumentation; the Institute of Impulse Technologies in Moscow, which will provide diagnostics for nuclear tests; the Institute of Measurement Systems in Nizhny Novgorod, which is responsible for the design of non-nuclear warhead components; the Design Bureau of Road Equipment in Mytischy, which will transport nuclear warheads and provide transportation and handling equipment; and the Urals Electromechanical Plant in Yekaterinburg, which will produce non-nuclear components for nuclear weapons.[115]

As of 2003, non-weapons work predominates at the five other closed nuclear cities. In Sarov, nuclear warhead assembly and disassembly work has ceased at Avanguard, and its approximately 3,500 employees have been transferred back to VNIIEF.[116] Zarechny is also out of the warhead assembly and disassembly business, and appears to have work only on the non-nuclear components of weapons.[117] Seversk, Novouralsk, and Zelenogorsk no longer do defense work, but have income due to nuclear fuel cycle services and blending down HEU under the HEU Purchase Agreement. Zheleznogorsk is also out of the weapons business, but provides spent fuel storage and reprocessing services.[118]

The fate of some 6,500–7,000 workers whose jobs were connected to Russia's last three plutonium producing reactors is unclear.[119] Two of those reactors, located in Seversk, shut down in August 2008 and the third, in Zheleznogorsk, was closed in 2010. Presumably, when the HEU Purchase Agreement is finished on or about 2013, there will be significantly less demand for workers in the cities that concentrate on HEU downblending work (Ozersk, Seversk, Zelenogorsk, and Novouralsk).[120] Because of the

---

114. Bukharin, et. al., *Helping Russia Downsize its Nuclear Complex: A Focus on the Closed Nuclear Cities*, pp. 40, 43, 45; and Podvig, *Consolidating Fissile Materials in Russia's Nuclear Complex*, p. 15.

115. Bukharin, *Russia's Nuclear Complex: Surviving the End of the Cold War*, p. 30.

116. Ibid., pp. 21–22; and Rumyantsev and Kholodov, "Conversion Challenges in Russian Nuclear Cities," p. 170.

117. Bukharin, *Russia's Nuclear Complex: Surviving the End of the Cold War*, pp. 21–22; Bukharin, et. al., *Helping Russia Downsize its Nuclear Complex: A Focus on the Closed Nuclear Cities*, p. 47; and Podvig, *Consolidating Fissile Materials in Russia's Nuclear Complex*, p. 16.

118. Bukharin, *Russia's Nuclear Complex: Surviving the End of the Cold War*, p. 20; and Bukharin, et. al., *Helping Russia Downsize its Nuclear Complex: A Focus on the Closed Nuclear Cities*, pp. 40–43.

119. Bukharin, "The Future of Russia's Plutonium Cities," p. 133.

120. According to an interview with Russian official 1 (January 23, 2009), Russia is unlikely to renew the HEU Purchase Agreement.

lack of defense work or alternative nuclear power–related employment, it would appear that Zarechny and Zheleznogorsk represent the most desperate places, along with those many institutes in open cities outside of Moscow that lost both defense-related work and federal money for basic research and development. Russia, however, continued to focus its conversion efforts on Sarov and Snezhinsk, with Zheleznogorsk receiving some, but significantly less, assistance.[121]

More downsizing was planned. The goal of Minatom's 1998 conversion plan was to cut 40,000 people, and this goal was reaffirmed in Russian statements in 2002–2003 about conversion plans for the nuclear complex.[122] But the deadline of 2005 came and went, and a significant number of these jobs and downsizing plans remained unrealized. Russia, instead, chose to concentrate on restructuring its nuclear power complex. It remained interested, however, in reducing the size of the nuclear weapons complex, partially in order to attract better workers by offering higher salaries and to retain a robust capability in weapons research and design in the absence of testing.[123] As of early 2009, downsizing was again a topic for discussion.

The Soviet Biological and Chemical Weapons Complexes

The Soviet Union had large biological weapons (BW) and chemical weapons (CW) complexes. Only the broad outlines of the fate of the Soviet biological weapons complex is understood; even less is known about the chemical complex. Partially, this is because of the dual-use nature of the biological and chemical weapons research, development, and production processes. Facilities with weapons relevance often have legitimate commercial or public uses. But secrecy and a lack of access to these facilities have created additional uncertainties. Some facilities are still off limits to the United States and Western collaborators, and others have opened up only slowly and on a piecemeal basis. The following section summarizes the available information about the Soviet BW and CW complexes and traces the fate of their workers.

The Soviet Union had robust BW and CW programs that included redundant facilities and the means to dramatically increase weapons production in the event of mobilization or war. In 1972, the Soviet Union signed the Biological and Toxin Weapons Convention, which prohibits any work on biological weapons that is not defensive in nature. However, in 1992, Yeltsin admitted that clandestine work on biological weapons had continued after that time, and he promised to dismantle all BW facilities

121. Presentations at "Downsizing Russia's Weapons Complex by Facilitating Economic Development in the Closed Nuclear Cities: New Opportunities for Nuclear Security Cooperation."

122. For details on the plan, see Rumyantsev and Kholodov, "Conversion Challenges in Russian Nuclear Cities," p. 174.

123. Interview with former Russian program manager 1, July 1, 2009; and *Atompressa*, interview of Ivan Kamenskikh, Deputy General Director, Rosatom, on the Future of the Russian Nuclear Complex, posted on http://www.atominfo.ru/news/air6252.htm.

in Russia. Because the Soviets had previously cheated under the Convention, and because Russia continues to refuse to grant the United States access to certain former BW facilities that fall under the jurisdiction of the Ministry of Defense, the United States has remained skeptical about Yeltsin's promise.

The Soviet BW program had three major components.[124] One part, consisting of four major microbiology facilities, fell under the jurisdiction of the Ministry of Defense (MOD) and remained under the Russian MOD as of 2008. The MOD's Main Directorate for Bio, Radiation, and Chemical Defense works on defensive capabilities and includes the Scientific Research Institute of Microbiology in Kirov, the Center of Military-Technical Programs of Biological Defense at Yekaterinburg, the Center for Virology at Sergiev Posad, and the Scientific Research Institute of Military Medicine in St. Petersburg. MOD facilities have remained off limits to foreigners and little is known about them.

The second and much larger part of the Soviet BW complex was a group of some 40–50 facilities that did civilian research, development, and production of human and animal medicines but also performed secret work, supervised by the MOD, on weaponization and advanced BW technology for the military. These facilities were known collectively as Biopreparat.[125] The most significant institutes in the Biopreparat complex were the State Scientific Center of Applied Microbiology at Obolensk, the Institute of Immunological Design at Lyubachany, and the Scientific Center of Virology and Biotechnology, or Vector, at Koltsovo near Novosibirsk.

The third part of the Soviet BW complex consisted of other institutes doing weapons-relevant work in the KGB, the Academy of Sciences, and the Ministries of Agriculture, Health, and Chemical Industry.[126] Plants

---

124. For a summary of Soviet and now Russian BW facilities, see Anthony Rimmington, "From Military to Industrial Complex? The Conversion of Biological Weapons' Facilities in the Russian Federation," *Contemporary Security Policy*, Vol. 17, No. 1 (April 1996), pp. 80–112; Amy E. Smithson, *Toxic Archipelago: Preventing Proliferation from the Former Soviet Chemical and Biological Weapons Complexes* (Washington, D.C.: The Henry L. Stimson Center, December 1999), p. 5–10; and Roger Roffey, Wilhelm Unge, Jenny Clevström and Kristina S. Westerdahl, *Support to Threat Reduction of the Russian Biological Weapons Legacy - Conversion, Biodefence and the Role of Biopreparat*, Swedish Defence Research Agency, FOI-R—0841—SE, April 2003.

125. Biopreparat was founded in 1973 as a spin off from the Ministry of Medium Machine Building. Its creation was in response to advances in genetic engineering, and it was to focus on molecular biology, genetics, and the development of advanced technologies for the military. For more information, see Roger Roffey, "The legacy of the former Soviet BW programme and need for enhanced support for redirecting to civilian commercial and R&D activities," Workshop on Building a Global Agenda for Bio-proliferation: Current Status and Future of Russian Biotechnology, Como, Italy, November 17–18, 2003; Jonathan B. Tucker, "Biological Weapons Proliferation from Russia: How Great a Threat?" Remarks at the Seventh Carnegie International Non-Proliferation Conference," Washington, D.C., January 11–12, 1999; and Testimony of Milton Leitenberg, Senior Fellow, Center for International and Security Studies, University of Maryland, U.S. Congress, Senate, Permanent Subcommittee on Investigations, Committee on Governmental Affairs, *Global Proliferation of Weapons of Mass Destruction,* Part I, 104th Cong, 1st Sess., S. Hrg. 104-422, October 31 and November 1, 1995, p. 295.

126. Jonathan B. Tucker and Kathleen M. Vogel, "Preventing the Proliferation of Chemical

for large-scale production and weaponization in wartime were located in Russia at Sergiev Posad, Kirov, Omutninsk, Kurgan, Bedsk, and at Stepnogorsk in Kazakhstan.[127] There were two additional small production facilities located at Pokrov, Russia, and Biocombinat in Almaty, Kazakhstan.

Those employed in the Soviet BW complex included scientists but also administrators, janitors, and a variety of specialties in between. Estimates of the total number of people employed range widely, from 15,000 to 65,000.[128] According to Milton Leitenberg, in 1994 the U.S. Defense Intelligence Agency produced an estimate of 6,500–25,000 BW-related workers.[129]

Estimates of those employed at civilian versus military facilities suggest that around 30,000–40,000 worked in Biopreparat facilities,[130] approximately 15,000 in the MOD,[131] and 15,000–25,000 in other institutes.[132] The number of top weaponeers is estimated at 7,000–9,000.[133] Similar to the nuclear cities, BW production and research sites were located in isolated areas, and the facilities were also the social, health, education, and leisure centers for their employees.[134]

---

and Biological Weapon Material and Know-How," *Nonproliferation Review*, Vol. 7, No. 1 (Spring 2000), p. 89.

127. Ibid.

128. For estimates of the size of the Soviet BW complex, see Smithson, *Toxic Archipelago*. Rimmington contains a higher estimate of 100,000 total employees. See Rimmington, "From Military to Industrial Complex? The Conversion of Biological Weapons' Facilities in the Russian Federation," p. 87. Lower estimates of around 15,000–20,000 can be found in Derek Averre, "From Co-Option to Cooperation: Reducing the Threat of Biological Agents and Weapons," in Robert J. Einhorn and Michele A. Flournoy, eds., *Protecting Against the Spread of Nuclear, Biological, and Chemical Weapons* (Washington, D.C.: Center for Strategic and International Studies, 2003), p. 42 and fn. 30; and Testimony of Milton Leitenberg, *Global Proliferation of Weapons of Mass Destruction*, p. 176.

129. Milton Leitenberg, "Biological Weapons Arms Control," Center for International and Security Studies at Maryland, October 25, 1995, reprinted in U.S. Congress, *Global Proliferation of Weapons of Mass Destruction*, p. 294, fn. 11.

130. Smithson, *Toxic Archipelago*, p. 9; and Jonathan B. Tucker, "Biological Weapons in the Former Soviet Union: An Interview with Dr. Kenneth Alibek," *Nonproliferation Review*, Vol. 6, No. 3 (Spring–Summer 1999), p. 5.

131. Ibid.

132. Ibid. According to the National Research Council, the total number of biological weapons experts in the Soviet program was 30,000–40,000. See National Research Council, Office for Central Europe and Eurasia, Committee on Prevention of Proliferation of Biological Weapons, *The Biological Threat Reduction Program of the Department of Defense: From Foreign Assistance to Sustainable Partnerships* (Washington, D.C.: National Academy Press, 2007), p. 16.

133. Roffey, "The legacy of the former Soviet BW programme"; and Smithson, *Toxic Archipelago*, p. 9.

134. Roger Roffey, "Need for enhanced support for threat reduction in the biological area for redirecting production facilities," Non-proliferation and Disarmament Cooperation Initiative (NDCI) Conference, London, March 4–5, 2004.

With respect to CW capabilities, Russia signed the 1992 Chemical Weapons Convention, which prohibits the development, production, and use of chemical weapons. Estimates of the number of Soviet chemical weapons production, testing, and research facilities range from 20 to 24.[135] The main CW enterprise was the State Union Scientific Research Institute of Organic Chemistry and Technology (GosNIIOKhT), which was located in Moscow. Russia inherited most of the Soviet Union's CW production facilities, key parts of which can be found in the cities of Chapayevsk, Kineshma, Shikhany, and Volgograd.[136] The CW complex was thought to employ at least 6,000, with over half of those considered to have critical weapons knowledge.[137]

The United States remains concerned that additional undeclared CW facilities exist and, because of the dual-use character of CW facilities, that some otherwise civilian chemical industries and institutions were also involved in weapons work. There are also concerns that post-Soviet states inherited CW-related facilities without realizing they once did weapons-relevant work.[138]

Workers in the BW and CW facilities, like those in the nuclear weapons complex, are thought to have suffered from low or no wages, with many people leaving the programs because of the collapse of government funding and no future in weapons-related work. There are no comprehensive statistics on this exodus from the BW and CW complexes; most of the data that do exist are about the BW complex. There are thought to be between twenty and fifty former biological weapons–related institutes, most of which are in Russia.[139] Thirty-three of these have remained federal research centers, with promises of future funding for civilian-related work. But even these centers have experienced low salaries, wage arrears, funding cuts, and personnel losses. Personnel cuts of 50 percent or more from 1990 to 1999 seem not to have been unusual.[140] For example, during

---

135. Jonathan B. Tucker and Kathleen M. Vogel, "Preventing the Proliferation of Chemical and Biological Weapon Materials and Know-How," p. 88; and Smithson, *Toxic Archipelago*, pp. 10–11.

136. Gulbarshyn Bozheyeva, "The Pavlodar Chemical Weapons Plant in Kazahkstan," *Nonproliferation Review*, Vol. 7, No. 2 (Summer 2000), p. 144, n. 1. Other production facilities located in Dzerzhinsk and Novocheboksarask are no longer as much of a concern due to their destruction. See Jonathan B. Tucker, "Viewpoint: Converting Former Soviet Chemical Weapons Plants," *Nonproliferation Review*, Vol. 4, No. 1 (Fall 1996), p. 79.

137. Smithson, *Toxic Archipelago*, pp. 11, 49.

138. Tucker and Vogel, "Preventing the Proliferation of Chemical and Biological Weapon Materials and Know-How," pp. 89–90.

139. General Accounting Office, *Biological Weapons: Efforts to Reduce Former Soviet Threat Offers Benefits, Poses New Risks*, Washington, D.C. (April 2000), p. 9. and Roffey, et. al., *Support to Threat Reduction of the Russian Biological Weapons Legacy*, p. 82.

140. For estimates of the personnel reductions at selected BW and CW facilities, see Smithson, *Toxic Archipelago*, p. 16. According to an investigation by the General Accounting Office (GAO) in 2000, the six institutes that the GAO visited claimed to have lost as much as half of their former workforce, but stated that they had let go administrative and technical support staff to try to retain their senior scientists. General Accounting Office, *Biological*

the 1990s, Vector lost 50 percent of its staff; Obolensk lost between one-half and two-thirds, including almost one-third of its top scientists.[141] Amy Smithson, then a senior associate at the Henry L. Stimson Center, has produced one of the more comprehensive analyses of the fate of the Soviet BW and CW complexes. According to her work, conditions in the BW and CW complexes seemed to mirror those in the nuclear cities:

> working conditions at the institutes became truly spartan. With economic circumstances so dire, one could enter a weapons institute as early as 1997 to find a scribbled message inviting the remaining staff "to pick potatoes on Thursday, when a truck will be available to transport them." In one Moscow-area facility, unpaid scientists worked through the winter of 1999 in unheated laboratories, with some equipment not functioning because the temperatures were below 50 degrees Fahrenheit.[142]

According to Smithson, in the mid-1990s, salaries in the former BW and CW complexes were on the order of $25–$50 per month;[143] by 1999 they ranged from $50–$70 for a technician or assistant to $200–$260 for a senior scientist or project manager.[144] Unlike in the nuclear weapons complex where, after the late 1990s, salaries tended to be higher than in the rest of Russia, workers in the former BW and CW complexes remained poorly paid. Moreover, there are some facilities that no longer receive government funding at all. According to one U.S.-based scientist who has worked with both Minatom and Biopreparat institutes, the Minatom facilities could at least pretend that weapons work would return in the future. This was not possible at Biopreparat, where many facilities were simply separated from the federal government and cut off from its funding.[145] Many institutes outside of Russia suffered a similar fate.

There are few data on conversion of the former Soviet BW complex, and even fewer about the CW complex. Conversion at both began in 1990, when Gorbachev started plans for some institutes to produce a range of

---

Weapons: Efforts to Reduce Former Soviet Threat Offers Benefits, Poses New Risks, p. 10.

141. Jonathan Tucker, "Biological Weapons Proliferation from Russia: How Great a Threat?"; Sergey V. Netesov and Lev S. Sandakhchiev, "The Contribution of International Collaboration to Strengthening Biosafety and Physical Security at Russian State Research Center of Virology and Biotechnology VECTOR," presentation at Workshop on Building a Global Agenda for Bio-proliferation: Current Status and Future of Russian Biotechnology, Como, Italy, November 17–18, 2003; and Derek Averre, "From Co-Option to Cooperation," p. 42 and fn. 30.

142. Smithson, *Toxic Archipelago*, pp. 16–17.

143. Ibid., p. 15.

144. Jonathan B. Tucker, "Bioweapons from Russia: Stemming the Flow," *Issues in Science and Technology* (Spring 1999) p. 35.

145. Interview with Pacific Northwest National Laboratory staffer 3, March 5, 2003.

antibiotics and vaccines.[146] In 1992, when Yeltsin announced the existence of the Soviet BW program, he also announced cuts of 30 percent in funding and 50 percent in personnel.[147] Biopreparat was moved from the MOD to Minzdravmedprom, which is shorthand for the Ministry of Health and the Medical Industry of the Russian Federation, and departments for conversion were created in both the MOD and Biopreparat.[148]

As with nuclear weapons institutes, early conversion projects sought to commercialize technology that had been developed as part of the weapons process. Biopreparat became a joint stock company with the purpose of spinning off converted facilities. And a new network of federal research centers, administered by the Russian Ministry of Science and Technology Policy, sought to turn Biopreparat facilities into 33 federal research centers that work on public health and related issues.[149] From 1999–2005, the Russian government had planned to spend 330 million rubles on conversion at selected Biopreparat facilities, but it is unclear how much of this money was actually delivered or what results were produced.[150] Where there has been success, it has largely been confined to producing vaccines, medicines, biotech products, and antibiotics for the domestic Russian market.[151] As of 2000, Biopreparat-associated facilities accounted for 30 percent of the Russian pharmaceutical market.[152] In particular, Vector has been very successful in this regard. In 1990, 78 percent of Vector's income was from the government, and 22 percent from other sources; in 2002, 10 percent of Vector's income was from the government, 72 percent from commercial activities and 18 percent from research funding through international cooperation.[153] Aside from these activities at Vector, however, most conversion efforts have been largely unsuccessful.[154]

---

146. Anthony Rimmington, "From Military to Industrial Complex," p. 81. According to Sergey Netesov, Vector started conversion in the late 1980s by focusing on pharmaceutical production. For example, Vector is the sole producer of Hepatitis A vaccine in Russia, and one of two producers of measles vaccine. However, even with this production, a significant percentage of funding for Vector comes from research grants from Western collaborative programs, particularly contracts from the ISTC and the Department of Defense. See Sergey Netesov, "Comments," at Workshop on Building a Global Agenda for Bio-Proliferation Prevention: Current Status and Future of Russian Biotechnology," Como, Italy, November 17–18, 2003.

147. Smithson, *Toxic Archipelago*, p. 7.

148. Rimmington, "From Military to Industrial Complex?" pp. 81, 88–89.

149. Ibid., p. 88.

150. Roffey, et. al., *Support to Threat Reduction of the Russian Biological Weapons Legacy*, pp. 115–118.

151. Vlad E. Genin, ed., *The Anatomy of Russian Defense Conversion* (Walnut Creek, Calif.: Vega Press, 2001), p. 475.

152. Roffey, et. al., *Support to Threat Reduction of the Russian Biological Weapons Legacy*, p. 81.

153. Tucker, "Biological Weapons Proliferation from Russia: How Great a Threat?"; and Netesov and Sandakhchiev, "The Contribution of International Collaboration to Strengthening Biosafety and Physical Security."

154. Roffey, et. al., *Support to Threat Reduction of the Russian Biological Weapons Legacy*, p. 60.

Unlike in the nuclear complex, where there are several examples of successful conversion activities that do not involve Western assistance, in the BW area, most of the discussion about conversion gives substantial credit to aid from abroad. The International Science and Technology Center (ISTC), for example, has concentrated on Vector and Obolensk; many smaller institutes, as well as facilities outside of Russia, continue to receive income only because of Western assistance.[155] Most U.S. funding, however, continues to go toward security upgrades rather than job creation activities.

Because of the lack of success at job creation, conversion efforts in the BW area have come to focus on the dismantlement of certain facilities and capabilities.[156] The Stepnogorsk BW production facility provides a good example that seems to illustrate a broader trend. Stepnogorsk, located in Kazakhstan, was composed of civilian facilities that focused on fighting plague and a military facility mainly tasked with the mass production of BW agents and, in particular, weaponized anthrax. It employed about 3,000 people in weapons-related activities at the end of the Cold War.[157] Soon after the Soviet Union collapsed, the Russian government closed down programs at Stepnogorsk, stopped government funding, and largely abandoned the site to the Kazakh government, which had only a limited understanding of the weapons work that had taken place there. Estimates are that 70–90 percent of the workforce, mostly ethnic Russians, returned to Russia.[158]

In the early 1990s, the Kazakh government tried several conversion efforts which were unsuccessful. One was to turn the Stepnogorsk complex into a much-needed national center for biotechnology and the production of pharmaceuticals.[159] Stepnogorsk was reorganized into a joint stock company called AO Biomedpreparat, and initial funding was provided by the Kazakhstan State Program on Conversion. Clean-up and maintenance of the buildings proved expensive, however, and these costs, combined with those for utilities, transportation, and salaries, meant that products were too expensive to be competitive in the local market.[160] In 1995, the government severely cut back on funding conversion at the facility.[161]

---

155. Ibid., p. 62.

156. Rimmington, "From Military to Industrial Complex?" p. 80.

157. Interview with State Department staffer 3, May 1, 2007.

158. Some workers apparently came back when they found no opportunities in Russia. See Sonia Ben Ouagrham and Kathleen M. Vogel, *Conversion at Stepnogorsk: What the Future Holds for Former Bioweapons Facilities*, Cornell University Peace Studies Program, Occasional Paper No. 28 (February 2003), p. 21.

159. The plan was to bring together all the former BW facilities in Kazakhstan. See Yerlan Kunakbayev, Gulbarshyn Bozheyeva, Dastan Yeleukenov, *Former Soviet Biological Weapons Facilities in Kazakhstan: Past, Present, and Future*, Center for Nonproliferation Studies, Monterey Institute of International Studies, Occasional Paper No. 1, 1999, p. 13.

160. Ibid., p. 14.

161. Ibid., p. 15.

This failure, plus the lack of success with earlier efforts, led to the belief that conversion at Stepnogorsk was not possible. U.S. government assistance came to focus on dismantlement, which was completed in 2007, and clean-up rather than new conversion projects. Since the mid-1990s, U.S. and Kazakh funds have been used to dismantle several buildings, including most of those that were previously devoted to weapons production. Although there have been U.S.-funded research contracts, the most successful of which led to the creation of an environmental monitoring center, there was no significant job creation.[162] As of 2007, about fifty scientists remained at Stepnogorsk.[163]

Conversion of CW enterprises was attempted under somewhat different conditions. According to the Chemical Weapons Convention, any former facilities that produced chemical weapons must be either destroyed, converted temporarily and then destroyed after ten years, or, in special cases and with the permission of the Organization for the Prohibition of Chemical Weapons, converted permanently to the production of goods and services that are not prohibited under the convention.[164] Although Russia undertook conversion efforts at a few facilities, the restrictions imposed by the Chemical Weapons Convention only added to the problems experienced at other WMD facilities. These included a Russian preference for conversion projects without considering their market potential, a lack of investment, and a hesitancy on the part of Western businesses to work with weapons facilities that either posed environmental and clean-up problems, or which carried the stigma of producing now-prohibited weapons.[165]

Missile Technology and Expertise

The former Soviet missile complex was a subset of the Soviet defense industry. Like the WMD complexes just discussed, the Soviet defense industry was based on the principles of redundancy and rapid mobilization. Therefore, there were oversized facilities, multiple places to perform the

162. Roffey, et. al., *Support to Threat Reduction of the Russian Biological Weapons Legacy.*

163. Interview with U.S. government official 1, April 9, 2007; interview with State Department staffer 3, May 1, 2007; and Kathleen Vogel, "Bioweapons Proliferation: Where Science Studies and Public Policy Collide," *Social Studies of Science*, Vol. 36, No. 5 (October 2006), pp. 667, 668.

164. Sonia Ben Ouagrham, "Conversion of Russian Chemical Weapons Production Facilities: Conflicts with the CWC," *Nonproliferation Review*, Vol. 7, No. 2 (Summer 2000), p. 46–47; Alexander Pikayev and Jonathan B. Tucker, eds., Monterey-Moscow Study Group Report, *Eliminating a Deadly Legacy of the Cold War: Overcoming Obstacles to Russian Chemical Disarmament* (Moscow: Committee on Critical Technologies and Nonproliferation, January 1998).

165. These problems are illustrated in Ben Ouagrham, "Conversion of Russian Chemical Weapons Production Facilities: Conflicts with the CWC," pp. 51–56, which looks at conversion efforts at the Khimprom chemical plant in Volgograd; and by Gulbarshyn Bozheyeva, who addresses conversion efforts at the Pavlodar Chemical Plant in Kazakhstan in "The Pavlodar Chemical Weapons Plant," pp. 136–145.

same function, and excess production capacity. Estimates of the size of the Soviet defense complex vary. According to John S. Earle and Ivan Komarov, most researchers put the number of Soviet defense enterprises at around 2,000, with an estimated 6–12 million employees.[166] Of these enterprises, approximately 1,200 were devoted to industrial production, and about 920–970 did research and development.[167] Some of these enterprises were devoted solely to military output, others had only civilian orders, and still others had a mix of both.[168]

Part of this complex consisted of approximately 70 "science cities," which revolved around institutes and facilities that were devoted to defense matters; some of these cities were ZATOs, like the closed nuclear cities. Similar to the nuclear cities, these ZATOs are located in isolated areas and often had very limited economic opportunities outside of government funding.

There were also sizeable defense facilities outside Russia; an estimated 75 percent of the Soviet missile industry was located elsewhere.[169] Ukraine, in particular, played a significant role in the Soviet military infrastructure and inherited 25 percent of its defense complex, including an estimated 2.7 million workers.[170] Many important missile facilities were located in Ukraine, including the largest and most significant ICBM development and production center, the Yuzmash complex in Dneepropetrovsk.[171]

Conversion of the defense complex began in the mid-1980s, when Gorbachev announced large reductions in military forces and spending. Even though the Soviet defense industry had always produced civilian goods, most of these early conversion efforts were impractical and unsuccessful.[172] The initial approach to conversion was to use the same

166. John S. Earle and Ivan Komarov, "Measuring Defense Conversion in Russian Industry," Center for International Security and Arms Control, Stanford University, September 1996, p. 6. Estimates vary because of both problems accessing information and differences in defining the people and enterprises to be included in the defense complex.

167. Teresa Pelton Johnson and Steven E. Miller, eds., *Russian Security after the Cold War: Seven Views from Moscow* (Washington, D.C.: Brassey's, 1994), p. 48; Earle and Komarov, "Measuring Defense Conversion in Russian Industry," p. 6; and Tarja Cronberg, *Transforming Russia: From a Military to a Peace Economy* (London: I.B. Tauris, 2003), p. 23.

168. According to Earle and Komarov, "Measuring Defense Conversion in Russian Industry," p. 7, about 50 percent of the defense complex was solely military, about 28 percent solely civilian, and the rest mixed.

169. Steven J. Zaloga, *The Kremlin's Nuclear Sword: The Rise and Fall of Russia's Strategic Nuclear Forces, 1945–2000* (Washington, D.C.: Smithsonian Institution Press, 2002), p. 220.

170. Perhaps more significantly, 40 percent of the total working population of Ukraine was employed by the Soviet defense industry. See Stacy Larsen, *An Overview of Defense Conversion in Ukraine*, Paper 9, Bonn International Center for Conversion (June 1997), p. 16.

171. Zaloga, *The Kremlin's Nuclear Sword*, p. 220.

172. In 1988, for example, civilian production accounted for 40 percent of defense industry production. See Kevin P. O'Prey, *A Farewell to Arms? Russia's Struggles with Defense Conversion* (New York: The Twentieth Century Fund Press, 1995), p. 29. In 1990, the defense complex produced 25.9 percent of all non-food consumer goods produced in the Soviet Union. See

top-down Soviet planning system whereby defense orders were executed; the system would simply be directed to convert to increased civilian production.[173] The plans even specified civilian production priorities. The other emphasis was on replacing state orders with foreign military sales.[174] The result of this initial conversion effort was that most defense enterprises produced more civilian goods than before, but there were few spin-offs and little conversion.

The next round of conversion focused more on moving enterprises away from the defense complex, and on making individual facilities responsible for their own fates. Under Yeltsin, the state's central planning role in conversion was eliminated. With the exception of a few hundred enterprises that were prohibited from converting, most were told to engage in quasi-independent activities and made responsible for their own conversion schemes and products.[175] The plan was to reduce the number of defense enterprises by one-third, with some becoming completely privatized and others assuming a dual state-private ownership.[176] Although there were conversion funds available from the state, these were given for individual projects and not as overall support.[177] For a short time, "new" enterprises were able to avoid both the market and restructuring by relying on traditional supplier connections and payment in promissory notes.[178] As expected, this type of conversion was not sustainable. This was reinforced by the hope that reform and economic troubles would simply go away and defense production would revert to previous levels.

In 1997, yet another attempt at conversion began. Similarly, the goal was to reduce the number of defense enterprises, but restructure the complex around a core of institutes that would remain devoted to defense production but also have commercial elements. The firms that were to be privatized would get some assistance from the state, but mostly in the form of business and market expertise, not financial assistance.[179] But in 2001, the plan seems to have changed. Under a defense conversion plan, announced by the Russian government in October 2001, the number of defense enterprises was to be further reduced to 600.[180] According to Vitaly

Johnson and Miller, *Russian Security after the Cold War: Seven Views from Moscow*, p. 45.

173. O'Prey, *A Farewell to Arms*, pp. 27–33; and Cronberg, *Transforming Russia*, p. 2. According to Cronberg, Yeltsin mandated that 474 enterprises would remain the property of the state and not be privatized. See Cronberg, p. 29.

174. *Russia's Defense Industry at the Turn of the Century*, Brief 17, Bonn International Center for Conversion (November 2000), p. 24.

175. O'Prey, *A Farewell to Arms?* pp. 32–40. Also Genin, *The Anatomy of Russian Defense Conversion*, p. 252.

176. *Russia's Defense Industry at the Turn of the Century*, p. 24.

177. O'Prey, *A Farewell to Arms?* p. 34.

178. Ibid., pp. 34–35.

179. *Russia's Defense Industry at the Turn of the Century*, p. 25.

180. Vitaly V. Shlykov, "The Economics of Defense in Russia and the Legacy of Structural Militarization," in Steven E. Miller and Dmitri Trenin, *The Russian Military* (Cambridge,

Shlykov, these 600 firms were to be restructured to include both research and production elements, and would be fully owned by the state.[181] The fate of workers in the remaining companies was uncertain, given that part of this new restructuring plan involved the transfer of all equipment and intellectual property to these 600 firms.[182]

The results of these successive conversion efforts have been sparse. Given uncertainty over the number of enterprises in the Soviet military-industrial complex, it is difficult to tell if there were significant reductions. Estimates of the number of defense-affiliated firms in Russia as of 1999–2000 ranged from 1,500 to 1,700, but by 2008 this had been reduced to 1,400.[183] The defense industry's share of civilian production declined but, within the defense industry, civilian production increased from 40 percent during the late 1980s to 60–80 percent by the mid-1990s.[184] Those facilities that were the most successful were production units, as opposed to research and design bureaus.[185] In particular, production units that pursued conversion through selling military technology and weapons abroad did better.[186] Similar to the nuclear and biological weapons complexes, those enterprises in closed cities fared worse and those near Moscow fared better.[187] Another commonality between weapons complexes is that the most frequent form of reduction was voluntary departure. People simply left.[188] From 1992 through 1999, the defense complex lost an average of

---

Mass.: The American Academy of Arts and Sciences and The MIT Press, 2004), p. 167.

181. Ibid.

182. Ibid.

183. *Russia's Defense Industry at the Turn of the Century*, p. 25; and Shlykov, "The Economics of Defense in Russia," p. 160. Shlykov claims that none of the 1,700 defense plants that Russian inherited in 1992 were closed (p. 177). In 2009, however, former defense minister Sergei Ivanov claimed that 1,400 enterprises existed, of which some forty were in "one company" towns that had little other form of employment. "Russia: Government Taking Action to Prevent Defense Industry Bankruptcies," *Rossiyskaya Gazeta*, March 8, 2009; and "Russia: S. Ivanov Details Benefits of Government Defense Procurement," *Rossiyskaya Gazeta*, February 27, 2009.

184. O'Prey, *A Farewell to Arms?* p. 29; *Russia's Defense Industry at the Turn of the Century*, p. 4; and Earle and Komarov, "Measuring Defense Conversion in Russian Industry," p. 7.

185. *Russia's Defense Industry at the Turn of the Century*, p. 29. This is because these units had something to sell and the profits, in turn, could be used for conversion. From 1995 through 1998, the number one source of conversion funding was profits from the enterprise itself. This funding was significantly more than that offered by the state. See *Russia's Defense Industry at the Turn of the Century*, p. 43.

186. See Victor Mizin, "Russia's Missile Industry and U.S. Nonproliferation Options," *Nonproliferation Review*, Vol. 5, No. 3 (Spring–Summer, 1998), p. 42, 18. Russian defense enterprises accounted for 80 percent of all Russian defense export revenue.

187. N.V. Zubarevich and A.G. Machrova, "Human Development and Intellectual Potential of Russia's Regions," in *Human Development Report for the Russian Federation, 2001* (United Nations Development Programme), p. 96.

188. According to Clifford Gaddy, many of the workers who seemed to leave voluntarily were perhaps forced out due to the social stigma of being laid off or fired. See Clifford G. Gaddy, *The Price of the Past: Russia's Struggle with the Legacy of a Militarized Economy* (Washington, D.C.: Brookings Institution Press, 1996), pp. 120–121.

15–20 percent of its personnel per year.[189] As of 2008, it is estimated that the Russian defense complex had approximately 1.5 million employees, down from a total of almost 8 million in the late 1980s.[190]

The defense industry, as of 2008, had not recovered its footing. In 2000, an estimated 40 percent of all defense enterprises were bankrupt and the rest were working at 15 percent of their capacity.[191] Under Putin, defense firms underwent a process of consolidation, and in 2000, a state-run export agency, Rosoboronexport, was created to coordinate arms sales abroad. Although such sales increased, there was no significant new investment in the defense industry and few increases in domestic Russian orders for conventional weapons. The 2008 economic downturn added problems. According to Sergei Chemezov of the Russian State Military-Industrial Commission, as of early 2009, one-third of the military-industrial complex was close to bankruptcy, and only one-third could be considered economically "stable."[192] Whereas in Soviet times defense workers tended to be paid more than their civilian counterparts, now the reverse was true. In 2004, for example, the average monthly wage in the arms production industry was 78 percent of the average industrial wage in Russia.[193] Vitaly V. Shlykov, who is an advisor to Russia's biggest engineering firm, wrote in 2004 that the notion of a Russian defense-industrial complex was "largely a myth"; Shlykov goes on to explain that rather than a government-funded and controlled set of enterprises, what existed was "essentially a loose collection of enterprises trying to survive on their own with very little state control or guidance."[194]

There has been little independent analysis of those enterprises devoted to missile technology. According to some estimates, 75 percent of the Soviet Union's missile industry was located outside of Russia, with significant facilities concentrated in Ukraine.[195] According to Victor Mizin, the Russian missile complex staff numbered close to 1 million, but this included employees ranging from support staff to scientists.[196] Other sources estimate that 40,000 were engaged in research and development within the Russian strategic missile program, and that Russia planned to lay off 8,000–10,000 of these workers in the future.[197] As of 2006–2007, wages in

---

189. *Russia's Defense Industry at the Turn of the Century*, p. 37.

190. Julian Cooper, "Appendix 9c. Developments in the Russian Arms Industry," *SIPRI Yearbook 2006, Armaments, Disarmament and International Security* (New York: Oxford University Press, 2006), p. 432; and "Russian Government Taking Action to Prevent Defense Industry Bankruptcies," *Rossiyskaya Gazeta*, March 8, 2009.

191. Bukharin, *Russia's Nuclear Complex: Surviving the End of the Cold War*, p. 6.

192. "Third of Arms Makers Face Bankruptcy," *St. Petersburg Times*, February 27, 2009.

193. Cooper, "Appendix 9c. Developments in the Russian Arms Industry," p. 432.

194. Shlykov, "The Economics of Defense in Russia," p. 173.

195. Zaloga, *The Kremlin's Nuclear Sword*, p. 220.

196. Mizin, "Russia's Missile Industry and U.S. Nonproliferation Options," p. 38.

197. *Russia's Defense Industry at the Turn of the Century*, p. 24.

the missile sector remained low, although experts disagreed on the size of the average salary. As part of his study of nuclear and missile experts, Valentin Tikhonov surveyed employees at the major missile enterprises in Russia. Based upon these surveys, Tikhonov reports that in 1999 the average salary among missile experts was about $50 a month, with wage delays of up to six months.[198] However, in an article published in 1998, Victor Mizin put the average monthly salary of missile workers at $150–$250.[199] Of those specialists surveyed by Tikhonov, 66–86 percent said they were worse off financially than before defense industry reforms and 79–92 percent said their financial situation was difficult or desperate.[200] The single exception was the Rocket and Space Corporation Energia in Korolev, a city close to Moscow, which had international contracts for work on the international space station and other activities.[201]

Proliferation?

It is clear that all former Soviet WMD institutes, and many missile and other conventional weapons facilities, faced trying times after the collapse of the Soviet Union. Most if not all workers suffered financially; the prestige associated with their work also plummeted. These circumstances persisted for many of these workers as late as 2008. However, to what extent did this situation lead to the proliferation of weapons expertise that was feared by the United States?

Evidence from surveys suggests room for concern about proliferation. In 2001, the Carnegie Endowment published a study by Valentin Tikhonov that looked at demographics and proliferation attitudes among nuclear weapons and missile experts.[202] Tikhonov surveyed 100 specialists working at each of the nuclear enterprises in the closed nuclear cities of Sarov, Snezhinsk, Seversk, Zarechny, and Trekhgorny, plus an additional fifty other former or potential employees.[203] Of those surveyed, 80 percent said that they would be willing to work in the military industry of a foreign country.[204] When asked about attitudes toward the emigration of their colleagues from Russia, 16 percent thought this was wrong, 21 percent envied or approved of those who had left, and 60 percent were neutral.[205] Tikhonov also reported that 60 percent of those surveyed were moonlight-

---

198. Tikhonov, *Russia's Nuclear and Missile Complex*, p. 13.

199. Mizin, "Russia's Missile Industry and U.S. Nonproliferation Options," p. 41. It is possible that this difference in salary can be explained by the 1998 devaluation and subsequent crash of the ruble.

200. Tikhonov, *Russia's Nuclear and Missile Complex*, p. 14.

201. Ibid., p. 13.

202. Ibid., p. 10.

203. For the specifics of his methodology, see ibid., p. 6.

204. Ibid., p. 10.

205. Ibid.

ing, and in most cases this additional income was the same or higher than salaries from the nuclear institutes.[206] Moreover, survey respondents estimated that the average monthly salary needed for "reasonable subsistence" was $160, yet the average monthly income of survey respondents was $43 per month and $74 per month for those with a second job.[207]

Tikhonov also surveyed 240 missile specialists from the cities of Miass, Votkinsk, and Korolev, each of which was home to a major missile-related enterprise.[208] Of those surveyed, 12–32 percent said they were willing to work abroad and of those, 5 percent are actually willing to take concrete action toward making this happen.[209] Twenty percent of the sample would be willing to work for another nation's military complex.[210] Salaries in the missile complex were considered low, and 28 percent of those surveyed moonlighted; an estimated 79–92 percent claimed their economic situation was difficult or desperate.[211]

In a 2005 article, Deborah Yarsike Ball and Theodore P. Gerber presented the results of a survey conducted in 2002–2003 of twenty former Soviet institutes that did both weapons and non-weapons–related research.[212] Of survey respondents, 18–24 percent would consider working in a "rogue" state, specified by the survey as either North Korea, Syria, Iran, or Iraq.[213] When asked specifically about WMD-related work, 10–15 percent found this acceptable; another 59 percent found possible dual-use work for a foreign company acceptable.[214]

Information about the actual proliferation of WMD experts from the former Soviet Union is sparse. It is certain that over the last two decades some former Soviet WMD experts have emigrated. Almost all have sought homes in the United States, Western Europe, or Israel.[215] There are anec-

---

206. Ibid., p. 9.

207. Ibid.

208. See ibid., pp. 6–7 for sample composition.

209. Ibid., p. 14. The percentage varies greatly by city.

210. Ibid.

211. Ibid., pp. 13–14.

212. For details, see Deborah Yarsike Ball and Theodore P. Gerber, "Russian Scientists and Rogue States," *International Security*, Vol. 29, No. 4 (Spring 2005), p. 59. The survey focused on scientists that had participated in projects through the International Science and Technology Center. It did not include nuclear weapons research institutes in the Rosatom (formerly Minatom) complex. Moreover, as the authors point out, the institutes surveyed were not those that were "exclusively committed to defense research," and this may limit the degree to which the survey results can be generalized to more weapons-centered places.

213. Ibid., p. 67. The survey did not specify that this work would necessarily be weapons-related. But, as the authors point out, in the case of some states it is fair to assume that weapons work was the concern.

214. Ibid., pp. 70–71. When asked about the acceptability of dual-use work for an otherwise unspecified authoritarian regime, 87 percent said this was not acceptable under any circumstances.

215. For example, according to a survey of missile experts in three Russian cities, of those

dotes about proliferation to "rogue" states, but the confirmed cases are very few. Obviously it is not possible to know how many cases have been overlooked or gone unreported, but it is clear that many of the initial fears about proliferation have not been realized.

Although Russia has consistently denied any brain drain on a large scale, there are confirmed cases of proliferation. Perhaps the most celebrated case is one that failed: in December 1992, some thirty Russian missile scientists from the Makeev Design Bureau, which makes Scud missiles, were stopped by Russian authorities en route to work in North Korea.[216] Other substantiated incidents include a report that in July 1998 the Russian government closed a training program for Iranian students at a St. Petersburg University on the grounds of national security,[217] and Russia's admission in 1998 that two firms that specialized in air-defense missiles sent employees to Iran.[218] The Russian government also officially cooperates with Iran by sharing expertise related to missiles and nuclear energy; the United States and Russia disagree as to whether this is dangerous knowledge proliferation.

If one moves into the area of unproven accusations, the list expands. In the late 1990s, the FSB accused two Russian missile enterprises (NPO Trud and NPO Polyas) of trying to sell missile engine parts and guidance components to Iran.[219] There are unsubstantiated reports of nuclear weapons–related personnel being approached by North Korea, and of some nuclear weapons or nuclear power experts working in Cuba, Iran, Iraq, Libya, Mexico, North Korea, South Korea, and Turkey.[220] In 1998, a

---

who have emigrated to other countries, 43 percent went to North America, 15 percent to Israel, 33 percent to Western Europe, and the rest to Australia and New Zealand. See Tikhonov, *Russia's Nuclear and Missile Complex*, p. 15.

216. See Mizin, "Russia's Missile Industry and U.S. Nonproliferation Options," p. 44. According to Dorothy S. Zinberg, *The Missing Link? Nuclear Proliferation and the International Mobility of Russian Nuclear Experts*, Research Paper No. 35, United Nations Institute for Disarmament Research (August 1995), pp. 12–13, other sources put the number of scientists at between 30 and 64. On January 27, 1994, a Japanese weekly reported that some 160 Russian nuclear scientists and missile experts had gone to work in North Korea and that North Korea developed two warheads with Russian assistance. There have been no independent confirmations of this, nor is this information widely cited.

217. Scott Parrish and Tamara Robinson, "Efforts to Strengthen Export Controls and Combat Illicit Trafficking and Brain Drain," *Nonproliferation Review*, Vol. 7, No. 1 (Spring 2000), p. 112.

218. According to Parrish and Robinson, the firms used falsified documents to get around travel restrictions for the employees; Ibid., p. 120.

219. Ibid., pp. 112–124. See also Mizin, "Russia's Missile Industry and U.S. Nonproliferation Options," p. 42.

220. Zinberg, *The Missing Link?* pp. 12–13; Zachary Davis, Warren H. Donnelly, *Nuclear Scientists of the Former Soviet Union: Nonproliferation Issues*, Congressional Research Service Issue Brief, March 20, 1992; and R. Adam Moody, "Report: Reexamining Brain Drain from the Former Soviet Union," *Nonproliferation Review*, Vol. 3, No. 3 (Spring–Summer 1996), p. 94. Scott Parrish and Tamara Robinson, "Efforts to Strengthen Export Controls," p. 120, mentions Chinese reports of missile experts from Ukraine helping with the 1998 North Korean test of a Taepodong missile.

VNIIEF employee was arrested for attempting to sell weapons design information to Iraq and Afghanistan, but it is unclear whether these documents related to nuclear or advanced conventional weapons.[221] Three chemical weapons experts are thought to have gone to Syria,[222] and it is rumored that the Aum Shinrikyo cult had visited the former Soviet Union looking for chemical weapons technology and may have gotten information about anthrax from Stepnogorsk in Kazakhstan.[223]

Two countries are often singled out for concern: Iran and China. Initially, the United States focused on Russian assistance to the Iranian nuclear power program and thus, on Iran's potential nuclear weapons efforts. In January 1995, Russia agreed to complete construction of a light-water nuclear reactor for Iran at Bushehr, a project that was originally started in 1974 in cooperation with a German firm. Since that time, exports of nuclear power–related equipment and rumors about additional exchanges of enrichment technology, nuclear reactor fuel, and training of nuclear energy specialists have raised proliferation concerns in the United States. Similar issues have been raised about Russian-Iranian cooperation with respect to missile technology.[224]

The United States began to focus on the connection between Iran, Russia, and biological weapons in 1997. According to the Government Accountability Office (then the General Accounting Office), Iran and other countries have attempted to get BW expertise and material from fifteen former Soviet institutes,[225] and multiple sources cite between five and "a number" of BW scientists who have an Iranian connection. Sources vary as to whether scientists actually went to Iran or were simply made offers to engage in what might have been weapons work.[226] Regardless of

---

221.   There is no discussion of whether these documents were significant or real. See Baker and Cutler, *A Report Card on the Department of Energy's Nonproliferation Programs with Russia*, p. vii, which claims the sale pertained to nuclear weapons design information. However, according to the Nuclear Threat Initiative, the sale was of advanced conventional weapons. See Nuclear Threat Initiative, "Russia: Sarov (Arzamas-16) Overview," http://www.nti.org/db/nisprofs/russia/weafacl/warhead/sarov.htm (accessed May 1, 2009).

222.   Tucker and Vogel, "Preventing the Proliferation of Chemical and Biological Weapon Materials and Know-How," p. 89.

223.   See, for example, Marilyn Chase, David S. Cloud, and John J. Fialka, "Soviet Germ Program is a Worry Once Again Amid Anthrax Scare," *Wall Street Journal*, October 15, 2001, p. A1; and Kathleen Vogel, "Viewpoint: Ensuring the Security of Russia's Chemical Weapons: A Lab-to-Lab Partnering Program," *Nonproliferation Review*, Vol. 6, No. 2 (Winter 1999), pp. 70–83.

224.   For details about accusations of Russian assistance to Iran's missile program, see Fred Wehling, "Russian Nuclear and Missile Exports to Iran," *Nonproliferation Review*, Vol. 6, No. 2 (Winter 1999), pp. 138–142.

225.   General Accounting Office, *Biological Weapons: Efforts to Reduce Former Soviet Threat Offers Benefits, Poses New Risks*, p. 14.

226.   Roffey, et. al, *Support to Threat Reduction of the Russian Biological Weapons Legacy*, p. 69; Chase, Cloud, and Fialka, "Soviet Germ Program is a Worry Once Again Amid Anthrax Scare"; and Jonathan B. Tucker, "Biological Weapons Proliferation from Russia: How Great a Threat?" Vogel, "Bioweapons Proliferation: Where Science Studies and Public Policy Collide," refers to a report that Iran recruited four scientists from the All-Russian Institute

the lack of publicly confirmed cases, both the Central Intelligence Agency and independent experts tend to agree that Russia has been an important source of biological weapons expertise for Iran.[227] It is important to remember, however, that many Russians may not consider this problematic in terms of national security because of Russia's past friendship with Iran and because of official cooperation between these countries in the biotech area.[228] For example, in 1997, the Russian Ministry of Science and Technology sponsored a biotech trade fair in Iran, and more than one hundred leading Russian biologists attended.[229]

Concern about China began in the early 1990s. Here the focus is mostly on nuclear experts. China is accused of recruiting between three experts and "on a large scale."[230] There are also reports that missile experts from Ukraine are helping supply MIRV technology for missiles.[231] Famously, when trying to motivate Congress to provide funding for Cooperative Threat Reduction in 1996, a Senate staffer claims to have obtained a flyer from China advertising the services of former Soviet experts:

> Perhaps the most shocking statement in the advertisement, though, is the following, where the company states, "We have detailed files of hundreds of former Soviet Union experts in the field of rocket, missile, and nuclear weapons. These weapons experts are willing to work in a country which needs their skills and can offer reasonable pay."[232]

There have been significantly fewer rumors since the mid-1990s. Moreover, as is the case with respect to Iran, there is no publicly confirmed evidence that China's WMD programs have benefited from former Soviet expertise.

---

of Phytopathology in Bolitsino who went to Iran on a "business trip" in 1997; see pp. 663, 683, and n. 12.

227. General Accounting Office, *Biological Weapons: Efforts to Reduce Former Soviet Threat Offers Benefits, Poses New Risks,* p. 14.

228. For example, the Russian Ministry of Science and Technology sponsored a biotech trade fare in Tehran, and more than 100 scientists from former BW institutes participated. Russia has also sold dual-use equipment to Iran. See Roffey, et. al., *Support to Threat Reduction of the Russian Biological Weapons Legacy,* p. 69.

229. Vogel, "Bioweapons Proliferation: Where Science Studies and Public Policy Collide," pp. 663, 683, and fn.12.

230. For estimates, see U.S. Congress, Office of Technology Assessment, *Proliferation and the Former Soviet Union,* OTA-ISS-605 (Washington, D.C.: Government Printing Office, September 1994), p. 67; John Fialka, "U.S. Fears China's Success in Skimming Cream of Weapons Experts from Russia," *Wall Street Journal,* October 14, 1993, p. 12; T.M. Cheung, "China's Buying Spree," *Far Eastern Economic Review,* July 8, 1993, p. 24; Parrish and Robinson, "Efforts to Strengthen Export Controls and Combat Illicit Trafficking and Brain Drain"; and Moody, "Report: Reexamining Brain Drain," p. 94.

231. Parrish and Robinson, "Efforts to Strengthen Export Controls," pp. 120–121.

232. U.S. Congress, *Global Proliferation of Weapons of Mass Destruction,* Part II, p. 139.

There are significantly more reports and rumors about the theft of weapons-related materials. There is also a bit of exaggeration. For example, many incidents involve nuclear material that is not useful for weapons purposes; in other cases, the amount of material is embellished. Because of common misunderstandings about the relevance of material for weapons, difficulties substantiating rumors, and the sensationalism that goes with stories of nuclear smuggling, it is often difficult to separate truth and fiction.

In 2002, two scholars attempted to do just that.[233] William C. Potter and Elena Sokova looked at ten years of reports of nuclear smuggling. With respect to the former Soviet Union, from 1992 to 1995 they found ten cases of nuclear smuggling, the majority of which involved material stolen by an employee of the facility who was acting alone and motivated by economic circumstances.[234] The authors could confirm no significant cases of smuggling from 1995 to 1998 and only a handful from 1998 to 2001.[235] According to their analysis, collectively these cases total approximately 370 grams of plutonium-239 and 40.5 kilograms of uranium, which had been enriched to varying degrees, not all of it bomb-quality.[236] Subsequent confirmed cases of smuggling from the former Soviet Union include the seizure of approximately 170 grams of highly-enriched uranium in 2003, another 100 grams of the same material in 2005, and 100 grams of weapons-grade material that a Russian was attempting to sell in Georgia in 2006.[237] The International Atomic Energy Agency (IAEA) assumes that 8 kilograms of plutonium and 25 kilograms of uranium-235, as highly-enriched uranium, would be needed to make a simple, first-generation nuclear weapon.[238]

Although cases of nuclear material smuggled from former Soviet states have declined, overall incidences of trafficking in nuclear and radiological material have increased. According to a December 2006 report from the Department of Homeland Security that was based on information from the IAEA, during the decade of the 1990s there were approximately 100 reports per year of trafficking in nuclear or radioactive materials worldwide. As of 2000, this had increased to 200–250 cases per

233. William C. Potter and Elena Sokova, "Illicit Nuclear Trafficking in the NIS: What's New? What's True?" *Nonproliferation Review*, Vol. 9, No. 2 (Summer 2002), pp. 112–120.

234. Ibid., p. 113.

235. Ibid. For comparison, see Lyudmila Zaitseva and Kevin Hand, "Nuclear Smuggling Chains," *American Behavioral Scientist*, Vol. 46, No. 6 (February 2003), pp. 822–844, which analyzes the Stanford Database on Nuclear Smuggling, Theft, and Orphan Radiation Sources (DSTO) and concludes that from 1991 to 2002 there are seven confirmed cases of the theft of weapons-usable fissile material.

236. Based on Potter and Sokova, "Illicit Nuclear Trafficking in the NIS," pp. 114–115.

237. Lawrence Scott Sheets and William J. Broad, "Smuggler's Plot Highlights Fear Over Uranium," *New York Times*, January 25, 2007, p. A1; and Justin Reed, "HEU Smuggling Sting Raises Security Concerns," *Arms Control Today*, March 2007.

238. International Atomic Energy Agency, *International Atomic Energy Agency Safeguards Glossary*, 2001 edition, International Nuclear Verification Series, No. 3, 2002, p. 19.

year.[239] These higher numbers were largely due to an increase in incidents involving radioactive materials, not nuclear materials useful for power plants or weapons. But the contrast with confirmed cases from the former Soviet Union has raised concerns that smuggling from this area has not declined but has simply been driven deeper underground, or perhaps now involves more sophisticated intermediaries and possibly also organized crime. Potter and Sokova, for example, note that since 1998, cases of nuclear smuggling are increasingly the result of actions by organized groups of employees rather than a single individual.[240]

Given these concerns, it is important to consider not just cases of nuclear smuggling, but also the process through which these cases are detected and reported. Unfortunately, this process is far from perfect. The "official" source for incidents about unauthorized transfers of nuclear materials is the IAEA, which maintains the Illicit Trafficking Database. This database, however, reports only those incidents that member states confirm and decide to make public. Moreover, the database has little authority for reconciling inconsistent reporting from member states.[241] Obviously, for reasons of national security and to avoid embarrassment, states have an incentive to underreport both the number of incidents and the material involved. For example, Friedrich Steinhauesler, a professor at the University of Salzburg, estimates that the database on nuclear trafficking that he maintains in conjunction with Stanford University (the Stanford Database on Nuclear Smuggling, Theft, and Orphan Radiation Sources, or DSTO) suggests that the IAEA's figures undercount the number of incidents by 100 percent.[242]

The unauthorized transfer of weapons expertise and services is tracked by two places. One is the Monterey Institute of International Studies, which relies mainly on media reports and does little to confirm cases. And, in late 2004, the IAEA established a division to track black market transactions in nuclear services.[243] An additional problem in documenting the proliferation of knowledge is that efforts tend to focus on the physical movement of weapons experts or the training of foreigners in key weapons-relevant specialties; it is obviously even more difficult to monitor exchanges over email. But there is anecdotal evidence that such transfers exist. For example, a 1995 article in *U.S. News and World Report* tells of a Russian physicist who solves ballistic missile problems for Iran

---

239.   Richard Willing, "Nuclear Traffic Doubles Since '90s," *USA Today*, December 26, 2006, p. 1.

240.   Potter and Sokova, "Illicit Nuclear Trafficking in the NIS," pp. 113, 116.

241.   For example, according to Potter and Sokova, "Illicit Nuclear Trafficking in the NIS," p. 117, Russia has made statements about incidents of nuclear smuggling that are inconsistent.

242.   Communication with Friedrich Steinhausler, February 22, 2007.

243.   This is the Nuclear Trade Analysis Unit (NUTRAN) in the IAEA Department of Safeguards.

over e-mail, originally because he needed money to buy a new notebook computer.[244]

This brief survey of the proliferation from the former Soviet Union yields several important conclusions. First, the feared mass exodus of weapons experts never occurred. For whatever reasons, most former Soviet WMD-related workers chose to endure economic hardships and uncertain futures, or seek alternative civilian employment at home rather than sell their professional skills abroad. Those experts that were interested in emigrating were predominantly interested in the West and Israel, not "rogue" states. However, most proven or alleged cases of knowledge proliferation date from 1994 or before. Trafficking in materials has also declined. This either means that there is less proliferation or that less proliferation is being detected. There is no agreement as to which is the answer. Survey data suggest that even if proliferation was not a problem from 1990 to 2008, a significant minority of weapons and weapons-related experts saw the sale of their expertise as a useful and proper means of increasing their income. Therefore, the potential for proliferation remained. And, given current detection schemes and their shortcomings, it is clear that confidence in detecting smuggling in materials or expertise is not warranted.

---

244. Alan Cooperman and Kyrill Belianinov, "Moonlighting by Modem in Russia. Hard-up Scientists Sell their Skills Abroad," *U.S. News and World Report*, April 17, 1995, pp. 45–48.

Chapter 3

The Domestic Political Context of Threat Reduction

U.S. fears about the proliferation of weapons of mass destruction (WMD) expertise date from the waning days of the Soviet Union in 1990. It was at this time that the U.S. government first became concerned about the security of Soviet WMD materials, experts, and the weapons themselves, an agenda which is frequently lumped together under the moniker of Cooperative Threat Reduction (CTR). To understand U.S. attempts to limit the proliferation of WMD expertise, it is necessary to understand the domestic U.S. political context in which CTR was negotiated and institutionalized. In this chapter, I provide that background.

The chapter begins by outlining the main disagreements about how the United States should respond to the collapse of the Soviet Union and the eventual political bargain that led to CTR. This debate centered on whether to view CTR as a defense program that worked to reduce threats and potential security problems faced by the United States, or whether such spending was really foreign assistance and done in the interest of charity rather than U.S. needs. Also included in this debate was the fate of the money that was expected to be saved due to the end of the Cold War military competition with the Soviets. Should this "peace dividend" be spent helping the Russians with pressing economic and social problems, or should it be targeted to domestic U.S. needs for jobs, training, and community development?

This debate matters because it was never firmly resolved. As the case studies in subsequent chapters show, programs that were less directly linked to reducing numbers of weapons, weapons delivery systems, or key WMD experts suffered from inconsistent political support. In turn, this insecurity constrained the ability of these efforts to implement policy and adapt over time in response to changes in the Soviet Union or to learn lessons from past experience.

The Defense Department was initially responsible in some way for all CTR and CTR-related activities, including scientist engagement and redirection efforts. Over time, however, CTR's core missions of WMD security, dismantlement, and destruction proved more politically popular than other tasks, especially programs aimed at defense conversion, job creation, and the engagement of former Soviet WMD experts. In 1996, the Defense Department finally succeeded in ridding itself of the parts of CTR that were considered more peripheral, less popular, and not properly part of defense spending. An agreement brokered with the State Department made it more fully responsible for the Science Centers; similarly, the Department of Energy got full responsibility for the Initiatives for Proliferation Prevention program, as well as other efforts involving the security of weapons-usable materials. Congress cancelled the Defense Conversion program. The politics and consequences of this splintering of CTR-related activities are also addressed here.

Regardless of which department managed CTR and CTR-related activities, a major influence on these programs has been the political backing and interest of the president. Therefore, this chapter also investigates the consequences of the initial reluctance of the first Bush administration to embrace CTR and how, despite early support from the Clinton administration, interest waned over time, in part due to challenges from a Republican-controlled Congress. In contrast, George W. Bush was initially skeptical of security cooperation with Russia but, partially at the insistence of Congress, his administration presided over increased spending in several areas. Although CTR programs continued or expanded, by 2005–2006, the Bush administration began to draw to a close many security assistance programs in Russia and, instead, offer such cooperation to states beyond those of the former Soviet Union.

Looking back over the political history of the CTR agenda, it becomes clear that policymakers shared certain assumptions about many of these programs. With respect to programs aimed at the proliferation of weapons knowledge, the congressional hearings and policy debates reveal a widely shared set of assumptions about why former Soviet experts might proliferate and how best to stop them. These assumptions, and their consequences, are explored in the penultimate section of this chapter.

The chapter concludes with a summary of how the dynamics of U.S. domestic politics influenced the CTR agenda. This, in turn, sets the stage for the case studies that follow.

Getting Started

In the late summer of 1991, concern about the fate of the Soviet nuclear arsenal caused two members of Congress, Senator Sam Nunn (D-Ga.) and Representative Les Aspin (D-Wisc.), to push for aid to the Soviet Union. Initially they failed. But the ensuing debate was a harbinger of the issues that would govern consideration of CTR, and it set the stage for passage of the Soviet Nuclear Threat Reduction Act in December 1991. This debate has its roots in the U.S. response to the collapse of the Soviet Union.

Soviet leader Mikhail Gorbachev's desire to restructure and strengthen the Soviet economy led him to seek a less confrontational relationship with the United States. Eventually, in combination with other factors, this resulted in the 1987 U.S.-Soviet treaty to eliminate intermediate range nuclear forces, which also produced opportunities for cooperation in other areas. One of the first to explore this new openness was Les Aspin, the chair of the House Armed Services Committee. Aspin led a congressional delegation on a visit to the Soviet Union, one result of which was an invitation to Marshal Sergey Akhromeyev, the former chief of the Soviet General Staff, to testify to Aspin's committee. Akhromeyev, along with officials from the Soviet Institute for the Study of the USA and Canada, took part in hearings on the U.S. defense budget in August 1989.

By early 1991, however, it was clear that Gorbachev had unleashed forces for change that were overpowering. When Soviet hard-liners attempted a coup against Gorbachev in August 1991, concern spread about the fate of democratic reforms. With the exception of President George H.W. Bush, who remained skeptical of the changes, many U.S. and European leaders began to discuss what the West should do in terms of humanitarian and other assistance to the Soviets.[1]

Soon after the coup, Senator Sam Nunn accepted an invitation to visit Moscow, where he met with Gorbachev and other Soviet leaders. This experience impressed upon Nunn the fragility of the Soviet economy and concerns about the safety and control of Soviet nuclear weapons.[2] Nunn left Moscow convinced that the United States should help in both areas.[3]

In late August 1991, Aspin announced a plan whereby $1 billion would be taken from the almost $300 billion defense budget and used to provide emergency humanitarian assistance to the Soviet Union. Soon thereafter, Aspin and Nunn joined forces. The result was a plan for humanitarian assistance and weapons security. The president would get authority to transfer up to $1 billion from the defense budget to provide humanitarian aid to the Soviet Union, and money would be made available for creation of a commission to make recommendations on how the Soviet Union could dismantle, convert, and retrain part of its military complex, especially its nuclear arsenal.[4] In lobbying for the aid, Aspin explained that the threats facing the United States had changed: "During the Cold War, the threat was deliberate Soviet attack; now the bigger threat seems to be chaos in a nation with 30,000 nuclear weapons."[5]

There were several reasons for taking funding from the defense budget. First was the need to find the money. In 1990, the Budget Enforcement Act had put caps on discretionary defense, foreign aid, and domestic spending. Any new spending in each category had to be offset

---

1. See, for example, R.W. Apple, Jr., "Soviet Turmoil; Even as Bush Counsels Prudence, West Seems Eager to Aid Soviets," *New York Times*, August 29, 1991, p. A1.

2. Sam Nunn and Richard Lugar, "The Nunn-Lugar Initiative: Cooperative Demilitarization of the Former Soviet Union," in Allan E. Goodman, ed., *The Diplomatic Record 1991–1993* (Boulder, Colo.: Westview, 1995), pp. 141–142.

3. Ibid.

4. Ibid., p. 143; and John Lancaster, "Defense Bill Includes Soviet Aid; Budget Conferees Design New Role for U.S. Military," *Washington Post*, November 2, 1991, p. A1.

5. Don Oberdorfer, "First Aid for Moscow: The Senate's Foreign Policy Rescue," *Washington Post*, December 1, 1991, p. C2.

by spending cuts. Further, the Act prohibited shifting funds between these categories until after fiscal year 1993. Second, supporters were convinced that aid to the Soviet Union rightly came from the defense budget because, as explained by Aspin, it was "defense by different means, but defense nevertheless."[6] Third, both Aspin and Nunn felt there was some urgency. The annual defense authorization bill had already been considered and was now in conference. To save the time required for separate legislation, Aspin and Nunn asked that their provision be included in that bill, despite that fact that it had not been formally considered by either house. In early November, the conference committee agreed.

At the time, the Aspin-Nunn measure was seen as part of a proposed "grand bargain" with the Soviet Union. In 1991, Graham Allison and Robert Blackwill proposed such a plan.[7] They called for the West to offer substantial financial grants and loans to the Soviet Union in exchange for reforms aimed at promoting democracy and a market economy. Aid would come in the form of a "bargain of Marshall Plan proportions"—quantified by the authors as $15–$20 billion in grants each year for three years.[8]

Opposition to the grand bargain arose on several fronts. One set of critics doubted whether U.S. or Western aid could really influence the outcome of events in the Soviet Union. For example, Representative Robert McEwen spoke for many when he argued that "all the money in all the wallets of all the taxpayers in America would never be enough to bail out a failed, centrally planned economy in the Soviet Union."[9] Others favored a "wait and see" attitude, arguing that it was safer to see how reforms would play out in the Soviet Union before providing any aid.[10]

Some questioned linking U.S. aid with support for Gorbachev. Former Reagan administration official Frank Gaffney, for example, argued that any money for reform would strengthen the old central authorities because they were still in positions of power.[11] In arguing against the Aspin-Nunn proposal, Gaffney explained that aid would eventually grow to become "undisciplined assistance to the Soviet central authorities" and would constitute a "slush fund" for Soviet leaders.[12] Others argued

---

6. Aspin is quoted in Adam Clymer, "Soviet Turmoil; U.S. Swords Into Plowshares for Soviets?" *New York Times*, August 29, 1991, p. A22.

7. Graham Allison and Robert Blackwill, "America's Stake in the Soviet Future," *Foreign Affairs*, Vol. 70, No. 3 (Summer 1991), pp. 77–97.

8. Ibid., pp. 95, 97.

9. U.S. Congress, *Congressional Record*, 102nd Cong., 1st sess., Vol. 137, No. 177, Part 3, p. H11496.

10. See, for example, Richard Wolf and Jessica Lee, "Lawmakers: Use Military Funds for Aid," *USA Today*, August 29, 1991, p. 4A.

11. Congressional Research Service, *The Future of Arms Control: New Opportunities*, report prepared for the House Committee on Foreign Affairs, 102nd Cong., 2nd sess., April 1992, p. 65.

12. Ibid., p. 67.

for aid, but only if given to democratically elected leaders in the Soviet republics.[13]

Another set of concerns revolved around using aid to leverage concessions from the Soviets. For example, some argued that U.S. assistance should come only in exchange for reductions in Soviet defense spending.[14] A 1991 article favored postponing assistance until the Soviet Union embraced key market reforms.[15] Senator Bill Bradley, a New Jersey Democrat, pressed his colleagues to link future agricultural credits to market, military, immigration, and other internal reforms.[16] Focusing on key ethnic minorities, Florida's Senator Dennis Deconcini argued that the United States should "keep its checkbook in its pocket" until the Soviet Union stopped human rights violations in Lithuania.[17]

Another point of contention was whether U.S. aid would free the Soviets to spend money in other areas. For example, Representative Dana Rohrabacher argued for forcing the Soviet Union to sell its gold, diamond, timber, and military assets "before taxing the American people out of theirs."[18] Others opposed helping the Soviets convert their military complex because doing so would only make their military more efficient and encourage them to compete with U.S. industries.[19]

Still others complained about process. By attaching the measure to a bill that was already in conference, it was not subject to the normal structures of debate in committee or on the floor of each chamber. This emphasis on proper process should not be underestimated. According to Jason Ellis, there was strong bipartisan support for aid, but members of Congress were concerned about protecting their turf.[20] Some objected to bypassing the committees, other committee chairs felt that aid fell within their jurisdiction. Still others said that the provision needed to come from the normal foreign assistance authorization process.[21]

---

13. U.S. Congress, *Congressional Record*, 102nd Cong., 1st sess., Vol. 137, No. 90, pp. H4356–H4357.

14. For example, Secretary of Defense Richard Cheney argued that the Soviets should reduce their nuclear arsenal and defense spending unilaterally before receiving U.S. aid. See U.S. Congress, *Congressional Record*, 102nd Cong., 1st sess., Vol. 137, No. 123, p. S12591. See also U.S. Congress, *Congressional Record*, 102nd Cong., 1st sess., Vol. 137, No. 124, p. E2972; and U.S. Congress, *Congressional Record*, 102nd Cong., 1st sess., Vol. 137, No. 176, p. S18001.

15. Editorial, "No bargain—Soviet request for American economic assistance in exchange for promised economic reforms," *National Review*, June 24, 1991.

16. U.S. Congress, *Congressional Record*, 102nd Cong., 1st sess., Vol. 137, No. 86, p. S7274.

17. U.S. Congress, *Congressional Record*, 102nd Cong., 1st sess., Vol. 137, No. 89, p. S7510.

18. U.S. Congress, *Congressional Record*, 102nd Cong., 1st sess., Vol. 137, No. 90, p. H4356.

19. U.S. Congress, Senate, Committee on Foreign Relations, *Soviet Crisis and the U.S. Interest: Future of the Soviet Military and Future of the Soviet Economy*, 102nd Cong., 1st sess., June 6, 19, 1991, S. Hrg. 102-283, p. 100.

20. Jason D. Ellis, *Defense by Other Means: The Politics of U.S.-NIS Threat Reduction and Nuclear Security Cooperation* (Westport, Conn.: Praeger, 2001), pp. 78–79.

21. Ibid.

The fatal event, however, was the election of Harris Wofford to Congress. Wofford, a Democrat from Pennsylvania, won a special election in November 1991 by running on a platform calling for national health care and "America first."[22] Wofford's campaign and victory sounded a cautionary note to those, including President Bush, who would be up for re-election in 1992. In arguing that the peace dividend should be spent at home and not overseas, Wofford's election put a damper not just on aid to the Soviet Union but on foreign aid across the board. According to Aspin, the Wofford victory was "an enormous buzz saw" that demolished their chances for success.[23] By discouraging spending on non-domestic issues, the election results reinforced the opposition of House Budget Committee Chair Leon Panetta, who opposed Aspin-Nunn because it threatened to unravel the budget agreement.[24]

Although the Aspin-Nunn measure was approved by the Senate Armed Services Committee, it was clear that it would face opposition on both the Senate floor and in the House. In an effort to save the measure, Aspin held a press conference, along with House Majority Leader Richard Gephardt and Lee Hamilton, the chair of the House Foreign Affairs Committee. They called on Bush to show support for the measure in order to save it.

Aspin and Nunn had worked with members of the Bush administration to develop their proposal, but no public support was forthcoming.[25] Although President Bush was largely silent, earlier he had gone on record in opposition to using the defense budget for helping the Soviets, claiming he would not sacrifice the U.S. defense effort until the outcome of reform was clearer.[26] Secretary of Defense Dick Cheney was more vocal. Skeptical of changes in the Soviet Union, initially Cheney labeled the Aspin-Nunn measure a "foolish proposal" and "serious mistake."[27] Later, he claimed not to be opposed as long as spending the money was discretionary.[28] Instead of supporting Aspin-Nunn, Bush joined British Prime Minister John Major in calling for large-scale financial aid in return for Soviet reductions

---

22. Wofford won the Senate seat formerly held by John Heinz, a Republican who was killed in a plane crash in May 1991.

23. U.S. Congress, House, Committee on Armed Services, *Potential Threats to American Security in the Post–Cold War Era*, 102nd Cong., 1st sess., December 10, 11, 13, 1991, p. 92.

24. Nunn and Lugar, "The Nunn-Lugar Initiative: Cooperative Demilitarization of the Former Soviet Union," p. 142.

25. According to Don Oberdorfer, Aspin worked closely with several members of the Bush administration, including Deputy Secretary of State Lawrence Eagleburger, Budget Director Richard Darman, National Security Advisor Brent Scowcroft, and Cheney. See Oberdorfer, "First Aid for Moscow."

26. Nunn and Lugar, "The Nunn-Lugar Initiative: Cooperative Demilitarization of the Former Soviet Union," p. 142.

27. John Lancaster and Barton Gellman, "Citing Soviet Strife, Cheney Resists Cuts; Possible Civil War, Famine Noted by Pentagon Chief," *Washington Post*, August 30, 1991, p. A1.

28. Helen Dewar, "Lawmakers Drop Aid For Soviets; Domestic Needs Turn Tide on Hill," *Washington Post*, November 14, 1991, p. A1.

in military spending.[29] Both leaders also called for IMF and World Bank assistance to Soviet republics to formulate economic reform plans.[30]

Faced with likely defeat and no support from the administration, Aspin and Nunn withdrew their measure from the defense authorization bill on November 13, 1991. However, less than a week later, mounting pressure to take some action resulted in Bush announcing $1.5 billion in food aid to the Soviet Union. Instead of taking the money from the defense budget, $1.25 billion of the package was in the form of loans for purchasing U.S. grain.[31] The rest was direct shipments of food and technical assistance.

But Nunn was determined to get more. Shortly after the failure of the Aspin-Nunn initiative, he joined forces with Senator Richard Lugar in another attempt to win approval for helping the Soviet Union. Although Nunn had been supportive of Aspin's humanitarian assistance package, his real concern was the safety of Soviet nuclear weapons. Lugar, who had been involved with arms control discussions with the Soviets for years, had similar concerns.[32] On November 21, 1991, a bipartisan group of sixteen senators met to hear Nunn and Lugar's pitch about providing aid to the Soviet Union.[33]

The Nunn-Lugar proposal called for $500 million to be made available from the defense budget for nuclear weapons security, dismantlement, and destruction in the Soviet Union. A separate proposal added another $200 million for humanitarian aid. The congressional appropriations committees cut each amount by $100 million. The resulting Soviet Nuclear Threat Reduction Act was approved by Congress as an attachment to the Treaty on Conventional Armed Forces in Europe (P.L. 102-228), the most expedient legislative vehicle available. President Bush signed it on December 12, 1991. The Soviet Union ceased to exist two weeks later.

The Soviet Nuclear Threat Reduction Act authorized the president, at his discretion, to transfer up to $400 million from Defense Department appropriations for fiscal year 1992. The money was to be used to help the Soviet Union destroy weapons and delivery systems in order to meet its treaty obligations, safely transport these weapons in connection with their destruction, and establish safeguards against proliferation. In the Act, Congress justifies this spending by noting that changes in the Soviet Union pose three dangers to U.S. security: new states may inherit Soviet nuclear weapons; nuclear weapons or their components may be stolen or sold; and nuclear weapons, components, or weapons expertise

29. Clifford Krauss, "Soviet Turmoil; Republics to Get Direct Aid in a New U.S.-Britain Plan," *New York Times*, August 30, 1991, p. A14.

30. Ann Devroy, "Bush: Defense Restructuring Possible; President Says Soviet Arsenal Appears Secure, Backs Non-Cash Aid," *Washington Post*, August 30, 1991, p. A1.

31. John E. Yang, "U.S. to Give Soviets New Food Aid; $1.5 Billion Package Will Go to Republics," *Washington Post*, November 19, 1991, p. A1.

32. Richard Lugar, "Foreword," in Ellis, *Defense by Other Means*, p. xii; and interview with congressional staffer 1, August 8, 2003.

33. Oberdorfer, "First Aid for Moscow."

may proliferate outside the Soviet Union.[34] Concern that political and economic instability might hurt the development of democracy also led Congress to authorize the additional transfer of up to $100 million in defense money for the airlift of food, medicine, and other humanitarian assistance to the Soviet Union.

But Congress did not give the president complete discretion.[35] Before any money could be spent, he had to make several "certifications" with respect to former Soviet republics. Each was required to make a "substantial investment" of its own in weapons destruction, forego military modernization that was beyond reasonable defense needs, not replace any destroyed weapons or use components or fissionable material from those weapons in new ones, be in compliance with all relevant arms control agreements, observe human rights and especially the protection of minorities, and help the United States verify the destruction of weapons to be carried out with funding from the Act. These certifications, which were added to appease congressional critics of the legislation, would prove to be problematic, especially in later years. Eventually, in 2007, Congress would eliminate these requirements.

In addition to adding certification requirements, the Soviet Nuclear Threat Reduction bill was changed in other ways, largely to meet concerns expressed by congressional Republicans. Of these changes, one—the "Buy American" provision—would prove significant for many CTR programs, including those aimed at the proliferation of expertise. The "Buy American" provision meant that whenever possible, CTR and CTR-related activities had to use U.S. technology, expertise, and businesses.[36]

Consider the following example. When the United States installed security monitors at Russian fissile material storage sites, it was often the case that such monitors had to be purchased from U.S. businesses and the work overseen and inspected by government contractors to insure against waste and fraud. Russia, however, was trying to develop and market its own monitors, partly to profit from their sales and partially to ensure access to replacement parts and technology. Insisting on U.S. products raised issues about profit and continuing dependence on the United States. Additionally, fissile material storage sites were highly sensitive national security assets. Demanding access for accountants and other non-technical personnel buttressed Russian concerns that the United States was actually

---

34. *Conventional Forces in Europe Treaty Implementation Act of 1991*, P.L. 102-228, December 12, 1991, Title II, Section 211.

35. For the impact of congressional restrictions on CTR overall, see Sharon K. Weiner, "The Evolution of Cooperative Threat Reduction," *Nonproliferation Review*, Vol. 16, No. 2 (July 2009), pp. 211–235.

36. This emphasis also extended to U.S. efforts to promote democratic and market reforms in Russia. From the early to mid-1990s, for example, the U.S. Agency for International Development's technical assistance program consisted almost exclusively of contracts to U.S. companies and non-governmental organizations to provide advice in Russia. Few Russian organizations or individuals benefited financially from this cooperation. See James M. Goldgeier and Michael McFaul, *Power and Purpose: U.S. Policy Toward Russia After the Cold War* (Washington, D.C.: Brookings Institution, 2003), p. 95.

spying. This was reinforced by the fact that stringent accounting and oversight regulations were usually lacking in Russia.

Some argued that the "conditions" should be waived because the national security benefits of CTR were more important than the objectives these conditions are intended to achieve. In other words, the security of nuclear weapons materials was more important than good bookkeeping. Such "Buy American" provisions persisted, however. In later years, the Clinton administration would feel similar pressure from Congress and private industry to orient non-security aid to the former Soviet Union so that it directed more money toward promoting the expansion of U.S. businesses, experts, and investments.[37] Although such "Buy American" requirements would eventually be relaxed for many CTR programs, they remained in place for some of the programs aimed at the proliferation of weapons expertise.

The Nunn-Lugar bill differed from the failed Aspin-Nunn measure in two important ways. First, and perhaps most significantly, the funds requested were cut in half. Second, there was no humanitarian assistance; this was provided for in a separate measure. There were also differences with respect to defense conversion, which were of little consequence at the time. Aspin-Nunn, while mostly humanitarian aid, also committed the United States over the longer term to help with defense conversion in the Soviet Union.[38] Nunn-Lugar said nothing on the subject.

According to Sam Nunn, the success of Nunn-Lugar was one of the biggest political turnarounds of his career in the Senate.[39] Coming barely one month after the defeat of the Aspin-Nunn measure, this change can be attributed to four factors. One, as discussed above, was the money.[40] Members of Congress were simply more willing to provide $500 million and to use that money to visibly reduce threats to the United States from Soviet nuclear weapons. They were less interested in winning post-Soviet hearts and minds through humanitarian assistance.

A second issue was internal congressional politics. Les Aspin was known for his willingness to tell other members of Congress what to do, not for his consensus-building skills.[41] He held no committee hearings on his $1 billion aid proposal. It is unclear if he even sought the advice

37. Doyle McManus, "Administration Reworks Russia Aid to Promote U.S. Business," *Los Angeles Times*, June 3, 1993, p. A4.

38. See Statement by Les Aspin, *Congressional Record*, 102nd Cong., 1st sess., Vol. 137, No. 168, November 14, 1991, E3835.

39. Helen Dewar, "The Senate's New Alliance: Nunn and Lugar; Lawmakers Choose Partnership over Partisanship and Score Success in Breaking Aid Logjam," *Washington Post*, March 7, 1993, p. A11.

40. Interview with congressional staffer 1, August 8, 2003; interview with congressional staffer 2, August 4, 2003; and interview with former Clinton administration official 1, September 17, 2003.

41. In 1987, Aspin lost the chairmanship of the House Armed Services Committee, partly due to his lack of consideration for the viewpoints of other members.

of other committee members.[42] Nunn and Lugar, in contrast, worked to convince other members of Congress and to build support for their proposal.[43] They hosted briefing sessions and bipartisan meetings, including some with important Soviet officials.

At these briefings, the results of an important study were presented. *Soviet Nuclear Fission*, which analyzed nuclear weapons security in the former Soviet Union, was produced by members of Harvard University's John F. Kennedy School of Government in 1991.[44] Later, this would be complemented by a study of the Soviet military-industrial complex and its relationship to economic growth and transformation. This analysis was produced by a group at the Center for International Security and Cooperation (CISAC) at Stanford.[45] Both studies received financial support from the Carnegie Corporation of New York and involved academics who would go on to implement CTR as officials in the Clinton administration.

Soviet Nuclear Fission was important because it highlighted the dangers the United States might face if the Soviet Union collapsed, and provided an analysis of what could reasonably be done in response.[46] The study highlighted three main risks: new nuclear powers in the form of post-Soviet states; the loss or theft of nuclear weapons; and proliferation due to the spread of fissionable materials and scientific expertise.[47] The CISAC study, which came later, focused more specifically on defense conversion in the former Soviet Union.[48] It argued that Soviet WMD scientists, faced with deteriorating standards of living and potential unemployment, were a proliferation risk. This risk could be mitigated by encouraging Western commercial businesses to partner with Soviet defense enterprises to create spin-offs. According to the CISAC study, such cooperation would promote economic reform overall, which in turn would enhance political reform and stability. It would also lower the pressure for Soviet

---

42.   Interview with congressional staffer 2, August 4, 2003.

43.   Ibid.

44.   Kurt M. Campbell, Ashton B. Carter, Steven E. Miller, and Charles A. Zraket, *Soviet Nuclear Fission* (Cambridge, Mass.: Center for Science and International Affairs, Harvard University, November 1991). Aspin credits Graham Allison and Ashton Carter for helping to save aid to the former Soviet Union. See U.S. Congress, *Potential Threats to American Security*, p. 120.

45.   David Bernstein and William J. Perry, "Defense Conversion in Russia: A Strategic Imperative," *Stanford Journal of International Affairs*, Vol. 2, No. 2 (Summer 1993).

46.   For the importance of this study in the thinking of Nunn and Lugar, see Richard Combs, "U.S. Domestic Politics and the Nunn-Lugar Program," in John M. Shields and William C. Potter, eds., *Dismantling the Cold War: U.S. and NIS Perspectives on the Nunn-Lugar Cooperative Threat Reduction Program* (Cambridge, Mass.: MIT Press, 1997), p. 43; Jess Hobart, "Gore Launches Inaugural Symposium of Belfer Center," *Harvard Gazette*, November 6, 1997; and Helen Dewar, "The Senate's New Alliance." This is also reinforced by comments from interview with congressional staffer 3, August 12, 2003.

47.   Congress considers these risks in U.S. Congress, *Potential Threats to American Security*, p. 124–125.

48.   Bernstein and Perry, *Defense Conversion in Russia: A Strategic Imperative*.

firms to make money by exporting arms and services, and would increase transparency at Soviet defense enterprises.[49] This study would form the basis of CTR's defense conversion efforts.

The fourth reason for the success of Nunn-Lugar was the increasing alarm coming from the Soviet Union. Shortly after the Aspin-Nunn measure was dropped, advisers to Gorbachev and other officials came to Washington, D.C., and raised concerns about Gorbachev's hold on power and the fate of Soviet nuclear weapons should he be deposed.[50] Earlier, members of the Senate had met with Viktor Mikhailov, the Soviet Deputy Minister for Atomic Energy. In a rare display of candor, Mikhailov asked for U.S. help in storing and dismantling Soviet tactical nuclear weapons and intimated that some of those weapons might be missing.[51]

THE BUSH RESPONSE

As Gorbachev was struggling with market and government reforms in the Soviet Union, the Bush administration did little besides offer advice. Leon Sigal chronicles the administration's lack of concrete support for what were, in terms of U.S. interests, quite positive developments in the Soviet Union.[52] There was little material support from the United States for German reunification; Bush convinced the G7 to exclude the Soviet Union from an upcoming summit; U.S. Cold War restrictions on trade, investment, and technology transfer remained in place. Moreover, Sigal explains that the United States treated the Soviet Union as a weakened enemy rather than a potential ally. Instead of mutually beneficial changes in conventional and nuclear weapons policies, the United States pressed for maximum advantage in terms of conventional force reductions in Eastern Europe, nuclear weapons reductions, and NATO expansion.[53] This hard line, in turn, limited Gorbachev's ability to undertake reform by reinforcing concerns among Communist party leaders that the United States was bent on destroying the Soviet Union.

In a slightly more sympathetic account, James M. Goldgeier and Michael McFaul argue that Bush's inaction can best be understood as the result of concern for global stability and U.S. security after the Cold War.[54] Rather than seek to influence changes within the Soviet Union, which Bush thought were a matter for the Soviets themselves, he instead sought to react to any changes in a way that would preserve the U.S. position as the world's sole superpower. By concentrating on the global balance of power, Bush missed key opportunities to encourage government and

---

49. Ibid., p. 130.

50. Oberdorfer, "First Aid for Moscow."

51. Ibid.

52. Leon V. Sigal, *Hang Separately: Cooperative Security between the United States and Russia, 1985–1994* (New York: The Century Foundation Press, 2000).

53. For examples, see ibid., pp. 81, 268, 290.

54. Goldgeier and McFaul, *Power and Purpose*, pp. 9–10.

economic reforms in the Soviet Union. Were it not for the aggressive lobbying of Secretary of State James Baker, the administration might also have opted out of CTR.[55]

The Soviet Nuclear Threat Reduction Act was initially greeted with little support from the Bush administration. Bush himself was not openly skeptical, and eventually accepted the idea of helping the Soviet Union once assured that he would have some discretion over the funding. Secretary of Defense Dick Cheney, as noted above, was openly critical of the Act. He remained unconvinced that changes in the Soviet Union, and later, Russia, were positive, or that the United States should provide aid. Other members of the administration were hesitant to work with Russia because of Boris Yeltsin, who was elected president of Russia in June 1991, and whom some considered a "demagogue."[56] As a result, the Bush administration made no move to spend the $500 million over which the Act gave them discretion.

Bush faced resounding criticism for his lack of action, both in implementing CTR and in supporting democracy and market reform. Some was expected. For example, Congressman Aspin complained that if Bush had spoken up, they would have gotten $1 billion instead of half of that amount.[57] Other criticism came from more unexpected sources. Jack Matlock, Bush's own ambassador to the Soviet Union, pushed for more active engagement, as did his successor, Robert Strauss, who was quite vocal in his disappointment with the administration's inaction.[58] Particularly pointed were statements from former President Richard Nixon. Using editorials and other statements, Nixon accused Bush of taking a "penny-ante" approach to the Soviet Union and warned him that history would identify him as the man who "lost Russia."[59]

Throughout the remainder of the Bush administration, CTR would languish without support from the executive branch. Rather than active resistance to the measure, it was more the case that the administration simply did not provide the cooperation necessary to insure timely implementation. There was little pressure on the Pentagon to reprogram money for CTR measures. The necessary presidential certifications required before CTR money could be spent in Russia were not forthcoming. Months went by with no money provided for implementing CTR. As explained by one former congressional staffer, the Bush administration treated CTR as a congressional initiative that would be tolerated but not enthusiastically

---

55. Ibid., p. 42.

56. Doyle McManus, "Baker Opens Fact-Finding Soviet Visit," *Los Angeles Times*, September 11, 1991, p. A6.

57. U.S. Congress, *Potential Threats to American Security*, p. 101.

58. See, for example, Robert Strauss's testimony in U.S. Congress, *Potential Threats to American Security*, pp. 89–92, 93.

59. Carroll Bogert and Margaret Garrard Warner, "The 'Who Lost Russia' Debate," *Newsweek*, March 23, 1992, p. 37; and Richard Nixon, "The Challenge We Face in Russia," *Wall Street Journal*, March 11, 1992, p. A14.

embraced.[60] With the exception of Secretary of State James Baker's efforts to establish the Science Centers, this lack of attention would not change until the election of Bill Clinton and his appointment to the Pentagon of some of CTR's strongest supporters.

INSTITUTIONALIZING CTR

In October 1992, the defense authorization bill for fiscal year 1993 included a reauthorization of Nunn-Lugar. In the form of the Former Soviet Union Demilitarization Act, Congress gave the president an additional $400 million in transfer authority from Defense Department funds. This Act differed from the 1991 Nunn-Lugar provision in that in addition to funding the transportation, storage, safeguarding, and destruction of nuclear and other weapons, it called for attention to the potential proliferation of weapons-related expertise, defense conversion, and military-to-military contacts between the United States and states of the former Soviet Union, as well as the creation of the Science Centers.[61]

The Act set spending limits on several individual items, including defense conversion. Although the conference report expresses confidence in the need to help with the demilitarization of former Soviet defense industries, the Act specifies that no more than $40 million can be spent on conversion and that, to the extent possible, the U.S. private sector should be involved in this effort.[62] The conference report explains that part of the reason for setting this limit was concern about the size and potential for inefficiency in such an effort.[63] Advanced notification of any conversion projects was also required.

The fiscal year 1994 defense budget introduced the term "Cooperative Threat Reduction" and created a Demilitarization Enterprise Fund (DEF) to make grants and loans to defense conversion projects. Funding for DEF was capped at $40 million.[64] Perhaps most importantly, for the first time CTR was given new money and no longer had to rely on transfers of funds between Defense Department accounts.[65]

Subsequent aid for WMD security and destruction, plus other related activities, have been considered as part of the annual defense budget process in every year since. In each year, the Defense Department's budget for

---

60. Interview with congressional staffer 3, August 12, 2003.

61. Title XIV, "Demilitarization of the Former Soviet Union," U.S. Congress, House, Committee on Armed Services, *National Defense Authorization Act for FY 1993*, Part 1, 102nd Cong., 2nd sess., October 1, 1992, H. Rpt. 102-966.

62. Ibid., pp. 782–783.

63. Ibid., p. 783.

64. U.S. Congress, House, Committee on Armed Services, *National Defense Authorization Act for Fiscal Year 1994*, 103rd Cong., 1st sess., November 10, 1993, H. Rpt. 103-357, Title XII, Cooperative Threat Reduction with the States of the Former Soviet Union, Sections Title XII 1204 and 1205.

65. According to interview with congressional staffer 3, August 12, 2003, CTR initially was not given its own budget line item due to concern that this would prompt additional resistance from the Bush administration.

CTR has remained around $400 million, a figure which was arbitrary in the first place.[66] CTR programs, however, grew significantly over time. As explained in more detail below, in 1996, CTR-related activities were split between the Departments of Defense, Energy, and State. Ten years later, the combined budgets for these programs was approximately $1.1 billion a year.

THE FREEDOM SUPPORT ACT AND THE SCIENCE CENTERS

Less than two months after Congress agreed to the Soviet Nuclear Threat Reduction Act, another initiative was announced. On February 17, 1992, during a trip to Russia, Secretary of State James Baker announced plans to create a multinational center for collaborative scientific research in Moscow in order to foster and manage cooperation between former Soviet WMD specialists and Western experts. By offering interesting non-weapons research, the goal was to engage former Soviet specialists temporarily, provide them with some income, and hopefully help them establish the skills and contacts needed to find permanent reemployment in the future.

Although Baker made his announcement in 1992, the idea of creating a science center seems to have been discussed in different places the previous year; it is unclear who originally formulated the plan. In 1991, German Foreign Minister Hans-Dietrich Genscher proposed an international program to provide financial support to weapons scientists.[67] This general idea seems to have been discussed in Europe for several years, but Genscher's proposal raised it to a more serious level.[68] In December 1991, the *Los Angeles Times* reported that the Bush administration was developing a plan to employ scientists.[69] Russian Foreign Minister Andrei Kozyrev is also thought to have discussed similar ideas in a November 1991 visit to Washington, D.C., and in a January 1992 meeting with Genscher.[70]

Regardless of where the plan originated, by early 1992, the United States, Germany, and Russia were discussing it seriously. Then, in February 1992, Baker visited Russia and made a side trip to Snezhinsk, a closed city that was home to one of the main Soviet nuclear weapons research and design institutes. There he met nuclear weapons scientists who were

66. Sarah Mendelson, *Domestic Politics and America's Russia Policy*, The Century Foundation and The Stanley Foundation, October 2002, pp. 24–25.

67. Office of International Affairs, National Research Council, *An Assessment of the International Science and Technology Center: Redirecting Expertise in Weapons of Mass Destruction in the Former Soviet Union* (Washington, D.C.: National Academy Press, 1996), pp. 5–6.

68. According to Glenn Schweitzer, *Moscow DMZ: The Story of the International Effort to Convert Russian Weapons* (Armonk, N.Y.: M.E. Sharpe, 1996), p. 18, the director of the Kurchatov Institute, which specializes in nuclear energy research, claims that several years earlier he started similar cooperation through a secretariat in Switzerland.

69. John M. Broder and Doyle McManus, "U.S. Gives Soviets Proposals to Block Nuclear Exports," *Los Angeles Times*, December 14, 1991, p. A10.

70. R. Adam Moody, "The International Science Center Initiative," in Shields and Potter, eds., *Dismantling the Cold War*, p. 260.

eager to turn their talents toward other work but who lacked the financing to do so. The next day, Baker and Yeltsin announced plans to create a science center. Eventually two centers were set up, one in Moscow and the other in Kiev.[71]

Funding and direction for the Science Centers came from the Freedom Support Act (FSA). Officially the Freedom for Russia and Emerging Eurasian Democracies and Open Markets Support Act of 1992, this was the Bush administration's first major legislative initiative aimed at influencing events in the former Soviet Union.[72] Submitted to Congress in April 1992, the Freedom Support Act was a wide-ranging aid package developed by Baker with input from Senators Nunn and Lugar. As amended by Congress, the Act authorized some $600 million in U.S. assistance to the states of the former Soviet Union. More specifically, $410 million was for humanitarian and technical assistance, $25 million went to State Department programs, $71 million was for educational and cultural programs, and $100 million for CTR programs in the Defense Department.[73] Other actions by Bush included a $12 billion increase in U.S. contributions to the International Monetary Fund specifically for former Soviet states and additional credits to purchase U.S. agricultural products.

Title V of the Act dealt with nonproliferation. It reiterated many of the same concerns expressed in the Soviet Nuclear Threat Reduction Act of 1991, and required most of the same presidential certifications to be made before money could be spent to address these concerns. But borrowing from the Former Soviet Union Demilitarization Act, it also specifically called for efforts aimed at the proliferation of WMD-related expertise from former Soviet states and the conversion of the Soviet military-industrial base.[74] Besides giving the president the authority to transfer money to fund these initiatives, Section 505 also limited spending for defense conversion in the former Soviet Union to no more than the president used for the purposes of converting installations inside the United States.

---

71. There are two different stories as to why two centers were established. According to interview with former State Department staffer 1, July 16, 2003, there was never an intention to establish a second center, but Secretary of State Baker agreed to do so after being approached by high-level Ukrainian officials. According to interview with Science and Technology Center in Ukraine staffer 2, October 26, 2005, there were always plans for a second center in Kiev because there were too many scientists for one center to handle, a significant number of WMD experts were in Ukraine, and Ukraine did not want to be seen as secondary to Russia.

72. *The Freedom for Russia and Emerging Eurasian Democracies and Open Markets Support Act of 1992*, P.L. 102-511. Prior to this, Bush had used his own authority to approve various agricultural and other credits that the Soviet Union could use to buy food and other supplies. Bush also authorized the U.S. Agency for International Development to provide some technical assistance, mostly with food distribution.

73. For a summary of legislative action on the Freedom Support Act, see Curt Tarnoff, *Freedom Support Act of 1992: A Foreign Aid Program for the Former Soviet Union*, Congressional Research Service, CRS Issue Brief, November 4, 1992.

74. Oddly, however, in the Former Soviet Union Demilitarization Act, the focus of the Science Centers is research pertaining to nuclear reactor safety issues.

Similar to congressional consideration of CTR, there was considerable debate about the provisions of the FSA. The main areas of disagreement were similar: spending the peace dividend on U.S. domestic needs versus overseas, whether the Soviet Union was still an enemy, forcing the Soviets to spend their own money in these areas, and an overall long-term strategy for the uses of any U.S. aid.[75]

Congressional action eventually led to an FSA that differed significantly from the Bush administration's initiative. The main differences were three.[76] First, Congress included more funding levels and specifications than in the original bill. Therefore, the president got significantly less flexibility in terms of what the FSA would fund and at what level. Second, similar to CTR money, funding under the FSA could be spent only if certain conditions were met by the recipient states. Eventually, Congress added eleven "conditions," including such foreign policy issues as the peaceful resolution of certain ethnic and regional conflicts, an end to Russia's support for the Castro regime in Cuba, and removal of Russian troops from the Baltics. Third, congressional amendments added specific programs, including the Science Centers and some defense conversion provisions.

Both Science Centers faced numerous delays before funding their first research collaborations. The International Science and Technology Center (ISTC), based in Moscow, was established by formal agreement between the United States, the European Union, Japan, and Russia. To come into force, this agreement needed the approval of several Russian ministers, as well as ratification by the Russian legislature, which at the time was the Supreme Soviet.[77] Somewhat unexpectedly, debate in the Supreme Soviet was intense and caused significant delays.

There were several key concerns expressed by the Russian legislators. First, members were concerned that the ISTC meant the influence of foreign governments in Russian security affairs.[78] Second, they were concerned about the influence of foreign governments on Russia's

75. For a discussion of these debates, see Curt Tarnoff, *The Former Soviet Union and U.S. Foreign Assistance in 1992: The Role of Congress*, Congressional Research Service, CRS Report for Congress, May 20, 2004.

76. This comparison is based upon Tarnoff, *The Former Soviet Union and U.S. Foreign Assistance in 1992: The Role of Congress*, which includes a more comprehensive discussion of congressional changes to Bush's original legislation.

77. Seventeen ministerial-level people in Russia had to sign off on the agreement, and this took time. See R. Adam Moody, "The International Science Center Initiative," in Shields and Potter, eds., *Dismantling the Cold War*, p. 267. Ratification by the Supreme Soviet involved five committees. See Office of International Affairs, National Research Council, *An Assessment of the International Science and Technology Center*, p. 6. The agreement was sent to the Supreme Soviet in early 1993 and had a first reading in the Committee on International Affairs. Although the Committee was not hostile, the votes on it were split, and with ratification not a burning issue, the Committee did not rush to push the measure through. The agreement was also sent to the Committee on the Budget, Taxes, and Finance. See Ildar A. Akhtamzian, "The International Science and Technology Center: Bureaucratic Games," *Nonproliferation Review*, Vol. 3, No. 1 (Fall 1995), pp. 79, 80.

78. Office of International Affairs, National Research Council, *An Assessment of the International Science and Technology Center*, p. 6.

scientific priorities.[79] The third issue was money. Partly, this was concern for intellectual property and the theft of Russia's top scientific expertise and findings.[80] But partly it was also a concern that the tax exemptions provided in the agreement were unacceptable; that, in effect, local Russian officials should be paid for access to the scientific establishments in their areas.[81] Money was also at issue in that some complained that the income tax exemptions for ISTC personnel were overly generous.[82] The fourth issue was the effect ISTC contracts would have on the Russian labs themselves. An ISTC contract could mean that some scientists were making significantly more money than others and receiving a regular paycheck; also, ISTC would mean that Russian institute directors would no longer have control over how money was distributed in their institutes.[83] In turn, this would cause problems with management and social cohesion. Of course, if the institute directors did not support ISTC, then they could do much to discourage participation in its projects.

There is evidence that some Russian institutes took a different perspective, coming out strongly in favor of ISTC because it was a much needed source of income and independence. One of the Russian negotiators, Eugeny Velikhov, wanted ISTC to be headquartered at the Kurchatov Institute, which was a key part of Russia's nuclear energy research infrastructure, but not under the authority of the Ministry of Atomic Energy (Minatom), which controlled Russia's nuclear weapons facilities. Scientists at key Russian nuclear weapons institutes, however, opposed this, arguing that locating the Center at an institute that was independent of Minatom would inhibit their access to the Center.[84] Also, the scientists saw ISTC as a way to exercise increasing autonomy from Minatom, which originally had controlled all foreign contacts at its institutes but was being forced to relax this authority because of the sheer volume of foreign visitors.[85] It is clear that the Russian nuclear institutes had by this time become convinced that the Russian government could not guarantee their continued funding, and that they would have to turn to the West. It is also clear that the decentralized contacts between institutes and the ISTC promised to reduce the overall power of Minatom.

---

79. Ibid.

80. Akhtamzian, "The International Science and Technology Center," p. 80.

81. Ibid. When ISTC was being considered, the value of the ruble was falling, and local officials no doubt saw the ISTC, and taxes on the equipment and supplies it would import, as a lucrative source of Western currency and wealth.

82. Ibid.

83. Ibid., p. 82; interview with Minatom official 1, July 24, 2002; and interview with Minatom official 2, July 24, 2002.

84. See Federation of American Scientists and the Natural Resources Defense Council, "Report on the Fourth International Workshop on Nuclear Warhead Elimination and Nonproliferation," Washington, D.C., February 26–27, 1992, p. 12.

85. Schweitzer, *Moscow DMZ*, p. 17.

As the legislation needed to create ISTC languished in the committees of the Supreme Soviet, Russian President Boris Yeltsin found himself embroiled in a wider struggle for power. As a result, in September 1993, Yeltsin disbanded the legislature. Claiming executive authority, on December 27, 1993, Yeltsin signed a protocol with the other ISTC founding parties that gave ISTC temporary status but allowed it to begin full operations. ISTC was officially established on March 2, 1994, and began funding research the next day, almost two years after the initiative was first announced by Baker.[86]

The Science and Technology Center in Ukraine (STCU), based in Kiev, also faced delays. Although the creation of STCU was announced on October 25, 1993, there were delays that arose from problems forming a post-Soviet government in Ukraine.[87] Ukraine finally authorized STCU through a decree by Ukrainian President Leonid Kravchuk on May 4, 1994, and the Center began operations in November 1995.

A THIRD INITIATIVE FOR SCIENTIFIC COOPERATION

These delays with the Science Centers led to concerns in Washington, especially among some in the U.S. nuclear weapons community. Based upon previous interactions, they knew that their counterparts in the former Soviet Union faced dire financial circumstances. This sense of urgency would eventually lead to the creation of the Initiatives for Proliferation Prevention Program (IPP), which involved the Department of Energy (DOE) and its national laboratories.

The history of DOE's involvement with Russian nuclear weapons scientists actually stretches back to the mid-1980s.[88] DOE oversees the U.S. nuclear weapons establishment, which includes the nuclear weapons research, design, and development laboratories of Los Alamos, Livermore, and Sandia.[89] These laboratories were given the task of verifying certain arms control agreements, and in 1986, they began cooperation with their Soviet counterparts under the Joint Verification Experiments, which were efforts to understand how to detect and remotely measure underground

---

86. According to R. Adam Moody, "The International Science Center Initiative," p. 265, the ISTC was originally supposed to be housed in Minsk, but because of communications and logistics issues and other political reasons it was placed in Moscow.

87. These included lack of experience and logistical resources, which were lost when the Soviet bureaucracy left, as well as inadequate communication and banking infrastructures. Also, this was one of the first international agreements negotiated by the now sovereign state of Ukraine, and there were issues about executive-legislative powers. R. Adam Moody, "The International Science Center Initiative," pp. 271–273.

88. The history of U.S. laboratory interaction, however, dates from 1959, when Soviet nuclear weapons scientists came to Los Alamos. Stalin's death created more freedom for Soviet scientists to interact with the West, and in 1959, Igor Kurchatov, the leader of the Soviet nuclear weapons program, proposed basic scientific cooperation between his laboratory and Los Alamos.

89. Sandia is considered a weapons lab, although its work is on the non-nuclear components of the weapons.

nuclear tests in support of a ban on nuclear testing.[90] Next came the Geneva talks on the Threshold Test Ban Treaty. By the late 1980s, the main U.S. and Soviet nuclear weapons laboratories had exchanged visitors, and the Soviets were offering further collaboration. These early exchanges, plus a history of reading each others' publications about common scientific issues, created an impetus for further interaction. Key U.S. laboratory personnel who had been involved in this early work reinforced this desire for future cooperation, because some believed that the Soviet complex had produced interesting technologies.[91] By 1991, U.S. and Soviet experts were working together to provide security upgrades for nuclear material at Soviet facilities. For the U.S. scientists, proliferation became a growing concern, because it was clear that key Soviet weapons personnel, as well as entire nuclear weapons institutes, were facing economic difficulties.[92]

In December 1991, at a meeting of U.S. laboratory directors, Secretary of Energy James Watkins raised an issue that had been troubling the White House and National Security Council: was there a danger that nuclear material or expertise was leaving Soviet nuclear weapons laboratories? Because the U.S. laboratories had experience working with their Soviet counterparts and, it was believed, had developed a certain level of mutual respect and trust, the DOE Secretary sent Siegfried Hecker, the director of Los Alamos, to visit his counterparts in the Soviet Union and assess the prospects for cooperation.[93] This visit confirmed that material security and the proliferation of expertise were critical problems that needed to be addressed.

DOE thus gave the green light for the U.S. laboratories to pursue further cooperation with a few key nuclear institutes in Russia. As the Science Centers struggled with various domestic legal and administrative issues, the hope was that U.S. laboratory personnel could expedite cooperation because of their past interaction with their Russian counterparts, as well as a shared scientific interest.[94] Indeed, by early 1992, U.S.

90. The history of this early interaction can be found in "Part I: Roots of the Lab-to-Lab Collaboration," *Los Alamos Science*, Number 24 (1996), pp. 3–18; and "Part II: The Lab to Lab Program in Scientific Conversion and Nuclear Materials Control," *Los Alamos Science*, Number 24 (1996), pp. 19–41.

91. Hugh Casey, "The New Independent States Industrial Partnering Program," *Los Alamos Science*, Number 24 (1996), pp. 85–86, mentions interest in high-powered gyrotrons. According to Steve Younger, Soviet scientists were five years ahead of the United States in pulsed power research; see Janet Bailey, *The Good Servant: Making Peace with the Bomb at Los Alamos* (New York: Simon and Schuster, 1995), p. 186. One early participant in such cooperation explained that the United States expected to find many interesting technologies and processes. Interview with Lawrence Livermore National Laboratory staffer 8, April 3, 2003.

92. Interview with Los Alamos National Laboratory staffer 3, April 29, 2003; and interview with Lawrence Livermore National Laboratory staffer 8, April 3, 2003.

93. "Part II: The Lab to Lab Program in Scientific Conversion and Nuclear Materials Control," p. 19.

94. Russian scientists in the closed cities pushed for IPP out of concern that the ISTC would not fund certain Russian nuclear weapons institutes. According to interview with Los Alamos National Laboratory staffer 3, April 29, 2003, the concern was that ISTC would

and Russian nuclear weapons scientists were already engaged in cooperative research projects. In March of that year, more than 100 scientists from the Kurchatov Institute were part of a $90,000 contract with DOE to do peaceful work related to nuclear fusion.[95] By the summer of 1993, Los Alamos, Livermore, and Sandia were involved in a handful of such contracts, totaling almost $2 million.[96]

These initial projects were paid for by discretionary funds at Los Alamos, Livermore, and Sandia Laboratories.[97] A team of U.S. scientists from these laboratories developed and proposed to DOE a plan to formalize this cooperation and expand funding and participation. And in 1993, Senator Pete Domenici, who represented New Mexico, where Los Alamos is located, sponsored legislation to create the Industrial Partnering Program, the original name for IPP. It began the following year with $35 million in funding.[98]

SPLITTING UP

Initially, all programs that in some way dealt with the destruction and safety of former Soviet WMD were funded under the rubric of CTR. This includes the programs in the Departments of Defense, Energy, and State that were aimed at engaging former WMD scientists. Overall, the Defense Department was the agency in charge of administering CTR.[99] This meant that the Defense Department was responsible for managing the annual budget authorization process for most CTR and CTR-related projects, including those that were actually implemented by the Departments of Energy and State. Funding for these efforts also came out of the defense budget and, for its first two years, CTR activities were funded by reprogramming previously authorized money from other Defense Department

neglect the nuclear cities because it was founded in cooperation with people from nuclear energy institutes in open cities. This concern proved unfounded, as ISTC soon provided significant project grants to the main Russian nuclear weapons research and development institutes in the closed cities of Sarov and Snezhinsk.

95.   Doyle McManus, "U.S. Will Fund Nuclear Fusion Research at Russian Lab," *Los Angeles Times*, March 6, 1992, p. A4.

96.   U.S. Congress, Office of Technology Assessment, *Proliferation and the Former Soviet Union* (Washington, D.C.: Government Printing Office, September 1994), p. 65.

97.   Ibid.

98.   This initial funding for IPP came in the form of the *Foreign Operations, Export Financing, and Related Programs Appropriations Act for Fiscal Year 1994*, P.L. 103-87, Section 575.

99.   According to Nunn, the Defense Department rather than the State Department was originally made the executive agent for CTR out of concern for expertise and timeliness. The State Department did not have expertise in WMD, proliferation, or the equipment needed to deliver humanitarian assistance. Moreover, there was concern that the State Department would get bogged down in negotiations. As Nunn explained, if the Soviets appointed their State Department in response, "before long, the people doing the controlling are the ones who have been negotiating for 9 and 10 years on every arms control agreement when we really do have some sense of urgency here." See U.S. Congress, Senate, Committee on Armed Services, *Assisting the Build-Down of the Former Soviet Military Establishment*, 102nd Cong., 2nd sess., February 5, 6, 1992, pp. 27–29.

accounts, not through new authorizations. Therefore, the Defense Department was also responsible for nurturing the political support needed to maintain adequate funding.

As might be expected, the Defense Department soon became reluctant to be responsible for efforts that were actually conducted by other agencies and were seen as a drain on its budget. Moreover, many of these activities were not directly related to the weapons transportation, dismantlement, and destruction projects at the heart of CTR. In 1995, the Defense Department sought to renegotiate responsibility for some CTR activities. In that year, John Deutch, Clinton's deputy secretary of defense from 1994–1995, brokered an agreement whereby the Departments of Energy and State assumed political and budgetary responsibility for their threat reduction programs.

Although this division of effort may seem logical, it was also political. According to Jason Ellis, one key disagreement between the Departments of Defense, Energy, and State was over priorities and strategies. The Defense Department favored weapons dismantlement, while the Departments of Energy and State increasingly emphasized the threat from the proliferation of weapons materials and experts.[100] This inevitably led to disputes over funding. According to Ellis, some at the Defense Department felt that the Departments of Energy and State were tapping the defense budget rather than making the case for their own programs in front of Congress.[101] Less charitably, some in the military felt that other agencies saw the defense budget as an easy source of funding for their projects.[102]

Taking a more critical view, Rose Gottemoeller, a deputy undersecretary of energy as well as a National Security Council staffer in the Clinton administration, argues that the Pentagon sought to get rid of the "less palatable" parts of CTR.[103] These divisions reinforced factions in Congress, particularly Republicans in the House, who believed that parts of CTR were really foreign aid and should not be funded out of the defense budget. Former congressional staffers echo this, claiming that many in Congress who were skeptical of CTR were especially critical of activities that did not directly contribute to the dismantlement and destruction of nuclear weapons.[104]

In 1996, the Department of Energy took over many of the material security programs and IPP, the State Department assumed full responsibility for the Science Centers, and the Defense Department was left with programs aimed at moving, dismantling, and destroying nuclear weapons and their delivery platforms. As a result, CTR became the label for the

---

100. Ellis, *Defense By Other Means*, p. 123.

101. Ibid., p. 124.

102. Ibid.

103. Rose Gottemoeller, "Presidential Priorities in Nuclear Policy," in Shields and Potter, eds., *Dismantling the Cold War*, p. 69–70.

104. Interview with congressional staffer 1, August 8, 2003; interview with congressional staffer 2, August 4, 2003; and interview with congressional staffer 3, August 12, 2003.

Defense Department's cooperative activities with the former Soviet Union, while related efforts continued in the Departments of Energy and State under the general umbrella of "threat reduction programs."[105]

The Politics of CTR Under Clinton and George W. Bush

As explained above, the first Bush administration greeted CTR with a combination of passionate disinterest and benign neglect. It also did little to embrace changes in the Soviet Union. Although the Clinton administration was much keener to pursue CTR, this interest often did not translate into the executive-level attention needed to solve persistent problems. This was especially true after the 1994 mid-term elections. Despite these problems, CTR and CTR-related programs managed to ingrain themselves within the U.S. government and become established fixtures in U.S. relations with the states of the former Soviet Union. This institutionalization helps to explain the programs' staying power under the second Bush administration. Although George W. Bush did much to pursue a harmonious relationship with Russia, his administration did not consistently champion the CTR agenda. His initial skepticism of these programs never gave way to whole-hearted support, even after the September 11, 2001, attacks raised concerns about terrorists equipped with WMD. Under Bush, CTR and CTR-related programs continued or expanded, largely due to the work of Congress. By 2005, however, the Bush administration had initiated efforts to wean Russia off of U.S. security assistance in favor of extending these programs beyond the states of the former Soviet Union. Congress, in general, went along with this plan.

CTR initially flourished under the Clinton administration. Within the Pentagon, Clinton's team had the commitment and energy to force CTR on a somewhat reluctant military bureaucracy. Initially, CTR was seen by many in the Defense Department as a potential competitor for other priorities. Some offered cooperation on CTR, but only in exchange for support for their own issues.[106] Eventually, authority over CTR became more centralized, and financial and staff resources became more secure.

Under Clinton, aid to the former Soviet Union increased across the board, although promises of aid often fell short of what was actually delivered. This zeal for engaging Russia did not, however, always translate into smooth sailing. CTR encountered the myriad problems that it takes to implement a national security initiative that depends upon cooperation between former enemies, yet lacks unified domestic political support in both Russia and the United States.

---

105. Amy F. Woolf, *Nonproliferation and Threat Reduction Assistance: U.S. Programs in the Former Soviet Union*, Congressional Research Service, Washington, D.C., February 11, 2009, p. 4.

106. According to interview with former Clinton administration official 1, September 17, 2003, in its first years the CTR office in the Pentagon was approached by a continuous stream of career bureaucrats and military officers who wanted to exchange their support for CTR for something else that they wanted on a quid pro quo basis.

During the early 1990s, CTR faced delays due to issues about access to former Soviet facilities, the reluctance of some republics to make the necessary legal changes to enable CTR, and problems with interagency cooperation in the United States. These problems could be expediently solved only through the direct attention of the president or vice president. For many issues, this was achieved through the Gore-Chernomyrdin Commission, which was established in 1993 to manage U.S.-Russian cooperation on a variety of issues.

This attention, however, began to drift during the mid-1990s. Partly, this was due to policy challenges after the 1994 elections, in which the Republicans gained control of Congress. This forced the Clinton administration to redirect its energy to other legislative priorities. But attacks on CTR itself also increased as program critics used their committee positions both to place limits on the program and to encourage new and further criticisms.

One of the most persistent conflicts was over funding and, in debates reminiscent of the early 1990s, whether CTR was defense or foreign aid.[107] Led by the House Armed Services Committee (which changed its name briefly in 1994 to the House National Security Committee), in fiscal year 1996, the House did not approve all of the President's requested CTR budget for the first time. The same thing happened again in 1997. Although the Senate was usually able to restore most of the requested money, the authorization and appropriations processes became much more contentious. Eventually, in October 1999, Clinton vetoed the Foreign Operations Appropriations Act, largely because of cuts in aid to Russia. Subsequent negotiations resulted in an $847 million appropriation, almost $200 billion below Clinton's initial request.

In addition to funding issues, Congress also attacked CTR by making it conditional on more aspects of behavior in the recipient state. Particular onerous was a requirement for the president to verify that Russia was no longer pursuing a biological weapons program, which threatened to derail CTR funding efforts in 1995. CTR was also linked to a variety of other more tangential issues, such as Russian military activity in Chechnya, Russia's proposed sale of weapons to India, and other foreign policy issues. Congress specifically targeted aspects of CTR that were not directly related to weapons dismantlement, and, in 1996, permanently banned several programs including defense conversion, environmental restoration, the construction of housing for Russian officers, and certain military-to-military contacts and training.

Clinton had only partial success in stopping the funding cuts and did little to counter congressional termination of defense conversion. Part of the problem was the lack of consensus in support of many CTR objectives. Although the Clinton administration had expended considerable energy to rally political support to the cause of nuclear weapons consolidation,

---

107. For examples, see U.S. Congress, *Congressional Record*, 104th Cong., 1st sess., June 13, 1995, pp. H5865, H5867, H5871; and U.S. Congress, *Congressional Record*, 105th Cong., 1st sess., June 23, 1997, pp. H4199.

dismantlement, and destruction, there was no comparable effort in support of other parts of the CTR agenda. As a result, material security, defense conversion, and other issues were subjected to persistent political attacks. Additionally, issues arising from inter-agency and bilateral state relations became significant obstacles because they lacked the presidential attention needed to resolve them.

Relations with Russia also suffered because of U.S. actions in the 1999 war over Kosovo. Political scientists James M. Goldgeier and Michael McFaul argue that the U.S. pursuit of military action in Kosovo was perceived by Russia as undue interference in its sphere of influence. This, in turn, reinforced Russian fears that U.S. plans to expand NATO were really an attempt to encircle Russia.[108] After Kosovo, Russia became much more wary of U.S. security cooperation and increasingly assertive of its own national interests.

For CTR, these political issues were also exacerbated because of a lack of coordination between programs. For example, programs with essentially similar mandates did little to share solutions to common problems or lessons learned. Different programs with projects at the same Russian institute would do little to coordinate or cooperate on site visits, thus raising concerns from Russia about spying and "nuclear tourism." Cooperative research programs had few mechanisms for insuring that they were not funding the same research from the same teams of former Soviet scientists. Those who paid attention to the overall CTR agenda criticized it for not harmonizing or prioritizing funding requests or program objectives.

By the mid-1990s, there were nineteen federal agencies involved in U.S. assistance to the former Soviet Union; five different agencies had a role in overseeing CTR spending.[109] Although the Freedom Support Act created a coordinator for assistance to the former Soviet states, this official often had little influence over other agencies, especially USAID, and had no authority over CTR programs.[110] As early as 1994, calls were heard for the appointment of a coordinator for CTR and CTR-related assistance, not only to manage inter-agency activities but also to lead the way in ordering priorities and establishing a strategic vision for U.S. assistance. One natural focal point, the National Security Council (NSC), was functionally divided on CTR, with responsibility for denuclearization going to the Russia, Ukraine, and Eurasia Directorate, and Material Protection, Control, and Accounting (MPC&A) programs going to the Nonproliferation Directorate.[111] Upon the recommendation of a 1995 report by the President's Committee of Advisers on Science and Technology, Clinton signed a

---

108. Goldgeier and McFaul, *Power and Purpose*, pp. 12–13, 247–249. Also, Clinton had repeatedly promised not to expand NATO, a pledge which was broken soon after he took office.

109. Katherine E. Johnson, "Sustaining Nuclear Threat Reduction Programs: The "Bottom-Up" Approach," in Shields and Potter, ed., *Dismantling the Cold War*, p. 235.

110. General Accounting Office, *Former Soviet Union: U.S. Bilateral Program Lacks Effective Coordination*, GAO/NSIAD-95-10, Washington, D.C. (February 1995), pp. 2–4.

111. Rose Gottemoeller, "Presidential Priorities in Nuclear Policy," p. 77.

national security directive making CTR activities a national security priority and making the NSC responsible for oversight and coordination. Problems, however, persisted. Despite the fact that the appointment of a coordinator or "czar" was one of the most frequently recommended improvements, one was not appointed by either Clinton or George W. Bush.[112]

Instead of better program coordination, the Clinton administration concentrated on a series of initiatives aimed at increasing funding for assistance to the former Soviet Union. The first, in 1997, was the Partnership for Freedom Initiative. Although Congress did not approve the level of funding requested, the initiative served to increase money for technical and other assistance to former Soviet states and especially to Central Asia.

Nunn-Lugar II came next, in the form of an amendment to the defense authorization bill for fiscal year 1997. A congressional initiative that was strongly supported by the administration, this measure provided $201 million in funding, with about half for domestic preparedness in the United States, and half for WMD security efforts in the former Soviet Union. Most specifically, the measure targeted Russian chemical and biological weapons facilities for dismantlement and the replacement of Russia's remaining plutonium-producing nuclear reactors with facilities using fossil fuels.

Then, prompted by the 1998–1999 collapse of the ruble and subsequent economic crisis in Russia, Clinton undertook two new efforts. One was the Nuclear Cities Initiative, which became a Department of Energy program focused on community development, conversion, and job creation in Russia's core nuclear cities.

The other was the Expanded Threat Reduction Initiative (ETRI), which Clinton announced in his 1999 State of the Union speech. Approved the next year, ETRI was to be part of a five-year, $4.5 billion program to enhance nuclear security efforts with the former Soviet Union. It provided additional funding to a variety of existing CTR efforts, including substantial increases to the Science Centers. Again, however, Congress funded ETRI at a lower level than requested by the administration. Targeted for cuts were the construction of a chemical weapons destruction facility near Shchuch'ye, Russia, and the IPP and NCI programs.

Although the Clinton administration saw considerable progress on the CTR agenda, after eight years there were also widely acknowledged

---

112. For example, Nunn-Lugar II and the Baker-Cutler Report emphasize the need for a coordinator. See Department of Energy, The Secretary of Energy Advisory Board, Howard Baker and Lloyd Cutler, *A Report Card on the Department of Energy's Nonproliferation Programs with Russia* (Washington, D.C.: Department of Energy, January 10, 2001). And in October 2000, Congress added a "sense of Congress" provision to the defense authorization bill calling for more coordination between CTR-related programs. U.S. Congress, House, Committee on Armed Services, *Enactment of Provisions of H.R. 5408, the Floyd D. Spence National Defense Authorization Act for FY 2001*, 106th Cong., 2nd sess., October 6, 2000, H. Rpt. 106-945, section 3174. In January 2009, President Barack Obama appointed Gary Samore as Special Assistant to the President and White House Coordinator for Arms Control and Weapons of Mass Destruction, Proliferation, and Terrorism.

problems, especially with respect to material security and nonproliferation programs. Many of these concerns were summed up in a report com-
missioned by Secretary of Energy Bill Richardson, and released in early
2001. The Baker-Cutler Report, so-named after its co-chairs, aimed to re-
mind policymakers that there was still significant danger in the former
Soviet WMD complex:

> The Task Force offers one major recommendation to the
> President and Congress. **The President, in consultation
> with Congress and in cooperation with the Russian
> Federation, should quickly formulate a strategic plan to
> secure and/or neutralize in the next eight to ten years
> all nuclear weapons-usage material located in Russia
> and to prevent the outflow from Russia of scientific ex-
> pertise that could be used for nuclear or other weapons
> of mass destruction.** Accomplishing this task will be re-
> garded by future generations as one of the greatest con-
> tributions the United States and Russia can make to their
> long-term security and that of the entire world.[113]

In addition to a resounding reaffirmation of the CTR agenda, the report went on to call for several changes.[114] These included broader program mandates and a strategic plan that would prioritize objectives;
specify goals and measurable objectives; and develop an exit strategy.
Some $30 billion in additional funding was suggested, but the report also
states that additional monies should be contingent on reasonable plans
for spending them productively. Yet another recommendation was for the
appointment of a high-level coordinator to prioritize issues and mobilize
public and congressional support. One final key proposal called for an
agreement with Russia to resolve enduring issues about access to facilities
and transparency.

Despite the assessment of the Baker-Cutler Report that CTR was important for U.S. national security, George W. Bush came into office with a
good degree of skepticism about the program and aid to Russia in general.
His first budget cut threat reduction funding by approximately 20 percent below 2001 levels.[115] The most severely effected were Energy Department programs, especially MPC&A, IPP, and NCI, which were reduced
by 32 percent, although Defense Department programs also took a 10 percent hit.[116] During the congressional appropriations process, much of the

---

113. Emphasis in the original. Baker and Cutler, *A Report Card on the Department of Energy's
Nonproliferation Programs with Russia*, p. iv.

114. Ibid., especially p. 25.

115. See Matthew Bunn and Anthony Wier, *Securing the Bomb: An Agenda for Action*
(Cambridge, Mass., and Washington, D.C.: Project on Managing the Atom at Harvard
University and Nuclear Threat Initiative, 2004), p. 96.

116. William Hoehn, "Analysis of the Bush Administration's Fiscal Year 2002 Budget
Requests for U.S.-Former Soviet Union Nuclear Security: Department of Energy Programs,"

Energy funding was restored, including an increase of about $13 million for IPP and NCI.[117]

In late March 2001, Bush announced that he would ask for a full review of threat reduction efforts in Russia, and reports of programs cuts soon surfaced.[118] IPP and NCI were considered particularly vulnerable. During my interviews with program managers both in Washington and in the field, this vulnerability took the form of two stories that were in wide circulation. One story told of a staffer in the U.S. Embassy in Moscow who had been asked by the Bush administration to write a report about Energy Department programs that was so scathing that most would be shut down. Another story was that a long-time critic of these efforts had been sent to the U.S. Embassy in Moscow to cause enough bureaucratic delays that IPP and NCI would be effectively stalled. Although both stories contained incorrect information and exaggerations, it was the case that the Bush administration undertook significant reviews of these programs and seemed disinclined to continue them. No terminations were forthcoming. In fact, most programs were endorsed, although this did not lead to significant funding increases.[119]

Many CTR supporters also assumed that September 11, 2001, would give Bush no choice but to fully embrace the CTR agenda in the name of preventing WMD terrorism. Congress approved an emergency spending proposal after the attack that included $20 billion for homeland security and recovery efforts plus another $20 billion, some of which was expected to go toward nuclear security efforts with Russia. When Bush did not move to spend this money in Russia, Congress allocated $226 million for Energy Department programs, specifically MPC&A, IPP, and NCI.[120] According to a 2004 analysis by Matthew Bunn and Anthony Wier of Harvard's Managing the Atom Project, when adjusted for inflation, the Bush administration proposed post–September 11 budgets for CTR activities that grew by approximately 2 percent per year, on average, but which were significantly less than the spending proposed under Clin-

---

Russian-American Nuclear Security Advisory Council (RANSAC), Washington, D.C., August 10, 2001, p. 1; and RANSAC, "Preliminary Report: Anticipated FY 2003 Budget Request for Department of Energy Cooperative Nuclear Security Programs in Russia," Washington, D.C., January 9, 2002, p. 1.

117. RANSAC, "Preliminary Report: Anticipated FY 2003 Budget Request for Department of Energy Cooperative Nuclear Security Programsin Russia," Washington, D.C., January 9, 2002, p. 1.

118. Philipp C. Bleek, "Bush Reviews Threat Reduction Programs, Contemplates Cuts," *Arms Control Today* (April 2001), p. 26.

119. Programs identified for "adjustment" or "refocusing" were all Department of Energy programs and specifically IPP, NCI, plutonium disposition, and border security initiatives. See White House, "Fact Sheet," http://www.whitehouse.gov/news/releases/2001/12/20011227.html.

120. RANSAC, "Preliminary Report: Anticipated FY 2003 Budget Request for Department of Energy Cooperative Nuclear Security Programs in Russia," Washington, D.C., January 9, 2002, p. 1.

ton's ETRI.[121] Moreover, for several years after 2001, Congress increased funding beyond that requested by the administration.[122] Therefore, to the extent that September 11, 2001, prompted the United States to spend more on nuclear security and nonproliferation in the former Soviet Union, this was due more to the work of Congress.

The Bush administration did, however, help coax other countries into contributing more. In a June 2002 meeting of the G8 countries in Kananaskis, Canada, the Global Partnership Against the Spread of WMD was announced. Brokered by the Canadian delegation, the G8 countries agreed to spend $20 billion over ten years to help Russia and other parts of the former Soviet Union reduce proliferation threats. Four priorities were identified: chemical weapons destruction, decommissioning nuclear submarines, disposing of fissile materials, and creating jobs for former WMD experts.

Although the United States pledged to provide half of the money for the Global Partnership, this $1 billion a year was approximately equal to U.S. spending on CTR and CTR-related programs at the time. In other words, the Global Partnership did not commit the United States to increased spending for this effort. Also in doubt was the extent to which the Global Partnership would eventually lead to more funding. By mid-2006, almost $8 billion had been pledged by the other G8 countries, including $2 billion from Russia. Most of this money was raised in the first two years after the Partnership was announced. Much of it represented new commitments, but some was a reaffirmation of annual spending for established programs. As of June 2005, however, only $3.5 billion had actually been spent on projects.[123]

Despite the Global Partnership, in other areas the Bush administration sought to wind down many CTR programs, especially those in Russia. Scaled back were nuclear weapons dismantlement efforts, biological weapons–focused threat reduction efforts in Russia, and a series of steps that would eventually result in the termination of NCI. But this shift could also be seen in several other ways. First, in its 2008 budget, the Bush administration requested lower funding for most major CTR programs. Activities at the Defense Department, for example, would decline by about 7 percent, and those at the Department of Energy would decline by 5 percent.[124] These reductions, although modest, included core

---

121. See Matthew Bunn and Anthony Wier, *Securing the Bomb: An Agenda for Action*, p. 99.

122. Matthew Bunn and Anthony Wier, *Securing the Bomb 2006* (Cambridge, Mass., and Washington, D.C.: Project on Managing the Atom at Harvard University and Nuclear Threat Initiative, July 2006), p. 106, fig. 4-1.

123. Center for Strategic and International Studies, "Assessing the G8 Global Partnership: From Kananaskis to St. Petersburg," Strengthening the Global Partnership Project, Washington, D.C., July 2006, p. 4.

124. Isabelle Williams, "Analysis of the U.S. Department of Defense's Fiscal Year 2008 Cooperative Threat Reduction Budget Request," Partnership for Global Security, Washington, D.C., March 19, 2007, p. 1; and Isabelle Williams and Kenneth Luongo, "Analysis of the U.S. Department of Energy's Fiscal Year 2008 International Nonproliferation Budget Request," Partnership for Global Security, Washington, D.C., February 26, 2007, p. 1.

efforts aimed at dismantling weapons and storing fissile materials. Funding for the Science Centers, which had proven remarkably stable at around $30 million annually since 2001, declined from this level for two years in a row. CTR's annual reports to Congress also began to project significantly less funding for most programs through 2011.[125]

Second, many programs, including most that enjoyed modest funding increases, were being expanded beyond the former Soviet Union.[126] In the fiscal year 2004 defense authorization bill, the administration requested authority to use up to $50 million in CTR funds for activities outside of the former Soviet Union.[127] In mid-2004, Bush used this authority for the first time in order to help with chemical weapons destruction in Albania.[128] At the State Department, scientist redirection efforts were expanded to Iraqi and Libyan WMD experts and its Export Control and Border Security (EXBS) programs included Africa, the Middle East, and South Asia. At the Department of Energy, the Global Initiatives for Proliferation Prevention (GIPP) program began to expand beyond the former Soviet Union, and the Global Threat Reduction Initiative, a program to find, move, secure, and destroy nuclear and other radioactive materials, developed beyond the former Soviet Union to be global in focus. These changes meant that even with constant budgets, programs had less money to spend in the former Soviet states or Russia.

More evidence that these programs were winding down can be found in target dates for program completion. Most CTR and CTR-related programs worked under a series of rolling deadlines and target dates for completing their work. Moreover, as work neared completion in one area, it was expected that additional opportunities for cooperative work would be negotiated with Russia. Increasingly, however, projected completion dates became less fungible. Further, programs increasingly discussed their exit and the transition of programs to Russian control and funding.[129]

---

125. See, for example, Department of Defense, Defense Threat Reduction Agency, "Cooperative Threat Reduction Annual Report to Congress," fiscal year 2007, Washington, D.C.

126. William Hoehn, "Preliminary Analysis of the U.S. Department of Energy's Fiscal Year 2006 Nonproliferation Budget Request," RANSAC, Washington, D.C., February 9, 2005, p. 1; and William Hoehn, "Preliminary Analysis of the U.S. State Department's Fiscal Year 2006 Budget Request for Global WMD Threat Reduction Programs," RANSAC, Washington, D.C., March 24, 2005, p. 1.

127. The previous year, the Senate had approved an amendment by Richard Lugar that would give the president this authority. Despite Senate approval and support from the president, the amendment was removed during conference at the insistence of the House.

128. Amy F. Woolf, *Nonproliferation and Threat Reduction Assistance: U.S. Programs in the Former Soviet Union*, Congressional Research Service, CRS Report for Congress, June 26, 2006, p. 54.

129. For example, the Departments of Defense and Energy planned to complete security upgrades at warhead and weapons material sites in Russia by the end of 2008. Their plan, however, did not include provisions for negotiating access to additional places where significant quantities of weapons-relevant materials were stored. See Government Accountability Office, *Nuclear Nonproliferation: Progress Made in Improving Security at Russian Nuclear Sites, but the Long-term Sustainability of U.S. Upgrades is Uncertain*, Washington, D.C.

Several major Energy Department projects were scheduled to end in 2008; programs in the Defense Department projected significant cutbacks after 2007.

Finally, certification and liability issues created problems for the CTR agenda. Certification refers to the need for the president to verify that former Soviet states are meeting certain criteria before funds can be spent in those countries. The original CTR legislation specified six such conditions; the Freedom Support Act echoed these and added a few more. Over time, Congress mandated several additional certifications. For each requirement, the president had to certify that states receiving aid were "committed to" the specified objectives, which included such things as investing their own money in weapons destruction, complying with relevant arms control agreements, and protecting minority rights.

Certification requirements for foreign aid versus CTR varied. Some foreign aid certifications were about concrete actions: Russia was seen as either helping or not helping Iran build nuclear reactors, having or not having passed laws protecting religious minorities, selling or not selling missile technology to India. From fiscal year 1996 through fiscal year 2003, each year some 60 percent of foreign aid to Russia was conditioned on a particular certification.[130] Certification requirements for CTR tended to be more vague. For example, although Russia was required to make a "substantial investment" of its own resources in weapons destruction, it was up to the president to define "substantial." The idea was for the president to exercise his political judgment about the value of compliance on specific issues relative to making progress through CTR.

In 2002, the Bush administration failed for the first time to certify Russian behavior as required for CTR assistance. At issue was Russia's compliance with the conventions banning biological and chemical weapons. Reportedly, Russia had refused to share requested information about its past biological and chemical weapons programs and to cooperate in providing access to some new strains of anthrax that had been developed by Russian scientists.[131] As a result, almost one-third of CTR-related assistance to Russia was held up.

Rather than make the necessary certifications, the Bush administration asked Congress to permanently waive the certification requirements for CTR. Congress refused, but did grant a temporary waiver for three years. In 2008, Congress eliminated the certification requirements for CTR. The Bush administration did lobby for permanent waiver authority, presumably to show its support for CTR. However, it is also the case that in 2002 the Bush administration held up CTR programs because it refused either to certify Russia for CTR assistance or to waive the need for certification.

(February 2007), p. 7.

130. Curt Tarnoff, *U.S. Assistance to the Former Soviet Union*, Congressional Research Service, CRS Report for Congress, March 16, 2006, p. 10.

131. Judith Miller, "U.S. to Help Reduce Threat of Russian Arms," *New York Times*, August 9, 2002, p. A8.

Using the same information and assurances, however, this certification had been approved every year by the Clinton administration.[132]

This willingness to stop some CTR programs due to other issues can also be seen in the Bush administration's attempts to resolve issues about liability. All CTR programs were governed by country-specific implementing agreements that spelled out the rights and responsibilities of all parties. The Departments of Defense, Energy, and State all had their own implementing agreements with Russia. In the original agreement with Russia that covered CTR programs at the Defense Department, Russia agreed to sole and unconditional liability for any accidents or damage resulting from CTR activities. The Energy Department negotiated a similar agreement for its projects in Russia. Subsequently, however, other countries and programs signed implementing agreements that limited Russia's liability burden. In 2003, when the Energy Department's implementing agreements for its NCI and Plutonium Disposition programs were set to expire, issues about liability prevented their renewal. Besides these two programs, at issue was the precedent any new liability agreement would set for the overall CTR umbrella agreement, which would need renewal in 2006.

Despite the fact that the Energy Department's program managers and contractors agreed to accept Russia's version of the liability provisions, the Bush administration would not. As a result, work under the plutonium disposition and NCI programs stopped. In July 2005, a liability agreement covering DOE programs was reached, and a similar one for CTR as a whole was agreed to in June 2006. In both cases, Russia assumed blanket liability for past and current projects, but the United States agreed to negotiate more limited liability rules in the future on a project-by-project basis.[133]

Although this disagreement over liability was eventually resolved, it did halt two Department of Energy programs for a period of about two years. One program, NCI, never recovered from this delay. It ceased operations in September 2006, the first CTR-related program to be terminated as a result of presidential actions.

Shared Assumptions

Since the early 1990s and the first debates over security cooperation with the former Soviet Union, congressional hearings, testimony, and public statements from policymakers have conveyed a widely shared set of assumptions about the danger of the proliferation of WMD expertise from the former Soviet Union. These assumptions, in turn, have influenced the design and implementation of U.S. brain drain programs, as well as the

---

132. Woolf, *Nonproliferation and Threat Reduction Assistance: U.S. Programs in the Former Soviet Union*, pp. 46–47.

133. Ibid., pp. 45–46.

political environment in which they are implemented. These assumptions can be grouped into three general categories.

One set of assumptions pertains to who is a danger and why. So-called brain drain was seen from the beginning as a danger on par with the proliferation of nuclear weapons and weapons-usable materials. Although Russia inherited the bulk of the Soviet WMD complex, all states of the former Soviet Union were a concern, as were all WMD experts, whether their skills are related to nuclear, biological, or chemical weapons or to missile technology. That said, until 1997, priority was given to working with nuclear weapons scientists. Assumptions were also made about who wanted to employ these experts. Initially, the concern was states that were traditionally seen as proliferation risks, but this shifted to include terrorist groups.[134]

Another set of assumptions served to define the problem by explaining why weapons experts might proliferate and how many should be targeted for engagement. Policymakers tended to share beliefs about why scientists might proliferate and how many were a proliferation risk. More specifically, the assumption was that proliferation was a likely response to economic desperation; as long as weapons experts had decent salaries and living conditions, they would not traffic in weapons technology or knowledge. But not all poor weapons experts are created equal. It was assumed that of those that might share their expertise, the most serious risk came from a pool of some 60,000 WMD experts who possessed the most weapons-relevant skills and knowledge. But there was also a tacit agreement that U.S. programs would never engage or reemploy such a large number.

A final assumption has to do with the relationship between programs and proof of proliferation. As Chapter 2 explains, between the collapse of the Soviet Union in 1990–1991 and 2008, there were few proven cases of the proliferation of expertise. Although suspicions grew about undocumented cases—mostly proliferation by electronic means—policymakers consistently assumed that the proliferation of WMD expertise to certain states would be so disastrous for U.S. interests that the potential alone was enough to justify U.S. efforts.

BRAIN DRAIN: WHO AND WHERE?

Although the notion of "loose nukes" grabbed the most attention in the early 1990s, initial proliferation fears focused mostly on the theft of nuclear weapons materials such as highly-enriched uranium and plutonium.[135]

---

134. Prior to the attacks on September 11, 2001, worries about terrorist acquisition of nuclear weapons had become a focus under the Clinton administration in the late 1990s.

135. During the early 1990s, the theft of nuclear weapons was widely discussed. But when the collapse of the Soviet Union did not bring predictions about widespread chaos to fruition, concern over the theft of weapons dissipated. In testimony in 1996, for example, Director of Central Intelligence John Deutch reports that the intelligence community sees the risk of weapons theft as "slight." See Prepared Statement for the Record, John Deutch, Director of Central Intelligence, U.S. Congress, Senate, Permanent Subcommittee on Investigations, Committee on Governmental Accountability, *Global Proliferation of Weapons of Mass Destruction*, Part II, 104th Cong., 2nd sess., March 13, 20 and 22, 1996, S. Hrg. 104-422,

Despite the attention given to fissile materials, concern over the proliferation of weapons expertise was consistently present. In 1992, CIA Director Robert Gates went so far as to testify to Congress that concern for brain drain was in fact greater than concern about the loss of materials or the weapons themselves, largely due to the desperate living conditions and lack of economic opportunity for weapons experts.[136] Despite this, hearings and reports addressing security in the former Soviet weapons complex in subsequent years often mention concern about the proliferation of expertise, but usually devote more space to materials and weapons-security concerns.[137]

Despite this focus on nuclear weapons, materials, and experts, plus the fact that Russia inherited the bulk of Soviet assets in these areas, policymakers were frequently reminded of the importance of other types of weapons and other former Soviet states. For example, in 1993, CIA Director R. James Woolsey cautioned Congress not to forget the many former WMD workers who remained outside of Russia.[138] Although brain drain programs were located in several other post-Soviet states, it was only in 1997–1998 that significant program activity took place outside of Russia. This shift was accelerated under George W. Bush because of an increasing reluctance to engage in difficult negotiations with Russia. It was simply easier, both bilaterally and within the United States, to make the case for important U.S. nonproliferation interests in other countries. For example, states in central Asia and the Caucasus region were seen as an important conduit for many forms of smuggling; the former had the added advantage of offering military bases close to Iraq and Afghanistan. Moreover, these countries had, in general, been much more willing to accept U.S. assistance programs with fewer concerns about reciprocity, liability, access, and the other problematic conditions that often went with working in Russia.

Similarly, attention shifted from nuclear experts to those with biological weapons–related skills. Policymakers tended to consider biological and chemical weapons important because they carried political clout as "weapons of mass destruction," yet were cheaper to develop that nuclear weapons. Despite this concern, expertise programs focused overwhelmingly on nuclear weapons.[139] However, concerns about continuing work on biological weapons in Russia persisted since Yeltsin admitted in

---

p. 312.

136. U.S. Congress, Senate, Committee on Governmental Affairs, *Weapons Proliferation in the New World Order*, 102nd Cong., 2nd sess., 1992, S. Hrg. 102-720, p. 21. Another early emphasis on brain drain can be found in John M. Deutch, "The New Nuclear Threat," *Foreign Affairs*, Vol. 71, No. 4 (Fall 1992), p. 129.

137. As an example, see U.S. Congress, *Global Proliferation of Weapons of Mass Destruction*, Part II. Although all three volumes of these hearings mention former Soviet and especially Russian nuclear security, Part II is more consistently devoted to these topics.

138. U.S. Congress, Committee on Governmental Affairs, *Proliferation Threats of the 1990s*, 103rd Cong., 1st sess., February 24, 1993, S. Hrg. 103-209, p. 11.

139. See, for example, ibid., p. 18.

1992 that the Soviet Union had not ended its offensive program, as specified by the Biological and Toxin Weapons Convention.[140] These fears were reinforced by repeated Russian refusals to allow cooperative work or even access to former biological weapons facilities that were controlled by the Ministry of Defense.

In 1997, stories surfaced about Iranian visits to the Russian cities of Obolensk and Koltsovo, where key former biological weapons institutes were located. The next year, President Clinton began to focus more on biological weapons proliferation, a concern that reportedly arose after he read a fictional account of a terrorist attack on New York City.[141]

According to the Government Accountability Office, much of the infrastructure for designing and making biological weapons was still in place at most former Soviet institutes in 2000.[142] Concern about Iran's interest in these facilities and their workers led to an expansion of funding for biological weapons–related cooperation as part of the Expanded Threat Reduction Initiative. Whereas from fiscal years 1994 through 1999, the United States allocated some $20 million for biological weapons–related collaborative research, spending for fiscal years 2000 through 2004 was to increase to $110 million.[143] As the case studies in subsequent chapters show, the result was a shift in focus at the Science Centers and IPP, as well as the creation of new efforts in the Defense and State Departments. The anthrax-laced letters that were sent to various media and congressional offices in September and October 2001 seemingly reinforced this change in emphasis.[144]

Finally, one other shift took place with respect to assumptions about the proliferation of WMD expertise. Initially, the chief concern was states seeking to augment their own WMD and chemical weapons programs by hiring former Soviet experts. Most suspicion was leveled at those states whose supposed nuclear ambitions the United States has traditionally opposed. These include Syria, North Korea, Iraq, Iran, and China.[145] Less

---

140. General Accounting Office, *Biological Weapons: Efforts to Reduce Former Soviet Threat Offers Benefits, Poses New Risks*, Washington, D.C. (April 2000), p. 16.

141. Judith Miller and William J. Broad, "Exercise Finds U.S. Unable to Handle Germ War Threat," *New York Times*, April 26, 1998, pp. A1, A10.

142. General Accounting Office, *Biological Weapons: Efforts to Reduce Former Soviet Threat Offers Benefits, Poses New Risks*, pp. 5–6.

143. Ibid., p. 6.

144. Bob Woodward reports that former CIA Director George Tenet, in a meeting with Secretary of Defense Donald Rumsfeld, speculated that renegade Russian scientists might have helped produce the anthrax. Bob Woodward, *Bush at War* (New York: Simon & Schuster, 2002), p. 248. In March 1995, Aum Shinrikyo's use of sarin gas on the Tokyo subway killed seven and injured five hundred, which led to considerable U.S. government interest in preventing terrorist use of chemical weapons. Oddly, this did not translate into a similar emphasis on former Soviet chemical weapons facilities.

145. For example, see Testimony of Robert M. Gates, Director, CIA, U.S. Congress, *Weapons Proliferation in the New World Order*, pp. 5–6; and U.S. Congress, *Proliferation Threats of the 1990s*, p. 41. These same states appear repeatedly in testimony over the years. For example, see Testimony of Glenn E. Schweitzer, Director, Office for Central Europe and Eurasia,

frequently mentioned were Cuba, Egypt, Algeria, India, Pakistan, and Libya.[146] Concern about terrorist groups recruiting former Soviet experts surfaced in 1995, after Aum Shinrikyo's sarin gas attack on the Tokyo subway.[147] Worry over terrorist access to WMD expertise increased significantly after September 11, 2001. As the case studies show, however, this shift in concern was not translated into a programmatic response.

SCIENTISTS AT RISK

With respect to the proliferation of expertise, most hearings, documents, and publications pointed to financial desperation as the problem.[148] Members of the armed forces and WMD experts at both military and civilian institutes in the former Soviet Union all suffered a severe decline in living standards. As prices for basic goods increased due to inflation, those on the state payroll found their salaries stagnant and usually unpaid for long periods. Crime was up, food supplies were down, and there were few if any opportunities for alternative employment. Policymakers, however, seldom if ever asked for these specifics. Congressional hearings and testimony talk in very broad terms, and sometimes offer quite vivid descriptions, but seem satisfied with generalities. Senator Sam Nunn's remarks at the start of a 1993 hearing are not atypical: "History has never before witnessed scientists, technicians, and military personnel highly skilled in building and operating nuclear weapons who must worry daily about finding food and housing for themselves and their families."[149]

Most policymakers also tended to discount the social factors working against proliferation. The one exception seems to be Glenn Schweitzer, the founding director of ISTC. While acknowledging that economic desperation can cause a change of heart, on several occasions he reminded policy-

National Academy of Sciences, Founding Director, International Science and Technology Center, Moscow, in U.S. Congress, *Global Proliferation of Weapons of Mass Destruction*, Part II, pp. 65–66.

146.   Testimony of Robert M. Gates, Director, CIA, U.S. Congress, *Weapons Proliferation in the New World Order*, pp. 5–6; and U.S. Congress, *Proliferation Threats of the 1990s*, p. 41.

147.   Testimony of John F. Sopko, Deputy Chief Counsel to the Minority, and Alan Edelman, Counsel to the Minority, U.S. Congress, Senate, Permanent Subcommittee on Investigations, Committee on Governmental Affairs, *Global Proliferation of Weapons of Mass Destruction*, Part III, 104th Cong., 2nd sess., March 27, 1996, S. Hrg. 104-422, p. 7.

148.   As examples, see U.S. Congress, Senate, Subcommittee on European Affairs, Committee on Foreign Relations, *Soviet Crisis and the U.S. Interest: Future of the Soviet Military and Future of the Soviet Economy*, 102nd Cong., 1st sess., June 6, June 19, 1991, p. 246; and U.S. Congress, *Potential Threats to American Security*, pp. 4–9, 67. For concern about the effect finances have on the safety of nuclear operations, see U.S. Congress, Senate, Committee on Armed Services, *Current Developments in the Former Soviet Union*, 103rd Cong., 1st sess., Feb. 3, 17, 24, March 3, 1993, S. Hrg. 103-242, p. 17.

149.   U.S. Congress, *Current Developments in the Former Soviet Union*, p. 2. For other examples, see U.S. Congress, Senate, Committee on Governmental Affairs, *International Organized Crime and Its Impact on the U.S.*, 103rd Cong., 2nd sess., May 25, 1994, S. Hrg. 103-899, p. 3; and U.S. Congress, *Potential Threats to American Security*, p. 92, in which Ambassador to the Former Soviet Union Robert Strauss cautions members of the House Armed Services Committee to be wary of "demagogues" who seek to take advantage of "homeless" weapons scientists.

makers of the patriotism of former Soviet weapons experts. Besides being proud of their roles in the Soviet defense program, Schweitzer argued that weapons experts remained loyal to their home countries and were very conscious of the dangers of WMD proliferation to other states.[150] Interviews with program workers in the United States confirm this tendency to downplay the patriotism of former Soviet experts. While assuming that most former Soviet experts would not proliferate except in dire circumstances, only a few interviewees suggested that patriotism would most likely always trump individual financial need. These few interviewees were always people with more than three years of experience working with former Soviet experts, and tended to be people who had participated in U.S. efforts during the early to mid-1990s. Perhaps more telling is the way they conveyed this conclusion: it was usually offered to me outside of our formal interviews and in hushed tones as if it were contrary to conventional wisdom.

It is also clear from hearings and testimony that not all WMD experts were equal in terms of proliferation concern. In general, the United States was more interested in the top WMD, especially nuclear, experts, and less interested in technicians and engineers with weapons-relevant skills.[151] During the early 1990s, this was usually quantified as a few thousand people or a few tens of thousands. For example, in 1992, CIA Director Robert Gates testified that an estimated one million people worked in the Soviet nuclear weapons program, but only a thousand or two knew how to design nuclear weapons; according to Gates, another "few thousand" had useful biological weapons–related skills.[152] In 1993, CIA Director R. James Woolsey referred to emigration concerns about "tens of thousands of former Soviet scientists [who] were involved in sensitive weapons programs."[153] According to Amy Smithson, the U.S. government estimated that there are about 2,000 critical nuclear weapons experts, 3,500 with

---

150. Testimony of Glenn E. Schweitzer, *Global Proliferation of Weapons of Mass Destruction,* Part II, p. 54.

151. The sole exception is a 1991 hearing that involved Ashton Carter, who would go on to supervise these programs as an assistant secretary in the Defense Department under Clinton. In 1991, Carter testified that the key experts were not the few people who could make bombs, but teams of other experts who together could help a state produce fissile materials or put together a weapons program. See U.S. Congress, *Potential Threats to American Security,* p. 151.

152. U.S. Congress, House, Committee on Foreign Affairs, *The Future of U.S. Foreign Policy in the Post–Cold War Era,* 102nd Cong., 2nd sess., February 6, 19, 20, 25, March 5, 24, April 30, 1992, p. 205. Other policymakers citing the "few thousand" number include Ashton Carter, former Assistant Secretary of Defense for International Security Policy under Clinton, Ashton Carter Testimony, U.S. Congress, Senate, Committee on Armed Services, *Department of Defense Authorization for Appropriations for FY 95 and the Future Years Defense Program, Part 7: Nuclear Deterrence, Arms Control and Defense Intelligence,* 103rd Cong., 2nd sess., April 21, 26, 28, May 3, 5, 11, 1994, S. Hrg. 103-765, pt. 7, p. 243; Robert Gallucci, former Assistant Secretary of State for Political-Military Affairs and Ambassador at Large, in Robert L. Gallucci, "Redirecting the Soviet Weapons Establishment," *Arms Control Today,* June 1992; and Senator Carl Levin in U.S. Congress, *Assisting the Build-Down of the Former Soviet Military Establishment,* p. 38.

153. U.S. Congress, *Proliferation Threats of the 1990s,* p. 11.

important chemical weapons–related knowledge, and 7,000 in the biological weapons area.[154]

In 1996, Schweitzer estimated that there were 60,000 WMD experts who deserved to be the focus of attention.[155] Of these, 30,000 were from the aerospace complex, 20,000 were from the nuclear weapons complex, and the rest were biological and chemical weapons experts.[156] Schweitzer's figures have subsequently become the most frequently cited estimates.[157]

Regardless of estimates of the number of critical WMD and chemical weapons experts, U.S. policymakers consistently made one other assumption: that only a small fraction of those experts would ever be involved in U.S. redirection programs. There was never an attempt to link funding to numbers of "critical" scientists in need of engagement or reemployment. Instead, there was the underlying assumption that reaching many or most WMD experts was at best unlikely and probably impractical, given the funding and security disclosures that would be required.[158] Rather, the goal was to work with as many WMD experts as possible, and in so doing discourage the proliferation both of selected highly capable experts as well as large numbers of people with weapons-relevant skills.[159]

POTENTIAL VERSUS PROOF

Finally, it is important to note one other assumption made by policymakers: that the potential for proliferation was enough to justify U.S. programs. In the late 1990s, the U.S. intelligence community began reporting that former Soviet weapons experts appeared to be staying at home while solving weapons-relevant problems remotely, presumably by email, for other countries.[160] Such reports, however, were unknown in the early 1990s. When the initial decisions were made to fund brain drain programs, there

---

154. Amy E. Smithson, *Toxic Archipelago: Preventing Proliferation from the Former Soviet Chemical and Biological Weapons Complexes,* (Washington, D.C.: The Henry L. Stimson Center, December 1999), p. 49.

155. Schweitzer, *Moscow DMZ,* p. 84.

156. Testimony of Glenn E. Schweitzer, Director, Office for Central Europe and Eurasia, National Academy of Sciences, Founding Director, International Science and Technology Center, Moscow, U.S. Congress, *Global Proliferation of Weapons of Mass Destruction,* Part II, p. 53.

157. According to a 2007 GAO report, the figure of 60,000 came from a 1991 National Academy of Sciences estimate. Also, according to the GAO in 2005, a RAND study reduced this number to 35,000. See Government Accountability Office, *Nuclear Nonproliferation: DOE's Program to Assist Weapons Scientists in Russia and Other Countries Needs to be Reassessed,* Washington, D.C. (December 2007), pp. 20–21.

158. It is highly unlikely that the former Soviet states, especially Russia, would have identified their top nuclear weapons experts for national security reasons. Also, biological and chemical weapons experts had an inherent incentive not to be identified because the production of such weapons is illegal under both Russian and international law.

159. Carla Anne Robbins, "The X Factor in the Proliferation Game," *U.S. News and World Report,* March 16, 1992, pp. 44–51.

160. U.S. Congress, Senate, Select Committee on Intelligence, *Current and Projected National Security Threats to the U.S.,* 105th Cong., 2nd sess., January 28, 1998, S. Hrg. 105-587, p. 135.

were confirmed cases of the theft and smuggling of nuclear weapons–relevant materials out of Russia. There were also horror stories about former Soviet experts moving to China, Iraq, and other countries. But there was almost no evidence that former Soviet weapons experts had emigrated to countries outside of the United States, Western Europe, and Israel. In 1992, for example, in response to queries about rumors of fifty ex-Soviet nuclear weapons scientists working in Iraq, CIA Director Woolsey reiterated to Congress that there was no evidence of brain drain from the former Soviet Union.[161] In 1996, Schweitzer confirmed that, in his opinion, the chances of a Russian weapons expert migrating to North Korea or the Middle East was "close to zero."[162] As the previous chapter notes, there were few confirmed cases of the proliferation of experts to such countries.

In contrast to this lack of emigration, there were stories, as well as hard evidence, both from the early 1990s, that certain countries—among them Iran, Iraq, North Korea and Libya—were interested in employing former Soviet experts with significant WMD-relevant skills.[163] Moreover, this was common knowledge among the relevant policymaking communities. U.S. brain drain programs thus appeared to be justified by the demand for former WMD specialists, but not by hard evidence that such experts were actually interested in proliferation.

Domestic Politics and CTR

The goal of this chapter has been to establish the overall domestic U.S. political context within which brain drain programs were implemented. There are three broad conclusions. First, CTR and CTR-related programs were never supported by a broad domestic political consensus. Instead, a debate endured about whether these programs were foreign aid or properly part of the U.S. defense effort. Annually, U.S. defense spending ranges in the neighborhood of 5–6 percent of gross national product; foreign aid usually is around 0.2 percent. The conclusion is obvious: programs that are labeled "foreign aid" should expect significantly smaller budgets and less political support. Although CTR-related programs consistently managed to ally themselves with other defense efforts, it remained the case that a persistent and significant group of policymakers questioned this relationship.

It is relatively easy to make the case that it is in the interest of U.S. national security to dismantle and destroy nuclear weapons that were

---

161. U.S. Congress, *Proliferation Threats of the 1990s*, p. 148. For similar assurances about the lack of proliferation, see U.S. Congress, *The Future of U.S. Foreign Policy in the Post–Cold War Era*, pp. 234, 236; and U.S. Congress, *Potential Threats to American Security in the Post–Cold War Era*, p. 105.

162. Schweitzer also added that scientists in countries such as Georgia might be more interested in emigrating to the Middle East, but the weapons knowledge of non-Russian experts is less dangerous. See Testimony of Glenn E. Schweitzer, *Global Proliferation of Weapons of Mass Destruction*, Part II, p. 65.

163. U.S. Congress, *Global Proliferation of Weapons of Mass Destruction*, Part II, p. 131.

once aimed at the United States. Moreover, CTR's denuclearization efforts could measure their progress by counting the number of nuclear weapons that had been dismantled and the number of bombers, missiles, and submarines that had been destroyed. Other programs were not so lucky; those aimed at the consolidation, inventory, and security of WMD-relevant materials faced critics who claimed that such activities should be financed by Russia. Furthermore, they argued, such aid only freed Russia to spend its own money on weapons research, development, and production. Programs to convert facilities, retrain, and create jobs for former Soviet weapons scientists faced these questions plus an additional one: why pay for these programs in Russia when there are unemployment problems at home? All CTR-related programs suffered from the "defense versus foreign aid" debate; programs that were less related to weapons dismantlement had a harder time convincing policymakers that they were, as described by Les Aspin, "defense by other means."

It would seem logical that the September 11, 2001, attacks on the United States would have shifted the "defense versus foreign aid" debate in favor of defense. Most policymakers and analysts assumed that terrorists would use nuclear weapons if they could only steal or build them. Therefore, programs aimed at securing WMD and relevant materials and expertise should clearly have been in the national security interest of the United States. But such was not the case. Although CTR and related programs enjoyed reasonably consistent budget increases over time, there was no significant jump due to the terrorist attack on the United States.

Moreover, there was general agreement that considerable work remained before the former Soviet WMD complex was secured. In 2006, security upgrades had been completed at fewer than half of Russian nuclear warhead storage sites; almost half of the Soviet Union's nuclear weapons–relevant materials were in facilities that needed additional security measures; Russia maintained considerable excess highly-enriched uranium and plutonium; and few WMD experts had been transitioned to sustainable civilian jobs.[164] Instead of redoubling its efforts in Russia, however, the Bush administration reduced CTR-related programs there in favor of modest expansion to other countries outside of the former Soviet Union.

Because spending for the CTR agenda was never completely justified on the basis of its contribution to national security, critics conditioned that spending on other goals and objectives. These included Russia's compliance with arms control treaties and defense-related commitments, as well as other domestic and foreign policy issues, "Buy American" provisions and other measures aimed at privileging U.S. business expansion into the former Soviet space, legal liability, and following standard accounting and oversight rules. These requirements often served to slow or stall program implementation, limit projects, and reinforce Russian criticisms.

---

164. For a widely respected analysis of progress in these areas, see Bunn and Wier, *Securing the Bomb 2006*. This report is updated annually.

The case studies in subsequent chapters illustrate how U.S. conditions on nonproliferation programs served to constrain opportunities, complicate cooperation with Russia, and limit program success.

The second overall conclusion of this chapter is that presidential support matters. With the exception of the first few years of the Clinton administration, CTR-related programs never enjoyed consistent presidential support and attention. Instead, this agenda was maintained by a few members of Congress, key personnel at the Departments of Defense, Energy, and State, supporters from academia and the National Academies of Science, and several non-governmental organizations such as the Partnership for Global Security and the Nuclear Threat Initiative. Although coalitions among these groups resulted in new initiatives and increased funding, they did not have the clout or authority to solve the important and persistent problems that are illustrated in the case studies in the following chapters.

The third conclusion is that programs aimed specifically at the proliferation of WMD expertise were all based on a widely shared set of assumptions about which scientists were the most dangerous, who wanted to hire them, and why they might be tempted to sell their skills. These assumptions initially led to a focus on nuclear weapons experts in Russia and their emigration to a small number of states, mostly in the Middle East, that were seen as posing significant challenges to U.S. interests. In fact, however, at the time there was almost no evidence that former Soviet weaponeers were emigrating, or even inclined toward proliferation. Brain drain programs went forward because of the potential for proliferation. While this potential problem was assumed to arise from economic desperation, it was never specifically defined in terms of the numbers of experts, the quality of their skills, or their locations. The result, as the case studies show, is that U.S. programs tended to target anyone who had an affiliation with former Soviet weapons efforts.

Chapter 4

Early Conversion Efforts at the Defense Department

After the collapse of the Soviet Union, the Defense Department funded three efforts aimed at addressing the proliferation of weapons knowledge. This chapter describes these conversion and redirection efforts, discusses the threats that came to be seen as their focus, and assesses their results, both in terms of their own goals and with respect to their impact on the proliferation of weapons of mass destruction (WMD) expertise.

Two of these programs date from the first years of Cooperative Threat Reduction (CTR). One, the Defense Conversion program, matched up U.S. companies and former Soviet weapons producers for conversion projects, with the U.S. government subsidizing initial investments. Never popular with Congress, legislation prohibited any additional funding for this effort in 1995. The second and related program, the Defense Enterprise Fund (DEF), was a government-subsidized investment fund that provided grants and loans directly to conversion projects. Most of DEF's resources were exhausted by the mid-1990s, and the fund was closed in 2003, largely due to management problems. The third effort, the Biological Threat Reduction Program (BTRP), is discussed in Chapter 5 within the context of the Science Centers, which administered BTRP projects.

In total, the Defense Conversion program and DEF cost almost $200 million, of which about $88 million was spent on the conversion projects themselves, with the rest going to administrative and other expenses in the United States. Thirty-four conversion projects resulted, of which twelve were at least initially successful, nineteen failed, and the fates of three are not known. Using the most favorable estimates, some 4,000 people were employed as a result, although it is not possible to know how many of these are former weapons experts.

It is often assumed that these conversion and job-creation programs did not perform better either because Congress did not provide enough funding or because the Russians would not cooperate. The history of Defense Department conversion efforts suggests a different conclusion. Although the state of Russia's economy, the mindset of former weapons workers, and the misperceptions those workers had of what was required for success in a market economy all caused problems for conversion programs, these were made worse by the inability of the Defense Department to select appropriate U.S. business partners that recognized these problems and were committed to working around them. Congress, in turn, saw poor results as additional evidence that conversion was a waste of money.

Most crucially, however, the Defense Department never embraced conversion as part of its accepted mission, or as a critical part of CTR. Therefore, there was no support within the organization for making the procedural changes that were necessary for greater success, or for using the political clout of the military to persuade Congress that conversion was worthwhile. Although conversion was supported by a few key Clinton administration appointees to the Defense Department, their influence was not sufficient enough and their battles were too many for them to convince both Congress and the Defense Department to embrace conversion as a critical means for countering the proliferation of WMD expertise.

The Defense Department and Cooperative Threat Reduction

Although the discussions that led to the creation of the CTR program referenced the danger of proliferation from under- and unemployed WMD workers, it was the 1992 Former Soviet Union Demilitarization Act that expanded CTR's agenda officially to include conversion. Conversion, however, was always a small part of the Defense Department's CTR efforts.

From its start in the early 1990s through 2007, about half of CTR funding went for weapons destruction and dismantlement activities, including the elimination of launch facilities, and of weapons delivery systems, including bombers, and land and sea-launched intercontinental ballistic missiles.[1] In Russia, CTR funding went toward helping with the destruction of nuclear warheads, and for designing and constructing a facility to destroy stockpiles of chemical weapons.[2] About two-thirds of the remaining money spent through CTR funded security improvements for weapons-relevant materials, specifically the design and construction of a

---

1. A tally of the numbers and types of destroyed launchers can be found at http://www. dtra.mil/toolbox/directorates/ctr/scorecard.cfm. A similar accounting that is updated more frequently is http://lugar.senate.gov/nunnlugar/scorecard.html.

2. Under CTR, the United States did not destroy Russian warheads. Rather, the United States helped fund the construction of facilities associated with this destruction. It would have been politically unpopular in Russia if U.S. funds were used to directly destroy warheads. The United States also worked with Russia to design and build a facility for destroying chemical weapons at Shchuch'ye, Russia. This project suffered from numerous delays due to U.S. concerns that Russia was not fully declaring its chemical weapons stockpile, and U.S.-Russian disagreements about cost-sharing. Although CTR had funded the Shchuch'ye facility since 1992, the design work was not yet finished and construction was only about 25 percent complete as of early 2006. See Amy F. Woolf, *Nonproliferation and Threat Reduction Assistance: U.S. Programs in the Former Soviet Union*, Congressional Research Service, CRS Report for Congress, Washington, D.C., updated April 6, 2006, pp. 17–20. The Shchuch'ye chemical weapons destruction facility finally opened in late May 2009.

fissile material storage facility at Mayak, in the southern Ural mountains.[3] A large part of remaining CTR funds were spent on the purchase of armored blankets, emergency response kits, security kits for railroad cars, and other items to enable nuclear weapons to be moved safely. Russia, Ukraine, Kazakhstan, and Belarus inherited the Soviet Union's nuclear weapons, and initially transportation security focused on moving these weapons to Russia. By mid-1992, all Soviet tactical nuclear weapons had been moved to Russia, and by the end of 1996, the same was true for all Soviet strategic nuclear warheads. After that, transportation security focused on weapons in Russia that were en route to dismantlement facilities.[4] Over time, the Defense Department's other CTR activities included environmental restoration at former defense sites, the construction of housing for demobilized military officers, and military-to-military contacts.

With the inception of CTR, the Defense Department also played a role in trying to limit the proliferation of weapons expertise. The first effort—the Defense Conversion program—dates from the founding of CTR. On a yearly basis, however, these conversion efforts seldom amounted to more than 12 percent of CTR's yearly budget. Conversion was never popular with Congress, and in 1996, Congress began what would eventually become a permanent ban on using CTR for conversion and job-retraining efforts. Housing construction and environmental restoration activities were also banned.

In 1998, however, the Defense Department once again began to use CTR to fund retraining efforts. This time, the focus was on biological weapons–related experts and facilities. Under the Biological Threat Reduction Program (BTRP), the Defense Department targeted funding toward dismantling former biological weapons production facilities, increasing safety and security at institutes that stored and handled biological weapons–related materials, developing surveillance and warning systems for those facilities, and engaging former biological weapons experts in collaborative research.[5] Through fiscal year 2007, Defense received approximately $434 million for BTRP, of which about 25 percent was targeted toward cooperative research projects.[6] Because BTRP lacked

---

3. Like the facility at Shchuch'ye, the Mayak storage facility for fissile material was delayed significantly and repeatedly, due to disagreements with Russia over cost-sharing and design. When the facility finally opened in late 2003, it had been reduced in size by one-half and remained empty for three years because of disagreement over how to determine that the material being stored there came from dismantled nuclear weapons as opposed to other fissile material.

4. For progress reports in these areas, see Matthew Bunn, *Securing the Bomb 2008* (Cambridge, Mass., and Washington, D.C.: Project on Managing the Atom, Harvard University, and Nuclear Threat Initiative), November 2008. This report is one in a series that is updated regularly.

5. Originally this program was named the Biological Weapons Proliferation Program (BWPP). It was changed to BTRP in 2007.

6. Department of Defense, Defense Threat Reduction Agency, "Cooperative Threat Reduction Annual Report to Congress," fiscal year 2009, Washington, D.C., pp. 32, 35. Although a total of $434 million was obligated for BTRP overall through fiscal year 2007,

an implementing agreement in Russia, the Defense Department funded cooperative research projects through the International Science and Technology Center (ISTC) in Moscow.

Conversion and the Defense Enterprise Fund

Conversion was largely the brainchild of Clinton administration Deputy Secretary and later Secretary of Defense William Perry, who had played a key role in the Stanford University study that informed Congress' initial decisions about CTR. This section of the chapter discusses the process by which defense conversion projects were selected and financed, and briefly describes the joint ventures that were funded. It also discusses the political environment that affected their implementation.

The Defense Conversion program matched up and provided seed capital for U.S. commercial firms seeking to establish joint ventures in the former Soviet Union. First, a list of candidates for conversion among the former Soviet weapons enterprises was developed by country-specific Defense Conversion Committees. Such committees were created for Russia, Ukraine, Kazakhstan, and Belarus, and were composed of officials from those countries, as well as representatives of the U.S. Defense Department. Based upon the list developed by each committee, Defense Department officials selected 150 target institutes.[7] To qualify, an institute was supposed to be slated for significant or complete closure but, as critics were to later point out, some had lost all of their defense orders in the late 1980s and already were standing idle.[8]

In order to convert, the former Soviet weapons institute was supposed to create a private spin-off enterprise, although this requirement was later relaxed. The preference for spin-offs was based on the desire to clearly separate military from civilian production, ideally through a privatized joint stock company, and to challenge central government control of an enterprise by allowing for employee ownership.[9] Then, U.S. commercial firms were invited to bid for the right to enter into joint ventures with one of these newly privatized entities. Winners received seed capital from the CTR budget and were also expected to make contributions of their own; most contributions were in-kind in the form of equipment or personnel. These U.S. firms would also be a source of additional capital, marketing training, and management training for the spin-offs.

The involvement of U.S. business was prompted by more than just a desire for burden-sharing and mentoring. Congress saw conversion as

---

only $333 million was actually spent during this period.

7. General Accounting Office, *Cooperative Threat Reduction: Status of Defense Conversion Efforts in the Former Soviet Union*, Washington, D.C. (April 1997), p. 2.

8. General Accounting Office, *Weapons of Mass Destruction. Reducing the Threat from the Former Soviet Union: An Update*, Washington, D.C. (June 1995), pp. 30, 51–52.

9. See David Bernstein and William J. Perry, "Defense Conversion in Russia: A Strategic Imperative," *Stanford Journal of International Affairs*, Vol. II, Issue 2 (Summer 1993), p. 114.

a means of giving U.S. businesses experience working in Russia and increasing U.S. access to domestic markets there.[10]

Implementation and oversight were initially assigned to the Defense Department's Defense Nuclear Agency (DNA), which was also responsible for supporting the military's nuclear weapons programs. In 1996, DNA became the Defense Special Weapons Agency (DSWA). In October 1998, the Defense Department announced that program authority for all CTR activities would be moved to the newly created Defense Threat Reduction Agency (DTRA), which was also made responsible for both U.S. efforts to detect and respond to WMD attacks and U.S. compliance with arms control treaties, in addition to the old DNA mission of maintaining and improving U.S. nuclear forces. As of 2008, DTRA remained the Defense Department organization responsible for CTR.

CTR program staff developed a separate, detailed project plan for each conversion effort and negotiated implementing agreements. Project proposals were forwarded for final review and selection to the Safety, Security, and Dismantlement (SSD) Working Group. The SSD Working Group was a product of U.S. negotiations with the newly independent states of the former Soviet Union that were necessary for implementing CTR. Housed at the National Security Council, the group included members from the Office of the Secretary of Defense, the Joint Chiefs of Staff, the Departments of Energy and State, and the CIA.[11] Overall responsibility for political guidance was initially divided between the assistant secretary of defense for atomic energy, who was responsible for acquisition-related issues, and the assistant secretary of defense for international security policy. This led to some confusion and coordination problems, and in April 1993 these responsibilities were formally shifted to the assistant secretary for international security policy.[12] Under Clinton, this position was held by Ashton Carter, who contributed to the work at Harvard University that proved so influential in convincing Congress to create CTR.

As CTR's agenda expanded, some members of Congress, Republicans in particular, were concerned that all of CTR's resources should be refocused on the dismantlement of nuclear weapons.[13] Conversion efforts proved particularly unpopular. Partly this was because conversion was often considered to be foreign assistance rather than legitimate defense spending.[14] Some politicians worried about the ramifications of fund-

---

10. U.S. Congress, House, Committee on Armed Services, *National Defense Authorization Act for FY 93*, 102nd Cong., 2nd sess., October 1, 1992, p. 782.

11. General Accounting Office, *Former Soviet Union: U.S. Bilateral Program Lacks Effective Coordination*, Washington, D.C. (February 1995), p. 15.

12. See Department of Defense, Office of the Inspector General, *Evaluation of the Defense Nuclear Agency's Cooperative Threat Reduction Office* (Washington, D.C.: National Technical Information Service, October 12, 1995), ADA371438, p. 3.

13. Interview with congressional source 1, August 8, 2003; interview with congressional source 2, August 4, 2003; and interview with former Clinton administration official 1, September 17, 2003.

14. See, for example, U.S. Congress, House, *Department of Defense Appropriations for 1995*,

ing job creation in the former Soviet Union when unemployment was a problem at home. There was also concern about funding conversion efforts in the United States. For example, in 1992, Congress specified that no funds could be used for conversion in the former Soviet Union unless the president also authorized an equal or greater amount for converting defense industries at home.[15] Even those who favored conversion noted that it was likely to be expensive and inefficient.[16]

For fiscal year 1993, Congress specified that the Defense Department could spend no more than $40 million on conversion efforts. Several subsequent reprogramming requests were also denied. Despite a persistent and robust defense of conversion programs by Clinton administration officials in the Defense Department, Congress prohibited the use of CTR funds for defense conversion after fiscal year 1996. Although this partly reflected opposition to conversion specifically, it was also due to a desire to refocus CTR spending on the elimination of weapons in general. As expressed by the House committee in charge of authorizing defense spending:

> The committee reiterates its belief that funding for CTR activities should be directed toward facilitating the safe transportation, storage and elimination of weapons of mass destruction, their delivery vehicles, and components, and for programs and activities designed to prevent proliferation. The committee does not support CTR funding for activities outside these basic purposes. For this reason, the committee recommends a provision (sec. 1103) that would maintain a prohibition on the use of CTR funds for peacekeeping-related activities, housing, environmental restoration, job retraining, and defense conversions.[17]

Over the life of the program, Congress approved approximately $126 million for conversion, of which approximately $60 million was actually spent on conversion projects in the former Soviet Union.[18] From fiscal years 1992 through 1995, CTR overall received funding of approximately

---

Part 4, 103rd Cong., 2nd sess., 1994, pp. 565–576.

15.   U.S. Congress, House, Committee on Foreign Affairs, *Freedom Support Act*, 102nd Cong., 2nd sess., October 1, 1992, p. 68.

16.   U.S. Congress, House, Committee on Armed Services, *National Defense Authorization Act for FY 93*, 102nd Cong., 2nd sess., October 1, 1992, p. 783; and General Accounting Office, *Weapons of Mass Destruction Reducing the Threat from the Former Soviet Union*, Washington, D.C. (October 1994), p. 13.

17.   U.S. Congress, House, Committee on National Security, *National Defense Authorization Act for Fiscal Year 1998*, 105th Cong., 1st sess., June 16, 1997, House Rpt. 105-132, p. 420.

18.   These totals are based on the spending figures presented in Table 4.1; and General Accounting Office, *Cooperative Threat Reduction: Status of Defense Conversion Efforts in the Former Soviet Union*, pp. 20–37.

$1.25 billion; thus conversion projects amounted to about 10 percent of CTR funding during this period.[19]

In total, the Defense Conversion program funded sixteen projects. Russia was the initial focus; attention there was centered on four projects—called the Fast Four—in an effort to get the program moving quickly and demonstrate success early. Ultimately, three projects were funded in Belarus, four others in Kazakhstan, and five in Ukraine. Preference was given to infrastructure projects, in the belief that these would provide the foundation for helping local companies be more competitive in world markets and ease the entry of U.S. businesses into Russia.[20] Table 4.1 briefly describes these conversion projects along with their U.S. and formerly Soviet partners.

In response to growing political criticism about defense conversion efforts, the Defense Department created the Demilitarization Enterprise Fund (DEF) in 1994.[21] William Perry, who became Secretary of Defense in February 1994, personally persuaded Congress in the summer of 1993 to create DEF as part of the CTR provisions in the fiscal year 1994 defense authorization bill.[22] To avoid the negative political baggage that was increasingly associated with conversion, the name was quickly changed to the Defense Enterprise Fund, although the acronym remained the same. In fiscal year 1995, CTR began shifting its defense conversion efforts to DEF.

Similar to the Defense Department's earlier conversion efforts, DEF's focus was also limited to enterprises that were associated with some part of production for weapons of mass destruction. Projects were also selected based on the likelihood of project success and profitability.[23]

DEF functioned like a private investment fund by providing loans or grants, sometimes in return for equity, to U.S. companies that would pursue joint ventures with spin-offs from former Soviet defense enterprises. DEF could also provide collateral for loan guarantees from the Export-Import Bank. Although DEF was initially supposed to receive grants from other government agencies and the private sector, it got two-thirds of its funding from the Defense Department. Also unfulfilled was the expectation that DEF would re-coup its loans, hopefully with additional profits, and use these to make future investments.

Although DEF was created by Congress to finance conversion in the former Soviet Union, it was run as a quasi-independent agency with its

---

19.   General Accounting Office, *Weapons of Mass Destruction: Reducing the Threat from the Former Soviet Union: An Update*, pp. 1, 31.

20.   Bernstein and Perry, "Defense Conversion in Russia: A Strategic Imperative," p. 114.

21.   Graham T. Allison, Owen R. Coté, Jr., Richard A. Falkenrath, and Steven E. Miller, *Avoiding Nuclear Anarchy: Containing the Threat of Loose Russian Nuclear Weapons and Fissile Material* (Cambridge, Mass.: MIT Press, 1996), pp. 91–92.

22.   Richard Combs, "U.S. Domestic Politics and the Nunn-Lugar Program," in John M. Shields and William C. Potter, eds., *Dismantling the Cold War: U.S. and NIS Perspectives on the Nunn-Lugar Cooperative Threat Reduction Program* (Cambridge, Mass.: MIT Press, 1997), p. 48.

23.   Kevin P. O'Prey, *A Farewell to Arms? Russia's Struggles with Defense Conversion* (New York: Twentieth Century Fund Press, 1995), p. 88.

own board of directors. Originally DEF was managed by its employees, but in 1997, the Pentagon transferred that responsibility to Global Partner Ventures, a private firm owned by two DEF employees. In 1999, DEF's management was transferred to Siguler Guff and Company of New York.

Table 4.1. CTR-Funded Conversion Projects.

FORMER SOVIET ENTERPRISE	MILITARY FUNCTION	U.S. BUSINESS PARTNER	JOINT VENTURE	CTR FUND-ING[a]
Belarus				
Belarussian Optical and Mechanical Association (Belomo)	Made optics for satellites, gun sights, and missile defense systems	Byelocorp	Laser pointers	$0.96
Integral Electronics	Made nuclear-hardened chips for command and control systems	Kras Corporation	Low-end integrated circuits	$5.75
Minsk Computer	Made mainframe computers for the military	Federal Systems Group	Battery chargers	$2.45
Kazakhstan				
BioMedPreparat	Research and production of biological weapons	Allen and Associates	Manufacture, package, and distribute vitamins	$2.69
Gidromash	Made missile and aircraft systems	Byelocorp	Valves and pressure vessels for cryogenic materials and gases	$3
Kazakhstan National Nuclear Center	Managed nuclear test site	Kras Corporation	Produce printed circuit boards	$4
Kazin, State Property Committee on Kazakhstan	Operated the Saryshaghan test site for surface to air and anti-ballistic missiles	Lucent Technologies/AT&T	Telecom and wireless services (KazInformtelecom)	$5
Russia				
Leninets	Designed missile guidance and radars	International American Products	Equipment for Russian dental facilities	$1.95

Table 4.1. *(continued)*

Scientific Production Association (NPO) Mashinostroyeniya	Designed satellites, cruise missiles, and ICBMs	Double Cola	Bottling soft drinks	$5.13
State Research Institute for Aviation Systems (GosNIIAS)	Designed bombers and aircraft	Rockwell International	Air traffic control systems	$4.1
State Scientific Production Enterprise (NPO) Istok	Designed radios, vacuum tubes, radars, and lasers for military use	Hearing Aids International	Hearing aids (Istok Audio International)	$5.6
Ukraine				
Kommunar Production Association	Made aerospace and military electronics equipment	Federal Systems Group	Manufacture and assemble cell phones	$3.25
Meridian	Designed and tested radio equipment and instruments for missiles	Die Casters International (second partner)	Die cast products	$4.1
Monolit	Made electronics for rocket control and guidance systems	ABB (Switzerland)	Advanced instrumentation and control systems for nuclear and conventional commercial power stations	$4.8
Orizon	Made precision guidance and control systems for satellites	American Industrial Development Corporation (AIDCO)	PVC multiple layered windows	$2.7
Scientific Production Association (NPO) Khartron	Made space and ballistic missile guidance systems	Westinghouse	Power plant instrumentation and control systems (Hartron Corporation)	$5

[a]These numbers are in millions of U.S. dollars.

SOURCES: Department of Defense, "Cooperative Threat Reduction Annual Reports to Congress," fiscal years 1994–1999, Washington, D.C.; Department of Defense, "Cooperative Threat Reduction Semi-Annual Reports to Congress," fiscal years 1994–1999, Washington, D.C.; and General Accounting Office, *Cooperative Threat Reduction: Status of Defense Conversion Efforts in the Former Soviet Union*, Washington, D.C. (April 1997).

The Defense Department eventually provided $52 million to DEF before congressional restrictions on conversion spending prohibited additional funding after fiscal year 1996. As a result, it was the State Department that gave DEF its last funding in 1997. Thereafter, Congress prohibited additional public financing.

But DEF's troubles were not over. In 1999, it was accused by a former employee of gross mismanagement of its investment portfolio, using money to buy political favors from Russian officials, and lavish spending by some Moscow-based employees.[24] That employee brought his concerns to Ambassador William Taylor, the State Department's Coordinator of U.S. Assistance to the Newly Independent States. Although the subsequent internal State Department investigation did not support these allegations, two investigations by the Department of Defense Inspector General did find evidence of poor management and questionable investments. The Inspector General found that DEF officials spent about half of the fund's money on managing the fund's affairs, about $1 million on unnecessary living expenses, and had made $38 million in investments that were subsequently worth only $15 million.[25] DEF was closed on December 31, 2003, due no doubt in part to its poor financial performance and recent scandals.

Over the course of its life, DEF invested a total of approximately $28 million in eighteen projects: fifteen in Russia, two in Kazakhstan, and one in Ukraine.[26] Initial plans to invest in Belarus were shelved due to problems related to privatization laws and human rights abuses. Table 4.2 describes DEF's investments. (See pp. 120–121.)

The Defense Department funded one additional conversion project, although it had little to do with the proliferation of weapons expertise. According to Russian law, members of the Strategic Rocket Forces and some other military officers could not be sent home unless they were provided with a place to live.[27] Therefore, to enable the demobilization and withdrawal of troops from various formerly Soviet states, houses had to be built for them. Removing Russian troops from Estonia, Lithuania, and Latvia was especially popular due to pressure from ethnic groups within the United States that supported the independence of these Baltic republics.[28] Because housing was in short supply throughout the former

24. Matt Bivens, "Shredded, ignored, exiled and penniless," *Moscow Times*, April 4, 2001, p. 7; and Matt Bivens, "Investing, Pentagon-Style," *Moscow Times*, April 4, 2001, p. 7.

25. Department of Defense, Office of the Inspector General, "Audit Report, Defense Enterprise Fund," Report No. D-2000-176, August 15, 2000; and Department of Defense, Office of the Inspector General, "Management Costs Associated with the Defense Enterprise Fund," Report No. D-2002-033, December 31, 2001.

26. Total investment is based on sources listed for Table 4.2, DEF's Investment Portfolio.

27. The U.S. Agency for International Development (USAID) also had a program for building houses for Russian troops returning from Estonia, Latvia, and Lithuania. As of February 1995, USAID had spent $39 million and obligated a total of $160 million for its housing program. See U.S. Congress, House, Committee on International Relations, *U.S. Assistance Programs for Economic and Political Reform and Dismantling of Weapons of Mass Destruction in the NIS*, 104th Cong., 1st sess., March 3, 1995, p. 82.

28. See U.S. Congress, Senate, Committee on Appropriations, *Foreign Operations, Export*

Soviet Union, private construction companies were considered good investments, and approximately $56 million in CTR money went to fund the conversion of four enterprises from weapons production to housing construction. Two of these housing conversion projects were in Ukraine, one in Russia, and another in Belarus.

Ultimately, like other conversion efforts, housing proved politically unpopular with Congress, especially at a time when the United States was closing some of its own military bases. After several rescinded reprogramming requests, Congress ended all CTR spending for housing construction after fiscal year 1996.

Defining the Threat

Congressional documents and testimony by Defense Department officials suggest that the Defense Department's conversion efforts were aimed at three distinct, albeit related threats. Moreover, focusing on other threats besides proliferation allowed the Defense Department to measure the success of its conversion efforts using much more favorable criteria.

Ostensibly, one of the main threats that conversion projects were designed to defeat was the proliferation of WMD expertise. To discourage this, the goal was to create jobs for excess or idle WMD-related workers who might otherwise be tempted to sell their skills to another country or to sell weapons for profit. According to the Defense Department, in order to be a candidate for conversion dollars, an enterprise was supposed to have contributed to Soviet WMD capabilities. In practice, however, this qualification was defined broadly. Besides firms involved in the production of nuclear, biological, or chemical weapons, the Defense Department also included those that had produced WMD delivery systems, such as bombers or missiles, as well as enterprises that were involved in command, control, and communications. This definition served to expand the list of candidate firms significantly. But this expanded list was also more likely to include firms with fewer security-related restrictions on access, thus making cooperation easier.

The initial candidates for conversion projects were developed by the bilateral commissions for each country. The firm's participation in WMD-related activities were then supposedly verified using a list put together by the U.S. intelligence community of WMD-related enterprises in the former Soviet Union.[29] From this list, a smaller subset of firms was selected and the Defense Special Weapons Agency, which administered CTR at the time, worked with each firm to put together plans for privatization.[30] Certainly, at the time key enterprises that were directly involved in making WMD could easily have been identified. But there is no evidence that

---

Financing, and Related Programs Appropriations, FY 95, 103rd Cong., 2nd sess., March 2, 8, 15, 22, April 12, 19, 26, May 17, 24, 1994, pp. 43–45.

29.   Interview with former Clinton administration official 3, March 31, 2003; and interview with former U.S. government official 2, April 4, 2003.

30.   Ibid.

Table 4.2. DEF's Investment Portfolio.

FORMER SOVIET ENTERPRISE	MILITARY FUNCTION	U.S. BUSINESS PARTNER	JOINT VENTURE
Kazakhstan			
Kazakhstan National Nuclear Center	Operated Kazakh nuclear weapons test site	Kras Corporation	Design, make, assemble and market printed circuit boards and consumer electronics (KK Interconnect)
Kazin, State Property Committee on Kazakhstan	Satellite tracking capability	Lucent/AT&T	Telephone carrier services (Nursat)
Russia			
Beryllium Institute in Kaluga	Made beryllium housings for missiles and nuclear weapons guidance systems	Beryllium Composite Technology, Inc.	Computer hard drives and CD-ROM disks from a beryllium aluminum alloy
Central Communications Station of the Russian Railways Ministry	None	EP-CDC (Cyprus-based company owned by DEF)	Modernize railway communications through fiber optic cable
Khlopin Radium Institute	Nuclear weapons design	REM Capital, Paine-Weber, Western Bulk Carriers (Norway)	Timber irradiation (RAIES International)
Kirovsky Zavod	Made propulsion systems for nuclear submarine, tanks, and other heavy equipment	Caterpillar	Excavating equipment
Metallugicheski Zavod Ametists	Firm composed of former defense workers	Valme Industries (France) and EBRD	Recovery of precious metals from electronic scrap
MNIIS	Command and control for Strategic Rocket Forces	NYROS Telecom Services	Commercial telephone services (RTN)

Table 4.2. (continued)

Moscow Institute of Communications Research and the Russian Tele-communications Network	Communications for strategic command and control	NYROS Telecom Services	Commercial telephone services (RUSNET Labs)
NPO Impuls	Variety of military research and development programs	Kent International	Assemble and distribute personal computers and office equipment (RAMEC)
NPO Istok	Designed radios, vacuum tubes, radars, and lasers for military use	Transcontinental Systems Development Group	Software programming
NPO Mashinostroyeniya	Military aerospace	U.S.-based software company	Software engineering and development services (ORBITSoft)
Scientific Production Association (NPO) Nauka	Made military aircraft environmental control systems	Hamilton-Standard	Environmental control systems for aircraft
Siberian Mining and Chemical Combine	Plutonium production	DEF	Production of polycrystalline silicon
Sukhoi Design Bureau	Military aircraft engineering	DEF	Develop and market a durable, heavy-duty oil pump for deep oil drilling
Svetlana Electron Devices	Military electronics production	R&G Inc.	Vacuum tubes
Two independent scientists	unknown affiliation	DEF	Solid lubricant to reduce friction and dust (Impregnated Abrasive Instruments)
Ukraine			
Dosvid Engineering Company	Former anti-tank grenade factory	DEF	Recycling of scrap aluminum (Liform)

SOURCES: General Accounting Office, *Weapons of Mass Destruction, Reducing the Threat from the Former Soviet Union: An Update*, Washington, D.C. (June 1995), p. 55; Department of Defense, "Cooperative Threat Reduction Annual Reports to Congress" fiscal years 1994–1999, Washington, D.C.; Department of Defense, "Cooperative Threat Reduction Semi-Annual Reports to Congress," fiscal years 1994–1999, Washington, D.C.; "DEF's Portfolio Today," *Moscow Times*, April 4, 2001, p. 10; and General Accounting Office, *Cooperative Threat Reduction: Status of Defense Conversion Efforts in the Former Soviet Union*, Washington, D.C. (April 1997), p. 49.

suggests that the Defense Department tried to focus on the most WMD-relevant firms or that it was dissatisfied with the firms that were selected for conversion.[31]

Moreover, there is no evidence that Defense Department officials or program managers made any effort to target key WMD experts at the facilities that were selected. Instead, they left decisions about who would become part of the spin-off to the host partner enterprise and the host country to make. Additionally, because most conversion efforts involved production rather than services, they necessarily employed a significant number of laborers, but fewer scientists and engineers.

This lack of attention to WMD relevance reinforces consistent sentiments expressed in interviews with former Defense Department officials that conversion was not predominantly motivated by the desire to reduce WMD proliferation.[32] As originally framed, defense conversion and job creation were an integral part of the overall CTR effort and included an emphasis on fighting proliferation. But in contrast to the Science Centers and Department of Energy programs, Defense Department conversion projects were also seen as an extension of CTR overall; that is, they were intended to reduce direct threats to the United States from Soviet legacy systems.[33] For Perry and his team, the collapse of the Soviet Union provided the United States with the opportunity to reduce the Soviet defense infrastructure, and with it the number of weapons that threatened the United States.

It was clear that the Soviet Union had significant excess defense production capability with respect to conventional weapons, weapons of mass destruction, and the means to deliver both. Similar to CTR's efforts to destroy Soviet nuclear weapons launchers, converting defense industries would directly reduce the ability of Russia and other post-Soviet states to target those weapons at the United States. There was, of course, also the danger that this excess capacity would be used to produce weapons and delivery systems that were not needed and could not be paid for by the Russian central government; therefore, institutes might seek to sell these weapons to other buyers.[34] Indeed, in the early 1990s, key officials in the Russian defense establishment proposed funding conversion through the sale of conventional weapons to other countries.[35] Although this pro-

31. Ibid.; and interview with U.S. government official 3, February 22, 2007.

32. Interview with former Clinton administration official 1, September 17, 2003; interview with former Clinton administration official 3, March 31, 2003; and interview with former U.S. government official 2, April 4, 2003.

33. See, for example, U.S. Congress, House, Committee on Appropriations, *Department of Defense Appropriations for 1995*, Part 4, 103rd Cong., 2nd sess., 1994, p. 565; and General Accounting Office, *Weapons of Mass Destruction: Reducing the Threat from the Former Soviet Union*, pp. 40–42.

34. According to interview with former Clinton administration official 3, March 31, 2003, this was a fear for the Clinton administration.

35. U.S. Congress, Senate, Committee on Armed Services, *Trip Report: A Visit to the Commonwealth of Independent States*, 102nd Cong., 2nd sess., March 10, 1992, p. 5.

liferation was a concern, it took a backseat to the overall goal of directly reducing the number of weapons aimed at the United States. This connection is illustrated in congressional testimony by Ashton Carter, Clinton's assistant secretary of defense for international security policy:

> We have felt from the beginning that the CTR program should take an end-to-end approach to threat reduction. That is, we would seek to eliminate deployed weapons, which you see over there in that silo, but we would also seek to assist in the shrinking and reorientation to peaceful purposes of the weapons of mass destruction–related industry of the former Soviet Union, so that if things take a turn for the worse in the future, that industry is smaller, less able to produce a renewed threat.[36]

Similar testimony can also be found about the relationship of DEF to CTR's overall goals of reducing weapons aimed at the United States. This connection between conversion projects and threat reduction can also be seen in CTR's housing construction projects, which were expressly intended to enable the demobilization of the approximately 164,000 excess strategic rocket forces troops that manned former Soviet strategic nuclear missile batteries, most of which were aimed at the United States.

Besides nonproliferation and threat reduction, there was another goal that was at least equally important. Conversion was seen as a means of helping Russia develop an economy that was more responsive to market forces than central government directives had been, and of encouraging economic integration with the West. This, in turn, would help stabilize the Russian economy and facilitate a relationship with Russia that was no longer premised on military confrontation.

According to this logic, defense conversion was seen as an opportunity to demonstrate the benefits of production for commercial benefit, the associated social and economic benefits, and to convince Russia to fund its own conversion efforts.[37] For these reasons, in terms of conversion candidates, the WMD expertise of a firm or individual was secondary to its commercial and conversion potential. For example, one of the criteria for the initial selection of institutes for conversion efforts—what would become the "Fast Four"—was preference for enterprises that were ripe for

---

36. U.S. Congress, House, Committee on Armed Services, *National Defense Authorization Act for FY 93*, 102nd Cong., 2nd sess., October 1, 1992, p. 1123. Similar connections can be found in the testimony of other Department of Defense officials. See also U.S. Congress, House, Committee on Appropriations, *Department of Defense Appropriations for 1995*, Part 4, 103rd Cong., 2nd sess., March 9, 15, 17, April 12, 13, 1994, p. 565; and General Accounting Office, *Weapons of Mass Destruction: Reducing the Threat from the Former Soviet Union*, pp. 40–42.

37. See comments of John D. Nowell, DEF President, General Accounting Office, *Cooperative Threat Reduction: Status of Defense Conversion Efforts*, p. 43; and U.S. Congress, Senate, Committee on Armed Services, *Department of Defense Authorization for Appropriations for FY 95 and the Future Years Defense Program, Part 7: Nuclear Deterrence, Arms Control and Defense Intelligence*, 103rd Cong., 2nd sess., April 21, 26, 28, May 3, 5, 11, 1994, S. Hrg. 103-765 Pt. 7, pp. 209–210.

conversion, with good business plans and chances for success, and an attitude and management that were pro-market.[38] The idea was to demonstrate the fruits of successful conversion to other defense enterprises.

This interest in commercial benefit can also be seen in the emphasis that defense conversion projects placed on partnerships that would build infrastructure, such as telecommunications, transportation, energy, and housing. In contrast, other programs at State and Energy focused on projects that were high-tech and scientifically intensive as a means of interesting top weapons experts. More defense conversion projects focused instead on what could be considered "public goods," reasoning that states would need a solid infrastructure to compete in and integrate with world markets and to allow for the expansion of U.S. business interests.[39] Moreover, since spin-offs were unlikely to be competitive in world markets in the short term, these conversion ventures should focus on domestic and regional markets.[40] This is an important distinction because projects that focused on production for Western or world markets were much less successful, as will be explained in later chapters.

There was one additional goal of defense conversion. According to one former U.S. government official involved in defense conversion efforts, in Kazakhstan, Belarus, and Ukraine, conversion projects were initiated partly as a carrot to convince those countries to give up the nuclear weapons they had inherited from the Soviet Union and to commit to a future status as non-nuclear weapons states.[41]

Tying conversion efforts to the twin goals of reducing the number of weapons that could be used against the United States and demonstrating the benefits of a decentralized market economy had two important benefits that would not as easily have resulted had conversion been linked solely to nonproliferation. First, it meant that it was possible to justify conversion programs and measure their progress without linking them to precise numbers or targets. If nonproliferation was the only goal, then all idle workers and excess defense capacity would be threats. Despite the Defense Department's insistence that it never intended to convert the entire former Soviet defense industry, it is the case that numbers of redundant workers and excess defense plants can both be measured and, given the size of the Soviet military machine, these numbers were quite large. Clearly it was beyond the capacity of U.S. conversion efforts to make more than token progress toward such a goal. And limited progress, even if it is expected, is often political suicide. Indeed, in the mid-1990s, when there was an effort to measure the amount of factory space that was now devoted to commercial production as a result of U.S. efforts, Defense

38. Interview with former Clinton administration official 1, September 17, 2003; and interview with former U.S. government official 2, April 4, 2003.

39. See Bernstein and Perry, "Defense Conversion in Russia: A Strategic Imperative," p. 114.

40. Ibid.

41. Interview with former U.S. government official 2, April 4, 2003.

Department officials tended to shy away from such figures.[42] This sort of quantification made it easy for CTR critics to show that conversion was inefficient, extremely costly, and liable to require U.S. funding for decades, if not longer.

If, however, the goal of conversion was to encourage Russia and other former Soviet states to fund their own conversion efforts, then the pool of potential projects was much smaller. Instead of the need to engage the many enterprises that were relevant to WMD production, the goal became to work with the much smaller number of such firms that were ripe for conversion. Focusing on only those firms that were ready to undertake conversion was more likely to lead to demonstrable success because the Defense Department could engage a significant number of the entire pool. In contrast, it was never likely that the Defense Department could convert any more than a very small number of the firms that were in excess of Russia's defense needs.

In a similar fashion, focusing on threat reduction led to better indicators of program success. If threat reduction was the goal, then any conversion project was useful because it eliminated weapons that were targeted at the United States. Nonproliferation, however, begs a measurement focused on the firms that had yet to be engaged or converted, a much larger number.

Measuring Progress

CTR's conversion efforts were initially aimed at reducing the chances of proliferation by reemploying WMD experts and reducing threats to the United States by eliminating weapons capacity in the former Soviet Union, especially Russia. Over time, the Defense Department also came to justify conversion as a means of demonstrating the economic benefit of converting excess defense industry. To what extent were these goals achieved?

REDUCING PROLIFERATION
With respect to discouraging proliferation by creating jobs for excess weapons workers, the results are not encouraging. The Defense Department did not keep comprehensive records of the people employed through its conversion projects, their WMD-related skills, or the fate of the projects after CTR involvement came to a close. According to my interviews, U.S. business participants were not asked how many people their projects employed, nor did the Defense Department attempt to keep independent records.[43] It is possible, however, to estimate jobs created based on CTR's annual reports to Congress and on audits by the Government Accountability Office (GAO). Based on these sources, and using the

---

42. Interview with U.S. government official 3, February 22, 2007; and interview with U.S. government official 4, February 22, 2007.

43. Ibid.; interview with former U.S. government official 2, April 4, 2003; interview with U.S. government official 5, January 29, 2007; and interview with U.S. business person 1, February 22, 2007.

highest estimates where there are discrepancies, the sixteen conversion projects that were funded by the Defense Department's Defense Conversion program initially employed some 1,900 people. If this pool is reduced to projects that succeeded for at least five years or whose fate is unclear, an estimated 1,122 were employed. Four of these projects led to sustainable businesses that still existed as of 2007: Istok Audio, the Byelcorp-Gidromash project, KK Interconnect, and Nursat. Initially their projects employed 614 people.[44] As of mid-2007, Istok Audio had 350 employees, of whom 80 originally transferred from the defense institute NPO Istok; KK Interconnect employed 150; Byelkamit had over 500 employees; and employee information for Nursat was not available.[45]

With respect to DEF-funded projects, estimates are that they reemployed 2,030 former defense workers.[46] However, an audit of DEF by the Defense Department's Inspector General expressed concern that DEF's totals do not reflect reductions in employment due to failed ventures or suspended production.[47]

There is a further problem of distinguishing between weapons and non-weapons workers. According to a 1997 study by the GAO, of twenty-four CTR-funded conversion projects (four DEF projects and twenty Defense Conversion projects), five projects did not employ any WMD-related workers, and the GAO was unable to determine if WMD workers were employed in eleven other projects.[48] Of the conversion projects that did prosper, it is not known how many of these employees were hired from outside the associated defense institute or had WMD-relevant skills.

Moreover, in no case did any conversion project employ a significant fraction of the total workforce at an institute. A typical example is that of NPO Istok, one of the successful conversion projects funded by CTR. Of the 8,000 people employed at Istok in 1994, 160 found jobs as part of the conversion project.[49]

The results are no less discouraging if the focus is on the institute rather than at the individual level. Initially, between 150 and 200 firms were identified for conversion, and there is no evidence that this list was subsequently updated or expanded. Conversion projects took place in only about 30 of these firms. Further conversion efforts engaged only small spin-offs, not entire enterprises. Therefore, it is clear that U.S.-funded conversion projects were of little or no consequence to the vast majority of

44. General Accounting Office, *Cooperative Threat Reduction: Status of Defense Conversion Efforts*, pp. 20–37.

45. Electronic communication from KK Interconnect on May 23, 2007; electronic communication from Istok-Audio on May 23, 2007 and May 24, 2007; and Byelkamit's website, http://www.kioge.kz/en/2004/oview/-1019706590/ (accessed June 13, 2007).

46. Department of Defense, *Defense Enterprise Fund*, p. 8.

47. Ibid.

48. General Accounting Office, *Cooperative Threat Reduction: Status of Defense Conversion Efforts in the Former Soviet Union*, pp. 3, 20–40.

49. Ibid, p. 28.

idle or potentially idle defense enterprises or workers in the former Soviet Union.

ELIMINATING WEAPONS THAT THREATENED THE UNITED STATES

In terms of the goal of reducing threats to the United States from former Soviet or Russian WMD, the results are also discouraging. Tables 4.1 and 4.2 list the projects that were funded by the defense conversion program and DEF. With respect to the most catastrophic threat—an attack using nuclear weapons—conversion programs had little impact. Of the thirty-four conversion projects that were funded, only a handful involved enterprises that were engaged in the research, design, development, or manufacture of nuclear weapons. The most WMD-relevant conversion projects involved the anthrax production facility at BioMedPreparat in Kazakhstan, St. Petersburg's Khlopin Radium Institute, which designed nuclear weapons, and the Siberian Mining and Chemical Combine in Zheleznogorsk, Russia, which made plutonium for nuclear weapons.

Although three projects involved converting two former weapons-testing sites and facilities in Kazakhstan, their contribution to threat re-duction was minimal. The Soviet Union declared a moratorium on nuclear testing in 1990, and the United States followed suit in 1992. In addition, Russia, which inherited all of the Soviet Union's nuclear weapons, still maintained a test site at Novaya Zemlya for conducting sub-critical nucle-ar tests. Because Kazakhstan returned its nuclear weapons to Russia and joined the Nuclear Non-Proliferation Treaty as a non-nuclear weapons state, it had already agreed to close the Semipalatinsk nuclear weapons test site and the anti-ballistic missile testing facility at Saryshagan.

Perhaps the most directly WMD-relevant enterprise that the Defense Department engaged was BioMedPreparat in Kazakhstan. Located in Stepnogorsk, the complex was one of the Soviet Union's largest biologi-cal weapons research and production facilities. In particular, Stepnogorsk was a major producer of weapons-grade anthrax. Under the conversion plan, $2.69 million in CTR money was invested in a partnership between Allen and Associates, Inc., and BioMedPreparat to make, package, and distribute vitamins and pharmaceuticals. The venture ended before any production began. The failure was largely due to the inexperience of the U.S. partner, Allen and Associates, which had little practice with the commercialization of bio-technology but good political connections in Washington.[50] There were also problems due to scheduling issues, build-ing maintenance costs, and the inability of the facility to pay its electric-ity and other infrastructure bills.[51] The Defense Department eventually spent another $1.3 million on other conversion projects at Stepnogorsk,

50. Michael Dobbs, "Soviet-Era Work on Bioweapons Still Worrisome; Stall in U.S. Dismantling Effort Could Pose Proliferation Threat," *Washington Post*, September 12, 2000, p. A1; and interview with U.S. government official 1, April 9, 2007.

51. Yerlan Kunakbayev, Gulbarshyn Bozheyeva, and Dastan Yeleukenov, "Former Soviet Biological Weapons Facilities in Kazakhstan: Past, Present and Future," Center for Nonproliferation Studies, Monterey, Calif., June 1999.

most of which also failed.[52] The most successful was the Environmental Monitoring Lab (EML), a project initially funded with $1 million from CTR. As of 2008, EML had contracts for environmental monitoring and testing, including some from the U.S. Environmental Protection Agency, and had International Organization for Standardization (ISO) certification for environmental testing.[53] In 2007, the Kazakh Ministry of Health took over the facility and pledged to continue paying for certain projects and to maintain the ISO certification.

The repeated failure of conversion, plus congressional prohibitions on spending CTR money for these projects after 1995, eventually resulted in a shift in emphasis to dismantling Stepnogorsk rather than converting it. CTR funding enabled the destruction of the facility's biological weapons–related equipment in 2003 and the dismantlement of weapons-related buildings in 2007.[54]

Stepnogorsk initially employed an estimated 3,000.[55] As of April 2007, an estimated 50–70 scientists with critical biological weapons knowledge worked there.[56] About 25 of these were at EML.[57] The fate of the remaining experts is unknown. Under the State Department's Bio-Chem Redirection Program, efforts continued as of 2008 to find employment for the scientists who remain at the facility and for the engineers who were employed doing dismantlement.

Besides illustrating the difficulties with conversion, Stepnogorsk is also an example of how defense conversion assistance might have had a negative impact. When the Soviet Union collapsed, many Russian biological weapons experts initially left the Stepnogorsk complex and returned to Russia. Some, however, no doubt stayed on due to the lure of potential jobs through conversion, and there is evidence that a few returned to Stepnogorsk from Russia because of promises of U.S. assistance. It is possible that some passed up opportunities for employment in the hope that U.S. interest would lead to jobs that made better use of their scientific skills, albeit in non-weapons work. When the United States stopped funding conversion, these experts were once again on their own. Certainly some participated in other U.S.-funded research efforts, but most had to find their own futures away from the complex. Additionally, according to one U.S. government official familiar with these conversion efforts, elevated expectations, unfulfilled promises, and the negative experience of

52. Dobbs, "Soviet Era Work on Bioweapons Still Worrisome," p. A1.

53. ISO certification is an indicator that products and performance consistently meet internationally recognized quality standards.

54. Department of Defense, Defense Threat Reduction Agency, "Cooperative Threat Reduction Annual Report to Congress," fiscal year 2007, Washington, D.C., p. 24.

55. Interview with State Department official 3, May 1, 2007.

56. Ibid.; and interview with U.S. government official 1, April 9, 2007.

57. Ibid.

working with Allen and Associates led to poor relations and poisoned the environment for future conversion efforts.[58]

Instead of redirecting experts who had critical WMD knowledge, most Defense Department conversion projects were with enterprises that had produced WMD command, control, and communications systems or weapons delivery platforms. At least one project, which involved an anti-tank grenade factory in Ukraine, had no WMD relevance at all. Had conversion been successful in all of these projects—and, as I argue in the next section, this is far from the case—this would not necessarily have reduced the risk faced by the United States from these particular weapons. This is because Russia, which remained the only post-Soviet state with the capability of challenging the U.S. military, was committed to defense downsizing. In the early 1990s, Russia took steps to close some defense production lines and begin the process of converting others. The former Soviet firms that were engaged by U.S. conversion efforts were mostly those that had already been declared excess. According to the GAO, most conversion projects involved facilities that were no longer in use.[59] In a 1997 study of twenty-four conversion projects, the GAO found that only one involved an enterprise that was still producing goods associated with weapons of mass destruction.[60] Russia's defense downsizing meant that conversion projects may have engaged former weapons workers, but did little to convince additional workers, firms, or the Russian government to further reduce its military capabilities.

Moreover, there were conflicts between the U.S. and Russian governments over which buildings to involve in conversion activities. The United States wanted to convert the spaces where the worst weapons were made. In contrast, the Russian government, as well as institute managers, wanted to keep these buildings in case they were needed for future defense requirements. Instead, they wanted to use buildings that had leaky roofs, broken windows, and which generally needed repair.[61]

Finally, in at least one instance, conversion may have inadvertently funded Russia's weapons capacity. According to the GAO, the Defense Department did not consistently require institutes to spin-off privatized entities for the purposes of conversion.[62] Because the notion of privatization was initially poorly understood by the Russian government, this created problems for conversion projects, and CTR agreed to work with

---

58. Ibid.

59. General Accounting Office, *Weapons of Mass Destruction: Reducing the Threat from the Former Soviet Union: An Update*, p. 30. The Defense Department, in response to the GAO report, pointed out that economic pressure may force the managers of dormant facilities to produce weapons for sale abroad, even if they no longer serve this function for the state. See pp. 51–52.

60. General Accounting Office, *Cooperative Threat Reduction: Status of Defense Conversion Efforts in the Former Soviet Union*, p. 3.

61. Interview with U.S. government official 4, February 22, 2007.

62. General Accounting Office, *Weapons of Mass Destruction: Reducing the Threat from the Former Soviet Union: An Update*, pp. 31–32.

joint ventures that would remain state owned.[63] In one case—a conversion project with GosNIIAS, a Russian institute that specialized in aviation and avionics— there was no privatized spin-off, and the institute was also actively filling military orders for the Russian government. Therefore, it is possible that any profits from the conversion project went to GosNIIAS and ended up subsidizing their military work for the Russian state. Although such profits were small compared to overall Russian military spending, the GAO report served to reinforce concerns raised by some CTR skeptics that the program was really a subsidy to the Russian defense program.

DEMONSTRATING THE BENEFITS OF CONVERSION

One of the main goals of conversion came to be demonstrating the benefits of commercial production, and thus convincing former Soviet states to fund their own conversion activities. As with the other measurements, however, the results in this case are also disappointing.

CTR was authorized $125 million, of which $60 million was actually spent on conversion projects in former Soviet states. There were sixteen projects in total. Five of those projects were successful, in that the joint venture that was established continued to exist after five years. Four of those projects continued at least until mid-2007. NPO-Istok and Hearing Aids International led to Istok Audio International, which had ISO certification to produce a variety of hearing aids, mostly for the domestic Russian market. The Byelkamit company was the result of the collaboration between Byelocorp, Gidromash, and an Italian company; it had ISO certification to produce pressure vessels. Also successful were both projects with test site managers. What was formerly the Kazakhstan National Nuclear Center became home to KK Interconnect, which assembled Samsung televisions for the domestic Kazakh market. And the partnership between Kazin and Lucent Technologies led to Nursat, the leading telecom operator in Kazakhstan. The fate of the fifth possible success is less clear. There is no evidence that the joint venture between Leninets and International American Products succeeded, although Leninets continued to pursue other joint ventures through a privatized holding company; this included, however, selling military equipment and technology to China and India.

Of the remaining eleven conversion projects, the fate of two is uncertain. Both the Westinghouse-Hatron and AIDCO-Orizon ventures demonstrated initial success, but there is no evidence documenting their continued existence.

The remaining nine projects either never got off the ground or failed after a few years. There are various reasons for these failures, most of which relate to unfavorable business conditions. For example, the Byelocorp-Belomo venture in Belarus was able to make laser pointers, but not at a competitive price. The vitamin-production project with BioMedPreparat

63. David Bernstein presentation, Russian-American Nuclear Security Advisory Council (RANSAC) and Russian Transition Initiatives (RTI), Strategies for Russian Nuclear Complex Downsizing and Redirection: Options for New Directions, Washington, D.C., March 25–26, 2003.

was terminated before work began due to scheduling and production difficulties related to the institute's inability to pay its utility bills. Test runs also indicated an inability to produce a quality product consistently. In at least one case, the Rockwell collaboration with GosNIIAS, the Russian Duma would not approve the legislation needed to move forward with the planned satellite-based air-traffic-control system.[64] Perhaps the most publicized failure involved NPO Mashinostroyeniya, whose experts had formerly designed satellites and space-launch vehicles. They were somewhat disappointed to find that their business partners expected them to produce soft drinks.

Of these projects, Stepnogorsk and the Fast Four in Russia were specifically targeted for attention and intended to demonstrate the benefits of conversion.[65] Of these showcase projects, only one was clearly a success: the partnership between NPO Istok and Hearing Aids International that resulted in Istok Audio International. At Stepnogorsk, cooperative ventures had to be abandoned in favor of dismantlement. Of the Fast Four conversion projects in Russia, one was never implemented; a second ran into difficulties with Russian law and began to look for a new Western partner in 1998; and the fate of a third is unclear. These projects, instead of modeling the benefits of conversion, clearly demonstrated the difficulties of both conversion and working with Western partners.

DEF had a somewhat better success rate. Table 4.2 contains information about the DEF-funded joint ventures.[66] Of the $72 million it was given, DEF eventually invested $28 million in 18 projects.[67] According to the GAO, based on the performance of other investment funds and defense conversion activities, the Defense Department estimated that 30–70 percent of DEF projects would fail. The more pessimistic projection ended up being the more accurate.

Of DEF's projects, seven were active, ten failed, and the fate of one was uncertain as of early 2009. Telecommunications proved to be a good bet. In addition to the success of Nursat and KK Interconnect, which were also funded by the first set of defense conversion efforts, two other DEF investments in Russian regional telecom providers, RTN and RUSNET Labs, were successful. Nevamash, the venture produced by Kirovsky Zavod's collaboration with Caterpillar, is now owned by Caterpillar and makes components for excavating equipment that is assembled in Europe. RAMEC, a partnership between NPO Impuls and Kent International, continues to assemble and distribute personal computers and office equipment in Russia, and Svetlana Electron Devices holds down a niche market

64. Interview with former U.S. government official 2, April 4, 2003.

65. For more on the role of Stepnogorsk as a showcase for conversion, see William Broad, Stephen Engelberg, and Judith Miller, *Germs: Biological Weapons and America's Secret War* (New York: Simon and Schuster, 2001), p. 182.

66. DEF intended to fund projects in Belarus, but eventually decided not to due to problems related to privatization laws and human rights abuses.

67. General Accounting Office, *Weapons of Mass Destruction: Reducing the Threat from the Former Soviet Union: An Update*, p. 33.

in older-style vacuum tubes, although it has now split from its original U.S. partner. Of the ten DEF projects that failed, it appears that most never got off the ground and were stymied due to concerns among the Western business partners about potential markets and intellectual property rights.

U.S. conversion efforts did encourage some post-Soviet states besides Russia to invest in conversion at key weapons enterprises that they had inherited. In general, the goal was not to create commercial products, but rather to maintain precious scientific resources and redirect them toward research and development in the public interest, most commonly in the area of public health. Even here the record was poor. Conversion in Russia was largely unsuccessful, whether it was funded by U.S. or indigenous government dollars. The result of these efforts was that teams of experts were maintained in place at institutes, many of which also retained their weapons-relevant equipment and research facilities. These institutes had few prospects for conversion.

MEETING DEADLINES

A final criterion for assessing CTR's conversion efforts is whether they succeeded within their own self-imposed deadlines. But not only did Congress terminate conversion in 1996, there is also no evidence that Defense Department officials set concrete timetables or deadlines for disengagement. Instead, they expressed the hope that eventually the Russian economy would revive and the government would come to take over these conversion efforts and fund its own more robust conversion program.[68] As explained in Chapter 3, this only began to happen in 2003–2006, and even then most evidence indicated that government spending was going to renewed weapons programs rather than conversion efforts.

Explaining Outcomes

Clearly, CTR's defense conversion programs did not meet their goals or redirect many former WMD experts to sustainable non-weapons work. What explains this failure?

The most obvious answer is that Congress killed CTR's defense conversion program and limited DEF's funding. Therefore, the program did not have a chance to succeed because of time and funding constraints. However, this logic begs the question of why defense conversion was curtailed. There are two answers: the political climate surrounding CTR and the Defense Department's support for conversion-type activities. Moreover, both of these issues are related.

CTR's conversion component was ended because Congress never definitively embraced conversion as a legitimate part of the defense effort. CTR overall was a creature of Congress. It was initiated by members of the House and Senate and forced on a Bush administration that, with the exception of Secretary of State James Baker, was skeptical of changes in the Soviet Union and reluctant to cooperate with Russia. This suspi-

---

68. Interview with former Clinton administration official 3, March 31, 2003.

cion was reinforced by factions in Congress that were primarily, but not totally, allied with a conservatism that saw little reason to cooperate with former Cold War enemies and remained convinced of threats to the United States from Russia. Even more members of Congress felt it was difficult to justify spending any "peace dividend" abroad instead of helping Americans first. Although the election of Bill Clinton promised more substantial presidential support for CTR, these sentiments still kept many members of Congress from fully embracing CTR's agenda. When the Republicans took control of the House in 1994, CTR faced renewed challenges.

As explained in Chapter 3, the debate over CTR centered on whether aid to the former Soviet Union was a legitimate part of the defense budget because it directly reduced threats faced by the United States. Critics questioned this connection, and sought either to end CTR since it was "charity" to an enemy, or to fund it from the foreign affairs budget. This question of whether CTR was a defense program or a form of foreign aid plagued the program; it was a persistent quarrel that dragged on for years after the collapse of the Soviet Union, and remained a consideration when Congress considered CTR funding as part of the annual defense appropriations and authorization processes for years after.[69]

Although all of CTR was criticized, the connection between U.S. security and CTR's efforts to eliminate, dismantle, and secure former Soviet WMD and related materials was more direct. It was harder to see how converting some former Soviet institutes and their employees were related to U.S. security. There were also competing domestic demands in this area, as U.S. bases were closed and relocated and the defense industry restructured in anticipation of significant reductions in defense spending. For example, during the mid-1990s, the Defense Department spent hundreds of millions of dollars to close, restructure, and convert U.S. military bases.[70] Similarly, CTR's funding of housing construction, environmental restoration, and military training programs were all challenged as aid rather than defense. These activities, along with conversion, were a casualty of the aid-versus-defense debate and were given up in the hopes of muting criticism of CTR overall.

But this story is not complete without also adding in the troubles CTR experienced in the Defense Department. Just as some politicians questioned CTR's relevance to national security, parts of the Pentagon believed the program was a drain on the defense budget, and that the Department of Defense was not the appropriate implementing agency. This was not simply a difference of opinion between civilians and the military. Certainly, members of both the military and the career civilian staff in the Pentagon accepted CTR as an assignment, and proceeded to implement its programs with good faith. But some also rejected CTR because it was foreign aid; others saw it as yet another competitor for a shrinking pool

---

69. Interview with congressional source 1, August 8, 2003.

70. General Accounting Office, *Military Base Closures: Detailed Budget Requests Could Improve Visibility*, Washington, D.C. (July 1997), pp. 1–2.

of defense dollars. And in the bureaucratic competition for funding and resources, CTR was the newcomer; it had no established champions or clientele. Moreover, no service stood to improve its combat capabilities as a result of CTR.

CTR had trouble establishing itself within the Pentagon. For its first two years, all funding came from reprogramming money that had originally been authorized for other programs. This made CTR unpopular, and identifying and transferring money to CTR programs was a difficult and slow process.[71] According to one former CTR official, this became a sort of shell game, whereby money for CTR would be identified one day only to go missing when the comptroller in charge of those funds would temporarily transfer it somewhere else rather than give it up to CTR.[72] According to another official, some Pentagon offices would try and trade assistance with CTR for support for their own programs or for future favors.[73] This lack of cooperation was reinforced by the Bush administration, whose lack of support for the program did little to convince the Pentagon bureaucracy to cooperate.

This struggle became easier when Congress authorized new money for CTR, and when CTR supporters moved to the Pentagon with the election of Bill Clinton.[74] Perversely, however, things also worsened. Wherever possible, CTR initially used excess equipment and other items that already existed in the Defense Department. This minimized the impact of the program on the defense budget.[75] But when this surplus was gone, concerns about the impact of CTR on regular defense spending surfaced. This was reinforced by pressures to reduce the defense budget after the Cold War, and by an alliance of CTR critics in the Pentagon and Congress.[76]

According to Rose Gottemoeller, who was director for Russia, Ukraine, and Eurasia at the National Security Council under Clinton, the Clinton administration tried to solve some of the problem by creating a bureaucratic home for CTR within the Pentagon.[77] CTR was assigned to the Defense Nuclear Agency, which had been given responsibility for coordinating implementation, centralizing negotiations and implementation with the post-Soviet states, and lobbying for CTR.[78] Prior to this,

---

71.   Jason D. Ellis, *Defense by Other Means: The Politics of US-NIS Threat Reduction and Nuclear Security Cooperation* (Westport, Conn.: Praeger, 2001), p. 117; interview with congressional source 2, August 4, 2003; interview with congressional source 3, August 12, 2003; and interview with former Clinton administration official 3, March 31, 2003.

72.   Interview with former Clinton administration official 3, March 31, 2003.

73.   Interview with former Clinton administration official 1, September 17, 2003.

74.   Interview with congressional source 2, August 4, 2003.

75.   Rose Gottemoeller, "Presidential Priorities in Nuclear Policy," in Shields and Potter, *Dismantling the Cold War*, p. 67.

76.   Ibid., p. 68.

77.   Ibid.

78.   Initially, Congress planned to give responsibility for CTR to the Pentagon's Advanced

there were multiple offices responsible for elements of CTR with little overall coordination.

But CTR never firmly established itself in the Pentagon. And, similar to the debate in Congress, the elements of the program that were not directly related to weapons destruction and dismantlement were even less popular. This, combined with critical debates in Congress, culminated in a decision to remove certain parts of CTR from the Defense Department, including conversion. In total, nine parts of CTR were transferred to other departments. There were some attempts to transfer DEF to the State Department, but Congress prohibited funding for conversion and allowed the State Department to fund DEF for only one additional year.

If conversion had continued as a part of CTR, it is still unlikely that there would have been significant additional results. It is tempting to blame this on either Congress or Russia. As later chapters also illustrate, the claim is often made that program results were limited because Congress did not authorize enough funding or because of problems getting the Russians to cooperate, usually on issues related to accessing facilities where conversion and employment activities were taking place. Neither of these proved to be limiting factors in the case of defense conversion. In terms of money, conversion programs consistently had more money authorized than they could spend on business ventures. During its first years, CTR ended the fiscal year in the black, and large unused balances led Congress to reduce CTR funding on more than one occasion.[79] Money went unspent partly due to the time needed to negotiate implementing agreements with the former Soviet states, especially Russia, and to follow normal contracting procedures.

Other programs also suffered due to problems getting access to the facilities and experts that they sought to reemploy. This did not prove to be a problem in the case of CTR's conversion efforts. This is largely because CTR only sought to convert portions of institutes rather than entire facilities, and because these facilities were already slated for closure and thus had fewer access restrictions. Access was seldom an issue, and the Russian Federal Security Service (FSB), which took over internal security matters from the KGB, was seldom formally involved in negotiating conversion projects.[80] In the few cases where cooperative ventures focused on buildings that were still part of the defense complex, other buildings were quickly identified that were suitable to both parties.

Instead of money shortages or access problems, the history of the Defense Department's conversion projects suggests other factors bear more

---

Research Project Administration (ARPA, now DARPA). ARPA, however, convinced Congress that it had no expertise in this area. Responsibility for CTR was subsequently shared by the assistant secretaries of defense for international security policy, acquisition, and atomic energy, as well as the Joint Chiefs of Staff.

79.   For example, CTR was authorized $800 million for its first two years, but managed to earmark only about 25 percent for projects. See Peter Grier, "US Effort to Aid Ex-USSR in Disarming Bogs Down," *Christian Science Monitor,* January 13, 1993, p. 1.

80.   Interview with former Clinton administration official 3, March 31, 2003.

of the burden for failure. These factors include Russia's poor economic performance and the economic and cultural shocks that occurred when the need for defense conversion coincided with the transition from a command to a market economy. These problems were magnified by the assumptions and inexperience of U.S. companies that were willing to enter into conversion ventures. In some ways this was hard to avoid. Most U.S. companies were unprepared to enter the Russian market, inexperienced in defense conversion, and unable to anticipate the idiosyncrasies of working with former weapons workers who were also products of the Soviet system. But the requirement for U.S. business participation in the first place, plus the process used to select participants, did little to mitigate these factors, and in many cases contributed new problems itself.

For many reasons, the state of the Russian economy and the legacy of the Soviet system made defense conversion extremely difficult. Throughout the 1990s, the average Russian consumer simply did not have the income to buy much beyond basic living requirements. Therefore, conversion projects geared toward domestic consumers suffered from a shortage of customers.

Ventures aimed at foreign markets had a different problem: a disconnect between what former Soviet scientists and U.S. businesses wanted to produce. The Soviet system of defense production was skewed toward military equipment that incorporated advanced technology, and experts were valued for their scientific abilities. Therefore, it is perhaps only natural that they sought conversion based on high-tech products and services. In contrast, U.S. business partners wanted ventures that would produce something with commercial potential or proven demand. Or they sought to offset the high cost of their production and services by hiring much cheaper employees in former Soviet states. In either case, the U.S. partners were predominantly interested in the production of low-tech consumer goods. The U.S. government was also more interested in lower-technology projects because these helped avoid some dual-use concerns.[81]

The consequences of this mismatch in expectations are illustrated by the partnership between Double Cola and Mashinostroyeniya. The latter was expecting a venture that took advantage of its technical prowess in space and missile technology. Instead, they were partnered in a project to bottle soft drinks. According to Ignor Postnikov of Mashinostroyeniya: "It was our absolute last choice.... Everyone is laughing at us. Imagine, one of Russia's most famous military-design bureaus making cola."[82]

Soviet defense workers were also notoriously proud of the role they had played in the defense of their country and of their skills in general. Asking them to make run-of-the-mill consumer products was a signifi-

81. David Bernstein and Nicholas Carlson, "The Cooperative Threat Reduction "Fast Four" Defense Conversion Projects in the Russian Federation," prepared for the U.S.-Russian Committee on Defense Industry Conversion, Gore-Chernomyrdin Commission, January 1997, p. 61.

82. Adi Ignatius, "U.S. Stirs Russian Resentment with Plans for Defense Conversion," *Wall Street Journal*, September 19, 1994, p. A10.

cant blow to their prestige. According to Chuck Vollmer of Booz Allen Hamilton, a firm that also bid on conversion contracts, the Double Cola–Mashinostroyeniya partnership was seen as the equivalent of asking the nuclear weapons physicists at Los Alamos to change careers and make baby diapers.[83] These differences of perspective led to protracted disagreements about which buildings to convert and the cost involved in refurbishing them.[84] As a result, in 1996, Double Cola asked the U.S. government to release it from the project. Despite these issues, Russian managers claimed they learned a great deal from the experience and were eager to search for and work with another Western partner.[85] It is unclear whether this was due to a genuine interest in cooperating with U.S. business or to the fact that, given the Russian central government's dictates about downsizing and conversion, they had few other choices.

A related problem was product quality and replicability. Typically, former Soviet managers undervalued aesthetic and cost issues. They also had problems understanding the need to consistently produce goods according to accepted international standards. For example, according to Frederick Kellett, who was the executive vice president of Byelocorp Scientific and actively involved in their joint project with Belomo in Belarus to make laser pointers, almost 20 percent of their products had to be rejected due to quality control problems.[86] Many of the joint ventures aimed at vitamins, medicines, and other pharmaceuticals, for example, ended because of their inability to get and maintain ISO certification. Issues of quality were particularly troublesome for consumables produced in former biological weapons facilities, because they played into public concern about contamination from former weapons agents, even though this was highly unlikely.

There were also significant economic and legal barriers associated with working in the former Soviet Union, especially Russia. First among these was a lack of capital. As a communist economy, there were few indigenous sources of capital. Business ventures had to rely on outside funding; because most sources of private capital in the United States were unfamiliar with and wary of the Russian economy, they were averse to financial ventures there.[87] For small businesses and individual entrepreneurs, there were few opportunities for loans. Second, even if ventures brought their own financing, most former Soviet states lacked legal protection for intellectual property or enforcement of contracts. Moreover, the rules for new patents were confusing or nonexistent. Third, there were

---

83. Ibid.

84. Department of Defense, "First-Half FY 1996 Semi-Annual Report," Washington, D.C., pp. 1–9.

85. Interview with U.S. government official 3, February 22, 2007.

86. Frederick Kellett, "Bankrolling Failure," *Bulletin of the Atomic Scientists,* Vol. 59, No. 5 (September/October 2003), p. 43.

87. Bernstein and Carlson, "The Cooperative Threat Reduction 'Fast Four' Defense Conversion Projects in the Russian Federation," January 1997, p. 9.

inconsistent and conflicting tax and customs regulations, and these were frequently exploited at the local or regional level. For example, even if federal legislation or rulings waived taxes on certain imports by foreign entities, local or regional officials might try to collect them anyway. Sometimes this was due to a lack of communication between government officials; local authorities were simply unaware of changes to the tax code and needed to be convinced before they would agree to a waiver. Other times, however, the motivation was personal gain. Most U.S. business partners were ill-equipped to tell the difference between the two. Finally, language differences and a lack of trust between partners led to delays and additional costs as materials were translated between Russian and English.

Frederick Kellett's assessment of his company's experience in Belarus also points to conflicts over control of money. According to Kellett, both their Belarusian partner and the government of Belarus agreed that the U.S. partner would manage all project funds. When the consequences of this became clear, however, the Belarusian entities tried to inflate local costs and thus funnel more money into accounts over which they had control.[88] Similar misunderstandings occurred in the Fast Four projects in Russia.[89] Many former Soviet managers were also resentful of money spent by U.S. partners on their own administrative and living expenses while in Russia or other states. In the mind of these weapons workers, these funds should rightly be spent only on enabling conversion and helping the impoverished workers.

Obviously it was beyond the power of the Defense Department to change the state of the Russian economy or mandate the legal and cultural changes that would have made the already difficult problem of defense conversion easier. But the Defense Department could have helped mitigate the impact of these problems through the selection of the U.S. conversion partner. Instead of choosing partners on the basis of their experience in Russia, their success in other developing market economies, or their past history with defense conversion, the Defense Department instead relied on standard acquisition procedures. This meant that conversion partnerships went to the lowest bidder in the contracting process, rather than the most experienced or most appropriate.[90] This, combined with occasional political pressure in Washington to favor some firms over others, led to several problems.

One problem was unrealistic expectations. Few of the U.S. firms selected had any experience in defense conversion, a difficult task in and of itself. But they had even less understanding of how defense enterprises had worked in the Soviet Union. Just as former Soviet enterprises had little experience producing for a market economy, U.S. conversion partners did not understand the role of informal networks and hierarchy that

---

88. Kellett, "Bankrolling Failure," p. 43.

89. Bernstein and Carlson, "The Cooperative Threat Reduction 'Fast Four' Defense Conversion Projects in the Russian Federation," p. 63.

90. Interview with former U.S. government official 2, April 4, 2003.

characterized the Soviet system. Despite the requirement for spin-offs as a prelude to conversion, in practice many privatized firms retained close connections with their parent state–owned enterprises. Besides personal and social ties, these enterprises were the only known source of materials and other inputs into the production process. Moreover, many former Soviet managers felt that despite the spin-off process, the state still had a claim to buildings, equipment, and workers it had paid for. It was unrealistic for the U.S. partner to expect privatization to sever these links, or for a sudden influx of funding from the U.S. government and partner not to create competing claims for these resources.

U.S. companies also expected to discover technological treasures in the former Soviet defense complex. There was a general feeling in the early 1990s that the quality of Soviet science and education meant that Soviet defense enterprises would have produced certain technologies that were unique and highly profitable. The reality, however, was that such technologies did not exist, were not made available for exploitation, or did not lead to marketable goods. Most conversion projects eventually produced low-tech consumer goods that had minimal profit margins.

Another problem was the motivation U.S. companies had for seeking conversion projects in the first place. Most U.S. partners were interested in earning money. They saw Defense Department projects as a subsidized way to test the Russian market.[91] There was no requirement for sustainability. And the Defense Department did a poor job of getting firms to buy into the goals of threat reduction and nonproliferation. The Russian counterparts, however, did not have the financial resources to consider cooperation a test; this was their lifeline. This led to misunderstandings about commitment, risk, and short-term profits, as well as feelings of betrayal when the U.S. partner sought to terminate involvement rather than spend more resources attempting to overcome significant obstacles to future success.[92]

According to David Bernstein, who participated in early Defense Department conversion efforts and has analyzed both Defense Department and privately funded business ventures in the former Soviet Union, commitment issues could have been mitigated if Defense Department conversion contracts had been given to smaller companies.[93] Although smaller companies did not necessarily understand Russia or conversion any better than larger companies, they were more resource-constrained. The resources they invested in the conversion ventures had greater marginal utility, and smaller companies knew this was likely to be their only shot at entering the Russian market. According to Bernstein, smaller

91. David Bernstein, "Analysis and Conclusions from Case Studies," in David Bernstein, editor, *Cooperative Business Ventures between U.S. Companies and Russian Defense Enterprises* (Palo Alto, Calif.: Institute for International Studies, Stanford University, April 1997), pp. 143–144.

92. See, for example, the legacy of defense conversion at Stepnogorsk, as described in Dobbs, "Soviet-Era Work on Bioweapons Still Worrisome," p. A01.

93. Interview with David Bernstein, April 4, 2003.

companies worked harder to overcome obstacles, and were less willing to give up and absorb the sunk costs. But Defense Department bidding practice did not take this into consideration.

Bernstein points out one additional problem. According to his experience with the Fast Four projects in Russia, he explains that selecting business partners through a lowest-bidder process also meant that there was little time for relationships to develop.[94] The U.S. and Russian partners had different ways of doing business, negotiating agreements, and identifying deliverables. These misunderstandings led to conflicts before the trust to resolve them had been established. Moreover, the Russians felt they were forced into relationships and had no say in selecting their own business partners.[95]

If the Defense Department's competitive bidding process led to poor choices about U.S. partners for conversion projects, the question remains as to whether there were better choices to be made. Defense Department officials did try to encourage certain businesses to offer bids, but in practice the U.S. business community saw conversion of former Soviet defense enterprises as a risky venture. There were problems finding businesses that were interested.[96] That said, it is also the case that simultaneous with the Defense Department's efforts, private companies were developing partnerships in Russia without U.S. government involvement. Some of these partnerships, especially those in the aerospace industry, were with formerly government-owned defense enterprises. And while many privately funded ventures failed, there were also numerous success stories. Therefore, it appears that even though investment in Russia was risky, there were willing business partners. The Defense Department's project development process, however, did little to find these companies or to encourage their involvement.

An argument can also be made that a better approach would have been to offer small-scale loans to small and medium-sized entrepreneurs in the former Soviet Union, or to organize larger financing through investment banks such as the European Bank for Reconstruction and Development. Another approach, used throughout the early 1990s by the U.S. Agency for International Development (USAID), was to fund local business centers to provide consulting services and training on subjects like business planning and development. But these options were not available to the Defense Department. To placate critics in Congress who saw defense conversion as foreign aid, the Defense Department was required to convert former Soviet defense enterprises only in conjunction with U.S. business partners. Although this requirement was eventually relaxed and the Defense Department switched its efforts to the DEF investment fund,

---

94. Ibid.

95. Bernstein and Carlson, "The Cooperative Threat Reduction 'Fast Four' Defense Conversion Projects in the Russian Federation," p. 8, 19.

96. David Bernstein presentation, Strategies for Russian Nuclear Complex Downsizing and Redirection: Options for New Directions.

congressional interest in conversion had soured and further U.S. government contributions to the fund were prohibited.

Organizational Interests and Defense Conversion

It is clear that the Defense Department's two job-creation programs reemployed few workers and even fewer WMD experts. Both the Defense Conversion program and DEF made only limited investments in conversion partnerships, and neither program focused on critical WMD facilities or experts. Although the Defense Conversion program was terminated in 1995, DEF continued for another seven years. There is little evidence, however, to suggest that DEF changed its investment strategy to take into account past experience or changes in the former Soviet WMD complex.

One explanation for this failure is the constraints imposed by Russia. But, although economic conditions in the former Soviet Union made the task of job creation difficult, the Defense Department's means of selecting business partners did little to overcome these problems. Instead of selecting companies that were familiar with Russia or other post-Soviet states, or were willing to invest in a high-risk venture, the Defense Department used standard contracting rules that awarded projects to the lowest bidder. As a result, U.S. partners were ill-prepared for the challenges they would face; former Soviet institutes were often insulted by the level of technology the project involved; and the partners from both sides had few incentives for building the relationships necessary for sustained involvement or eventual success. There is no evidence to support the argument that Russia or other states caused problems by limiting access to institutes or workers.

A more convincing explanation can be found in constraints imposed by Congress. Never enamored with the notion of conversion as a tool for countering proliferation, Congress increasingly imposed funding limits and other constraints on the Defense Department's conversion programs, eventually ending all new funding for one program in 1996 and the other in 1997.

But the Defense Department did little to dissuade Congress from this action. There is virtually no evidence to suggest that efforts were made to select more appropriate U.S. business partners and thus win support by demonstrating greater success. Such remedies were not undertaken because there was no backing from the Defense Department for fixing defense conversion programs. Although parts of the Defense Department eventually embraced CTR's weapons dismantlement and destruction activities as worthy goals, conversion remained a priority only for a select few presidential appointees in the Clinton administration. Despite efforts to sell conversion as another example of threat reduction, this definition was rejected by the Defense Department, which eventually tried to rid itself of all aspects of CTR that were not central to the core goals of taking apart and permanently eliminating WMD and WMD-delivery systems. The Defense Department's reluctance, plus a Congress that was at best disinterested and at times hostile, left the supporters of defense conversion with little choice but to agree to its demise and shift their energy and resources to ensuring the success of CTR.

Chapter 5

The Science Centers

In early 1992, U.S. Secretary of State James Baker announced plans to create a center in Moscow that would help former Soviet experts with skills relevant to weapons of mass destruction (WMD) and missiles redirect their skills to non-military work. In 1993, a second center was added in Kiev. Funded jointly by the United States and several other nations, the centers were to facilitate collaborative research by helping to match teams of former Soviet weapons experts with Western partners. The short-term goals were to provide these weapons experts with some income and to begin the process of integrating them into the broader international scientific community, thus mentoring them in standards about nonproliferation and transparency; in addition, they would be educated about how to apply their skills to commercial opportunities. Later, the goal became more explicitly to help these workers find sustainable jobs outside of the weapons complex.

Both Science Centers—the International Science and Technology Center (ISTC), based in Moscow, and the Science and Technology Center (STCU) in Kiev, Ukraine—shared these goals of engagement and reemployment and pursued them through similar processes. U.S. participation in both centers was managed by the State Department, which coordinated the project proposal review and funding processes in the United States. Each Science Center maintained its own international staff, one based in Moscow and the other in Kiev, that helped former weapons workers develop research proposals and that oversaw the projects that were funded.

In this chapter, I argue that both Science Centers deserve praise for their efforts at engagement; that is, for the short-term research projects that provided income to former weapons experts and introduced them to collaboration with U.S., Canadian, European, and other experts. Between the early 1990s and 2008, over 70,000 former Soviet defense workers participated in Science Center projects. For some, this was their only source of income. This was especially true immediately after the collapse of the Soviet Union, when economic woes and government wage arrears combined to reduce monthly incomes to below subsistence levels. But even fifteen years later, engagement with the Science Centers remained the main or only source of income for some people, especially those who were employed at former weapons institutes outside of Russia or at institutes that were once devoted to biological or chemical weapons work.

Despite this level of engagement, there are several reasons to question the contribution of the Science Centers to U.S. nonproliferation goals. As I argue below, only about half of the 85,000 people who participated in projects from 1994–2008 were actually former weapons experts. And neither the Science Centers nor U.S. participation in them did much to distinguish between the former weapons experts who were a proliferation concern and other people employed at or recently hired to work at current and former weapons institutes. Moreover, in seeking to engage weapons experts, the Science Centers also kept in place teams of former weapons workers at some institutes, mostly those not directly involved in weapons work, that otherwise would have dissolved due to lack of funding or to take advantage of other employment opportunities.

In terms of the second goal—the redirection of former weapons experts to sustainable non-weapons employment—the results are disappointing. After almost a decade during which "sustainability" was a top priority at both Science Centers, neither could claim to have helped create more than a few thousand jobs, if that.

What explains this combination of success and failure? I argue that there is little evidence to suggest that Russian or U.S. domestic political actors are to blame. Instead, more of the responsibility falls to organizational interests, most specifically the mismatch between the activities of the Science Centers and the traditional missions and procedures of the U.S. State Department. I argue that this disconnect led to problems with funding, goal definition, and the evolution of Science Center projects from engagement to redirection.

In making this argument, I begin by outlining the history and main activities of the Science Centers from their beginning until the end of 2008. Next I discuss Science Center goals, how they changed through 2008, and any progress made toward achieving them. This is followed by an analysis of how Science Center goals and project development were influenced by Russia, the U.S. Congress, and the U.S. State Department. Finally, in the last section of this chapter, I turn to the issue of the expansion of the Science Centers. Beginning in 2005, the United States began to consider expanding Science Center activities beyond the countries of the former Soviet Union. I argue that this change had inherent implications for the success of nonproliferation efforts in Russia.

ISTC and STCU

Soon after Congress passed the legislation authorizing Cooperative Threat Reduction (CTR) in 1991, the Bush administration introduced a plan to provide humanitarian and other aid to the Soviet Union. Part of this package included an initiative for collaborative research with WMD experts which had been announced previously by Secretary Baker. The idea for an international program to combat the proliferation of WMD expertise had been discussed the previous year in European capitals and was greeted with enthusiasm when Baker visited the closed nuclear city of Snezhinsk in early 1992. Later that year, funding for the Science Centers was authorized as part of the Freedom Support Act, which also included money for educational and cultural programs, humanitarian and technical assistance, and CTR.

As of 2006, Freedom Support Act programs concentrated on bilateral economic and business development assistance, exchanges aimed at promoting democracy, and initiatives to increase or develop civil society. Under the Act, the United States continued to promote the development of democracy and a market economy and to encourage the integration of former Soviet states with Western economic and political institutes. From 1992 through mid-2006, approximately 11 percent of U.S. assistance to the states of the former Soviet Union went toward Freedom Support Act programs, which, as of 2006, amounted to $500–$600 million annually.[1]

The State Department also played a role in CTR activities. According to analysis by Curt Tarnoff of the Congressional Research Service, from 1992 through mid-2006, approximately 22 percent of such U.S. assistance to the former Soviet Union came from Foreign Operations appropriations for State Department programs.[2] The bulk of this went toward programs to engage and reemploy WMD experts. Through fiscal year 2008, the United States funded the Science Centers at $415.2 million, with annual funding ranging from a high of $59 million in 2000 to $12 million in 2008.

Two additional efforts were added in later years. In 1999, the Bio-Chem Redirection Program began; it used money from the State Department to fund projects at the Moscow-based Science Center that were of interest to other U.S. government agencies, including the U.S. Department of Health and Human Services, the Department of Agriculture, and the Environmental Protection Agency. Initially funded at between $22 million and $45 million per year, from 2005–2008 the program received $17 million annually.[3] The other effort, started in 2002, was the BioIndustry Initiative (BII). BII also provided funding for the Departments of Health and Human Services, Agriculture, and the Environmental Protection Agency to engage in projects through the Science Centers and especially in the area of developing vaccines for highly infectious diseases. BII also included funds for security upgrades and conversion of former biological weapons–

1. Curt Tarnoff, *U.S. Assistance to the Former Soviet Union*, Congressional Research Service, CRS Report for Congress, Washington, D.C., March 16, 2006, pp. 1–2.

2. Ibid.

3. Amy F. Woolf, *Nonproliferation and Threat Reduction Assistance: U.S. Programs in the Former Soviet Union*, Congressional Research Service, CRS Report for Congress, Washington, D.C., updated June 26, 2006, p. 24; Amy F. Woolf, *Nonproliferation and Threat Reduction Assistance: U.S. Programs in the Former Soviet Union*, Congressional Research Service, Washington, D.C., February 11, 2009, p. 24; and State Department,Office of the Coordinator of U.S. Assistance to Europe and Eurasia, "U.S. Government Assistance to and Cooperative Activities with Eurasia, Annual Reports," 1999–2005, Washington, D.C.

related institutes. In fiscal year 2002, BII was funded through a $30 million transfer to the State Department from the Defense Department; as of 2008, it had received between $3 million and $13 million annually in funding.[4] Both programs fell under the Biosecurity Engagement Program (BEP) and, like the Defense Department's efforts, as of 2006 were being directed away from Russia in favor of a focus on other states outside of the former Soviet Union.

The other main security-focused program at the State Department was an effort aimed at increasing border security and export controls in former Soviet states. As of 2007, this program claimed $7–$8 million per year.[5]

Finally, there was one other anti–brain drain initiative that was launched due to concerns about the proliferation of WMD and related expertise from the former Soviet Union. In 1992, Congress passed the Soviet Scientists Immigration Act, which permitted up to 750 scientists with WMD expertise to immigrate to the United States without the normal requirement of securing a job offer prior to entry. According to Heather Wilson, who later became a member of Congress, the U.S. Immigration and Naturalization Service had problems writing the regulations to enable this immigration and subsequently few scientists were able to take advantage of the Act.[6] Motivated in part by an interest in providing permanent jobs for key biological weapons experts, in 2003 the Act was renewed for four additional years, and the total number of scientists allowed into the United States was raised to 950.[7]

SCIENCE CENTER ACTIVITIES

Unlike the other scientist-focused nonproliferation programs, the Science Centers were multinational efforts, each of which targeted a different part of the former Soviet Union. The Moscow-based ISTC initially supported collaborative research with former weapons experts in Russia, but this grew to include Armenia, Belarus, Georgia, Kazakhstan, Kyrgyzstan, and Tajikistan. Similarly, STCU in Kiev began funding research projects in Ukraine, but also came to work with former WMD experts in Georgia, Uzbekistan, Azerbaijan, and Moldova. All of these countries provided in-kind and other support, including donating

4. Woolf, *Nonproliferation and Threat Reduction Assistance: U.S. Programs in the Former Soviet Union*, June 26, 2006, p. 24; Woolf, *Nonproliferation and Threat Reduction Assistance,* February 11, 2009, p. 24; State Department, Office of the Coordinator of U.S. Assistance to Europe and Eurasia, "U.S. Government Assistance to and Cooperative Activities with Eurasia, Annual Reports," 1999–2005; and Michelle Marchesano, "Funding Analysis of FY09 International WMD Security Programs," Partnership for Global Security, Washington, D.C., April 2009, p. 8.

5. For more information see Woolf, *Nonproliferation and Threat Reduction Assistance*, February 11, 2009, p. 26.

6. Heather Wilson, "Beyond the Cold War—Foreign Policy in the 21st Century: Nuclear Threat—Leadership Wanted," *Wall Street Journal*, December 8, 1993, p. A14.

7. For the text of the original bill, see U.S. Congress, House, Committee on the Judiciary, *Immigration in the National Interest Act of 1995*, 104th Cong., 2nd sess., March 4, 1996, H. Rpt. 104-469.

facilities and utilities. Administrative costs for each center plus funding for research projects were paid for by various member states. In the case of ISTC, initially this was the United States, the European Union, and Japan, but expanded to include Canada, Norway, and South Korea. STCU's "funding parties" originally were the United States, Sweden, and Canada, but Sweden was eventually replaced by the European Union.

More than any other funding party, money for both research projects and administrative costs for the centers came from the United States. According to a 2001 analysis by the Government Accountability Office (GAO), the United States paid for approximately one-third of ISTC's operating expenses and two-thirds of those at STCU.[8] In terms of project money, U.S. funding was also significant. Table 5.1 shows ISTC project funding for basic science projects by country per year. At ISTC, the United States traditionally provided between one-third and one-half of project funding. Beginning in 2004, however, U.S. contributions began to decline significantly, falling for the first time below both E.U. and other country contributions.

Table 5.1. ISTC Project Funding by Funding Country (in millions of current U.S. dollars).

	Total Funding	U.S. Funding	EU Funding	Funding from Other Countries
1994	$46.7	$22.5	$13.9	$10.3
1995	$34	$12	$15.5	$6.5
1996	$39.2	$20.4	$12	$6.8
1997	$33.4	$11	$14.4	$7.9
1998	$33.2	$11.7	$17	$4.5
1999	$33.3	$14.8	$14.5	$4.1
2000	$62	$37.7	$15.3	$9
2001	$45.6	$21.9	$13.3	$10.4
2002	$43.5	$21.1	$15.9	$6.5
2003	$47	$25	$20.2	$1.8
2004	$35.4	$7.9	$17.6	$9.9
2005	$29.9	$7.1	$15.9	$6.9
2006	$29.2	$4.1	$14.2	$10.9
2007[a]	$16.3	$0.114	$14.6	$1.6

[a]Reflects totals as of July 2007.

SOURCE: Based upon data provided by ISTC, electronic communication, July 11, 2007. Columns may not add up due to rounding.

8.   General Accounting Office, *Weapons of Mass Destruction: State Department Oversight of Science Centers Program*, Washington, D.C. (May 2001), p. 5.

With respect to STCU, the United States consistently provided the bulk of the funding. As of December 2, 2005, the United States had provided approximately 54 percent of project funding, with the EU providing 17 percent, and other partner countries 3 percent.[9] Additional funding came from commercial and other project partners.

Each Science Center oversaw two types of projects. Basic science projects involved temporary collaboration between teams of former weapons experts at an institute in a former Soviet state and one or more international collaborators, typically someone from a university or private scientific or technical institute in the United States, Canada, Europe, South Korea, or Japan. These projects were intended first and foremost to provide income to scientists. But this partnership was also supposed to help the weapons experts learn about the research interests and quality standards of a broader scientific community, and also begin the process of reorienting their skills toward non-weapons work. Basic science projects consistently made up the bulk of Science Center efforts, as shown in Tables 5.2 and 5.3.

Table 5.2. New Projects and New Project Funding per Year—ISTC (in millions of U.S. dollars).

	Funding for Basic Science Projects	New Basic Science Projects per year	Funding for Partner Projects	New Partner Projects per year
1994	$46.7	91	0	0
1995	$34	109	$0.9	2
1996	$39.2	127	$0.3	1
1997	$33.4	157	$0.7	8
1998	$33.2	146	$3.1	13
1999	$33.3	145	$9.5	43
2000	$62	235	$34.9	78
2001	$45.6	178	$35.5	198
2002	$43.5	154	$47.4	91
2003	$47	153	$28.1	68
2004	$35.4	129	$24.3	62
2005	$29.9	107	$19.6	54
2006	$29.2	106	$21.8	76
2007	$27.4	73	$21.8	74
2008	$26.2	79	$6.7	21

SOURCES: International Science and Technology Center, "Annual Reports," 1994–2008, Moscow; and electronic communications with ISTC on June 15, 2007 and June 20, 2007.

9. Based on data from Science and Technology Center in Ukraine, "Annual Reports," 2000–2005, Kiev; and Science and Technology Center in Ukraine, "Governing Board Minutes," 1995–2008, Kiev.

Table 5.3. New Projects and New Project Funding per Year—STCU (in millions of U.S. dollars).

	Funding for Basic Science Projects	New Basic Science Projects per year	Funding for Partner Projects[a]	New Partner Projects per year
1995	$1.7	12	$0	0
1996	$8.7	73	$0	0
1997	$6.5	57	$1.1	11
1998	$7.4	65	$0.56	8
1999	$7.6	54	$0.69	8
2000	$14.2	96	$2.1	20
2001	$12.4	85	$3	24
2002	$9.5	53	$11.2	17
2003	$9.7	68	$7.3	23
2004	$9.2	67	$5.8	17
2005	$8.6	51	$4.5	21
2006	$8.9	52	$7.2	33
2007	$6.7	38	$7.6	47
2008	$6.8	40	$4.3	24

[a]Does not include funding for the extension of partner projects.

SOURCES: Based on information provided in Science and Technology Center in Ukraine, "Annual Reports," 2000–2005, Kiev; and Science and Technology Center in Ukraine, "Governing Board Minutes," 1995–2008, Kiev.

Basic science projects typically involved teams of 30–60 researchers, although some could be larger. Starting in the early 2000s, the average amount of funding for a project was about $320,000 at ISTC and $300,000 at STCU, and projects took between two and three years to complete.[10] A typical basic science project was ISTC Project No. 1567. This project involved a team of experts at Russia's Bochvar Institute for Inorganic Materials in partnership with Sandia, Brookhaven, and Argonne National Laboratories in the United States, Washington State University, and additional collaborators in the United States, Germany, and Japan. The scientists at Bochvar had been working on a way to clean up radioactive contamination in the soil. Through the ISTC project, they did additional basic and applied research and developed a product that, when sprayed on contaminated soil, binds and immobilizes the radioactive materials.

10. Victor Alessi and Ronald F. Lehman II, "Science in the Pursuit of Peace: The Success and Future of the ISTC," *Arms Control Today*, June/July 1998, p. 20; interview with Science and Technology Center in Ukraine staffer 7, October 27, 2005; and interview with Science and Technology Center in Ukraine staffer 14, October 31, 2005.

In the United States, radioactive clean-up often involves removing and storing large amounts of earth. By enabling the contaminated material to concentrate in the topsoil, the Bochvar method would require less soil to be removed and thus reduce the cost of both remediation and storage.[11]

In addition to engaging scientists through basic and applied research, both Science Centers also emphasized projects that were commercially viable and could lead to permanent reemployment.[12] To foster such projects, the ISTC began its Partners Program effort in 1996; STCU followed suit the next year. Through Partner Projects, companies and government agencies funded research conducted by teams of former weapons experts. The idea was to fund projects that tested whether a particular new technology or process was viable or potentially profitable. Ideally, once this test was complete, successful projects and their research teams would transition to private sector employment. Partners used the Science Centers as a means of administering projects and getting salary checks to researchers. Because the centers had tax-free status, partners could also use them for sending equipment and supplies to their collaborators.

An example of a Partner Project was the $330,000 agreement between Mobile Technology and VNIITF to model oil flow through porous media.[13] Mobile needed experts in applied math and computational science and found it was cheaper to hire people in Russia than to bring them to the United States and train them, or compete with other industries for the few people who graduate each year with the necessary skills. The capabilities of VNIITF's workforce were recommended by a Russian émigré who was already working at Mobile and who subsequently helped in facilitating language, cultural, and business communication between the two partners.

Although Partner Projects were originally started as a way to encourage funding from the private sector and to further sustainable reemployment, "partners" were overwhelmingly government entities, particularly U.S. government agencies. For example, the Department of Energy (DOE) paid Russian scientists to help evaluate methods of storing the waste products that result from the production of nuclear weapons. In particular, the team studied the merits of depositing radioactive material in various rock formations. U.S. government agencies that funded Partner Projects include the Defense Threat Reduction Agency, the Environmental Protection Agency, the Department of Agriculture, the National Institutes of Health, and various U.S. national laboratories, among others. With the exception of some efforts directed at former biological weapons experts,

---

11. This description is based on interview with Los Alamos National Laboratory staffer 7, May 1, 2002; and interview with Bochvar Institute staffer 1, June 4, 2003.

12. This emphasis on permanent reemployment was part of the U.S. agenda for the Science Centers from the start. See, for example, Federation of American Scientists and the Natural Resources Defense Council, "Report on the Fourth International Workshop on Nuclear Warhead Elimination and Nonproliferation," Washington, D.C.: February 26–27, 1992, p. 12.

13. International Science and Technology Center, "ISTC News/Mobil Technology and VNIITF Press Release," September 16, 1999.

U.S. government partners funded Partner Projects out of their own or other appropriations, not from funds allocated by the United States to the Science Centers.

Government Partner Projects were more common at the ISTC. But the prevalence of U.S. government partners upset country participants from the European Union.[14] In the European Union's view, ISTC party states should be equal partners. U.S. government partners created a separate government-specific income stream at ISTC which led to greater importance for U.S. government funding, rather than the multilateralism that was supposed to be reflected at ISTC. Because of the tension this caused at ISTC, STCU tried to avoid significant government sponsorship of Partner Projects.

PROJECT LOGISTICS

Although the Science Centers were largely independent of each other, they worked according to similar processes. Each center had its own executive director, representatives from each funding country, and a staff, mostly Russian or Ukrainian, to encourage scientists to participate, supervise projects, and administer review and auditing processes. In the late 1990s, ISTC expanded to include contractors hired to manage portfolios of Partner Projects.[15] For example, an ISTC staffer from the United States would oversee all of the Department of Energy's Partner Projects.[16] In contrast, STCU employed one person who was in charge of all Partner Projects with government partners. The life of a basic science project was similar but not identical at both Science Centers. Here the ISTC process is described with significant STCU differences noted.

At the ISTC, basic science projects usually got their start at a former Soviet WMD or missile institute. Although the process varied by country, in most cases the former weapons experts submitted project proposals through their research institutes to their government, which then had to approve the project and certify the expertise of the senior weapons scientists who were involved.[17] Some institutes had special proposal vetting requirements of their own. According to Amy Smithson, Biopreparat required some proposals for ISTC to go through their own screening process to make sure they did not reveal national security secrets; projects

14. Interview with former State Department staffer 2, July 9, 2007; and interview with former U.S. government official 4, October 2, 2007.

15. At the U.S. Embassy in Moscow, there were also employees of other U.S. government agencies (for example, the Department of Energy, the Defense Threat Reduction Agency, and the Department of Agriculture) who were employees of those agencies and were at the embassy to help manage agency programs in Russia. Interview with Department of Energy staffer 3, June 3, 2003.

16. According to interview with former State Department staffer 2, July 9, 2007, this was prompted by a request from the U.S. interagency coordination process. Agencies wanted more of a management and oversight role in their ISTC projects and especially those that dealt with former biological weapons institutes and experts.

17. General Accounting Office, *Weapons of Mass Destruction: State Department Oversight of Science Centers Program*, p. 9.

with former biological and chemical weapons experts were also vetted by the Ministry of Science and Technology.[18] In Russia, ISTC projects required the approval of the Russian Federal Atomic Energy Agency (Rosatom) or the Russian Academy of Sciences.[19] Despite claims from Rosatom, there is some evidence to suggest that it favored projects that involved its own nuclear-energy and weapons-related institutes and believed that ISTC funded too many non-nuclear projects.[20] At STCU, it appears that neither the institutes nor the government pressured the scientists to do any particular kind of project; they approved everything they got.[21] Partly, this was because an STCU project gave them prestige and access to equipment but also because it was a "lottery ticket to more money."[22]

Next, the proposal was submitted to the ISTC, where program staff made sure it met the requirements of a basic science project proposal. These requirements included a short description of the project, the project location, the expected duration, projected scientific and commercial results, measures to safeguard both intellectual property rights and national security secrets, and cost. Cost was subdivided into salaries, equipment, supplies, travel, and overhead, and there were restrictions on how much could be spent in each category. Equipment and supplies that were imported into Russia were supposed to be tax-exempt, although in practice there were some problems enforcing this.

Project proposals also had to identify the project manager and all participants. This was to help member states and the ISTC assess the degree to which projects involved people with weapons-relevant expertise and to ensure that all participants had skills that were important to the project.[23] Project participants were asked to describe their former weapons work according to a list supplied by ISTC that asked them to classify their skills in terms of five weapons specialties (missile technology, chemical, biological, or nuclear weapons, and other) and subspecialties.[24] For example, nuclear weapons experts were given a choice of delineating relevant

18. Amy E. Smithson, *Toxic Archipelago: Preventing Proliferation from the Former Soviet Chemical and Biological Weapons Complexes* (Washington, D.C.: Henry L. Stimson Center, December 1999), pp. 23–24.

19. Some U.S. government agencies and partners used the Civilian Research & Development Foundation (CRDF) to administer their projects rather than ISTC. Projects that went through CRDF were not required to have the approval of Rosatom.

20. Interview with Institute for Physics and Power Engineering staffer 1, July 23, 2002; interview with Minatom official 1, July 24, 2002; and interview with International Science and Technology Center staffer 4, July 24, 2007.

21. Interview with Science and Technology Center in Ukraine staffer 7, October 27, 2005; and interview with Science and Technology Center in Ukraine staffer 14, October 31, 2005.

22. Interview with Science and Technology Center in Ukraine staffer 14, October 31, 2005.

23. For example, there is evidence that project teams were sometimes pressured to include institute managers, relatives, or other people even if they would not be involved in the project.

24. International Science and Technology Center, "Weapon Expertise Areas," November 2000.

experience as basic knowledge of nuclear weapons design, construction, or effects characteristics; or as expertise related to the design, construction, or performance of missile warheads, equipment, and components for uranium and plutonium separation, equipment connected with Heavy Water production, equipment for the development of detonators, explosive substances, nuclear testing, breeder reactors, or nuclear reactors for use in submarines or military space programs.[25] This self-identification was not necessarily a trivial requirement, because the names and skill sets of Soviet WMD and especially nuclear weapons experts were initially considered secret and remained sensitive information.

Finally, all projects were required to have a Western collaborator. The purpose of the collaborator was to mentor former Soviet scientists in the research, funding, and publication process used among the international scientific community and to help Science Center funding countries learn about the skills and research capabilities of former Soviet scientists and organizations. The collaborator was also the judge of a project's merit. Before a project could go forward, it had to have a letter of support from a Western collaborator, who evaluated the final project report. In practice, only a handful of collaborators ever met the other project participants, although thanks to travel grants this increased over time. It remained the case, however, that most collaboration involved reading an initial proposal and then a final report; some joint publications resulted, but little joint research.

The process of getting approval for a project could take a long time and required much back and forth between the ISTC staff and the institute and scientists. For example, interviews at ISTC and STCU suggested that five or more revisions per proposal were not uncommon. Only when the project had satisfied the requirements of each center was it forwarded to individual countries for their consideration. Each ISTC funding party had its own review process; the U.S. process is explained in more detail below.

Once the funding countries conducted their reviews and made their decisions, the project then returned to ISTC. At this point, ISTC had 45 days either to ask for further revisions in the proposal or to forward it on to the Center's Governing Board.[26] Each Science Center had a Governing Board that met from two to four times a year and whose membership included representatives from each funding country and a rotating seat for host country participation.[27] For those proposals that reached the Governing Board, this was the place where funding countries announced their

25. Ibid.

26. The Governing Board also made decisions about policy, set funding and project targets, and considered other issues. Prior to meetings, a Coordination Committee reviewed and prepared issues for consideration by the Governing Board.

27. ISTC differed from STCU in the way that the call for proposals was administered. ISTC employed an open rolling call for proposals and quarterly meetings were held to review as many proposals as possible. STCU used a semi-annual proposal process. Proposals were submitted only during a finite period of time. STCU held a minimum of two board meetings per year, ISTC usually held four. The difference was largely due to STCU's smaller staff and the small number of proposals it gets.

intentions to invest in a project. Rather than allocating resources from a common pool, each country made its own decisions and used its own resources to fund projects.[28] Since the Board made decisions by consensus, however, in practice one member could veto another's funding decisions, although this rarely happened.[29]

If a project was funded at a Governing Board meeting, then the work could begin. Although the Governing Board at ISTC considered all projects that met the guidelines, it tended to fund only half of the projects it received.[30] At STCU, the same was true initially, although later it funded one out of every ten to fifteen project proposals.[31]

The time it took to go from proposal submission to the first paycheck could be quite lengthy. Between twelve and eighteen months was typical, although the process could take as long as three years or more.[32] This delay contributed to a sense of frustration among ISTC staff and to resentment on the part of some scientists. According to one former ISTC participant from Russia's Kurchatov Institute, he counseled colleagues to invest their time in trying to get Initiatives for Proliferation Prevention (IPP) projects instead of going through the ISTC.[33] Similarly, in interviews from 2001 to 2007 with IPP project managers at the U.S. national laboratories, it was not uncommon for them to explain that they chose to administer their projects through the Civilian Research and Development Foundation (CRDF) rather than ISTC because they felt the latter was slow and overly bureaucratic.

STCU solved part of this problem by adopting a web-based proposal submission and review process which decreased the time between project submission and Governing Board consideration. STCU also developed

28. According to Office of International Affairs, National Research Council, *An Assessment of the International Science and Technology Center: Redirecting Expertise in Weapons of Mass Destruction in the Former Soviet Union* (Washington, D.C.: National Academy Press, 1996), p. 6, this decision to allocate funds on an individual basis rather than a pool was reached early in ISTC's history.

29. Interview with former State Department staffer 2, July 9, 2007. At this stage, project review might also involve the ISTC Scientific Advisory Board (SAB), which was composed of up to two representatives from each of the four founding members. (The STCU did not have a similar scientific review board.) The role of the SAB was to advise the Governing Board about the quality of project proposals, help determine new directions for project activity, and evaluate on-going projects. Interview with Science and Technology Center in Ukraine staffer 2, October 26, 2005; and interview with Los Alamos National Laboratory staffer 10, June 2, 2003.

30. Scott Parrish and Tamara Robinson, "Efforts to Strengthen Export Controls and Combat Illicit Trafficking and Brain Drain," *Nonproliferation Review*, Vol. 7, No. 1 (Spring 2000), p. 121.

31. Interview with Science and Technology Center in Ukraine staffer 7, October 27, 2005; and interview with Science and Technology Center in Ukraine staffer 8, October 27, 2005.

32. Interview with Science and Technology Center in Ukraine staffer 1, October 26, 2005; interview with Science and Technology Center in Ukraine staffer 7, October 27, 2005; interview with Science and Technology Center in Ukraine staffer 10, October 28, 2005; interview with International Science and Technology Center staffer 12, Oct. 22, 1999; and Smithson, *Toxic Archipelago*, p. 29.

33. Interview with Kurchatov Institute staffer 1, August 1, 2002.

outreach materials for helping scientists understand how to develop their business plans and presentation skills and incorporate these into their initial proposals.

Project participants got paid according to a standardized schedule. Their paychecks were automatically deposited into individual bank accounts in U.S. dollars for ISTC participants and in Ukrainian hryvenas for those at STCU.[34] In theory this was supposed to give scientists more control over their money and help them avoid pressure to share their paychecks with former supervisors or colleagues.

Finally, each project was subject to specific monitoring and evaluation requirements. In theory, ISTC staff oversaw all projects on a quarterly basis and conducted additional technical and financial audits once a year.[35] ISTC had the right to audit any project for two years after its completion.[36] In practice, the bulk of ISTC audits were financial; staff did not have the scientific expertise to conduct technical audits on every project.[37] Moreover, time was also an issue. A 1996 study by the National Academy of Science found that ISTC project managers were stretched too thin, with each having, on average, responsibility for sixteen projects.[38] This load seemed to grow significantly after that point. For example, during my interviews at ISTC, project managers routinely talked of responsibility for thirty-five to fifty projects and sometimes more. Additionally, with multiple projects to oversee, in practice some ISTC staff claimed they monitored projects only irregularly instead of quarterly, and some project sites were not visited once a year.[39]

Besides time, project oversight required access to people and facilities. Sometimes this meant getting into places where access was restricted for national security reasons. Under the terms of ISTC project agreements, staff were supposed to have access to the locations where research was conducted and to the relevant personnel, equipment and documentation. And, although Russia did not object to the idea that projects should be monitored, initially there were issues about access.[40] Many of these problems were resolved and ISTC staff generally got access to facilities with

34. Interview with International Science and Technology Center staffer 1, October 18, 1999; and interview with Science and Technology Center in Ukraine staffer 2, October 26, 2005.

35. Interview with International Science and Technology Center staffer 1, June 2, 2003.

36. Interview with International Science and Technology Center staffer 4, July 24, 2007.

37. Interview with Pacific Northwest National Laboratory staffer 1, March 12, 2003; and interview with Lawrence Livermore National Laboratory staffer 4, April 7, 2003.

38. Office of International Affairs, National Research Council, *An Assessment of the International Science and Technology Center*, p. 11.

39. General Accounting Office, *Weapons of Mass Destruction. Reducing the Threat from the Former Soviet Union: An Update*, Washington, D.C. (June 1995), p. 30; interview with International Science and Technology Center staffer 10, October 22, 1999; and interview with International Science and Technology Center staffer 11, October 22, 1999.

40. Glenn Schweitzer, *Moscow DMZ: The Story of the International Effort to Convert Russian Weapons* (Armonk, N.Y.: M.E. Sharpe, 1996), p. 28.

twenty days advanced notice, and thirty-five days in the case of closed cities.[41]

The STCU monitoring process was a bit different. Projects were monitored four times. The initial visit was during the first six months, when the rules about STCU and its practices were explained to participants. Then, projects were reviewed after one year and then again after an additional year. The last review happened when the project was completed and took the form of a final evaluation and discussion about possible follow-on activities of interest to commercial partners. STCU staff overall expressed much less frustration with the demands of oversight. Typically, STCU staff had a portfolio of about twenty projects, down from a high of around thirty-five in previous years, and seemed able to keep to the timetable described above.[42]

The life cycle of a Partner Project was different. First, the partner negotiated a work plan and all financial matters with the project participants. Then, the partner provided a letter of intent and registered the project at ISTC. After the ISTC staff made sure that the proposal contained all the required information, it was forwarded to the funding countries, which then had 100 days to object to the project; this seldom happened.[43] Partner Projects in Russia also had to be approved by Rosatom or the Russian Academy of Sciences.[44] Partners and project teams had to submit quarterly cost statements and progress reports as well. For their efforts, both Science Centers charged private partners an overhead of 5 percent of total project costs.[45]

Based on the assumption that a partner would not engage in a project unless it promised some reward, Partner Projects received less scrutiny than basic science projects. Besides less input from center staff, the funding parties were given less information due to concerns about intellectual property rights and other proprietary issues. For example, at STCU, a Partner Project was typically a general technical description and lacked

---

41. Representatives from funding countries were supposed to be allowed access to closed cities with 45 days advanced notice. Apparently, however, despite these rules, there was often broad variation in access arrangements for specific projects. Interview with International Science and Technology Center staffer 4, July 24, 2007.

42. Interview with Science and Technology Center in Ukraine staffer 1, October 26, 2005; and interview with Science and Technology Center in Ukraine staffer 7, October 27, 2005.

43. International Science and Technology Center, "ISTC," briefing slides, September 16, 1999. At STCU, the funding countries have 45 days to express their disapproval for a project.

44. Interview with International Science and Technology Center staffer 1, June 2, 2003; and Interview with International Science and Technology Center staffer 4, July 24, 2007.

45. Interview with International Science and Technology Center staffer 4, July 24, 2007; interview with Science and Technology Center in Ukraine staffer 1, July 9, 2007; Science and Technology Center in Ukraine, http://www.stcu.int/partnershipprogram (accessed October 24, 2005); and "Conditions for Approval of Partner Project Proposals," partners.istc.ru/media/for-partners/Conditions-For-Approval-Of-Partner-Project-Proposals.pdf (accessed June 11, 2007). Government partners were not charged an overhead fee.

the specifics about research, schedules, and deliverables that were found in a basic science project.[46]

In response to concerns from partners about paperwork and delays, ISTC implemented a streamlined process for dealing with these projects in 2003. A Partnering and Sustainability Department was created that focused on serving partners. Each partner was assigned a Partner Project manager who acted as the main point of contact, helped accomplish project aims, and coordinated with other ISTC units.[47] Several government agencies had dedicated staff members that focused on their projects. STCU, which had a much smaller staff, hired one person to manage all government partners and another that dealt with non-governmental ones.

Both Science Centers also engaged in a variety of other smaller activities aimed at encouraging participation from commercial partners or helping scientists develop business skills. These included ISTC's Seminar Program and the Promising Research Abstracts program, funded by Japan, both of which were attempts to interest the business community in former Soviet experts. Other activities were aimed at helping scientists understand patents and intellectual property issues, develop business and management skills, or get travel grants for visiting their collaborators.

U.S. PARTICIPATION

Each Science Center funding country established its own practices for project requirements, review, and funding. In the United States, this process was managed by the State Department. As of 2008, the Science Centers fell under the Office of Cooperative Threat Reduction in the Bureau of International Security and Nonproliferation.[48]

Initially the Science Centers were funded, as were all CTR activities, out of transfers from the Department of Defense budget. But in 1996, when CTR's activities were split, funding responsibility shifted fully to the State Department. Through 2002, the Science Centers were funded through the Freedom Support Act but were then shifted to the Nonproliferation, Anti-Terrorism, Demining and Related (NADR) issues account.[49] Congress, as part of its consideration of the Foreign Operations Budget, authorized money for these accounts and then the State Department had discretion over specifically how to divide funding between programs. Table 5.4 shows U.S. funding for both Science Centers over time.

46. Interview with Science and Technology Center in Ukraine staffer 2, October 26, 2005.

47. International Science and Technology Center, "ISTC Partner News," 4th Quarter 2003, p. 1.

48. Initially, the Science Centers were under the State Department Bureau of Political-Military Affairs. The Office of Cooperative Threat Reduction was created in a 2005 reorganization of the State Department by President George W. Bush.

49. Within the Nonproliferation, Anti-Terrorism, Demining and Related (NADR) account, the Science Centers fell under the line for Nonproliferation of WMD Expertise until 2008, when the account was changed to Global Threat Reduction Programs.

Table 5.4. U.S. Funding for the Science Centers (in millions of U.S. dollars).

Fiscal Year	Funding
FY 1994	$35
FY 1995	$29
FY 1996	$15.5
FY 1997	$14
FY 1998	$17.5
FY 1999	$22
FY 2000	$59
FY 2001	$35
FY 2002	$37
FY 2003	$32
FY 2004	$28.5
FY 2005	$34.5
FY 2006	$21.5
FY 2007	$22.7
FY 2008	$12

SOURCES: Department of State, "Science Centers Program," briefing slides; U.S. Congress, House, Committee on International Relations, *Report on the Expanded Threat Reduction Initiative, Message from the President,* 106th Cong., 2nd sess., June 28, 2000, House Doc. 106-263, p. 5; William Hoehn, "Analysis of the Bush Administration's Fiscal Year 2003 Budget Requests for U.S.-Former Soviet Union Nonproliferation Programs," Russian-American Nuclear Security Advisory Council (RANSAC), Washington, D.C. (April 2002); William Hoehn, "Preliminary Analysis of the U.S. State Department's Fiscal Year 2005 Budget Request for Nonproliferation Programs in Russia and the FSU," RANSAC, Washington, D.C., March 11, 2004; Amy F. Woolf, *Nonproliferation and Threat Reduction Assistance: U.S. Programs in the Former Soviet Union,* Congressional Research Service, CRS Report to Congress, Washington, D.C., updated June 26, 2006., p. 24; Department of State, "Annual Report on Assistance to the Former Soviet Union," Fiscal Years 1994–2006, Washington, D.C., especially fiscal years 2000 and 2005; Isabelle Williams, "Preliminary Analysis of the U.S. State Department's Fiscal year 2008 Budget Request for Global WMD Threat Reduction Programs," Partnership for Global Security Policy Update, Washington, D.C. (April 2007); and Michelle Marchesano, "Funding Analysis of FY 09 International WMD Security Programs, Partnership for Global Security, Washington, D.C. (April 2009), p. 8. Through 2000, the State Department budgeted for the Science Centers separately, but from 2001 on the Science Center budget was frequently lumped together with the Bio-Chem Redirection Program and the BioIndustry Initiative, making it difficult to parse out the funding for the Science Centers.

Before each ISTC Board meeting, proposals for basic science projects were evaluated and rated for suitability of U.S. funding. There were several review processes, including those that dealt with scientific merit, involvement of WMD experts, practicality, and consistency with U.S. non-proliferation and other policies.[50] Partner Projects went through the same policy

---

50. Alessi and Lehman, "Science in the Pursuit of Peace: The Success and Future of the ISTC," p. 19.

review process but did not have a technical review.[51] All of these activities were coordinated by the Office of Cooperative Threat Reduction in the State Department.

Technical reviews were done by a team of science advisers, mostly at the Department of Energy national laboratories and CRDF.[52] Science advisers forwarded proposals to two or three other scientists with relevant expertise, and based on those reviews, the advisers developed a consensus opinion on the merits of the proposal and whether or not to recommend funding. Reviewers were supposed to focus on scientific merit and assess whether the project involved a significant number of former weapons experts. It was U.S. policy to reject proposals where less than half of the participants were not former senior weapons experts. The United States did, however, co-fund projects that did not meet these criteria.[53] In general, advisers relied on the scientists' own identification of their expertise, as required by the Science Center proposal development process. The science advisers also considered the commercial potential of a project.

The rigor with which these requirements were enforced is a subject for debate. Some U.S. project reviewers claimed that they had their own criteria for evaluating projects and that when project selection was discussed, everyone deferred to each other's top priorities.[54] Another reviewer with years of experience with the ISTC noted that the technical description contained in project proposals was too sparse to know what the scientists planned to do, much less evaluate the merit.[55] The most frequent problem, however, appeared to be that reviewers lacked the time to do a thorough analysis. Most project reviewers were U.S. national laboratory personnel who had technical expertise that was relevant to Science Center projects. Usually, however, these reviewers were not paid for their time, and in interviews this was almost universally mentioned as the number one problem with helping the Science Centers.[56] Although most people expressed a personal commitment to engaging former Soviet scientists, many felt pressured to be involved in Science Center projects because it "looks good," yet discouraged from spending time on this work because hours were not billable to any contract. Project collaborators tended to

---

51. Interview with Science and Technology Center in Ukraine staffer 2, October 26, 2005.

52. This section is based on General Accounting Office, *Weapons of Mass Destruction: State Department Oversight of Science Centers Program*, pp. 11–12; and Alessi and Lehman, "Science in the Pursuit of Peace: TheSuccess and Future of the ISTC," pp. 19–20.

53. General Accounting Office, *Weapons of Mass Destruction: State Department Oversight of Science Centers Program*, p. 12, fn. 11.

54. Interview with Los Alamos National Laboratory staffer 7, May 1, 2002; interview with Los Alamos National Laboratory staffer 10, June 2, 2003; interview with Lawrence Livermore National Laboratory staffer 4, April 7, 2003; interview with former U.S. government official 3, December 8, 1999; and interview with former U.S. government official 7, October 10, 2003.

55. Interview with former U.S. government official 3, December 8, 1999.

56. Sometimes U.S. lab employees could be paid for this work through a small grant from CRDF.

favor working through IPP, because they felt they had greater intellectual control over their project and they were compensated for their time.

Policy review was done through an interagency process that involved the Departments of Defense and Energy as well as other groups that were responsible for U.S. nonproliferation interests and objectives.[57] Here the aim was to identify projects that contradicted U.S. policy, posed a proliferation risk, or had the potential to contribute to their host country's military capabilities, and to look for projects that involved institutes with a history of working with Iran or other suspected proliferant states. This was also the point at which IPP and other scientist redirection programs were supposed to make sure that the proposed project was not something they were already funding.[58]

After the various review processes, representatives from the Departments of Defense, Energy, and State met to develop the official U.S. decision about what projects to fund. In addition to the information and recommendations developed in the review process, the group considered past experience with institutes and scientists as well as goals of engaging new or specific institutes. Then the Science Center staff worked with the project team to make any necessary changes to the official project agreement.

Proposal review for projects involving biological and chemical weapons experts was slightly different. According to Amy Smithson, who at the time was with the Henry L. Stimson Center, most proposals involving chemical weapons experts were reviewed by both the Departments of Defense and Energy.[59] Proposals involving biological weapons experts usually went to the Defense Department's Office of Threat Reduction Policy, the U.S. Army Medical Research Institute of Infectious Diseases, the Department of Agriculture, or the Department of Health and Human Services.[60] These technical evaluations then went to the monthly Nonproliferation Interagency Roundtable, where a final ranking was assigned to each proposal.[61] For projects with biological weapons experts, the State Department had a tracking system to help coordinate proposals under consideration by ISTC, STCU, and IPP.[62]

---

57. Alessi and Lehman, "Science in the Pursuit of Peace: The Success and Future of the ISTC," p. 19.

58. General Accounting Office, *Weapons of Mass Destruction: State Department Oversight of Science Centers Program*, p. 10. According to interview with former State Department staffer 2, July 9, 2007, the interagency review process was probably not robust enough to prevent the Science Centers, IPP, or the Nuclear Cities Initiative from sometimes funding the same proposal. This official went on to say that the process did, however, do a good job of making sure that the Science Centers did not fund the same proposal twice.

59. Smithson, *Toxic Archipelago*, p. 26.

60. Ibid.

61. Ibid.

62. Ibid., p. 96.

The other form of project review happened through project collabora-tors. The U.S. government encouraged government scientists and techni-cal experts to be collaborators for Science Center projects, even though no compensation was provided for this.[63] In theory, the results of projects were supposed to inform the collaborator's own work for the U.S. govern-ment. In practice, as is explained in more detail below, there were few checks to make sure that this happened. At the U.S. national laboratories, managers strongly encouraged people to be collaborators, and this sense of buy-in to the program encouraged people to take part, even though there was no compensation. People were also motivated by the chance to get money to travel to Russia or other former Soviet states to verify projects.[64]

The United States conducted additional audits of Science Center proj-ects, which were done by the Defense Contract Audit Agency (DCAA).[65] Each year, the State Department selected a number of projects for review, mostly of accounting and financial matters. In 1996, for example, DCAA audited seventeen ISTC projects, all in the cities of Sarov and Snezhinsk.

In interviews, some Science Center staff and collaborators expressed a sense of frustration about these audits, claiming that they emphasized bookkeeping issues over science and innovation. The following story, told by one staff member at STCU, illustrates these concerns.[66] According to this staffer, a DCAA auditor asked a project scientist what he was doing. "I'm thinking," was the reply. Then the scientist went on to explain that for the last two to three months he had worked on an important calculation that could be written on a single piece of paper. Despite the research sig-nificance of this equation, the auditor reported that the project had wasted valuable time with too few results.

Defining Goals and Threats

Since their founding, U.S. participation in the Science Centers consistently focused on two primary goals.[67] The short-term goal—engagement—was aimed at discouraging proliferation by providing additional income to as many WMD and missile technology experts as possible. The long-term goal, sometimes called redirection or sustainability, was to reemploy these people permanently in non-weapons work. Additionally, the centers had

---

63. There were limited funds available for collaborators to travel to the former Soviet Union to visit project teams.

64. Interview with Lawrence Livermore National Laboratory staffer 1, April 1, 2003.

65. According to interview with former U.S. government official 4, October 2, 2007, this practice originated with the Defense Department. Reasoning that the Science Centers were funded with Defense Department dollars, Defense insisted that they have accounting and audit rules similar to other defense programs.

66. Interview with Science and Technology Center in Ukraine staffer 14, October 31, 2005.

67. Each Science Center funding party set its own project selection criteria. Here I focus on U.S. criteria, although in general all other funding countries shared these goals.

a variety of other less important goals that included helping support the transition to a market economy in former Soviet states, promoting the integration of scientists into the wider international scientific community, and helping to preserve the skills and knowledge base to solve scientific problems of public, national, or international importance.[68] These goals are discussed in more detail below.

ENGAGEMENT

The threat that prompted the creation of the Science Centers was the fear that economic desperation would lead weapons experts to sell their skills and knowledge. Similar to the concerns that prompted CTR, the Science Centers were based on the assumption that financial worries might lead to proliferation. Because of economic circumstances in the Soviet Union, and then Russia and the other post-Soviet states, weapons workers were paid very little, and even those salary payments were often months late. Further, the Soviet nuclear complex was oversized, and it was clear that the Russian government would have no choice but to lay off weapons workers in the future. There were also rumors that certain states, such as Iran, Iraq, and North Korea, were actively recruiting at WMD institutes.

Just days before Secretary of State James Baker announced plans to create ISTC in February 1992, he made a well-publicized trip to the Russian nuclear city of Snezhinsk. While there, he was told that monthly salaries ranged from 857 rubles (about $6) for technicians to 1,500 rubles (about $10) for a top bomb designer, and that even with bonuses, housing, and subsidized food, the scientists were having a hard time making ends meet.[69] The scientists told Baker that they were eager to turn their scientific skills into civilian work, but that the Russian government lacked the necessary funding to help.[70]

Based upon the assumption that weapons workers were "almost desperate," the first goal of the Science Centers was to provide income to these experts as soon as possible by engaging them in short-term research contracts.[71] Similar to the conversion projects implemented by the Depart-

---

68. ISTC Statute, Article II, http://www.istc.ru (accessed May 30, 2007); and STCU Mission Statement, http://www.stcu.int (accessed May 30, 2007).

69. Thomas L. Friedman, "Ex-Soviet Atom Scientists Ask Baker for West's Help," *New York Times*, February 15, 1992, pp. 1, 4. During 1992, the ruble first became legally convertible to dollars. The exchange rate varied from around 150 rubles to the dollar initially to over 400 rubles to the dollar by the end of the year.

70. David Hoffman, "Baker Reassures Elite of Ex-Soviet Scientists; Russians at Nuclear Complex Plead for Commercial Work," *International Herald Tribune*, February 15–16, 1992, p. 1.

71. Friedman, "Ex-Soviet Atom Scientists Ask Baker for West's Help," p. 1. Interestingly, the state of this desperation may have been a bit overblown. It is not in dispute that economic conditions were bad. During the first years of the Science Centers, the State Department summarized this situation with a briefing slide that appeared frequently in presentations and was subsequently referenced by other programs. The slide compared the salary of a bus driver in Moscow to that of a weapons designer in a closed nuclear city. According to the slide, which cited as its source an article from the February 26, 1994 edition of *The Moscow*

ment of Defense, the goal was to mitigate the problem of brain drain as quickly as possible. There were no presumptions that the Science Centers would reach every weapons expert or guarantee that none would facilitate proliferation. Rather, the goal was to alleviate the chances of proliferation as much as possible and to encourage the Russian government to do more to discourage proliferation from its weapons institutes. Engaging as many weapons experts and institutes as possible remained one of the core missions of both Science Centers.

Although the number one priority was to engage weapons experts, the Science Centers also tried to fund projects that emphasized interesting research and made use of relevant knowledge and skills. For example, the U.S. evaluation process for proposals from both centers included scientific merit as one of several criteria for selection. The presumption was that scientists would be more motivated to participate if the work was interesting, and that it was important to preserve the scientists' sense of dignity, as well as provide them with income.

Finally, the motivation behind engaging scientists in research becomes clearer when one understands that such activities were called "engagement" and not "employment." Although the Science Centers paid scientists each month for their labor on projects, senior staff, especially those working with ISTC would vigorously correct me when I referred to this as a salary. According to them, because the Science Centers were never intended to serve as employers, the Science Centers gave "grants."[72] Whereas "salary" was taken to imply that scientists were employed by the Science Centers, "grants" suggested that workers remained affiliated with their home institutes and that their future employment lay elsewhere. Additionally, because payments to project scientists were supposed to be tax-free, they were initially called grants as a way of encouraging host countries to respect this status.[73]

REDIRECTION AND SUSTAINABILITY

The second major goal of the Science Centers was to create sustainable jobs for weapons workers that permanently redirected them away from the defense complex.[74] Although both Science Centers started programs

---

Times, the bus driver earned significantly more money. According to my own research into salaries, however, this is unlikely to have been the case. Moreover, despite repeated searches for the cited *Moscow Times* article, I have not been able to find any article during this time period that allows for comparisons between the salaries of bus drivers and nuclear weapons designers.

72. Interview with Los Alamos National Laboratory staffer 10, June 2, 2003; interview with International Science and Technology Center staffer 1, February 6, 2002; interview with International Science and Technology Center staffer 3, June 4, 2003; interview with International Science and Technology Center staffer 11, October 22, 1999; and interview with International Science and Technology Center staffer 14, October 22, 1999.

73. Schweitzer, *Moscow DMZ*, p. 87.

74. According to Alessi and Lehman, all ISTC funding parties placed an emphasis on funding projects with commercial potential. See Alessi and Lehman, "Science in the Pursuit of Peace: The Success and Future of the ISTC," p. 21.

to promote sustainability in the mid-1990s, the interest in this goal was present from the beginning. For example, in making the case for ISTC in 1992, Robert Gallucci, the State Department's senior coordinator for nonproliferation initiatives with the former Soviet Union and later an assistant secretary of state, argued that research projects should have commercial potential and help pave the way for converting weapons experts to peaceful employment.[75] According to Glenn Schweitzer, the first ISTC executive director, most countries encouraged their private industries to get involved on the assumption that many products for the commercial market would result from ISTC's efforts.[76] Also, U.S. selection criteria for both ISTC and STCU projects always included a ranking for commercial potential.[77] Commercialization was also seen as a means of burden-sharing. Countering proliferation was too big a challenge for U.S. government funding alone; therefore the idea was to also encourage involvement from private businesses and foundations.[78]

Initially, however, the Science Centers focused on projects that engaged weapons experts first and foremost. According to Glenn Schweitzer, of the first projects, fewer than 5 percent would be considered relevant to commercial applications.[79]

The emphasis on sustainability started in 1997. Initially, however, the Science Centers created the Partners Program as a way of getting additional project funding because country contributions were not enough to match the number of interesting projects that were available.[80] By involving other government agencies, the Science Centers leveraged additional resources. Later, Partner Projects became a way to transition from providing short-term emergency assistance to a more long-term focus on redirection. Partially, the change was due to the realization that the immediate crisis was over, and economic circumstances had improved enough to make commercialization more likely to be successful.[81] But it was also the case that focusing on sustainability helped placate increasing concern

---

75. Robert Gallucci, "Redirecting the Soviet Weapons Establishment," *Arms Control Today*, June 1992, p. 3.

76. Schweitzer, *Moscow DMZ*, p. 108.

77. Interview with Los Alamos National Laboratory staffer 10, June 2, 2003; and interview with Science and Technology Center in Ukraine staffer 2, October 26, 2005.

78. Federation of American Scientists and the Natural Resources Defense Council, "Report on the Fourth International Workshop," p. 12; Statement of Robert Gallucci, Senior Coordinator in the Office of the Deputy Secretary of State, U.S. Congress, House, Defense Policy Panel and the Department of Energy Defense Nuclear Facilities Panel of the Committee on Armed Services, *Regional Threats and Defense Options for the 1990s*, 102nd Cong., 2nd sess., March 10, 11, 17, 19, 24, 26, 27, 31, April 2, 8, 9, and May 5, 1992, p. 326; and U.S. Congress, Senate, Committee on Armed Services, *Assisting the Build-Down of the Former Soviet Military Establishment*, 102nd Cong., 2nd sess., February 5, 6, 1992, pp. 50, 58.

79. Schweitzer, *Moscow DMZ*, p. 108.

80. Interview with former State Department staffer 2, July 9, 2007; and interview with former U.S. government official 4, October 2, 2007.

81. Interview with Science and Technology Center in Ukraine staffer 2, October 26, 2005.

among program skeptics that the program needed a path that would wean scientists off U.S. assistance.[82] By December 2007, the State Department had developed a measurement for assessing whether former Soviet institutes could "graduate" from Science Center funding.[83]

The Partners Program allowed government and private entities to fund collaborative research projects. The presumption was that private businesses would only fund research if they saw potential for future commercialization or other advantages. Moreover, the collaborative process involved in the research would help scientists and businesses to develop a relationship that might lead to future projects or longer-term employment. ISTC initially hired additional staff to evaluate past projects for commercial potential, then contracted with a marketing company to do an analysis of the most promising projects and to help promote their potential among the business community.[84] Later, projects came to be evaluated for possible licensing agreements, patents, and other ways to steer scientists into commercial activities.[85] Scientists were given opportunities for business training and skill development and strongly encouraged to seek out domestic companies that were interested in the services or products they produced through a basic science project. ISTC also offered a service whereby it would search its database of scientists and projects for specific skills of interest to a company. According to one interviewee in 1999, the mantra at ISTC was "sustainability, sustainability, sustainability."[86]

STCU began its Partners Program in 1997 as well. In addition to hiring staff to provide business training, STCU began the process of developing performance measures for evaluating projects in terms of sustainability and outlining criteria for identifying commercial potential. The goal was to eventually have a scientist in charge of commercialization at each institute.[87] As of April 2003, all projects were required to have a "sustainability statement" in which they specified how they would link the project to future funding and collaboration beyond STCU. To complete this section, project scientists usually either turned to STCU staff for help or used the Internet and did literature searches for relevant companies. In interviews with project managers, however, there was no consistent agreement as to what "sustainability" meant in the STCU context. Although all agreed that sustainability was a project requirement, few managers were able to explain how scientists could realistically expect to guide their projects in this

---

82. Woolf, *Nonproliferation and Threat Reduction Assistance*, June 26, 2006, p. 25.

83. Government Accountability Office, *Nuclear Nonproliferation: DOE's Program to Assist Weapons Scientists in Russia and Other Countries Needs to be Reassessed*, Washington, D.C. (December 2007), p. 24.

84. Interview with International Science and Technology Center staffer 1, October 23, 1999; and interview with International Science and Technology Center staffer 11, October 22, 1999.

85. Interview with International Science and Technology Center staffer 3, June 4, 2003; and interview with International Science and Technology Center staffer 11, October 22, 1999.

86. Interview with International Science and Technology Center staffer 1, October 18, 1999.

87. Interview with Science and Technology Center in Ukraine staffer 3, October 26, 2005.

direction. The sentiments expressed by one project manager were common: "sustainability is a focus, whatever that means."[88]

Despite the similar emphasis on sustainability at both ISTC and STCU, there was little communication between the centers on how to achieve this. Staff in charge of sustainability were not familiar with the procedures or staff at the other center. Moreover, "sustainability" meant slightly different things at each place. At ISTC, the emphasis was much more on individual scientists or teams. The exception was former biological weapons workers, where the goal was to keep them in place at their institutes and sustain those institutes through government- or foreign-funded research related to public health, bio-defense, and infectious disease issues. STCU tended to share the latter emphasis and focused on how to sustain institutes but wean them off a reliance on STCU funding streams.

There was one agreement about sustainability, however: it was never meant to replace engagement. Although there was a concern that scientists might become dependent on Science Center projects for their income, there was also the recognition that some mostly older scientists might never transition away from these grants. Rather than leave these scientists without an income, scientists at certain key institutes and in some of the places served by STCU were encouraged to participate in projects until they retired or died. According to estimates at STCU, of the 7,000 people who had been involved in projects as of 2005, about 10 percent were expected always to work on STCU projects.[89]

Regardless of the merits of sustainability as a goal, it was also the case that it might lead to tension with other Science Center objectives. For example, as explained in Chapter 4's case study of defense conversion projects, there was a persistent disconnect between what former weapons workers saw as interesting science and what the market rewarded with profit. In the case of defense conversion projects, scientists were disappointed that they were asked to make simple commercial goods rather than high-tech products. Increasingly, however, former Soviet scientists came to realize the commercial potential of low-tech goods and services. But the loans needed to advance such efforts were difficult to get at reasonable rates. The Science Centers, however, required their projects to involve some form of science that would be interesting to weapons experts and did not, as a rule, fund low-tech projects even if they involved such experts. For example, in interviews with U.S. project managers and reviewers, I asked if they would fund a proposal that was highly likely to be profitable, and involved WMD experts, but focused on the low-tech project of building a hotel. In all cases, project managers said that such a project would not be eligible for funding.[90] In this sense, the Science

88. One interviewee (Science and Technology Center in Ukraine staffer 8, October 27, 2005) said this section was "silly," and scientists were encouraged to just write something vague about their commercialization plans.

89. Interview with Science and Technology Center in Ukraine staffer 1, October 26, 2005.

90. Such low-tech projects would, however, be funded by the Nuclear Cities Initiative. For example, hotels were built in several cities that were home to important defense institutes

Center emphasis on interesting science may have caused it to reject efforts that would have led to sustainable reemployment.

Another conflict existed between the goal of sustaining institutes and that of nonproliferation. While a few key experts could lead a WMD project, it generally takes teams of people to build a bomb. Sustaining institutes served to preserve weapons teams in the same place with facilities and equipment. Sustaining individuals, however, split up these teams or removed key members from the equipment and facilities they used in their days of weapons work. It was, however, also the case that for many people outside of Russia or major cities, there were few opportunities for reemployment. Thus the trade-off was between the danger of proliferation as these institutes were forced to close and their experts dispersed, versus the danger of future proliferation if these institutes were kept intact. For those institutes that were lucky enough to transition to other sources of government funding, this was less likely to be a problem. But aside from a few former biological weapons facilities, there were few institutes that made this transition.

Former biological weapons institutes also prove an exception to this trade-off for another reason. The dual-use nature of most former biological weapons facilities, plus the substantial weapons-relevant skills of individual scientists, meant that for proliferation reasons there was an incentive to keep teams of researchers in place at institutes and use repeated international cooperation to monitor their activities until the researchers found permanent reemployment or died.

TARGET POPULATIONS

Chapter 2 discusses estimates of the number of former weapons workers and various ways of determining which experts were the biggest proliferation concern. With respect to the Science Centers, the goal was to engage former WMD and missile experts. There were no official statements that narrowed the population further or made claims about certain groups being more at risk for proliferation. Informally, however, and with respect to individual funding countries, it is possible to be more specific about the population the Science Centers were intended to target.

With respect to the pool of scientists available for engagement, the largest estimate was that of Glenn Schweitzer, the first ISTC director, who put the number of people who participated in Soviet WMD programs at more than one million, of whom 60,000 were a proliferation concern.[91] Schweitzer, however, stopped short of arguing that the Science Centers

---

and which were therefore involved in numerous collaborative programs with the United States and other countries. Scientists reasoned, correctly as it turned out, that U.S. program managers would pay to stay in a hotel with more Western-oriented services and standards. These "hotel projects" did not involve interesting science but did lead to reemployment for some weapons workers.

91.   U.S. Congress, Senate, *Committee on Governmental Affairs, Global Proliferation of Weapons of Mass Destruction*, Part II, March 13, 20, 22, 1996, p. 53. Also, Schweitzer, *Moscow DMZ*, pp. 84, 101.

should use 60,000 as the target for engagement. According to a senior U.S. ISTC staffer interviewed in 1999, the ISTC target population was 35,000.[92] A study by the National Research Council offered a higher number, claiming that ISTC used estimates for Russia alone of 10,000–20,000, plus an additional 40,000–50,000 others with less directly WMD-relevant knowledge or experience.[93] However, according to a 2001 comment from the State Department on a pending report by the Government Accountability Office, the U.S. national security community never established a definitive estimate of the total WMD scientific population in the former Soviet Union.[94]

Estimates of STCU's target population varied even more. On the low end were the estimates given during interviews at STCU: in the mid-1990s, the target population was 20,000, of whom 10,000 were in Ukraine.[95] However, according to STCU slides dating from 2005, STCU had "available" more than 300,000 scientists at 1,000 scientific and technical institutes.[96] Presumably, all of these scientists constituted a proliferation threat in some way, or they would not qualify for STCU assistance. That said, STCU saw as a goal the maintenance of a robust science and technology infrastructure that could be handed over to Ukraine when STCU ended its commitment. Therefore, its target population included anyone who could potentially be part of this infrastructure. Also, STCU had a broader definition of what it meant to be a proliferation risk with respect to biological weapons. In contrast to ISTC, which tended to identify biological weapons–relevant experts based upon institutes where such work was performed, at STCU, according to one project manager, they considered any scientist with an advanced degree in a biological science to be a potential proliferation risk.[97]

The decision about which scientists to target was left up to each Science Center funding party. Overall, most countries showed a preference for projects involving weapons experts. In U.S. project selection, this was referred to as the POO factor, or Purity of Objective. Project reviewers in the United States were supposed to rank projects in terms of several criteria, including technical or scientific merit, the level of international collaboration, previous work experience with ISTC, clearly specified project results, financial structure, potential market applications of the results, and cost per person-month of the project. But the number one selection criterion was the number of former weapons workers who would be

92.   Interview with former State Department staffer 3, February 20, 2003.

93.   Office of International Affairs, National Research Council, *An Assessment of the International Science and Technology Center*, p. 7.

94.   General Accounting Office, *Weapons of Mass Destruction: State Department Oversight of Science Centers Program*, p. 25.

95.   Interview with Science and Technology Center in Ukraine staffer 2, October 26, 2005.

96.   Science and Technology Center in Ukraine, "Overhead Slides," *Nanophotonics* (computer CD), September 2005.

97.   Interview with Science and Technology Center in Ukraine staffer 13, October 31, 2005.

involved in the project. The degree to which a project satisfied these criteria was its POO factor.

For basic science projects, the United States required project teams to be at least 50 percent former weapons workers, with a preference for at least 60 percent.[98] These requirements could be relaxed for the purposes of engaging institutes that had been earmarked for funding, such as those where previous engagement had been limited, or where there were specific concerns about key personnel. Moreover, the United States had no POO factor for Partner Projects at ISTC, although STCU had its own rule of not approving projects where fewer than 30 percent of the members were weapons scientists.[99]

In terms of types of workers, the Science Centers were directed specifically at nuclear, biological, and chemical weapons and missile delivery experts, but most early projects focused on specialists in nuclear weapons or nuclear energy. For example, during its first two years of operations, about two-thirds of ISTC projects were directed toward nuclear weapons experts, with less than 10 percent of project funding going to the biological or chemical expertise areas.[100] This was partly because the largest funder of basic science projects, the United States, focused its spending in this area.[101] U.S. project selection emphasized nuclear-related research until 1997, when the emphasis shifted to working with former biological weapons experts. But this emphasis on nuclear-related workers was also reinforced by the Russian Ministry of Atomic Energy (Minatom), which was given the lead in selecting institutes for engagement and project approval. Initially Minatom favored projects that involved their own experts, although this did not appear to be the case with Rosatom.[102]

The United States also focused its Science Center funding on weapons-relevant scientists, engineers, and technicians and left the danger of administrative, custodial, or other staff stealing weapons or materials to programs that focused on detection, border controls, or material security and accounting.

Finally, in terms of which individuals to target, U.S. policy toward the Science Centers suggests three contradictions. First, the United States did not fund proposals from individuals or institutes that were thought to be involved in offensive biological or chemical weapons work, both of which are illegal under international law.[103] Yet if nonproliferation was the

98. General Accounting Office, *Weapons of Mass Destruction: State Department Oversight of Science Centers Program*, p. 12.

99. Interview with Science and Technology Center in Ukraine staffer 10, October 28, 2005.

100. Office of International Affairs, National Research Council, *An Assessment of the International Science and Technology Center*, p. 7.

101. Statement of Robert Gallucci, Senior Coordinator in the Office of the Deputy Secretary of State, U.S. Congress, *Regional Threats and Defense Options for the 1990s*, p. 348; Gallucci, "Redirecting the Soviet Weapons Establishment," p. 4.

102. Interview with Minatom official 1, July 24, 2002; and interview with former State Department staffer, 3, February 20, 2003.

103. Smithson, *Toxic Archipelago*, p. 27, fn. 89.

goal, these should have been precisely the institutes that the United States wanted to engage, because this offered alternatives to making money through proliferation. In addition, engagement led to more transparency at those institutes. Similarly, the United States would not fund projects with people or institutes that had engaged in proliferation in the past. Yet this was also counterproductive for the same reasons. Third, if an individual was fired or laid off by their institute, that individual could no longer participate in Science Center projects.[104] The centers had no means of involving weapons experts except as members of an institution, yet it was scientists that were facing economic difficulties, such as those brought on by unemployment, that the Science Centers were created to help.

Measuring Progress

How well did the Science Centers do at meeting their two main goals of engagement and redirection?[105] In terms of engagement, the results are encouraging. Collectively, Science Center projects involved a large number of people at hundreds of institutes in all corners of the former Soviet Union. Moreover, during the difficult years of the early 1990s, for many people and institutes the Science Centers were their only sources of income. Even as late as 2008, Science Center "grants" remained a significant contribution to most participants' annual take-home pay. However, it is also the case that many Science Center participants were not former weapons workers. Additionally, engagement totals included a significant number of people who worked fifty days or less per year on a Science Center project. The Science Centers also paid little attention to whether they were engaging older workers with no future in the complex or new people who would spend their careers doing weapons work. These issues suggest that in terms of progress toward nonproliferation goals, the number of people "engaged" was not necessarily a good measurement.

With respect to permanent redirection, the results are less encouraging. Few scientists got sustainable jobs through Science Center projects. Moreover, the Partners Program that was started with the intention of increasing sustainable redirection was composed of mostly government rather than private sector partners. Therefore, Partner Projects offered little promise of long-term work.

---

104. I thank Science and Technology Center in Ukraine staffer 10, October 28, 2005, for bringing this to my attention.

105. With respect to the other goals of the Science Centers, the Department of Defense asked the National Academies of Science (NAS) to report on ISTC's progress in May 1995. In its 1996 review, the NAS found that ISTC was successful at providing meaningful non-weapons work through its projects, was contributing to the solution of important technical problems in host states, and had helped former Soviet weapons experts integrate into the Western scientific community. The NAS study also concluded that ISTC had made only limited progress in helping former Soviet states transition to a market economy. As of 2008, there had been no subsequent external evaluations of progress toward these goals. See Office of International Affairs, National Research Council, *An Assessment of the International Science and Technology Center*, pp. 11–14.

The following section explains these and other conclusions in more detail and discusses the metrics the Science Centers and the United States used for judging the success of this effort.

ENGAGING FORMER WEAPONS EXPERTS

As of the end of 2008, the Science Centers had collectively engaged almost 85,000 people. According to ISTC, from its beginning in 1994 through the end of 2008, a total of approximately 71,400 people participated in its projects.[106] During a similar period, the STCU reported a total of 13,300.[107] The number of scientists engaged in projects grew from 3,000 during ISTC's first year of operation to almost 25,000 at ISTC in 2005 and nearly 5,000 at STCU.[108]

It is difficult to overestimate the importance of Science Center projects in the early to mid-1990s, when financial circumstances were the most desperate for workers throughout the former Soviet Union. Before ISTC was officially up and running in Moscow, its staff were visiting former weapons institutes, describing the program to scientists, and encouraging them to apply. Within six months there were 3,000 people involved in funded projects; a year later there were 11,500.[109] This is impressive given that few former Soviet WMD institutes were readily accessible to foreigners, and that both the project teams and the institute directors who needed to approve their involvement had almost no experience with international collaboration. Many were also suspicious of working with the United States, revealing national security secrets, or concerned that their best ideas would be stolen by foreigners.

The Science Centers also reached out to a wide variety of institutes. After little more than a year of operation, ISTC had projects at over 150 institutes in Russia, Belarus, and Kazakhstan.[110] By 2004, it had worked with

---

106.   International Science and Technology Center, "Annual Report," 2008, Moscow, p. 5.

107.   STCU did not regularly report the total number of scientists engaged. According to STCU, it had engaged 12,000 scientists through September 2005. See Science and Technology Center in Ukraine, "Overhead Slides," *Nanophotonics*. According to another STCU document, STCU had engaged 13,300. See Science and Technology Center in Ukraine, "Science and Technology Center in Ukraine, (STCU)," overhead briefing slides, March 2008. The 13,300 total is consistent with that reported by Olena Levytska of STCU in a presentation at "Perspective Materials, Devices and Structure For Space Applications," ISTC Workshop, Yerevan, Armenia, May 26–29, 2009.

108.   General Accounting Office, *Weapons of Mass Destruction: Reducing the Threat from the Former Soviet Union*, Washington, D.C. (October 1994), p. 11; International Science and Technology Center, "Annual Report," 2005, Moscow, p. 1; Science and Technology Center in Ukraine, "Annual Report," 2005, Kiev, p. 13; and Science and Technology Center in Ukraine, "Annual Report," 2007, Kiev, p. 13.

109.   Department of State, Office of the Coordinator of U.S. Assistance to the NIS, "FY 1995: U.S. Government Assistance to and Cooperative Activities with the New Independent States of the Former Soviet Union," April 1996, p. 113.

110.   Ibid.

over 750 institutes in 9 countries.[111] STCU engaged some 400 institutes.[112] During the critical years of 1994–1998, ISTC funded over $33 million in projects at Russia's two main nuclear weapons research and design institutes, the All-Russian Research Institute of Experimental Physics (VNIIEF) and the All-Russian Research Institute of Technical Physics (VNIITF), and was crucial in providing income to their nuclear weapons workforce.[113] Certain institutes got most of their income from working on Science Center projects. For example, in 1990, 78 percent of funding at Vector came from the state; in 2000, it got more than twice as much funding from ISTC projects as from the Russian federal budget.[114] The Science Centers became particularly important at facilities that were formerly engaged in biological weapons work.[115]

Although almost 85,000 people were engaged, this total represents every person in the former Soviet Union who ever participated in a Science Center project without regard for their skills or time spent on a project. Further delineation of project participants along these lines brings into question the degree to which engagement reflects counterproliferation goals.

First, the total number of people engaged in projects is not the same as the number of weapons scientists. All projects involved other personnel. For example, most projects employed non-weapons workers to provide necessary technical, administrative, computer, or other skills. This begs the question of how many of the 85,000 who were engaged were actually

---

111. Michael Roston, "Reported Accomplishments of Threat Reduction and Nonproliferation Programs, by Agency," Policy Update, Russian-American Nuclear Security Advisory Council (RANSAC), Washington, D.C. (July 2004), p. 11; and interview with International Science and Technology Center staffer 4, July 24, 2007.

112. Interview with Science and Technology Center in Ukraine staffer 2, July 9, 2007.

113. Interview with International Science and Technology Center staffer 15, April 16, 1998. For example, during its first two years of operations, ISTC projects employed some 1,200 scientists at VNIIEF, about 5 percent of the workforce. See National Research Council, *An Assessment of the International Science and Technology Center*, p. 11; and Oleg Bukharin, Frank N. von Hippel, and Sharon K. Weiner, *Conversion and Job Creation in Russia's Closed Nuclear Cities* (Princeton, N.J.: Program on Nuclear Policy Alternatives, Center for Energy and Environmental Studies, Princeton University, 2000), p. 13.

114. Derek Averre, "From Co-Option to Cooperation: Reducing the Threat of Biological Agents and Weapons," in Robert J. Einhorn and Michele A. Flournoy, eds., *Protecting Against the Spread of Nuclear, Biological, and Chemical Weapons* (Washington, D.C.: Center for Strategic and International Studies, 2003), p. 34. According to interview with Science and Technology Center in Ukraine staffer 2, July 9, 2007, based on survey data, STCU understood that the institutes it served got about 50 percent of their funding from non-government sources. Of that 50 percent, STCU provided just over 60 percent. In some countries, however, such as Uzbekistan, STCU provided 80 percent or more of all funding. In general, institutes outside of Russia and Ukraine got more of their income from the Science Centers.

115. For example, in 1996, 10 percent of the budget at the Russian Institute of Applied Microbiology came from ISTC projects. See National Research Council, *An Assessment of the International Science and Technology Center*, p. 11. Amy Smithson offers specifics about the importance of Science Center grants at key former biological weapons institutes in *Toxic Archipelago*, pp. 48–50.

former weapons workers. With respect to STCU, this is a straightforward issue. As of September 2005, STCU reported that of the 12,000 people its projects had engaged up to that point, a total of 7,000 were former weapons scientists, about 58 percent of all participants.[116] In 2008, STCU reported that through 2007 it had engaged 83,000 weapons experts and 5,000 others, and thus 62 percent of project participants were former WMD scientists.[117] ISTC did not provide details about the number of weapons-related experts involved in projects in its annual reports. Assuming that all ISTC projects met the requirement of 50 percent weapons scientists, that would suggest that the ISTC employed approximately 35,700 weapons experts through the end of 2008. In another study from 2001, the Government Accountability Office reported that together the Science Centers engaged about 21,000 weapons experts, which is about 53 percent of total participant levels for that time.[118] Therefore, roughly half seems to be a good estimate of the number of weapons experts involved in projects.

Of course, not all weapons-relevant skills are alike. Certain scientists, for example, may be of particular proliferation concern or have critical weapons skills. Therefore, Science Center projects that included these people would have significant nonproliferation value, even if the total number of weapons experts in the project was low. While it may be the case that early Science Center projects did target such individuals, by 1999, there was little evidence that this practice had persisted. My interviews with Science Center personnel from 1999 through 2007 provide evidence that some institutes, particularly those involved in past biological weapons efforts, continued to be targeted for involvement, but that this did not extend to individual scientists. Indeed, "weapons scientists" tended to be treated as a homogeneous group in terms of their nonproliferation value.

The Science Centers determined the number of weapons experts involved in their projects by asking project participants to identify their level of expertise in terms of a standardized list of areas broken down into nuclear, biological, or chemical weapons knowledge, missile technology, or nuclear energy skills. Staff at both Science Centers claimed they knew the scientists involved and over time could validate their claims to expertise through informal networks and contacts. Neither of the Science Centers, nor the U.S. government, made a rigorous attempt

---

116. Science and Technology Center in Ukraine, "Overhead Slides," *Nanophotonics*.

117. "Science and Technology Center in Ukraine (STCU)," overhead briefing slides, March 2008; and presentation by Levytska, "Perspective Materials, Devices and Structure for Space Applications."

118. General Accounting Office, *Weapons of Mass Destruction: State Department Oversight of Science Centers Program*, p. 15. This comparison is based upon State Department, Office of the Coordinator of U.S. Assistance to the New Independent States, "U.S. Government Assistance to and Cooperative Activities with the New Independent States of the Former Soviet Union, FY 2000 Annual Report," Washington, D.C. (January 2001), p. 243, which reports that as of the end of fiscal year 2000, the Science Centers had a total of almost 40,000 participants in their projects.

to independently verify weapons expertise.[119] Instead, for two main reasons they argued for confidence in the self-identification method.

First, the project approval process was designed to encourage research that would be of interest to people who used to earn their living making weapons. Therefore, projects required tasks that could only be accomplished by people with certain skills or experience. For nuclear weapons experts, this presumptive match between project research and participants' skills was probably a reasonable indicator of whether former weapons experts were involved. Scientists who used to make nuclear weapons were concentrated in institutes that were devoted to that purpose. Although parts of the former Soviet nuclear weapons complex were also engaged in commercial activities, it is a fair bet that any Science Center projects at these institutes that also involved interesting physics, materials science, or selected other areas, would involve some former weapons workers.

But this relationship breaks down when former biological or chemical weapons experts are involved. Because of the broad overlap between militarily useful skills and those needed for legitimate civilian research, it would be difficult to design research projects that involved only former biological or chemical weapons experts unless those research projects had military applications. Furthermore, most former Soviet institutes that worked on biological or chemical weapons also did significant civilian work.[120] Therefore, simply involving people with certain skills who worked at these institutes is not a reliable indicator of past weapons work. Moreover, these institutes were among the most likely to be cut off from government funding, and workers there had fewer alternative sources of income. Because participation in a Science Center project provided significant income, scientists had an incentive to inflate their weapons credentials to encourage project approval.

One response to this critique about self-identification is that in dual-use areas, scientists without any experience in the weapons process could still be of value to a proliferant. This, however, begs the question of whether the goal of the Science Centers was to counter the proliferation risk posed by the relatively small number of former weapons workers or the danger due to the much larger population of civilian employees with potentially weapons-relevant skills.[121] There is no evidence that ISTC, STCU,

119. General Accounting Office, *Weapons of Mass Destruction: State Department Oversight of Science Centers Program*, p. 2; and interview with International Science and Technology Center staffer 3, June 4, 2003. According to the Government Accountability Office, *Nuclear Nonproliferation: DOE's Program to Assist*, p. 15, ISTC and STCU asked the directors of the former Soviet institute to verify the weapons credentials of project participants.

120. In the Soviet Union there were institutes that were devoted more exclusively to work on biological or chemical weapons. In Russia these places fell under the Ministry of Defense and remained off-limits to foreign collaboration as of 2008.

121. Another interesting question pertains to the role of experience in weapons-relevancy. In "Bioweapons Proliferation: Where Science Studies and Public Policy Collide," *Social Studies of Science*, Vol. 36, No. 5 (October 2006), Kathleen Vogel explores the relationship between tacit knowledge and weapons skills. She argues that it may be the case that the ability to

or U.S. policymakers considered this distinction or its consequences. If weapons scientists were the target, then self-identification was a reliable indicator only if project participants had no incentives to lie or inflate their resumes. If people with no experience but relevant skills were the target, then the Science Centers should have engaged a much larger number of institutes and experts.

The Science Centers argued that a second reason to trust self-identification of weapons skills was that host institutes and countries had to sign off on projects. The presumption was that they would not agree to inaccurate classifications of expertise by project scientists. However, it is also the case that institutes got overhead and equipment for projects. In the case of ISTC projects, 10 percent of project funding went to the institute for overhead, and 50 percent or more generally went toward the purchase of equipment and supplies.[122] At STCU, overhead costs were 10 percent, and 20–30 percent went for equipment purchases.[123] Because institutes got much-needed income and supplies from projects and because project proposals were more likely to be successful if they involved at least 50 percent weapons scientists, there was an incentive for participants to inflate their WMD relevance.

This discussion is not to suggest that scientists or institutes lied. Rather, the purpose is to understand the degree of confidence the Science Centers had in their ability to measure the involvement of weapons scientists, given the incentives for both scientists and institutes to misrepresent their skills. Although the Science Centers claimed confidence in the self-identification method, backed up by informal networking and relationship building, this confidence was misplaced. In the 1990s, it would have been virtually impossible to double-check weapons credentials, given the level of suspicion left over from the Cold War, the novelty of international collaboration, and the sensitive security issues that go with identifying bomb makers. But the importance of these issues lessened significantly over time, and it became possible to get additional verification of weapons skills.

Additional evidence that "engagement" came to replace more proliferation-oriented goals can be found in the way engagement came to mean almost any degree of involvement with the Science Centers. For example,

---

contribute to a biological weapons program may decline as scientists lose direct experience making such weapons. Vogel explains that if this is the case, scientist redirection programs should have been aimed at a much smaller pool of people and only for a shorter period of time. For a similar argument about nuclear weapons experts, see Donald MacKenzie and Graham Spinardi, "Tacit Knowledge, Weapons Design, and the Uninvention of Nuclear Weapons," *American Journal of Sociology*, Vol. 101, No. 1 (July 1995), pp. 44–99.

122. Interview with International Science and Technology Center staffer 1, October 18, 1999; interview with International Science and Technology Center staffer 12, October 22, 1999; and General Accounting Office, *Weapons of Mass Destruction: State Department Oversight of Science Centers Program*, p. 5. According to one ISTC project reviewer, the percentage of money going to equipment and supplies versus personnel made it look like ISTC projects were really a welfare vehicle for beefing up institutes.

123. Interview with Science and Technology Center in Ukraine staffer 2, October 26, 2005.

according to the ISTC annual reports for 1998–2005, on average about 50 percent of project participants worked 50 or fewer days per year on an ISTC project.[124] On average, 31 percent worked fewer than 25 days per year.[125] STCU annual reports for 2004 and 2005 show that, for these two years, about half of all participants worked fewer than 75 days a year on a project.[126] From these figures, it is clear that most project participants spent small percentages of their time working for the Science Centers, yet all project participants counted equally in terms of the "engagement" metric. Moreover, the Science Centers made few attempts to understand how scientists spent the rest of their time, including whether or not they remained involved in weapons work.[127]

Another way to consider engagement is in terms of income to participants. If financial insecurity is presumed to be an incentive to proliferate, then engagement matters based on the income it provided rather than the days worked. Using this metric, "engagement" with the Science Centers was much more relevant to counterproliferation goals, because even working 50 or fewer days on a project meant a significant increase in income for almost all participants.

For example, ISTC salaries for project participants were originally based on what was being paid at relevant institutes and firms.[128] As of 2007, salaries ranged from about $16 a day for less skilled employees to $35 a day for a highly skilled project manager.[129] Salaries at STCU were similar.[130] Despite considerable changes in Russia's economic situation and salaries at relevant institutes, salaries for basic science projects did

---

124. Based upon information in International Science and Technology Center, "Annual Reports," 1998–2005, Moscow. According to some interviewees, the number of days devoted to ISTC projects may also have been limited because of tensions between those who worked for ISTC and those who did not. ISTC participants got higher salaries and also they got to manage the procurement of their own equipment and supplies. This led to tension with "old school Soviet" managers who needed resources and who wanted to maximize their control over activities at their institutes. Apparently this tension was greatest in the early 1990s, when Science Center participants made significantly more than others at their institutes, but as salaries equalized this tension was reduced. Interview with International Science and Technology Center staffer 1, October 23, 1999; interview with International Science and Technology Center staffer 12, October 22, 1999; interview with Science and Technology Center in Ukraine staffer 8, October 27, 2005; and interview with Institute for Physics and Power Engineering staffer 1, July 23, 2002.

125. This is based upon information in International Science and Technology Center, "Annual Reports," 1998–2005, Moscow.

126. Science and Technology Center in Ukraine, "Annual Reports," 2004 and 2005, Kiev.

127. General Accounting Office, *Weapons of Mass Destruction: State Department Oversight of Science Centers Program*, p. 29.

128. Schweitzer, *Moscow DMZ*, pp. 43–44.

129. Interview with International Science and Technology Center staffer 1, October 18, 1999, and subsequent electronic communication on February 6, 2002; interview with International Science and Technology Center staffer 3, June 4, 2003; and interview with International Science and Technology Center staffer 4, July 24, 2007.

130. Interview with Science and Technology Center in Ukraine staffer 8, October 27, 2005; and interview with former State Department staffer 2, July 9, 2007.

not change significantly over time.[131] The goal was to keep salaries attractive but, as economies improved, to encourage scientists to take advantage of other opportunities.[132] Although payment for Partner Projects was determined differently—it was negotiated between partners and scientists—participants in these projects tended to have higher salaries, and could also be paid performance bonuses.[133] If salaries are averaged among all participants, the average daily wage working on an ISTC project was $22.55.[134] This means that half of all ISTC participants earned about $1100 or more per year through ISTC. Compared to the Russian average wage for this time period, it is clear that working even 50 days a year on an ISTC project was still a significant salary boost, even for people at the best paid nuclear weapons institutes in Russia.[135]

One caveat: scientists may not have kept all of their paychecks. In some cases, project teams got together and decided how to split up the money among themselves, but also within the larger networks of managers and suppliers who enabled them to do their projects.[136] According to one interviewee who participated in Science Center projects, it was a common practice for institutes to deduct time spent on Science Center projects from participants' salaries. Although this evidence is anecdotal, neither Science Center had mechanisms for insuring that these problems were not widespread.

Finally, "engagement" was a questionable metric because it did not differentiate between old and new workers. For some institutes, such as those outside of Russia and many that were part of the biological and chemical weapons complexes, there was clearly no prospect for government funding in the future and no reason to hire new workers. At some places, however, the goal was to return to the host government a converted weapons institute that then played a role in doing science for the public interest. Such institutes might well hire new employees with additional skills. In Russia, for example, the nuclear weapons institutes eventually began to hire new people for weapons work.

The Science Centers allowed all of these workers to participate in projects, and this calls into question the degree to which engagement reflected progress toward nonproliferation goals. The Science Centers were prompted by the fear that poorly paid weapons scientists might

---

131.   Interview with International Science and Technology Center staffer 3, June 4, 2003.

132.   Ibid.

133.   Interview with former State Department staffer 3, February 20, 2003.

134.   Electronic communication with International Science and Technology Center staffer 1, February 6, 2002.

135.   In Chapter 2, I explain that the average salary in Russia in 2005 was $260 a month or $3,120 per year, so 50 days with ISTC would have increased one's salary by about one-third. The average yearly salary for an employee at the Kurchatov Institute in Moscow around this same time was approximately $3,000 per year and about $4,500 at institutes in the nuclear cities.

136.   Interview with Oak Ridge National Laboratory staffer 4, February 19, 2003; and interview with Science and Technology Center in Ukraine staffer 8, October 27, 2005.

proliferate. According to this logic, the centers should have engaged those scientists who lacked a secure employment future, not workers who were recently hired and who had every reason to assume their job was protected. Moreover, because of U.S. concerns about indirect subsidies to the Russian defense industry, ISTC should also have avoided newly hired workers.

One counterargument is that allowing newly hired workers to participate in projects promoted transparency at institutes. And while there is evidence to support this claim, transparency as a goal begets a long-term commitment—one focused on information-gathering in addition to nonproliferation. Both are beyond the original mission of the Science Centers and U.S. goals for participation.

Another counterargument is that new workers were also a proliferation risk. Although there was no mass exodus of weapons workers from the Soviet Union, newer workers were being hired into a system that lacked the nationalistic, social, and family bonds that made proliferation unthinkable for formerly Soviet workers. Few ties to institutes meant that workers were more likely to find proliferation acceptable. The Science Centers fought this problem by rewarding those who stayed in place.

There is some evidence to support this claim. According to a 2001 survey of Russian scientists by Deborah Yarsike Ball and Theodore P. Gerber, participating in cooperative research projects such as those funded by ISTC resulted in scientists who were less inclined to work for rogue states.[137] But it was also the case that targeting new workers for this reason was a deviation from the original mission of the Science Centers. The centers were premised on the presumption of a proliferation risk due to the collapse of the Soviet Union. Hiring new workers in the name of counterproliferation suggests that Russia and other post-Soviet states constituted a long-term and possibly permanent proliferation risk—one that arose from issues other than financial desperation.

In summary, although the Science Centers deserve credit for engaging a large number of people during years when financial desperation was at its highest, there are reasons to doubt the degree to which engagement reflected progress toward reducing the danger of proliferation in later years. Although some 85,000 people were involved in Science Center projects, there is strong evidence that only about half of these people were former weapons workers. There are additional reasons to question whether the label "weapons worker" reflected people with significant weapons-related, especially biological and chemical weapons–related, experience. Additionally, the number of people engaged included people who had future careers in the weapons complex, as well as workers who spent most of their time doing something other than projects for the Science Centers. All of these caveats suggest that "engagement" came to reflect an expanded definition of who was a proliferation danger and why, and perhaps

---

137.   Deborah Yarsike Ball and Theodore P. Gerber, "Russian Scientists and Rogue States: Does Western Assistance Reduce the Proliferation Threat?" *International Security*, Vol. 29, No. 4 (Spring 2005), pp. 72–75.

even entirely new, more long-term goals. Moreover, there is no evidence that the U.S. Congress, the United States, or any other funding party approved or formally considered this expansion of mission beyond original Science Center goals.

PERMANENT REDIRECTION

It is difficult to determine how many scientists found permanent reemployment as a result of the Science Centers. Although both Centers published "success stories," neither officially measured the number of jobs created or scientists redirected. According to senior staff at both ISTC and STCU, it was unlikely that many jobs resulted from Science Center projects.[138] Queries of project managers at ISTC and STCU routinely yielded responses that they either knew of no one who had gotten jobs as a result of Center projects, or that perhaps ten to fifteen people had found reemployment. One manager explained that even in cases where jobs were created, they sometimes failed because the product was not competitive.[139] Because Soviet institutes provided a variety of social benefits for their workers, the private spin-offs tried to do the same. However, this made the price of their product or service too expensive.

Instead, the centers measured the number of partners, Partner Projects, and spending on these efforts. Having a Partner Project was, however, no guarantee of permanent reemployment or even of an additional Partner Project. Moreover, one STCU project manager claimed that because Partner Projects had fewer reporting requirements than regular science projects, often little was known about the partner's future plans or level of interest in sustainability.[140] Another project manager at ISTC said that often they did not even know the deliverables for Partner Projects, and therefore could not assess whether they were working on commercializing technologies.[141]

The centers also measured the number of people who were involved in attempts to commercialize technologies. In the fall of 2001, ISTC surveyed the managers of all completed or nearly completed projects and found that one-third were engaged in some form of technology commercialization as a result of their projects.[142] Most had collaborations in place for future Science Center projects, but twenty-two reported small enterprises, four reported joint ventures, and thirty-two said they had contracts for future joint activities.[143] Further study, however, showed that most of

138.   Interview with International Science and Technology Center staffer 1, October 18, 1999; and interview with Science and Technology Center in Ukraine staffer 2, October 26, 2005.

139.   Interview with Science and Technology Center in Ukraine staffer 9, October 28, 2005.

140.   Interview with Science and Technology Center in Ukraine staffer 9, October 31, 2005.

141.   Interview with International Science and Technology Center in Ukraine staffer 2, June 2, 2003.

142.   Maria Douglas and Peter Falatyn, "More than Money: Small Technology Spin-Offs of the WMD Complex," *JRL Research & Analytical Supplement*, No. 10 (July 2002).

143.   Ibid.

the twenty-two small enterprises existed before the ISTC project began, and many were still connected to the parent institutes of the workers.[144]

Most Partner Projects could not lead to permanent reemployment because they involved contracts with government agencies. As of the end of 2008, ISTC had a cumulative total of 705 Partner Projects, of which 559 were with government partners.[145] Government partners also accounted for 91.5 percent of all Partner Project funding.[146] Moreover, most government Partner Projects were with U.S. agencies. Through July 2007, funding from U.S. government partners accounted for almost 80 percent of all Partner Project funding at ISTC.[147] There is evidence to suggest that government partner funding at STCU was also significant. From 2000 to 2007, STCU had a total of $50.38 million in Partner Projects, of which 64 percent, or $32.03 million, was from government partners.[148]

The Science Centers did attempt to interest businesses in Partner Projects; although their efforts were limited, they did improve over time. Initially, the centers focused on helping scientists develop their business and presentation skills and made them responsible for finding commercial partners. To the extent that the centers looked for business partners, they were not very proactive. For example, the centers would post the results of promising projects on the web or in other promotional materials and either wait for interested businesses to find these listings or for project collaborators or scientists to make connections to partners.[149] The centers also hosted job fairs where they presented certain interesting technologies and brought in former Soviet scientists to explain their research and its potential. But these events tended to be "fishing expeditions," according to one STCU staffer, where the location was advertised but little effort was

---

144. Ibid.

145. International Science and Technology Center, "Annual Report," 2005, p. 14; "Annual Report," 2006, p. 4; "Annual Report," 2007, p. 5; and "Annual Report," 2008, p. 6.

146. This is based on information from International Science and Technology Center, "Annual Report," 2005, p. 14; "Annual Report," 2006, p. 4; "Annual Report," 2007, p. 5; and "Annual Report," 2008, p. 6.

147. Based on information provided by ISTC, electronic communication, July 22, 2007.

148. Science and Technology Center in Ukraine, "Annual Report," 2005, p. 12; Department of State, Office of the Coordinator of U.S. Assistance to Europe and Eurasia, "FY 2000 U.S. Assistance to the NIS: Annual Report on U.S. Government Assistance to and Cooperative Activities with the New Independent States of the Former Soviet Union," Washington, D.C. (January 2001), p. 243; and Science and Technology Center in Ukraine, "Annual Report," 2007, p. 12.

149. According to International Science and Technology Center, "ISTC," briefing slides, September 16, 1999, there were three models for industry participation, all of which put the onus on the business to find ISTC rather than the other way around. One Russian interviewee expressed what he claimed was a wide spread frustration with ISTC's emphasis on commercialization while providing few guidelines for doing this. Interview with Institute for Physics and Power Engineering staffer 1, July 23, 2002. Several project collaborators at the U.S. national laboratories also expressed a sense of being "left on their own" to find commercial partners. Interview with Lawrence Livermore National Laboratory staffer 1, April 1, 2003; interview with Los Alamos National Laboratory staffer 7, May 1, 2002; and interview with Sandia National Laboratory staffer 1, May 2, 2003.

made to target specific businesses or develop connections in advance.[150] Also, in the beginning, the focus at these job fairs tended to be on the nonproliferation benefits of Partner Projects. Later, however, the emphasis shifted to explaining how projects could be used to access interesting technologies or mitigate the risk of entering new markets in former Soviet states.[151] Project managers and collaborators tended to extol the latter issues in their search for business partners. In addition, they also emphasized how Partner Projects offered an opportunity to subcontract services to a highly competent and extremely cheap labor force.[152]

By 2005, the Science Centers had inaugurated a much more targeted approach. Both hosted job fairs and conferences that came to focus on specific groups of technologies such as, for example, fuel cells, nanotechnology, or environmental remediation. One of the activities that staffs, scientists, and collaborators spoke highly of was the matchmaking activity funded largely by the Canadian government. Canada paid for trade missions where the focus was on demand pull; that is, on discussing particular technical needs with a group of businesses and then finding the scientific teams to fulfill those needs.[153] Most Science Center efforts were technology push; they tried to sell business on a technology that had already been developed. The Canadians also provided funding for businesses to travel to Ukraine to check out scientific teams and institutes. According to one interviewee, it helped that Canada had a significant Ukrainian population, and most of the businesses who expressed an interest had staff with a cultural connection.[154]

Explaining Outcomes

Collectively, the Science Centers have engaged over 85,000 people, but only about half of these may have been WMD experts. Together the centers also created jobs for, at most, a few thousand. Furthermore, over time, the goal of "engaging" WMD experts came to replace reemployment and job creation. What explains this mismatch between the number of people engaged and reemployed by the Science Centers and U.S. nonproliferation goals?

In this section of the chapter I consider several answers, including lack of cooperation from Russia, the role of Congress in restricting U.S. participation in and funding of the centers, and organizational interests,

---

150.   Interview with Science and Technology Center in Ukraine staffer 9, October 28, 2005.

151.   See STCU training CDs. In the late 1990s I attended several of these job fairs, where the nonproliferation and national security benefits of U.S. cooperation with the Science Centers was emphasized but little was said about the business benefits of partnership.

152.   Interview with Science and Technology Center in Ukraine staffer 9, October 28, 2005; and interview with Lawrence Livermore National Laboratory staffer 1, April 1, 2003.

153.   This description is based on interview with Science and Technology Center in Ukraine staffer 11, October 28, 2005.

154.   Ibid.

including the possibility of conflict between the Science Centers and the State Department. Although each of these factors had some impact, organizational variables offer the most persuasive explanation for Science Center results.

More specifically, while it is the case that neither the United States nor the Science Centers had the budget to fund all worthy projects, the State Department did not request significant increases in funding for the centers. Moreover, in the absence of revised project development criteria, additional funding and more projects would have made only minimal progress toward achieving U.S. nonproliferation goals. Below I make the case that while organizational interest was responsible for the initial success of the Science Centers and their ability to engage large numbers of people, it was also responsible for diverting the centers away from greater success in responding to the danger of proliferation as it evolved after 1994.

WORKING WITH THE RUSSIANS

Despite ISTC's initial problems getting official sanction to begin operations, there is no evidence that the Russian government created significant or persistent roadblocks for the Center. STCU had even fewer difficulties with the Ukrainian government.

Similar to the Defense Department's conversion projects, one initial problem faced by ISTC was that the Russian government and scientists focused on projects that were "interesting science" but not necessarily commercially or politically feasible. For example, in the early 1990s, some Russian nuclear weapons experts wanted to promote the peaceful uses of nuclear explosions and were very enthusiastic about working through ISTC.[155] But, according to Robert Gallucci, ISTC quickly convinced them this was a non-starter: "It is not surprising that the first thing they think of is peaceful nuclear explosions. That is the last thing we think of. We don't think of it at all, and we've made that very clear."[156] Similarly, ISTC also had to convince workers that research projects had to have some commercial potential. Over time a shift in attitude took place, although it remained the case that some older scientists still tended to focus only on the science involved in a project. Without commercial potential, however, few of these projects were approved. This was also a problem at STCU in Ukraine, but scientists came around more quickly due to the fact that they had fewer alternatives. In 2005, STCU claimed that they were getting better quality projects and also projects that were market-oriented.[157]

Another potential problem was access. The Nuclear Cities Initiative, in particular, had problems convincing the Russians to allow commer-

---

155. Gallucci, "Redirecting the Soviet Weapons Establishment," p. 6.

156. Ibid.

157. Interview with Science and Technology Center in Ukraine staffer 1, October 26, 2005; interview with Science and Technology Center in Ukraine staffer 2, October 26, 2005; and interview with Science and Technology Center in Ukraine staffer 7, October 27, 2005.

cial partners sufficient access to facilities in the closed nuclear cities. For ISTC, however, access was not an issue. Rules about access to institutes and the closed cities were written into ISTC's implementing agreement. Although these rules were sometimes contested at the local level, there is little evidence that they significantly hindered ISTC activities. Further, in my interviews with ISTC staff, I found little dissatisfaction with respect to access. The one exception was that, beginning in 2005, the FSB became much more strict about access and, according to one interviewee, this was because the Russian government felt it had outgrown ISTC's assistance.[158]

Taxes were a much larger issue. ISTC salaries and project-related supplies and equipment were supposed to be tax-free in Russia, according to the ISTC implementing agreement. But, as explained above, there is evidence that some salaries were taxed in unofficial ways. Also, projects were periodically stalled because federal, regional, or local officials inappropriately insisted on taxing imports or misunderstood the rules. According to the Government Accountability Office, from 1994 to 1999, ISTC paid about $270,000 in value-added taxes on equipment and services purchased in Russia.[159] In some cases, however, ISTC was able to negotiate refunds.

With respect to Partner Projects, taxes were more problematic. Although Partner Projects were allowed the same tax exemptions, there is some evidence that Russia believed that business partners were less interested in creating jobs for weapons workers than in using the ISTC to avoid customs duties for their business in Russia.[160] According to ISTC rules, however, a business could only use Partner Projects to investigate technologies and make prototypes. Once it began sustained production, it was no longer eligible for participation, and therefore lost ISTC's tax benefits.

In general, ISTC did not have as many significant problems with Russia as did other scientist redirection efforts. According to R. Adam Moody, who has written widely on the early history of the Science Centers, this is partly because ISTC's rules and procedures were specified in an intergovernmental agreement and not established at the institute or ministry level or on an ad-hoc basis.[161] This helped increase understanding and transparency and therefore trust in ISTC. Another argument is that ISTC treated Russia as a partner rather than an aid recipient. Russia invested resources in ISTC and was involved in decision-making and planning. Furthermore, numerous Russian employees held oversight

---

158. Interview with International Science and Technology Center staffer 4, July 24, 2007.

159. General Accounting Office, *Weapons of Mass Destruction: Some U.S. Assistance to Redirect Russian Scientists Taxed by Russia,* Washington, D.C., April 28, 2000, p. 3.

160. Interview with Lawrence Livermore National Laboratory staffer 1, April 1, 2003; interview with Minatom official 1, July 24, 2002; and interview with former Minatom official 1, July 30, 2002.

161. R. Adam Moody, "The International Science Center Initiative," in John M. Shields and William C. Potter, eds., *Dismantling the Cold War: U.S. and NIS Perspectives on the Nunn-Lugar Cooperative Threat Reduction Program,* (Cambridge, Mass.: MIT Press, 1997), pp. 279–280.

as well as other positions in ISTC.[162] Finally, it is also the case that ISTC projects led to income for scientists more quickly and on a larger scale than any other redirection effort.

THE ROLE OF CONGRESS

Congressional hearings and legislation show consistent but largely silent support for the Science Centers. The Science Centers were initially approved without much debate, and there were few restrictions on how the Science Centers operated or spent their funds. Mild or approving comments were more typical. For example, in February 2000, Congress approved funding for the Science Centers as long as the participation of former Soviet weapons scientists "predominates."[163] In the Expanded Threat Reduction Initiative in the same year, the House urged the Science Centers to focus more on permanent redirection and commercial activities.[164] Various measures called for more effective coordination between all scientist redirection efforts and between programs that focused on CTR in general. At one point Congress also suggested that a few more U.S. citizens should work in-country on U.S. funded programs. But in no case was funding made contingent upon meeting these objectives.

Scientist redirection efforts at the Departments of Defense and Energy suffered because of congressional rules that made U.S. programs contingent on Russian behavior. For CTR and many related programs, the U.S. president had to certify that the Russian government was abiding by certain arms control, human rights, and other agreements. Initially the U.S. president had to certify Russian compliance, but in 2008, Congress cancelled the need for certification. With one exception, judgments about broad U.S. policy issues with Russia had little impact on U.S. participation in the Science Centers.

That exception was in 1999–2001, when Congress linked funding for several programs to Russian cooperation with Iran. Because the Science Centers were funded out of the Freedom Support Act, which was one of the affected accounts, the State Department had to significantly revise its project funding plans. Of the $14 million that was originally allocated for ISTC activities in Russia for fiscal year 1999, only $8.5 million was allowed due to the congressional restrictions.[165] At the March 2001 ISTC Board Meeting, the United States instructed its representatives to withhold funding from any projects involving Minatom institutes in retaliation for Russian assistance to Iran.[166] Officially, the cause was a high-level

---

162. Alessi and Lehman, "Science in the Pursuit of Peace: The Success and Future of the ISTC," pp. 20–21.

163. RANSAC, "Russian Nuclear Security and the Clinton Administration's Fiscal Year 2000 Expanded Threat Reduction Initiative. A Summary of Congressional Action," Washington, D.C. (February 2000), p. 27.

164. Ibid.

165. United States Department of State, "Annual Report," fiscal year 1999, Washington, D.C.

166. Electronic communication with former U.S. government official 5, April 16, 2001; and

policy review, but political pressure was the intended result.[167] Moreover, this reduced project funding came on the heels of the 1998 financial crisis brought on by Russia's devaluation of the ruble, and therefore at a time when salaries for former weapons workers were among their lowest.

But cooperation was soon restored. Moreover, in 2002, the State Department determined that certain activities funded through the NADR account in the Foreign Operations budget were not affected by presidential certification.[168] This included the Science Centers, which were funded under the NADR account staring in fiscal year 2003.

ORGANIZATIONAL ISSUES

Another possible explanation for the lack of results is that the State Department, which administered U.S. participation in the centers, found the program to be incompatible with its mission and, as result, the program suffered. Chapter 4, for example, explains how the Defense Department saw defense conversion and CTR as outside of its normal responsibilities for sustaining U.S. military capabilities, and how various agencies sought to limit CTR's ability to reprogram funds. In the case of the Science Centers, the State Department found them to be an odd fit with traditional State Department missions and, as a consequence, was ineffective at securing consistent or significant funding increases for the program.

The Science Centers were a small part of a larger set of programs administered by the State Department that focused on the former Soviet Union. Over time these programs included technical, economic, and civil society programs funded by the Freedom Support Act, money for weapons dismantlement and demilitarization assistance that came from CTR, food aid provided by the Department of Agriculture, and humanitarian assistance provided by private and U.S. government sources. The State Department was also home to an ambassador-rank coordinator for U.S. assistance to the former Soviet Union, a position that was created by the Freedom Support Act and subsequently strengthened by Congress.

In contrast to the Science Centers, which focused on a specific issue, most of the State Department is organized according to regions or other geographically defined responsibilities. This distinction—between a functional program and a geographic one—made the Science Centers an anomaly in terms of both their mission and the process by which they put together budgets. Moreover, State generally oversees few cooperative programs like the centers. Finally, the Science Centers had more rigorous oversight and accounting rules, a legacy of their original association with the Defense Department. The result was an "unnatural relationship," as

---

electronic communication with former U.S. government official 6, April 16, 2001.

167. Ibid.

168. William Hoehn, "Update on Congressional Activity Affecting U.S.-Russian Cooperative Nonproliferation Programs," RANSAC, Washington, D.C., July 26, 2002, p. 3.

phrased by one interviewee, that had consequences for general support, personnel, and budgets.[169]

In terms of general support, the State Department often had a hard time understanding or justifying the Science Centers. This is not to suggest that the State Department actively sought to restrict the Science Centers. Rather, it is more the case that relevant parts of the State Department did not coordinate with them. For example, the State Department publishes a "Country Commercial Guide" to Russia, which looks at the commercial and investment climate and provides information about investment opportunities. The Guide did not, however, mention ISTC or any other scientist redirection programs, even though ISTC claimed its projects could help businesses evaluate expansion into the Russian market. Similarly, there was little interaction with the U.S. Agency for International Development (USAID), which receives guidance from the State Department. Despite its considerable experience with business development in Russia, including areas that should be of interest to the Science Centers, USAID did not specifically target cities that were home to significant WMD institutes, nor did the Science Centers mine USAID for its advice or lessons learned. For example, in 1994, USAID was working with Merck and Lederle to remedy problems with vaccine supply and production in Russia, but there is no evidence that they coordinated or involved the Science Centers and their biological weapons worker redirection efforts.[170] USAID also funds various different business development and training programs but, again, there is no evidence that these involved the Science Centers, or any other scientist redirection effort. Furthermore, even among parts of the State Department that were geared toward foreign assistance, there was a feeling that the nonproliferation mission of the Science Centers was more about U.S. national security.[171]

As a result of this mismatch, working for the Science Centers was not considered career-enhancing by foreign service officers. According to two interviewees, each of whom had a long history with the Science Centers, the centers had a hard time recruiting foreign service officers.[172] There was also some concern that key Science Center personnel were not promoted due to persistent rivalry between civil service employees and foreign service officers.[173] Finally, some interviewees complained that over time, newer people assigned to the Science Center program in the State Department were ill-informed about the program's activities, unaware of the history of its accomplishments, and lacked the context for appreciating

---

169. Interview with former U.S. government official 4, October 2, 2007.

170. Department of State, "Annual Report on Assistance to the NIS," 1994, Washington, D.C.

171. Interview with former U.S. government official 4, October 2, 2007; and interview with former State Department staffer 2, July 9, 2007.

172. Ibid.

173. Interview with former State Department staffer 1, July 16, 2003.

the centers' role in U.S. diplomacy.[174] Therefore, in inter-agency battles for resources, this lack of experience with the Science Centers hurt.

The third area that was affected by this mission mismatch was the budget. Congress consistently approved budget requests for the Science Centers. But, with the exception of fiscal year 2000, the State Department flat-lined Science Center budgets at around $35 million. According to one interviewee, the functional focus of the Science Centers made their budget process different from the norm at the State Department.[175] Furthermore, the overall budget for assistance to Russia was significant compared to many traditional State Department programs, making it a tempting target for those in search of money to redistribute to other efforts. Additionally, when the centers were funded out of the Freedom Support Act, there was resentment at providing money for what many considered a mission that was not foreign assistance. Partly as a result of these problems, the centers were shifted to the NADR account in 2002. This change brought new issues. The State Department's NADR account included funding for other WMD proliferation–related activities, such as export controls and border security.[176] Within the account's subcategories, the State Department was free to distribute funding as it saw fit. Although funding requests for the NADR account increased, the portion of money that was allotted to the Science Centers began to decline during the early 2000s. Moreover, Science Center funding was increasingly squeezed to increase funding for other programs aimed at cooperation with former biological weapons experts. Additionally, in 2007, the United States expanded its participation in the Science Centers to include other countries beyond the former Soviet Union. This expansion, however, was not accompanied by additional funding. Therefore, it could only be accomplished with the sacrifice of program activity in Russia.

In summary, the State Department's support for the Science Centers is called into question in three ways. First, other relevant State Department programs did not historically include the Science Centers in their activities. Second, there were concerns that a rotation with the Science Centers was not career-enhancing at the State Department and, later, that the centers were assigned inexperienced personnel who were not committed to the program. Third, the Science Centers were increasingly forced to share budget allocations with several different programs. This, plus expansion of the centers' mandate, meant less money and support for activities in Russia. Despite the importance of these issues, as the next section argues, there are additional organizational reasons that explain

---

174. Interview with former State Department staffer 2, July 9, 2007; interview with International Science and Technology Center staffer 4, July 24, 2007; and interview with State Department official 1, May 1, 2007.

175. Interview with former U.S. government official 4, October 2, 2007.

176. For more detail, see Isabelle Williams, "Preliminary Analysis of the U.S. State Department's Fiscal Year 2008 Budget Request for Global WMD Threat Reduction Programs," Policy Update, Partnership for Global Security, Washington, D.C. (April 2007).

more fully the failure of the Science Centers to deal permanently with the threat of the proliferation of WMD expertise.

PROCESS, PROCESS, PROCESS

As discussed above, the Science Centers established a rather elaborate set of rules and procedures for conducting their activities. Although those activities were always supposed to include both engagement and redirection, over time they focused on the former. Moreover, the Science Centers increasingly came to measure success in terms of activities that were not necessarily a good indicator of progress toward nonproliferation goals. According to this logic, if lots of people were involved, and if processes were standardized and followed rigorously, the centers were doing their job. Much less effort was spent considering whether, after almost fifteen years of operations, these processes still led to projects that maximized the involvement of former weapons experts. Because of the displacement of goals to focus more on due process and engagement, more funding for more projects did not necessarily translate into less danger of proliferation.

From the beginning, the Science Centers faced two critical tasks. They had to develop a rapport with former Soviet weapons workers so that they would apply for projects and encourage their co-workers to do so. Second, as multinational organizations, the centers had to orient their activities toward a common goal that was shared by all members, yet still leave room for individual states to assert their own priorities. Process filled both needs.

For former weapons workers, standardized project requirements, selection, and oversight meant transparency and predictability. Scientists need not master the priorities of individual funding countries, or even understand market economics, business development, or commercialization. They only had to learn the Science Center routine. As a result, the Science Centers were able to engage a larger number of scientists quickly and to expand to other scientists and institutes more efficiently. Without this emphasis on process, the early success of the Science Centers would not have been possible.

Moreover, in the early years, it was not possible to query scientists more directly about their weapons-relevant skills. Because of security issues and a lingering history of distrust, it was impolitic for the United States to push Russia on some sensitive matters. Self-identification of weapons skills, according to a standard list, was developed as a means of providing reasonable assurances about skills without being unduly intrusive. The United States explicitly traded greater certainty about weapons skills for increased cooperation from the Russian government. Over time, however, it became possible to verify weapons skills in other ways. For example, in 1998, the U.S. Congress asked for and received from the Departments of Defense, Energy, and State a report on the number and expertise of former WMD and missile experts in the former Soviet Union, as well as an analysis of which expertise levels were most important with respect to U.S. nonproliferation goals.[177] Also, as the Russian economy improved during the early 2000s, and the United States sought to wind down its threat reduction programs there, it also became possible to push Russia for more specifics about its weapons experts. But despite these changes, the United States never re-evaluated the initial trade-off it made between efficiency and relevance.

Nor is it the case that the Science Centers relied on self-identification because they wanted to avoid micromanaging project teams. Initially, there was concern that project teams would be inflated to include institute managers, co-workers, or relatives. These potential problems led the Science Centers to try and control project teams by limiting the involvement of senior managers and institute directors, allowing spouses to work on the same project only if they had relevant publications, and other rules.[178]

Process also enabled cooperation between funding countries. Concern over knowledge proliferation was predominantly an issue for the United States. Other countries were convinced to contribute to the centers because they shared this concern, but also because they were allowed to set their own priorities. Center participation did not require accepting a U.S.-focused modus operandi. Instead, the project-selection process allowed countries to determine their own funding levels and priorities while providing reasonable assurances that these resources would be used as intended. Moreover, funding countries got economies of scale. Rather than each country dealing with issues such as access, taxes, and how to pay salaries, the Science Centers provided these services. By focusing on project management, the Science Centers enabled more countries to contribute to more projects in former Soviet states.

U.S. participation in the Science Centers reinforced this focus on process over proliferation. Through its participation and funding, the United States played a preeminent role in the Science Centers, and other funding countries tended to follow its cues. While it encouraged center projects to focus on weapons workers through the "POO factor" in project selection, the United States did not push for a re-evaluation of how weapons workers were identified or an analysis of how proliferation potential changed as a result of social and economic changes in the former Soviet Union, especially Russia. Instead, the United States focused on engagement for

---

177. U.S. Congress, House, Committee on Armed Services, *Fiscal Year 1999 Defense Authorization Bill*, 105th Cong., 2nd sess., H. Rpt. 105-736, p. 253.

178. Interview with Institute for Physics and Power Engineering staffer 1, July 23, 2002; interview with Science and Technology Center in Ukraine staffer 2, October 26, 2005; interview with International Science and Technology Center staffer 10, October 22, 1999; interview with International Science and Technology Center staffer 12, October 22, 1999; and interview with International Science and Technology Center staffer 11, October 22, 1999. Interestingly, one project participant expressed a different frustration about project teams. Usually, the project participants that were listed on the project proposal were required to stay in place once the project was approved. This resulted in an inability to remove people from the approved list of staff if they did not do the work, did inferior work, or died. Interview with Lawrence Livermore National Laboratory staffer 10, April 2, 2003.

the sake of engagement, while ignoring opportunities to focus its limited resources on the most serious problems.

The impact on permanent redirection efforts has been greater. Initially, the purpose of the Partners Program was to find additional streams of revenue for Science Center projects. Later on, the goal became more specifically to re-energize original plans in order to involve businesses in permanent reemployment efforts. Willing business participants, however, proved few. Moreover, at the time, other U.S. programs in Russia were having problems with taxes, implementation, and congressional restrictions due to presidential certification requirements. Later, the United States implemented efforts aimed specifically at former biological weapons experts. All of these programs turned to the ISTC, because it had an established mechanism for paying salaries and importing equipment and supplies in Russia. For these reasons, plus the need for additional funding, ISTC's Partners Program came to involve significant numbers of U.S. government partners, and to focus more on the administrative needs of these projects and less on soliciting commercial relationships. Moreover, there is no evidence to suggest that the United States or ISTC re-evaluated the Partners Program in an attempt to focus it more on permanent redirection.

In this chapter, I have argued that the initial processes and metrics used by the Science Centers were sound. As conditions in the former Soviet Union and U.S. resource commitments changed, however, these processes and metrics became increasingly removed from proliferation goals. Yet neither the Science Centers nor the United States sought to re-establish this connection. What explains this inertia?

Perhaps the most logical argument is that the Science Centers were widely considered the most successful of all the U.S.-funded scientist redirection efforts. The centers had larger budgets, better relations with Russia, more programs in more former Soviet states, and they boasted impressive sounding results that could be quantified. This appearance of success served to isolate them from criticism and limit pressure for change. Additionally, the centers were valued by other U.S. government programs for their ability to manage projects in a neutral way. To pursue their goals in Russia, many U.S. government agencies needed the administrative capacity of ISTC. These same agencies, however, had little stake in whether the Science Centers themselves made progress toward their own nonproliferation goals.

Ending or Expanding?

When the Science Centers began, there was no official discussion of how long they would be needed or what cues would suggest their mission had been accomplished. Instead, the assumption was of a multi-year effort that would persist until the former Soviet states transitioned to more sustainable market economies. Informally, however, it seems that the State Department expected to wind down its participation in the centers after five to seven years and, by 2003, transition funding to non-governmental sources and other U.S. agencies.[179] Although metrics to determine whether institutes could "graduate" from Science Center assistance were established, concerns about proliferation were still evident in 2008. Despite this, the Bush administration began to move away from threat reduction programs in Russia, including the Science Centers.

As the Bush administration drew to a close, the future looked different depending on whether one was at ISTC or STCU. By 2005, many in the Kiev center privately admitted that their work was almost over. Although many former weapons workers still did not have jobs, the presumption was that they were extremely unlikely to cooperate with terrorists, and that the STCU had done all it could to tide them over until government funding resumed. The presumption was that some institutes would fade away, but the hope was that others would be funded by the government of Ukraine and become sources of research, development, and innovation that the government could use to solve public problems and encourage foreign investment. At a select number of other institutes, salaries seemed to be increasing beyond those offered by STCU, and this suggested that the Center was no longer necessary or an attractive source of income.

At ISTC, however, the future looked different. In large part due to U.S. prompting, the Center seemed poised to expand its activities beyond the former Soviet Union and serve as a permanent administrative mechanism for working with WMD and other scientists in states of concern to the United States such as Yemen, Libya, and Iraq. The idea of allowing the ISTC to be used for activities beyond the former Soviet Union was considered in a closed session of ISTC member states, and the decision was made to allow this expansion, although as of summer 2007, the details had yet to be approved.[180] Russia, as might be expected, was strongly opposed to sharing ISTC resources beyond the former Soviet Union.

Few ISTC funding countries besides the United States expressed an interest in using ISTC as a mechanism for working with other countries, and several ISTC project managers and collaborators expressed what they claimed was a widely shared view: the United States sought to use engagement through the ISTC as a political quid pro quo with which to entice cooperation on other U.S. policy objectives. According to one long-time U.S. participant, the future of ISTC was not nonproliferation, but buying influence for the United States by offering scientific engagement and cooperation.[181]

In 2003, Congress officially sanctioned expanded U.S. participation and funding for the Science Centers to include Iraq and Libya. In 2007, the State Department proposed extending this to South Asia, the Middle East,

---

179. Office of International Affairs, National Research Council, *An Assessment of the International Science and Technology Center*, p. 19; and General Accounting Office, *Weapons of Mass Destruction. Reducing the Threat from the Former Soviet Union: An Update*, p. 29.

180. Interview with International Science and Technology Center staffer 1, June 2, 2003; and interview with International Science and Technology Center staffer 4, July 24, 2007.

181. Interview with Lawrence Livermore National Laboratory staffer 13, April 3, 2003.

and North Korea.[182] In its fiscal year 2008 budget request, the State Department changed the name and scope of the budget account that includes the Science Centers to Nonproliferation of Weapons of Mass Destruction Expertise (NWMDE) to reflect a more global focus.[183] As of 2008, however, this expansion had not been accompanied by increases in funding.

Regardless of the merits of scientific engagement as a tool to increase transparency or a lever for further cooperation on broader political goals, expanding ISTC beyond the former Soviet Union will have costs. One is simply money; without new funding, the U.S. expansion of its participation in ISTC inherently comes at the expense of money for traditional Science Center activities in the former Soviet Union. Second, less support for ISTC will do little to bolster U.S.-Russian relations, which, as of 2008, were increasingly strained. Finally, it is also the case that proliferation concerns remain in Russia, as well as other parts of the former Soviet Union. Therefore, diluting ISTC's influence there may well jeopardize U.S. national security in the future.

Organizational Interest and the Science Centers

In summary, although relations with Russia were not always optimal, there is little evidence to suggest they posed a significant impediment. The same can be said for the U.S. President and Congress. The Science Centers were not affected by the same requirements for presidential certification that were imposed on other threat reduction programs. Moreover, aside from a short period in the late 1990s, when U.S. participation in the Science Centers was stalled because of congressional concerns over Russian assistance to Iran, Congress was quite supportive. It is organizational interest, I argue, that has had more of an influence on the activities of the Science Centers.

One area where organizational interest mattered is funding. Whereas Congress tended to approve the State Department's budgets, the State Department itself was a poor advocate for the centers. Largely because they did not fit into the traditional mold of State Department programs, the Science Centers did not have the staff or resources to win the intra-agency battle for larger budgets. In turn, one of the reasons the centers came to focus on Partner Projects with government agencies was to make up for this lack of funding.

However, while it is the case that more money would have led to more projects, this does not necessarily translate into greater progress toward nonproliferation goals. I argue that this is because organizational interest led to two additional problems for the Science Centers.

---

182. Department of State, "Congressional Justification," fiscal year 2007, Washington, D.C., p. 139.

183. In its fiscal year 2004 consideration of State Department appropriations, the House also tried unsuccessfully to reduce Science Center funding and redirect it toward Iraq. See William Hoehn, "Update on Activity in the 108th Congress Affecting U.S.-Former Soviet Union Cooperative Nonproliferation Programs," RANSAC, Washington, D.C., November 4, 2003, p. 24.

First, like the U.S. State Department, which was so influential in their evolution, the Science Centers came to concentrate on process. The State Department focuses on the routines and practices of carrying out foreign policy decisions. The purpose to which those decisions are directed is determined elsewhere. Similarly, the Science Centers evolved to focus on due process; as long as projects were selected and overseen according to agreed-upon rules and procedures, the centers were being successful. I argue that this process-centered behavior led to the transparency that was necessary for the centers to work at sensitive facilities in the former Soviet Union and to the consensus needed to insure continued funding from a variety of states that did not necessarily share the same nonproliferation goals. I also argue, however, that these processes, which were initially designed to foster access and agreement, did a poor job of focusing resources on critical WMD experts. Concerns about future funding and the past legacy of successful cooperation meant that it later became both necessary and possible to be more exclusive about who took part in projects. Yet neither the Science Centers nor the State Department reevaluated the process by which they selected projects, participants, or the relationship between these and the original goal of fighting proliferation.

The second additional problem that can be traced to organizational interest is goal displacement. More specifically, the goal of creating permanent jobs for WMD experts was replaced by an emphasis on documenting training efforts, technologies with commercial potential, and the number of partners and Partner Projects. Neither center measured the number of jobs created, or devoted as many resources to actually convincing private businesses to make use of the skills and products of WMD experts. I argue that part of this failure can also be explained by the partners that each center brought into its redirection efforts. Rather than pair former weapons experts with commercial businesses, most "Partner Projects" involved U.S. government agencies. Although the resulting collaborations sometimes contributed to solving problems that were in the public interest, or to helping the U. S. government do research at a lower cost, such projects seldom offered permanent reemployment. As a result, they fell short of the original nonproliferation goals they were created to achieve.

Chapter 6

Initiatives for Proliferation Prevention

In the early 1990s, as the State Department struggled to get the necessary Russian and Ukrainian approval for the Science Centers, the U.S. nuclear weapons laboratories became involved in a parallel effort to create their own program to engage and eventually to reemploy former Soviet weapons of mass destruction (WMD) experts, especially those with nuclear knowledge. It is largely the work of Los Alamos, Livermore, and Sandia National Laboratories that led, in 1994, to the creation of the Initiatives for Proliferation Prevention program (IPP) in the Department of Energy (DOE). Almost a decade later, the name was changed to Global Initiatives for Proliferation Prevention (GIPP) when, like the Science Centers, the program expanded beyond the former Soviet Union.

IPP's original goals focused on fighting the proliferation of WMD expertise via job creation. In the short term, the program funded cooperative research projects; over time, the plan was to leverage business interests to create permanent civilian jobs and to cherry-pick Russian technologies. Like the basic science projects funded by the Science Centers, IPP's initial collaborations provided much-needed income to former Soviet WMD workers, especially throughout the 1990s, when economic circumstances were the most grim. Moreover, IPP targeted a special group of experts: nuclear weapons scientists. Based upon their similar scientific training and work, U.S. nuclear weapons experts from the national laboratory system were able to convince their Soviet counterparts to take part in these projects and to persuade the Russian government, nuclear weapons institutes, and security services to enable this cooperation, despite the legacy of mistrust left over from the Cold War. From its beginning in 1994 through 2008, some 17,000 former Soviet workers were involved in IPP projects. However, as with the Science Center projects, there is reason to doubt whether these workers were all weapons experts.

IPP was less successful at permanent reemployment. Despite a shift in the mid-1990s that reinforced commercial involvement in IPP projects, job creation totals remained low. By most estimates, IPP projects led to fewer than 3,000 jobs. Furthermore, IPP increasingly focused its efforts on former biological and chemical weapons experts, as well as scientists outside of the former Soviet Union. These trends, plus reductions in funding for projects in Russia, meant less of an emphasis on and even fewer jobs for nuclear weapons scientists.

I argue that these meager results are a consequence of institutional interests and culture. IPP relied heavily on scientists and other experts from the U.S. national laboratories to develop and manage cooperative research between teams of former Soviet weapons experts and U.S. businesses. The U.S. labs, however, have traditionally enjoyed a decentralized power structure that gives them considerable independence from each other as well as their nominal boss, DOE. This system is what initially enabled U.S. nuclear weapons experts to bypass normal diplomatic processes and pursue an innovative strategy for engaging their Russian counterparts.

This same tenacity, however, also led to problems with program adaptation, management, and oversight. Each U.S. lab engaged in IPP according to its own interests. As a result, IPP resources were not consistently targeted toward the areas of greatest proliferation concern. Furthermore, the program suffered because of a lack of centralized control and direction, but also due to insufficient outreach to other programs and potential supporters.

The IPP Program

Through 2008, about one-half of security-related assistance to the former Soviet Union was managed by DOE.[1] IPP and the Nuclear Cities Initiative (NCI), DOE's second knowledge nonproliferation program which started in 1998, together were funded at between $20 million and $40 million annually during this time period. This amounts to less than 5 percent of DOE's spending on Cooperative Threat Reduction (CTR) assistance to the former Soviet Union. The bulk of DOE's contributions came in the form of efforts to secure and reduce nuclear weapons–relevant materials.

When the CTR program began, it included funding for discouraging the proliferation of weapons-usable materials such as uranium and plutonium by upgrading fences and perimeter security around the buildings where this material was stored; improving the methods and systems used to account for and track the movement of these materials; and enhancing security measures at ports and borders. Collectively, these activities came to be known as Materials Protection, Control and Accounting (MPC&A). Initially, the Defense Department engaged in MPC&A activities with the Russian military and DOE worked with the Russian Ministry of Atomic Energy, but in 1997, more of this work began to be done by DOE. DOE's

---

1. Through the early 2000s, the Department of Energy (DOE) accounted for about one-third of CTR-related efforts, but after that a larger role in securing WMD materials increased DOE's share of CTR spending. For a summary of CTR budgets over time by department, see Nuclear Threat Initiative, "Interactive Threat Reduction Budget Database," http://www.nti.org/e_research/cnwm/charts/cnm_funding_interactive.asp.

budget for MPC&A work steadily expanded from about $3 million a year in 1993 to almost $370 million a year in 2008.

DOE also headed up several efforts aimed at converting or destroying fissile materials. These included a global effort to convert nuclear reactors from highly-enriched uranium fuel to the less weapons-usable low-enriched uranium, and a project to close Russia's three remaining plutonium-producing reactors and replace them with thermal power plants. Over time, funding for these programs increased significantly, and as of 2008, was in the neighborhood of $200 million. DOE was also involved in a plan to build a facility to turn Russia's stocks of weapons-usable plutonium into fuel for nuclear reactors.

HISTORY AND MISSION

The international scientific cooperation at the heart of IPP got its start in U.S.-Soviet arms control negotiations during the Cold War. Although there are earlier examples, it was during the 1980s that the U.S. and Soviet nuclear weapons establishments developed a relationship, based upon research, to solve technical issues relating to arms control verification and transparency. After the Soviet collapse, the U.S. nuclear weapons laboratories were among the first to raise concerns about the financial situation of their former Soviet counterparts and the proliferation dangers this raised. When the effort to establish the Science Centers appeared to stall, the U.S. labs asked for permission to engage Russian nuclear weapons experts in short-term research contracts as a means of tiding them over financially. These initial research contracts in 1992 led to the Industrial Partnering Program (IPP) in 1994.

In an attempt to distinguish itself from the Science Centers, IPP focused on pairing former Soviet experts with U.S.-based commercial companies as a means of creating a path to permanent reemployment. Some critics of the program, however, saw this as corporate welfare, arguing that IPP used national security to unfairly subsidize private interests. In 1994, when the Republicans gained control of Congress, such concerns played a role in congressional action to terminate CTR's defense conversion efforts. To protect itself from a similar fate, IPP changed its name to Initiatives for Proliferation Prevention, keeping the same acronym.[2]

In 1998, a second knowledge nonproliferation program—NCI—was created at DOE. In 2002, Congress required IPP and NCI to be merged into one program: Russian Transition Initiatives (RTI). NCI and IPP were to remain separate programs, but would report to one director. Officially, under the RTI umbrella, IPP was to focus on engaging scientists, while NCI would concentrate on helping Russia reduce the size of its nuclear

2.   Interview with Los Alamos National Laboratory staffer 4, June 23, 2003; interview with Lawrence Livermore National Laboratory staffer 8, April 3, 2003; and interview with Lawrence Livermore National Laboratory staffer 11, April 7, 2003.

weapons complex.[3] In practice, however, both programs remained separate and continued much as before.

In 2003, NCI's five-year implementing agreement with Russia expired. Because of its lack of results and troubled past, the United States did not seek to renew the agreement, and NCI was given until September 2006 to complete its unfinished projects in Russia. In September 2006, all NCI activities were terminated. That same year, RTI underwent a name change—to Global Initiatives for Proliferation Prevention (GIPP)—to reflect the program's plan to expand activities to include Libya and Iraq. This move was prompted in part by revelations that Pakistan's A. Q. Khan had engaged in illicit sales of weapons-relevant materials to a variety of countries, including Libya, and reports that Al Qaeda was recruiting Iraqi WMD experts.[4]

Like the Science Centers, the main mission of IPP was nonproliferation. Since its beginning, the program included former nuclear, biological, and chemical weapons experts, and IPP's scope of operations came to include Russia, Ukraine, Kazakhstan, Armenia, Georgia, Belarus, and Uzbekistan. In practice, however, most activities were with Russian nuclear weapons scientists.[5]

In addition to the former Soviet experts, there were two key groups of players in IPP projects: U.S. laboratory personnel and Western commercial partners. The U.S. national laboratory complex is composed of numerous research and development facilities, production sites, and other institutes, half of which took part in IPP. Although Los Alamos, Livermore, and Sandia were the most instrumental in the creation of IPP, six labs were originally part of the effort, and eventually twelve were involved. By 2008, the biggest players in IPP were Sandia and Pacific Northwest, followed by Oak Ridge, Livermore, Los Alamos, and Brookhaven. Table 6.1 gives the locations and areas of specialization of the labs that were part of IPP. (See pp. 200–201.) Most of these same facilities also contributed to NCI and provided project review and collaboration for the Science Centers.

Coordination between the U.S. labs was accomplished by means of the Inter-Laboratory Advisory Board (ILAB), which consisted of a chair and a representative from each facility. Additionally, the IPP program had a director and small administrative staff located in Washington, D.C. at the National Nuclear Security Administration (NNSA), a semi-autonomous part of DOE that oversees the U.S. laboratory complex. This staff provided overall coordination, oversight, and liaison work with DOE and Congress, but the bulk of programmatic power resided at the

3. Department of Energy, National Nuclear Security Administration, "Russian Transition Initiatives," promotional literature, undated.

4. Monte Mallin, Director of the Office of Global Security Engagement and Cooperation, National Nuclear Security Administration, Department of Energy, Remarks for the United States Industry Coalition Annual Conference, March 7, 2007.

5. In early 2007, IPP claimed that over 80 percent of its projects were in Russia. See Government Accountability Office, *Nuclear Nonproliferation: DOE's Program to Assist Weapons Scientists in Russia and Other Countries Needs to be Reassessed*, Washington, D.C. (December 2007), p. 2.

individual U.S. laboratories. This division created numerous issues and problems, which are discussed below.

Most IPP projects were required to have a commercial partner. Finding these partners was the job of IPP staff at the U.S. laboratories, who turned to USIC, the United States Industry Coalition, for help. In 1994, when IPP was created, DOE also funded USIC, an association of businesses and research institutes whose role was to facilitate the goals of IPP by matching promising technology and former Soviet weapons experts with interested companies and investment banks. USIC also reviewed business plans for some IPP projects and lobbied Congress on behalf of the program. All commercial partners in IPP projects had to be members of USIC, which was accomplished by payment of a small yearly fee.

IPP PROJECTS

From 1994 to 2008, IPP funded projects at an estimated two hundred institutes.[6] The IPP process was intended to work as follows. First, scientists from the U.S. national laboratories worked with their counterparts at former Soviet institutes to identify and evaluate promising technologies from those institutes. In a Thrust 1 project (or T1, in IPP parlance), the U.S. government paid teams of former Soviet experts to verify and validate this technology. Progress was overseen and the results confirmed by U.S. laboratory experts. If a technology was deemed to have sufficient commercial potential, it became a Thrust 2 (T2) project, in which former Soviet experts worked with both U.S. laboratory personnel and a U.S. commercial partner to move the technology or its product further toward a marketable good or service. Thrust 2 projects required equal cost-sharing between the U.S. government and the commercial partner, although in practice the commercial partner's contribution was usually mostly in-kind, in the form of labor, materials, or facilities. Ideally, after Thrust 2, the next step was full collaboration between industry and the former Soviet team without U.S. government participation. In a few cases, however, U.S. funding paid for U.S. laboratory personnel to monitor further work in the form of a Thrust 3 (T3) project.

One Thrust 1 project, for example, involved cooperation between Sandia National Laboratory and the All-Russian Research Institute of Technical Physics (VNIITF), one of Russia's main nuclear weapons research and design institutes.[7] With $250,000 in funding from IPP, the project involved cooperative research into technologies for a prosthetic leg that would more closely mimic the movement abilities of natural limbs. After research and testing of a prototype, the project was able to attract investment from the Seattle Orthopedic Group as a Thrust 2 project.

---

6. Ibid.; and United States Industry Coalition, "Annual Report," 2005–2006, Washington, D.C.

7. Sandia National Laboratories, "Prosthetics: An IPP Success Story," *International Security News*, Vol. 1, No. 2 (March 2001), p. 9; and General Accounting Office, *Nuclear Proliferation: Concerns with DOE's Efforts to Reduce the Risks Posed by Russia's Unemployed Weapons Scientists*, Washington, D.C. (February 1999), p. 72.

A typical Thrust 2 project is illustrated by the cooperation between DuPont, Lawrence Berkeley National Laboratory, and Vector, previously a key part of Russia's biological weapons program.[8] Initially, a microbiologist at Lawrence Berkeley became interested in some of Vector's work on microbiology in extreme climates. In this case, the work was done in the Lake Baikal region of Siberia. This led to a Thrust 1 project between the scientist and experts at Vector, who had done the initial research. The goal was to explore the ability to culture certain unique microbes found in the area and then use them for various medical and therapeutic applications. Based on a presentation of the research results at a conference, DuPont became interested. The result was a Thrust 2 project involving funding from DuPont and cooperation between Berkeley and Vector in screening microbes to find out which ones had industrial applications.

Table 6.1. The U.S. National Laboratory Complex.

U.S. National Laboratory	Location	Main Research Areas
Argonne	Argonne, IL	Multidisciplinary basic science research, energy research and development, environmental management, national security work on the nuclear fuel cycle, and detecting biological, chemical, and radiological threats
Brookhaven	Upton, NY	Nanotechnology, life sciences, high energy and nuclear physics, space radiation, and homeland security
Idaho National Engineering and Environmental Laboratory	Idaho Falls, ID	Nuclear energy, the nuclear fuel cycle, and homeland security
Kansas City Plant	Kansas City, MO	Production of non-nuclear components for nuclear weapons
Lawrence Berkeley	Berkeley, CA	Space, quantitative biology, nanoscience, energy, and environmental management
Livermore	Livermore, CA	Nuclear weapons design and maintenance, nuclear material security, energy, environment, and life sciences

8. This summary is based upon interview with Lawrence Berkeley National Laboratory staffer 1, March 31, 2003; interview with Lawrence Berkeley National Laboratory staffer 2, March 31, 2003; and "A DOE Program is Turning Swords into Ploughshares," *Electronic Design*, August 21, 2000, http://www.elecdesign.com/Articles/ArticleID/4633/4633.html (accessed June 15, 2007).

Table 6.1. *(continued)*

Los Alamos	Los Alamos, NM	Nuclear weapons design and maintenance, nanotechnology, biology, materials science, and physics
National Renewable Energy Laboratory	Golden, CO	Alternative and renewable energy
Oak Ridge	Oak Ridge, TN	Nuclear energy, neutron science, supercomputing, biology, and materials science
Pacific Northwest	Richland, WA	Environment, microbial and cellular biology, chemistry, radiological science, computational science, and measurement technologies
Sandia	Albuquerque, NM	Nuclear weapons engineering and maintenance, nuclear accident response, energy, conventional military systems, other basic sciences and engineering[a]
Savannah River Site	Aiken, SC	Plutonium disposition, chemical and radiochemical processing, computational science, environmental science and biotechnology

[a]Los Alamos, Livermore, and Sandia are considered the core nuclear weapons labs. Sandia, however, works on the non-nuclear components of weapons.

SOURCES: This chart is based on the mission statements and core competencies listed on the website for each laboratory.

IPP's last project category was Thrust 3. Although IPP funded only three of these projects, the general idea can be understood by looking at "Silicon of Siberia," located in the Russian city of Zheleznogorsk, which produced plutonium for Soviet nuclear weapons. This project explored the possibilities of turning part of Zheleznogorsk's facilities into a plant for making isotopically-pure silicon for use in semiconductors. At the time the project was first considered, Japan produced 75 percent of this type of silicon, and Germany was the only other significant producer. Russia would bring a much needed third supplier to the world market. Originally funded by the Defense Enterprise Fund, IPP was involved in the project for almost a decade.[9] Its initial investment of $200,000

9. The Defense Enterprise Fund gave about $500,000 to the IPP Silicon of Siberia project. See U.S. Congress, House, Committee on Appropriations, *Energy and Water Development Appropriations, FY 2000, Part 6: Department of Energy*, 106th Cong., 1st sess., March 16, 18,

grew to $1.9 million by 2005.[10] Under IPP, funds were given to Sandia to manage a feasibility study at the Mining and Chemical Combine in Zheleznogorsk. IPP also paid for U.S. companies to do a business plan and market analysis.[11] Eventually the Isonics Corporation was brought in to work with Lawrence Berkeley lab and the Zheleznogorsk workers to produce the silicon. Despite success at producing small amounts of quality material, foreign investment proved difficult. A polysilicon plant eventually opened in September 2008, due in large part to financing from the Russian Federal Agency for Atomic Energy.

These projects illustrate the basic differences between types of IPP projects. Thrust 1 projects involved lab-to-lab collaboration to identify an interesting technology and test its potential; they typically received between $50,000 and $250,000 over a two-year period.[12] Like all IPP projects, they had to meet certain criteria. These included engaging former weapons experts and complementing ongoing research at a U.S. national laboratory, which supplied a Principal Investigator (PI) who collaborated on the project and provided oversight. Projects also had to have strong commercial potential, a plan for protecting the intellectual property rights of all parties, no significant dual-use issues or weapons relevance; be in compliance with export control rules; and not duplicate projects that were currently funded by the Science Centers or other U.S. government-funded scientist redirection efforts.[13] In addition, 50 percent of project funds were supposed to be spent in the former Soviet Union, but in 2001 the goal was changed to 70 percent.[14]

Initially, most IPP projects were Thrust 1, but as pressure to demonstrate job creation increased, IPP funded more Thrust 2 collaborations. After 1999, IPP funded only Thrust 2 or Thrust 3 efforts, unless the project engaged an institute that was of particular interest to the U.S. government.[15] Thrust 2 projects had to meet the same criteria outlined above, but also required a business partner who had to match U.S. government funding. This "matching financing," however, could come in the form of in-kind contributions and include, for example, billable hours for time spent managing projects, rather than investment dollars. The obligations and

1999, p. 533.

10. Department of Energy, Initiatives for Proliferation Prevention program, "IPP," program brochure; and "Isonics Corporation (Closter, N.J.) Utilizing Silicon Isotopes to Improve Thermo-Conductivity," interview by Alise Coen, August 1, 2005, Henry L. Stimson Center, http://www.stimson.org/cnp/?SN=CT20050826903 (accessed June 15, 2007).

11. Department of Energy, Initiatives for Proliferation Prevention, "IPP," Program Brochure, unknown date.

12. Based on funding of projects listed in Appendix II, General Accounting Office, *Nuclear Proliferation: Concerns with DOE's Efforts*, pp. 68–72.

13. Projects could be co-funded with the Nuclear Cities Initiative.

14. Interview with Brookhaven National Laboratory staffer 1, March 19, 2003; and interview with Brookhaven National Laboratory staffer 2, March 19, 2003.

15. Ibid.; and interview with Initiatives for Proliferation Prevention staffer IPP 1, February 13, 2002.

responsibilities for all parties in a Thrust 2 project were usually spelled out in the form of two legal agreements: a Cooperative Research and Development Agreement (CRADA) that specified the relationship between the lab, the former Soviet institute, and the company, and a contract that outlined the former Soviet workers' costs and deliverables.[16] Thrust 2 projects were usually funded at between $250,000 and $1 million over a two-year period.[17]

Thrust 3 projects were intended to be grants to bridge the gap from U.S. to private sector funding.[18] In these projects, U.S. government funding was supposed to be limited to providing for the continued involvement of a few U.S. laboratory personnel; eventually project financing was to come from the commercial partner.[19] After Thrust 2, however, IPP preferred to terminate all U.S. government involvement. There were only three Thrust 3 projects, the last of which finished in 2001.[20]

THE LIFE OF AN IPP PROJECT

IPP projects, which typically took nine to eighteen months to put together, started out at the U.S. national laboratories. The labs employed PIs who were, in turn, supervised by higher-level managers at each lab who might also oversee the lab's involvement in the Science Centers or NCI.[21] The PIs, who usually became collaborators on the projects, had to have relevant scientific and technical skills, and were almost always lab employees who continued to be involved in their own research but who also billed part of their time to the IPP program. This was one of the key differences between the Science Centers and IPP. IPP paid U.S. lab personnel for the time they spent with project management and oversight, whereas the Science Centers did not pay for project review and evaluation.

PIs were responsible for soliciting proposals from former Soviet WMD institutes, mostly in Russia, and collaborators at the U.S. labs. Often, the PI would sit down with teams of Russian experts and go through their list of proposed projects, but ideas could also come from other contacts or

16.   Interview with Pacific Northwest National Laboratory staffer 1, March 12, 2003; and interview with Pacific Northwest National Laboratory staffer 6, March 5, 2003. Also, under the 1989 Technology Transfer Act, one of the main missions of the U.S. labs became technology transfer. The Act made it possible for labs that are operated by contractors to work directly with universities, state and local governments, and businesses to jointly sponsor research and development activities. The contractual mechanisms for such agreements was the Cooperative Research and Development Agreement.

17.   Based on funding of projects listed in Appendix II, General Accounting Office, *Nuclear Proliferation: Concerns with DOE's Efforts*, pp. 68–72.

18.   Electronic communication with Initiatives for Proliferation Prevention staffer 2, October 18, 2000. Thrust 3 grants were intended to be small, in the range of $100,000 or less.

19.   Interview with Brookhaven National Laboratory staffer 1, March 19, 2003; and interview with Brookhaven National Laboratory staffer 2, March 19, 2003.

20.   Government Accountability Office, *Nuclear Nonproliferation: DOE's Program to Assist Weapons Scientists*, p. 9.

21.   Interview with Lawrence Livermore National Laboratory staffer 12, April 3, 2003; and interview with Initiatives for Proliferation Prevention staffer IPP 2, July 16, 2003.

requests from companies that were looking for a particular technology or capability.[22] According to the interviews I conducted with lab PIs, project development was much easier if you started with the needs of a company and then found a former Soviet institute that fit the bill. By focusing on the technology first, commercialization was more likely to result. Also, the former Soviet experts often did not have realistic ideas for projects, although this improved over time and with the requirement that all projects had to have a commercial partner before they could begin.[23] The PI also estimated how much money was likely to be required for further research.

PIs were also responsible for finding the commercial partners for their projects. In theory, they went to USIC, which was partially funded by IPP at around $1 million per year.[24] In practice, most PIs explained that USIC was of marginal or no use. This is confirmed by a study of IPP participating companies conducted by Frederick Kellett for the Henry L. Stimson Center. Of thirty-six companies surveyed, none said they had been recruited by USIC.[25] Instead, PIs found their own commercial partners who, in turn, were required to join USIC before they could participate in IPP. While most PIs expressed disdain for USIC's role, a few credited the organization with providing assistance with business plans and reviews and with promoting IPP to the public and especially to Congress. A few others explained that USIC's value had more to do with providing equal access and opportunity for interested commercial partners, thus allowing the PIs to avoid the normal government contracting rules designed to insure fair competition.

There were also complaints about USIC from industry members. According to the survey work of Frederick Kellett, industry partners usually did not understand USIC's role in IPP or have much contact with it.[26] Rather than USIC, companies preferred instead to turn to the U.S. labs for help in resolving project problems.[27] Although companies recommended improvements and ways that USIC could play a greater role, many were disappointed that change was not forthcoming.[28]

Instead of relying on USIC, almost all of the PIs I interviewed claimed they relied first and foremost on their own contacts and networking. As scientists at the U.S. labs, many PIs had considerable contact with indus-

---

22. Interview with Lawrence Livermore National Laboratory staffer 12, April 3, 2003.

23. Ibid.; interview with Pacific Northwest National Laboratory staffer 6, March 5, 2003; interview with Sandia National Laboratory staffer 3, May 5, 2003; and interview with Sandia National Laboratory staffer 4, May 5, 2003.

24. Interview with Initiatives for Proliferation Prevention staffer 1, July 16, 2003.

25. Frederick P. Kellett, "USIC and the Initiatives for Proliferation Prevention: A Survey of Companies Doing Business in the Former Soviet Union," Report No. 60, Henry L. Stimson Center, Washington, D.C. (March 2007), p. 11.

26. Ibid., pp. 16, 21.

27. Ibid., p. 16.

28. Interview, Frederick Kellett, February 22, 2007.

tries through their own work. Others relied on Internet searches, conferences, and informal connections. Most PIs favored small or medium-sized companies, claiming that they were more innovative and committed to projects because the resources were more important to them.[29] Few PIs expressed problems finding companies that were interested in testing the skills and technologies offered by former Soviet weapons workers.

Once a potential project had a team of experts from a former Soviet institute and an interested commercial partner, the PI then needed approval from their own lab as well as DOE.[30] At the lab, the PI and sometimes a program manager would help pull together the necessary business plan, statement of commitment from the former Soviet experts, and description of the work to be accomplished. The PI would then submit this to the IPP program office in Washington, D.C., where IPP had a small administrative staff including an overall manager, support staff, and a technical staff of scientists who evaluated projects for technical merit and nonproliferation value. This staff also served as the liaison with the Science Centers and other U.S. government programs, and was responsible for promoting the program to Congress.

The proposal then went to USIC, which rated the business plan and suggested improvements, and to the ILAB, which was composed of representatives of each of the U.S. laboratories. ILAB was responsible for making sure the project complemented ongoing research at a U.S. laboratory, coordinating the review and evaluation of the technical capabilities of the former Soviet partners, and reviewing projects for nonproliferation merit.[31] ILAB's other responsibilities included working with USIC to evaluate technologies for commercial potential, suggesting IPP program strategy and activities, and promoting the program at the U.S. labs.[32]

Next came technical and dual-use reviews done internally by the U.S. labs. At this point, if the project still met with approval, it was sent for external interagency reviews for dual-use and export control concerns, nonproliferation issues, and consistency with other U.S. policies.[33] According to a 1999 investigation of IPP by the U.S. Government Accountability Office (GAO), reviews of projects that involved former biological or chemical weapons experts were problematic. The GAO's audit found that

---

29.   Interview with Pacific Northwest National Laboratory staffer 9, March 6, 2003; interview with Pacific Northwest National Laboratory staffer 10, March 6, 2003; interview with Sandia National Laboratory staffer 3, May 5, 2003; and interview with Sandia National Laboratory staffer 4, May 5, 2003.

30.   The project review process described here is based upon Department of Energy, Initiatives for Proliferation Prevention, "Annual Report for Fiscal Year 2000," September 30, 2000, pp. 1–2; and interviews conducted at the U.S. laboratories and IPP from 2001–2005.

31.   Department of Energy, Initiatives for Proliferation Prevention, "Program Strategy," November 1999, p. 7.

32.   Ibid., pp. 12–13.

33.   For example, the State Department looked at whether the project would contradict other U.S. policy goals, the Defense Department focused on whether the project would enhance Russian military capabilities, and the intelligence agencies tried to determine whether the project would reach key biological or chemical weapons institutes.

IPP provided inconsistent or no criteria for conducting these reviews or collecting the comments.[34]

Concerns and suggestions were fed back to the PI, and the project might be revised several times until it was finally ready to be considered for funding.[35] Funding decisions were made by IPP headquarters staff and by the Inter-Laboratory Board. Decision-making criteria included the likely commercial success of the project, priorities for engaging certain institutes or teams of former weapons experts, and individual U.S. laboratory project priorities. Although the PIs I interviewed usually praised the project review process for providing detailed comments about what was needed for a project to be approved, they were less satisfied with the logic behind funding decisions. Several PIs expressed concerns that funding decisions were a function of the need to distribute resources among the labs, rather than based on the merits of individual projects.[36]

If a project was approved and funded, the PI then wrote the Cooperative Research and Development Agreement between the business partner and the U.S. lab, as well as the contract for deliverables with the former Soviet weapons institute.[37] IPP issued paychecks only upon satisfactory receipt of the items that were specified in this initial contract, in contrast to the Science Centers, which paid former weapons workers according to a regular schedule.

For projects in Russia, the next step was to decide whether to move forward through the International Science and Technology Center (ISTC) as a Partner Project or through the Civilian Research and Development Foundation (CRDF). Because IPP did not have its own tax-exempt status in Russia, it had to use an intermediary administrative organization for importing equipment and supplies and paying salaries. Projects involving institutes of Rosatom had to go through ISTC. In addition, some PIs preferred the Science Center, claiming that the process was quicker, the administrative fee cheaper, and ISTC staff provided important oversight functions.[38] Most, however, favored CRDF, claiming that it was faster, required less paperwork, and they were able to retain more control of their projects, including linking salary payment to deliverables.[39]

---

34. General Accounting Office, *Nuclear Nonproliferation. Concerns with DOE's Efforts*, pp. 46–47.

35. According to the Department of Energy, Initiatives for Proliferation Prevention, "Annual Report for Fiscal Year 2000," pp. 1–2, about 60 percent of proposals were sent back for revision.

36. Interview with Lawrence Livermore National Laboratory staffer 5, April 1, 2003; interview with Lawrence Livermore National Laboratory staffer 12, April 3, 2003; and interview with Oak Ridge National Laboratory staffer 1, February 19, 2003.

37. This contract also specified the intellectual property rights for all parties.

38. Interview with Lawrence Livermore National Laboratory staffer 11, April 7, 2003; and interview with Oak Ridge National Laboratory staffer 1, February 20, 2003.

39. Interview with Lawrence Livermore National Laboratory staffer 5, April 1, 2003; interview with Lawrence Livermore National Laboratory staffer 12, April 3, 2003; interview with Pacific Northwest National Laboratory staffer 3, March 5, 2003; interview with Pacific

Although a PI might typically spend nine to eighteen months getting to this point in a project, most PIs were only allowed to bill for their time once the project was approved by DOE.[40] Besides relying on the pro bono work of the PI, IPP provided almost no money for project development; this worked to discourage U.S. lab personnel from participating in the program.[41] This had three consequences. One is that some PIs favored big projects over small ones. PIs and their labs tended to get paid around 30 percent of the total cost of a project, and since most projects took about the same amount of time to put together, the PI had an incentive to favor projects with bigger budgets.[42] Second, once PIs invested time in a project, they tended to pursue that project until it was approved. Rather than start over again with a new and perhaps better project idea, PIs had an incentive to make any project work once they had invested time in it. The third outcome is that some of the smaller U.S. labs felt disadvantaged by IPP. They argued that Los Alamos, Livermore, and Sandia had their own funds to pay their PIs for project development, whereas the smaller labs did not have these resources.[43] Problems with delays were echoed by both the Russian participants I interviewed, who complained about the long time lag between their original proposal and the first paycheck, and by U.S. industry participants.[44]

Once work on a project began, the PI monitored progress, encouraged the on-time delivery of results, and sometimes did independent testing

---

Northwest National Laboratory staffer 9, March 6, 2003; interview with Pacific Northwest National Laboratory staffer 10, March 6, 2003; interview with Brookhaven National Laboratory staffer 1, March 19, 2003; interview with Brookhaven National Laboratory staffer 2, March 19, 2003; interview with Sandia National Laboratory staffer 3, May 5, 2003; interview with Sandia National Laboratory staffer 4, May 5, 2003; interview with Lawrence Berkeley National Laboratory staffer 1, March 31, 2003; and interview with Lawrence Berkeley National Laboratory staffer 2, March 31, 2003. Some interviewees complained that the ISTC regular payment schedule did not allow the PIs to use salary payments as an incentive for getting former Soviet experts to do quality work in a timely fashion. They preferred CRDF, which issued salary payments only when told to by the PIs. According to Kellett, "USIC and the Initiatives for Proliferation Prevention," p. 15, industry participants in IPP also found the Science Centers excessively bureaucratic.

40. Interview with Lawrence Livermore National Laboratory staffer 5, April 1, 2003; interview with Lawrence Livermore National Laboratory staffer 8, April 3, 2003; interview with Lawrence Livermore National Laboratory staffer 11, April 7, 2003; and interview with Pacific Northwest National Laboratory staffer 1, March 12, 2003.

41. Interview with Lawrence Livermore National Laboratory staffer 11, April 7, 2003.

42. Interview with Lawrence Livermore National Laboratory staffer 5, April 1, 2003; and Kellett, "USIC and the Initiatives for Proliferation Prevention," p. 19.

43. Interview with Brookhaven National Laboratory staffer 1, March 19, 2003; and interview with Brookhaven National Laboratory staffer 2, March 19, 2003.

44. Interview with Kurchatov Institute staffer 1, August 1, 2002; interview with Institute for Physics and Power Engineering staffer 1, July 23, 2002; and Kellett, "USIC and the Initiatives for Proliferation Prevention," pp. 7, 18. According to the GAO, IPP project participants reported delays of up to one year in getting paid for their work. See Government Accountability Office, *Nuclear Nonproliferation: DOE's Program to Assist Weapons Scientists*, p. 8.

of materials or ideas. If IPP required additional reviews or audits, none of the PIs I interviewed were aware of these; most said they relied on the schedule of deliverables negotiated in the contract as their form of oversight.[45] This is problematic, however, because according to a 2005 GAO report, of the six IPP projects examined, five lacked complete records of contracts, deliverables, and payments.[46]

Defining Goals and Threats

IPP's mission focused on three goals: engaging former weapons experts, creating more permanent reemployment outside the WMD complex, and, in the process, seeking commercial advantage for U.S. businesses. Although these three goals were consistent over time, the emphasis placed on each varied. A 1997 investigation by the GAO resulted in a fourth goal: spending more money at former Soviet WMD institutes and less at the U.S. national labs.

Although IPP was created to foster cooperation with former Soviet states for the purposes of nonproliferation, over time this main mission underwent a subtle shift. As the Russian economy improved and evidence of proliferation remained sparse, the emphasis increasingly moved to cooperation for the sake of transparency.

ENGAGEMENT

The first goal, and the one that received priority until the late 1990s, was to engage former Soviet WMD experts in cooperative research as a way of discouraging them from selling their skills. Similar to the Science Centers, this proliferation was a concern because of the economic desperation in the former Soviet Union, combined with few prospects for legitimate alternative employment. Moreover, by the mid-1990s, the danger of proliferation had expanded beyond the initial focus on the emigration of experts to include proliferation in-place; that is, workers who share WMD-relevant information without ever leaving home. For example, in 1996, Charles B. Curtis, then Deputy Secretary of Energy, warned in testimony before Congress that "a desperate technician...is only a fax machine away from aiding proliferators."[47]

To measure progress toward its goal of engagement, IPP adopted the metric of counting the number of former Soviet workers who receive income from IPP cooperative research projects. With respect to numbers and types of WMD experts, IPP was initially intended to include nuclear,

---

45. Interview with Lawrence Livermore National Laboratory staffer 5, April 1, 2003; and General Accounting Office, *Nuclear Nonproliferation: Concerns with DOE's Efforts*, p. 40.

46. General Accounting Office, *Nuclear Nonproliferation: Better Management Controls Needed for Some DOE Projects in Russia and Other Countries*, Washington, D.C. (August 2005), p. 6.

47. Statement of Charles B. Curtis, Deputy Secretary of Energy, U.S. Congress, Senate, Committee on Governmental Affairs, *Global Proliferation of Weapons of Mass Destruction*, Part II, 104th Cong., 2nd sess., March 13, 20, 22, 1996, S. Hrg. 104-442, p. 454. See also Department of Energy, Initiatives for Proliferation Prevention, "Annual Report for Fiscal Year 2000," p. 1.

biological, and chemical weapons scientists, engineers, and technicians.[48] Most early projects involved nuclear energy and weapons-related institutes. In the mid-1990s, however, revelations about Iran's recruiting efforts in Russia caused a shift, and it became official U.S. government policy to focus more on former biological weapons experts.[49] In 1996, for example, the Defense and State Departments transferred money to IPP specifically to fund projects at Stepnogorsk, Kazakhstan, and at the Khimprom chemical weapons production facility in Volgograd, Russia.[50] By 1999, IPP's goal was to spend 30 percent of project funding on cooperation involving biological and chemical weapons experts.[51]

As for target numbers, IPP tended to adopt the same figures used by the Science Centers: 60,000–70,000 weapons experts throughout the former Soviet Union, of whom some 30,000 had experience with nuclear weapons.[52] In later years, IPP cited the figure of 35,000 nuclear-relevant workers, which is the number of people the Russian government claimed were excess to its needs in the weapons complex.[53] The lower figure was the result of a 2005 RAND study that had been requested by DOE, but was never translated into revised program or budgeting guidance.[54]

JOB CREATION

The second part of IPP's mission was to reduce the danger of proliferation by creating jobs. Although the program initially concentrated on quickly engaging scientists, especially nuclear weapons experts, IPP always focused on the generation of sustainable non-weapons work.[55] By partner-

48. U.S. Congress, House, Committee on Appropriations, *Energy and Water Development Appropriations for 1998, Part 6: Department of Energy*, 105th Cong., 1st sess., March 12, April 9, 1997, p. 625.

49. Interview with Brookhaven National Laboratory staffer 1, March 19, 2003; interview with Brookhaven National Laboratory staffer 2, March 19, 2003; and Department of Energy, Initiatives for Proliferation Prevention, "New Independent States Industrial Partnering Program—Reducing the Nuclear Danger," submitted as part of U.S. Congress, *Global Proliferation of Weapons of Mass Destruction*, Part II, pp. 404–410.

50. U.S. Congress, House, Committee on Appropriations, *Energy and Water Development Appropriations for 1999, Part 6: Department of Energy*, 105th Cong., 2nd sess., March 12, 17, 18, 1998, pp. 573, 557.

51. Department of Energy, Initiatives for Proliferation Prevention, "Program Strategy," November 1999, p. 19.

52. Department of Energy, Initiatives for Proliferation Prevention, "Annual Report for Fiscal Year 2000," p. 1; and U.S. Congress, *Energy and Water Development Appropriations, FY 2000*, p. 295.

53. Department of Energy, Office of the Administrator, Weapons Activities, Defense Nuclear Nonproliferation, Naval Reactors, "Fiscal Year 2006 Congressional Budget Request," Vol. 1., Washington, D.C., p. 496.

54. Government Accountability Office, *Nuclear Nonproliferation: DOE's Program to Assist Weapons Scientists*, p. 21.

55. U.S. Congress, *Global Proliferation of Weapons of Mass Destruction*, p. 404; Department of Energy, Industrial Partnering Program, "New Independent States Industrial Partnering Program—Reducing the Nuclear Danger," March 7, 1996, p. 405; General Accounting

ing with U.S. businesses, IPP would share the financial and technical risk of working in the former Soviet Union. In helping companies evaluate former Soviet workers and their technologies, the program would help create viable commercial opportunities that would hopefully lead to a successful permanent relationship that no longer required U.S. government support.[56]

Due to mounting congressional pressure for more results and a 1997 GAO investigation that highlighted other problems, IPP officially shifted its priorities from engagement to job creation.[57] This took the form of a move away from projects involving basic research in favor of those that validated technologies or that had commercial potential. As a result, after 1999, IPP stopped funding Thrust 1 projects unless they engaged institutes that were of specific nonproliferation interest to the U.S. government.[58]

In terms of metrics, IPP initially put little emphasis on counting the number of jobs created as a result of its projects. Although in later years the program did report on the numbers of jobs created, it is unclear how these results were collected or measured. Instead, IPP tended to favor other metrics, most of which were considered indicators of commercial success and therefore proxies for job creation. These metrics varied over time and included, for example, the number of Thrust 2 and Thrust 3 projects; the number of commercial partners involved in IPP projects; the number of Cooperative Research and Development Agreements signed; the number of license and patent applications; the number of projects to reach the stage of "commercial take-off"; and the amount of money invested in IPP projects by commercial partners.[59] As explained in the next section, many of these metrics were not consistently reported. These metrics also raise questions about whether they reflect the sustainable reemployment of WMD experts.

Office, *Nuclear Nonproliferation: Concerns with DOE's Efforts*, p. 42; Gore-Chernomyrdin Commission, Eighth Session, Energy Policy Committee, Background Papers, January 1997, p. 19; Gore-Chernomyrdin Commission, Eighth Session, February 5–8, 1997, DOE briefing book, Tab 8 b.; Department of Energy, Initiatives for Proliferation Prevention, "Program Strategy," November 1999, pp. 16–17; and Department of Energy, Initiatives for Proliferation Prevention, "Annual Report for Fiscal Year 2001," Washington, D.C., September 30, 2001.

56. Department of Energy, Initiatives for Proliferation Prevention, "Annual Report for Fiscal Year 2001." According to Gore-Chernomyrdin Commission, Eighth Session, February 5–8, 1997, DOE briefing book, Tab 8 b., at one time, the requirement was to create one job in the United States for every job created in the former Soviet Union.

57. Department of Energy, Initiatives for Proliferation Prevention, "Program Strategy," November 1999, p. 1; and U.S. Congress, *Energy and Water Development Appropriations, FY 2000*, p. 359.

58. Most such institutes involved former biological weapons activities.

59. Department of Energy, Initiatives for Proliferation Prevention, "Program Strategy," November 1999, p. 17–18; Department of Energy, Initiatives for Proliferation Prevention, "Overhead Slides," December 11, 1997; and General Accounting Office, *Nuclear Nonproliferation: Concerns with DOE's Efforts*, p. 35.

HELPING U.S. BUSINESSES

The third part of IPP's mission was to fund projects that were beneficial to U.S. industry by helping companies take advantage of technologies and services offered in the former Soviet Union and enhancing their position within emerging markets in these states.[60] Therefore, IPP over time also included as a performance metric the annual revenues generated by IPP projects for industry participants.

There is some evidence that IPP's goal, at least initially, was to cherry-pick interesting technologies for use not only by U.S. industry, but also for the work of the U.S. laboratories too. For example, based on cooperation in 1998, Los Alamos became interested in high-powered gyrotrons produced in the Soviet Union.[61] After the Soviet collapse, Los Alamos convinced DOE to fund the lab and a consortium of manufacturing industries to evaluate and then acquire this technology.[62] Based upon this and other past experiences, combined with the respect U.S. scientists had for Soviet experts, there was a general feeling that the WMD complex had potentially lucrative services or technologies just waiting to be discovered.[63]

Although this goal was not initially translated into metrics, in the early to mid-2000s, IPP began to report U.S. revenues generated by its projects, as well as job creation in the United States.

ONE ADDITIONAL GOAL: MONEY

Originally, IPP intended to spend half of its budget on projects at former Soviet institutes.[64] In 1999, however, the GAO released the results of an investigation which showed that only about 37 percent of IPP's project funding had actually gone to former Soviet institutes.[65] In contrast, about 12 percent had been used to support business participation in IPP, but over half, 51 percent, had been spent at the U.S. national laboratories.[66] Of the part retained by the U.S. labs, most went for administrative support fees, including overhead, salaries for PIs and managers, and travel expenses.[67] In particular, salaries for U.S. lab employees consumed about 70 percent of the money spent in the United States.

---

60. Department of Energy, Initiatives for Proliferation Prevention, "Overhead Slides," December 11, 1997.

61. Gyrotrons are tubes that can deliver bursts of microwave energy. They are useful for experimental physics in, for example, particle accelerators.

62. Hugh Casey, "The New Independent States Industrial Partnering Program," *Los Alamos Science*, No. 24, 1996, pp. 85–86.

63. Interview with Lawrence Livermore National Laboratory staffer 8, April 3, 2003; interview with Los Alamos National Laboratory staffer 4, June 23, 2003; and Janet Bailey, *The Good Servant: Making Peace with the Bomb at Los Alamos* (New York: Simon and Schuster, 1995), pp. 186–187.

64. Interview with Initiatives for Proliferation Prevention staffer 2, October 18, 2000.

65. General Accounting Office, *Nuclear Nonproliferation: Concerns with DOE's Efforts*, p. 4.

66. Ibid.

67. Ibid., p. 29.

These findings resulted in a funding struggle in Congress that affect-ed IPP, and also NCI. Both programs were cut. For fiscal year 2000, IPP's budget was reduced by 25 percent; NCI suffered a 75 percent cut. Further-more, Congress required that in subsequent years, IPP could spend no more than 35 percent of its budget at the U.S. labs.[68] For fiscal year 2002, Congress reduced this further when it merged IPP and NCI. The resulting RTI had to limit its expenses at the U.S. labs to 25 percent.[69] As a result of these concerns, IPP adopted for itself the target of spending at least 70 percent of its funding in the former Soviet Union.[70]

PROLIFERATION OR TRANSPARENCY?
From its beginning in 1994 through 2008, IPP claimed that its overall goal was nonproliferation. IPP guidance specified that projects should involve a "preponderance" of weapons workers, which was defined as 60 percent or more of project participants.[71]

Some U.S. project participants, however, expressed doubts that scientists were a proliferation concern. By the mid-1990s, several people who were instrumental in initial IPP activities came to believe that the patriotism of Russian nuclear weapons scientists would prevent them from engaging in proliferation.[72] In my interviews with PIs who came to the program later, it was not uncommon for the same belief to be expressed. This was particularly true for PIs who had been involved with Russian nuclear weapons scientists for more than three years through IPP, the Science Centers, or other activities. Nevertheless, most continued to argue that the program was still valuable because working with the Russians fostered transparency. In other words, engagement increased U.S. confidence that it understood the state of the Russian nuclear weap-ons complex and likely activities taking place there.

This same argument about engagement for the sake of transparen-cy, not nonproliferation, was used to justify IPP's expansion beyond the former Soviet Union. Transparency was also the basis for arguments for

68. U.S. Congress, House, Committee on Appropriations, *Energy and Water Development Appropriations for 2001, Part 6: Department of Energy*, 106th Cong., 2nd sess., March 21, 23, 2000, p. 561.

69. William Hoehn, "Analysis of the Bush Administration's Fiscal Year 2002 Budget Requests for U.S.-Former Soviet Union Nuclear Security: Department of Energy Programs," Russian-American Nuclear Security Advisory Council (RANSAC), Washington, D.C., August 10, 2001.

70. Interview with Initiatives for Proliferation Prevention staffer 2, October 18, 2000. IPP had also been criticized for not keeping track of how the labs were spending program funds.

71. Department of Energy, Initiatives for Proliferation Prevention, "Guidance for Evaluating Weapons Scientists, Engineers, and Technicians," June 2002, p. 1, http://www.usic.net (accessed June 29, 2007).

72. Interview with Los Alamos National Laboratory staffer 3, April 29, 2003; interview with Los Alamos National Laboratory staffer 8, May 1, 2003; interview with Lawrence Livermore National Laboratory staffer 2, April 1, 2003; interview with Lawrence Livermore National Laboratory staffer 8, April 3, 2003; interview with Sandia National Laboratory staffer 6, May 5, 2003; and interview with Sandia National Laboratory staffer 7, May 5, 2003.

continued engagement in Russia, despite improvements in the economy and reinvigorated funding of the Russian nuclear weapons complex. This shift, however, created some inconsistencies with the assumptions that were at the core of IPP's mission. Congressional funding and Russia's cooperation in IPP were also premised on slightly different assumptions.

Transparency contradicted the initial assumption that IPP was intended to be finite. The program often prided itself on having an exit strategy, in that its projects were intended to transition WMD experts to a permanent relationship with businesses and thus wean them off U.S. government funding. More precisely, according to DOE officials, IPP was intended to phase out its operations in the mid-2000s, finishing its work by 2007.[73] A shift in goals from nonproliferation to transparency, however, implied an open-ended commitment to continued funding and U.S.-Russian cooperation.

Transparency also suggested focusing on different WMD institutes. Initially, IPP targeted WMD experts and institutes based upon concern for proliferation. Transparency, however, called for funneling U.S. dollars and participation toward former Soviet institutes that would remain part of the nuclear weapons complex. As a result, some vulnerable institutes, such as those with little or no funding from their governments or other sources, would be neglected. Furthermore, transparency meant working with people who remained part of the Russian defense infrastructure, thus using U.S. funds to contribute to Russia's weapon programs, an outcome that many PIs acknowledged.[74]

Regardless of the shift toward engagement for the sake of transparency, some of IPP's rules and procedures inherently undercut its nonproliferation goal. One example is the IPP focus on high-tech projects. Like the Science Centers, IPP projects emphasized work that required the advanced scientific skills of former weapons workers. This meant that projects such as hotels, breweries, and other low-tech endeavors were not eligible for IPP funding, regardless of their potential for creating jobs. Another example is that in an attempt to deter proliferation, IPP excluded some of the most vulnerable WMD experts from participating in its projects. Like the Science Centers, IPP was prohibited by Congress from working with institutes that had been involved in proliferation in the past or had

---

73. Electronic communication with William Hoehn, RANSAC, March 8, 2000; General Accounting Office, *Nuclear Nonproliferation: Concerns with DOE's Efforts*, p. 27; General Accounting Office, *Biological Weapons: Effort to Reduce Former Soviet Threat Offers Benefits, Poses New Risks*, Washington, D.C. (April 2000), p. 31; and U.S. Congress, *Energy and Water Development Appropriations for 1999*, p. 573. The GAO, however, faulted the program in its 2007 audit for not having a means to determine when institutes could "graduate" from IPP assistance. See Government Accountability Office, *Nuclear Nonproliferation: DOE's Program to Assist Weapons Scientists*, pp. 6–7.

74. Interview with Brookhaven National Laboratory staffer 2, March 19, 2003; interview with Los Alamos National Laboratory staffer 6, April 29, 2003; interview with Lawrence Livermore National Laboratory staffer 1, April 1, 2003; interview with Pacific Northwest National Laboratory staffer 9, March 6, 2003; interview with Pacific Northwest National Laboratory staffer 11, March 6, 2003; and interview with Sandia National Laboratory staffer 7, May 5, 2003.

taken part in offensive biological or chemical weapons work. Moreover, even if an institute or project team repented, there was no mechanism for removing them from IPP's blacklist.[75] Therefore, potential or proven proliferants, because they were excluded from participation, had even fewer alternatives. Unlike the Science Centers, however, IPP would work with people who had already left their weapons institute and formed their own companies.[76]

Measuring Progress

Like the Science Centers, IPP deserves credit for its initial engagement of former Soviet weapons workers. Also like the Science Centers, there were problems verifying the weapons credentials of these workers, and there are good reasons to believe that many of the people engaged through IPP projects were not WMD experts.

IPP is similar to the Science Centers in yet a third way: neither program created significant numbers of permanent jobs. Instead of job creation, IPP emphasized a variety of other metrics. But these measurements offered little evidence that IPP was embedding former weapons workers in sustainable commercial partnerships.

Finally, with respect to its efforts to spend more money in the former Soviet Union and less in the United States, there was clear success. However, requirements to spend more money abroad had other adverse consequences on IPP project development and did not necessarily result in more projects or project participants.

ENGAGING WEAPONS WORKERS

IPP quickly engaged key nuclear weapons scientists. Within a year of beginning operations, IPP projects had involved about 2,000 people, some of whom were in Russia's hard-to-access nuclear cities.[77] Through IPP, U.S. lab personnel were able to reciprocate overtures from key Russian and other former Soviet WMD personnel and not only fund projects, but also establish the precedent and procedures for future cooperation. Moreover, although this collaboration went forward only with the approval of the Russian government and key federal ministries, it was largely decentralized. Project proposals were not dictated by the state. In many respects, they were also independent of institute control. Instead, IPP projects were developed by teams of scientists acting largely on their own initiative.

As of April 2007, IPP claimed to have worked with 16,770 workers at approximately 200 institutes in the former Soviet Union.[78] However,

75. Interview with Initiatives for Proliferation Prevention staffer 1, July 16, 2003.

76. Ibid.; and interview with Brookhaven National Laboratory staffer 1, March 19, 2003.

77. Department of Energy, Initiatives for Proliferation Prevention, "New Independent States Industrial Partnering Program—Reducing the Nuclear Danger," March 7, 1996, submitted as part of U.S. Congress, *Global Proliferation of Weapons of Mass Destruction*, p. 404.

78. See Government Accountability Office, *Nuclear Nonproliferation: DOE's Program to Assist*

determining how many of them were weapons scientists is problematic. One reason is that both DOE and the U.S. labs had inadequate record-keeping with respect to IPP. In a 1999 report, the GAO found numerous problems, including deficiencies in tracking funds received at former Soviet institutes; problems identifying projects with weapons potential; vague and inconsistent methods of determining the weapons credentials of project participants; and insufficient documentation to establish the number of participants in projects.[79] According to the GAO, some U.S. labs found it unnecessary to keep track of the number of weapons experts or verify their credentials, and others made estimates based upon project salaries without any external verification.[80] In response to these concerns, in April 2000, IPP asked all of its PIs to identify the numbers of scientists and technicians involved in their projects since the program started.[81] The result was 7,996.[82] That same year, IPP's annual report stated that projects had involved over 13,000 people, suggesting that 62 percent of project participants were weapons experts.[83] IPP's official policy was that project teams should be at least 60 percent weapons experts. If this guidance was put into practice, then IPP engaged just over 10,000 weapons workers between 1994 and early 2007.

My research provides additional reasons for concern about IPP record-keeping. During 1999–2002, I was given access to the IPP project database. The database asked PIs to provide estimates of Full Time Equivalents (FTEs) for each project. An FTE would be an estimate of the total number of person-hours required to complete a project. To calculate the number of people involved, one needed to know the length of the work week and that the average participant worked half or three-quarters of their time for IPP.[84] During frequent visits to the database, I found that the FTE estimates were either missing or obviously inaccurate.[85] In interviews, some PIs admitted that their FTE estimates were either wild guesses or back of the envelope calculations. In response to my queries to IPP's main office about how to determine the number of project participants, I was told to ignore the FTEs listed in the database.[86] Instead, it was suggested I

Weapons Scientists, p. 2.

79. See General Accounting Office, *Nuclear Nonproliferation: Concerns with DOE's Efforts.*

80. Ibid., pp. 42–43.

81. Department of Energy, Internal Report on Programs in Russia, 2001.

82. Ibid.

83. Department of Energy, Initiatives for Proliferation Prevention, "Annual Report for Fiscal Year 2000," pp. 1–2.

84. Interview with Los Alamos National Laboratory staffer 12, July 15, 1999; and interview with Initiatives for Proliferation Prevention staffer 3, July 17, 1999.

85. For example, the database figures for a project would suggest that thousands were employed or that all employees were making almost no salary.

86. Interview with Initiatives for Proliferation Prevention staffer 1, February 13, 2002; interview with Initiatives for Proliferation Prevention staffer 2, July 21, 1999; interview with Initiatives for Proliferation Prevention staffer 3, July 17, 1999; and interview with Los Alamos

estimate the number of participants by dividing total project funds by $5,400, the average salary for a year's participation in an IPP project; 70 percent of the result, according to IPP, could be assumed to be weapons workers.

Additional evidence suggests that IPP did not improve its record-keeping. In 2005, the GAO audited several contracts at DOE's National Nuclear Security Administration, including six with IPP. Although the audit focused on the record-keeping associated with contracts and deliverables and not numbers of scientists involved, the GAO found that records were complete for only one IPP project.[87] Another audit in 2007 focused more specifically on IPP. The GAO accused the program of "overstating" its results when an examination of a subset of current IPP projects revealed that less than half of the former Soviet participants had claimed to have WMD experience.[88]

A second area of concern involves the definition of "weapons scientist" and how PIs verify weapons credentials. Initially, "weapons scientist" was defined as someone with direct experience in the design, development, production, or testing of WMD.[89] No further instructions were provided for refining this definition.[90] As of 2000, however, all new IPP projects were required to list the people who would be involved, along with the nature of their involvement with WMD "during Soviet times."[91] This requirement was accompanied by new program guidance that asked PIs to break down the weapons expertise of project participants into three categories: direct involvement with WMD production or testing, involvement with research on WMD technologies, or no involvement with WMD.[92]

Formally, weapons credentials were determined by self-declaration and then verification by project PIs.[93] In my interviews, some PIs claimed they used their own contacts and personal judgment.[94] Still others said they did not verify weapons expertise, claiming this was not their respon-

National Laboratory staffer 12, July 15, 1999.

87.   General Accounting Office, *Nuclear Nonproliferation: Better Management Controls Needed*, pp. 6, 20.

88.   Government Accountability Office, *Nuclear Nonproliferation: DOE's Program to Assist Weapons Scientists*, pp. 5–6.

89.   General Accounting Office, *Nuclear Nonproliferation: Concerns with DOE's Efforts*, p. 15.

90.   Electronic communication with Initiatives for Proliferation Prevention staffer 2, November 20, 2000.

91.   Department of Energy, Internal Report on Programs in Russia, 2001.

92.   Ibid.; and Department of Energy, Initiatives for Proliferation Prevention, "Guidance for Evaluating Weapons Scientists, Engineers, and Technicians," June 2002, http://www.usic.net (accessed June 29, 2007).

93.   General Accounting Office, *Nuclear Nonproliferation: Concerns with DOE's Efforts*, p. 15.

94.   Electronic communication with Initiatives for Proliferation Prevention staffer 2, November 20, 2000; interview with Initiatives for Proliferation Prevention staffer 1, July 16, 2003; interview with Lawrence Livermore National Laboratory staffer 12, April 3, 2003; interview with Brookhaven National Laboratory staffer 1, March 19, 2003; and interview with Pacific Northwest National Laboratory staffer 9, March 6, 2003.

sibility or that there was an interagency procedure or other mechanism for verifying weapons credentials.[95] In other cases, PIs claimed to rely on the institute; if it was involved in WMD activities, then they felt it was reasonable to assume that the people who worked there had WMD credentials.[96]

IPP's guidance dating from 2002 suggests that PIs relied on age; more specifically, all senior staff who were old enough to have been "professionally employed" during Soviet times were to be assumed to have experience with weapons of mass destruction.[97] This emphasis on Soviet-era workers is consistent with the original intention of the program, which was to minimize the risk of proliferation from Soviet-era experts, who were presumably more likely to lose their jobs than younger workers. Indeed, my interviews suggested that some PIs did rely on age as a means of verification. The GAO's 2007 audit, however, found that about 15 percent of project participants were too young to have worked in the Soviet Union, and that several WMD institutes actually used the possibility of working on an IPP project to recruit new scientists into their current weapons workforce.[98]

Another area of uncertainty is the degree to which IPP projects sustained project participants. Given differences in wages and time worked, the average participant made about $5,400 a year during the early to mid-2000s.[99] Salaries tended to reflect those paid by the Science Centers, but the average IPP participant spent a greater percentage of the work week on IPP projects.[100] Compared to average wages throughout Russia, it is clear that IPP project salaries were quite lucrative. One PI, however, reported in

---

95.   For claims that PIs were not responsible for verifying the weapons expertise of program participants, see General Accounting Office, *Nuclear Nonproliferation: Concerns with DOE's Efforts*, pp. 39–40. During interviews with PIs at Pacific Northwest, Oak Ridge, Los Alamos, and Livermore, I had at least one PI or more at each lab claim there was a master list of all WMD experts from the former Soviet Union that was maintained by U.S. intelligence services. According to these PIs, their project participants are double-checked against this list for weapons credentials. Most program managers, many PIs, and other participants that I interviewed with IPP, the Science Centers, and the Nuclear Cities Initiative denied that such a list existed. According to General Accounting Office, *Nuclear Nonproliferation: Concerns with DOE's Efforts*, p. 41, there was no comprehensive list of critical institutes or people to engage.

96.   Interview with Brookhaven National Laboratory staffer 1, March 19, 2003; interview with Brookhaven National Laboratory staffer 2, March 19, 2003; and interview with Pacific Northwest National Laboratory staffer 1, March 12, 2003.

97.   Department of Energy, Initiatives for Proliferation Prevention, "Guidance for Evaluating Weapons Scientists, Engineers, and Technicians," June 2002, http://www.usic.net (accessed June 29, 2007).

98.   Government Accountability Office, *Nuclear Nonproliferation: DOE's Program to Assist Weapons Scientists*, p. 6.

99.   Interview with Initiatives for Proliferation Prevention staffer 1, February 13, 2002; interview with Initiatives for Proliferation Prevention staffer 2, July 21, 1999; and interview with Initiatives for Proliferation Prevention staffer 1, July 16, 2003.

100.   Interview with Pacific Northwest National Laboratory staffer 6, March 5, 2003; and U.S. Congress, *Energy and Water Development Appropriations, FY 2000*, p. 310.

2003 that Russian wages for software programmers had increased to the point that it was difficult to convince them to participate in IPP projects.[101]

However, there is some reason to question whether IPP participants got the average wage. In the GAO's 1999 investigation into IPP, it found that PIs often did not know whether project participants received all the promised wages.[102] The GAO found deductions due to wire transfer fees, taxes, and institute overhead, as well as other variables. The result was that the average IPP recipient only took home about 47 percent of the salary paid by IPP.[103]

Finally, with respect to the type of WMD expert engaged, IPP saw significant movement toward working with more people who were formerly part of the Soviet biological weapons program. By virtue of the U.S. and Russian experts who helped create the program, IPP initially focused almost exclusively on the nuclear side, and engaged in only two to three projects per year with biological weapons experts.[104] Beginning in 1997, as a result of U.S. concerns about Iran and others seeking biological weapons capabilities, this area received a higher priority and IPP's goal became to spend 30 percent of its project funds there.

Because IPP budgets did not increase proportionally, the result was a shift away from nuclear weapons experts. Whereas projects with former biological weapons experts averaged less than $500,000 per year in 1994–1996, they rose to over $3 million per year in 1997–1999.[105] The number of projects also increased to around fifteen annually during this same period, and by fiscal year 2001, 30 percent of IPP's budget was going toward projects with former biological and chemical weapons experts.[106] In 2003, however, this was reduced to 20 percent and remained near that level as of 2008.[107]

JOB CREATION

Initially, IPP did not require PIs to report on jobs created, and it is unclear if a uniform means for assessing this was ever developed. For example, none of the PIs I interviewed claimed to keep a record of the jobs created by their projects, and few had personal knowledge of any permanent re-

---

101. Interview with Lawrence Livermore National Laboratory staffer 5, April 1, 2003.

102. General Accounting Office, *Nuclear Nonproliferation: Concerns with DOE's Efforts*, p. 30.

103. Ibid., p. 31.

104. General Accounting Office, *Biological Weapons. Effort to Reduce Former Soviet Threat Offers Benefits, Poses New Risks*, pp. 20–21.

105. Ibid., p. 20.

106. Department of Energy, "Performance and Accountability Report," fiscal year 2001, p. A68; fiscal year 2002, p. 90; and fiscal year 2003, p. 98, Washington, D.C.

107. National Research Council, Office for Central Europe and Eurasia, Committee on Prevention of Proliferation of Biological Weapons, *The Biological Threat Reduction Program of the Department of Defense: From Foreign Assistance to Sustainable Partnerships* (Washington, D.C.: National Academy Press, 2007), pp. 50–51.

employment. Moreover, IPP did not investigate the fate of former Soviet workers or IPP projects once U.S. government funding ended.

As of April 2007, IPP claimed to have created 2,790 long-term jobs.[108] As might be expected, the number of jobs accelerated in later years as projects became more mature. For example, in 2000, IPP reported cumulative job creation totals of approximately 700; by 2002, this had grown to almost 900, and to over 1,000 in 2003.[109] Assuming that IPP's target of 60 percent weapons experts per project was met, then 1,670 of these jobs went to WMD personnel. The GAO's 2007 audit, however, suggests that the actual number was much lower. The GAO examined 50 projects that IPP identified as having created long-term jobs and was not able to find "many"; moreover, it did find evidence that some jobs were either part-time or were in existence prior to the start of the IPP project.[110]

In addition to job creation, IPP reported a variety of other measures that were meant to indicate commercial success, and thus the potential for future reemployment. Here I focus on the two that were most consistently employed in IPP's Annual Report, DOE's yearly *Performance and Accountability* reports, and their budget requests to Congress. The first metric was commercialization. According to IPP's Annual Report, from 1994 through 2001, ten projects reached the stage of "commercial takeoff."[111] After that point, IPP referred to technologies that had been commercialized or businesses that had been expanded as a direct result of IPP projects, and reported twenty for fiscal year 2003 and thirty-six for fiscal year 2004.[112] In 2007, USIC claimed that 20 percent of IPP projects resulted in commercialization.[113]

Another metric used to indicate commercial potential was the percentage of industry contributions to IPP projects. It was IPP policy for Thrust 2 projects, which made up most of the program's portfolio, to require equal cost-sharing between the U.S. government and private business partners. Here, however, the results are mixed.

---

108. Government Accountability Office, *Nuclear Nonproliferation: DOE's Program to Assist Weapons Scientists*, p. 6.

109. Robert J. Einhorn and Michele A. Flournoy, eds., *Protecting Against the Spread of Nuclear, Biological, and Chemical Weapons: An Action Agenda for the Global Partnership, Volume 1: Agenda for Action* (Washington, D.C.: Center for Strategic and International Studies), January 2003, p. 30; and United States Industry Coalition, "Annual Report," 2004–2005, Washington, D.C., p. 8.

110. Government Accountability Office, *Nuclear Nonproliferation: DOE's Program to Assist Weapons Scientists*, p. 6.

111. Department of Energy, Initiatives for Proliferation Prevention, "Annual Report for Fiscal Year 2001," p. 4.

112. Department of Energy, National Nuclear Security Administration, Office of the Administrator, Weapons Activities, Defense Nuclear Nonproliferation, Naval Reactors, "FY 2006 Congressional Budget Request," Vol. 1, Washington, D.C. (February 2006), p. 495. Unfortunately, the number of technologies commercialized or businesses expanded was not reported after fiscal year 2004.

113. United States Industry Coalition, "Annual Report," 2007, Washington, D.C., p. 11.

On one hand, there was consistent cost-sharing. According to the United States Industry Coalition, between 1994 and 2007, business contributions to IPP project funding equaled that of the U.S. government.[114] However, according to DOE's congressional budget documents, business contributions equaled 50 percent of U.S. government funding in fiscal year 2003 and climbed steadily to the point that, in fiscal year 2006, they reached 70 percent.[115]

On the other hand, however, these figures do not reflect burden-sharing. The requirement for cost-sharing from commercial partners was intended to ensure that companies were more committed to IPP projects and to the weapons experts involved, and that they would use IPP to establish a partnership that would lead to future, non-U.S. government-funded collaboration. In practice, however, there is room to doubt that such relationships developed. Most cost-sharing involved in-kind contributions such as labor, materials, and facilities used for project participation in the United States. Companies typically did not invest financial resources or provide contributions that increased their own expenses.[116] IPP had no policy for policing company contributions, and in my interviews PIs reported companies getting credit for activities that were part of their normal business functions, for projects that were already underway, and for counting the salary the person designated to oversee the project would normally receive anyway. Few PIs claimed knowledge of industry contributions of money, equipment, or supplies that were actually shipped to the former Soviet teams, although such transfers were supposed to occur.

Furthermore, the business partner often did not meet the former Soviet workers it was employing until well into the project. It was the U.S. labs that were responsible for finding companies and negotiating project agreements. As a result, it might be close to two years before a company had any significant interaction with the former weapons workers, and by that time all the critical issues had been resolved.[117] As a result of this missed opportunity, and because companies usually provided contributions that had a limited opportunity cost, there was little basis for building a relationship that could last beyond U.S. government involvement.

---

114. United States Industry Coalition, *Commercial Partnerships in the Former Soviet Union*, Spring 2007, p. 1; and United States Industry Coalition, "Annual Report," 2007, p. 6.

115. Department of Energy, National Nuclear Security Administration, Office of the Administrator, Weapons Activities, Defense Nuclear Nonproliferation, Naval Reactors," FY 2008 Congressional Budget Request," Vol. 1, Washington, D.C. (February 2007), p. 458.

116. Kellett, *USIC and the Initiatives for Proliferation Prevention*, p. 20, fn. 2.

117. Interview with Lawrence Livermore National Laboratory staffer 5, April 1, 2003; interview with Sandia National Laboratory staffer 6, May 5, 2003; interview with U.S. businessperson 1, February 22, 2007; and interview with non-governmental organization staffer 10, July 24, 2007.

FUNDING THE U.S. LABS

According to both congressional statute and IPP policy, 70 percent of program funding had to be spent on projects in the former Soviet Union. However, the percentage of money spent in the U.S. labs versus former Soviet ones was not reported consistently by IPP, DOE, or the United States Industry Coalition. The most recent figure, cited by DOE for projects in fiscal year 2000, claims that 57 percent of its funds were spent in the former Soviet Union.[118] In its annual report for 2007, however, USIC provided additional information. According to USIC, once a project was approved, 70 percent of project funds would go to the former Soviet partner.[119] It is unclear, however, whether this figure included only project funding or IPP budgets overall. Moreover, in 2007, the GAO discovered that, with respect to IPP projects in Libya, 97 percent of funding went to the U.S. national labs.[120]

It is clear, however, that project responsibilities shifted in an attempt to spend less in the United States. For example, to avoid paying the higher salaries of PIs in the U.S. labs, more project responsibilities were taken over by IPP's administrative office at DOE.[121] Money spent there was not counted as part of what the U.S. labs received. Second, IPP began to make more use of ISTC and its administrative capabilities in Russia. Finally, more IPP projects were given to the U.S. labs that had the lowest overhead and other rates for contracting.[122]

Explaining Outcomes

IPP has been the subject of various evaluations, including several by the GAO, an internal review conducted for IPP by Booz Allen Hamilton, and assessments conducted by other parts of the executive branch. These evaluations all had one common finding: the main IPP office had inadequate control over the U.S. lab employees who formed the backbone of the IPP project process. In combination, these reviews provide snapshots over time of what was in reality a set of persistent problems, all tied to the traditional independence the U.S. labs enjoyed under DOE. The following section explains how the U.S. labs were the source of IPP's success, but were also responsible for problems that limited program funding, undercut opportunities for sustainable reemployment, injured relations with

118. Department of Energy, "Performance and Accountability Report," fiscal year 2000, Washington, D.C., p. A70.

119. United States Industry Coalition, "Annual Report," 2007, p. 5.

120. Government Accountability Office, *Nuclear Nonproliferation: DOE's Program to Assist Weapons Scientists*, p. 7.

121. Department of Energy, The Secretary of Energy Advisory Board, Howard Baker and Lloyd Cutler, *A Report Card on the Department of Energy's Nonproliferation Programs with Russia* (Washington, D.C.: Department of Energy, January 20, 2001), p. 149; and Department of Energy, Initiatives for Proliferation Prevention, "Annual Report for Fiscal Year 1999," Washington, D.C.

122. Baker and Cutler, *A Report Card*, p. 149.

the State Department, and bred a permissive culture that raised concerns about program accountability.[123]

As was the case with the Science Centers, relations with both Russia and the U.S. Congress contributed their share of problems. In general, however, IPP developed successful solutions to problems with access and taxes in Russia. As for Congress, it often acted to increase IPP's budget beyond the president's original request. Moreover, if IPP budgets had been significantly higher, it is reasonable to assume that more former weapons experts would have been involved in the program, but far from clear that many additional jobs would have been the result.

RUSSIA

Similar to what other programs experienced in their early cooperation with former Soviet experts, IPP had problems convincing scientists and institutes to focus on commercialization rather than on pet projects or interesting science. IPP's requirement for a commercial partner in most projects after the mid-1990s, plus repeated emphasis on this issue over time, largely did away with this issue. More serious were problems due to access and taxes, both of which were exacerbated due to IPP's decentralized approach to working in former Soviet states. In contrast to the Defense Department's conversion efforts, the Science Centers and NCI, each of which established implementing agreements with the governments hosting their projects, DOE's IPP favored a decentralized approach that focused on institutes or, in some cases, individual project teams.

Access was more of an issue for IPP, mostly with respect to projects in Russia's nuclear cities. Not only did the closed nuclear cities have special restrictions on admitting foreigners, but also it was the case that projects with institutes in these cities had to deal more with the Russian Ministry of Atomic Energy (Minatom), and its successor, the Federal Agency for Atomic Energy (Rosatom), which tried to exert more influence not only on access but also on the content of projects.[124] The Russian Federal Security Services (FSB) also became a player. Moreover, the power of the FSB increased under President Vladimir Putin, whereas Boris Yeltsin had often been willing to reign in the FSB in exchange for international cooperation. Because of problems in the nuclear cities, in some cases PIs transferred their projects to nearby open cities or arranged to meet project teams there.[125] Although access may have slowed projects, project PIs generally proved to be willing and able to work around such issues.

123. For a comparison of the role of the labs in NCI and IPP, see Sharon K. Weiner, "Organizational Interest, Nuclear Weapons Scientists, and Nonproliferation," *Political Science Quarterly*, Vol. 124, No. 4 (Winter 2009–10), pp. 655–679.

124. Landau Network—Centro Volta, International Working Group, General Secretariat, "Analysis. International Cooperation Programs and Russian Nuclear Cities: Future Initiatives, Drawbacks, Strategies and Europe's Role," February 11, 2002, p. 4.

125. Interview with Lawrence Livermore National Laboratory staffer 5, April 1, 2003; and interview with Lawrence Livermore National Laboratory staffer 12, April 3, 2003.

IPP lacked the detailed implementing agreement that, in the case of the Science Centers, also established standard procedures, oversight rules, and requirements for access to project sites and participants. Because of this difference, IPP tended to negotiate project agreements, as well as solutions to problems, on a case-by-case or institute-specific basis. Therefore, there was more variation between IPP projects in terms of contract specifics, payment schedules, and oversight rules. Moreover, the PI had considerable discretion to determine these. As a result, when institutes or federal agencies such as Rosatom become involved in decision-making about IPP projects, there was often confusion and a slow learning curve.

This decentralized approach to project management had both positive and negative consequences. On the positive side, it meant that IPP could leverage the desire of former weapons workers to work with the U.S. labs to coerce institutes for their approval. For example, early cooperation with Biopreparat institutes was stalled because of Biopreparat's insistence on overhead fees for all IPP projects. Thanks to stoic resistance from IPP's headquarters and internal pressure from former weapons workers who wanted to cooperate, Biopreparat had to back down. Similarly, scientists in the nuclear cities had in some cases established relationships with local FSB officers or applied pressure through their connections at Rosatom in an attempt to reduce resistance to their international collaboration.[126]

But there is also a negative side to this decentralization. Often, PIs at different U.S. labs confronted similar problems, but dealt with them independently. As explained below, there were few attempts to share solutions or lessons from past experience. Also, this decentralization allowed individual institutes to "tax" projects by charging overhead, or for project teams to demand unreasonable salaries.[127] Improper taxes, too, might be applied to equipment and salaries, despite a 1992 bilateral agreement between the United States and Russia stating that equipment, supplies, and property used in connection with bilateral assistance programs were to be tax-free.[128] According to people familiar with IPP, this did not solve the problem, because institute, city, and regional officials each had their own definitions for what constituted project necessities and justifiable overhead. Estimates are that between 50 percent and 75 percent of U.S. assistance to certain institutes had, at times, been diverted because of these problems.[129] Funneling IPP projects through the International Science and Technology Center and the Civilian Research and Development Foundation helped mitigate this problem, although PIs still encoun-

---

126. Interview with Lawrence Livermore National Laboratory staffer 11, April 7, 2003.

127. Gore-Chernomyrdin Commission, Eighth Session, Energy Policy Committee, Background Papers, January 1997, p. 19. For the pervasiveness of the problem of corruption, see Kellett, "USIC and the Initiatives for Proliferation Prevention," p. 27.

128. General Accounting Office, *Weapons of Mass Destruction: Some U.S. Assistance to Redirect Russian Scientists Taxed by Russia*, Washington, D.C., April 28, 2000, p. 3.

129. Michael S. Lelyveld, "Skimming Cuts Aid to Russian Scientists. DOE," *Journal of Commerce*, May 13, 1997, p. 1; General Accounting Office, *Weapons of Mass Destruction: Some U.S. Assistance to Redirect Russian Scientists Taxed by Russia*, p. 2.

tered some difficulties. For projects outside of Russia, in some cases IPP projects were suspended for a time to pressure host governments to intercede with local authorities to stop unreasonable or illegal taxation.[130]

The decentralized approach also opened the door for federal-level disputes between agencies in Russia. It was the FSB and not Rosatom that determined access rules to institutes and the nuclear cities. When an individual project ran into trouble and the issue had to be elevated to the federal level, this gave the FSB an opportunity to trade access for other unrelated concessions from Rosatom. For these and other reasons, officials from Rosatom's predecessor, Minatom, tended to favor the International Science and Technology Center over IPP.[131]

Several PIs mentioned another downside: project-sharing. Because former Soviet experts at similar institutes knew each other, there were attempts to submit the same project to IPP or to submit a project that had already been completed through the Science Centers.[132]

CONGRESSIONAL RESTRICTIONS

Although Congress was generally supportive of IPP, it took a much more active role than was true for the Science Centers. Congress influenced IPP mainly through funding and program restructuring and other administrative changes. The presidential certification requirements that applied to many Cooperative Threat Reduction activities until 2008 never applied to IPP and were therefore not problematic.

While PIs and the United States Industry Coalition frequently complained that IPP had more good projects than it could fund, Congress was generally supportive of IPP's budgets. Initially, funding for the program received strong bipartisan support and, over time, Congress acted to increase IPP's budget over the amount requested by the Administration on numerous occasions. Table 6.2 shows the relationship over time between IPP budget requests and congressional authorizations.

With only a few exceptions, Congress maintained or increased IPP's funding beyond what was requested. The first such exception dates from 1995, when the program did not receive additional money because its implementation was delayed and it was unable to spend most of its original $35 million authorization. The other exceptions were due to concerns that IPP was spending too much of its money in the U.S. labs. For example, in fiscal year 1998, Congress reduced IPP's funding because too little of it

---

130. Department of Energy, Initiatives for Proliferation Prevention, "Annual Report for Fiscal Year 2001." In particular, activities in Ukraine and Kazakhstan were suspended for a long time due to the threat of taxes by local authorities. Agreements were reached with both countries in fiscal year 2000.

131. Interview with Minatom official 1, July 24, 2002; and interview with Minatom official 3, July 24, 2002.

132. Interview with Brookhaven National Laboratory staffer 1, March 19, 2003; interview with Brookhaven National Laboratory staffer 2, March 19, 2003; interview with Los Alamos National Laboratory staffer 10, June 2, 2003; and interview with Institute for Physics and Power Engineering staffer 1, July 23, 2002.

was going to former Soviet institutes.[133] Most of the cuts proposed the next year for the same reason were ultimately reversed. During consideration of the fiscal year 2000 budget, however, Congress decreased the budget by some $2 million, and required that in the future, 65 percent of program funds be spent in the former Soviet Union.[134]

In addition to funding, Congress also influenced IPP by requiring changes in its organization and structure. In response to GAO investigations that raised concerns about the power of the U.S. labs, Congress encouraged DOE to invest more responsibility for IPP in DOE's main office in Washington, D.C., a move which is discussed in more detail in the next section. Congress also required the program to merge with NCI in 2002, creating RTI. The official story behind this change is that Congress was concerned about potential duplication between IPP and NCI. Therefore, RTI was created to force the programs to work more closely together; NCI would concentrate on helping Russia downsize its nuclear weapons complex, while IPP would focus on conversion through commercialization projects. The alternative story, told by many in the U.S. labs and at DOE, is that RTI was a recognition of political reality. NCI had always been a politically troubled program, and its future was in doubt. Because NCI relied on U.S. national laboratory personnel and was administered out of the same DOE office as IPP, any problems with NCI inherently reflected on IPP as well. RTI was an attempt to protect IPP by removing NCI and its problems from the spotlight.[135]

Regardless of the reasons behind RTI, its creation made little difference to IPP or NCI. At the U.S. labs, a significant number of personnel had always been involved in both programs, and lab program directors were usually in charge of both efforts. Lab PIs reported few changes as a result of the merger, including no additional cooperation with NCI.[136] During my interviews at the U.S. labs during the two years immediately following RTI's creation, many PIs were not even aware of the new name or changes. At IPP's headquarters in DOE, there was also little evidence that RTI led to significant changes. IPP's director, program management, and reporting requirements remained the same. Initial fears that NCI would become a drain on IPP's budget were not realized, even though under RTI, Energy Department officials were given more discretion to divide authorized funding between the programs.

---

133. RANSAC, "House of Representatives, U.S. Energy and Water Appropriations Act," December 31, 1997, p. 1.

134. U.S. Congress, House, Committee on Appropriations, *Energy and Water Development Appropriations Bill, 1998*, 105th Cong., 1st sess., July 21, 1997, 105 H. Rpt. 190, p. 123; and U.S. Congress, House, *Making Appropriations for Energy and Water Development for the Fiscal Year Ending September 30, 1998, and Other Purposes*, 105th Cong., 1st sess., September 26, 1997, 105 H. Rpt. 271, p. 95.

135. Interview with U.S. government official 6, May 28, 2002; and interview with Initiatives for Proliferation Prevention staffer 1, July 16, 2003.

136. Interview with Lawrence Berkeley National Laboratory staffer 1, March 31, 2003; interview with Sandia National Laboratory staffer 7, May 5, 2003; and interview with Oak Ridge National Laboratory staffer 1, February 20, 2003.

Table 6.2. IPP Funding (in millions of U.S. dollars).

Fiscal Year	IPP Request	Congressional Authorization
IPP		
1994		$35[d]
1995		$0
1996	$10[c]	$20
1997	$29.6	$29.6
1998	$30	$29.6
1999	$29.6	$22.5
2000	$22.5	$20.7
2001	$22.5	$24.1
RTI[a]		
2002	$28.8	$57 (includes additional funds from 9/11 supplemental spending measures)
2003	$39.3	$39.3
2004	$39.8	$39.8
2005	$41	$40.7
GIPP		
2006	$37.9	$39.6
2007[b]	$28.1	$28.1
2008[b]	$20.2	$30.9

[a]Funding for RTI and GIPP includes both the IPP program and the Nuclear Cities Initiative. Because the Nuclear Cities Initiative received little new funding after its implementing agreement expired in September 2003, after that date most RTI and GIPP funding went to the IPP program.

[b]Funding for 2007 and 2008 includes activities in Libya and Iraq.

[c]As part of the redistribution of CTR activities, responsibility for IPP was given to the Department of Energy; for fiscal year 1996, IPP received $10 million from DOE and $10 million from the Defense Department.

[d]Initially, the Senate Appropriations Committee recommended that IPP be given $50 million, even though only $35 million was approved by Congress. See U.S. Congress, Committee on Appropriations, *Foreign Operations, Export Financing, and Related Programs Appropriations Bill,* 1994, 103rd Cong., 1st sess., S. Rpt. 103-142, September 14, 1993.

SOURCES: Department of Energy, National Nuclear Security Administration, Office of the Administrator, Weapons Activities, Defense Nuclear Nonproliferation, Naval Reactors, "FY 2008 Congressional Budget Request," Vol. 1, February 2007, p. 458; General Accounting Office, *Nuclear Proliferation: Concerns with DOE's Efforts to Reduce the Risks Posed by Russia's Unemployed Weapons Scientists,* Washington, D.C. (February 1999), p. 33; U.S. Congress, House, Committee on Appropriations, *Energy and Water Development Appropriations for 1998, Part 6: Department of Energy,* 105th Cong., 1st sess., March 12, April 9, 1997, p. 610; U.S. Congress, House, Committee on Appropriations, *Energy and Water Development Appropriations Bill, 1998,* 105th Cong., 1st sess., July 21, 1997, 105 H. Rpt. 190, p. 123; U.S. Congress, House, *Making Appropriations for Energy and Water Development for the Fiscal Year Ending September 30, 1998, and Other Purposes,* 105th Cong., 1st sess., September 26, 1997, 105 H. Rpt. 271, p. 95; U.S. Congress, House, Committee on

International Relations, *Report on the Expanded Threat Reduction Initiative, Message from the President*, 106th Cong., 2nd sess., June 28, 2000, House Doc.106-263; Amy F. Woolf, *Nonproliferation and Threat Reduction Assistance: U.S. Programs in the Former Soviet Union*, Congressional Research Service, CRS Report for Congress, Washington, D.C., updated June 26, 2006, p. 38; Amy F. Woolf, *Nuclear Weapons in Russia: Safety, Security, and Control Issues*, Congressional Research Service, Issue Brief for Congress, November 21, 2000), p. 11; Matthew Bunn, Anthony Wier, and John P. Holdren, *Controlling Nuclear Warheads and Materials: A Report Card and Action Plan*, (Cambridge, Mass., and Washington, D.C.: Project on Managing the Atom, Harvard University, and Nuclear Threat Initiative, March 2003), p. 56; Russian-American Nuclear Security Advisory Council (RANSAC), "Russian Nuclear Security and the Clinton Administration's Fiscal Year 2000 Expanded Threat Reduction Initiative. A Summary of Congressional Action," Washington, D.C. (February 2000); William Hoehn, "Update on Congressional Activity Affecting U.S.-Russian Cooperative Nonproliferation Programs," RANSAC, Washington, D.C., July 26, 2002, p. 34; RANSAC, "Preliminary Report: Anticipated FY 2003 Budget Request for Department of Energy Cooperative Nuclear Security Programs in Russia," Washington, D.C., January 9, 2002, p. 2; William Hoehn, "Observations on the President's Fiscal Year 2004 Budget Request for Nonproliferation Programs in Russia and the Former Soviet Union," RANSAC, Washington, D.C., February 11, 2003, p. 5; William Hoehn, "Policy Update, Preliminary Analysis of the U.S. Department of Energy's Fiscal Year 2006 Nonproliferation Budget Request," RANSAC, Washington, D.C. (February 2005), p. 4; William Hoehn, "Final Report of Congressional Activity Affecting U.S. Global Threat Reduction Programs in 2005," RANSAC, Washington, D.C. (February 2005), p. 46; William Hoehn, "Preliminary Analysis of the U.S. Department of Energy's Fiscal Year 2007 Nonproliferation Budget Request," RANSAC, Washington, D.C. (February 2006), p. 4; Isabelle Williams and Kenneth Luongo, "Analysis of the U.S. Department of Energy's Fiscal Year 2008 International Nonproliferation Budget Request," Partnership for Global Security, Washington, D.C., February 26, 2007, pp. 1, 3; United States Industry Coalition, E-Notes, Vol. 8, No. 4, May 4, 2007, p. 2; Electronic communication with Initiatives for Proliferation Prevention staffer 3, May 23, 2001; U.S. Department of Energy, Defense Nuclear Nonproliferation, "Executive Budget Summary," Congressional Budget Request, fiscal year 2001, p. 89; and Department of Energy, National Nuclear Security Administration, Office of the Administrator, Weapons Activities, Defense Nuclear Nonproliferation, Naval Reactors, "FY 2009 Congressional Budget Request," Vol. 1, Washington, D.C. (February 2008), p. 486.

Finally, as a result of IPP's expansion beyond the former Soviet Union, RTI's name was changed to Global Initiatives for Proliferation Prevention (GIPP). Because NCI's implementing agreement with Russia expired in September 2003 and was not renewed, for all practical purposes GIPP became the new name for what used to be the IPP program.

INSTITUTIONAL CULTURE

It should be clear at this point that IPP was a child of the U.S. national laboratories. However, this made it hostage to the overall relationship between the labs and DOE. The department itself has been accused of being a dysfunctional organization.[137] It is composed of diverse missions that

---

137.   There have been numerous studies documenting problems with the Department of Energy's management and organization. The main ones are General Accounting Office, *Department of Energy. Need to Address Longstanding Management Weaknesses*, Testimony of Victor S. Rezendes, GAO, to Subcommittee on Energy and Environment, House Committee on Commerce, July 13, 1999; *Science at its Best, Security at its Worst: A Report on*

sometimes work at cross-purposes and it suffers from "stovepiping"; that is, from a lack of coordination or cooperation across organizational units. Moreover, DOE's defense and nuclear weapons programs are housed in a quasi-autonomous agency—the National Nuclear Security Administration (NNSA)—which has been faulted for insufficient control over the U.S. nuclear weapons laboratories and for tolerating rivalry, insufficient coordination, inefficiency, and arrogance.[138] Because of the power of the individual nuclear weapons labs, and especially Los Alamos, Livermore, and Sandia, both NNSA and DOE often have problems reaching decisions or enforcing trade-offs. According to former Deputy Secretary of Energy Charles Curtis, the labs play off parts of DOE against each other or threaten to appeal to Congress if the department does not agree to their priorities.[139]

NNSA is further divided into organizations with responsibility for nonproliferation, threat reduction, material control, and international cooperation, among others. NNSA has been reorganized several times in the last decade. As of 2008, GIPP could be found in NNSA's NA-24: Office of Nonproliferation and International Security, in the Office of Global Security Engagement and Cooperation. DOE also maintained its own office at the U.S. Embassy in Moscow in order to provide help in implementing all of the department's programs in Russia.

The institutional culture and politics that is the result of this decentralized power structure had profound consequences for IPP. On one hand, it gave the U.S. labs the independence to forge relationships with their sister institutions in the former Soviet Union. However, as explained below, this same autonomy also led to a program that was significantly hamstrung due to insufficient coordination, competition and distrust between the labs, problems with overall program management and oversight, and relations with other agencies, particularly the State Department.

Security Problems at the U.S. Department of Energy, A Special Investigative Panel, President's Foreign Intelligence Advisory Board, June 1999 (The Rudman Report); and U.S. Congress Commission on Maintaining the Expertise to Manage the U.S. Nuclear and Weapons Stockpile (Chiles Commission), Washington, D.C., 1997–1999. For an illustration of these problems, see Notra Trulock, *Code Name Kindred Spirit: Inside the Chinese Nuclear Espionage Scandal* (San Francisco, Calif.: Encounter Books, 2003). Several lab PIs, including those at Los Alamos, where Trulock used to work, recommended this book, claiming that while they did not necessarily agree with its presentation of the Chinese espionage case, they did believe it was a good description of management by the Department of Energy.

138. For NNSA's missions, see Department of Energy, National Nuclear Security Administration, Report to Congress on the Organization and Operations of the National Nuclear Security Administration, February 25, 2002. For a summary of management issues, see General Accounting Office, *Nuclear Security: Security Issues at DOE and Its Newly Created National Nuclear Security Administration*, Washington, D.C., March 14, 2000; and General Accounting Office, *Department of Energy. Views on DOE's Plan to Establish the National Nuclear Security Administration*, Washington, D.C., March 2, 2000.

139. See, for example, Sydney J. Freedberg, Jr., "Beating Swords into Plowshares," *National Journal*, Vol. 30, No. 50 (December 12, 1998), pp. 2936–2937.

THE ROLE OF THE U.S. LABS. To the extent that IPP made inroads into engaging former weapons workers and creating jobs, credit belongs to the U.S. national laboratories. U.S. lab scientists shared a common language with their former Soviet counterparts and used this as the basis for building trust. This trust, in turn, helped both U.S. and former Soviet experts form an alliance to combat the skepticism and secrecy that was a legacy of not only the Cold War but also of both U.S. and Soviet national security programs. Not only did the Soviet, and later Russian, government need to be convinced of the value of cooperation, but many U.S. policymakers were also initially skeptical. Although members of Congress, especially Les Aspin, Sam Nunn, and Richard Lugar, are frequently credited with creating Cooperative Threat Reduction, several U.S. lab experts were also critical in providing information and incentives, and in lobbying for cooperation. And over the life of IPP, it was the U.S. labs that pushed policymakers in Washington, D.C. to make the compromises necessary for cooperation to continue, despite broader disagreements between Russia and the United States.

The labs also remained important resources for validating the skills and products of former weapons experts in the former Soviet Union, not only for IPP, but also for the Science Centers, NCI, and the U.S. business partners in these programs.

Moreover, U.S. lab experts were extremely enthusiastic about the opportunity to meet, work with, and help their Soviet counterparts. Part of this excitement grew out of the opportunity to discover new technologies and to learn how Soviet scientists had approached common scientific problems. It is also the case that some U.S. experts were inspired by the excitement of working with former enemies and the realization that, with the end of the Cold War, their own weapons jobs were perhaps in jeopardy.[140]

But some of the motivation of U.S. lab experts can only be explained by altruism. The respect U.S. scientists had for Soviet science and accomplishments, plus their ability to understand the dire economic circumstances faced by their colleagues, led many U.S. experts to give up their own work, time, and, in some cases, funding to enable their IPP projects to go forward.[141] Also, at a time when they had every reason to expect budget reductions, Los Alamos, Livermore, and Sandia used their own discretionary funds to begin the lab-to-lab cooperation that would become IPP.

Yet it was also the case that the involvement of the U.S. labs served to make IPP more expensive. In terms of money, it has already been

---

140. Interview with Oak Ridge National Laboratory staffer 8, February 19, 2003; and interview with Pacific Northwest National Laboratory staffer 10, March 6, 2003. The budgets of the U.S. nuclear weapons labs were reduced in the early 1990s. For example, from 1992 to 1994, Livermore's operating budget fell by 12.5 percent; budgets for core nuclear weapons research fell by 29 percent, and 10 percent of employees took early retirement. See Jonathan Weisman, "Early Retirement for Weaponeers?" *Bulletin of Atomic Scientists*, Vol. 50, No. 4 (July/August 1994), pp. 16–22.

141. One U.S. lab expert eventually mortgaged his home when U.S. government funding for his project was terminated.

established that during its first years, half of IPP funding went to the U.S. labs. Although as of 2002, Congress capped IPP spending in the U.S. labs at 35 percent, it remained the case that the costs of involving the labs constrained the program. This is mostly because lab employees were expensive. For example, in 2000, the average cost of a national lab employee (the Full Time Equivalent) for one year was $230,000–$250,000, and slightly more at the nuclear weapons laboratories.[142] Besides PIs, who were needed to develop and manage projects as IPP became institutionalized, most labs created administrative positions to oversee projects with IPP, NCI, and the Science Centers. It was also the case that more PIs depended upon IPP to pay for a significant portion of their salaries, whereas initially most PIs supervised only one or two projects and remained mostly involved in other work.[143]

The combination of the high cost of lab labor, plus limitations on how much program money could be spent at the labs, resulted in several constraints. Some labs reevaluated their future involvement in IPP. Others came to favor fewer and larger projects.[144] Some labs tried to compensate by hiring postdoctoral fellows, non-governmental organizations, DOE's office in Moscow, or employees in Russia to perform certain project responsibilities.[145] Others used the same PIs for both IPP and NCI projects. Funding constraints also served to skew project selection toward those that contributed to ongoing lab research or other programs.[146] According to Frederick Kellett's analysis, congressionally mandated spending limits also resulted in three other undesirable outcomes: lab employees did work they were not paid for; they neglected work that was required for project success; and project spending in the former Soviet Union was increased beyond what was justified in order to increase absolute spending at the U.S. labs.[147]

More significantly, the U.S. labs contributed to coordination problems within IPP. The U.S. labs were accustomed to setting their own priorities and operating largely independent of each other. The Inter-Laboratory

---

142. Electronic communication with Initiatives for Proliferation Prevention staffer 2, October 18, 2000; and Department of Energy, Initiatives for Proliferation Prevention, "The Role of the U.S. Department of Energy National Laboratories in the Initiatives for Proliferation Prevention Program," p. 9.

143. Interview with Oak Ridge National Laboratory staffer 1, February 19, 2003; interview with Oak Ridge National Laboratory staffer 8, February 19, 2003; interview with Sandia National Laboratory staffer 7, May 5, 2003; interview with Los Alamos National Laboratory staffer 3, April 29, 2003; and interview with Lawrence Livermore National Laboratory staffer 11, April 7, 2003.

144. Interview with Oak Ridge National Laboratory staffer 1, February 19, 2003.

145. Ibid.; interview with Lawrence Berkeley National Laboratory staffer 1, March 31, 2003; and interview with Department of Energy official, August 12, 2003.

146. Department of Energy, Initiatives for Proliferation Prevention, "The Role of the U.S. Department of Energy National Laboratories in the Initiatives for Proliferation Prevention Program," July 1999, pp. 12–13.

147. Kellett, "USIC and the Initiatives for Proliferation Prevention," pp. 19, 25.

Board, in theory, was supposed to coordinate IPP activities between the labs and distribute funding according to the merits of project proposals. The Board's decisions, however, often reflected negotiations and trade-offs between the labs, rather than overall priorities for IPP.[148] This was due to the fact that the Board used consensus decision-making and lacked independent oversight, and because IPP's program office was unable to enforce trade-offs between the labs. For example, project funds were sometimes distributed on the basis of what was needed to keep IPP active at a particular U.S. lab, rather than according to project merit.

The role played by the Inter-Laboratory Board in resource allocation represents the apex of lab coordination. There was no similar relationship with respect to program direction, evaluation, or information-sharing. For example, the labs did not have a formal mechanism for communicating solutions to common problems. Moreover, even though there was widespread agreement about the importance of good PIs to project success, there was little exchange of information about how to train and recruit good ones. In general, the labs did a poor job of educating PIs, and the PIs I interviewed repeatedly explained that they learned by doing. There are two exceptions. Sandia National Laboratory had an extensive training manual that it put together for IPP project managers. Sandia, however, considered this manual to be proprietary information and a source of advantage over other labs in the competition for IPP resources.[149] The other exception was the Y-12 Plant at Oak Ridge, Tennessee, which had a program guide for both NCI and IPP, but did not share this guidance with other labs or with Oak Ridge National Laboratory, its sister facility.[150]

In his analysis of survey data from interviews with members of the United States Industry Coalition and lab employees, Frederick Kellett points out three reasons why IPP projects were skewed away from long-term commercial success. All three reasons can be traced to the experiences of the U.S. labs and their routine relations with U.S. companies. The first factor was intellectual property rights. According to Kellett, the U.S. labs retained intellectual property rights to IPP project technologies.[151] The labs claimed that this was part of their role in protecting their former Soviet colleagues from exploitation. Kellett, however, points out that this

148.   Interview with Los Alamos National Laboratory staffer 4, June 23, 2003; interview with Brookhaven National Laboratory staffer 1, March 19, 2003; interview with Brookhaven National Laboratory staffer 2, March 19, 2003; interview with Oak Ridge National Laboratory staffer 1, February 19, 2003; and interview with Initiatives for Proliferation Prevention staffer 2, July 16, 2003.

149.   Interview with Sandia National Laboratory staffer 3, May 5, 2003; interview with Sandia National Laboratory staffer 4, May 5, 2003; and interview with Sandia National Laboratory staffer 7, May 5, 2003.

150.   Interview with Oak Ridge National Laboratory staffer 1, February 19, 2003; interview with Oak Ridge National Laboratory staffer 4, February 19, 2003; interview with Oak Ridge National Laboratory staffer 10, February 19, 2003; interview with Oak Ridge National Laboratory staffer 3, February 19, 2003; and interview with Oak Ridge National Laboratory staffer 5.

151.   Interview with Rick Kellett, February 22, 2007.

may have raised concerns about a company's ability to commercialize products for which the labs owned the intellectual property rights.[152]

Second, Kellett explains that IPP treated business partners as customers of former Soviet experts rather than their employers. According to Kellett, this meant that IPP selected companies that were interested in temporary services rather than long-term relationships. Instead of focusing on validating a future workforce, the companies used IPP to prove the benefits of a technology.[153] Moreover, the U.S. lab remained in the middle, performing various administrative and oversight functions. As a result, companies did not develop closer relations with the former Soviet experts, nor did they focus on job creation or sustainable involvement.

The third factor relates to projects that provided services, as opposed to engaging in production. The U.S. labs did research and development for companies; they did not produce items for sale. Similarly, most IPP projects focused on validating technologies using the skills of former Soviet experts, rather than converting facilities to the production of goods. Kellett, however, argues that sustainable reemployment for former Soviet experts was more likely to result if IPP focused on production as well as research and development. Kellett found that, of the businesses in his survey, few focused on the possibility of employment.[154] Moreover, IPP business partners tended to move away from relationships with former Soviet institutes once a technology had been validated.[155] Because production work had proven problematic in the former Soviet Union, and because of the assumption that former weapons workers were not interested in such jobs, IPP provided few ways for companies to develop relationships with production workers and no investment options for U.S. companies to transition their projects to production. Once a technology was validated, U.S. companies tended to terminate their involvement with IPP unless they were interested in testing another technology. IPP did not focus on opportunities to employ former Soviet workers in private business ventures that made their profit through services rather than production. Therefore, there was less of a basis for an ongoing relationship.

THREE GORILLAS AND SEVEN DWARFS. The role of the labs in IPP was further complicated by the fact that the labs were not equal partners. Over time, ten laboratories, the Kansas City Plant, and the Savannah River Site were involved in IPP projects. Traditionally, the labs getting the largest share of IPP funding were Los Alamos, Livermore, and Sandia, but the redirection of IPP toward more work with former biological weapons experts meant that Pacific Northwest and Brookhaven came to be includ-

---

152. Kellett, "USIC and the Initiatives for Proliferation Prevention," p. 18.

153. Ibid., p. 29.

154. Ibid., p. 7.

155. Ibid., p. 12.

ed in this list.[156] It is no coincidence that the three labs with the most projects were also the ones most involved in U.S. nuclear weapons research, design, and development. Therefore, they traditionally carried more clout and commanded more resources within the U.S. national laboratory system.

Because of their predominance, the other labs who were involved in IPP referred to Los Alamos, Livermore, and Sandia as the "Three Gorillas."[157] With respect to IPP, the other labs tended to be envious of the Three Gorillas' claim on resources, at times inflating their power and budgets. But they also claimed that the Three Gorillas used their clout to claim more IPP resources than were justified by the merits of the projects they proposed, and that these three labs had a more influential relationship with IPP headquarters and within DOE overall; therefore, they played a bigger role in setting IPP strategic priorities and policy. The smaller labs tended to see themselves as underdogs in the competition for IPP resources.

There was also a presumption among the smaller labs that the Three Gorillas preferred large IPP projects that involved advanced technology and thus soaked up more funding. The smaller labs saw such projects as highly unlikely to lead to successful commercialization, a conclusion that tended to be supported by success stories from the Science Centers and IPP. In contrast, the smaller labs tended to prefer less expensive projects that focused on small and medium-sized businesses or might include Russian business partners. Even though all of the U.S. labs worked with commercial partners, the smaller labs believed that their relationship with industry was more developed and closely knit. Because the larger labs focused on nuclear weapons, they had fewer ties to the commercial world.

The Three Gorillas tended to see the other labs as "Seven Dwarfs."[158] Even though IPP originally intended to involve all the labs, the nuclear weapons facilities tended to see the other labs as peripheral to IPP's purpose because they were not involved as extensively in nuclear weapons science. According to this logic, preventing the proliferation of nuclear weapons knowledge was IPP's number one priority, and therefore more of IPP's resources should go to the experts who could work most closely with the former Soviet nuclear weapons community. Furthermore, this meant that the U.S. nuclear weapons labs should have a predominant

---

156. U.S. Congress, House, Committee on Appropriations, *Energy and Water Development Appropriations for 2002, Part 6: Department of Energy*, 107th Cong., 1st sess., May 3, 9, 2001, p. 159; and Department of Energy, National Nuclear Security Administration, Office of the Administrator, Weapons Activities, Defense Nuclear Nonproliferation, Naval Reactors, "FY 2004 Congressional Budget Request," Vol. 1, Washington, D.C., pp. 666–667.

157. This phrasing was used repeatedly during interviews I conducted at Oak Ridge, Pacific Northwest, and Brookhaven National Laboratories.

158. This was reinforced during my interviews at Los Alamos, Livermore, and Sandia National Laboratories, but my interviews also suggest that the smaller labs tended to see themselves as underdogs.

role in IPP that included program planning, strategy, and implementation guidelines, in addition to project development and management.

The nuclear weapons labs, especially Los Alamos, chastised the smaller labs for "sneaking around their backs" to DOE and IPP headquarters with complaints, rather than confronting the issues directly.[159] Also, whereas the big labs saw their place in IPP as legitimate and their participation as a public service, they believed that the Seven Dwarfs took part as a means of earning money.[160]

There was also a dynamic that pitted Los Alamos against everyone else. For example, most of the labs saw Los Alamos as claiming more resources and publicity than it deserved. Livermore tended to claim that its role in IPP was altruistic, whereas Los Alamos was trying to claim fame and glory that it could then turn against Livermore in the competition for resources within DOE. Also, many blamed Los Alamos for creating problems within Russia. In particular, Los Alamos was faulted for making repeated trips to Russia's nuclear cities and promising jobs that it could not deliver, especially as part of NCI. As a result, the Russian government and especially the security services became suspicious, calling such visits "nuclear tourism" and claiming that U.S. cooperation was geared more toward spying that conversion or job creation.

Finally, each of the labs believed it had a unique contribution to make to IPP. Los Alamos and Livermore stressed their nuclear weapons credentials. In contrast, Oak Ridge claimed better connections to nuclear-relevant industries. Pacific Northwest saw itself as the expert on projects with former biological weapons experts. And Sandia saw its advantage not in a specific expertise, but in its integrated program structure which pulled together various cooperative programs according to their location.

Because the labs had different interests, needs, and amounts of political clout, their participation in IPP became part of their competition with each other. Additionally, the decentralized power structure of IPP, especially the inability of the program office to adequately influence lab behavior, resulted in a program whose strategy, design, and implementation responded to the needs of the labs, often at the expense of IPP's nonproliferation goals.

THE LABS VERSUS THE DEPARTMENT OF ENERGY. Given the institutional structure and culture of DOE and its laboratories, it is no surprise that IPP's administrative office had frequent problems exercising control.

---

159. Interview with Los Alamos National Laboratory staffer 1, May 21, 2002; interview with Los Alamos National Laboratory staffer 2, May 28, 2002; interview with Los Alamos National Laboratory staffer 3, April 29, 2003; interview with Lawrence Livermore National Laboratory staffer 7, April 2, 2003; interview with Lawrence Livermore National Laboratory staffer 8, April 3, 2003; interview with Sandia National Laboratory staffer 4, May 5, 2003; and interview with Sandia National Laboratory staffer 7, May 5, 2003.

160. Interview with Lawrence Livermore National Laboratory staffer 8, April 3, 2003; interview with Lawrence Livermore National Laboratory staffer 12, April 3, 2003; and interview with Sandia National Laboratory staffer 5, May 5, 2003.

There were three predominant issues from the beginning. One was that IPP was disenfranchised from the rest of DOE. The program had often been seen as alien to DOE's mission and, as a consequence, was not supported by department management.[161] According to the GAO, IPP's director had also complained of inadequate political and material support from the Department in dealing with the labs and with the State Department.[162]

A second problem was the inability of IPP headquarters to coordinate and lead the individual programs at each lab. When IPP was initially created, the labs were in charge. Headquarters was a small office with little power that served mainly as a liaison between the labs and DOE. PIs were free to pursue projects that interested them, and to use their own resources and intuition to make cooperation happen.[163] The labs merely kept DOE informed about their activities. Moreover, Los Alamos, Livermore, and Sandia held the most power and tended to see DOE and IPP's administrative office as an infringement on their authority. This lack of coordination led to different understandings about IPP's mission both within and between U.S. labs. According to analysis by Frederick Kellett, some labs and PIs saw IPP's mission as engagement, others focused on job creation, and still others saw their goal as keeping tabs on activities at former Soviet institutes.[164] As a consequence, different IPP projects engaged companies for different reasons and with divergent long-term consequences.

A third problem stemmed from interagency relations. As several different agencies were seeking to implement new programs in the former Soviet Union in the early 1990s, the labs pursued IPP with little coordination with the Defense Department, the Science Centers, or the National Security Council. Many other U.S. cooperative programs with Russia found the lab people to be irresponsible and self-centered in their dealings with the Russians.[165]

In the fall of 1997, IPP got a new program director, who was charged with improving relations with the State Department and the National Security Council and getting better control over IPP's finances, a task that was reinforced by the GAO's subsequent investigation of the program. This new director was William Desmond. One of Desmond's first changes was to strengthen IPP's headquarters by giving it a greater role in funding distribution. Previously, IPP funding was dispersed

---

161. U.S. Congress, *Energy and Water Development Appropriations for 1999*, p. 684.

162. General Accounting Office, *Nuclear Nonproliferation: Concerns with DOE's Efforts*, p. 22.

163. Interview with Lawrence Livermore National Laboratory staffer 2, April 1, 2003; interview with Lawrence Livermore National Laboratory staffer 8, April 3, 2003; interview with Los Alamos National Laboratory staffer 3, April 29, 2003; and interview with Los Alamos National Laboratory staffer 8, May 1, 2003.

164. Kellett, *USIC and the Initiatives for Proliferation Prevention*, pp. 7, 23.

165. Interview with Los Alamos National Laboratory staffer 3, April 29, 2003; interview with former U.S. government official 4; June 2, 2003; interview with non-governmental organization staffer 1, Feb. 22, 2007; and interview with Department of Energy official 5, August 12, 2003.

from a DOE field office in Albuquerque, New Mexico. In 1998, this function was shifted to IPP's Washington, D.C. office and additional staff were hired to provide auditing and oversight.[166] Previous IPP projects were audited, and a stricter financial accounting system was imposed on the labs. The Inter-Laboratory Board was reorganized to include more representation from smaller labs, and Thrust 1 projects were discouraged. IPP's headquarters was also relocated to DOE's Office of Arms Control and Nonproliferation, which also housed other programs with similar missions.[167] Dedicated staff and a new director also were hired for the United States Industry Coalition, which was also relocated to Washington, D.C. from Albuquerque, New Mexico.

Although the changes seemed to improve both accountability and interagency relations, the cost came in support from the labs. Some of the PIs I interviewed accused Desmond of delaying projects for which he could not claim credit.[168] Others believed he hated Russia and because of this he wanted IPP to fail, or that the Russians hated him because he promised more than he could deliver.[169] Most PIs, with some legitimacy, felt that the labs created IPP and used their own energy and money to forge relationships with Russia that were now being taken away from them by bureaucrats in Washington, D.C.

The increased power and responsibility vested in IPP's headquarters, plus congressional restrictions on spending at the U.S. labs, combined to create resentment among the labs and individual PIs, even after Desmond's departure. Most PIs complained of too much bureaucracy and delay. Because of this, a significant number of people I interviewed claimed that they would cease to be involved with IPP once their current projects were finished. Some saw IPP's headquarters as siding too often with DOE rather than the labs in disputes over policies and resources.[170] Others saw headquarters as imposing rules on all the labs in response to a transgression from only one.[171]

There was one additional consequence of this troubled relationship between the labs and DOE: building support for IPP. The U.S. national laboratories are not supposed to lobby. Instead, DOE is responsible for building support for programs in Congress and with the public. Because of the independence of the labs and concerns about

---

166. U.S. Congress, *Energy and Water Development Appropriations for 1999*, p. 683.

167. Ibid., p. 684.

168. Interview with Los Alamos National Laboratory staffer 4, June 23, 2003; interview with Lawrence Livermore National Laboratory staffer 8, April 3, 2003; and interview with Oak Ridge National Laboratory staffer 8, February 20, 2003.

169. Interview with Lawrence Livermore National Laboratory staffer 8, April 3, 2003; and interview with Los Alamos National Laboratory staffer 3, April 29, 2003.

170. Ibid.; interview with Oak Ridge National Laboratory staffer 1, February 19, 2003; and interview with Oak Ridge National Laboratory staffer 10, February 19, 2003.

171. One interviewee (Sandia National Laboratory staffer 8, May 5, 2003) illustrated this with the claim that IPP took the approach that if one person gets cancer, everyone should go on chemotherapy.

speaking "off the script," however, the Department hesitated to ask PIs and IPP managers to present the IPP program to Congress.[172] This is unfortunate, given that most PIs were enthusiastic supporters of their projects and could explain them in great detail, often brandishing examples of products their projects have produced. The United States Industry Coalition was also charged with this public outreach, but it was generally seen as uninterested in providing the "information" that would be useful for advocacy purposes and, given USIC's lack of technical expertise, ineffective at presenting the unique abilities of the labs or their IPP projects.[173] USIC also had significant trouble getting lab PIs to share the project information, stories, and photos that would form the basis of a campaign for more public and congressional support.[174]

THE LABS VERSUS THE STATE DEPARTMENT. In many ways, IPP and the Science Centers, especially Science Center Partner Projects, performed duplicate functions. Initially, when both IPP and the Science Centers were being developed, there was some competition between them, as well as problems with coordination, policy development, and administrative matters, such as State Department clearance for U.S. lab employees to travel to Russia. There were also disputes over money. Originally, Senator Pete Domenici's proposal for IPP requested $50 million in funding, but this was reduced to $35 million, largely due to pressure from the State Department.[175] Because of State Department reluctance to make this money available, Los Alamos and Livermore accused the Science Centers of trying to steal funds that were meant for IPP. Some in the Departments of Defense and State felt that the U.S. lab scientists sought to distinguish IPP by making grandiose claims about their projects and their own abilities. The labs, in turn, thought that the State Department was partially responsible for the GAO's negative review of IPP in 1999. There were also personality clashes that complicated matters.

After that time, however, relations improved, largely because each program continued with minimal interference from the other. Most coordination happened through interagency reviews that focused on dual-use issues, overall policy goals, and specific nonproliferation interests. Also, the Science Centers began to administer some IPP collaborations as Partner Projects. But there was no review that aimed at coordinating

---

172. Interview with U.S. government official 6, May 28, 2002; interview with non-governmental organization staffer 10, July 24, 2007; and interview with Lawrence Livermore National Laboratory staffer 11, April 7, 2003.

173. Interview with Lawrence Berkeley National Laboratory staffer 1, March 31, 2003; interview with Sandia National Laboratory staffer 3, May 5, 2003; and interview with Los Alamos National Laboratory staffer 3, April 29, 2003.

174. The United States Industry Coalition published a periodic newsletter called E-Notes which frequently asked the labs for such information. However, according to my interviews at the Coalition, the labs almost never responded.

175. Interview with Lawrence Livermore National Laboratory staffer 8, April 3, 2003; and interview with former State Department staffer 1, July 16, 2003.

similar projects or insuring that the same project was not funded by two different programs.[176] Similarly, as of 2007, IPP continued to fund projects at institutes that the Science Centers considered to have sufficient enough support to "graduate" from U.S. financing.[177]

There appeared to be more substantive coordination with respect to projects with former biological weapons experts. Some PIs that I interviewed said they worked with the International Science and Technology Center to fund what would otherwise be Thrust 1 projects, returning them to IPP as Thrust 2 projects when a commercial partner was secured.[178] However, there appeared to be no formal or routine method for cooperation on project development or funding between IPP and State, or for that matter, collaborative research with former biological weapons experts that was funded by the Defense Department programs.

Many PIs, however, were convinced there was greater competition between IPP and the Science Centers, and this was especially true at Los Alamos and Livermore. Even in 2003, a few PIs still claimed that the State Department was trying to sabotage IPP.[179] More claimed that the State Department added people to IPP delegations or required debriefings after trips as a means of gathering intelligence about interesting projects that could be pursued through the Science Centers.[180] The most frequent complaint I heard during my interviews was that the State Department delayed approval for U.S. lab employees to travel to Russia or canceled their trips at the last minute, largely as a means of harassing IPP. According to my interviews with former State Department employees, the U.S. labs often ignored U.S. government rules and procedures for visiting

---

176. In interviews, PIs acknowledged that this lack of review was problematic because they suspected a small number of former Soviet experts submitted the same projects to the Science Centers, IPP, and sometimes also the Nuclear Cities Initiative. One former weapons designer at Livermore suggested that such duplication should be expected. According to this interviewee, the U.S. nuclear weapons labs submit their own duplicate projects to the Defense Nuclear Agency and the Defense Threat Reduction Agency because the staffs change every few years and therefore they do not recognize the duplication. Interview with Lawrence Livermore National Laboratory staffer 8, April 3, 2003.

177. Government Accountability Office, *Nuclear Nonproliferation: DOE's Program to Assist Weapons Scientists*, p. 7.

178. Interview with Pacific Northwest National Laboratory staffer 1, March 12, 2003; interview with Pacific Northwest National Laboratory staffer 9, March 6, 2003; interview with Pacific Northwest National Laboratory staffer 10, March 6, 2003; and interview with Los Alamos National Laboratory staffer 10, June 2, 2003.

179. Interview with Sandia National Laboratory staffer 6, May 5, 2003; and interview with Lawrence Livermore National Laboratory staffer 5, April 1, 2003.

180. Interview with Lawrence Livermore National Laboratory staffer 5, April 1, 2003; interview with Lawrence Livermore National Laboratory staffer 8, April 3, 2003; interview with Oak Ridge National Laboratory staffer 8, February 20, 2003; and interview with Los Alamos National Laboratory staffer 3, April 29, 2003. Even though the United States denies that IPP and the Nuclear Cities Initiative used their trips to Russia to gather intelligence for the CIA, two PIs told me that they were approached by the CIA and that they went out of their way to look for specific information during their trips to Russia.

Russia, and the State Department sought to enforce these rules, in some cases perhaps with a vengeance.[181]

Regardless of the degree to which these complaints were exaggerated, or personality-dependent, it is the case that relations between the Science Centers and IPP were never close. The cooperation that did exist was largely the result of personal networking or ad hoc relationships. However, this underlying animosity was also seldom translated into direct competition between the programs for funding or public support. In fact, it was hard to find congressional testimony or other public statements in which program officials directly criticized each other. Instead, cooperation seemed to be governed by a truce under which each program went its separate way, avoiding both competition but also the prioritization of issues and projects that would have been necessary for better coordination.

Organizational Interest and IPP

IPP was intimately tied to the U.S. national labs. Laboratory PIs were responsible for project design and implementation. The labs convinced U.S. businesses to take part in IPP. Laboratory personnel bore most of the burden for trouble-shooting problems in Russia and convincing institutes and their WMD experts to participate in the program. And, within the United States, the political clout and pressure of the labs was largely responsible for domestic support and funding for IPP.

It was the organizational interests of the labs that started and enabled IPP. The special skills and technical nature of nuclear weapons compelled lab experts to reach out to their counterparts in the Soviet Union. Drawn together by their common scientific interests, the nuclear weapons labs on both sides combined to push their institutes and governments toward mutually beneficial cooperation. They did so despite a legacy of mistrust from the Cold War, and in the absence of higher-level rapprochement between the United States and Russia.

But allowing the labs such discretion also led to liabilities. IPP strategy and funding tended to be a consequence of logrolling between the labs, rather than overall program priorities and guidance. IPP's headquarters was unable to impose accounting and recordkeeping improvements. As a result, the program suffered because of excess spending in the United States, poor accounting and recordkeeping, and an inability to clearly demonstrate engagement and job creation for WMD experts. The labs treated Russian institutes as their own subcontractors and, in the process, inhibited the relationships that were critical to sustained cooperation between Russian WMD experts and their U.S. business partners. Cooperation with other U.S. government programs, especially the State Department, also suffered. And the desire to continue U.S.-Russian col-

---

181. Interview with State Department official 1, May 1, 2007; interview with Department of Energy official 5, August 12, 2003; interview with former U.S. government official 4, October 2, 2007; and interview with former State Department official 4, May 5, 2007.

laboration eventually resulted in a shift toward engagement for the sake of transparency.[182]

Each of these problems had its roots in the decentralized power structure within DOE and the traditional independence of and competition between the U.S. national laboratories, especially the nuclear weapons institutes. To fit in, IPP had to become subordinate to the organizational interests of the U.S. labs. In the process, it sacrificed its ability to achieve its original nonproliferation goals.

---

182. The GAO, in 2007, uncovered evidence that another shift in goals might be taking place. They discovered that IPP had joined with DOE's Global Nuclear Energy Partnership and was using its program money to fund projects aimed at expanding commercial nuclear power, despite having no congressional authorization to do so. See Government Accountability Office, *Nuclear Nonproliferation: DOE's Program to Assist Weapons Scientists*, p. 7.

Chapter 7

The Nuclear Cities Initiative

Despite the activities of the Science Centers and Initiatives for Proliferation Prevention (IPP), by the mid-1990s, there was growing concern about economic conditions in Russia's ten "closed nuclear cities."[1] Seeking a decidedly different approach, the United States launched the Nuclear Cities Initiative (NCI) in 1998. NCI focused on the cities at the heart of Russia's nuclear weapons complex and aimed not just to create jobs for weapons experts, but also to improve job opportunities, economic conditions, and the social welfare of entire communities. The program also was supposed to help Russia reduce the physical size of its weapons complex and convert the freed-up buildings and space to commercial development.

NCI proved to be quite controversial. For many in Washington who were already skeptical of Cooperative Threat Reduction, the program looked too much like welfare. Some in the U.S. labs lobbied against any projects that were not focused on weapons expertise. And when NCI failed to meet expectations for funding and job creation, relations with Russia also became more problematic. By 2003, the program had created fewer than 2,000 jobs, had been the subject of two critical investigations by the Government Accountability Office (GAO), and had seen several of its most high-profile efforts fail. These events reinforced the concerns of George W. Bush's administration about the value of the program. In September 2003, an argument with Russia over who would assume liability for such cooperation became the excuse to stop activities, and the program was given three years to wind up its operations.

Like the Defense Department's early conversion projects, which are the subject of Chapter 4, much of the responsibility for NCI's poor performance can be explained by domestic politics in the United States. Relations with Russia also deserve some of the blame. Both of these factors put considerable pressure on NCI to demonstrate unambiguously that its projects could result in jobs for weapons workers.

---

1. See, for example, U.S. Congress, Senate, Committee on Governmental Affairs, Permanent Subcommittee on Investigations, *Global Proliferation of Weapons of Mass Destruction*, Part II, March 13, 20 and 22, 1996, 104th Cong., 2nd sess., S. Hrg. 104-422 Part II, p. 176.

However, I argue that this explanation is incomplete. NCI made choices about how to appease its critics that were a reflection of its organizational environment. In particular, the program lacked the support of its parent agency—the Department of Energy (DOE)—and was unable to control or marshal the resources of its partners—the U.S. national labs. As a result, NCI could do little to protect itself from domestic political forces in both the United States and Russia that were growing weary of the compromises needed for cooperation. In a last-ditch attempt to prove itself, NCI focused its resources and attention on two projects, both of which were favored by key U.S. and Russian players. With their failure, NCI exhausted its financial and political resources and therefore its ability to continue operations.

The Nuclear Cities Initiative

Russia's nuclear cities were home to the bulk of the Soviet Union's nuclear weapons and nuclear energy resources They were governed as "closed administrative territories"; that is, they were funded directly by the Ministry of Atomic Energy (Minatom), existed only for their nuclear-related functions, and movements to or from them were tightly controlled by Russia's internal security forces. This isolation brought a measure of security, but also meant limited economic opportunities. In the post–Cold War years, they were hit hard by wage delays from the Russian federal government, and the result was dire economic conditions for the scientists, engineers, and technicians in these cities, who had few alternative opportunities. The August 1998 collapse of the ruble made the situation much worse.

Concern about the Soviet Union's core nuclear weapon experts manifested itself within a small network of academics, policy experts, and U.S. laboratory personnel. Some of these individuals knew each other from previous stints in government, others from common academic pursuits. They also had connections to academic and technical experts in Russia, as well as to Lev Ryabev, the deputy minister in charge of Russia's nuclear cities.

The genesis of NCI was a 1995 workshop in Moscow that focused on plutonium management. At that workshop, members of Princeton University's Center for Energy and Environmental Studies (CEES) had informal discussions with people from several of the cities in Russia's plutonium production complex.[2] Experts from Zheleznogorsk, in particular, were interested in converting part of their facilities to make industrial silicon, and the Princeton group introduced them to scientists from the U.S. labs at Los Alamos and Sandia to investigate possibilities.[3] Anatoli

---

2. The nuclear policy research group at the Center for Energy and Environmental Studies (CEES) became the Program on Science and Global Security at Princeton University's Woodrow Wilson School of Public and International Affairs.

3. This would eventually become Silicon of Siberia, a job-creation project that received funding from both the Defense Enterprise Fund and the Initiatives for Proliferation

Diakov, a Russian physicist based at the Moscow Physical Technical Institute (MPTI) who had also worked for a time at Princeton, helped facilitate cooperation with Minatom.

In May 1997, and again in 1998, the Princeton group, along with members of the U.S.-based Russian-American Nuclear Security Advisory Council, met with Ryabev, who in turn introduced them to municipal and institute leaders in the nuclear cities.[4] The Russians were very candid about the economic problems facing the cities and their need for outside help.[5] Together, this group formulated a program that would focus specifically on three nuclear cities: Sarov, Snezhinsk, and Zheleznogorsk.

The idea for NCI got a further boost from people in the U.S. national labs and IPP who were frustrated with what they saw as a growing and heavy-handed bureaucracy at DOE headquarters in Washington, D.C.[6] Separately, the Pacific Northwest lab proposed sharing the results of its own conversion efforts with the Russians, and approached DOE about arranging such a visit in 1997.[7] The proposal won the support of Rose Gottemoeller, who at the time was director of the Office of Nonproliferation and National Security at DOE, and was thus in a position to help leverage department and lab resources. When the Gore-Chernomyrdin Commission met in March 1998, creating NCI was on the agenda.[8] The United States and Russia signed an agreement to start the program on September 22, 1998.

Although NCI's goal was first and foremost to create new civilian jobs for former Soviet nuclear workers, from the start its mission was significantly different from other knowledge nonproliferation efforts. Most obviously, NCI's focus was solely on nuclear weapons scientists, and only on those found in the closed nuclear cities. Second, NCI's mission was broader than simply the creation of permanent civilian jobs for nuclear weapons workers. It was also responsible for helping the nuclear cities improve their living standards and create more hospitable business environments. Therefore, NCI took part in efforts to improve health care, support drug treatment programs, develop Internet connections, and establish business support and training activities. Third, NCI's job-creation efforts

---

Prevention program.

4.   Kenneth Luongo, the director of this group, was a former Clinton administration official with ties to the CEES group at Princeton. The Russian-American Nuclear Security Advisory Council (RANSAC) has since changed its name to the Partnership for Global Security.

5.   Interview with non-governmental organization staffer 4, June 3, 2004; and interview with Los Alamos National Laboratory staffer 3, April 29, 2003.

6.   Interview with Los Alamos National Laboratory staffer 3, April 29, 2003; interview with Lawrence Livermore National Laboratory staffer 8, April 3, 2003; and interview with Lawrence Livermore National Laboratory staffer 2, April 1, 2003.

7.   Interview with Pacific Northwest National Laboratory staffer 2, March 23, 2003.

8.   The Gore-Chernomyrdin Commission brought together senior U.S. and Russian officials to discuss key issues in U.S.-Russian relations. It was established in April 1993, originally to focus on cooperation on space and energy issues, but its mandate was soon extended to a number of areas, especially issues of economic and technical cooperation.

were limited to the open parts of the nuclear cities; that is, to buildings and facilities that were outside of the security perimeter surrounding the weapons institutes. Therefore, NCI was responsible for brokering agreements with Russia to reduce the size of its nuclear weapons complex by handing over facilities to the municipal governments in the nuclear cities and making that space available for commercial businesses. Finally, NCI was charged with encouraging other U.S. government and multilateral agencies to focus their resources on projects in the nuclear cities.

NCI faced political trouble from the start. Unlike other scientist engagement and redirection efforts, NCI did not enjoy the full support of Congress. In particular, in agreeing to create NCI, the House of Representatives required the Secretary of Energy to report on the program's objectives, processes, milestones, and timeline, and then wait twenty legislative days before receiving any funds.[9] NCI was also the subject of one investigation by the Government Accountability Office that began almost before NCI had started work, and another after the program was only two years old.[10] In 2002, the political unpopularity of aid for "community development" forced NCI to eliminate all of its projects that did not focus on job creation and complex downsizing.

In a move that was partially intended to forestall possible closure, NCI was merged with IPP to form Russian Transition Initiatives in 2002. That same year, DOE directed the program to wind down its activities in Snezhinsk and Zheleznogorsk in favor of concentrating on work in Sarov. In 2003, however, the Bush administration announced that NCI would cease operations altogether by the end of the year. The excuse was the expiration of NCI's implementing agreement with Russia. At the time, the United States and Russia were engaged in a disagreement about who would assume liability for any accidents or acts of sabotage in cooperative national security programs. The United States wanted Russia to assume all responsibility; Russia balked. Although eventually a compromise was reached, both NCI and DOE's plutonium disposition program were stalled. NCI never recovered. In September 2003, it was given three years to finish its current projects in Russia. For all practical purposes, NCI ceased operations in September 2006.[11]

NCI PROJECTS AND PROCESSES
Over time, NCI engaged in several types of activities including job creation, conversion, and downsizing of the Russian nuclear complex, community development projects, and efforts to leverage other U.S.

---

9. See U.S. Congress, House, *Strom Thurmond National Defense Authorization Act for Fiscal Year 1999*, 105th Cong., 2nd sess., September 22, 1998, House Rpt. 105-736, Section 3133 (B).

10. General Accounting Office, *Nuclear Nonproliferation: Concerns with DOE's Efforts to Reduce the Risks Posed by Russia's Unemployed Weapons Scientists*, Washington, D.C. (February 1999); and General Accounting Office, *Nuclear Nonproliferation: DOE's Efforts to Assist Weapons Scientists in Russia's Nuclear Cities Face Challenges*, Washington, D.C. (May 2001).

11. For a time, a staff member did remain at the office the program had shared with Initiatives for Proliferation Prevention.

government programs to spend their resources in Russia's nuclear cities. Moreover, as will become clear below, many of these areas were inter-related. Various examples of these projects are described below, along with the processes by which NCI put together, implemented, and oversaw them. Like IPP, NCI relied heavily on personnel from the U.S. national laboratories. However, in the case of NCI, its headquarters in Washington, D.C. tended to assume a much greater role in strategic direction for the program and in managing U.S. lab involvement.

NCI PROJECTS. Most of NCI's activities were directed at job-creation projects. Job creation under NCI was different from other scientist redirection efforts in a variety of ways. Most obviously, NCI job-creation efforts were confined to the closed cities of Sarov, Snezhinsk, and Zheleznogorsk. Accounts vary as to why these three cities were selected among the ten closed nuclear cities that were part of the Russian nuclear complex. According to perhaps the most plausible story, the choice was based upon an analysis of need.[12] Of these ten cities, four had significant income from their participation in the U.S. agreement to purchase highly-enriched uranium from Russia, and also sold services associated with the nuclear fuel cycle. Three other cities were closed to foreigners because of their sensitive security functions: they manufactured and dismantled nuclear warheads. That left the cities of Sarov, Snezhinsk, and Zhelez-nogorsk. The other story is that Minatom chose these cities for various reasons ranging, in the opinion of some, from whim to plans for their own conversion efforts.[13]

Regardless of why the cities were chosen, it is clear that Minatom made NCI's expansion contingent on first demonstrating success at Sarov, Snezhinsk, and Zheleznogorsk.[14] Moreover, these three cities were not treated equally. Because of Minatom's preferences, the greater promi-nence of Sarov and Snezhinsk in Russia's future nuclear weapons com-plex, and the relative clout of the U.S. labs they were partnered with under NCI, more job creation funds and projects went to Sarov and Snezhinsk, leaving Zheleznogorsk a somewhat distant third.[15]

---

12. This account is based on Jill Cetina, Oleg Bukharin, and Frank von Hippel, *Defense Conversion and Small Business Development: A Proposal for Two IFC Projects in Three of Russia's Closed Nuclear Cities* (Princeton, N.J.: Center for Energy and Environmental Studies, Princeton University), PU/CEES Report 306, March 1998, p. 11; "New Opportunities for Nuclear Security Cooperation," Russian-American Nuclear Security Advisory Council (RANSAC) meeting, Moscow, April 7–11, 1998; interview with Los Alamos National Laboratory staffer 1, May 21, 2002; and interview with non-governmental organization staffer 4, June 3, 2004.

13. Interview with Nuclear Cities Initiative staffer 1, May 29, 2002; interview with Lawrence Livermore National Laboratory staffer 2, April 1, 2003; and interview with Los Alamos National Laboratory staffer 3, April 29, 2003.

14. Interview with Nuclear Cities Initiative staffer 1, May 29, 2002.

15. Interview with Pacific Northwest National Laboratory staffer 4, March 4, 2003; interview with Pacific Northwest National Laboratory staffer 7, March 5, 2003; interview with Department of Energy official 4, May 29, 2002; interview with Sandia National Laboratory staffer 1, May 2, 2003; and interview with Los Alamos National Laboratory staffer 1, May 21,

Besides working in only three locations, NCI job-creation efforts were different from the Science Centers and IPP in other important ways. First, NCI was not limited to recruiting only U.S. partners, and worked with a variety of enterprises, including companies based in Russia. In Zheleznogorsk, for example, NCI sponsored a project with the Russian company Razvitie to employ former weapons workers in the production of satellite antennas for Internet connections.[16] NCI also funded Russian businesses that were interested in regional expansion, such as one project involving a pre-existing company in Krasnoyarsk that wanted to expand its production of pre-insulated pipes.[17] NCI projects also had a greater focus on marketing to local or regional Russian markets, rather than foreign ones. For example, several projects involved the development of local Internet and telecom services and the production of medical supplies for local use.

NCI job-creation activities also tended to be biased in favor of low-tech projects and, in contrast to IPP, projects involving production rather than services. Although NCI initially flirted with larger, more high-tech projects such as Silicon of Siberia—an effort to convert a weapons facility in Zheleznogorsk to make isotopically-pure silicon—most projects involved items on par with canola packaging and processing, making simple PET scanners, and manufacturing construction supplies. Projects that involved the provision of services emphasized weaning the provider off of U.S. government contracts and diversifying their customer bases. For example, both the Sarov Open Computing Center (sometimes called Sarov Labs) and the Snezhinsk Open Computing Center (called Strela in Russia) initially subsisted on contracts from the U.S. labs, but expanded to include work for U.S. companies as well as contracts with Russian entities.

Also, job-creation efforts tended to favor community needs or public goods. For example, with a project manager from the Savannah River Site and $20,000 from NCI, a Sarov group was able to win a $250,000 contract with the Nizhny Novgorod regional government for the development and use of their innovative road-repair truck technology.[18] Another example is a project with a Spokane-based wood importer and the city of Zheleznogorsk that focused on manufacturing energy-efficient windows.[19]

Additionally, because of NCI's dual focus on conversion and job creation, it worked with former weapons experts to create spin-off enterprises, rather than engaging experts who remained employed by

---

2002. According to Department of Energy, Nuclear Cities Initiative, "Nuclear Cities Initiative Accomplishments," September 16, 1999, during its first two years when it was most active, NCI started an estimated 21 projects in Sarov, 22 in Snezhinsk and 15 in Zheleznogorsk. At the time, Zheleznogorsk received less than 15 percent of NCI project spending.

16. Interview with Pacific Northwest National Laboratory staffer 7, March 5, 2003.

17. Ibid.

18. Interview with Nuclear Cities Initiative staffer 3, May 29, 2002; and interview with Savannah River Site staffer 2, May 29, 2002. Apparently, the truck does a good job of patching small pot holes and cracks in the highway.

19. Interview with Pacific Northwest National Laboratory staffer, March 5, 2003.

their parent weapons laboratories. This led, for example, to the creation of computer programming and software development centers, independent think tanks doing research on arms control and other policy issues, and private companies that acted as subcontractors for NCI and provided market analysis, business development, and audits in support of other NCI projects.

Finally, many of NCI's larger job-creation efforts were duplicated in more than one nuclear city. For example, there were two job-training centers, two computing services centers, and, initially, NCI funded three research centers aimed at nonproliferation issues.[20]

The spirit of NCI's job-creation efforts is perhaps best illustrated by the activities of Itek, a Russian company created by six former weapons workers in Snezhinsk.[21] Through previous work with the United States on nuclear materials security, some of these workers became interested in the application of bar code technology for the Russian market. A colleague at the U.S. laboratory of Oak Ridge helped them formulate a proposal to NCI to support efforts to market U.S. bar code technology in Russia. With $395,000 in funding from NCI, Itek formulated a marketing strategy and subsequently adapted this technology for the Russian market by developing Cyrillic bar codes and readers. The company sold its products and services to the United States for use in nuclear materials security activities with Russia. After three years in operation, Itek had grown to twenty-one full-time and twenty-three part-time workers and was consistently profitable.

Besides job creation, NCI's other main emphasis was facilitating reductions in the size of the Russian nuclear weapons complex. Here, the focus was almost exclusively on Sarov. The first major downsizing effort was aimed at the Avangard Electromechanical Plant. This facility, which used to employ some 2,700 in the assembly and disassembly of nuclear warheads, was scheduled by Minatom for complete closure in 2003.[22] NCI negotiated with Minatom to remove the security fences that surrounded some of Avangard's buildings, and renovate and return these buildings to the city for use as a commercial technopark. After NCI spent some $1.5 million, the technopark opened in 2000; it used four buildings which together made up 500,000 square feet of space that used to be part of Avangard's weapons work.[23] NCI then spent additional funds creating seven

20. Of these centers, only the Analytic Center for Nonproliferation at Sarov remained in existence as of 2008.

21. This summary is based on interview with Oak Ridge National Laboratory staffer 6, February 20, 2003; interview with Oak Ridge National Laboratory staffer 1, February 19, 2003; and General Accounting Office, *Nuclear Nonproliferation: DOE's Efforts to Assist Weapons Scientists in Russia's Nuclear Cities Face Challenges*. Itek was actually co-owned by the workers and the city administration of Snezhinsk and Itek workers were required to leave the employment of VNIITF.

22. Department of Energy, Nuclear Cities Initiative, "Nuclear Cities Initiative Program Status," July 19, 2000.

23. Ibid.; and General Accounting Office, *Nuclear Nonproliferation: Concerns with DOE's Efforts to Reduce the Risks Posed by Russia's Unemployed Weapons Scientists*, p. 18.

projects at the technopark. These projects included the production of shock absorbers for cars, high voltage switches, oil and gas instruments, sheet metal, pumps for contaminated drains, and work on a metro light rail system.

Originally, part of the space in the technopark was intended to go to Fresenius, a U.S. company that manufactured kidney dialysis equipment and supplies. But, due to delays, the Russians gave the space to another company.[24] Fresenius reached an agreement with NCI and Avangard to remove an additional building from Avangard's secure area and convert it for use in the development, production, and marketing of kidney dialysis equipment. Jobs estimated as a result of this project ranged from two hundred to one thousand.[25] IPP was to invest $3 million, NCI $1.5 million, Fresenius would provide $6 million in equipment, and Russia would contribute an additional $500,000 in financing.[26] By the end of 2001, the security fence at Avangard had been moved and the building was ready for renovation. But, for various reasons that are explained more fully below, there were delays and disagreements and the venture never materialized.

The other main downsizing activity was the development of a strategic plan for accelerated conversion at Sarov. Based upon suggestions from the city administration of Sarov and the All-Russian Research Institute of Experimental Physics (VNIIEF), its main nuclear weapons research and development institute, Los Alamos proposed a portfolio of ideas for quick-start conversion projects and an investment fund for the city in 1999.[27] NCI, however, delayed consideration of the plan. In 2000, the plan was revived, and the United States and Russia agreed to create a working group to identify the kinds of jobs required for the city, strategize on how to create those jobs, estimate the costs, and coordinate implementation through NCI.[28] DOE, however, never made the resources available to implement the plan or asked Congress to include the cost in NCI's budget. As a result, only a few ad hoc projects went forward.

Another part of NCI's resources were directed toward community development projects. Because the nuclear cities were in remote areas and designed to be isolated, NCI funded a variety of activities to encourage business development and improve local living standards. One area focused on infrastructure, specifically telecommunications and Internet improvements. Another initiative aimed to improve health care. For

---

24. Some of these delays were due to disagreements about financing and ownership of the new facility and whether the project should involve NCI, IPP, or both. Interview with Nuclear Cities Initiative staffer 5, May 29, 2002.

25. Department of Energy, Nuclear Cities Initiative, "Fresenius," undated internal document.

26. Interview with Nuclear Cities Initiative staffer 5, May 29, 2002.

27. Interview with Los Alamos National Laboratory staffer 1, May 21, 2002.

28. James W. Toevs, "Sarov, Russia: The Sarov Demonstration Project," Forum on European Nuclear Cities Initiative, December 12–13, 1999, Rome.

example, NCI supplied equipment for a Sarov Telemedicine Center in order to enable Sarov medical specialists to communicate in real time with experts at the Medical College of Georgia and hospitals in Nizhny Novgorod.[29] There were also training programs for health care providers, drug rehabilitation services, and the purchase of equipment for specific procedures such as laparoscopy. To bolster civil society, the mayors of U.S. cities that were home to nuclear weapons facilities exchanged visits with their Russian counterparts to discuss common problems with conversion and other issues.[30] A Rotary Club was created in Snezhinsk. Programs were initiated to discuss drug and alcohol dependence, retirement, and child welfare.

The highest profile community development activities were the International Development Centers (IDCs). The IDCs involved representatives from NCI or its designate, the local city administration, and the nuclear facility.[31] Besides encouraging these groups to cooperate on the economic development of the city, the IDCs helped local entrepreneurs to improve their business skills and plans, offered English language lessons and computer training, provided a service center for foreigners visiting the cities to check out opportunities for investment or business development, and scouted for other potentially interested businesses. The IDCs also provided market analysis, planning, and other advice for NCI projects. IDCs were established in Snezhinsk and Zheleznogorsk; Sarov already had other organizations that essentially served the same functions as an IDC, and it feared increased U.S. involvement in the city's strategic planning and financial decision-making.[32]

The fourth category of NCI activities was leveraging other programs to spend some of their own resources in the nuclear cities. Here, the two main efforts were Sister Cities and a loan program through the European Bank for Reconstruction and Development (EBRD). Until it was reorganized in 1999, the United States Information Agency funded exchanges under its Sister Cities program, whereby foreign and U.S. cities were paired for cultural, social, and educational exchanges.[33] Through this program, the State Department funded Sister Cities programs between Los Alamos and Sarov, Livermore and Snezhinsk and Maryville, Tennessee (home to Oak Ridge Laboratory) and Zheleznogorsk. As Sister Cities, Los Alamos and Sarov, for example, had exchange visits of teachers, students, medical professionals, and newspaper reporters. At one point,

29. Department of Energy, "Russian Transition Initiatives," *Transitions*, Vol. 1, No. 1 (2002), pp. 1–4.

30. Interview with Nuclear Cities Initiative staffer 1, May 29, 2002.

31. NCI participation in the IDC in Zheleznogorsk was administered by the Foundation for Russian-American Economic Cooperation (FRAEC), a non-governmental organization based in Seattle.

32. Interview with non-governmental organization staffer 5, March 4, 2003; and interview with Pacific Northwest National Laboratory staffer 4, March 4, 2003.

33. In 1999, such exchanges were moved to the State Department's Bureau of Educational and Cultural Affairs.

Los Alamos scientists, who reported on the financial hardships in Sarov, used the relationship to collect assistance funds from Los Alamos residents.[34]

NCI also worked with EBRD to expand its loan services to the nuclear cities. EBRD provided small loans for local entrepreneurs in Central Europe and the former Soviet Union. In Russia, it was very difficult to get access to such financing, and to do so for a reasonable interest rate. NCI approached the bank because it wanted to encourage grassroots economic activities in the cities that would respond to local demand. As a result, NCI gave $1.5 million to EBRD in December 1999 to establish loan offices in the nuclear cities and thus make it easier for local residents to access the bank's funding opportunities.

NCI PROCESSES. Similar to IPP, NCI project generation and implementation involved personnel from the U.S. national laboratories working with their counterparts in Russia's nuclear weapons complex. In contrast to the decentralized structure of IPP, overall program direction, oversight, and funding allocations in NCI were determined by a staff based in Washington, D.C., at DOE's National Nuclear Security Administration (NNSA) in the Office of Defense Nuclear Nonproliferation. Until NCI ceased new activity in September 2003, its D.C.-based staff included a program director, technical and administrative staff, and desk officers who focused specifically on individual Russian nuclear cities as well as functional activities, such as community development, that occurred in more than one city.

The U.S. labs had Principal Investigators (PIs) who oversaw portfolios of projects, usually in one particular nuclear city. The vast majority of NCI activities were concentrated at Los Alamos, which was the lead lab on projects in Sarov; Livermore, which was partnered with Snezhinsk; and Sandia, which was most involved with Zheleznogorsk.[35] The other U.S. labs that were involved in NCI also tended to concentrate on one Russian city, although there were exceptions. For example, Pacific Northwest at one time managed the IDCs in both Snezhinsk and Zheleznogorsk, and Oak Ridge had projects in all three Russian cities. Some projects, such as the nonproliferation research centers, were overseen directly by NCI headquarters, not by personnel from the U.S. labs.

Cooperation between NCI's headquarters and U.S. lab participants was mostly accomplished by periodic teleconferences and working group meetings. There were meetings specific to individual cities, functions, and also particular projects. Cooperation between the U.S. and Russian

---

34. "Los Alamos and Arzamas-16: The "Sister Cities" Relationship," *Los Alamos Science*, No. 24 (1996), pp. 44–47.

35. For example, in fiscal year 2001, NCI spent some $10 million at Los Alamos, Livermore, and Sandia combined, $1.7 million at Oak Ridge, another $838,000 at Pacific Northwest, and less than $1 million at all the other labs combined. See U.S. Congress, House, Committee on Appropriations, *Energy and Water Development Appropriations for 2002, Part 6: Department of Energy*, 107th Cong., 1st sess., May 3, 9, 2001, pp. 156–157.

governments with respect to NCI happened in the form of the U.S.-Russian Joint Steering Committee, which was composed of senior officials from U.S. and Russian agencies and, in particular, DOE, the Ministry of Atomic Energy, and its successor, the Federal Agency for Atomic Energy (Rosatom). The Steering Committee met twice a year to review recent activities, map out future strategies and priorities, and settle any disagreements or other problems.

NCI projects originated from personnel at the U.S. labs, Russian weapons institutes, the local governments of the nuclear cities, or NCI's headquarters. Ideas were put on a list of possible projects and further developed by teams of PIs and former weapons experts in Russia, then circulated among NCI headquarters and lab staff to gauge the level of interest and determine whether the project had been tried before, and then set baseline estimates for funding. If a private company needed to be involved in the project, the U.S. and Russian lab experts used networks they had developed through their own research to find and draw in such businesses.[36] Job-creation and conversion projects also involved business plans and market analysis, which were put together by NCI staff in conjunction with private business consultants, or occasionally the IDCs in the cities themselves.[37] Projects involved negotiations about the plan of work, funding levels, and the roles of all participants; before they were finalized, projects also required the concurrence of the Russian partners, Rosatom, and DOE.[38]

While project development in the United States was mostly a task for lab and NCI headquarters personnel, most project-selection decisions fell to NCI headquarters, in cooperation with Russian institute and city managers. NCI based project selection on a variety of criteria. Overall guidelines included the numbers of jobs created for weapons experts, the cost per job, maximizing benefits per dollar spent in the nuclear cities, the ability to replicate projects in more than one city, and the amount of industry involvement.[39] More specific criteria were then applied to different categories of projects.

The most elaborate criteria were for job-creation projects. Here an emphasis was placed on avoiding dual-use issues and, in particular, the degree to which the resulting enterprise and its profits would be independent of the Russian weapons institute. Other factors included the total

---

36. Interview with Lawrence Livermore National Laboratory staffer 6, April 2, 2003; and interview with Los Alamos National Laboratory staffer 9, May 1, 2003. According to some project managers, if the goal was commercialization or research services, the best partners were in the West. If the goal was to produce something, then the best partners were local Russian ones.

37. Interview with Lawrence Livermore National Laboratory staffer 6, April 2, 2003. From my interviews, it seems that the detail provided by these business and market analyses varied widely. Also, some PIs used the International Development Centers and paid a few thousand dollars, while other paid tens of thousands to international management consulting firms.

38. Department of Energy, Nuclear Cities Initiative, "Draft Program Guide," October 2002.

39. Nuclear Cities Initiative website, http://www.nci.nn.doe.gov (accessed March 1, 2000).

cost and number of jobs created, any resulting ancillary job creation, the number of former weapons experts who would be employed, the status and quality of the project's business and market plans, equipment and infrastructure costs, intellectual property rights, expected duration and size of U.S. funding, and the role of Russian and other participant funding and resource commitments.[40] Sustainability was also an important criterion. NCI would also fund job creation through a variety of models, including start-ups working with already proven technology, research to test or improve a technology of commercial interest, and small businesses in need of initial help.[41] In all cases, however, Congress required the project to become economically viable within three years after initial receipt of NCI funding.[42]

Community development projects were selected according to slightly different criteria. These included whether the project satisfied a critical need in the local community, the project's impact on the community, the time needed for implementation, the degree to which local community resources would be involved, the number of jobs created, and whether the project could be duplicated in other cities.[43]

In practice, however, NCI's project selection was, at times, skewed toward other variables. For example, there is some evidence that DOE and the U.S. interagency process were more likely to approve job creation rather than community development projects, regardless of merit.[44] At times, NCI also approved projects in order to split work more evenly among the U.S. labs.[45] Partly, this was because it was inefficient for any one lab to have only one or a few projects, and partly because PIs needed more than one project in order to have a credible presence in a Russian nuclear city.[46] Because of a preference for projects that could be imple-

---

40. Department of Energy, Nuclear Cities Initiative, "Business Workshop: NCI Project Selection Criteria," September 21, 1999; Department of Energy, Nuclear Cities Initiative, "Draft Program Guide," October 2001; and Department of Energy, Nuclear Cities Initiative, "Program Guide," October 2002.

41. Department of Energy, Nuclear Cities Initiative, "Program Guide," October 2001.

42. The requirement for sustainability within three years is specified in U.S. Congress, *Floyd D. Spence National Defense Authorization Act for FY 2001* (PL 106-398), 106th Cong., 2nd sess., sections 3172 (d)(2)(c) and (e)(2)(b)(iii). Concern over sustainability figured into NCI's project selection criteria. Projects needed to specify cost, sales, and revenue projections showing they would no longer need U.S. government funding within three years. Also, NCI evaluated business partners to determine whether they were likely to achieve these goals. See Department of Energy, Nuclear Cities Initiative, "Draft Program Guide," October 2001; and Department of Energy, Nuclear Cities Initiative, "Program Guide," October 2002.

43. According to NCI's guidelines, the size of the impact on the community was more important than the cost of the project, and there was a preference for projects that could be implemented quickly. See Department of Energy, Nuclear Cities Initiative, "Community Development Working Group (CDWG) Briefing Update," July 23, 1999.

44. See, for example, Department of Energy, Nuclear Cities Initiative, "Community Development Working Group (CDWG) Briefing Update," July 23, 1999.

45. Interview with Department of Energy official 4, May 29, 2002.

46. Ibid.

mented quickly, NCI also funded ideas that had been recycled from the Science Centers or IPP, or agreed to pursue the pet ideas of Russian institute directors regardless of their job creation or nonproliferation merit.[47] Additionally, it is also the case that in its early years NCI did a poor job of developing long-term strategies for engagement. As a result, it tended to fund projects as they came up rather than according to a game plan.[48]

After selection, both job creation and community development projects entered the same interagency review process.[49] First was a technical review that, in general, involved mostly U.S. lab personnel, but which may also have included other government agencies with relevant expertise.[50] It is at this point that NCI considered whether the project overlapped with other U.S. government programs and whether NCI could draw upon their experience or entice them to cooperate.[51] Next was a review for dual-use issues and the degree to which the project might contribute to Russia's military capabilities. This was done by NCI, along with DOE's Division of Nuclear Transfer and Supplier Policy, U.S. lab experts, the Defense Threat Reduction Agency, and, for export control issues, the Department of Commerce. The State Department also looked at projects to make sure that they were consistent with other U.S. goals and, in particular, nonproliferation policy.

After a project finished with all these steps, NCI negotiated any changes needed to get approval from the relevant Russian institutes and agencies, and the project was put on the list for final approval by the U.S.-Russia Joint Steering Committee.[52] Once underway, a project was typically funded for only one year, after which it had to demonstrate progress to receive additional money.[53] NCI projects were monitored through monthly financial reports and quarterly progress reports submitted by U.S. lab PIs.[54]

In contrast to this process, downsizing plans and proposals took a different route. They involved direct negotiations between NCI, U.S. laboratory personnel, and, in Russia, representatives from Rosatom, the relevant nuclear weapons institute, the city administration, and at times the FSB.

---

47. Interview with Oak Ridge National Laboratory staffer 4, February 19, 2003; and interview with Nuclear Cities Initiative staffer 1, May 29, 2002.

48. Interview with Nuclear Cities Initiative staffer 1, May 29, 2002.

49. This description is taken from Department of Energy, Nuclear Cities Initiative, "Draft Program Guide," October 2001; and Department of Energy, Nuclear Cities Initiative, "Program Guide," October 2002.

50. Nuclear Cities Initiative website, http://www.nci.nn.doe.gov (accessed March 1, 2000).

51. Ibid.

52. Department of Energy, Nuclear Cities Initiative, "Draft Program Guide," October 2002.

53. Ibid.

54. Ibid.; and Department of Energy, Nuclear Cities Initiative, "Program Guide," October 2001.

Goals

Over time, NCI focused on four main goals: job creation, downsizing, community development, and leveraging other programs and groups to spend program funds in Russia's nuclear cities. More significantly, NCI sought to differentiate itself from other programs and secure its own future by arguing that all of these goals were interrelated. In what it considered a "holistic" approach, NCI's overall goal was not just the redirection and employment of former weapons experts, but also the transition of Russia's closed nuclear cities from one-product towns to diversified communities with vibrant social services, a variety of civilian economic opportunities, and a civil society that is independent of the nuclear weapons complex. Because of these broader goals, NCI's targets were not just weapons workers but their families, friends, and indeed any resident of the nuclear cities. The key was to embed weapons workers within robust economic and social environments, so they could avoid the temptation of selling their knowledge for financial gain.

Although NCI's goals were interrelated, the relative emphasis on each one changed considerably over time. Despite NCI's vision, for various political reasons it was emphasizing the goals of job creation and downsizing by 2000, and, by 2001, had almost ceased to pursue new opportunities with respect to community development or leveraging. Thanks to the problems IPP had with spending too much money in the U.S. labs and not enough in Russia, NCI adopted the goal of spending 65 percent of its program funds in Russia. Furthermore, because it started off in only three of ten closed nuclear cities, NCI also sought to establish a schedule for completing activities in one place and moving on to eventually work in all of the cities, except for one. Ozersk was excluded because it was thought to have sufficient income from the nuclear fuel storage services at Mayak.[55]

NCI also came to specify detailed metrics for measuring its own progress. Partly this was a legacy of the criticism that NCI faced from the beginning. As a result, the program knew that future funding depended upon a concrete demonstration of success. Such measurements would also help to convince Russia that NCI should be allowed to expand to other cities. Regardless of the reason, NCI's metrics focused on measuring the success of projects that had already been selected, rather than testing whether NCI's project choices or overall approach were valid in the first place. For example, once NCI established the International Development Centers and charged them with providing business training, it focused on measuring the number of people who received business training, rather than trying to understand the impact this training had on entrepreneurship and successful business development in the nuclear cities. Each of these goals is discussed in more detail below.

---

55. Department of Energy, Nuclear Cities Initiative, "Nuclear Cities Initiative Program Status," July 19, 2000; and Department of Energy, Nuclear Cities Initiative, "Program Overview," overhead slides, June 2001. The low number of jobs planned for Snezhinsk was justified by its continued role in the nuclear weapons complex.

JOB CREATION

Job creation was consistently one of NCI's main missions.[56] It had two motivations, both connected to reducing threats faced by the United States. The original goal was to reduce the danger that economically desperate or soon-to-be-unemployed nuclear weapons experts would sell their skills to the highest bidder or steal weapons-relevant materials.[57] In contrast to other U.S. government programs that were initially motivated by fears of emigration, however, from the beginning NCI focused on proliferation via telephone, email, and other means, and on the danger that institute directors would encourage their scientists to market their skills as a means of keeping teams in place and institutes afloat.[58] Also, NCI was unique in that it focused not solely on employment of weapons experts but also on the security of their families. Therefore, in addition to creating jobs for former weapons workers, as a way to encourage those experts to remain in the nuclear cities, NCI also thought it was legitimate to try to create jobs for relatives, friends, and other residents of the nuclear cities.[59]

The second motivation behind job creation was to encourage Russia to reduce the size of its nuclear weapons complex. The Russian government, especially Minatom, was hesitant to dump excess workers into an economy with few job prospects. By creating civilian jobs in the nuclear cities, NCI would encourage such downsizing.[60] Similar to other CTR efforts, the goal was to directly reduce threats faced by the United States, but instead of destroying weapons and launchers, NCI would permanently destroy part of the nuclear weapons production complex.

Although threat reduction due to proliferation and downsizing were both initially part of NCI's mission, the emphasis had shifted to the need for jobs by 2000. Partly, this was due to the fact that by then there had been few documented cases of proliferation via brain drain. But this change was also a consequence of the difficulty of measuring success at countering proliferation. Aside from emigration or proven proliferation, it was very difficult to measure the degree to which NCI had an impact on attitudes toward proliferation. In contrast, NCI followed the example of the Defense Department's Cooperative Threat Reduction activities, the suc-

---

56. For example, one of NCI's first strategy documents highlights the centrality of job creation to NCI's mission. See Department of Energy, Nuclear Cities Initiative, "Program Strategy," August 1999.

57. Interview with Los Alamos National Laboratory staffer 3, April 29, 2003; Department of Energy, Nuclear Cities Initiative, "Nuclear Cities Initiative"; and Walter Pincus, "Funds to Hire Russian Atom Scientists Cut," *Washington Post*, November 12, 1999, p. A08.

58. For example, see Siegfried S. Hecker, "Thoughts About an Integrated Strategy for Nuclear Cooperation with Russia," *Nonproliferation Review*, Vol. 8, No. 2 (Summer 2001), pp. 1–24.

59. General Accounting Office, *U.S. Nuclear Nonproliferation: Concerns with DOE's Efforts to Reduce the Risks Posed by Russia's Unemployed Weapons Scientists*, p. 56.

60. For example, this was a stated mission of NCI by 1999. See Department of Energy, Nuclear Cities Initiative, "Nuclear Cities Initiative (NCI) Status Report and Program Plans," October 1999; and Department of Energy, Nuclear Cities Initiative, "Program Overview," overhead slides, June 2001.

cess of which was widely attributed to the ability to clearly measure how programs reduced direct threats to U.S. security by destroying former Soviet weapons platforms.

It was this desire for downsizing that drove NCI's specific job creation goals. According to NCI, in the late 1990s, the Russian Ministry of Atomic Energy had plans to reduce its work force by 70,000, of whom 30,000–50,000 would be in the nuclear cities, and this became NCI's long-term goal with respect to job creation.[61] The number of jobs needed was further broken down by city, largely on the basis of planned layoffs in each. As a result, job-creation goals were estimated at 6,000–7,000 for Sarov, 2,000 for Snezhinsk, 5,000 for Zheleznogorsk, 10,000 for Seversk, 3,000 for Trekhgorny, 6,000 for Novouralsk, and 4,000 each for Zarechny, Lesnoy, and Zelenogorsk.[62] Of particular importance was the Avangard facility in Sarov. Russia planned to end defense work there entirely, and 2,700 of the jobs projected for Sarov were aimed at redundant defense workers from Avangard.[63]

NCI, however, never intended to create all the necessary jobs on its own. Some job creation in the nuclear cities would come from the Science Centers and IPP. But NCI also focused on ancillary job creation and what it considered to be a more "holistic" strategy.[64] Because of the state of the Russian economy, especially the isolated location and history of the nuclear cities, creating jobs directly would be tremendously expensive and difficult. Therefore, NCI's original plan included community and infrastructure development and job-training activities as a means of making the nuclear cities more attractive to private companies, who might expand or invest there even without subsidies or other assistance from the U.S. government.[65]

Additionally, job creation came to embody a different goal for some in NCI over time, particularly PIs from the U.S. labs. As happened in IPP, many came to see the real value of job creation as a mechanism for engaging Russian nuclear weapons workers. This engagement, in turn, would

61. U.S. Congress, House, *Committee on Appropriations, Energy and Water Development Appropriations, FY 2000. Part 6: Department of Energy,* 106th Cong., 1st sess., March 16, 18, 1999, p. 295; Department of Energy, Nuclear Cities Initiative, "Program Strategy," August 1999; Department of Energy, Nuclear Cities Initiative, "Program Overview," overhead slides, June 2001; and General Accounting Office, Testimony before the Subcommittee on Emerging Threats and Capabilities, Committee on Armed Services, Senate by Gary L. Jones, *Nuclear Nonproliferation: DOE's Efforts to Secure Nuclear Materials and Employ Weapons Scientists,* GAO-01-726T, Washington, D.C., May 15, 2001, p. 3.

62. Department of Energy, Nuclear Cities Initiative, "Nuclear Cities Initiative Program Status," July 19, 2000; Department of Energy, Nuclear Cities Initiative, "Program Overview," overhead slides, June 2001; and U.S. Congress, *Energy and Water Development Appropriations for 2002,* pp. 155–156.

63. Department of Energy, Nuclear Cities Initiative, "Nuclear Cities Initiative Program Status," July 19, 2000.

64. Interview with U.S. government official 6, May 28, 2002.

65. Department of Energy, Nuclear Cities Initiative, "Program Strategy," August 1999. See also U.S. Congress, *Energy and Water Development Appropriations, FY 2000,* p. 360.

help the United States to better understand activities in the Russian nuclear weapons complex and would make that complex more transparent to the outside world.[66]

Regardless of the motivations behind job creation, under NCI these activities were intimately linked to community development. In trying to differentiate itself from other programs, NCI focused on community development activities and how these would build relationships, not just with the directors of the weapons institutes, but also with community and regional governments, and local leaders and entrepreneurs. These relationships, plus NCI's focus on low-tech projects, services, and small to medium-sized business partners, were seen as the key to creating more jobs and doing so more quickly than through IPP.[67]

Soon after its first funding was authorized, NCI came under criticism from members of Congress, backed up by an investigation by the GAO, for having few ways to gauge progress or measure success. In response, by 2000, NCI had developed a series of metrics.[68] With respect to job creation, these included the number of jobs created both directly and indirectly, the number of businesses established or expanded, the number of commercial firms investing in the nuclear cities, the size and type of that investment, and the number of new businesses started, along with their growth in revenue.[69]

By 2002, job creation metrics also included the cost per job created.[70] Based upon U.S. and Russian experience in Sarov, NCI's analysis concluded that it costs $10,000–$11,000 in U.S. funds to create one sustainable job in a nuclear city, with additional funding needed from both Russia and the business partner.[71] Assuming this analysis was correct, NCI would need at least $450 million to create 45,000 jobs in the ten nuclear cities.

DOWNSIZING THE RUSSIAN NUCLEAR COMPLEX

In addition to job creation, NCI's original mission also included negotiating with Russia to close parts of its nuclear weapons complex and

---

66. Interview with Los Alamos National Laboratory staffer 1, April 29, 2003; interview with Lawrence Livermore National Laboratory staffer 11, April 7, 2003; and interview with Lawrence Livermore National Laboratory staffer 6, April 2, 2003.

67. General Accounting Office, *Nuclear Nonproliferation: Concerns with DOE's Efforts to Reduce the Risks Posed by Russia's Unemployed Weapons Scientists*, pp. 52–53; and interview with non-governmental organization staffer 4, June 3, 2004.

68. Interview with Nuclear Cities Initiative staffer 5, May 29, 2002.

69. Department of Energy, Nuclear Cities Initiative, "Report to Congress Pursuant to Section 3172(d) of the National Defense Authorization Act for FY 2001," December 2000; Department of Energy, Nuclear Cities Initiative, "Nuclear Cities Initiative Program Plan," October 2000; Department of Energy, Nuclear Cities Initiative, "Program Guide," Draft, October 2002; and General Accounting Office, *Nuclear Nonproliferation: DOE's Efforts to Assist Weapons Scientists In Russia's Nuclear Cities Face Challenges*, p. 51.

70. Department of Energy, Nuclear Cities Initiative, "Program Guide," Draft, October 2002.

71. General Accounting Office, *Nuclear Nonproliferation: Concerns with DOE's Efforts to Reduce the Risks Posed by Russia's Unemployed Weapons Scientists*, p. 57.

convert them for civilian use. This meant reaching formal agreements for reductions, removing facilities and equipment from the complex to the cities and making these available for commercial development, and then encouraging businesses to take advantage of these facilities and workers.[72] Whereas job creation was an immediate need, downsizing was seen as a more long-term goal.[73]

In addition to reducing threats faced by the United States, the goal was to "right-size" the Russian nuclear weapons complex. During the Cold War, the Soviet nuclear weapons complex had included excess production capacity, as well as redundant facilities. According to U.S. logic, Russia's post–Cold War budgets and its relationship with the United States meant that it needed to and could have a much smaller complex.[74] More specifically, the U.S. opinion was that Russia's nuclear weapons complex should be about the same size and have capabilities similar to that of the U.S. nuclear weapons complex.[75] This symmetry, in turn, would foster more rapid progress in future arms reductions and agreements.[76]

Similar to job creation, the goal of downsizing was closely linked to NCI's other objectives. For example, the purpose of community development activities was to help improve the civilian-based economic opportunities of the cities and, by making Minatom less concerned about the fate of any redundant workers, encourage it to realize its plans for complex downsizing and structuring.[77] Job-creation projects were intended to provide similar encouragement.

Within two years of its beginning, however, NCI began to focus more exclusively on the goal of downsizing, at first only in terms of declared policy, but later this shift was also reflected in NCI's activities. Partly this was due to the unpopularity of community development and infrastructure projects, a change that is described in more detail below. But the goal of downsizing also served to distract from problems with job creation.[78] Although two years was a very short time in which to show progress, NCI was under considerable political pressure in the United States to

---

72. Department of Energy, Nuclear Cities Initiative, "Nuclear Cities Initiative (NCI) Status Report and Program Plans," October 1999; Department of Energy, Nuclear Cities Initiative, "NCI Program Overview," overhead slides, June 2001; and interview with Los Alamos National Laboratory staffer 3, April 29, 2003.

73. Department of Energy, Nuclear Cities Initiative, "NCI," overhead slides, June 1999.

74. General Accounting Office, *Nuclear Nonproliferation: Concerns with DOE's Efforts to Reduce the Risks Posed by Russia's Unemployed Weapons Scientists*, p. 54.

75. Department of Energy, Nuclear Cities Initiative, "Nuclear Cities Initiative Program Plan," October 2000; and Department of Energy, Nuclear Cities Initiative, "Complex Reduction and Russia's Nuclear Cities: Progress with the Nuclear Cities Initiative," April 2002.

76. Department of Energy, Nuclear Cities Initiative, "Nuclear Cities Initiative Program Plan," October 2000.

77. Department of Energy, Nuclear Cities Initiative, "Program Guide," October 2002.

78. Interview with Los Alamos National Laboratory staffer 3, April 29, 2003; and interview with Nuclear Cities Initiative staffer 5, May 29, 2002.

demonstrate success early. Yet not only were few jobs created, but also the U.S. labs involved in NCI often did not agree on the appropriate job-creation strategies. Furthermore, focusing on downsizing as opposed to job creation helped placate congressional and other critics who saw downsizing as a national security strategy, but who continued to think of job creation as welfare or foreign aid.

Downsizing was also more in sync with the goals of key people at Los Alamos and the Russian Ministry of Atomic Energy. Although several Los Alamos experts had played a key role in establishing NCI, many of those who had been involved were becoming disillusioned with the program by early 2000. Some favored more emphasis on cooperating with Russia to secure weapons-relevant materials. Other concerns included what was considered excess or wasted spending on community development projects and the growing realization that access and cooperation with the nuclear cities was becoming harder as Russia's economy improved and the clout of the Russian security forces increased. In an attempt to salvage NCI, Siegfried Hecker, at the time the director of Los Alamos, proposed a plan for accelerated conversion at Sarov.[79] Of all of the nuclear cities, Sarov had the closest connections to Los Alamos. Moreover, Sarov was the focus of Russia's own conversion efforts, and the idea was supported by Minatom's First Deputy Minister, Lev Ryabev.[80] Minatom felt that NCI needed to demonstrate success soon, or it would risk losing the support of the Russian government. Therefore, accelerated conversion was seen as a way of leveraging NCI in support of Russia's own goals, therefore demonstrating the program's continued value to Russia.

In May 2000, NCI was authorized to establish a joint working group on accelerated conversion at Sarov. Although Sarov continued to remain the focus, soon NCI was planning to develop similar plans for each of the nuclear cities.[81] In 2000, NCI planned on completing studies for Sarov, Snezhinsk, and Zheleznogorsk.[82] The next year, NCI's goals included a study that would compare the process of conversion in Russia to that of the U.S. nuclear weapons complex, and apply its lessons to conversion in Russia.[83]

As with job creation, NCI developed specific metrics for downsizing. These were facility closure, which came to be measured in terms of the

79. Interview with Los Alamos National Laboratory staffer 3, April 29, 2003; and Department of Energy, Nuclear Cities Initiative, "Sarov, Russia: Accelerated Conversion and the Open Computing Center," January 17, 2001.

80. Interview with Los Alamos National Laboratory staffer 3, April 29, 2003; and interview with Nuclear Cities Initiative staffer 5, May 29, 2002.

81. Department of Energy, Nuclear Cities Initiative, "Nuclear Cities Initiative Program Plan," October 2000; and Department of Energy, Nuclear Cities Initiative, "Nuclear Cities Initiative (NCI) Status Report and Program Plans, FY 2000."

82. Department of Energy, Nuclear Cities Initiative, "Nuclear Cities Initiative (NCI) Status Report and Program Plans, FY 2000."

83. Department of Energy, "Internal DOE Report on Programs in Russia, 2001"; and Department of Energy, Nuclear Cities Initiative, "Program Overview," overhead slides, June 2001.

number of buildings and square feet that were removed from the weapons complex, reductions in the number of employees in the complex, and the amount of infrastructure that had been upgraded or created for use in civilian commercial activities.[84]

COMMUNITY DEVELOPMENT

Although downsizing came to be seen as NCI's unique contribution to U.S. nonproliferation efforts, initially NCI saw its comparative advantage in community development.[85] Community development was a key means by which NCI would reach its goal of having a significant positive impact on both the economic and social lives of the nuclear cities.[86] Also, because job creation and downsizing were more long-term activities, community development was seen as a means of making a more immediate positive impact on the cities.[87]

NCI engaged in community development with several goals in mind. Infrastructure improvements, such as better telecommunications, Internet access, industrial parks, and business development and business services centers, were aimed at making it easier, cheaper, and thus more attractive for businesses to employ residents of the nuclear cities, relocate part of their activities there, or initiate new investments.[88] These activities would also make it easier for local entrepreneurs to start their own commercial ventures. By offering training in marketing, management, and other business skills, NCI hoped to serve as a catalyst for these local entrepreneurs, whether they were weapons workers seeking civilian jobs or friends and family of these workers.

A third goal for community development projects was to increase the strength of civil society in the nuclear cities. Throughout their existence, almost all aspects of city life had been dominated by the nuclear weapons institutes and Minatom. Community development activities were designed to increase the role of city administrations and others in planning for the future of the cities and diversifying the city's business activities beyond those that were authorized by or connected to the nuclear weapons institutes.[89] The hope was that building civil society

---

84. Department of Energy, Nuclear Cities Initiative, "Report to Congress Pursuant to Section 3172(d) of the National Defense Authorization Act for FY 2001," December 2000; Department of Energy, Nuclear Cities Initiative, "Program Guide," October 2001; Department of Energy, Nuclear Cities Initiative, "Program Guide," Draft, October 2002; and General Accounting Office, *Nuclear Nonproliferation: DOE's Efforts to Assist Weapons Scientists In Russia's Nuclear Cities Face Challenges*, p. 51.

85. Community development activities were part of the government-to-government agreement establishing NCI. See Department of Energy, Nuclear Cities Initiative, "Nuclear Cities Initiative Program Plan," October 2000.

86. Department of Energy, Nuclear Cities Initiative, "Program Plan," May 18, 1999.

87. Interview with U.S. government official 6, May 28, 2002.

88. Department of Energy, Nuclear Cities Initiative, "Community Development and Jobs Creation."

89. Department of Energy, Nuclear Cities Initiative, "Nuclear Cities Initiative Program

would, in turn, help create networks between the cities and political and economic interests in surrounding communities and at the regional level.

Finally, community development was also a path to downsizing. In the Russian nuclear complex, workers received a variety of health, educational, and social benefits through the workplace. By duplicating some of these activities in the cities, the goal was to encourage more workers to retire or relocate, and to reduce stress among those who had already been laid off and might be tempted to share their weapons knowledge as a means of improving their living standards.[90]

Metrics to measure the success of community development efforts centered on the number of training courses offered and the number of people who took advantage of them, but also included factors such as whether there was a project found to match significant needs in each community, the size of the impact on the community, the amount of credit and investment provided by the European Bank for Reconstruction and Development and other lenders to local businesses, and the number of people using the services of the International Development Centers.[91]

Community development activities soon proved problematic. Overall, they raised issues within Congress about whether NCI was just welfare for weapons scientists.[92] Community development was also unpopular with many U.S. lab PIs, who saw these projects as a waste of money and time because they did not involve nuclear weapons experts or activities for which lab skills were necessary.[93] In particular, there were complaints from Los Alamos, Livermore, and Sandia that community development activities were really an excuse for the other U.S. nonnuclear weapons labs to be involved in NCI.[94] Los Alamos, which was a major driving force in NCI, also tended to favor the IPP approach, which

---

Plan," October 2000; and Department of Energy, Nuclear Cities Initiative, "Program Overview," June 2001.

90.   Interview with U.S. government official 6, May 28, 2002; and Department of Energy, Nuclear Cities Initiative, "Community Development and Jobs Creation."

91.   Department of Energy, Nuclear Cities Initiative, "Nuclear Cities Initiative Program Plan," October 2000; Department of Energy, Nuclear Cities Initiative, "Report to Congress Pursuant to Section 3172(d) of the National Defense Authorization Act for FY 2001," December 2000; Department of Energy, Nuclear Cities Initiative, "Program Guide," October 2001; Department of Energy, Nuclear Cities Initiative, "Program Guide," October 2002; General Accounting Office, *Nuclear Nonproliferation: Concerns with DOE's Efforts to Reduce the Risks Posed by Russia's Unemployed Weapons Scientists*, pp. 53–55; and General Accounting Office, *Nuclear Nonproliferation: DOE's Efforts to Assist Weapons Scientists In Russia's Nuclear Cities Face Challenges*, p. 51.

92.   Interview with Nuclear Cities Initiative staffer 1, May 29, 2002.

93.   For example, PIs opposed NCI financing loans in the nuclear cities from the European Bank for Reconstruction and Development, reasoning that this project took money away from "real" NCI projects and the people in the cities could always get loans elsewhere, a claim which was often stated but greatly exaggerated given the high interest rates charged at local banks.

94.   Interview with Sandia National Laboratory staffer 6, May 5, 2003; interview with Oak Ridge National Laboratory staffer 1, February 20, 2003; and interview with Lawrence Livermore National Laboratory staffer 6, April 2, 2003.

focused on high-tech research and development projects, and not the more multi-pronged efforts, supported by NCI headquarters, that included substantial emphasis on community development activities.[95] Finally, the Russian government and Minatom also disliked community development projects, and considered them a diversion of money that would otherwise go toward job creation.

The unpopularity of community development projects came to a head in 2001, when the GAO issued a report that was highly critical of NCI's current activities and its ability to succeed in the future. As a result, NCI cancelled many of its future community development projects, although it did continue to fund the IDCs.[96] Additionally, it was around this time that Rose Gottemoeller, who had long been a champion of both NCI and community development, left her position as deputy undersecretary for defense nuclear nonproliferation at DOE, and support for these projects was further eroded.[97]

LEVERAGING MONEY

Because of the size of the problem it was created to address, it was unlikely that NCI would receive enough funding to make more than a dent. Therefore, one of NCI's core goals was to "lead, link, and leverage" other U.S. government, non-government, and Russian groups to spend some of their own program funds in the nuclear cities.[98] Early efforts focused on DOE, Science Center, and later European programs such as the European Nuclear Cities Initiative and Technical Aid to the Commonwealth of Independent States (TACIS), the European Union's technical and foreign assistance program. But NCI's biggest successes were with EBRD, the U.S. Information Agency, and an alliance of non-profit organizations and universities that provided funding for the Analytical Center for Non-Proliferation in Sarov.

To measure the success of its leverage efforts, NCI looked at the level of external financing coming into the cities, the amount of funds other programs spent in the nuclear cities, Russia's own investment and in-kind contributions and, at one time, the ratio of total projects in the nuclear cities to NCI-funded projects.[99]

95. Interview with Nuclear Cities Initiative staffer 5, May 29, 2002.

96. Ibid.; interview with U.S. government official 6, May 28, 2002; and interview with Savannah River Site staffer 1, February 21, 2003.

97. Interview with U.S. government official 6, May 28, 2002; interview with Lawrence Livermore National Laboratory staffer 2, April 1, 2003; and interview with Los Alamos National Laboratory staffer 1, April 29, 2003.

98. Department of Energy, Nuclear Cities Initiative, "Nuclear Cities Initiative Program Status," August 15, 2000; and Department of Energy, Nuclear Cities Initiative, "Nuclear Cities Initiative Program Plan," October 2000.

99. Department of Energy, Nuclear Cities Initiative, "Report to Congress Pursuant to Section 3172(d) of the National Defense Authorization Act for FY 2001," December 2000; Department of Energy, Nuclear Cities Initiative, "Program Guide," October 2001; and Department of Energy, Nuclear Cities Initiative, "Program Guide," October 2002.

Because it was seen to take money and time away from job creation and downsizing, NCI's leveraging goals were unpopular with program critics, many U.S. lab PIs, and Minatom. Therefore, NCI eventually was forced to move away from these projects. Also, according to NCI, it did a poor job of exploiting contacts and its own experiences leveraging money, and overcoming donor hesitation about working on nuclear issues or in the nuclear cities.[100]

SPENDING IN RUSSIA

Because of the criticism leveled at IPP for the amount of project funds going to the U.S. labs, NCI began to focus more on the goal of spending a certain amount of its program funds in Russia. In the fiscal year 2000 defense authorization bill, Congress specified that at least 51 percent of program funds had to be spent in Russia. As a result, NCI adopted this goal for 2001 and increased the amount to 65 percent for 2002.[101] The amount of money spent in Russia subsequently became a metric for the program.

TIME FRAME

In terms of realizing its overall goals, NCI's initial expectation was that it would show "significant results" in five to ten years, assuming it received the necessary funding.[102] More specifically, NCI planned to expand to additional nuclear cities, creating a specified number of jobs in each one and 45,000 overall. Initially, the assumption was that within three to four years, NCI could demonstrate significant progress in downsizing activities in Sarov, Snezhinsk, and Zheleznogorsk.[103] Then, NCI's plan was to add a new city per year, starting with Zarechny and eventually expanding to include all the cities except Ozersk. Originally, the timeline had NCI working in an additional city by 2000, in all nine cities by 2008, and closing up operations by 2011.[104] However, these plans were consistently pushed back due to limited progress in the original three

---

100. Department of Energy, Nuclear Cities Initiative, "A Chronicle of Outreach for Alternative Funding Sources for the Nuclear Cities Initiative—1998–2001," June 2001.

101. General Accounting Office, Testimony by Gary L. Jones, *Nuclear Nonproliferation: DOE's Efforts to Secure Nuclear Materials and Employ Weapons Scientists*, p. 2.; and Department of Energy, Nuclear Cities Initiative, "Program Guide," October 2001. Initially, NCI claimed that it would spend 75 percent of project funds in Russia but, according to one person I interviewed, this figure was included for political reasons and NCI immediately backed away from it, adopting what it considered the more realistic goal of spending 65 percent of all funding in Russia. Interview with Department of Energy official 4, May 29, 2002.

102. "Nuclear Cities Initiative," http://www.nci.nn.doe.gov (accessed March 1, 2000).

103. U.S. Congress, *Energy and Water Development Appropriations for 2002*, pp. 156–157, 159; U.S. Congress, House, Committee on Appropriations, *Energy and Water Development Appropriations for 2001. Part 6: Department of Energy*, 106th Cong., 2nd sess., March 21, 23, 2000, p. 553; and interview with U.S. government official 6, May 28, 2002.

104. Department of Energy, Nuclear Cities Initiative, "Nuclear Cities Initiative (NCI) Status Report and Program Plans"; and Department of Energy, Nuclear Cities Initiative, "Nuclear Cities Initiative Program Status," August 15, 2000.

cities. Eventually, because of funding and other restrictions, the target was narrowed to Sarov, where the original goal of completing work by 2004 was eventually extended to 2008.[105]

Measuring Progress

Similar to the Defense Department's early conversion efforts, NCI had a short life. Its first project funding became available in March 1999; new funding ended in September 2003; and it essentially ceased operations in September 2006.[106] Despite this abbreviated time frame, NCI had significant success at job creation, with its projects leading to employment for 1,600 people. It is also directly responsible for negotiating the closure of the Avangard facility in Sarov in 2003 and converting some 550,000 square feet to civilian use as a technology park.

Other indicators of success, however, proved elusive. NCI did a poor job of analyzing and documenting the results of its efforts. Progress toward many of its goals was inherently difficult to measure, and the program invested little time in trying to prove its impact on such ambiguous areas as economic improvement and social life. Instead, NCI chose to report data on individual projects, such as bank loans or individuals trained at NCI-funded business centers. And, even here, NCI did not consistently publicize its results. NCI argued that many of its activities would likely have an indirect influence on job creation. Yet, while NCI did report the results of its job-creation projects, it made no effort to document jobs created tangentially through other activities. Finally, the quarterly reports from the U.S. labs that served as the source for much of NCI's data collection followed no consistent guidelines, often contained little that was useful for assessing progress toward goals, or were the product of gross estimates. As a result, NCI was unable to clearly demonstrate progress or contradict the claims of its critics that it was unfocused, had too many broad goals, and was a waste of money.

JOBS CREATED

Initially, NCI's activities focused on community development and downsizing, rather than job creation. For example, of the approximately 26 projects NCI initiated during its first two years, less than half were devoted to job creation.[107] Despite the significant barriers to starting a new program and doing work in the nuclear cities, during those two years NCI started projects that led to an estimated 370 jobs.[108] Most of these jobs were

105.   Department of Energy, Nuclear Cities Initiative, "Program Overview," June 2001.

106.   Department of Energy, Nuclear Cities Initiative, "Nuclear Cities Initiative Program Status," August 15, 2000.

107.   General Accounting Office, *Nuclear Nonproliferation: DOE's Efforts to Assist Weapons Scientists in Russia's Nuclear Cities Face Challenges*, pp. 3–4, 19–20.

108.   General Accounting Office, Testimony by Gary L. Jones, *Nuclear Nonproliferation: DOE's Efforts to Secure Nuclear Materials and Employ Weapons Scientists*, p. 2.

concentrated in Sarov at the Open Computing Center, which employed 100, and the Analytical Center for Non-Proliferation, which had a staff of 30.[109] As many as 25 people were employed in each of eight other job-creation projects scattered between the cities.[110] By 2005, NCI reported creating approximately 1,600 jobs in the nuclear cities, far below the 13,000–14,000 jobs that the program had hoped to create in Sarov, Snezhinsk, and Zheleznogorsk.[111]

These job-creation totals refer to people employed through projects in which NCI had a direct financial investment. NCI, however, also aimed to create jobs in a variety of indirect ways, including business training, a loan program through the European Bank for Reconstruction and Development, and other activities. It is unclear, however, whether NCI ever monitored or recorded jobs created through these activities, even though such numbers were consistently a metric by which NCI claimed to judge success. There is, however, anecdotal evidence. For example, in 2003, NCI claimed that of the 4,000 workers who had been laid off at the All-Russian Research Institute of Technical Physics (VNIITF) since 1998, NCI had helped Russia find jobs for all of them using job-creation projects (most specifically the Strela Open Computing Center, the Itek company, and SPEKTR-Conversia, VNIITF's own conversion-directed spin-off); training and other support so that local businesses could employ additional workers; and redirecting some functions to the city government.[112] There is also evidence of small-business creation and expansion through the NCI-funded loan program.

Furthermore, NCI did a poor job of following up on its job-creation activities, and it is unclear whether it ever collected information about the fate of its projects once NCI involvement ended or after funding for new projects was terminated in September 2003.[113] Although NCI received quarterly reports from the U.S. labs about their NCI projects, there is no evidence that NCI consistently collected data on its projects, had a comprehensive database, or gathered information in a systematic

---

109. Department of Energy, Nuclear Cities Initiative, "Nuclear Cities Initiative (NCI) Status Report and Program Plans."

110. Ibid.

111. Matthew Bunn and Anthony Wier, *Securing the Bomb 2005: The New Global Imperatives* (Cambridge, Mass., and Washington, D.C.: Project on Managing the Atom at Harvard University and Nuclear Threat Initiative, May 2005), p. 55; and Fred Weir and Mark Clayton, "US-Russia Effort to Contain Nuclear Experts Fades," *Christian Science Monitor*, September 20, 2006, p. 1. According to Analytical Center for Non-Proliferation, "Quarterly Information Bulletin," Issue 25 (2005), Sarov, Russia, p. 12, NCI created 1,000 jobs in Sarov alone.

112. "Visible Impact on the Cities," http://www.nnsa.doe.gov/na-20/nci/about_impact. shtml (accessed August 2, 2007).

113. NCI's estimates for job creation in projects were often very ambiguous. Even though the collaboration between Fresenius and Avangard was a critical NCI project on which much attention and resources were focused, job estimates for the project ranged from 200 to over 3,000. See Department of Energy, Nuclear Cities Initiative, "Fresenius." Additionally, in my interviews with U.S. lab PIs, many were uncertain of the jobs that had been created through their projects, and several did not consider it their responsibility to find this information.

fashion. Using NCI documentation and reports from DOE, it appears that NCI eventually funded an estimated seventy projects that would have resulted either directly or indirectly in job creation.[114] Many of these projects, however, never got off the ground. Others, such as SPEKTR-Conversia, were initially promising, but then later failed or significantly cut back on their activities.[115] Therefore, with the exception of a few favored projects, it is unclear how many people found sustainable jobs as a result of NCI.

NCI also did a poor job of reporting its other metrics for job creation. For example, there were almost no reports of the cost per job created or the number of commercial firms with new investments in the nuclear cities. And there were only a few reports about the number of businesses created or expanded.[116]

Finally, it is unclear how many of these jobs went to former weapons workers. Officially, NCI defined its mission as fighting proliferation by improving the quality of life in the nuclear cities. Therefore, most NCI officials and PIs were content to create jobs for anyone who lived in these cities, reasoning that eventually the benefits would trickle down to the weapons workers.[117] My interviews suggest that very few PIs asked for lists of people that would be involved in their projects, and even fewer made attempts to validate their weapons skills. Also, according to work by the GAO, during NCI's first two years, most weapons experts worked on projects part-time, and therefore continued to work at their original jobs in the Russian nuclear weapons complex. Therefore, NCI may have been indirectly subsidizing weapons research and development in Russia.[118]

---

114. NCI eventually was involved in an estimated 34 projects in Sarov, 13 in Snezhinsk, and 23 in Zheleznogorsk. Many of these are described in Department of Energy, Nuclear Cities Initiative, "Ongoing Projects," http://www.nnsa.doe.gov/na-20/nci/projects.shtml (accessed on August 2, 2007).

115. SPEKTR-Conversia was intended as a contract research and development center that would employ VNIITF workers in developing and testing technologies for civilian businesses and institutes. After a promising start, SPEKTR eventually employed an estimated 357 people. After August 2000, however, VNIITF stopped providing funding to the center and gave its employees a choice of returning to work in the weapons complex or going it alone. About 60 people chose to stay on with SPEKTR and were sustained largely through grants from NCI and IPP. As of 2002, the company had grown to 80–103 full-time workers, but its future was uncertain. See Department of Energy, Nuclear Cities Initiative, "Annual Report," fiscal year 2002, Washington, D.C.; Yuriy Rumyantsev and Aleksey Kholodov, "Conversion Challenges in Russian Nuclear Cities," *Nonproliferation Review*, Vol. 10, No. 3 (Fall–Winter 2003), p. 175; and Department of Energy, Russian Transition Initiatives, "Focus on Spektr-Conversia, *Transitions*, Vol. 1, No. 2 (Fall 2002), p. 3.

116. For example, NCI reported that it had helped create or expand fifteen businesses in 2003. See Department of Energy, Nuclear Cities Initiative, "NCI Program," July 2003.

117. This attitude was widespread at the eight U.S. labs where I conducted interviews.

118. General Accounting Office, Testimony by Gary L. Jones, *Nuclear Nonproliferation: DOE's Efforts to Secure Nuclear Materials and Employ Weapons Scientists*, p. 2.

DOWNSIZING THE RUSSIAN NUCLEAR WEAPONS COMPLEX

Because of the persistence and diligence of NCI, Russia eventually made good on its commitment to close the Avangard Electromechanical Plant in Sarov in 2003. With funds from both NCI and the Russian Ministry of Atomic Energy, the security fence around the facility was moved, and several buildings were cleaned out and refurbished to form a technopark on 550,000 square feet of converted space. NCI's only other major downsizing success was in Zheleznogorsk, where, in 2004, some equipment that had previously been used to process plutonium for nuclear weapons was converted for use in a commercial niobium producing project.[119]

NCI's other downsizing goals included implementing accelerated conversion plans in the nuclear cities. Although such plans were completed in 2000, only the one for Sarov was eventually signed and partially implemented.[120]

COMMUNITY DEVELOPMENT

NCI undertook community development activities to help improve the economic and social lives of the nuclear cities, strengthen civil society, lessen the monopoly influence of Minatom on decision-making in the cities, and encourage downsizing by making a variety of benefits available through means other than employment in the nuclear complex. Unfortunately, only anecdotal evidence is available about progress toward these goals. For example, the Sarov city administration developed more independence from the nuclear complex and increased its interaction with regional political and economic authorities. Zheleznogorsk also experienced similar changes, although to a lesser degree.[121] Snezhinsk remained more firmly tied to the federal government and the nuclear complex. It is unclear what role, if any, NCI played in these transitions, however. NCI did little to analyze its influence in these areas, and few independent measures are available. One exception was the "Quarterly Information Bulletin" put together by the Analytical Center for Non-Proliferation at Sarov, which routinely published information about demographics in the city, services, and interaction with regional authorities.[122] The other was improvement of the telecommunications infrastructure, especially

---

119. Department of Energy, "Performance and Accountability Report," Washington, D.C., fiscal year 2004, p. 132.

120. Department of Energy, "Internal DOE Report on Programs in Russia, 2001," pp. 18–19.

121. For example, because of the limited defense work in Zheleznogorsk, the Russian Ministry of Atomic Energy interfered less in the city's administration. As a result, the NCI-funded International Development Center was left largely on its own; it was able to develop a close relationship with the city administration and implement standard decision-making rules that emphasized consensus. Interview with Pacific Northwest National Laboratory staffer 4, March 4, 2003; and interview with non-governmental organization staffer 5, March 4, 2003.

122. The Analytical Center for Non-Proliferation at Sarov published its "Quarterly Information Bulletin" from 1999 to 2006. In February 2006, however, NCI ended funding for the program. The bulletins can be found on the web through http://www.ransac.org.

Internet services in all three cities, which was completed in 2003 and funded mostly by NCI.[123]

NCI's own metrics for measuring progress in community development instead focused on the narrow indices of numbers of training courses, people who attended them, people using the services of the International Development Centers, and the amount of credit and investment provided through the European Bank for Reconstruction and Development. Even here, NCI did not consistently report results. What is known is that during its first eighteen months of operations, NCI spent about $1 million on community development and funded about twelve projects.[124] As of May 2004, NCI had provided business-related training to an estimated 2,000 people, mostly through the International Development Centers.[125] During 2000, these Centers provided services to, on average, 40 people a month.[126] And through 2000, the lending program made some 250 loans in the nuclear cities.[127] Little else is known about progress in achieving NCI's community development goals.

LEVERAGING MONEY

NCI eventually convinced other organizations and government agencies to commit some $1.38 million of their own program funds to activities in the nuclear cities.[128] Also, as of May 2003, NCI reported industry contributions of $24.7 million, plus an additional $55 million for conversion and job-creation projects from the Russian Ministry of Atomic Energy.[129] The nuclear cities themselves also made in-kind contributions, such as paying rent and utilities for buildings, paying city employees to help develop and oversee NCI projects, and paying travel expenses for some personnel.[130]

PROGRESS TOWARD OTHER GOALS

Like IPP, NCI eventually had to adopt as a metric the amount of funding spent in Russia versus in the United States at the U.S. national labora-

---

123. Michael Roston, "Reported Accomplishments of Threat Reduction and Nonproliferation Programs, By Agency," Policy Update, RANSAC, Washington, D.C. (July 2004), p. 10.

124. General Accounting Office, *Nuclear Nonproliferation: DOE's Efforts to Assist Weapons Scientists in Russia's Nuclear Cities Face Challenges*, p. 20.

125. Roston, "Reported Accomplishments of Threat Reduction and Nonproliferation Programs, By Agency," p. 10.

126. Department of Energy, "Performance and Accountability Report," Washington, D.C., fiscal year 2000, p. A70.

127. Department of Energy, Nuclear Cities Initiative, "Program Overview," February 2001.

128. Department of Energy, Nuclear Cities Initiative, "Nuclear Cities Initiative Program Status," August 15, 2000.

129. Michael Roston and David Smigielski, "Accomplishments of Selected Threat Reduction and Nonproliferation Programs in Russia, By Agency," RANSAC, Washington, D.C., June 10, 2003, p. 10.

130. U.S. Congress, *Energy and Water Development Appropriations, FY 2000*, p. 156.

tories. During its first two years, over 70 percent of NCI's funding was spent in the United States, mostly for overhead and labor costs.[131] Soon thereafter, however, the program was merged with IPP into Russian Transition Initiatives, which was required to limit U.S. expenses to 25 percent. Subsequently, no additional information about NCI's spending patterns was made available.

Also, NCI had plans to expand its activities to six other nuclear cities. Although it did discuss with Minatom the possibility of activities in Zarechny, NCI remained confined to its three cities until it ceased new project funding in 2003. Moreover, NCI operations in Snezhinsk began to wind down before this, largely due to rejuvenated Russian defense funding. Needless to say, NCI did not meet its goal of completing its work in either Sarov by 2008 or in all nine cities by 2011.

Explaining Outcomes

More than any other engagement and redirection program, NCI was influenced by domestic politics in the United States and Russia. Partly, the program was a victim of the times. Soon after NCI was created in 1998, the Russian economy began to recover, and the government grew weary of the compromises needed for such cooperation. As the power of the FSB grew, the Ministry of Atomic Energy became less able to ensure access to the nuclear cities and less inclined to expend its political clout for a program that did not quickly demonstrate success. In the United States, the Republican-controlled Congress disliked NCI's community development projects, and tightly linked future funding to success at job creation and conversion. This linkage, however, was so strict that it made it even more difficult for NCI to successfully implement its projects.

This story is not complete, however, without understanding the organizational context within which NCI was asked to function. The program was caught between the proverbial rock and a hard place. On one side was a department that found NCI's goals anomalous and was often embarrassed by its lack of success. Therefore, it was slow to approve NCI's projects, did little to maintain or increase budgets, and was a poor public advocate for the program. On the other side were the U.S. nuclear weapons labs, which initially fought any NCI projects that did not involve scientific cooperation and increasingly became disillusioned with the program. As a result, NCI held more closely to its previous decisions and strategies. Rather than engage in a battle for more money or public support, the program chose to concentrate on a small number of projects and make the case that success with these would vindicate its strategy. Unfortunately, given the circumstances in Russia, the U.S.

---

131. According to the GAO, 96 percent of NCI's money that was spent in the United States went to the U.S. national labs, and of this 75 percent was spent on overhead and labor. See General Accounting Office, Testimony by Gary L. Jones, *Nuclear Nonproliferation: DOE's Efforts to Secure Nuclear Materials and Employ Weapons Scientists*, pp. 2, 10; and Department of Energy, Nuclear Cities Initiative, "Program Overview," February 2001.

Congress, and DOE, NCI no longer commanded the resources necessary to ensure this success. With the failure of these projects, NCI's future was increasingly called into question.

PROBLEMS WITH RUSSIA

More than any other job-creation program, some of NCI's problems can clearly be traced to Russia. There were important differences between the types of projects the Ministry of Atomic Energy wanted and those favored by NCI. Focusing on the closed nuclear cities also inherently meant problems with economic diversification and access to facilities and workers. Because NCI's mandate involved work in these cities and direct cooperation with Minatom, many of these problems could not be avoided. However, NCI made choices about goals and projects partly in response to the political circumstances it had to negotiate in the United States. As a result, it is likely that many of the problems that arose from having to work with the closed cities in Russia were exacerbated by choices made by NCI.

Similar to other programs, NCI had problems convincing the Russians to focus on technologies for which there was proven demand or that involved marketable items.[132] Many Russian ideas focused on projects that involved interesting science or technologies and services that were pet projects of institute directors. Another problem was the Russian preference for large projects for which there was insufficient demand for the products, not enough investment, or both.[133]

Although all U.S. government programs experienced problems convincing the Russians to focus on commercialization, this was particularly acute with NCI. This is odd, given that NCI did not start its operations until 1999, by which point IPP and the Science Centers had made good progress toward convincing the Russians that success lay in projects with proven market demand. However, these other programs also developed their projects directly with the scientists who would be employed by the project and would gain or lose depending on the outcome. In contrast, NCI job-creation projects usually had more active involvement from institute directors and department managers. These are the very people who had been marginalized by many other job-creation efforts and who would still retain their original jobs even if a job-creation project failed. In bypassing the workers, NCI also deprived itself of the relationships and adaptability that were required to make projects successful. As a result, the people with the least stake in the outcome of any one project were more involved in designing it.

For example, one of NCI's most high-profile projects was an effort involving Avangard and Fresenius Medical Care to produce kidney

132. Interview with Lawrence Livermore National Laboratory staffer 2, April 1, 2003; interview with U.S. government official 6, May 28, 2002; interview with Pacific Northwest National Laboratory staffer 4, March 4, 2003; and interview with Nuclear Cities Initiative staffer 1, May 29, 2002.

133. Department of Energy, Nuclear Cities Initiative, "Economic Diversification in the Closed Nuclear Cities of Russia," pp. 2–3.

dialysis equipment. Part of the reason for the ultimate failure of the project can be traced to what some PIs referred to as the "Soviet mentality" of Avangard's leadership, referring to the tendency to be inflexible about project specifics and to their insistence on using Avangard dialysis technologies, which were widely considered to be old-fashioned. There were also complaints from Avangard managers that it was beneath the dignity of their workers to manufacture such simple equipment.

Access was also an issue confronted by other job-creation programs, but for NCI this became a significant problem.[134] The access restrictions on Russia's closed administrative territories, or ZATOs, made the costs of doing business in the nuclear cities more expensive, more complicated, and riskier. Eventually, it created five types of problems for NCI.

The first overarching issue was the mechanism by which access was provided for NCI. NCI was based on a government-to-government agreement with Russia, part of which included overall rules about access to the nuclear cities, including the number of visits during a specified period that would be granted to NCI personnel and their business contacts. In late 1999 and early 2000, both NCI and DOE's nuclear material security program had to curtail some of their activities in Russia due to disagreements about access. Although the U.S. and Russian governments reached an agreement in 2002, subsequent issues about access were usually elevated to the level of government-to-government negotiations, and NCI was eventually allowed fewer total visits to the nuclear cities than it had requested.[135]

The International Science and Technology Center (ISTC) and IPP both largely avoided this problem. IPP did so because it was not based on a government-to-government agreement, and was free to negotiate access with individual institutes and with teams of workers who would directly benefit from this access. IPP also approached access as a problem with multiple solutions. For example, some IPP projects brought Russian workers to the United States or other open Russian cities; others took pictures of equipment and facilities or hired Russians to inspect them when access for Western business partners proved problematic.[136] NCI,

---

134. Most NCI staff I interviewed and most, but not all, of the lab PIs mentioned access as their number one problem. Access was also cited as a significant setback in the Department of Energy's 2001 evaluation of NCI, as well as in the Baker-Cutler report. See Department of Energy, The Secretary of Energy Advisory Board, Howard Baker and Lloyd Cutler, *A Report Card on the Department of Energy's Nonproliferation Programs with Russia* (Washington, D.C.: Department of Energy, January 10, 2001).

135. Interview with Nuclear Cities Initiative staffer 4, May 29, 2002; interview with Department of Energy official 4, May 29, 2002; interview with Nuclear Cities Initiative staffer 2, May 30, 2002; and Lev Ryabev, First Deputy Minister, Russian Ministry of Atomic Energy, Letter to Linton F. Brooks, Deputy Administrator for Defense Nuclear Nonproliferation, Department of Energy, May 16, 2002.

136. The Department of Energy's Material Protection, Control, and Accountability program had also used similar tactics to satisfy U.S. requirements for oversight and accountability of U.S. tax dollars.

however, remained focused on a universal solution to access issues that was negotiated at the highest levels.

At ISTC, part of its government-to-government agreement included a much more liberal access arrangement that allowed program personnel and associated parties into the nuclear cities with forty-five days of advance notice, and sometimes less. Because this agreement was part of the ISTC implementing statute, it was not subject to interpretation or renegotiation.

The second access-related issue had to do with getting specific people cleared to visit the cities within a reasonable amount of time. NCI submitted to the Russian government a list of personnel who, with a specified amount of advance notice, were to be pre-approved for access to Sarov, Snezhinsk, and Zheleznogorsk. Additionally, NCI would request access for representatives from businesses interested in job-creation projects who wanted to meet the workers they would employ or inspect the facilities that would be involved. At times, however, entire delegations would be cancelled, sometimes at the last minute and without justification from the Russian government. More often, specific individuals would be denied access. According to my interviews with PIs from the U.S. labs, it was usually impossible to know the reasons behind these decisions.

One category of visitors often enjoyed more success: Russians. The U.S. labs employed a few PIs who were émigrés from Russia. The Science Center in Moscow also tended to send Russian staff to the closed cities for project oversight. Russian businesses also had more liberal access arrangements.[137] In general, Russians who were employed by U.S. programs reported few access problems. In my interviews, it was also true that these Russian employees were more aware of or spoke more openly about corruption, the need for bribes, pressure from the FSB, and other specifics about what were in many ways normal business practices in Russia.[138] Unlike other programs, however, NCI did not seek out Russian nationals to act as its emissaries in the nuclear cities.

A third set of problems was associated with negotiating access arrangements for individual job-creation projects. According to the U.S.-Russian agreement on NCI, all projects had to take place in the municipal areas of the nuclear cities; therefore, any job creation involving former weapons facilities had to be preceded by the removal of those facilities

---

137. For example, non-Russian businesses could not invest in serial production facilities such as Avangard. For the purposes of business development, these facilities had to be removed from the security area for there to be any access for non-Russians. Also, businesses had to negotiate access arrangements on a case-by-case basis and, in general, Russian businesses were allowed access with less advance notice.

138. For example, I spoke with one Russian-born PI at a U.S. lab who paid "overhead" to institute directors and managers so they would remove some of the obstacles to getting access to equipment and facilities. Another such PI communicated directly with the local FSB representatives in a closed city and offered to personally give them communications with project scientists as a way of making the project more transparent. Yet another PI told the project accountant to call the bribes necessary for doing business "storage fees."

from the secure area of the weapons complex. Even access to the municipal parts of the cities was, however, still governed by rules about access to the ZATOS. When job-creation projects involved non-Russian business partners, these requirements often did not meet the expectations of companies that were used to visiting their employees and facilities at will.[139]

The case of Fresenius and Avangard illustrates this problem.[140] In return for its investment, Fresenius wanted guarantees about access. There was no disagreement about the right to visit facilities with the forty-five day advance notice that was required for all ZATOs. There was also eventually agreement about access for pre-identified staff with only fourteen days notice.

At issue was access with shorter notice of a few days, which was requested in anticipation of equipment breakdown or other production problems. Even here there had been a verbal agreement to provide such access for one or two engineers on an emergency basis. Fresenius, however, wanted this as part of a formal agreement. Minatom, meanwhile, was under pressure from the FSB for what it saw as too many foreigners who were already visiting Sarov. Moreover, there were already Western businesses that had set up manufacturing facilities in Sarov yet had not requested such immediate access or which had arranged for local engineers or other personnel to deal with any production problems temporarily until foreigners could be cleared for access to the facility.

As a demonstration of good faith, Minatom proposed that Fresenius begin operations with the promise that any emerging issues about access would eventually be resolved. As a result, Minatom could use the jobs created by the project as evidence to convince the FSB to agree to an access arrangement. Fresenius, however, was facing a crucial meeting of its board and needed a final decision. So far, it had no proof of the development or manufacturing capabilities at Avangard and had previous problems negotiating licensing and leasing agreements. Plus, the estimated cost of renovating facilities for production had grown from $3.5 million to $4.5–$8 million. With Minatom unable to formalize an access agreement beforehand, Fresenius pulled out of the project.

Access clearly played a role in the demise of the Fresenius project. Less clear is who should be assigned responsibility. Certainly the company

---

139. Lev Ryabev, First Deputy Minister, Russian Ministry of Atomic Energy, Letter to Linton F. Brooks, Deputy Administrator for Defense Nuclear Nonproliferation, U.S. Department of Energy, May 16, 2002; interview with Oak Ridge National Laboratory staffer 2, February 19, 2003; interview with Oak Ridge National Laboratory staffer 4, February 19, 2003; interview with Lawrence Livermore National Laboratory staffer 6, April 2, 2003; and interview with Minatom official 1, July 24, 2002.

140. This story is based on the following resources: interview with Lawrence Livermore National Laboratory staffer 2, April 1, 2003; interview with Minatom official 1, July 24, 2002; interview with Lawrence Livermore National Laboratory staffer 11, April 7, 2003; interview with Nuclear Cities Initiative staffer 3, May 29, 2002; interview with Oak Ridge National Laboratory staffer 5, February 19, 2003; interview with Nuclear Cities Initiative staffer 5, May 29, 2002; interview with Nuclear Cities Initiative staffer 4, May 29, 2002; and interview with Nuclear Cities Initiative staffer 2, May 30, 2002.

had every right to expect access to its investment and to doubt Minatom's verbal assurances. But the FSB also had plenty of evidence to suggest that the security risks associated with access were unlikely to be outweighed by successful job creation. It was, however, NCI's actions that tilted the balance in favor of the FSB. NCI's focus was on resolving the problem with a formal agreement that was specific to Fresenius, and doing so before the project started. Yet formal agreements often prove difficult to change and, in the case of Fresenius, there was no evidence to suggest that immediate access would have been necessary. Moreover, if the FSB granted immediate access to Fresenius, this would set a precedent for further job-creation projects in the nuclear cities.

In contrast, both ISTC and IPP had job-creation projects in the nuclear cities, yet they avoided similar problems. For both programs, access rules were negotiated on a case-by-case basis. However, they also tended to negotiate similar agreements for all businesses and to deal with the issue of immediate access by encouraging companies to hire local Russian representatives, a solution that was not considered by NCI. Finally, these other programs had proven track records in the nuclear cities. Although they had created few jobs, they had provided considerable income in the form of short-term research and development funding, much of which had included equipment and supply purchases for the nuclear weapons institutes. NCI, however, could make no such claims. These differences suggest that access arrangements that would have satisfied Fresenius and the FSB could have been made.

Fourth, access also became problematic for NCI because it got caught up in larger political disputes between the United States and Russia.[141] Most significantly, after September 11, 2001, the United States increased both the information and fees required to get a visa. People who had skills or backgrounds that associated them with weapons of mass destruction, often only tangentially, were required to undergo additional and often lengthy screening processes before receiving permission to visit the United States. The Russian government resented having these rules applied to its citizens and personnel from Russian nuclear weapons institutes, many of whom had been visiting the United States for years, and found the new U.S. rules and delays an unnecessary insult. In response, Russia adopted visa application procedures and rules that mimicked those of the United States. As a result, NCI staff and any associated business personnel were saddled with onerous and often intrusive requirements for information about their backgrounds, skills, and past travel. My interviews suggested that most people involved with NCI projects understood the larger political motives that were driving these new requirements, and many even sympathized with the Russian government. In practice,

---

141. Interview with Nuclear Cities Initiative staffer 3, May 29, 2002; interview with Minatom official 1, July 24, 2002; and Lev Ryabev, First Deputy Minister, Russian Ministry of Atomic Energy, Letter to Linton F. Brooks, Deputy Administrator for Defense Nuclear Nonproliferation, U.S. Department of Energy, May 16, 2002.

however, the new rules caused additional delays and raised the cost of trying to create jobs in Russia, and even more so in the nuclear cities.

Access problems also resulted from a fifth issue: by virtue of working in the nuclear cities, NCI got caught up in power struggles between the FSB, Minatom, and local and regional Russian officials. Even though Minatom generally supported NCI and its job-creation efforts, it did not control the FSB. The FSB contested Minatom's authority with respect to the nuclear cities, partly because conversion and access by foreigners directly challenged the FSB's own mission to guarantee internal security. Minatom's task was to convince the FSB that U.S. access to the nuclear cities was in Russia's own interest and not aimed at intelligence collection. This became increasingly difficult as more and more U.S. lab PIs requested access to the nuclear cities, yet comparatively little money was spent there and few jobs were created.[142] This was further exacerbated by what many saw as big promises from NCI that were never delivered.[143] Both NCI and IPP were also accused of "nuclear tourism"; that is, making repeated visits to the closed cities with no subsequent results. These issues became more important as the FSB gained political clout under Putin during the late 1990s, and Minatom and its successor, Rosatom, found it increasingly difficult to counter the FSB's restrictive attitude toward access or prove the benefits of international cooperation.

NCI also created problems for the FSB because its community development and infrastructure projects made the nuclear cities less dependent on the nuclear weapons complex. In the nuclear cities, the local internal security forces traditionally had a close relationship with the weapons institutes. If the nuclear weapons institute saw the growing independence of city officials as a threat, then so would the local FSB.[144] In closed cities, such as Sarov, where there was a harmonious relationship between city and institute officials, often the local FSB got into disagreements with FSB headquarters in Moscow, which did not appreciate the need for diversification in such communities.[145] Similarly, regional FSB offices became involved as NCI encouraged the nuclear cities to become more integrated with their neighbors and at the regional level.[146] For these reasons, NCI's access needs became part of local and intergovernmental power struggles.

142. Interview with Minatom official 1, July 24, 2002; interview with Oak Ridge National Laboratory staffer 2, February 19, 2003; and interview with Sandia National Laboratory staffer 1, May 2, 2003.

143. Interview with Sandia National Laboratory staffer 1, May 2, 2003; interview with Minatom official 1, July 24, 2002; interview with Minatom official 3, July 24, 2002; and interview with Los Alamos National Laboratory staffer 1, May 21, 2002.

144. Interview with Los Alamos National Laboratory staffer 1, May 21, 2002; interview with Sandia National Laboratory staffer 6, May 5, 2003; and interview with former Clinton administration official 2, May 21, 2002.

145. Interview with former Clinton administration official 2, May 21, 2002; interview with Nuclear Cities Initiative staffer 5, May 29, 2002; and interview with Lawrence Livermore National Laboratory staffer 11, April 7, 2003.

146. Interview with non-governmental organization staffer 3, May 21, 2002.

It is also the case that by the time NCI was created in 1998, Russia had close to ten years of experience with U.S. cooperation and was growing weary of giving in to U.S. demands. The United States, in turn, was poised to ask Russia to assume more of the burden for cooperative nonproliferation efforts. Therefore, NCI suffered because it was in the wrong place at the wrong time. However, this problem was intensified by fundamental disagreements between the United States and Russia over NCI's goals. As one U.S. lab PI explained, access was a problem not because it was a hard issue to resolve, but because it was NCI that was involved.[147]

NCI and Minatom agreed on two important goals: job creation and downsizing. They disagreed, however, on the best means of achieving each. Moreover, each needed the other to be successful but, because of this disagreement over the means to these goals, NCI and Minatom found themselves increasingly at odds with each other.

Although NCI's goal was job creation, the underlying rationale was nonproliferation: its projects were all aimed at convincing nuclear weapons workers that they could make a viable living without selling their skills. Minatom, which also focused on the goal of job creation, had a different mission: it wanted to downsize its nuclear weapons complex responsibly, and could do so only when workers could be reasonably assured of jobs elsewhere.

NCI, however, initially focused on community development rather than job-creation projects. Doing so was consistent with its nonproliferation goals; improving the infrastructure and life in the nuclear cities would hopefully encourage scientists to stay there and make the communities more attractive to potential investors. But community development projects also solved another problem for NCI. It was clear from the experiences of the Science Centers and IPP that job creation involving former weapons workers in Russia was difficult. Moreover, NCI was under considerable pressure in the United States to show results even before it had spent its first dollar. Community development projects promised demonstrated results that had the added benefit of setting the stage for future job creation. As a result, much of NCI's initial funding was channeled into community development and other projects that held promise, but did not lead to direct job creation.

Minatom did not share this enthusiasm for community development. There were two underlying reasons. First, in agreeing to NCI, Minatom inherently agreed to open up its most sensitive facilities to increased cooperation with the United States and to reduce its control over conversion. In return, it needed job creation as proof that this risk-taking was warranted. Instead, during its first two years, NCI funded Internet connections, drug rehabilitation programs, medical exchanges, loan schemes, and very low-tech job-creation projects that employed only a few people in activities

---

147. Interview with Los Alamos National Laboratory staffer 9, May 1, 2003. According to more than one PI, if they requested access to a nuclear city for a project with IPP, it was usually not a problem. Access to the same city for an NCI project, however, was much more likely to create trouble.

that Minatom saw as beneath the dignity of nuclear weapons experts.[148] Second, during NCI's first years, it became increasingly clear that a signifi- cant amount of NCI funding was being spent in the U.S. nuclear weapons complex rather than the Russian one. Although Minatom seems to have made unreasonable assumptions about the amount of money NCI would involve, and about Minatom's ability to control those funds, it is the case that Minatom felt NCI had not delivered on its promises.[149] Moreover, Minatom needed jobs created in order to demonstrate to the FSB that allowing NCI access to the nuclear cities was a worthy risk.

Although eventually Minatom would come to value any job, regard- less of the level of technology or expertise involved, NCI was forced to change its strategy. Under political pressure at home to demonstrate success quickly and in a way that was clearly beneficial for U.S. national security, NCI abandoned its community development efforts and came to concentrate more fully on its other main mission: conversion of the Russian nuclear weapons complex.[150]

Minatom also shared this goal, but again the two parties focused on different processes. Minatom's main focus remained on job creation, but over time it hoped to learn from the conversion experiences of the U.S. nu- clear weapons complex.[151] Once NCI had demonstrated its ability to create jobs, Minatom would be more able to cooperate in downsizing.[152] NCI, which promised eventually to arrange for a joint study of conversion, ad- opted downsizing as its primary goal. Moreover, NCI focused on identify- ing specific facilities for removal from the weapons complex. Then, after downsizing had occurred, it would help create jobs for workers who had already left the complex because of this conversion.

Although NCI and Minatom agreed on both the goals of job creation and downsizing, their domestic political environments forced them to place a different priority on each. According to one NCI official, the result was that NCI was forced to focus on downsizing for its U.S. audience while talking about job creation in Russia.[153] As a result, it could achieve neither goal. Moreover, because they pursued these goals for

---

148. According to officials at Minatom, the FSB pointed to Minatom's own job-creation efforts during 1999–2000 and argued that during this timeframe Minatom had created some 2,500 jobs, while NCI had produced less than 100.

149. Interview with Nuclear Cities Initiative staffer 1, May 29, 2002; interview with former U.S. government official 6, April 12, 2001; interview with Minatom official 2, July 24, 2002; and interview with Minatom official 1, July 24, 2002.

150. Interview with Nuclear Cities Initiative staffer 5, May 29, 2002; and interview with Los Alamos National Laboratory staffer 1, April 29, 2003.

151. Interview with Nuclear Cities Initiative staffer 1, May 29, 2002; and interview with Los Alamos National Laboratory staffer 9, April 8, 2002.

152. Lack of progress in job creation, especially high-tech job creation, also created problems between Minatom officials and local institute directors. For example, officials at Avangard are rumored to have begged Minatom for more defense work rather than taking uninteresting jobs or remaining in an under-utilized complex.

153. Interview with Nuclear Cities Initiative staffer 1, May 29, 2002.

different reasons, both NCI and Minatom engaged in activities that seemed designed to antagonize the other. This problem is illustrated by Yevgeny Adamov, who, as Minister of Minatom in 2000, told a delegation of U.S. officials from DOE that NCI was the least efficient U.S.-Russian cooperative program:

> We were counting, rather, on the expertise of your people, involved in the military production conversion programs and development of civil projects on their basis. We were thinking about your people who would teach how to write marketing plans and implement them.... Efficiency of this program up to date is 100 jobs. It is zilch, my dear sirs.... What is worse, is that the worst expectations come true. Here I should be open with you, gentlemen (and excuse me for being so frank)—the NCI is seen by many here as an opportunity to get an uncon-ditioned access to the confidential information on our nuclear weapons complex. And every time, when any project under the NCI is preceded by the unconditional leadership of the access team I see that these assumptions do have some grounds. A project is not there yet, but dozens of people are already demanding access to the closed areas.[154]

There was one other source of disagreement inherent in NCI's mission. NCI was unique in that unlike other scientist-focused efforts, NCI would work with city officials as well as people from the nuclear weapons complex. In the nuclear cities, however, Minatom had tradi-tionally had a predominant influence over decision-making at both the defense institutes and the city administrations. By working with the city, NCI threatened to reduce Minatom's freedom of action, as well as the influence of the nuclear weapons institutes in city decision-making.

In general, Minatom was supportive of NCI's efforts, and had little trouble convincing the directors of its institutes to cooperate.[155] And, in some cases, NCI was able to leverage greater participation from the nuclear weapons institutes by threatening to cooperate instead with groups in the city.[156] Disputes, however, did arise in the city of Snezhinsk. In contrast to Sarov, where Minatom made it a priority to convert certain well-defined parts of the weapons institute, Snezhinsk held on to the promise of future weapons work. As a result, VNIITF, the

---

154. Y. O. Adamov, Speech of the Minister of Nuclear Energy of the Russian Federation before the SEAB Delegation, July 24, 2000.

155. Interview with Minatom official 1, July 24, 2002.

156. According to interview with Brookhaven National Laboratory staffer 4, March 19, 2003, it was also possible to encourage greater cooperation by having groups compete for work under either NCI or IPP. IPP would work with the weapons institutes and NCI would offer to work with the city.

weapons institute in the city, often fought against the city administration and its efforts to cooperate with NCI or take a more active role in conversion.[157] In the early 2000s, when Russia's nuclear weapons complex started to see increases in funding, it became much more difficult to convince Snezhinsk to take part in NCI projects.

U.S. DOMESTIC POLITICS

Many of NCI's troubles can be attributed to domestic political problems in the United States. It is certainly the case that Congress was more critical of NCI than of any other CTR program. For example, members of Congress requested one investigation by the GAO before NCI had started, and another after only two years of operations. These were used as a basis for criticizing the program for not showing results, when in reality it had had no time to do so. Also, NCI seems to have accrued more negative attention from President George W. Bush, who was widely seen as opposed to U.S. cooperative programs with Russia. Bush, in turn, allowed issues about liability and presidential certification to stall activities. NCI, which was struggling to show results, was particularly affected by these work stoppages.

However, these problems were made worse by a series of critical choices made by NCI. Most specifically, at a time when the program desperately needed to demonstrate results, it focused on a small number of potentially risky projects. When these failed, there was little evidence to show that these setbacks were anomalies, rather than further proof that the concerns of program critics were justified.

CONGRESS AND FUNDING. Initially, NCI significantly overestimated the money it would receive, expecting budgets of $500–$600 million over a five-year period.[158] Budgets of this size were necessary because the costs for completing activities in each city ranged from $40 million to $75 million, depending on the number of workers and the facilities that needed to be shut down or converted.[159] Later, NCI's expectations were reduced to about $30 million in funding per year, with activities stretching out over a longer time frame.[160] Even this proved to be optimistic.

---

157.   Interview with Nuclear Cities Initiative staffer 1, May 29, 2002; interview with U.S. government official 6, May 28, 2002; interview with Lawrence Livermore National Laboratory staffer 11, April 7, 2003; and interview with former Clinton administration official 2, May 21, 2002. According to one interviewee, VNIITF also charged huge overhead for projects in the city and diverted some funding to its own use as "tax" for agreeing to such cooperation. Interview with Brookhaven National Laboratory staffer 4, March 19, 2003.

158.   Interview with U.S. government official 6, May 28, 2002; interview with Lawrence Livermore National Laboratory staffer 2, April 1, 2003; and General Accounting Office, *Nuclear Nonproliferation: Concerns with DOE's Efforts to Reduce the Risks Posed by Russia's Unemployed Weapons Scientists*, p. 6.

159.   U.S. Congress, *Energy and Water Development Appropriations for 2002*, pp. 156–157, 159; and U.S. Congress, *Energy and Water Development Appropriations for 2001*, p. 553.

160.   Interview with Nuclear Cities Initiative staffer 1, May 29, 2002.

More than any other program, NCI's budget involved struggles between the Senate and the House, usually with Senate Democrats requesting more funding, and between a supportive Congress pushing a higher budget on a reluctant Bush administration. Even with the additional support, however, Congress usually conditioned NCI's ability to spend money on a variety of measures that were most often aimed at forcing NCI to demonstrate success at its main goals of job creation and downsizing. Table 7.1 provides administration requests and congressional authorizations for NCI.

NCI's funding struggles began in its first year, when DOE's initial transfers to fund the program fell short of what was authorized by Congress. The department was given the authority to transfer up to $15 million from other programs but in the end, only $12.5 million was reprogrammed. Of that money, $7.5 million came from the Material Protection, Control, and Accounting program, and $5 million came from IPP.

For fiscal year 2000, when NCI received its first appropriations of new money, the Clinton administration's request was cut 75 percent by the House, in large part due to a February 1999 GAO report showing that more money in IPP was being spent in U.S. rather than Russian labs. Similar to the restrictions put on IPP, Congress directed NCI to spend no more than 49 percent of its funding in the United States in fiscal year 2001. There was also some concern that NCI would duplicate IPP, and Congress pushed NCI to provide more details about its own mission.[161]

Although Congress increased NCI's funding the next year, there were strings attached. Of the $27.5 million authorized, $10 million was contingent upon receiving a written agreement from Russia that it would downsize some facilities within five years, and no more than $8.75 million could be spent until NCI implemented a project-review process that, among other things, assessed projects for commercial viability.[162] All NCI projects were also required to become commercially viable after three years, a criterion that was almost certainly impossible to meet.[163]

---

161.   U.S. Congress, Senate, Committee on Appropriations, *Energy and Water Development Appropriations, FY 2000*, 106th Cong., 1st sess., March 9, 11, 18, April 13, 1999, p. 262.

162.   U.S. Congress, *Enactment of Provisions of H.R. 5408*, title XXXI, section 3172. In requiring NCI to conclude an agreement on downsizing with Minatom, it was the intent of Congress to encourage NCI to end its community development efforts and focus on downsizing and job creation only for excess weapons workers. This requirement was also intended to limit NCI activities to its three original nuclear cities until it could demonstrate success there. See RANSAC, "Russian Nuclear Security and the Clinton Administration's Fiscal Year 2000 Expanded Threat Reduction Initiative. A Summary of Congressional Action," Washington, D.C. (February 2000).

163.   General Accounting Office, *Nuclear Nonproliferation: DOE's Efforts to Assist Weapons Scientists in Russia's Nuclear Cities Face Challenges*, p. 25. There were also concerns in Congress that NCI was funding very low-level job-creation projects that resulted in only a few positions. For example, Rose Gottemoeller (acting deputy administrator, defense nuclear nonproliferation, department of energy) testified about NCI projects in front of the Emerging Threats Subcommittee of the Senate Armed Services Committee in March 2000. According to one observer, as Gottemoeller explained NCI's projects, she mentioned a butcher shop, which

Table 7.1. NCI Funding (in millions of U.S. dollars).

Fiscal Year	Administration Request	Congressional Funding
1999	$0	$15
2000	$30	$7.5
2001	$17.5	$27.5
2002	$6.6	$21
2003	$16.7	$17

SOURCES: Russian-American Nuclear Security Advisory Council (RANSAC), "Russian Nuclear Security and the Clinton Administration's Fiscal Year 2000 Expanded Threat Reduction Initiative. A Summary of Congressional Action," Washington, D.C. (February 2000); Department of Energy, Nuclear Cities Initiative, "Annual Report," fiscal year 1999, Washington, D.C.; U.S. Congress, House, Committee on Armed Services, *Enactment of Provisions of H.R. 5408, the Floyd D. Spence National Defense Authorization Act for FY 2001*, 106th Cong., 2nd sess., October 6, 2000, H. Rpt. 106-945, title XXXI, section 3172; William Hoehn, "Analysis of the Bush Administration's Fiscal Year 2002 Budget Requests for US-Former Soviet Union Nuclear Security: Department of Energy Programs," RANSAC, Washington, D.C., April 18, 2001; U.S. Congress, House, Committee on Appropriations, *Energy and Water Development Appropriations for 2002, Part 6: Department of Energy*, Hearings, 107th Cong., 1st sess., May 3, 9, 2001, p. 152; and Department of Energy, National Nuclear Security Administration, "Budget Request," Washington, D.C., fiscal year 2003.

Eventually Minatom's Deputy Minister, Lev Ryabev, sent a letter to U.S. Secretary of Energy Spencer Abraham stating that the Avangard facility at Sarov would be closed. DOE, however, did not free up the money due to concerns that some buildings would be transferred to the Sarov nuclear weapons institute and thus not converted, and because Ryabev's letter fell short of the "written agreement" specified by Congress.[164] Eventually, however, the issue was resolved, and the additional money was made available for use by NCI.

The September 11, 2001, attacks on the United States brought a flurry of supplemental spending requests. The Bush administration, however, did not include increases for either IPP or NCI, which had just been merged together under the label Russian Transition Initiatives (RTI). Although initially Congress seemed reluctant to include additional money, it eventually increased funding for RTI by $15 million. A simi-

employed five people as the result of a loan from the European Bank for Reconstruction and Development. According to this observer, this was followed by a painful five to ten seconds of silence during which members of Congress were clearly dumbfounded at the idea that Russian scientists had gone from weapons production to butchering meat, or that this was being touted as a successful conversion story. Interview with non-governmental organization staffer 11, March 8, 2000.

164. Interview with Los Alamos National Laboratory staffer 9, May 1, 2003; and interview with Nuclear Cities Initiative staffer 2, May 30, 2002.

lar sequence played out during consideration of the 2002 budget. The Bush administration, which had ordered a review of all cooperative security programs in March 2001, requested less money for most DOE programs in Russia, including NCI, whose budget saw a 75 percent reduction compared to the previous year. The House Appropriations Committee added $10 million to Bush's request, and the Senate figure, which eventually prevailed, more than tripled it.[165]

As part of RTI, NCI and IPP were considered jointly by Congress in subsequent years, with individual funding levels determined by DOE within the overall appropriations provided by Congress.[166] Although the Senate expressed support for NCI's unique contributions to U.S. security, the Bush administration took actions that eventually resulted in the program's demise.[167]

THE PRESIDENT AND NCI. The second Bush administration had repeatedly expressed skepticism about cooperative security programs with Russia. After his first election, Bush ordered the National Security Council to conduct an evaluation of all DOE programs with Russia, the results of which were critical in general but especially damaging to NCI.[168] When I conducted interviews early in the Bush administration, many NCI program personnel expressed concern about the future of the program, and there was a widespread belief that the Bush administration took office committed to ending it. There was, however, disagreement over whether this was due to the Bush administration's dislike for cooperative security with Russia, or because NCI was considered to be an initiative of the Clinton administration.[169] Although eventually the president decided to continue NCI in a restructured form, the issue of the program's future came up again in 2003, and coalesced around the issue of liability.

Under the initial CTR agreement, Russia assumed all liability for accidents, including those resulting from sabotage. The Bush administration sought a similar agreement to cover the plutonium disposition program and NCI, even though NCI projects seldom involved dealing with hazardous radioactive materials. Russia, however, refused to accept

---

165. William Hoehn, "Analysis of the Bush Administration's Fiscal Year 2002 Budget Requests for U.S.-Former Soviet Union Nuclear Security: Department of Energy Programs," RANSAC, Washington, D.C., August 10, 2001.

166. RTI was authorized a total of $57 million in fiscal year 2002 and $39 million in fiscal year 2003.

167. For Senate support, see William Hoehn, "Update on Congressional Activity Affecting U.S.-Russian Cooperative Nonproliferation Programs," RANSAC, Washington, D.C., July 26, 2002, pp. 5–6.

168. See, for example, Mike Allen, "Bush Pledges More Aid for Russian Arms Cuts," *Washington Post*, December 28, 2001, p. A1.

169. Interview with U.S. government official 6, May 28, 2002; interview with Nuclear Cities Initiative staffer 2, May 30, 2002; and interview with Nuclear Cities Initiative staffer 5, May 29, 2002.

such broad responsibility.[170] NCI's implementing agreement was set to expire in September 2003, and the Bush administration used the liability dispute as an excuse not to seek renewal.

Although the program was terminated, there remained some small signs of interest in its approach. In considering fiscal year 2008 appropriations for DOE, the House Appropriations Committee recommended $10 million to restore NCI's funding.[171] However, no additional support for the program was forthcoming.

NCI supporters tended to see the program's demise either as an intentional and premeditated action on the part of the Bush administration, or as the result of being misunderstood by Congress because it had been less able to measure concrete results or was too "mushy" for members to understand.[172] There is more evidence, however, to support the argument that NCI was caught up in a broader political dynamic. When Cooperative Threat Reduction began in the early 1990s, there were detractors, mostly congressional Republicans, who argued that such programs were foreign aid rather than national security and that Russia was not an appropriate focus of such cooperation. NCI was singled out because it was the most recent example of such activity, and because it began operations at a time when Republicans had more political clout in Congress.

Although the Bush administration was expected to be critical of cooperative security programs and NCI, its review served to restructure but not eliminate these programs.[173] It was only after two more years of experience that the Bush administration seemed committed to terminating the program. And during those two critical years, NCI made decisions that helped seal its own fate. In particular, the program chose to emphasize a small number of risky projects, all of which eventually failed.

A FEW KEY PROJECTS. Many of NCI's efforts were successful at creating handfuls of low-tech jobs, but for a variety of reasons, NCI quickly came to concentrate on only a few projects. Because these projects were selected without rigorous review, or to satisfy imperatives other than job creation,

170. For a more detailed discussion of the liability dispute, see Henry L. Stimson Center, "Liability Issues in Cooperative Nonproliferation Programs in Russia," http://www.stimson.org/cnp/?SN=CT200706011307 (accessed June 1, 2007). Eventually the issue was resolved in 2005, when an agreement was reached that assigned liability to Russia, except in cases of intentional injury or death.

171. U.S. Congress, House, Committee on Appropriations, *Energy and Water Development Appropriations Bill, 2008*, 110th Cong., 1st sess., Rept. 110-185, p. 110.

172. Pete V. Domenici, "Issues in US/NIS Non-proliferation Cooperation," Remarks, Assessing U.S. Dismantlement and Nonproliferation Assistance Programs in the Newly Independent States, Monterey, California, December 11–13, 1999; interview with U.S. government official 6, May 28, 2002; and interview with Nuclear Cities Initiative staffer 1, May 29, 2002.

173. Department of Energy, "Internal DOE Report on Programs in Russia, 2001."

their chances for success were lessened.[174] When they failed, NCI had nothing to fall back on to demonstrate success.

One problem was that the involvement of the U.S. labs skewed project selection in several ways. The Open Computing Centers provide one example. Initially, NCI started a computer services center in Sarov because a U.S. company had inadvertently sold some computers to VNIIEF, the nuclear weapons institute, in violation of U.S. Department of Commerce export rules.[175] Although the computers were soon outdated, they could not be used by the lab. In order to find a legal resting place for the equipment, NCI invested in a computer center in the open section of Sarov and duplicated the project in Snezhinsk. Los Alamos, which was paired with Sarov under NCI, strongly supported their computer center and, similarly, Livermore lobbied for the project in Snezhinsk.[176] However, despite good starts and job-creation predictions in excess of five hundred, neither computer center proved to be a commercial success story, although the one in Sarov continued to get some commercial contracts as of December 2008.[177] Despite this, Livermore and Los Alamos, both of which had considerable clout in NCI, continued to demand funding for the centers, and, once so much had been invested, NCI was embarrassed to turn away.[178] As a result of concentrating funding in the Open Computing Centers, funding for other project ideas was limited.

The U.S. labs also skewed NCI projects because their involvement was expensive. Similar to IPP, NCI was under pressure to spend more money in Russia and less money at the U.S. labs. For these reasons, NCI preferred funding projects that could be administered out of its headquarters at DOE and required less input from the U.S. labs.

More significant, however, was the influence of domestic politics. Because higher levels of funding never materialized, and because it was under pressure from both the U.S. and Russian governments to demonstrate results quickly, NCI reoriented its strategy after 2001 to focus on two key projects: the job-creation effort involving the Fresenius company and Avangard, and a package of measures designed for the accelerated conversion of Sarov. Moreover, because these projects had high price tags, they consumed much of NCI's meager budget. Perhaps

---

174. For example, in 2001, the GAO criticized NCI for not having a rigorous screening process by which to select projects. See General Accounting Office, *Nuclear Nonproliferation: DOE's Efforts to Assist Weapons Scientists in Russia's Nuclear Cities Face Challenges*, pp. 15–16.

175. Twice in 1996, the Texas-based Jet Info Systems International shipped computers from Germany to VNIIEF without the required authorization.

176. One interviewee went so far as to call these U.S. labs the "sugar daddies" of the Open Computing Centers.

177. Interview with Lawrence Livermore National Laboratory staffer 2, April 1, 2003; interview with Lawrence Livermore National Laboratory staffer 7, April 2, 2003; interview with Brookhaven National Laboratory staffer 4, March 19, 2003; interview with Lawrence Livermore National Laboratory staffer 11, April 7, 2003; interview with Nuclear Cities Initiative staffer 1, May 29, 2002; and interview with Minatom official 1, July 24, 2002.

178. Interview with U.S. government official 9, May 30, 2002.

even more important, because the program did not receive increases in funding, these two efforts forced NCI to mortgage its future funds. As a result, there was almost no money left in later years to fund new projects.

Fresenius, the focus of one of NCI's first efforts, was estimated to create anywhere from 200 to 1,000 jobs. The project was seen as an enticement for Minatom to close the Avangard plant in Sarov, which had manufactured nuclear weapons.[179] NCI's future, in turn, rested on its ability to demonstrate that it could negotiate such downsizing agreements with the Russian government. Because of disagreements about access and the level of technology to be involved, however, both Fresenius and Minatom began to walk away from the project. By this time, however, NCI had widely touted the collaboration, claiming that it would vindicate its program strategy.[180] In an attempt to save the project, NCI increasingly committed more of its own funding to renovate the facilities, leaving less money for other NCI projects and, more importantly, reducing the commitment of Fresenius. According to one person who was involved in the project, the company came to see NCI as a "cash cow."[181] Although eventually NCI persuaded Minatom to make good on its pledge to close Avangard, by that time delays, costs, and other uncertainties had forced Fresenius to abandon the project.

A somewhat similar scenario played out with respect to a project for "accelerated conversion" at Sarov. Under pressure from the Russian federal government and the FSB to justify continued cooperation with NCI, Minatom began to push the program to concentrate in Sarov and invest its time and resources in a set of efforts designed to quickly result in job creation.[182] NCI focused on a strategic plan that had been developed earlier at Los Alamos, but which DOE was unable or unwilling to promote. As a result, accelerated conversion was never fully funded, and NCI instead implemented a few ad hoc projects. When few jobs resulted, Russia became further disillusioned with NCI.

ORGANIZATIONAL INTEREST

Although the decision to focus on a few key projects clearly shows the influence of organizational interest and survival in NCI's decision-making, organizational interests influenced NCI in other ways. Initially, NCI had the support of Rose Gottemoeller, who, as a deputy undersecretary, helped champion the program and cut through the bureaucratic red tape for which DOE is famous. After she left, and especially with the

179. Department of Energy, Nuclear Cities Initiative, "Fresenius"; interview with Los Alamos National Laboratory staffer 9, May 1, 2003; and interview with Lawrence Livermore National Laboratory staffer 6, April 2, 2003.

180. Interview with Nuclear Cities Initiative staffer 5, May 29, 2002; interview with Nuclear Cities Initiative staffer 2, May 30, 2002; interview with U.S. government official 9, May 30, 2002; and interview with Oak Ridge National Laboratory staffer 5, February 19, 2003.

181. Interview with U.S. government official 9, May 30, 2002.

182. Interview with Los Alamos National Laboratory staffer 1, April 29, 2003; and interview with Nuclear Cities Initiative staffer 5, May 29, 2002.

coming of the Bush administration, the program had to rely on its own devices for budgetary support, paperwork, and advocacy needs. Whereas IPP could turn to the lab PIs for support, NCI was less able to do so.[183] The U.S. nuclear weapons labs, which had the most political clout in DOE and Congress, had moved away from NCI because of a general turn toward other efforts that was fueled by disagreements with NCI over funding priorities. As a result, NCI was left to its own devices. Instead of reexamining its activities or seeking external allies, NCI kept to itself and chose to concentrate on its project with Fresenius and accelerated conversion at Sarov, both of which failed to renew faith in the program.

NCI AND THE DEPARTMENT OF ENERGY. NCI was managed by a small staff located in the Office of Defense Nuclear Nonproliferation in DOE's semi-autonomous National Nuclear Security Administration. In general, NCI's relationship with the rest of the department can be described at best as a poor fit and at worst as an embarrassment.

NCI had a rather tightly-knit staff that saw itself as a community working toward worthy goals. Despite this, DOE never embraced NCI. The core base of support for the program came from a small network of non-governmental experts, academics, and a few members of Congress, most of whom concentrated on fighting attempts in Congress to cut the program's funding or end it altogether. Gottemoeller had been a strong advocate of the program, but she left in October 2000.

Because NCI's headquarters also held most programmatic and budgetary authority, at times it ran into conflict with the U.S. national labs, especially Los Alamos. Furthermore, NCI's own staff lacked personal clout in the DOE bureaucracy, and at times the program's supporters were at odds with upper-level political appointees.[184]

As a result, DOE often proved unwilling to intercede with Congress, in the executive branch, or with the U.S. labs to help NCI reinforce its priorities, better control the distribution of its resources, or make the case for higher budgets. In addition, as NCI's troubles increased, staff were strongly discouraged from approaching members of Congress even to provide information about the program.[185] This was reinforced by concerns that NCI's negative publicity might spill over and create problems for IPP or other DOE projects in Russia. It was not uncommon in my interviews

183. This argument is elaborated in Sharon K. Weiner, "Organizational Interest, Nuclear Weapons Scientists, and Nonproliferation," *Political Science Quarterly*, Vol. 124, No. 4 (Winter 2009–10), pp. 655–679.

184. Interview with Nuclear Cities Initiative staffer 2, May 30, 2002; interview with U.S. government official 6, May 28, 2002; interview with Nuclear Cities Initiative staffer 4, May 29, 2002; interview with Los Alamos National Laboratory staffer 9, May 1, 2003; and interview with Lawrence Livermore National Laboratory staffer 8, April 3, 2003.

185. Interview with U.S. government official 6, May 28, 2002; interview with Lawrence Livermore National Laboratory staffer 2, April 1, 2003; interview with Pacific Northwest National Laboratory staffer 2, March 23, 2003; interview with Nuclear Cities Initiative staffer 2, May 30, 2002; interview with Nuclear Cities Initiative staffer 5, May 29, 2002; and interview with Nuclear Cities Initiative staffer 1, May 29, 2002.

to hear the claim that DOE considered NCI to be a "problem child" that could not be trusted and was best kept out of sight.[186]

NCI's relations with other agencies also suffered. Because most NCI projects required travel to Russia, NCI trips required clearance not only from DOE but also from the Department of State. Often this was a lengthy process that involved moving through multiple decision channels. Although this was complicated by the rigid hierarchy and lack of communication between programs at DOE, NCI also suffered because department officials proved unwilling to intercede on the program's behalf to streamline or speed up the travel clearance process.[187]

THE ROLE OF THE U.S. NATIONAL LABS. NCI, like IPP, relied heavily on personnel from the U.S. labs to develop and manage its projects. In NCI, however, much greater authority resided in the program's administrative office at DOE. As a result, the U.S. labs often had less influence over NCI's funding priorities, project design, and relations with Russia than they had with IPP, and would have preferred with NCI. There were several consequences to this relationship.

A key issue was funding priorities. NCI initially favored spending on community development, enabling bank loans, and job creation through low-tech projects. The labs, however, tended to favor high-tech projects that made use of the skills of nuclear weapons experts. This led, for example, to disagreements about funding for the International Development Centers.[188] The labs also preferred initiatives that were controlled by lab PIs, rather than by NCI's main office in Washington.[189]

Los Alamos and Livermore, in particular, pushed for projects that involved more science and could be controlled at the labs. Because of its emphasis on only high-tech projects, many of the PIs I interviewed preferred to spend their time working on projects for IPP. There was also some concern that community development and other low-tech efforts were created so that the non-nuclear weapons labs could also play a role

---

186. Interview with U.S. government official 9, May 30, 2002; and interview with Nuclear Cities Initiative staffer 2, May 30, 2002.

187. Interview with Nuclear Cities Initiative staffer 1, May 29, 2002; interview with Nuclear Cities Initiative staffer 2, May 30, 2002; interview with Nuclear Cities Initiative staffer 5, May 29, 2002; interview with Department of Energy official 4, May 29, 2002; interview with Lawrence Livermore National Laboratory staffer 2, April 1, 2003; interview with Los Alamos National Laboratory staffer 9, May 1, 2003; interview with U.S. government official 6, May 28, 2002; and interview with Los Alamos National Laboratory staffer 1, April 19, 2001.

188. Interview with Lawrence Livermore National Laboratory staffer 8, April 3, 2003; interview with Sandia National Laboratory staffer 6, May 5, 2003; interview with Lawrence Livermore National Laboratory staffer 6, April 2, 2003; and interview with Los Alamos National Laboratory staffer 9, May 1, 2003.

189. Interview with Brookhaven National Laboratory staffer 4, March 19, 2003; interview with Lawrence Livermore National Laboratory staffer 8, April 3, 2003; interview with Sandia National Laboratory staffer 6, May 5, 2003; interview with Lawrence Livermore National Laboratory staffer 6, April 2, 2003; and interview with Oak Ridge National Laboratory staffer 1, February 20, 2003.

in NCI.[190] In turn, some in the non-weapons labs would argue that Los Alamos, because it had been instrumental in starting NCI, laid claim to the best projects and resources.[191]

As a consequence of these disagreements, NCI could not always count on the support of Los Alamos and Livermore, the labs with the most political clout in both DOE and in Washington. Moreover, many of NCI's biggest projects, like the International Development Centers, were managed either out of the Washington office or by other organizations. Therefore, the big labs had less of a financial stake in the outcome of these projects.

Finally, personality also played a role in establishing lab relations with NCI. The previous chapter on IPP explains how William Desmond had responded to criticism of the program by tightening control over activities at the labs and requiring increasing accountability for project recordkeeping and budgets. Desmond was not popular among the program's PIs. He also became the first director of NCI; this personal dislike for him, combined with his efforts to centralize more authority in Washington, translated into skepticism about NCI.[192] As a result, NCI's headquarters office in DOE often found itself deprived of political support from key U.S. labs.

Organizational Interest and NCI

More than any other scientist engagement or redirection program, NCI's activities were influenced by problems with the Russians, an often skeptical Congress, and tepid support from the president. These constraints, however, were exacerbated by organizational interests.

NCI's mission was often met with skepticism in DOE. Moreover, by retaining power in its headquarters office, the program alienated some of the U.S. labs and lost their support. This was especially true during its first years, when NCI's funding priorities included community development activities. As a result, NCI was left largely to its own devices to navigate a dysfunctional and sometimes hostile DOE. Perhaps more important, NCI

190. Interview with Lawrence Livermore National Laboratory staffer 8, April 3, 2003; interview with Sandia National Laboratory staffer 6, May 5, 2003; interview with Nuclear Cities Initiative staffer 5, May 29, 2002; and interview with Oak Ridge National Laboratory staffer 1, February 20, 2003.

191. Interview with Savannah River Site staffer 1, February 21, 2003; interview with Lawrence Livermore National Laboratory staffer 2, April 1, 2003; interview with Los Alamos National Laboratory staffer 3, April 29, 2003; interview with Oak Ridge National Laboratory staffer 1, February 20, 2003; interview with Los Alamos National Laboratory staffer 9, May 1, 2003; interview with Oak Ridge National Laboratory staffer 6, February 20, 2003; and interview with Pacific Northwest National Laboratory staffer 2, March 23, 2003.

192. Interview with Nuclear Cities Initiative staffer 5, May 29, 2002; interview with Lawrence Livermore National Laboratory staffer 2, April 1, 2003; interview with Nuclear Cities Initiative staffer 2, May 30, 2002; interview with U.S. government official 6, May 28, 2002; interview with Department of Energy official 5, August 12, 2003; interview with U.S. government official 9, May 30, 2002; interview with Los Alamos National Laboratory staffer 1, April 29, 2003; and interview with Lawrence Livermore National Laboratory staffer 8, April 3, 2003.

was deprived of the political support that DOE and the U.S. labs would have provided in Congress and for future funding.

As a result of finding itself increasingly constrained by congressional and Russian expectations, and with few powerful allies in Congress, DOE, or the U.S. labs, NCI fell back on two projects that had been strongly supported by Livermore and Los Alamos and were also favored by Minatom. Unfortunately, the program did not control the things needed to make these projects successful. When these projects failed, NCI seemingly demonstrated the shortcomings of its strategy, and did so in an environment that was already seriously skeptical about the program.

Chapter 8

Conclusion

U.S. National Security, Institutional
Interests, and the Proliferation of Nuclear
Weapons Expertise

Students of public policy are well aware of the importance of institutional interest. Yet it is often assumed that the gravity of national security and "high politics" causes organizational imperatives to fade away. The case studies in this book prove otherwise.

Each case study examined a different program with its own unique approach for dealing with the threat of the proliferation of expertise from the former Soviet weapons of mass destruction (WMD) complex. And each case study also examined how this approach changed from the founding of each program through 2008. Despite the different programs, departments, and actors, the four case studies exhibit numerous similarities. One key commonality is the role of institutional self-interest in the design, goal-setting, implementation, and adaptation of efforts to engage and reemploy scientists.

More specifically, institutional interest created three problems that are common across all the cases examined here; I discuss these in the first section of this chapter. The first is goal displacement. Over time, each program came to focus on measuring progress toward goals other than nonproliferation. Second, it matters how much a program differs from the main norms, routines, and dynamics of its parent organization. Two of the programs studied here had short lives because they failed to "fit in" at their parent departments. In all four cases, each program adopted decision-making rules, program designs, and other adaptations over time that were motivated by a need to harmonize their activities with the norms of their home department. Third, each program struggled to prove its worth in a domestic political environment characterized by a lack of consistent support and potential challenges from a vocal minority. As a result, institutional interest led each program to refrain from competing with other brain drain efforts, but also to eschew cooperation. Using cross-case comparisons, I explain each of these problems in more detail in the first section of this chapter.

But highlighting the role of organizational interest in nonproliferation policy is not the whole story. Although the case studies show that few permanent jobs were created for former weapons experts, it is also the case that U.S. programs to engage and reemploy scientists provided important support to former Soviet WMD institutes and experts, often at critical times. Furthermore, through enabling and channeling the language of science, these programs brought the United States and Russia closer, forced Russia to be more open, and increased U.S. confidence in post-Soviet WMD activities. As a result, the United States is safer and, I argue, had a more open, intimate, and productive dialogue with Russia than would otherwise have been the case. The problems and potential of scientific cooperation as a tool of U.S. policy are discussed in the second section of this chapter.

The third section addresses the future of U.S. brain drain programs. The proliferation threat from Russia has changed since the early 1990s. In some ways the threat has lessened but in other ways it persists, albeit in a different form. The expansion of cooperative nonproliferation efforts, such as the Science Centers and Initiative for Proliferation Prevention (IPP), is likely to come at the expense of projects in the former Soviet Union. But it is unclear if such a shift best serves U.S. national security interests. Additionally, Russia's own interests and priorities, as well as the state of the economy, have increasingly come to influence threat reduction efforts. Combined with a domestic political environment in Washington, D.C. that questions whether brain drain is "defense by other means" or foreign charity, it is unclear how "cooperative" future threat reduction will be. All of these factors point toward a reevaluation of the Cooperative Threat Reduction agenda and U.S.-Russian burden-sharing.

Institutions, Interests, and Outcomes

Regardless of whether the goal is the expansion of brain drain programs to other countries, building a political consensus to support them in the United States, or renewing cooperation with Russia, future success at fighting the proliferation of WMD expertise depends upon learning lessons from past experience. The histories of Defense Department conversion efforts, the Science Centers, IPP, and the Nuclear Cities Initiative (NCI) provide valuable lessons about the role of organizational interest in U.S. brain drain programs. These case studies also point to an important link between organizational interest and program success and failure. Looking across these cases, several common themes emerge about the role of organizational interest and its influence on program goals, implementation, and metrics.

GOAL DISPLACEMENT

Organizations have an incentive to take the policy tasks they have been given and manipulate them such that they come to reflect the organization's own sense of mission, its definition of the task it was assigned, or results that are easier or more beneficial to measure. The four case studies here are no exception. In each case, programs came to measure progress toward goals that diverged from their original mission: the permanent redirection of former WMD experts.[1]

Perhaps the most obvious goal displacement was in the reluctance to measure job creation for WMD experts directly. Neither the Defense Department nor the Science Centers kept track of jobs created through their activities. The Defense Department preferred to focus on the overall number of institutes engaged in U.S.-funded conversion projects. But it collected little data that would indicate the success of such conversion; for example, it did not track revenues, patents, copyrights, or any of the other indicators used by the Science Centers and IPP. The Science Centers collected some of these measurements, but they did not do so consistently. For example, the Science Center in Moscow surveyed project managers about efforts to commercialize technologies, but they did so infrequently and on an ad hoc basis. Instead, as an indicator of commercial success, the Science Centers routinely reported numbers of Partner Projects and partners, as well as spending on these activities. Most Science Center partners were U.S. government agencies, however, and such collaboration offered little hope of permanent reemployment for former WMD experts.

IPP and NCI did report job creation totals. After 1997, IPP moved away from basic research collaboration and funded projects that required contributions from commercial partners. NCI's job-creation projects also involved business collaborators, although sometimes these were individual or small groups of Russian entrepreneurs in the nuclear cities rather than pre-established businesses. Therefore, for both IPP and NCI, the number of project participants was a better indicator of reemployment potential. However, both programs, and IPP in particular, were criticized for poor recordkeeping, including statistics about project participants. Initially, IPP did not require project managers to report job-creation totals, preferring instead to focus on U.S. industry contributions to projects, which were often in-kind rather than in the form of investment, equipment, or salaries for former Soviet workers. At NCI, estimates were often imprecise. And although both programs did start reporting job-creation totals starting in 2000, the accuracy of these figures is unclear.

Moreover, none of these four programs tracked the fate of its project participants once they stopped funding them. Therefore, the numbers of sustainable jobs that resulted from U.S. efforts is unknown. Instead, the Science Centers, IPP, and, to a lesser extent, NCI argued that sustainable job creation could be measured by looking at abstract indicators such as patents, commercialized technologies, or projects that reach the stage of "commercial takeoff." Despite the official focus on permanent redirection of WMD experts, each program argued that its responsibility for monitoring outcomes was done when a research collaboration or reemployment effort stopped receiving U.S. government funding.

---

1. The role of goal displacement in scientist redirection efforts is elaborated in Sharon K. Weiner, "Reconsidering Cooperative Threat Reduction: Russian Nuclear Weapons Scientists and Non-Proliferation," *Contemporary Security Policy*, Vol. 29, No. 3 (December 2008), pp. 477–501.

Finally, although each program was created to focus on WMD expertise, none developed rigorous criteria for verifying the WMD credentials of project participants, opting instead to accept self-declarations or, in the case of the Defense Department and NCI, no identification of WMD skills at all. Further, there is no evidence that any of the four programs focused on identifying WMD experts who were a particular proliferation concern, although at the request of the U.S. intelligence community, the Science Centers and IPP did engage particular institutes that were involved with the Soviet biological weapons program.

Goal displacement can also be seen in the shift in focus from engagement for the sake of discouraging proliferation to collaboration for the purposes of transparency. Although Defense Department conversion efforts and NCI both had short histories, IPP and the Science Centers came to emphasize transparency over the longer term, using this not only as justification for continued operations in Russia but also for expansion beyond the former Soviet Union. As argued in Chapter 6, IPP increasingly saw cooperative research as a way of keeping tabs on activities at institutes with dual-use potential and as a means of increasing U.S. confidence in its intelligence assessments of who was doing WMD-relevant work. The Science Center in Moscow used a similar justification for funding Partner Projects with U.S. government rather than business partners. Similarly, transparency was the justification often given for Defense and State Department-funded collaborations with former biological weapons institutes.

Transparency, however, contradicts some of the original assumptions behind the engagement and redirection of former WMD workers. First, such collaboration was intended to be of limited duration. Each of the four programs studied here, for example, had an estimated end date. U.S. funding was supposed to end when former Soviet states could take over financial responsibility for converting or redirecting the institutes they inherited from the Soviet Union. Transparency, on the other hand, implies engagement, as long as a country's WMD activities are viewed with suspicion. Transparency also suggests a shift from focusing on institutes that are proliferation concerns to those that will remain a part of the weapons establishment. Finally, the goal of transparency inherently raises issues about U.S. cooperation for the purposes of spying, an activity that all U.S. engagement and redirection programs vigorously denied.

FITTING IN AT HOME

Organizations that are given new tasks are more likely to embrace them if they fit into the organization's culture and sense of purpose. Activities that contradict accepted routines or require significant changes are likely to be marginalized or, if possible, transferred to other organizations or terminated altogether. The four programs studied here were not exceptions. Each case study tells the story of an established department that was given a new program that was at odds with its normal mission or activities. The process of trying to fit in with its parent organization's norms resulted in programmatic changes and adaptations. I argue that these changes help to explain the poor results of U.S. efforts to discourage proliferation through sustainable job creation.

Defense Department conversion efforts and NCI illustrate what happens to programs that fail to adapt to the norms of their parent organizations. The Defense Department was initially hesitant about playing a role in Cooperative Threat Reduction (CTR) and related activities. During the first years of CTR, money for reprogramming was hard to find, and support for CTR was sometimes offered only in exchange for backing other priorities. The Department of Defense remained unenthusiastic about CTR-related activities that were not directly linked to the destruction of Russian weapons. In 1996, the Defense Department brokered a deal to rid itself of such functions. And, with the exception of a couple of Clinton appointees, the department did nothing to save its defense conversion program from termination by Congress.

NCI suffered a similar fate. It found itself in a department that catered to the interests and priorities of the U.S. nuclear weapons laboratories. Although these labs were instrumental in bringing about cooperation with Russia, they strongly favored high-tech research projects with nuclear weapons scientists. In contrast, NCI initially focused on community development, infrastructure improvements, and low-tech job-creation efforts such as butcher shops, bars, and small loans to local entrepreneurs. Moreover, NCI attempted to rein in the role of the labs in setting program priorities and allocating funds. As a result, it found itself deprived of crucial political support in both the Department of Energy and Congress. The department was slow to approve NCI travel requests, did not encourage budget increases, and fell behind in efforts to create public support for the program. With no love for NCI, the Department of Energy did little to protect it from congressional opponents, refute the skepticism of the George W. Bush administration, or reinvigorate Russia's commitment to the program. NCI was terminated in 2003. Both it and the Defense Department's conversion efforts lasted less than six years.

The Science Centers and IPP fared better. As a multinational initiative, the Science Centers were embraced by the State Department as a diplomatic activity, although some in the Department saw them as a defense program that was at odds with State's traditional foreign assistance activities. However, the Science Centers were organized around a functional issue, and therefore did not fit into the standard State Department categorization of activities in terms of country or geographic region. Also, the State Department oversaw few such cooperative programs and, furthermore, the Science Centers had abnormal oversight and accounting rules that were inherited from their early years under the jurisdiction of the Defense Department. As a result, the Science Centers did not fit into normal State Department routines and processes. Although the Centers were tolerated, other relevant activities at the State Department were not coordinated with them, Science Center budgets tended to remain constant rather than increase, and little was done to make working there career-enhancing for foreign service officers.

As for IPP, of the four programs studied here, it enjoyed the best fit within its parent organization. IPP originated in the U.S. nuclear weapons laboratories, which, thanks to a decentralized power structure, have traditionally enjoyed considerable independence within the Department of Energy. Similarly, the U.S. labs had preponderant influence on IPP strategy and funding priorities, and in discussions with Russia. However, as explained below, this close fit between IPP and the U.S. labs caused the program to take on some of the characteristics that in the past have proven detrimental for the Department of Energy, and which also limited IPP's success.

In addition to possible conflicts due to differences in characteristics, routines, or missions, organizational interest can also mean that new programs take on some of the characteristics of their parent organizations in an attempt to better fit in. For example, the Defense Department's conversion efforts adopted the department's rules about contracting through competitive bidding, with a preference to the lowest bidder. As a result, many conversion projects were partnered with inexperienced, uncommitted, or ill-suited businesses; this led not only to the failure of individual projects, but also to creating an atmosphere among Russian defense institutes that was at times hostile to conversion and made collaboration with the United States more difficult. Instead, conversion projects could have been exempted from normal contracting rules in favor of selecting appropriate business partners that were more prepared for the risks and requirements associated with defense conversion in Russia.

For the Science Centers, fitting in meant a focus on process. The Science Centers established an elaborate set of rules and procedures for project development, selection, and oversight. This was partly due to the need to facilitate cooperation between Science Center funding countries, each of which had its own project selection criteria. But this emphasis on process was reinforced by the preeminent U.S. role in Science Center activities and policy which, over time, came to emphasize Partner Projects with U.S. government agencies. Instead of encouraging the centers to re-evaluate the institutes and experts they engaged or refocus their activities on sustainable redirection, U.S. involvement turned them into administrative mechanisms that were valued for their ability to adhere to due process rather than their progress toward their original nonproliferation goals.

At NCI, fitting in meant abandoning community development and infrastructure projects and concentrating on job creation and downsizing. Furthermore, in a desperate attempt to demonstrate results, the program came to focus on two projects that had the support of Los Alamos and Livermore National Labs, key sources of political clout in the Department of Energy. However, NCI's activities and lack of progress toward job creation and downsizing had already caused problems in both the United States and Russia. In addition, the U.S. nuclear weapons labs tended to favor IPP, within which they had more independent power and authority. When its final projects failed, NCI was left with few allies in Russia, the U.S. Congress, or the Department of Energy.

As for IPP, allowing the U.S. national labs the same independence and decentralized power they enjoyed under the Department of Energy resulted in a more harmonious relationship, but poor results in terms of job creation. For example, because the labs often did not coordinate their activities in Russia, they did not share solutions to similar problems. This reinforced concerns in Russia about "nuclear tourism" and spying, and created acrimony with the State Department, which was responsible for managing travel to Russia by U.S. officials. Within the United States, the labs involved in IPP often made decisions by trading votes with each other, rather than rank-ordering priorities and the allocation of resources. There was also competition and distrust between the seven small non-weapons labs and the nuclear weapons research institutes at Los Alamos, Livermore, and Sandia. The IPP program office at DOE also had problems imposing various recordkeeping and accounting rules on U.S. lab participants and, as a result, the program had problems documenting its results. In addition, IPP adopted lab procedures for contracting with business partners that may have worked in the United States, but did little to help U.S. companies and former Soviet WMD experts build the relationships necessary for sustained cooperation. And both IPP and NCI suffered because paying the salaries of U.S. lab participants skewed resource allocation toward the United States and away from Russia.

COOPERATION VERSUS COMPETITION

Organizations with similar missions sometimes choose to cooperate, but more often they prefer autonomy. At times, this desire for independence turns into a competition for budgets, program expansion, or other perks. But similar organizations may also agree to collude. For example, the history of the U.S. defense budget suggests that the Army, Navy, and Air Force prefer collusion, having learned under Secretary of Defense Robert McNamara that when they argued with each other, the secretary of defense might use this information to reward some and punish others. In terms of efforts to engage and reemploy scientists, the case studies presented in this book show a persistent pattern of collusion but not cooperation.[2]

Despite the fact that Defense Conversion efforts, the Science Centers, IPP, and NCI all shared a similar mission, there was little cooperation between them. This also holds true for relations between the Science Centers in Moscow and Kiev, and for IPP and NCI, which for a time were co-located in the Department of Energy. Although there is evidence that project ideas were shared between the Science Centers, IPP, and NCI, this took place on an ad hoc basis or as the result of personal networking, not as a matter of routine. The norm was compartmentalization. Programs

---

2. This lack of cooperation is not limited to scientist redirection efforts under CTR. For a brief history of the persistence of coordination problems in U.S. nonproliferation policy, see Amy B. Zegart, "Running in Place: An Institutional Analysis of U.S. Nonproliferation Organization Since the Cold War," *Nonproliferation Review*, Vol. 10, No. 2 (Summer 2003), pp. 30–50.

that faced common obstacles in Russia did not routinely share solutions. There were no inter-program discussions about how to improve job-creation efforts. Different programs aimed at retraining weapons experts unknowingly funded the same projects. And efficiency, planning, and communication suffered due to a lack of cooperation.

Initially, inter-program cooperation was facilitated at the National Security Council (NSC), where country and topic-specific groups met to coordinate activities. But the NSC stopped fulfilling this role early in the first Clinton administration. Repeated calls for a high-level coordinator for CTR and related activities went unheeded. And although at the NSC there was a monthly Nonproliferation Interagency Roundtable, it only reviewed proposals. It did not coordinate activities between programs or departments.[3]

Within this void, organizational interest produced a tacit truce. Although people involved with Defense Department conversion efforts, the Science Centers, IPP, and NCI would privately complain bitterly about the inadequacies of their sister programs, especially the role of the U.S. national labs, silence was the norm in public. This was largely a strategic solution to a problem faced by all of these programs. They shared a political environment in the United States that never strongly or consistently supported scientist redirection efforts. Periodically, factions in Congress revisited debates from the early 1990s about whether such programs should be funded because of their national security benefits or conditioned, cut, or eliminated because they were foreign aid. Furthermore, each program felt a degree of insecurity because it could neither report significant job creation for former WMD experts, nor concretely measure the benefits provided to U.S. national security. Given the experts who were involved in redirection efforts, it was inevitable that people who participated in U.S. programs were also still employed by the Russian nuclear or defense complexes. And indeed, defense conversion efforts, the Science Centers, and IPP each suffered political embarrassment due to investigations or accusations claiming they indirectly "subsidized" Russian weapons programs or, in the case of IPP, Iran's nuclear program via the work of Russian scientists on the nuclear power reactor at Bushehr.[4] In spite of persistent or exaggerated attacks on individual programs, they did not attack each other. Organizational interest dictated that when everyone was weak, all should keep silent.

As a result of these incentives to avoid competing, these programs went without the cooperation necessary to secure a more widely shared sense of political investment in this agenda among executive agencies,

---

3. National Research Council, Office for Central Europe and Eurasia, Committee on Prevention of Proliferation of Biological Weapons, *The Biological Threat Reduction Program of the Department of Defense: From Foreign Assistance to Sustainable Partnerships* (Washington, D.C.: National Academy Press, 2007), p. 51

4. See, for example, U.S. Congress, House Committee on Energy and Water, "Department of Energy Program Funds Russian Nuclear Work in Iran," Press Release, February 5, 2008.

Congress, and the public.[5] Extolling the importance of efforts to combat the proliferation of WMD expertise would have helped end the "defense versus foreign aid" debate and encouraged U.S. politicians to limit the degree to which concerns about accounting, liability, and other policy issues got in the way of funding these efforts. Additionally, reaffirming the importance of this agenda would have helped retain a focus on completing work with Russia before diluting efforts by moving on to other less immediately important states and activities. Greater cooperation would also have lessened concerns in Russia about spying, provided more overall coherence to U.S. engagement and redirection efforts, and, in the process, helped overpower forces that were skeptical of or opposed to CTR.

The Problems and Possibilities of Cooperation

The programs studied here all shared a common mission: to make the United States safer by reducing the proliferation of WMD expertise. Some programs focused on the conversion of buildings or institutes as the key to reducing proliferation; others emphasized the reemployment of individuals or teams of WMD experts. As the case studies show, however, no program came close to finding reemployment for more than a handful of the WMD experts it considered its target population. Using optimistic assumptions, Defense Department conversion projects created some 4,000 jobs. The Science Centers added at best a few thousand more. IPP reported some 3,000 long-term jobs, and NCI claimed an additional 1,600. Together, this amounts to the permanent redirection of fewer than one in five of the 60,000 "experts of concern," the target most frequently cited by U.S. government officials from 1991–2008.

Moreover, it is clear that not all of these jobs went to WMD experts. Most Defense Department conversion projects targeted institutes that had only a tangential affiliation with WMD technology. The Science Centers and IPP allowed up to 40 percent of project participants to be non-WMD experts, and anyone living in a nuclear city was eligible for NCI activities. No program made significant efforts to verify the WMD credentials claimed by project participants, although the Science Centers, and through them the Defense Department and IPP, made efforts to engage former biological weapons institutes of specific concern to the U.S. government. Furthermore, aside from the early 1990s, there is little evidence that programs targeted specific individuals.

While it is clear that relatively few WMD experts were reemployed through U.S. efforts, it is also equally apparent that measuring only job creation underestimates the contributions these programs made to U.S. national security. During the early 1990s, when former Soviet WMD experts were suffering from wage arrears, low salaries, and a significant and abrupt decline in their prestige and standard of living, the United

---

5. For an examination of how each program came to adopt similar coping strategies, see Sharon K. Weiner, "Looking Out, Looking In: Competing Organizational Interests and the Proliferation of Soviet WMD Expertise," *Daedalus*, Vol. 138, No. 2 (Spring 2009), pp. 105–114.

States befriended and supported key WMD institutes and personnel. In particular, funding from U.S. programs was crucial for several core nuclear weapons institutes, such as the weapons research and design facilities at Sarov and Snezhinsk. Several former biological weapons institutes that fell under the direction of Biopreparat also claimed that U.S. support was crucial. After the ruble crash of 1998, NCI helped rejuvenate three closed nuclear cities in Russia by providing income, improving social services, and encouraging conversion and the transfer of municipal functions from the federal Ministry of Atomic Energy to local city governments.

More broadly, U.S. engagement and redirection efforts, as well as other CTR activities, also made important contributions to U.S. foreign policy. Despite the opportunities offered by the end of the Cold War, the United States was quite hesitant to embrace Russia as an ex-enemy, much less an ally. Throughout most of the 1990s, the United States held Russia at arms length. Furthermore, winning individual policy battles such as NATO expansion, the development of missile defenses, and curtailing Russian military sales trumped the value of establishing a long-term cooperative relationship. When Russia's position in the international community was weak and it needed U.S. support, the United States appeared to treat Russia as a defeated adversary of whom advantage could be taken. Russia expert Stephen Cohen goes even further, claiming that both Democrats and Republicans waged an "undeclared cold war" on Russia during this time.[6] As a result, the United States did not establish the trust, dialogue, and relationships that would be necessary for a cooperative partnership once Russia was able once again to more strongly assert its own priorities.

In contrast, the case studies illustrate the rapid development of intense institutional and personal bonds. By exploiting a common appreciation for scientific inquiry, U.S. nuclear weapons scientists were able to convince Russian scientists and institute directors to take a chance on cooperation with the West. In turn, these scientists and directors were able to pressure Russian political leaders to ameliorate the political, legal, and other barriers that stood in the way of cooperation.[7] As a result, the United States developed a cooperative working relationship with Russian nuclear weapons scientists and institutes that was largely missing at higher political levels. More bluntly stated, to a large extent, the United States and Russia were allies rather than enemies because of these initiatives. It

---

6. Stephen F. Cohen, "The New American Cold War," *The Nation*, July 10, 2006, p. 9.

7. A similar relationship is credited with helping material security efforts. See Matthew Bunn, "Cooperation to Secure Nuclear Stockpiles," *Innovations*, Vol. 1, No. 2 (Winter 2006), pp. 115–137; and Caitlin Talmadge, "Striking a Balance: The Lessons of U.S.-Russian Materials Security Cooperation," *Nonproliferation Review*, Vol. 12, No. 1 (March 2005), pp. 1–35. More broadly, according to Matthew Evangelista, *Unarmed Forces:The Transnational Movement to End the Cold War* (Ithaca, N.Y.: Cornell University Press, 2002), such epistemic communities of scientists resulted in arms control advocates in both the United States and the Soviet Union pressuring their governments to agree to arms reductions and restrictions that neither government would have embraced on its own.

remains to be seen, however, whether these bonds are strong enough to help mitigate broader political disputes between the two countries in the decades to come.

Additionally, the benefits of this dialogue between scientists led to calls to expand engagement and reemployment. The notion that CTR could be a global program became reality in the fiscal year 2004 defense authorization bill, when Congress authorized the president to use CTR funds from the Defense Department outside of the former Soviet Union. The George W. Bush administration would eventually use this authority to help Albania dispose of some chemical weapons. The goal for the future is to make the United States safer by having the ability to take advantage of opportunities to secure, remove, or dispose of excess weapons-relevant materials around the world. In 2003, Congress authorized the Department of State to expand the use of some of its nonproliferation budget outside of the former Soviet Union; it began to use collaborative research to engage former weapons experts in Iraq in 2003, and in Libya the next year. Similarly, in 2004, IPP expanded its operations to include Iraqi and Libyan WMD experts. There were also plans to extend Science Center activities beyond the states of the former Soviet Union, but as of 2008, this had not been approved by Russia.

Working with scientists in other countries, especially those who are potentially interested in WMD, promises several benefits to the United States. One is transparency. By engaging scientists, the U.S. government can understand the incentives, abilities, and progress of other states with respect to WMD with greater certainty. But perhaps a more important contribution is suggested by the use of scientific cooperation as a form of "soft power." Although the United States remains concerned about terrorist use of WMD and the development of such capabilities by "states of concern," most such states find themselves preoccupied by problems of development, including pressing public health concerns. By funding cooperation with scientists, especially experts in the biological and health sciences, the United States can discourage the development of indigenous WMD programs while at the same time helping states to develop the skills and institutional capacity to meet public health and other needs that, left on their own, they would be unable to address, at least in the short term. In such a manner, scientific collaboration helps the United States achieve its own goals—but through cooperation rather than coercion.

As of 2008, however, such cooperation had yet to receive significant political support in the United States. As the case studies illustrate, there remained many skeptics who believed that such activities are not part of U.S. national security efforts, but rather constitute foreign aid. Therefore, some argue, such spending should be conditioned on a variety of other behaviors by the receiving state, or redirected to job creation, education, development, and other activities in the United States. This unresolved political debate over the value of foreign assistance, especially aid given to states that are not clearly allies, has been reinforced by a lack of metrics that prove the value of such activities. But it is hard to measure scientists who do not proliferate, weapons that are not built, and conflicts that are averted. This inability to concretely demonstrate the benefits of scientific engagement, combined with persistent and significant skepticism toward such efforts, resulted in congressional termination of the Defense Department's conversion efforts and the end of NCI under the second Bush administration. It is likely that funding and support for the Science Centers and IPP were also limited for these reasons.

Despite the attractiveness of using scientific cooperation as a tool to further U.S. national security goals, in the absence of a U.S. domestic political consensus that supports such policy initiatives, it is unlikely that they will receive the political support and funding necessary to succeed. Moreover, the case studies show that the expansion of scientist engagement programs, combined with the reassertion by Russia of its own interests, has meant less funding for such nonproliferation work in Russia. This begs the question of whether nonproliferation concerns in Russia have indeed been ameliorated, or whether the United States is poised to neglect pressing or even more dangerous threats.

The Changing Threat of Proliferation

During the almost two decades since the end of the Cold War, there have been changes in the former Soviet nuclear, biological, chemical, and missile complexes; Russia has mounted its own conversion efforts; and there have been important economic and political changes in both Russia and the United States. In combination, these factors suggest that the threat of proliferation of weapons expertise is not the same as it was when the Soviet Union collapsed in 1991, or when the ruble was devalued in 1998, and that post-2008, it will be significantly different; programs will need to adapt to be effective. Moreover, the United States is likely to be forced to reevaluate its commitment to such efforts and the goals it seeks to achieve through them.

FORMER SOVIET WEAPONS WORKERS

Scientists, technicians, and engineers who were part of the Soviet WMD complex still exist in Russia and other parts of the former Soviet Union. If the United States remains concerned that they are a proliferation threat, then it is necessary to acknowledge changes in both their circumstances and the ability to engagement them in job-creation efforts.[8] First, the WMD experts who were the easiest to reemploy left the former Soviet weapons complex, mostly during the early to mid-1990s, and the remaining workers are likely to be harder to place in market-based jobs. Second, the means to proliferate has changed. Instead of concern about people physically moving to "rogue" countries, the threat has evolved to include e-mail communications, conference presentations and networking, and other exchanges of information that are harder to detect and

---

8. Part of the argument that follows is based upon work previously published in Sharon K. Weiner, "Preventing Nuclear Entrepreneurship in Russia's Nuclear Cities," *International Security*, Vol. 27, No. 2 (Fall 2002), pp. 126–158.

control. Moreover, U.S. concern about WMD acquisition has expanded beyond states to include non-state actors, specifically terrorist groups. Compared to governments, these non-state actors have different weapons interests and priorities. As a result, the problem of knowledge proliferation has become broader.

Demographic changes in the Soviet WMD complex constitute one of the key evolutions in the threat of proliferation of weapons expertise. The most overwhelming way that downsizing was accomplished was through the voluntary exodus of workers from the weapons community. These workers were predominantly younger people who left willingly because they saw a lack of future in the weapons complex, and because they had either the entrepreneurial skills, business acumen, or personality to take the risks posed by moving into the market economy.[9] This meant two things: the most qualified workers left the defense complex, and those who remained were not necessarily the ones the government would have preferred to do the job of future weapons work; and, secondly, those who remained were inherently less interested in or adaptable to market-driven work in the private sector. As of 2008, some of these older workers remain throughout the WMD complex, as well as the defense industry.

This results in an interesting problem for U.S. programs. The people who were interested in such collaborations have already participated. There remains, however, a small but still existent cohort of weapons scientists who were not initially drawn to foreign collaborations. Rather than luring these people into collaborations, U.S. programs have instead come to focus on younger workers who have only recently joined the Russian weapons complex, and who have every reason to believe they have a secure future doing weapons work. This same tendency toward hiring new workers instead of older Soviet ones has also been true for commercial ventures that took place outside of U.S. programs. Intel developed software programming and other computer services in conjunction with the All-Russian Research Institute of Experimental Physics (VNIIEF), the nuclear weapons research and design institute in Sarov. Intel initially employed older workers from VNIIEF's math division, but by 2004 they were attracting younger people who either had been recently hired into the weapons complex or had never worked there at all.[10] However, this emphasis on new workers who were never part of the Soviet complex contradicts stated U.S. policy goals.

If the United States remains interested in reaching this last cohort of Soviet workers, it needs to understand the consequences of their age. The remaining experts who resisted civilian employment are older. Older

9. Presentations from "Reorientation of Defense Enterprises, Scientific and Engineering Staff to Civil Production," Russian-U.S. Training and Consulting Workshop, Obninsk, Russia, June 27–29, 2000; and Valentin Tikhonov, *Russia's Nuclear and Missile Complex: The Human Factor in Proliferation* (Washington, D.C.: Carnegie Endowment for International Peace, 2001), pp. 30–36.

10. Analytical Center for Non-Proliferation, "An Overview of VNIIEF-STL Experience and Projects," Sarov, Russia, 2004, p. 30–31.

workers present several problems. First, although the Russian pension system has improved, for most retirees, as of 2008, it still did not provide a comfortable retirement wage. Outside of Russia, pensions often mean poverty. Therefore, people resist retiring or seek to supplement their retirement pension. This means they are looking for work. If Russia realizes its future plans to reduce the size of the weapons complex, it is likely to seek to retire these older workers first. Thus, they constitute a possible proliferation problem, along with the former weapons experts who remain at institutes and facilities that have no future weapons role.

Second, there appears to be a close correlation between the age of workers and their lack of interest in transitioning to commercial-based employment. Older workers, as a group, are more set in their ways and resist the dramatic changes posed by a switch to market-based employment. They also have a greater sense of entitlement and less interest in changing jobs because of their personal investment in the old Soviet system. Besides enjoying prestige based on their positions, older workers are more likely to remember the hardships they endured for the sake of the nation. Some of the scientists who initially came to the nuclear cities were often greeted with little more than an open field and a shovel; they literally built the cities from scratch. Moreover, workers who lived in closed cities took part in a system where paternalistic bonds between workers and their employers were the norm.[11] Their jobs were their ticket to housing, health care, day care, and a variety of other perks. They lived, played, and raised their children in a community of coworkers. Leaving this system means, in a very real sense, a betrayal of the nation and of their social network. Finally, older workers are a poor investment for businesses in that they will work fewer years in any new job, and thus promise less of a return on the retraining that has been invested in them.

Older workers in Russia's closed cities present a particularly challenging problem. From the mid-1990s through 2006, there were changes in the rules and demographics in Russia's closed administrative territories, or ZATOs, that have had and will continue to have ramifications. In particular, these changes had the effect of discouraging business development and making hiring competition more intense. Although oil revenues and increased trade with China have improved living conditions in many parts of Russia, the business environment of the closed cities remains stifled. First, the legal status of the ZATOs changed. In 1992, the Duma created the ZATO system when it passed a law that gave special status to Russia's ten nuclear cities and approximately thirty other closed cities with defense-related functions. Special security requirements were applied to these ZATOS because of the security-related work that went on within their borders.[12] As of 2009, these cities remain closed in the

---

11. For a discussion of these bonds, see Kimberly Zisk, *Weapons, Culture and Self Interest: Soviet Defense Managers in the New Russia* (New York: Columbia University Press, 1998), pp. 35–39.

12. See Richard H. Rowland, "Russia's Secret Cities," *Post-Soviet Geography and Economics*, Vol. 37, No. 7 (September 1996), p. 427.

sense that movement in or out was still controlled by the FSB, although foreign visitors were usually allowed. For example, each of the ten nuclear ZATOs had been visited by foreigners, though some of their nuclear facilities remained off-limits.[13] But this admittance often took time; in addition to a visa to enter Russia, foreign visitors to ZATOs had to have an official letter of invitation from the appropriate government ministry or other government-affiliated organization. In the case of the nuclear ZATOs, entry permission had to be requested forty-five days in advance, although in some cases multiple-entry permits were issued that required only two weeks advance notice. Foreign visitors were usually escorted at all times. In the case of the nuclear cities, additional permission was also required to visit the nuclear weapons facilities themselves. In practical terms, this meant that potential employers could easily meet prospective employees only if those employees left their facilities or came outside the ZATOs. If employers were interested in converting existing facilities, often they could not inspect those facilities directly, or could do so only with lengthy delays.[14] Both private companies and U.S. government programs cited access problems as a major impediment to investment and hiring.[15] Obviously, the ZATO rules that were meant to protect Russian national security had the added effect of deterring economic diversification and development.

Access to many ZATOs, including the nuclear cities, was liberalized, but this also created additional problems for the reemployment of weapons experts. Because of their security restrictions, the ZATOs were seen as safer and more removed from problems in the "new" Russia, including petty crime, organized crime, and drugs. Moreover, ZATOs cities traditionally had better quality housing, schools, and public services.[16] For

13. The databases of various governmental and nongovernmental programs show cooperative work being initiated in all ten cities. See also L. Saratova, "Freedom for the Free: Regime in Sarov," *Gorodskoy Kuryer*, April 2, 1998, quoted in Oleg Bukharin, Appendix 3, "What are Russia's Closed Nuclear Cities?" in Oleg Bukharin, Frank N. von Hippel, and Sharon K. Weiner, *Conversion and Job Creation in Russia's Closed Nuclear Cities* (Princeton, N.J.: Program on Nuclear Policy Alternatives, Center for Energy and Environmental Studies, Princeton University, 2000), p. 74.

14. The rules for private employers are often different from the rules for foreign government–funded research. But all require some form of agreement with the Russian government about access to the facilities and the ZATO where they are housed. One exception was the Avangard facility in Sarov, where an "open" technopark was constructed. The U.S. government, under the Nuclear Cities Initiative, spent more than $1 million to relocate the security fences so that four buildings would be outside the nuclear facilities. However, these buildings are still inside the city of Sarov and thus still governed by all the access restrictions that apply to nuclear ZATOs.

15. Interviews with program managers frequently cited problems with access or rumors of problems with access. See also Department of Energy, The Secretary of Energy Advisory Board, Howard Baker and Lloyd Cutler, *A Report Card on the Department of Energy's Nonproliferation Programs with Russia* (Washington, D.C.: Department of Energy, January 10, 2001), pp. ix, 22–23.

16. Bukharin, "What are Russia's Closed Cities?" p. 75; and Glenn Schweitzer, *Swords into Market Shares: Technology, Economics, and Security in the New Russia* (Washington, D.C.: Joseph Henry Press, 2000), p. 186.

these reasons, ZATO residents overwhelmingly favored keeping the cities closed.[17] These conditions not only discouraged workers from leaving the ZATOs, but also they made them attractive places for emigration; people could move into the ZATOs if they were offered employment by the government facilities there or if they were relatives of current residents.[18] This meant that the population of the ZATOs actually increased. For example, during the 1990s, when Russia's urban population was in decline, the population of the nuclear ZATOs increased by approximately 8.5 percent.[19] These additional 60,000 people entered the competition for jobs in the nuclear cities. More specifically, this meant that at precisely the time when Russia was seeking to lay off additional workers in the early 2000s, there were more people competing for jobs. Whereas the unemployment rate in the nuclear cities was about the same as throughout Russia as a whole, from 2000 to 2008, the working-age population of the nuclear cities was expected to increase by an estimated 50 percent, thus causing significant increases in unemployment during this time and decades into the future.[20]

Besides demographic and legal changes in Russia, the danger of weapons expertise proliferation has also changed because of the increased ability of scientists to interact with the outside world. One of the goals of the United States has been to increase the international exposure of these experts and, in particular, to encourage them to interact more regularly with colleagues from the West. The rationale is that this interaction encourages scientists to adopt Western norms, including that of nonproliferation, provides scientists with more opportunities for peaceful collaboration, and creates networks between Russia and the West, so that more scientists in the West know what their Russian colleagues are doing. But the United States has also taught scientists the nature of capitalism, comparative advantage, and profit-making from selling weapons-relevant skills. These lessons, plus the easing of travel restrictions in Russia, especially with respect to weapons scientists, have meant that scientists are increasingly willing and able to attend international conferences and to leave Russia to do collaborative research with colleagues. Forgotten, however, is that there are few controls over conference topics, or that some of Russia's allies are considered U.S. enemies.[21] For example, speaking at a

---

17. According to Russian officials, in 1995, 95 percent of those living in the nuclear cities voted against opening them. Judith Perera, "Opening the Closed Towns," *Nuclear Engineering International* (June 1995), p. 44.

18. N. Kocheshkova, "Foreigners in Sarov," *Gordskoy Kuryer*, February 2001.

19. Alexander Pikayev, "Russian Nuclear Insecurity," *Proliferation Brief*, Vol. 2, No. 3 (Washington, D.C.: Carnegie Endowment for International Peace, February 19, 1999); and Richard H. Rowland, "Secret Cities of Russia and Kazakhstan in 1998," *Post-Soviet Geography and Economics*, Vol. 40, No. 4 (June 1999), p. 290.

20. Tikhonov, *Russia's Nuclear and Missile Complex*, pp. 25, 28.

21. The director of Vector, for example, claimed he was certain that proliferation did not occur at the Vector facilities, but also said he did not know what Russian specialists did at conferences and meetings. See "Building a Global Agenda for Bio-Proliferation Prevention: Current Status and Future of Russian Biotechnology," workshop sponsored by the Russian-

conference in Tehran on missile engine technology is seen very differently by the U.S. and Russian governments.

Moreover, in the name of increased communication and openness with former Soviet colleagues, the United States and private entities (for example, the Soros Foundation) helped to install Internet connections, including connections in remote areas. This, however, opened up the possibility of "moonlighting by modem"—that is, doing work for others that involves interaction only over email. The problem, of course, is that it is difficult to monitor the content of email communication, although the Russian internal security forces claim to monitor all Internet users online.[22]

The threat from weapons expertise has also changed in a way that was dramatically illustrated on September 11, 2001. The key U.S. proliferation concern has now changed from states developing WMD programs to weapons in the hands of terrorists. This change should also beget a shift in focus. States are probably interested in the ability to make their own weapons or, perhaps, to buy them from reliable suppliers. Deterrence is more robust if your enemies know you have a significant weapons capability or cannot be easily disarmed. States seeking a nuclear weapons program would likely want to employ experts who know how to manage a team to build a bomb. Such states would also be interested in select expertise that they do not possess. For example, if uranium enrichment is the chosen path to a nuclear bomb, then a state would be interested in people who understand centrifuge technology, even if those experts are of little use in actually constructing the bomb itself. If state actors are the key concern, then it is important to keep tabs on top weapons experts, but also on those with expertise in selected critical parts of the weapons process. This also means a concern about missile experts, since states are more likely to seek to deploy their weapons in a reliable and controlled way that signals to their enemies their intentions and capabilities.

Terrorists, however, are likely to seek the weapons themselves or the materials to build them, but not necessarily the capabilities to repeatedly make the weapons from scratch. In other words, the terrorist wants a bomb, not a bomb program. This suggests a different proliferation concern: security of weapons and materials instead of experts. It also sends a mixed message about the expertise of most concern. Certainly, top scientists and engineers who could lead a team to build a bomb using stolen or purchased materials are still worrisome. But so is anyone with access to the locks, windows, doors, and computer codes that lead to weapons-usable materials. Suddenly, the janitors and construction workers in the weapons complex are on an equal footing with the top scientists: All

---

American Nuclear Security Advisory Council (RANSAC), the Landau Network—Centro Volta, The International Center for Genetic Engineering and Biotechnology, The Analysis and Policy Planning Unit of the Italian Ministry of Foreign Affairs, and the International Science and Technology Center, Como, Italy, November 17–18, 2003.

22.   Roger Roffey, Wilhelm Unge, Jenny Clevström and Kristina S. Westerdahl, "Support to Threat Reduction of the Russian Biological Weapons Legacy—Conversion, Biodefence and the Role of Biopreparat," Swedish Defence Research Agency, FOI-R-0841-SE (April 2003), p. 66.

must be kept economically sound in order to discourage proliferation.[23]

If the United States continues to see former Soviet WMD experts as a proliferation risk, or if concerns arise about the activities of current workers, then it is important to understand changes in their incentives and abilities to proliferate, as well as their motivations for cooperating with the United States in threat reduction efforts. However, as explained in the next section, it is by no means clear that the United States will continue to see these workers as a proliferation threat that justifies the expenditure of U.S. dollars.

A NEW POLITICAL ENVIRONMENT

The U.S.-Russian relationship is obviously very different than it was at the end of the Cold War. Russia has become more economically secure, and has sought to translate this greater financial stability into a rejuvenated weapons complex. The economic crisis of 2008, however, has raised questions about Russia's ability to sustain its economic growth and turn it into improved living standards for its population. Russia has also become more willing to assert its own political priorities, and no longer feels as compelled to pretend to share U.S. concerns about proliferation. Meanwhile, there is domestic political pressure in the United States to translate Russia's economic success into increased responsibility for funding and sustaining threat reduction efforts. Russia, however, has few additional incentives to comply. Besides taking account of the new political realities in this relationship, any future cooperative nonproliferation efforts will also have to acknowledge the legacy of the past two decades of interaction.

Perhaps the biggest change since the collapse of the Soviet Union is the Russian economy. During the early to mid-2000s, Russia has been on a more secure financial trajectory, and can afford to assume more of the burden for the security of its own WMD personnel. When U.S. involvement began in the 1990s, the concern was that Russia's economic woes would mean that it had to lay off workers, could not pay the ones it had, and had insufficient resources to devote to conversion and job creation. But by the early 2000s, this was no longer the case.

The transition from a centrally planned economy to a market economy certainly took its toll. Although most post-Soviet states continue to struggle economically, the Russian economy has become much stronger since 2000. Whereas Russian GDP usually fell every year during the 1990s, growth became the norm by 1999, and the Russian economy has continued to grow by 3–9 percent per year.[24] Although the Russian economy

---

23. An argument similar to this is made by Laura S. H. Holgate, Nuclear Threat Initiative, "Linking Nuclear Expertise and Nuclear Security," Fifth International Working Group Meeting, Como, Italy, April 2005. She correctly points out that retirees also become more of an issue because they may maintain continued access to weapons and materials.

24. The worst year for the Russian economy was 1994, when GDP fell by over 12.5 percent. In the mid-1990s, GDP fell by an annual rate of 4–5 percent. See Stuart D. Goldman, "Russia," Congressional Research Service, April 9, 2004, p. 6.

has increased its production of retail goods and services and diversified beyond agriculture and heavy industry, one of the keys to Russia's economic recovery is the sale of oil and natural gas.[25] An estimated 40 percent of the Russian federal budget is from oil and gas sales and the taxes associated with them.[26]

Although these trends do not necessarily mean that Russia is certain to enjoy long-term economic growth, Russian government revenues have increased, and the government is making more long-term investments. In particular, Russian spending on defense and nuclear weapons has increased and is likely to continue to do so. Since the late 1990s, Russian defense spending has outpaced increases in Russian GDP, sometimes by close to 20 percent.[27] For 2007, the Russian defense budget was predicted to rise to over $32 billion.[28]

Spending on nuclear weapons has also increased. In 1994, the Russian federal budget for the nuclear weapons complex was just over $291 million and, because of revaluations of the ruble, it had decreased to some $70 million by the end of the decade.[29] By 2000, budgets began to recover, and spending for the nuclear weapons complex climbed from $211 million in 2001 to over $400 million in 2006.[30]

There are other indicators that the Russian nuclear weapons complex is becoming more robust. Salaries in core parts of the complex are

25.   Stephen Kotkin, in *Armageddon Averted: The Soviet Collapse 1970–2000* (Oxford: Oxford University Press, 2008), pp. 199–200, argues that Russia's economy is also buoyed by demand from China for Russian products and services.

26.   Department of Energy, Energy Information Administration, "Major, Non-OPEC Countries' Oil Revenues," June 2005.

27.   Based on a comparison of changes in Russian GDP and defense spending taken from Central Intelligence Agency, *World Fact Book*, Washington, D.C., various years; SIPRI Military Expenditure Database on the web at http://www.sipri.org; and Petter Stalenheim, Damien Fruchart, Wuyi Omitoogun, and Catalina Perdomo, "Appendix 8A. Tables of Military Expenditure," in Stockholm International Peace Research Institute, *SIPRI Yearbook 2006* (Oxford University Press, 2006), p. 341.

28.   Fred Weir, "Russia Intensifies Efforts to Rebuild Its Military Machine," *Christian Science Monitor*, February 12, 2007, p. 4.

29.   These figures are taken from Peter Romashkin, "Analysis of Federal Budgets of the Russian Federation in the National Defense Section of Spending," Subsection on the Nuclear Weapons Complex, IMEMO, May 25, 2006, p. 2. According to Ivan Safranchuk of the World Security Institute, the Russian federal budget for nuclear weapons activities is notoriously hard to interpret. Electronic communication with the author, March 17, 2006. In addition to complications due to secrecy over defense spending figures in Russia, official budget figures may or may not include funding for nuclear energy and non-weapons–related construction. Additional funding for the nuclear weapons can come from a variety of sources that may or may not be consistently reflected in the budget, including international assistance, legitimate commercial activities of individual enterprises, money from tax exemption schemes, especially for the nuclear cities, and income under the HEU Purchase Agreement. Add into this mix variances due to assumptions about constant versus current monetary values and ruble conversion rates. But, even with these caveats in mind, it is clear that budgets for the nuclear weapons complex are increasing, although not as consistently as the overall Russian federal budget.

30.   Romashkin, "Analysis of Federal Budgets of the Russian Federation," p. 2.

significantly above the Russian national average, there are no longer salary delays, and both VNIIEF and the All-Russian Research Institute of Technical Physics (VNIITF) are hiring several hundred young scientists each year. Additionally, in March 2003, Putin announced plans to reform and modernize the Russian military, including completing work on a "next generation" of nuclear weapons.[31]

Although Russia is clearly increasing spending on defense and nuclear weapons, these systems also deteriorated significantly throughout the 1990s; many are in need of replacement parts and repair. Spending increases, especially those in the nuclear weapons complex, are partly for improvements above and beyond simple recovery or maintenance. Therefore, this leads inevitably to the question of whether Russia is spending money to improve its military capabilities and letting the United States assume the burden for conversion and job creation. This has been a persistent argument by the U.S. Congress against aid to Russia.

U.S. pressure for Russia to assume more of the burden for conversion, proliferation, and brain drain programs is likely to increase as Russia improves its military and nuclear complexes. This pressure, however, takes place within a political context that is likely to make future U.S.-Russian cooperation more contentious. The United States places a high priority on nonproliferation, and is especially concerned about nuclear and biological materials in the hands of terrorists. The former Soviet Union is seen as the most likely source of these materials. Although it is unfair to say that Russia is not worried about proliferation, its national priorities focus on economic rejuvenation and regaining status as a great power. When Russia thinks of terrorism, it focuses on Chechnya, not Iran, Iraq, or Al Qaeda, although some see a connection between the latter and violence in Chechnya. This means that the United States and Russia have different motivations for pursuing cooperation, and different priorities for reaching agreement. As the United States seeks to put more of the economic burden for conversion on Russia, pressure Russia to grant more liberal access to weapons facilities, request sensitive information about additional facilities, and increase reporting requirements that involve national security related–information, Russia's own national security priorities provide little incentive to be more cooperative. Moreover, Russia can point to the hypocrisy of U.S. spending efforts: about 0.1 percent of an approximately $500 billion annual defense budget is spent on efforts to control terrorist access to WMD materials and expertise.

The political context within which proliferation programs will be renegotiated also includes two other important factors. First, Russia is increasingly willing to assert its own authority. It remembers that since the end of the Cold War, the United States has at times flaunted its wealth, superpower status, and authority in an attempt to tell Russia how to behave, democratize, and generally change its economy and political system to be more like that of the United States. Russia, however, still sees itself

---

31. Paul Webster, "Nuclear Weapons: Russia Revives Sagging Research Program," *Science*, Vol. 301, No. 5629 (July 4, 2003), p. 34.

as a great power, and will increasingly assert its own priorities. Moreover, within Russia there is a strong feeling that post–Cold War institutions and politics should properly follow neither European nor Asian models, but rather a "third way" which is distinctly Russian. In turn, this reassertion of Russian nationalism and increasing willingness to challenge U.S. leadership is interpreted by some in the United States as a rejuvenated Russian threat, which should be met with a tougher stance and, increasingly, sticks rather than carrots.[32] Furthermore, in many past threat reduction efforts, Russia feels that the United States has dictated the terms and conditions of what were supposed to be cooperative programs. In short, at precisely the time when the United States seeks to renegotiate the burden for cooperative nonproliferation efforts, domestic forces in both Russia and the United States will be increasingly less likely to compromise.

This situation is made worse by a second factor: the economic crisis that began in 2008. The United States sees future CTR projects as part of "right sizing" the Russian weapons complex, and expects Russia to assume more of the burden both to fund future projects and to sustain current efforts once U.S. assistance ends. Russia, however, prefers to continue investments aimed at modernizing its weapons complex, reasoning that because proliferation issues matter more to the United States, it should assume the burden for funding them.[33] Therefore, it is especially unlikely that Russia will agree to assume more of the financial burden for cooperative nonproliferation programs, and the United States may well be faced with a choice between abandoning some efforts or pursuing them on Russia's terms.

A similar quandary is posed by bilateral arms control discussions that have resumed with the start of the Obama administration. Even after the "New START" treaty, concluded in 2010, the leaders of both countries continue to talk about large reductions in their nuclear arsenals, and also the eventual elimination of nuclear weapons. Arms reductions will mean fewer jobs for Russian nuclear weapons experts. At the same time, Russia is also committed to the modernization and maintenance of a smaller weapons complex and to providing financial incentives for younger experts to seek jobs there. This will create redundant older weapons experts who might pose a proliferation risk. The question for the United States is whether this proliferation risk, and significant reductions in nuclear weapons, justify assuming a financial burden for funding scientist engagement and reemployment efforts that can easily be borne by Russia.

The United States may choose to reevaluate the goals it seeks to achieve through CTR, or the price it is willing to pay to achieve those goals. It may also decide to give up work with Russia in favor of non-

---

32. For example, in 2006, the Council on Foreign Relations released a report urging President Bush to be more forceful in relations with Russia and to see Russia as an authoritarian regime rather than a strategic partner. See Peter Baker, "Task Force Urges Bush to be Tougher With Russia," *Washington Post*, March 5, 2006, p. 16.

33. Interview with Russian government official 1, January 13, 2009.

proliferation programs and problems in other countries. Regardless, the resulting policies must contend with two political realities. One arises from the parochial interests of organizations. The case studies examined here show how far policy goals and successes can be influenced by an organization's attempts to get new policy assignments to fit in with the goals, routines, and values of its parent agency. The second reality is that even in the midst of what looks like consensus and support, domestic political disagreements matter. As the case studies show, such disagreements can result in program metrics that focus on measurable outcomes but not necessarily policy goals, a lack of cooperation between programs, and restrictions on innovation and risk-taking. Without paying attention to these lessons from past cooperative nonproliferation efforts, the United States runs the risk that in Russia, and perhaps in the future in other countries of proliferation concern, it will undercut the possibilities for deeper cooperative nonproliferation efforts. This may be a high price to pay for letting domestic politics and organizational interests prevail over national security.

Bibliography

BOOKS

Allison, Graham T., Owen R. Coté, Jr., Richard A. Falkenrath, and Steven E. Miller. *Avoiding Nuclear Anarchy: Containing the Threat of Loose Russian Nuclear Weapons and Fissile Material* (Cambridge: MIT Press, 1996).

Bailey, Janet. *The Good Servant: Making Peace with the Bomb at Los Alamos* (New York: Simon and Schuster, 1995).

Blau, Peter, and W. Richard Scott. *Formal Organizations* (San Francisco: Chandler, 1962).

Broad, William, Stephen Engelberg, and Judith Miller. *Germs: Biological Weapons and America's Secret War* (New York: Simon and Schuster, 2001).

Campbell, Kurt M., Ashton B. Carter, Steven E. Miller, and Charles A. Zraket. *Soviet Nuclear Fission* (Cambridge, Mass.: Center for Science and International Affairs, Harvard University, November 1991).

Cochran, Thomas B., Robert S. Norris, and Oleg A. Bukharin. *Making the Russian Bomb From Stalin to Yeltsin* (Boulder, Colo.: Westview Press, 1995).

Cronberg, Tarja. *Transforming Russia: From a Military to a Peace Economy* (London: I.B. Tauris, 2003).

Downs, Anthony. *Inside Bureaucracy* (Boston: Little Brown, 1967).

Eden, Lynn. *Whole World on Fire: Organizations, Knowledge, and Nuclear Weapons Devastation* (Ithaca, N.Y.: Cornell University Press, 2004).

Ellis, Jason D. *Defense by Other Means: The Politics of U.S.-NIS Threat Reduction and Nuclear Security Cooperation* (Westport, Conn.: Praeger, 2001).

Evangelista, Matthew. *Unarmed Forces: The Transnational Movement to End the Cold War* (Ithaca, N.Y.: Cornell University Press, 2002).

Gaddy, Clifford G. *The Price of the Past: Russia's Struggle with the Legacy of a Militarized Economy* (Washington, D.C.: Brookings Institution, 1996).

Genin, Vlad E., ed. *The Anatomy of Russian Defense Conversion* (Walnut Creek, Calif.: Vega Press, 2001).

Goldgeier, James M., and Michael McFaul. *Power and Purpose: U.S. Policy Toward Russia After the Cold War* (Washington, D.C.: Brookings Institution, 2003).

Goodman, Allan E., ed. *The Diplomatic Record 1991–1993* (Boulder, Colo.: Westview Press, 1995).

Johnson, Teresa Pelton, and Steven E. Miller, eds. *Russian Security after the Cold War: Seven Views from Moscow* (Washington, D.C.: Brassey's, 1994).

Kotkin, Stephen. *Armageddon Averted: The Soviet Collapse, 1970–2000* (Oxford: Oxford University Press, 2008).

Miller, Steven E., and Dmitri Trenin, eds. *The Russian Military* (Cambridge, Mass: American Academy of Arts and Sciences and MIT Press, 2004).

O'Prey, Kevin P. *A Farewell to Arms? Russia's Struggles with Defense Conversion* (New York: Twentieth Century Fund Press, 1995).

Perera, Judith. *The Nuclear Industry in the Former Soviet Union: Transition from Crisis to Opportunity*, Vol. 2 (London: Financial Times Energy Publishing, 1997).

Perrow, Charles. *Complex Organizations* (New York: McGraw-Hill, 1986).

Sapolsky, Harvey M. *The Polaris System Development: Bureaucratic and Programmatic Success in Government* (Cambridge, Mass.: Harvard University Press, 1972).

Schweitzer, Glenn E. *Moscow DMZ: The Story of the International Effort to Convert Russian Weapons* (Armonk, N.Y.: M.E. Sharpe, 1996).

_____. *Swords into Market Shares: Technology. Economics. and Security in the New Russia* (Washington, D.C.: Joseph Henry Press. 2000).

Selznick, Philip. *TVA and the Grass Roots: Study of the Sociology of Formal Organization* (Berkeley: University of California Press, 1949).

Shields, John M., and William C. Potter, eds. *Dismantling the Cold War: U.S. and NIS Perspectives on the Nunn-Lugar Cooperative Threat Reduction Program* (Cambridge, Mass.: MIT Press, 1997).

Sigal, Leon V. *Hang Separately: Cooperative Security between the United States and Russia, 1985–1994* (New York: Century Foundation Press, 2000).

Trulock, Notra. *Code Name Kindred Spirit: Inside the Chinese Nuclear Espionage Scandal* (San Francisco: Encounter Books, 2003).

Wallin, Lars B., ed. *Lectures and Contributions to East European Studies at FOA* (Stockholm: Swedish National Defence Establishment, 1996).

Woodward, Bob. *Bush at War* (New York: Simon and Schuster, 2002).

Zaloga, Steven J. *The Kremlin's Nuclear Sword: The Rise and Fall of Russia's Strategic Nuclear Forces, 1945–2000* (Washington, D.C.: Smithsonian Institution Press, 2002).

Zegart, Amy B. *Flawed By Design: The Evolution of the CIA, JCS, and NSC* (Stanford: Stanford University Press, 1999).

Zisk, Kimberly. *Weapons, Culture and Self Interest: Soviet Defense Managers in the New Russia* (New York: Columbia University Press, 1998).

ARTICLES

"A DOE Program is Turning Swords into Ploughshares," *Electronic Design*, August 21, 2000, www.elecdesign.com/Articles/ArticleID/4633/4633.html (accessed June 15, 2007).

Akhtamzian, Ildar A. "The International Science and Technology Center: Bureaucratic Games," *Nonproliferation Review*, Vol. 3, No. 1 (Fall 1995), pp. 79–83.

Alessi, Victor, and Ronald F. Lehman II. "Science in the Pursuit of Peace: The Success and Future of the ISTC," *Arms Control Today*, June/July 1998.

Allen, Mike. "Bush Pledges More Aid for Russian Arms Cuts," *Washington Post*, December 28, 2001, p. A1.

Allison, Graham, and Robert Blackwill. "America's Stake in the Soviet Future," *Foreign Affairs*, Vol. 70, No. 3 (Summer 1991), pp. 77–97.

Apple, R.W., Jr. "Soviet Turmoil; Even as Bush Counsels Prudence, West Seems Eager to Aid Soviets," *New York Times*, August 29, 1991, p. A1.

Baker, Peter, "Task Force Urges Bush to be Tougher With Russia," *Washington Post*, March 5, 2006, p. 16.

Ball, Deborah Yarsike, and Theodore P. Gerber. "Russian Scientists and Rogue States: Does Western Assistance Reduce the Proliferation Threat?" *International Security*, Vol. 29, No. 4 (Spring 2005), pp. 50–77.

Ben Ouagrham, Sonia. "Conversion of Russian Chemical Weapons Production Facilities: Conflicts with the CWC," *Nonproliferation Review*, Vol. 7, No. 2 (Summer 2000), pp. 44–62.

Bernstein, David, and William J. Perry. "Defense Conversion in Russia: A Strategic Imperative," *Stanford Journal of International Affairs*, Vol. 2, No. 2 (Summer 1993).

Bhattacharjee, Yudhijit. "Rising Asian Threat Leaves Russia in the Lurch," *Science*, Vol. 317, No. 5838 (August 3, 2007), p. 581.

Bivens, Matt. "Investing, Pentagon-Style," *Moscow Times*, April 4, 2001, p. 7.

————. "Shredded, Ignored, Exiled and Penniless," *Moscow Times*, April 4, 2001, p. 7.

Bleek, Philipp C. "Bush Reviews Threat Reduction Programs, Contemplates Cuts," *Arms Control Today*, April 2001.

Bogert, Carroll, and Margaret Garrard Warner. "The 'Who Lost Russia' Debate," *Newsweek*, March 23, 1992.

Bozheyeva, Gulbarshyn. "The Pavlodar Chemical Weapons Plant in Kazahkstan," *Nonproliferation Review*, Vol. 7, No. 2 (Summer 2000), pp. 136–145.

Broder, John M., and Doyle McManus. "U.S. Gives Soviets Proposals to Block Nuclear Exports," *Los Angeles Times*, December 14, 1991, p. A-10.

Brock, Gregory. "The ZATO Archipelago Revisited—Is the Federal Government Loosening Its Grip? A Research Note," *Europe-Asia Studies*, Vol. 52, No. 7 (November 2000), pp. 1349–1360.

Bukharin, Oleg. "Downsizing Russia's Nuclear Warhead Production Infrastructure," *Nonproliferation Review*, Vol. 8, No. 1 (Spring 2001), pp. 116–130.

_____. "The Future of Russia's Plutonium Cities," *International Security*, Vol. 21, No. 4 (Spring 1997), pp. 126–158.

_____. "Stewards and Custodians: Tomorrow's Crisis for the Russian Nuclear Weapons Complex?" *Nonproliferation Review*, Vol. 6, No. 4 (Fall 1999), pp. 128–138.

Bunn, Matthew. "Cooperation to Secure Nuclear Stockpiles," *Innovations*, Vol. 1, No. 2 (Winter 2006), pp. 115–137.

Bunn, Matthew, Oleg Bukharin, Jill Cetina, Kenneth N. Luongo, and Frank N. von Hippel. "Retooling Russia's Nuclear Cities," *Bulletin of the Atomic Scientists*, Vol. 54, No. 4 (September/October 1998), pp. 44–50.

Chase, Marilyn, David S. Cloud, and John J. Fialka. "Soviet Germ Program is a Worry Once Again Amidst Anthrax Scare," *Wall Street Journal*, October 15, 2001, p. A1.

Clymer, Adam. "Soviet Turmoil: U.S. Swords Into Plowshares for Soviets?" *New York Times*, August 29, 1991, p. A22.

Cohen, Stephen F. "The New American Cold War," *The Nation*, July 10, 2006.

Cooperman, Alan, and Kyrill Belianinov. "Moonlighting by Modem in Russia: Hard-up Scientists Sell their Skills Abroad," *U.S. News and World Report*, April 17, 1995, pp. 45–48.

de Wall, Thomas. "Security Falters in Decaying Atomic City," *Moscow Times*, August 25, 1994, pp. 1–2.

"DEF's Portfolio Today," *Moscow Times*, April 4, 2001, p. 10.

Deutch, John M. "The New Nuclear Threat," *Foreign Affairs*, Vol. 71, No. 4 (Fall 1992), pp. 120–134.

Devroy, Ann. "Bush: Defense Restructuring Possible; President Says Soviet Arsenal Appears Secure, Backs Non-Cash Aid," *Washington Post*, August 30, 1991, p. A1.

Dewar, Helen. "Lawmakers Drop Aid For Soviets; Domestic Needs Turn Tide on Hill," *Washington Post*, November 14, 1991, p. A1.

_____. "The Senate's New Alliance: Nunn and Lugar; Lawmakers Choose Partnership Over Partisanship and Score Success in Breaking Aid Logjam," *Washington Post*, March 7, 1993, p. A11.

Dobbs, Michael. "Soviet-Era Work on Bioweapons Still Worrisome; Stall in U.S. Dismantling Effort Could Pose Proliferation Threat," *Washington Post*, September 12, 2000, p. A01.

Douglas, Maria, and Peter Falatyn. "More than Money: Small Technology Spin-Offs of the WMD Complex," *JRL Research & Analytical Supplement*, No. 10 (July 2002).

Editorial. "No bargain—Soviet request for American economic assistance in exchange for promised economic reforms," *National Review*, June 2, 1991.

Fialka, John. "U.S. Fears China's Success in Skimming Cream of Weapons Experts from Russia," *Wall Street Journal*, October 14, 1993, p. 12.

Freedberg, Sydney J., Jr. "Beating Swords into Plowshares," *National Journal*, Vol. 30, No. 50 (December 12, 1998), pp. 2936–2937.

Friedman, Thomas L. "Ex-Soviet Atom Scientists Ask Baker for West's Help," *New York Times*, February 15, 1992, pp. 1, 4.

Gallucci, Robert L. "Redirecting the Soviet Weapons Establishment," *Arms Control Today,* June 1992.

Grier, Peter "US Effort to Aid Ex-USSR in Disarming Bogs Down," *Christian Science Monitor,* January 13, 1993, p. 1.

Hecker, Charles. "Payment Crisis Hits Elite Nuclear Center," *Moscow Times,* June 16, 1995, p. 4.

Hecker, Siegfried S. "Thoughts About an Integrated Strategy for Nuclear Cooperation with Russia," *Nonproliferation Review,* Vol. 8, No. 2 (Summer 2001), pp. 1–24.

Hobart, Jess. "Gore Launches Inaugural Symposium of Belfer Center," *Harvard University Gazette,* November 6, 1997.

Hoffman, David. "Baker Reassures Elite of Ex-Soviet Scientists; Russians at Nuclear Complex Plead for Commercial Work," *International Herald Tribune,* February 15–16, 1992, p. 1.

Ignatius, Adi. "U.S. Stirs Russian Resentment with Plans for Defense Conversion," *Wall Street Journal,* September 19, 1994, p. A10.

"Interview of Ivan Kamenskikh, Deputy General Director, Rosatom, on the Future of the Russian Nuclear Complex," *Atompressa,* posted on http://www.atominfo.ru/news/air6252. htm (accessed July 1, 2009).

Kellett, Frederick. "Bankrolling Failure," *Bulletin of the Atomic Scientists,* Vol. 59, No. 5 (September/October 2003), pp. 42–45.

Khripunov, Igor. "Russia's Minatom Struggles for Survival: Implications for US-Russian Relations," *Security Dialogue,* Vol. 31, No. 1 (March 2000), pp. 55–69.

Klugman, Jeni, and Jeanine Braithwaite. "Poverty in Russia during the Transition: An Overview," *World Bank Research Observer,* Vol. 13, No. 1 (February 1998), pp. 37–58.

Kocheshkova, N. "Foreigners in Sarov," *Gordskoy Kuryer,* February 2001.

Krauss, Clifford. "Soviet Turmoil: Republics to Get Direct Aid in a New U.S.-Britain Plan," *New York Times,* August 30, 1991, p. A14.

Lancaster, John. "Defense Bill Includes Soviet Aid; Budget Conferees Design New Role for U.S. Military," *Washington Post,* November 2, 1991, p. A1.

Lancaster, John, and Barton Gellman. "Citing Soviet Strife, Cheney Resists Cuts; Possible Civil War, Famine Noted by Pentagon Chief," *Washington Post,* August 30, 1991, p. A1.

Lelyveld, Michael S. "Skimming Cuts Aid to Russian Scientists. DOE: Duties, Taxes, Payoffs Siphon Off US Funds," *Journal of Commerce,* May 13, 1997, p. 1.

Leskov, Sergey. "Uchenogo-atomshika doveli do svintsovoy tochki," *Izvestiya,* November 1, 1996, p. 1, quoted on www.nti.org (accessed July 24, 2005).

Lodahl, Maria. "The Housing Market in Russia: Disappointing Results," *Economic Bulletin,* German Institute for Economic Research, Vol. 6 (2001).

MacKenzie, Donald, and Graham Spinardi. "Tacit Knowledge, Weapons Design, and the Uninvention of Nuclear Weapons," *American Journal of Sociology,* Vol. 101, No. 1 (July 1995), pp. 44–99.

McManus, Doyle. "Administration Reworks Russia Aid to Promote U.S. Business," *Los Angeles Times*, June 3, 1993, p. A4.

_____. "Baker Opens Fact-Finding Soviet Visit," *Los Angeles Times*, September 11, 1991, p. A6.

_____. "U.S. Will Fund Nuclear Fusion Research at Russian Lab," *Los Angeles Times*, March 6, 1992, p. A4.

Miller, Judith. "U.S. to Help Reduce Threat of Russian Arms." *New York Times*. August 9, 2002, p. A8.

Miller, Judith, and William J. Broad. "Exercise Finds U.S. Unable to Handle Germ War Threat," *New York Times*, April 26, 1998, pp. A1, A10.

"Minatom Rising," *Nukem*, April 2002.

Mizin, Victor. "Russia's Missile Industry and U.S. Nonproliferation Options," *Nonproliferation Review*, Vol. 5, No. 3 (Spring–Summer 1998), pp. 36–47.

Moe, Terry. "Political Institutions: The Neglected Side of the Story," *Journal of Law, Economics and Organization*, Vol. 6 (1990), pp. 213–254.

Moody, R. Adam. "Report: Reexamining Brain Drain from the Former Soviet Union," *Nonproliferation Review*, Vol. 3, No. 3 (Spring–Summer 1996), pp. 92–97.

Nixon, Richard. "The Challenge We Face in Russia," *Wall Street Journal*, March 11, 1992, p. A14.

Oberdorfer, Don. "First Aid for Moscow: The Senate's Foreign Policy Rescue," *Washington Post*, December 1, 1991, p. C2.

Panofsky, Wolfgang K.H. "A Damaging Designation," *Bulletin of the Atomic Scientists*, Vol. 63, No. 4 (January/February 2007), pp. 37–39.

Parrish, Scott, and Tamara Robinson. "Efforts to Strengthen Export Controls and Combat Illicit Trafficking and Brain Drain," *Nonproliferation Review*, Vol. 7, No. 1 (Spring 2000), pp. 112–124.

Perera, Judith. "Opening the Closed Towns," *Nuclear Engineering International*, June 1995, p. 264.

Pincus, Walter. "Funds to Hire Russian Atom Scientists Cut," *Washington Post*, November 12, 1999, p. A8.

Potter, William C., and Elena Sokova. "Illicit Nuclear Trafficking in the NIS: What's New? What's True?" *Nonproliferation Review*, Vol. 9, No. 2 (Summer 2002), pp. 112–120.

Reed, Justin. "HEU Smuggling Sting Raises Security Concerns," *Arms Control Today*, March 2007.

Rimmington, Anthony. "From Military to Industrial Complex? The Conversion of Biological Weapons' Facilities in the Russian Federation," *Contemporary Security Policy*, Vol. 17. No. 1 (April 1996), pp. 80–112.

Robbins, Carla Anne. "The X Factor in the Proliferation Game," *U.S. News and World Report*, March 16, 1992, pp. 44–51.

Rosenberg, David Alan. "The Origins of Overkill: Nuclear Weapons and American Strategy, 1945–1960," *International Security,* Vol. 7, No. 4 (Spring 1983), pp. 3–71.

Rowland, Richard H. "Russia's Secret Cities," *Post-Soviet Geography and Economics,* Vol. 37, No. 7 (September 1996), pp. 426–462.

_____. "Secret Cities of Russia and Kazakhstan in 1998," *Post-Soviet Geography and Economics,* Vol. 40, No. 4 (June 1999), pp. 281–304.

Rumyantsev, Yuriy, and Aleksey Kholodov. "Conversion Challenges in Russian Nuclear Cities," *Nonproliferation Review,* Vol. 10, No. 3 (Fall–Winter 2003), pp. 167–182.

"Russia: Government Taking Action to Prevent Defense Industry Bankruptcies," *Rossiyskaya Gazeta,* March 8, 2009.

"Russia: S. Ivanov Details Benefits of Government Defense Procurement," *Rossiyskaya Gazeta,* February 27, 2009.

Russia—OSC Summary. "Summary of Key Developments at Russia's Nuclear Institutes," August 30, 2007.

_____. "Summary of Reporting on Russian & FSU Nuclear Issues," January 17, 2008.

_____. "Summary of Reporting on Russian & FSU Nuclear Issues," January 31, 2008.

_____. "Summary of Reporting on Russian & FSU Nuclear Issues," September 26, 2008.

"Russia to Increase State Pensions by 14 Percent," *Russia Today* (Internet edition), September 24, 1999.

Sagan, Scott D. "The Perils of Proliferation: Organization Theory, Deterrence Theory, and the Spread of Nuclear Weapons," *International Security,* Vol. 18, No. 4 (Spring 1994), pp. 66–108.

Sheets, Lawrence Scott, and William J. Broad. "Smuggler's Plot Highlights Fear Over Uranium," *New York Times,* January 25, 2007, p. A1.

Tai Ming Cheung. "China's Buying Spree," *Far Eastern Economic Review,* July 8, 1993, p. 24.

Talmadge, Caitlin. "Striking a Balance: The Lessons of U.S.-Russian Materials Security Cooperation," *Nonproliferation Review,* Vol. 12, No. 1 (March 2005), pp. 1–35.

"Third of Arms Makers Face Bankruptcy," *St. Petersburg Times,* February 27, 2009.

Tucker, Jonathan B. "Bioweapons from Russia: Stemming the Flow," *Issues in Science and Technology* (Spring 1999), pp. 34–38.

_____. "Biological Weapons in the Former Soviet Union: An Interview with Dr. Kenneth Alibek," *Nonproliferation Review,* Vol. 6, No. 3 (Spring–Summer 1999), pp. 1–10.

_____. "Viewpoint: Converting Former Soviet Chemical Weapons Plants," *Nonproliferation Review,* Vol. 4, No. 1 (Fall 1996), pp. 78–89.

Tucker, Jonathan B., and Kathleen M. Vogel. "Preventing the Proliferation of Chemical and Biological Weapon Materials and Know-How," *Nonproliferation Review,* Vol. 7, No. 1 (Spring 2000), pp. 88–96.

Vogel, Kathleen. "Bioweapons Proliferation: Where Science Studies and Public Policy Collide," *Social Studies of Science,* Vol. 36, No. 5 (October 2006), pp. 659–690.

_____. "Viewpoint: Ensuring the Security of Russia's Chemical Weapons: A Lab-to-Lab Partnering Program," *Nonproliferation Review*, Vol. 6, No. 2 (Winter 1999), pp. 70–83.

Webster, Paul. "Nuclear Weapons: Russia Revives Sagging Research Program," *Science*, Vol. 301, No. 5629 (July 4, 2003), p. 34.

Wehling, Fred. "Russian Nuclear and Missile Exports to Iran," *Nonproliferation Review*, Vol. 6, No. 2 (Winter 1999), pp. 134–143.

Weiner, Sharon K. "Looking Out, Looking In: Competing Organizational Interests and the Proliferation of Soviet WMD Expertise," *Daedalus*, Vol. 138, No. 2 (Spring 2009), pp. 105–114.

_____. "Organizational Interest, Nuclear Weapons Scientists, and Nonproliferation," *Political Science Quarterly*, Vol. 124, No. 4 (Winter 2009–10), pp. 655–679.

_____. "Preventing Nuclear Entrepreneurship in Russia's Nuclear Cities," *International Security*, Vol. 27, No. 2 (Fall 2002), pp. 126–158.

_____. "Reconsidering Cooperative Threat Reduction: Russian Nuclear Weapons Scientists and Non-Proliferation," *Contemporary Security Policy*, Vol. 29, No. 3 (December 2008), pp. 477–501.

_____. "The Evolution of Cooperative Threat Reduction," *Nonproliferation Review*, Vol. 16, No. 2 (July 2009), pp. 211–235.

Weir, Fred. "Russia Intensifies Efforts to Rebuild Its Military Machine," *Christian Science Monitor*, February 12, 2007, p. 4.

Weir, Fred, and Mark Clayton. "US-Russia Effort to Contain Nuclear Experts Fades," *Christian Science Monitor*, September 20, 2006, p. 1.

Weisman, Jonathan. "Early Retirement for Weaponeers?" *Bulletin of Atomic Scientists*, Vol. 50, No. 4 (July/August 1994), pp. 16–22.

Willing, Richard. "Nuclear Traffic Doubles Since '90s," *USA Today*, December 26, 2006, p. 1.

Wilson, Heather. "Beyond the Cold War—Foreign Policy in the 21st Century: Nuclear Threat—Leadership Wanted," *Wall Street Journal*, December 8, 1993, p. A14.

Wolf, Richard, and Jessica Lee. "Lawmakers: Use Military Funds for Aid," *USA Today*, August 29, 1991, p. A4.

Yang, John E. "U.S. to Give Soviets New Food Aid: $1.5 Billion Package Will Go to Republics," *Washington Post*, November 19, 1991, p. A1.

Zaitseva, Lyudmila, and Kevin Haud. "Nuclear Smuggling Chains," *American Behavioral Scientist*, Vol. 46, No. 6 (February 2003), pp. 822–844.

Zegart, Amy B. "Running in Place: An Institutional Analysis of U.S. Nonproliferation Organization Since the Cold War," *Nonproliferation Review*, Vol. 10, No. 2 (Summer 2003), pp. 1–21.

FOREIGN GOVERNMENTS AND INTERNATIONAL ORGANIZATIONS

International Atomic Energy Agency. *International Atomic Energy Agency Safeguards Glossary* (International Nuclear Verification Series, No. 3., 2001.

International Science and Technology Center. "Annual Report," 1994.
_____. "Annual Report," 1995.
_____. "Annual Report," 1996.
_____. "Annual Report," 1997.
_____. "Annual Report," 1998.
_____. "Annual Report," 1999.
_____. "Annual Report," 2000.
_____. "Annual Report," 2001.
_____. "Annual Report," 2002.
_____. "Annual Report," 2003.
_____. "Annual Report," 2004.
_____. "Annual Report," 2005.
_____. "Annual Report," 2006.
_____. "Annual Report," 2007.
_____. "Annual Report," 2008.
_____. "Conditions for Approval of Partner Project Proposals," Partners.istc.ru/media/for-partners/Conditions-For-Approval-Of-Partner-Project-Proposals.pdf (accessed June 11, 2007).
_____. "ISTC," Briefing Slides, September 16, 1999.
_____. "ISTC News/Mobil Technology and VNIITF Press Release," September 16, 1999.
_____. "ISTC Partner News," 4th Quarter 2003.
_____. ISTC Statute, Article II, www.istc.ru (accessed May 30, 2007).
_____. "Weapon Expertise Areas," November 2000.

Russian Federation. Central Bank of the Russian Federation. Social and Economic Situation in January–February 2005, www.cbr.ru/eng/analytics/macro/print.asp?file=macroeconomics_jan-feb_05.htm (accessed February 17, 2006).
_____. Ministry of Atomic Energy of the Russian Federation. "Primary Objectives and Tasks," undated internal document.
_____. Ministry of Atomic Energy of the Russian Federation. Department for Conversion of Atomic Industry (DCAI). "Major Results of Conversion in Defense Complex Enterprises of Minatom, Russia, in 1998–2001," undated internal document.
_____. Ministry of Atomic Energy of the Russian Federation. Y. O. Adamov. Speech of the Minister of Nuclear Energy of the Russian Federation before the SEAB Delegation, July 24, 2000.
_____. Ministry of Atomic Energy of the Russian Federation. Lev Ryabev, First Deputy Minister. Letter to Linton F. Brooks, Deputy Administrator for Defense Nuclear Nonproliferation, U.S. Department of Energy, May 16, 2002.
_____. Russian Federal State Statistics Service. "Main Socio-Economic Indicators of Living Standard of Population," www.gks.ru/bgd/regl/b08_12/IssWWW.exe/stg/d01/07-01.htm (accessed on May 5, 2009).
_____. Russian Federal State Statistics Service. "Subsistence Minimum Level," www.gks.ru/bgd/regl/b08_12/IssWWW.exe/stg/d01/07-01.htm (accessed on May 5, 2009).

Science and Technology Center in Ukraine. "Annual Report," 2000.
_____. "Annual Report," 2001.
_____. "Annual Report," 2002.
_____. "Annual Report," 2003.
_____. "Annual Report," 2004.
_____. "Annual Report," 2005.
_____. "Annual Report," 2006.
_____. "Annual Report," 2007.
_____. "Governing Board Meeting," Board 1, December 15–16, 1995.
_____. "Governing Board Meeting," Board 2, May 10–11, 1996.
_____. "Governing Board Meeting," Board 3, December 15, 1996.
_____. "Governing Board Meeting," Board 4, May 15–16, 1997.
_____. "Governing Board Meeting," Board 5, December 15–16, 1997.
_____. "Governing Board Meeting," Board 6, June 8–9, 1998.
_____. "Governing Board Meeting," Board 7, December 10, 1998.

_____. "Governing Board Meeting," Board 8, May 27, 1999.
_____. "Governing Board Meeting," Board 9, December 15, 1999.
_____. "Governing Board Meeting," Board 10, June 1, 2000.
_____. "Governing Board Meeting," Board 11, December 7, 2000.
_____. "Governing Board Meeting," Board 12, June 6–7, 2001.
_____. "Governing Board Meeting," Board 13, December 5–6, 2001.
_____. "Governing Board Meeting," Board 14, June 11, 2002.
_____. "Governing Board Meeting," Board 15, December 12, 2002.
_____. "Governing Board Meeting," Board 16, June 12, 2003.
_____. "Governing Board Meeting," Board 17, December 4, 2003.
_____. "Governing Board Meeting," Board 18, June 17, 2004.
_____. "Governing Board Meeting," Board 19, February 10, 2005.
_____. "Governing Board Meeting," Board 20, June 16, 2005.
_____. "Governing Board Meeting," Board 21, December 2, 2005.
_____. "Governing Board Meeting," Board 22, May 18, 2006.
_____. "Governing Board Meeting," Board 23, November 16, 2006.
_____. "Governing Board Meeting," Board 24, May 31, 2007.
_____. "Governing Board Meeting," Board 25, November 15, 2007.
_____. "Governing Board Meeting," Board 26, June 19, 2008.
_____. "Governing Board Meeting," Board 27, November 20, 2008.
_____. Levytska, Olena. "Perspective Materials, Devices and Structure for Space Applications," presented at ISTC Workshop, Yerevan, Armenia, May 26–29, 2009.
_____. "Science and Technology Center in Ukraine (STCU)," Briefing Slides, March 2008.
_____. STCU Mission Statement, www.stcu.int (accessed May 30, 2007).
_____. STCU Training CDs, undated.

United Kingdom. Department of Trade and Industry. "United Kingdom–Russia Closed Nuclear Cities Partnership (CNCP)," www.pe-international.ru/eng.

United Nations Conference on Trade and Development. "Statistical Annex," *World Investment Report 1994* (New York: United Nations, 1994).
_____. "Statistical Annex," *World Investment Report 1995* (New York: United Nations, 1995).
_____. "Statistical Annex," *World Investment Report 1996* (New York: United Nations, 1996).
_____. "Statistical Annex," *World Investment Report 1997* (New York: United Nations, 1997).
_____. "Statistical Annex," *World Investment Report 1998* (New York: United Nations, 1998).
_____. "Statistical Annex," *World Investment Report 1999* (New York: United Nations, 1999).
_____. "Statistical Annex," *World Investment Report 2000* (New York: United Nations, 2000).
_____. "Statistical Annex," *World Investment Report 2001* (New York: United Nations, 2001).
_____. "Statistical Annex," *World Investment Report 2000* (New York: United Nations, 2000).
_____. "Statistical Annex," *World Investment Report 2001* (New York: United Nations, 2001).
_____. "Statistical Annex," *World Investment Report 2002* (New York: United Nations, 2002).
_____. "Statistical Annex," *World Investment Report 2003* (New York: United Nations, 2003).
_____. "Statistical Annex," *World Investment Report 2004* (New York: United Nations, 2004).
_____. "Statistical Annex," *World Investment Report 2005* (New York: United Nations, 2005).
_____. "Statistical Annex," *World Investment Report 2006* (New York: United Nations, 2006).
_____. "Statistical Annex," *World Investment Report 2007* (New York: United Nations, 2007).

Zinberg, Dorothy S. *The Missing Link? Nuclear Proliferation and the International Mobility of Russian Nuclear Experts,* Research Paper No. 35, UNIDIR, August 1995.

Zubarevich, N. V., and A.G. Machrova. "Human Development and Intellectual Potential of Russia's Regions," *Human Development Report for the Russian Federation 2001* (Moscow: United Nations Development Programme, 2001).

_____. "Human Development and Intellectual Potential of Russia's Regions," *Human Development Report for the Russian Federation 2004* (Moscow: United Nations Development Programme, 2004).

NON-GOVERNMENTAL ORGANIZATIONS AND UNIVERSITIES

Analytical Center for Non-Proliferation. Sarov, Russia. "An Overview of VNIIEF-STL Experiences and Projects," 2004.
_____. "RFNC-VNIIEF Quarterly Information Bulletin," Number 1, 1999.
_____. "RFNC-VNIIEF Quarterly Information Bulletin," Number 2, 1999.
_____. "RFNC-VNIIEF Quarterly Information Bulletin," Number 3, 2000.
_____. "RFNC-VNIIEF Quarterly Information Bulletin," Number 4, 2000.
_____. "Quarterly Information Bulletin," Number 5, 2000.
_____. "Quarterly Information Bulletin," Number 6, 2000.
_____. "Quarterly Information Bulletin," Number 7, 2001.
_____. "Quarterly Information Bulletin," Number 8, 2001.
_____. "Quarterly Information Bulletin," Number 9, 2001.
_____. "Quarterly Information Bulletin," Number 10, 2001.
_____. "Quarterly Information Bulletin," Number 11, 2002.
_____. "Quarterly Information Bulletin," Number 12, 2002.
_____. "Quarterly Information Bulletin," Number 13, 2002.
_____. "Quarterly Information Bulletin," Number 14, 2002.
_____. "Quarterly Information Bulletin," Number 15, 2003.
_____. "Quarterly Information Bulletin," Number 16, 2003.
_____. "Quarterly Information Bulletin," Number 17, 2003.
_____. "Quarterly Information Bulletin," Number 18, 2003.
_____. "Quarterly Information Bulletin," Number 19, 2004.
_____. "Quarterly Information Bulletin," Number 20, 2004.
_____. "Quarterly Information Bulletin," Number 21, 2004.
_____. "Quarterly Information Bulletin," Number 22, 2004.
_____. "Quarterly Information Bulletin," Number 23, 2005.
_____. "Quarterly Information Bulletin," Number 24, 2005.
_____. "Quarterly Information Bulletin," Number 25, 2005.
_____. "Quarterly Information Bulletin," Number 26, 2006.

Antonov, Alexander. "Comments," Presentation at the Second International Working Group Meeting of the European Nuclear Cities Initiative, Brussels, Belgium, February 25–26, 2002.

Averre, Derek. "From Co-Option to Cooperation: Reducing the Threat of Biological Agents and Weapons," Center for Strategic and International Studies, *Protecting Against the Spread of Nuclear, Biological, and Chemical Weapons: An Action Agenda for the Global Partnership, Volume 1: Agenda for Action*, Washington, D.C., January 2003.

Ben Ouagrham, Sonia, and Kathleen M. Vogel. *Conversion at Stepnogorsk: What the Future Holds for Former Bioweapons Facilities,* Cornell University Peace Studies Program, Occasional Paper No. 28, Ithaca, N.Y., February 2003.

Bernstein, David. "Analysis and Conclusions from Case Studies," *Cooperative Business Ventures between U.S. Companies and Russian Defense Enterprises* (Stanford: Institute for International Studies, Stanford University, April 1997).

_____. Presentation at "Strategies for Russian Nuclear Complex Downsizing and Redirection: Options for New Directions," Russian-American Nuclear Security Advisory Council (RANSAC) and Russian Transition Initiatives (RTI), March 25–26, 2003.

Bonn International Center for Conversion. *Russia's Defense Industry at the Turn of the Century*, Brief 17, November 2000.

Bukharin, Oleg. *Downsizing of Russia's Nuclear Warhead Production Infrastructure*, Center for Energy and Environmental Studies, PU/CEES Report No. 323, Princeton University, Princeton, N.J., May 2000.

_____. *Russia's Nuclear Complex: Surviving the End of the Cold War*, Program on Science and Global Security, Woodrow Wilson School of Public and International Affairs, Princeton University, Princeton, N.J., May 2004.

Bukharin, Oleg, Frank N. von Hippel, and Sharon K. Weiner. *Conversion and Job Creation in Russia's Closed Nuclear Cities* (Princeton, N.J.: Program on Nuclear Policy Alternatives, Center for Energy and Environmental Studies, Princeton University, November 2000).

Bukharin, Oleg, Harold Feiveson, Frank von Hippel, Sharon K. Weiner, Matthew Bunn, William Hoehn, and Kenneth Luongo. *Helping Russia Downsize its Nuclear Complex: A Focus on the Closed Nuclear Cities*, conference report, Princeton University, Princeton, N.J., March 14–15, 2000.

Bunn, Matthew. *Securing the Bomb 2007* (Cambridge, Mass., and Washington, D.C.: Project on Managing the Atom, Harvard University and the Nuclear Threat Initiative, September 2007).

_____. *Securing the Bomb 2008* (Cambridge, Mass., and Washington, D.C.: Project on Managing the Atom, Harvard University and the Nuclear Threat Initiative, November 2008).

Bunn, Matthew and Anthony Wier. *Securing the Bomb: An Agenda for Action* (Cambridge, Mass., and Washington, D.C.: Project on Managing the Atom, Harvard University and the Nuclear Threat Initiative, May 2004).

_____. *Securing the Bomb 2005: The New Global Imperatives* (Cambridge, Mass., and Washington, D.C.: Project on Managing the Atom, Harvard University and the Nuclear Threat Initiative, May 2005).

_____. *Securing the Bomb 2006* (Cambridge, Mass., and Washington, D.C.: Project on Managing the Atom, Harvard University and the Nuclear Threat Initiative, July 2006).

Bunn, Matthew, Anthony Wier, and John P. Holdren. *Controlling Nuclear Warheads and Materials: A Report Card and Action Plan* (Cambridge, Mass., and Washington, D.C.: Project on Managing the Atom, Harvard University and the Nuclear Threat Initiative, March 2003).

Center for Strategic and International Studies. "Assessing the G8 Global Partnership: From Kananaskis to St. Petersburg," *Strengthening the Global Partnership Project*, Washington, D.C., July 2006.

Cetina, Jill, Oleg Bukharin, and Frank von Hippel. *Defense Conversion and Small Business Development: A Proposal for Two IFC Projects in Three of Russia's Closed Nuclear Cities*, Center for Energy and Environmental Studies, Report 306, Princeton University, Princeton, N.J., March 1998.

Coen, Alise. "Isonics Corporation (Closter, N.J.) Utilizing silicon isotopes to improve thermoconductivity," Henry L. Stimson Center, Washington, D.C., August 1, 2005, www.stimson.org/cnp/?SN=CT20050826903 (accessed June 15, 2007).

Cooper, Julian. "Appendix 9c. Developments in the Russian Arms Industry," *SIPRI Yearbook 2006: Armaments, Disarmament and International Security* (Stockholm: Stockholm International Peace Research Institute, 2006).

Diakov, Anatoli S. "Conversion of the Russian Nuclear Weapons Complex," presentation at the Conference on Helping Russia Down-Size its Nuclear Weapons Complex, Princeton University, Princeton, N.J., March 14–15, 2000.

Domenici, Pete V. "Issues in US/NIS Non-proliferation Cooperation," remarks, Assessing U.S. Dismantlement and Nonproliferation Assistance Programs in the Newly Independent States, Monterey, California, December 11–13, 1999.

Earle, John S., and Ivan Komarov. "Measuring Defense Conversion in Russian Industry," Center for International Security and Arms Control, Stanford University, Stanford, California, September 1996.

Einhorn, Robert J., and Michele A. Flournoy. *Protecting Against the Spread of Nuclear, Biological and Chemical Weapons: An Action Agenda for Global Leadership, Volume 1: Agenda for Action* (Washington, D.C.: Center for Strategic and International Studies, January 2003).

Federation of American Scientists and the Natural Resources Defense Council. "Report on the Fourth International Workshop on Nuclear Warhead Elimination and Nonproliferation," (Washington, D.C.: February 26–27, 1992).

Henry L. Stimson Center. "Liability Issues in Cooperative Nonproliferation Programs in Russia," www.stimson.org/cnp/?SN=CT200706011307 (accessed June 1, 2007).

Hoehn, William. "Analysis of the Bush Administration's Fiscal Year 2002 Budget Requests for U.S.-Former Soviet Union Nuclear Security: Department of Energy Programs," Russian-American Nuclear Security Advisory Council, April 18, 2001.

_____. "Analysis of the Bush Administration's Fiscal Year 2002 Budget Requests for U.S.-Former Soviet Union Nuclear Security: Department of Energy Programs," Russian-American Nuclear Security Advisory Council, August 10, 2001.

_____. "Analysis of the Bush Administration's Fiscal Year 2003 Budget Requests for U.S.-Former Soviet Union Nonproliferation Programs," Russian-American Nuclear Security Advisory Council, April 2002.

_____. "Final Report of Congressional Activity Affecting U.S. Global Threat Reduction Programs in 2005," Russian-American Nuclear Security Advisory Council, February 2005.

_____. "Observations on the President's Fiscal Year 2004 Budget Request for Nonproliferation Programs in Russia and the Former Soviet Union," Russian-American Nuclear Security Advisory Council, February 11, 2003.

_____. "Preliminary Analysis of the U.S. Department of Energy's Fiscal Year 2006 Nonproliferation Budget Request," Russian-American Nuclear Security Advisory Council, February 9, 2005.

_____. "Preliminary Analysis of the U.S. Department of Energy's Fiscal Year 2007 Nonproliferation Budget Request," Russian-American Nuclear Security Advisory Council, February 2006.

_____. "Preliminary Analysis of the U.S. State Department's Fiscal Year 2005 Budget Request for Nonproliferation Programs in Russia and the FSU," Russian-American Nuclear Security Advisory Council, March 11, 2004.

_____. "Preliminary Analysis of the U.S. State Department's Fiscal Year 2006 Budget Request for Global WMD Threat Reduction Programs," Russian-American Nuclear Security Advisory Council, March 24, 2005.

_____. "Update on Activity in the 108th Congress Affecting U.S.-Former Soviet Union Cooperative Nonproliferation Programs," Russian-American Nuclear Security Advisory Council, November 4, 2003.

_____. "Update on Congressional Activity Affecting U.S.-Russian Cooperative Nonproliferation Programs," Russian-American Nuclear Security Advisory Council, July 26, 2002.

Holgate, Laura S. H. "Linking Nuclear Expertise and Nuclear Security," Fifth International Working Group Meeting, Nuclear Threat Initiative, Como, Italy, April 2005.

Kearney, A. T. *Foreign Direct Investment Confidence Index for 1998–2005*, Global Business Policy Council, Vienna, Va.

Kellett, Frederick P. "USIC and the Initiatives for Proliferation Prevention: A Survey of Companies Doing Business in the Former Soviet Union," Report No. 60 (Washington, D.C.: Henry L. Stimson Center), March 2007.

Kunakbayev, Yerlan, Gulbarshyn Bozheyeva, and Dastan Yeleukenov. "Former Soviet Biological Weapons Facilities in Kazakhstan: Past, Present and Future" (Monterey, California: Center for Nonproliferation Studies, June 1999).

Landau Network—Centro Volta. "International Cooperation Programs and Russian Nuclear Cities: Future Initiatives, Drawbacks, Strategies and Europe's Role," February 11, 2002.

Larsen, Stacy. *An Overview of Defense Conversion in Ukraine*, No. 9 (Bonn: Bonn International Center for Conversion, June 1997).

Marchesano, Michelle. "Funding Analysis of FY09 International WMD Security Programs," Partnership for Global Security, Washington, D.C., April 2009.

Mendelson, Sarah. *Domestic Politics and America's Russia Policy* (The Century Foundation and The Stanley Foundation, October 2002).

Mroz, T., D. Mancini, and B. Popkin. "Monitoring Economic Conditions in the Russian Federation: The Russia Longitudinal Monitoring Survey 1992–98," report submitted to the U.S. Agency for International Development, Carolina Population Center, University of North Carolina at Chapel Hill, North Carolina, March 1999.

National Academies of Sciences. Institute of Medicine and National Research Council. U.S.-Russian Collaborative Program for Research and Monitoring of Pathogens of Global Importance Committee. *Controlling Dangerous Pathogens: A Blueprint for U.S.-Russian Cooperation: A Report to the Cooperative Threat Reduction Program of the U.S. Department of Defense* (Washington, D.C.: National Academy Press, 1997).

National Academies. National Research Council. *Successes and Difficulties of Small Innovative Firms in Russian Nuclear Cities* (Washington, D.C.: National Academy Press, 2002).

_____. National Research Council. *Biological Science and Biotechnology in Russia: Controlling Diseases and Enhancing Security* (Washington, D.C.: National Academy Press, 2005).

_____. National Research Council. Office for Central Europe and Eurasia. Committee on Prevention of Proliferation of Biological Weapons. *The Biological Threat Reduction Program of the Department of Defense: From Foreign Assistance to Sustainable Partnerships* (Washington, D.C.: National Academy Press, 2007).

_____. National Research Council. Office of International Affairs. *An Assessment of the International Science and Technology Center: Redirecting Expertise in Weapons of Mass Destruction in the Former Soviet Union* (Washington, D.C.: National Academy Press, 1996).

_____. National Research Council. Office of International Affairs. *Protecting Nuclear Weapons Material in Russia* (Washington, D.C.: National Academy Press, 1999).

_____. *The Nuclear Weapons Complex: Management for Health, Safety, and the Environment* (Washington, D.C.: National Academy of Sciences, 1989).

Netesov, Sergey V., and Lev S. Sandakhchiev. "The Contribution of International Collaboration to Strengthening Biosafety and Physical Security at Russian State Research Center of Virology and Biotechnology VECTOR," Workshop on Building a Global Agenda for Bio-proliferation: Current Status and Future of Russian Biotechnology, Russian American Nuclear Security Advisory Council (RANSAC), Landau Network—Centro Volta, International Center for Genetic Engineering and Biotechnology, Analysis and Policy Planning Unit of the Italian Ministry of Foreign Affairs, and International Science and Technology Center, Como, Italy, November 17–18, 2003.

Netesov, Sergey V. "Comments on Building a Global Agenda for Bio-Proliferation Prevention: Current Status and Future of Russian Biotechnology," Workshop on Building a Global Agenda for Bio-proliferation: Current Status and Future of Russian Biotechnology, Russian American Nuclear Security Advisory Council (RANSAC), Landau Network—Centro Volta, International Center for Genetic Engineering and Biotechnology, Analysis and Policy Planning Unit of the Italian Ministry of Foreign Affairs, and International Science and Technology Center, Como, Italy, November 17–18, 2003.

Nuclear Threat Initiative. "Interactive Threat Reduction Budget Database," www.nti.org/e_ research/cnwm/charts/cnm_funding_interactive.asp.

_____. "Russia: Sarov (Arzamas-16) Overview," www.nti.org/db/nisprofs/russia/weafacl/ warheadd/sarov.htm (accessed May 1, 2009.)

Parachini, John V., David E. Moser, John Baker, Keith Crane, Michael Chase, and Michael Daugherty. *Diversion of Nuclear, Biological, and Chemical Weapons Expertise from the Former Soviet Union: Understanding an Evolving Problem* (National Security Research Division, Santa Monica, Calif.: RAND, 2005).

Pikayev, Alexander. "Russian Nuclear Insecurity," *Proliferation Brief*, Vol. 2, No. 3 (Washington, D.C.: Carnegie Endowment for International Peace, February 19, 1999).

Pikayev, Alexander, and Jonathan B. Tucker, eds. Monterey-Moscow Study Group Report, *Eliminating a Deadly Legacy of the Cold War: Overcoming Obstacles to Russian Chemical Disarmament* (Moscow: Committee on Critical Technologies and Nonproliferation, January 1998).

Podvig, Pavel. *Consolidating Fissile Materials in Russia's Nuclear Complex* (Princeton, N.J.: International Panel on Fissile Materials, May 2009).

"Reorientation of Defense Enterprises, Scientific and Engineering Staff to Civil Production," Russian-U.S. Training and Consulting Workshop, Obninsk, Russia, June 27–29, 2000.

Roffey, Roger. "The legacy of the former Soviet BW programme and need for enhanced support for redirecting to civilian commercial and R&D activities," Workshop on Building a Global Agenda for Bio-proliferation: Current Status and Future of Russian Biotechnology, Como, Italy, November 17–18, 2003.

_____. "Need for enhanced support for threat reduction in the biological area for redirecting production facilities," Presentation at the Non-proliferation and Disarmament Cooperation Initiative (NDCI) conference, London, March 4–5, 2004.

Roffey, Roger, Wilhelm Unge, Jenny Clevström, and Kristina S. Westerdahl. *Support to Threat Reduction of the Russian Biological Weapons Legacy—Conversion, Biodefence and the Role of Biopreparat*, Swedish Defence Research Agency, FOI-R—0841—SE, April 2003.

Romashkin, Peter. "Analysis of Federal Budgets of the Russian Federation in the National Defense Section of Spending: Subsection of the Nuclear Weapons Complex," Institute of World Economy and International Relations (IMEMO), May 25, 2006.

Roston, Michael. "Reported Accomplishments of Threat Reduction and Nonproliferation Programs, by Agency," RANSAC Policy Update, July 2004.

Roston, Michael, and David Smigielski. "Accomplishments of Selected Threat Reduction and Nonproliferation Programs in Russia, by Agency," RANSAC Policy Update, June 10, 2003.

Russian-American Nuclear Security Advisory Council (RANSAC). "Downsizing Russian Weapons Complex by Facilitating Economic Development in the Closed Nuclear Cities: New Opportunities for Nuclear Security Cooperation," Moscow, April 7–11, 1998.

_____. "House of Representatives, U.S. Energy and Water Appropriations Act," December 31, 1997.

_____. "New Opportunities for Nuclear Security Cooperation," Moscow, April 7–11, 1998.

_____. "Preliminary Report: Anticipated FY 2003 Budget Request for Department of Energy Cooperative Nuclear Security Programs in Russia," January 9, 2002.

_____. "Russian Nuclear Security and the Clinton Administration's Fiscal Year 2000 Expanded Threat Reduction Initiative: A Summary of Congressional Action," (February 2000).

Ryabev, Lev. "Downsizing of the Nuclear Complex and Defense Conversion Programs," Presentation at the Conference on Helping Russia Down-Size its Nuclear Weapons Complex, Princeton, N.J., March 14–15, 2000.

_____. "Russia's Down-Sizing and Conversion Programs," Presentation at the Sam Nunn/ Bank of America Policy Forum, Atlanta, Georgia, March 26–27, 2001.

Safranchuk, Ivan. "Nuclear Regionalism in the Volga Federal Okrug: Nizhny Novgorod Oblast and the Closed City of Sarov," unpublished paper prepared for the workshop on "Russian 'Nuclear Regionalism' and Challenges for U.S. Nonproliferation Assistance Programs," Center for Nonproliferation Studies, Monterey Institute, Monterey, Calif., April 5, 2002.

SIPRI Military Expenditure Database, www.sipri.org.

Smithson, Amy E. *Toxic Archipelago: Preventing Proliferation from the Former Soviet Chemical and Biological Weapons Complexes* (Washington, D.C.: Henry L. Stimson Center, December 1999).

Stalenheim, Petter, Damien Fruchart, Wuyi Omitoogun, and Catalina Perdomo. "Appendix 8A. Tables of Military Expenditure," *SIPRI Yearbook 2006* (Stockholm: Stockholm International Peace Research Institute, 2006).

Tikhonov, Valentin. *Russia's Nuclear and Missile Complex: The Human Factor in Proliferation* (Washington, D.C.: Carnegie Endowment for International Peace, 2001).

Toevs, James W. "Sarov, Russia: The Sarov Demonstration Project," Forum on European Nuclear Cities Initiative, Rome, December 12–13, 1999.

Tucker, Jonathan B. "Biological Weapons Proliferation from Russia: How Great a Threat? 7th Carnegie International Non-Proliferation Conference" (Washington, D.C.: January 11–12, 1999).

Weiner, Sharon K. "Nuclear Cities News," Center for Energy and Environmental Studies, Princeton University and the Russian-American Nuclear Security Advisory Council (RANSAC), Vol. 1, December 1999.

Williams, Isabelle. "Analysis of the U.S. Department of Defense's Fiscal Year 2008 Cooperative Threat Reduction Budget Request," Partnership for Global Security, Washington, D.C., March 19, 2007.

Williams, Isabelle, and Kenneth Luongo. "Analysis of the U.S. Department of Energy's Fiscal Year 2008 International Nonproliferation Budget Request," Partnership for Global Security, Washington, D.C., February 26, 2007.

U.S. GOVERNMENT PUBLICATIONS

Central Intelligence Agency. *World Fact Book, 1994.*
_____. *World Fact Book, 1995.*
_____. *World Fact Book, 1996.*
_____. *World Fact Book, 1997.*
_____. *World Fact Book, 1998.*
_____. *World Fact Book, 1999.*
_____. *World Fact Book, 2000.*
_____. *World Fact Book, 2001.*
_____. *World Fact Book, 2002.*
_____. *World Fact Book, 2003.*
_____. *World Fact Book, 2004.*
_____. *World Fact Book, 2005.*
_____. *World Fact Book, 2006.*
_____. *World Fact Book, 2007.*

Gore-Chernomyrdin Commission. Bernstein, David, and Nicholas Carlson. "The Cooperative Threat Reduction 'Fast Four' Defense Conversion Projects in the Russian Federation," Prepared for the U.S.-Russian Committee on Defense Industry Conversion of the Gore-Chernomyrdin Commission, January 1997.

_____. DOE Briefing Book, VIII session, February 5–8, 1997.

Los Alamos National Laboratory. Casey, Hugh. "The New Independent States Industrial Partnering Program," *Los Alamos Science*, No. 24, 1996.

Los Alamos National Laboratory. "Los Alamos and Arzamas-16: The 'Sister Cities' Relationship," *Los Alamos Science*, No. 24, 1996.

_____. "Part I: Roots of the Lab-to-Lab Collaboration," *Los Alamos Science*, No. 24, 1996.

_____. "Part II: The Lab to Lab Program in Scientific Conversion and Nuclear Materials Control," *Los Alamos Science*, No. 24, 1996.

Sandia National Laboratory. "Prosthetics: An IPP Success Story," *International Security News*, Vol. 1. No. 2 (March 2001).

U.S. Civilian Research and Development Foundation. *2005 Annual Report.*

U.S. Congress. Commission on Maintaining the Expertise to Manage the U.S. Nuclear Weapons Stockpile (Chiles Commission). *Science at its Best, Security at its Worst: A Report on Security Problems at the U.S. Department of Energy*, June 1999.

U.S. Congress—*Congressional Record*. 102nd Cong., 1st sess., Vol. 137, No. 86, p. S7274.
_____. 102nd Cong., 1st sess., Vol. 137, No. 89, p. S7510.
_____. 102nd Cong., 1st sess., Vol. 137, No. 90, pp. H4356–H4357.
_____. 102nd Cong., 1st sess., Vol. 137, No. 123, p. S12591.
_____. 102nd Cong., 1st sess., Vol. 137, No. 124, p. E2972.
_____. 102nd Cong., 1st sess., Vol. 137, No. 168, p. E3835, Extension of Remarks, Statement by Les Aspin, November 14, 1991.
_____. 102nd Cong., 1st sess., Vol. 137, No. 176, p. S18001.

_____. 102nd Cong., 1st sess., Vol. 137, No. 177, Part 3, p. H11496.
_____. 104th Cong., 1st sess., June 13. 1995, pp. H5865, H5867, H5871.
_____. 105th Cong., 1st sess., June 23. 1997, p. H4199.

U.S. Congress—Congressional Research Service. Davis, Zachary and Warren H. Donnelly. *Nuclear Scientists of the Former Soviet Union: Nonproliferation Issues,* Issue Brief, March 20, 1992.

_____. *The Future of Arms Control: New Opportunities,* report prepared for the House Committee on Foreign Affairs, 102nd Cong., 2nd sess., April 1992.

_____. Goldman, Stuart D. "Russia," April 9, 2004.

_____. Tarnoff, Curt. *Freedom Support Act of 1992: A Foreign Aid Program for the Former Soviet Union,* CRS Issue Brief, November 4, 1992.

_____. Tarnoff, Curt, *The Former Soviet Union and U.S. Foreign Assistance in 1992: The Role of Congress,* CRS Report for Congress, May 20, 2004.

_____. Tarnoff, Curt. *U.S. Assistance to the Former Soviet Union,* CRS Report for Congress, March 16, 2006.

_____. Woolf, Amy F. *Nonproliferation and Threat Reduction Assistance: U.S. Programs in the Former Soviet Union,* CRS Report for Congress, Washington, D.C.: Congressional Research Service, updated April 6, 2006.

_____. Woolf, Amy F. *Nonproliferation and Threat Reduction Assistance: U.S. Programs in the Former Soviet Union,* CRS Report for Congress, Washington, D.C.: Congressional Research Service, updated June 26, 2006.

_____. Woolf, Amy F. *Nonproliferation and Threat Reduction Assistance: U.S. Programs in the Former Soviet Union,* CRS Report for Congress, Washington, D.C.: Congressional Research Service, February 11, 2009.

_____. Woolf, Amy F. *Nuclear Weapons in Russia: Safety, Security, and Control Issues,* Issue Brief for Congress, November 21, 2000.

U.S. Congress—House. Committee on Appropriations. *Department of Defense Appropriations for 1995, Part 4,* 103rd Cong., 2nd sess., 1994.
_____. Committee on Appropriations. *Energy and Water Development Appropriations Bill, 1998,* 105 H. Rpt. 190, July 21, 1997.
_____. Committee on Appropriations. *Energy and Water Development Appropriations for 1998, Part 6: Department of Energy,* March 12, April 9, 1997.
_____. Committee on Appropriations. *Energy and Water Development Appropriations for 1999, Part 6: Department of Energy,* March 12, 17, 18, 1998.
_____. Committee on Appropriations. *Energy and Water Development Appropriations, FY 2000, Part 6: Department of Energy,* March 16, 18, 1999.
_____. Committee on Appropriations. *Energy and Water Development Appropriations for 2001, Part 6: Department of Energy,* March 21, 23, 2000.
_____. Committee on Appropriations. *Energy and Water Development Appropriations for 2002, Part 6: Department of Energy,* 107th Cong., 1st sess., May 3, 9, 2001.
_____. Committee on Appropriations. *Energy and Water Development Appropriations for 2002, Part 6: Department of Energy,* September 2001.
_____. Committee on Appropriations. *Energy and Water Development Appropriations Bill, 2008,* Report 110-185, 110th Cong., 1st sess.
_____. Committee on Armed Services. *Enactment of Provisions of H.R. 5408, The Floyd D. Spence National Defense Authorization Act for FY 2001,* H. Rpt. 106-945, 106th Cong., 2nd sess., Section 3174, October 6, 2000.
_____. Committee on Armed Services. *Fiscal Year 1999 Defense Authorization Bill,* H. Rpt. 105-736.

_____. Committee on Armed Services. *National Defense Authorization Act for FY 1993*, H. Rpt. 102-966, Part 1, 102nd Cong., 2nd sess., October 1, 1992.

_____. Committee on Armed Services. *National Defense Authorization Act for Fiscal Year 1994*, H. Rpt. 103-357, 103rd Cong., 1st sess., November 10, 1993.

_____. Committee on Armed Services. *Potential Threats to American Security in the Post–Cold War Era*, 102nd Cong., 1st sess., December 10, 11, 13, 1991.

_____. Committee on Armed Services. Defense Policy Panel and the Department of Energy Defense Nuclear Facilities Panel. *Regional Threats and Defense Options for the 1990s*, 102nd Cong., 2nd sess., Part I: March 10, 11, 17, 19, 24, April 2, 8, 9; Part II: March 18, 26, 27, 31, April 8, and May 5, 1992.

_____. Committee on Energy and Water. "Department of Energy Program Funds Russian Nuclear Work in Iran," Press Release, February 5, 2008.

_____. Committee on Foreign Affairs. *Freedom Support Act*, October 1, 1992.

_____. Committee on Foreign Affairs. *The Future of U.S. Foreign Policy in the Post–Cold War Era*, 102nd Cong., 2nd sess., Feb. 6, 19, 20, 25, March 5, 24, April 30, 1992.

_____. Committee on International Relations, *Report on the Expanded Threat Reduction Initiative, Message from the President*, 106th Cong., 2nd sess., House Doc. 106-263, June 28, 2000.

_____. Committee on International Relations. *U.S. Assistance Programs for Economic and Political Reform and Dismantling of Weapons of Mass Destruction in the NIS*, March 3, 1995.

_____. Committee on the Judiciary. *Immigration in the National Interest Act of 1995*, H. Rpt. 104-469, 104th Cong., 2nd sess., March 4, 1996.

_____. Committee on National Security. *National Defense Authorization Act for Fiscal Year 1998*, H. Rpt. 105-132, 105th Cong., 1st sess., June 16, 1997.

_____. *Department of Defense Appropriations for 1995*, Part 4, 103rd Cong., 2nd sess., 1994.

_____. *Making Appropriations for Energy and Water Development for the Fiscal Year Ending September 30, 1998, and Other Purposes*, 105 H. Rpt. 271, September 26, 1997.

U.S. Congress—Office of Technology Assessment. *Proliferation and the Former Soviet Union*, (Washington, D.C.: U.S. Government Printing Office, September 1994).

_____. *Proliferation of Weapons of Mass Destruction: Assessing the Risks* (Washington, D.C.: U.S. Government Printing Office, August 1993).

U.S. Congress—Senate. Committee on Appropriations. *Foreign Operations, Export Financing, and Related Programs Appropriations Bill, 1994*, S. Rpt. 103-142, September 14, 1993.

_____. Committee on Appropriations. *Foreign Operations, Export Financing, and Related Programs Appropriations, FY 95*, March 2, 8, 15, 22, April 12, 19, 26, May 17, 24, 1994.

_____. Committee on Appropriations. *Energy and Water Development Appropriations, FY 2000*, March 9, 11, 18, April 13, 1999.

_____. Committee on Armed Services. *Assisting the Build-down of the Former Soviet Military Establishment*, 102nd Cong., 2nd sess., February 5, 6, 1992.

_____. Committee on Armed Services. *Current Developments in the Former Soviet Union*, S. Hrg. 103-242, 103rd Cong., 1st sess., Feb, 3, 17, 24, March 3, 1993.

_____. Committee on Armed Services. *Department of Defense Authorization for Appropriations for FY 95 and the Future Years Defense Program, Part 7: Nuclear Deterrence, Arms Control and Defense Intelligence*, S. Hrg. 103-765 Pt. 7, April 21, 26, 28, May 3, 5, 11,1994.

_____. Committee on Armed Services. *Trip Report: A Visit to the Commonwealth of Independent States*, March 10, 1992.

_____. Committee on Foreign Relations. Subcommittee on European Affairs. *Soviet Crisis and the U.S. Interest: Future of the Soviet Military and Future of the Soviet Economy*, 102nd Cong., 1st sess., June 6, June 19, 1991.

_____. Committee on Governmental Affairs. *International Organized Crime and Its Impact on the U.S.*, S. Hrg. 103-899. 103rd Cong., 2nd sess., May 25, 1994.

_____. Committee on Governmental Affairs. *Proliferation Threats of the 1990s*, S. Hrg. 103-209, 103rd Cong., 1st sess., February 24, 1993.

_____. Committee on Governmental Affairs. *Weapons Proliferation in the New World Order*, S. Hrg. 102-720, 102nd Cong., 2nd sess., January 15, 1992.

_____. Committee on Governmental Affairs. Permanent Subcommittee on Investigations. *Global Proliferation of Weapons of Mass Destruction*, S. Hrg. 104-422, Part I, 104th Cong., 1st sess., October 31 and November 1, 1995.

_____. Committee on Governmental Affairs. Permanent Subcommittee on Investigations. *Global Proliferation of Weapons of Mass Destruction*, S. Hrg. 104-422, Part II, 104th Cong., 2nd sess., March 13, 20, and 22, 1996.

_____. Committee on Governmental Affairs. Permanent Subcommittee on Investigations. *Global Proliferation of Weapons of Mass Destruction*, S. Hrg. 104-422, Part III, 104th Cong., 2nd sess., March 27, 1996.

_____. *Ensuring Implementation of the 9/11 Commission Report Act*, S. 328, January 2007.

_____. Select Committee on Intelligence. *Current and Projected National Security Threats to the U.S.*, S. Hrg. 105-587, 105th Cong., 2nd sess., January 28, 1998.

U.S. Department of Defense. "Cooperative Threat Reduction, Semi-Annual Report to Congress," First-Half FY 1994.

_____. "Cooperative Threat Reduction, Semi-Annual Report to Congress," Second-Half FY 1994.

_____. "Cooperative Threat Reduction, Semi-Annual Report to Congress," First-Half FY 1995.

_____. "Cooperative Threat Reduction, Semi-Annual Report to Congress," Second-Half FY 1995.

_____. "Cooperative Threat Reduction, Semi-Annual Report to Congress," First-Half FY 1996.

_____. "Cooperative Threat Reduction, Semi-Annual Report to Congress," Second-Half FY 1996.

_____. Secretary of Defense. Cooperative Threat Reduction Annual Report to Congress for Fiscal Year 1997.

_____. Secretary of Defense. Cooperative Threat Reduction Annual Report to Congress for Fiscal Year 1998.

_____. Defense Threat Reduction Agency. Cooperative Threat Reduction Annual Report to Congress for Fiscal Year 1999.

_____. Defense Threat Reduction Agency. Cooperative Threat Reduction Annual Report to Congress for Fiscal Year 2000.

_____. Defense Threat Reduction Agency. Cooperative Threat Reduction Annual Report to Congress for Fiscal Year 2001.

_____. Defense Threat Reduction Agency. Cooperative Threat Reduction Annual Report to Congress for Fiscal Year 2002.

_____. Defense Threat Reduction Agency. Cooperative Threat Reduction Annual Report to Congress for Fiscal Year 2003.

_____. Defense Threat Reduction Agency. Cooperative Threat Reduction Annual Report to Congress for Fiscal Year 2004.

_____. Defense Threat Reduction Agency. Cooperative Threat Reduction Annual Report to Congress for Fiscal Year 2005.

_____. Defense Threat Reduction Agency. Cooperative Threat Reduction Annual Report to Congress for Fiscal Year 2006.

_____. Defense Threat Reduction Agency. Cooperative Threat Reduction Annual Report to Congress for Fiscal Year 2007.

_____. Defense Threat Reduction Agency. Cooperative Threat Reduction Annual Report to Congress for Fiscal Year 2008.

_____. Defense Threat Reduction Agency. Cooperative Threat Reduction Annual Report to Congress Fiscal Year for 2009.

_____. Office of the Inspector General. "Defense Enterprise Fund, Audit Report," Report No. D-2000-176, August 15, 2000.

_____. Office of the Inspector General. "Evaluation of the Defense Nuclear Agency's Cooperative Threat Reduction Office" (U.S. Department of Commerce, NTIS, October 12, 1995).

_____. Office of the Inspector General. "Management Costs Associated with the Defense Enterprise Fund," Report No. D-2002-033, December 31, 2001.

U.S. Department of Energy. Energy Information Administration. "Major Non-OPEC Countries' Oil Revenues," June 2005.

_____. Internal DOE Report on Programs in Russia, 2001.

_____. Mallin, Monte. Director of the Office of Global Security Engagement and Cooperation. National Nuclear Security Administration. U.S. Department of Energy. Remarks for the United States Industry Coalition Annual Conference, March 7, 2007.

_____. National Nuclear Security Administration. Office of the Administrator. Weapons Activities. Defense Nuclear Nonproliferation. Naval Reactors. *Fiscal Year 2001 Congressional Budget Request, Volume 1: National Nuclear Security Administration.*

_____. National Nuclear Security Administration. Office of the Administrator. Weapons Activities. Defense Nuclear Nonproliferation. Naval Reactors. *Fiscal Year 2003 Congressional Budget Request, Volume 1: National Nuclear Security Administration.*

_____. National Nuclear Security Administration. Office of the Administrator. Weapons Activities. Defense Nuclear Nonproliferation. Naval Reactors. *Fiscal Year 2004 Congressional Budget Request, Volume 1: National Nuclear Security Administration.*

_____. National Nuclear Security Administration. Office of the Administrator. Weapons Activities. Defense Nuclear Nonproliferation. Naval Reactors. *Fiscal Year 2006 Congressional Budget Request. Volume 1: National Nuclear Security Administration.*

_____. National Nuclear Security Administration. Office of the Administrator. Weapons Activities. Defense Nuclear Nonproliferation. Naval Reactors. *FY 2008 Congressional Budget Request, Volume 1: National Nuclear Security Administration,* February 2007.

_____. National Nuclear Security Administration. Office of the Administrator. Weapons Activities. Defense Nuclear Nonproliferation. Naval Reactors. *FY 2009 Congressional Budget Request, Volume 1: National Nuclear Security Administration,* February 2008.

_____. National Nuclear Security Administration. *Report to Congress on the Organization and Operations of the National Nuclear Security Administration,* February 25, 2002.

_____. Office of Legacy Management. *The Legacy Story* (U.S. Department of Energy, 1997).

_____. *Performance and Accountability Report,* Fiscal Year 2000.

_____. *Performance and Accountability Report,* Fiscal Year 2001.

_____. *Performance and Accountability Report,* Fiscal Year 2002.

_____. *Performance and Accountability Report,* Fiscal Year 2003.

_____. *Performance and Accountability Report,* Fiscal Year 2004.

_____. The Secretary of Energy Advisory Board. Howard Baker and Lloyd Cutler, Co-Chairs. *A Report Card on the Department of Energy's Nonproliferation Programs with Russia,* January 10, 2001.

U.S. Department of Energy—Initiatives for Proliferation Prevention Program. *Annual Report, Fiscal Year 1999.*

_____. *Annual Report, Fiscal Year 2000,* September 30, 2000.

_____. *Annual Report, Fiscal Year 2001,* September 30, 2001.

_____. "Guidance for Evaluating Weapons Scientists, Engineers, and Technicians," June 2002, www.usic.net (accessed June 29, 2007).

_____. Industrial Partnering Program. "New Independent States Industrial Partnering Program—Reducing the Nuclear Danger," March 7, 1996.

_____. "IPP," Program Brochure, undated.

_____. "Overhead Slides," December 11, 1997.

_____. "Program Strategy," November 1999.

_____. "The Role of the U.S. Department of Energy National Laboratories in the Initiatives for Proliferation Prevention Program," July 1999.

U.S. Department of Energy—Nuclear Cities Initiative. "A Chronicle of Outreach for Alternative Funding Sources for the Nuclear Cities Initiative—1998–2001," June 2001.

_____. "Business Workshop: NCI Project Selection Criteria," September 21, 1999.

_____. "Community Development and Jobs Creation," undated internal memo.

_____. "Community Development Working Group (CDWG) Briefing Update," July 23, 1999.

_____. "Complex Reduction and Russia's Nuclear Cities: Progress with the Nuclear Cities Initiative," April 2002.

_____. "Draft Program Guide," October 2001.

_____. "Draft Program Guide," October 2002.

_____. "Economic Diversification in the Closed Nuclear Cities of Russia," undated.

_____. "Fresenius," undated internal document.

_____. FY 1999 Annual Report.

_____. FY 2002 Annual Report.

_____. "NCI," overhead slides, June 1999.

_____. "NCI Program," July 2003.

_____. "Nuclear Cities Initiative," undated internal memo.

_____. "Nuclear Cities Initiative Accomplishments," September 16, 1999.

_____. "Nuclear Cities Initiative Program Plan," October 2000.

_____. "Nuclear Cities Initiative Program Status," July 19, 2000.

_____. "Nuclear Cities Initiative Program Status," August 15, 2000.

_____. "Nuclear Cities Initiative (NCI) Status Report and Program Plans," October 1999.

_____. "Nuclear Cities Initiative (NCI) Status Report and Program Plans, FY 2000."

_____. Nuclear Cities Initiative website, nci.nn.doe.gov (accessed March 1, 2000).

_____. "Ongoing Projects," www.nnsa.doe.gov/na-20/nci/projects.shtml (accessed on August 2, 2007).

_____. "Program Guide," October 2001.

_____. "Program Guide," October 2002.

_____. "Program Overview," February 2001.

_____. "Program Overview," overhead slides, June 2001.

_____. "Program Plan," May 18, 1999.

_____. "Program Strategy," August 1999.

_____. "Report to Congress Pursuant to Section 3172(d) of the National Defense Authorization Act for FY 2001," December 2000.

_____. "Sarov, Russia: Accelerated Conversion and the Open Computing Center," January 17, 2001.

_____. "Visible Impact on the Cities," www.nnsa.doe.gov/na-20/nci/about_impact.shtml (accessed August 2, 2007).

U.S. Department of Energy—Russian Transition Initiatives. "Focus on Spektr-Conversia," *Transitions*, Vol. 1, No. 2 (Fall 2002).

_____. "Russian Transition Initiatives," promotional literature, undated.

_____. *Transitions*, Vol. 1, No. 1, 2002.

U.S. Department of State. *Annual Report on U.S. Assistance to the Newly Independent States of the Former Soviet Union*, Fiscal Year 1994.

_____. *Annual Report on U.S. Assistance to the Newly Independent States of the Former Soviet Union*, Fiscal Year 1995.

_____. *Annual Report on U.S. Assistance to the Newly Independent States of the Former Soviet Union*, Fiscal Year 1996.

_____. *Annual Report on U.S. Assistance to the Newly Independent States of the Former Soviet Union*, Fiscal Year 1997.

_____. *Annual Report on U.S. Assistance to the Newly Independent States of the Former Soviet Union*, Fiscal Year 1998.

_____. Bureau of Economic and Business Affairs. *Russia: 1994 Country Report on Economic Policy and Trade Practices*.

_____. Bureau of Political-Military Affairs. "Nonproliferation through Science Cooperation," briefing slides, October 13, 1994.

_____. Congressional Budget Justification, FY 2007.

_____. Office of the Coordinator of U.S. Assistance to Europe and Eurasia. *U.S. Government Assistance to and Cooperative Activities with Eurasia*, Annual Report for 1999.

_____. Office of the Coordinator of U.S. Assistance to Europe and Eurasia. *U.S. Government Assistance to and Cooperative Activities with Eurasia*, Annual Report for 2000.

_____. Office of the Coordinator of U.S. Assistance to Europe and Eurasia. *U.S. Government Assistance to and Cooperative Activities with Eurasia*, Annual Report for 2001.

_____. Office of the Coordinator of U.S. Assistance to Europe and Eurasia. *U.S. Government Assistance to and Cooperative Activities with Eurasia*, Annual Report for 2002.

_____. Office of the Coordinator of U.S. Assistance to Europe and Eurasia. *U.S. Government Assistance to and Cooperative Activities with Eurasia*, Annual Report for 2003.

_____. Office of the Coordinator of U.S. Assistance to Europe and Eurasia. *U.S. Government*

Assistance to and Cooperative Activities with Eurasia, Annual Report for 2004.
_____. Office of the Coordinator of U.S. Assistance to Europe and Eurasia. *U.S. Government Assistance to and Cooperative Activities with Eurasia,* Annual Report for 2005.
_____. Office of the Coordinator of U.S. Assistance to Europe and Eurasia. *U.S. Government Assistance to and Cooperative Activities with Eurasia,* Annual Report for 2006.
_____. "Russia Economic Policy and Trade Practices," February 1994.
_____. "Science Centers Program," briefing slides, undated.

United States Enrichment Corporation. U.S.-Russian Megatons to Megawatts Program. "Fact Sheet."

U.S. General Accounting Office. *Biological Weapons: Efforts to Reduce Former Soviet Threat Offers Benefits, Poses New Risks* (Washington, D.C.: U.S. General Accounting Office, April 2000).
_____. *Cooperative Threat Reduction: Status of Defense Conversion Efforts in the Former Soviet Union* (Washington, D.C.: U.S. General Accounting Office, April 1997), NSIAD-97-101.
_____. *Department of Energy, Need to Address Longstanding Management Weaknesses,* Testimony of Victor S. Rezendes, U.S. General Accounting Office, to Subcommittee on Energy and Environment, House Committee on Commerce, July 13, 1999.
_____. *Department of Energy, Views on DOE's Plan to Establish the National Nuclear Security Administration* (Washington, D.C.: U.S. General Accounting Office, March 2, 2000), GAO/T-RCED-00-113.
_____. *Former Soviet Union: U.S. Bilateral Program Lacks Effective Coordination* (Washington, D.C.: U.S. General Accounting Office, February 1995), GAO/NSIAD-95-10.
_____. *Military Base Closures: Detailed Budget Requests Could Improve Visibility* (Washington, D.C.: U.S. General Accounting Office, July 1997).
_____. *Nuclear Nonproliferation: Better Management Controls Needed for Some DOE Projects in Russia and Other Countries* (Washington, D.C.: U.S. General Accounting Office, August 2005), GAO-05-828.
_____. *Nuclear Nonproliferation: Concerns with DOE's Efforts to Reduce the Risks Posed by Russia's Unemployed Weapons Scientists* (Washington, D.C.: U.S. General Accounting Office, February 1999), GAO/RCED-99-54.
_____. *Nuclear Nonproliferation: DOE's Efforts to Assist Weapons Scientists in Russia's Nuclear Cities Face Challenges* (Washington, D.C.: U.S. General Accounting Office, May 2001).
_____. *Nuclear Nonproliferation: DOE's Efforts to Secure Nuclear Materials and Employ Weapons Scientists,* Testimony by Gary L. Jones before the Subcommittee on Emerging Threats and Capabilities, Committee on Armed Services, May 15, 2001, GAO-01-726T.
_____. *Nuclear Security, Security Issues at DOE and Its Newly Created National Nuclear Security Administration* (Washington, D.C.: U.S. General Accounting Office, March 14, 2000), GAO/T-RCED-00-123.
_____. *Weapons of Mass Destruction: Reducing the Threat from the Former Soviet Union* (Washington, D.C.: U.S. General Accounting Office, October 1994).
_____. *Weapons of Mass Destruction: Reducing the Threat from the Former Soviet Union: An Update* (Washington, D.C.: U.S. General Accounting Office, June 9, 1995), NSIAD-95-165.
_____. *Weapons of Mass Destruction: Some U.S. Assistance to Redirect Russian Scientists Taxed by Russia* (Washington, D.C.: U.S. General Accounting Office, April 28, 2000).
_____. *Weapons of Mass Destruction: State Department Oversight of Science Centers Program* (Washington, D.C.: U.S. General Accounting Office, May 2001), GAO-01-582.
_____. *Weapons of Mass Destruction: Status of the Cooperative Threat Reduction Program* (Washington, D.C.: U.S. General Accounting Office, September 1996), GAO/NSIAD-96-222.

U.S. Government Accountability Office. *Cooperative Threat Reduction: DOD Has Improved Its Management and Internal Controls but Challenges Remain* (Washington, D.C.: U.S. Government Accountability Office, June 2005), GAO-05-329.
_____. *Nuclear Nonproliferation: DOE's Program to Assist Weapons Scientists in Russia and Other Countries Needs to be Reassessed* (Washington, D.C.: U.S. Government Accountability Program, December 2007).
_____. *Nuclear Nonproliferation: Progress Made in Improving Security at Russian Nuclear Sites, but the Long-term Sustainability of U.S. Upgrades is Uncertain* (Washington, D.C.: U.S. Government Accountability Office, February 2007), GAO-07-404.

United States Industry Coalition. *Annual Report for 2004–2005.*
_____. *Annual Report for 2005–2006.*
_____. *Annual Report for 2007.*
_____. *Commercial Partnerships in the Former Soviet Union*, Spring 2007.
_____. *E-Notes*, Vol. 8, No. 4 (May 4, 2007).

U.S. Statutes. *Conventional Forces in Europe Treaty Implementation Act of 1991*, P.L. 102-228.
_____. *Floyd D. Spence National Defense Authorization Act for FY2001*, P.L. 106-398.
_____. *Foreign Operations, Export Financing, and Related Programs Appropriations Act for Fiscal Year 1994*, P.L. 103-87.
_____. *The Freedom for Russia and Emerging Eurasian Democracies and Open Markets Support Act of 1992*, P.L. 102-511.

White House. "Fact Sheet," www.whitehouse.gov/news/releases/2001/12/20011227.html.

_____. Office of the Press Secretary. "Remarks by President Barack Obama," Prague, April 5, 2009, http://www.whitehouse.gov/the_press_office/Remarks-By-President-Barack-Obama-In-Prague-As-Delivered/ (accessed on May 1, 2009).

INTERVIEWS AND PERSONAL COMMUNICATION

Electronic communication, CRDF, August 22, 2007.
Electronic communication, former U.S. government official 5, April 16, 2001.
Electronic communication, former U.S. government official 6, April 16, 2001.
Electronic communication, William Hoehn, RANSAC, March 8, 2000.
Electronic communication, Initiatives for Proliferation Prevention staffer 2, October 18, 2000.
Electronic communication, Initiatives for Proliferation Prevention staffer 2, November 20, 2000.
Electronic communication, Initiatives for Proliferation Prevention staffer 3, May 23, 2001.
Electronic communication, ISTC, June 15 and 20, 2007, and July 11 and 22, 2007.
Electronic communication, International Science and Technology Center staffer 1, February 6, 2002.
Electronic communication, Istok-Audio, May 23, 2007 and May 24, 2007.
Electronic communication, KK Interconnect, May 23, 2007.
Electronic communication, Friedrich Steinhausler, February 22, 2007.
Electronic communication, Ivan Safranchuk, Center for Defense Information, March 17, 2006.

Interviews — Brookhaven National Laboratory
Brookhaven National Laboratory staffer 1, March 19, 2003.
Brookhaven National Laboratory staffer 2, March 19, 2003.
Brookhaven National Laboratory staffer 3, March 19, 2003.
Brookhaven National Laboratory staffer 4, March 19, 2003.

Interviews — Businesses
U.S. business person 1, February 22, 2007.
U.S. business person 2, April 12, 2002.
U.S. business person 3, April 12, 2002.
U.S. business person 4, April 12, 2002.

Interviews — Individuals
David Bernstein, April 4, 2003.
Frederick Kellett, February 22, 2007.

Interviews — Initiatives for Proliferation Prevention
Initiatives for Proliferation Prevention staffer 1, February 13, 2002.
Initiatives for Proliferation Prevention staffer 1, July 16, 2003.
Initiatives for Proliferation Prevention staffer 2, July 21, 1999.
Initiatives for Proliferation Prevention staffer 2, October 18, 2000.

Initiatives for Proliferation Prevention staffer 2, July 16, 2003.
Initiatives for Proliferation Prevention staffer 3, July 17, 1999.

Interviews—International Science and Technology Center
International Science and Technology Center staffer 1, October 18, 1999.
International Science and Technology Center staffer 1, October 23, 1999.
International Science and Technology Center staffer 1, February 6, 2002.
International Science and Technology Center staffer 1, June 2, 2003.
International Science and Technology Center staffer 2, June 2, 2003.
International Science and Technology Center staffer 3, June 2, 2003.
International Science and Technology Center staffer 4, July 24, 2007.
International Science and Technology Center staffer 5, July 24, 2007.
International Science and Technology Center staffer 6, March 25, 2003.
International Science and Technology Center staffer 7, March 25, 2003.
International Science and Technology Center staffer 8, March 26, 2003.
International Science and Technology Center staffer 9, November 9, 1999.
International Science and Technology Center staffer 10, October 22, 1999.
International Science and Technology Center staffer 11, October 22, 1999.
International Science and Technology Center staffer 12, October 22, 1999.
International Science and Technology Center staffer 13, October 22, 1999.
International Science and Technology Center staffer 14, October 22, 1999.
International Science and Technology Center staffer 15, April 16, 1998.
International Science and Technology Center staffer 15, October 22, 1999.

Interviews—Kansas City Plant
Kansas City Plant staffer 1, October 24, 1999.

Interviews—Lawrence Berkeley National Laboratory
Lawrence Berkeley National Laboratory staffer 1, March 31, 2003.
Lawrence Berkeley National Laboratory staffer 2, March 31, 2003.

Interviews—Lawrence Livermore National Laboratory
Lawrence Livermore National Laboratory staffer 1, April 1, 2003.
Lawrence Livermore National Laboratory staffer 2, April 1, 2003.
Lawrence Livermore National Laboratory staffer 3, May 21, 2002.
Lawrence Livermore National Laboratory staffer 4, April 7, 2003.
Lawrence Livermore National Laboratory staffer 5, April 1, 2003.
Lawrence Livermore National Laboratory staffer 6, April 2, 2003.
Lawrence Livermore National Laboratory staffer 7, April 2, 2003.
Lawrence Livermore National Laboratory staffer 8, April 3, 2003.
Lawrence Livermore National Laboratory staffer 9, April 3, 2003.
Lawrence Livermore National Laboratory staffer 10, April 2, 2003.
Lawrence Livermore National Laboratory staffer 11, April 7, 2003.
Lawrence Livermore National Laboratory staffer 12, April 3, 2003.
Lawrence Livermore National Laboratory staffer 13, April 3, 2003.

Interviews—Los Alamos National Laboratory
Los Alamos National Laboratory staffer 1, May 21, 2002.
Los Alamos National Laboratory staffer 1, April 29, 2003.
Los Alamos National Laboratory staffer 2, May 28, 2002.
Los Alamos National Laboratory staffer 3, April 29, 2003.
Los Alamos National Laboratory staffer 4, June 23, 2003.
Los Alamos National Laboratory staffer 5, April 28, 2003.
Los Alamos National Laboratory staffer 6, April 29, 2003.
Los Alamos National Laboratory staffer 7, May 1, 2002.
Los Alamos National Laboratory staffer 8, May 1, 2003.
Los Alamos National Laboratory staffer 9, May 1, 2003.
Los Alamos National Laboratory staffer 10, June 2, 2003.

Los Alamos National Laboratory staffer 11, July 15, 1999.
Los Alamos National Laboratory staffer 12, July 15, 1999.

Interviews—Non-Governmental Organizations
Non-governmental organization staffer 1, February 22, 2007.
Non-governmental organization staffer 2, February 22, 2007.
Non-governmental organization staffer 3, May 21, 2002.
Non-governmental organization staffer 4, June 3, 2004.
Non-governmental organization staffer 5, March 4, 2003.
Non-governmental organization staffer 6, October 21, 1999.
Non-governmental organization staffer 7, October 21, 1999.
Non-governmental organization staffer 7, June 3, 2004.
Non-governmental organization staffer 8, June 8, 2006.
Non-governmental organization staffer 9, September 27, 2000.
Non-governmental organization staffer 10, July 24, 2007.
Non-governmental organization staffer 11, March 8, 2000.

Interviews—Nuclear Cities Initiative
Nuclear Cities Initiative staffer 1, May 29, 2002.
Nuclear Cities Initiative staffer 2, May 30, 2002.
Nuclear Cities Initiative staffer 3, May 29, 2002.
Nuclear Cities Initiative staffer 4, May 29, 2002.
Nuclear Cities Initiative staffer 5, May 29, 2002.

Interviews—Oak Ridge National Laboratory
Oak Ridge National Laboratory staffer 1, February 19, 2003.
Oak Ridge National Laboratory staffer 1, February 20, 2003.
Oak Ridge National Laboratory staffer 2, February 19, 2003.
Oak Ridge National Laboratory staffer 3, February 19, 2003.
Oak Ridge National Laboratory staffer 4, February 19, 2003.
Oak Ridge National Laboratory staffer 5, February 19, 2003.
Oak Ridge National Laboratory staffer 6, February 20, 2003
Oak Ridge National Laboratory staffer 7, February 20, 2003.
Oak Ridge National Laboratory staffer 8, February 20, 2003.
Oak Ridge National Laboratory staffer 9, February 20, 2003.
Oak Ridge National Laboratory staffer 10, February 19, 2003.
Oak Ridge National Laboratory staffer 11, February 21, 2003.
Oak Ridge National Laboratory staffer 12, October 20, 1999.

Interviews—Pacific Northwest National Laboratory
Pacific Northwest National Laboratory staffer 1, March 12, 2003.
Pacific Northwest National Laboratory staffer 2, March 23, 2003.
Pacific Northwest National Laboratory staffer 3, March 5, 2003.
Pacific Northwest National Laboratory staffer 4, March 4, 2003.
Pacific Northwest National Laboratory staffer 5, March 5, 2003.
Pacific Northwest National Laboratory staffer 6, March 5, 2003.
Pacific Northwest National Laboratory staffer 7, March 5, 2003.
Pacific Northwest National Laboratory staffer 8, March 5, 2003.
Pacific Northwest National Laboratory staffer 9, March 6, 2003.
Pacific Northwest National Laboratory staffer 10, March 6, 2003.
Pacific Northwest National Laboratory staffer 11, March 6, 2003.

Interviews—Russian Officials
Minatom official 1, July 24, 2002.
Minatom official 2, July 24, 2002.
Minatom official 3, July 24, 2002.
Russian official 1, January 23, 2009.
Former Minatom official 1, July 30, 2002.
Former Russian Program Manager 1, July 1, 2009.

Bochvar Institute staffer 1, June 4, 2003.
Kurchatov Institute staffer 1, August 1, 2002.
Kurchatov Institute staffer 2, August 2, 2002.
Institute for Physics and Power Engineering staffer 1, July 23, 2002.
Institute for Physics and Power Engineering staffer 2, July 23, 2002.
Institute for Physics and Power Engineering staffer 3, July 23, 2002.

Interviews — Sandia National Laboratory
Sandia National Laboratory staffer 1, May 2, 2003.
Sandia National Laboratory staffer 2, May 21, 2002.
Sandia National Laboratory staffer 3, May 5, 2003.
Sandia National Laboratory staffer 4, May 5, 2003.
Sandia National Laboratory staffer 5, May 5, 2003.
Sandia National Laboratory staffer 6, May 5, 2003.
Sandia National Laboratory staffer 7, May 5, 2003.
Sandia National Laboratory staffer 8, May 5. 2003.

Interviews — Savannah River Site
Savannah River Site staffer 1, February 21, 2003.
Savannah River Site staffer 2, May 29, 2002.

Interviews — Science and Technology Center in Ukraine
Science and Technology Center in Ukraine staffer 1, October 26, 2005.
Science and Technology Center in Ukraine staffer 2, October 26, 2005.
Science and Technology Center in Ukraine staffer 2, July 9, 2007.
Science and Technology Center in Ukraine staffer 3, October 26, 2005.
Science and Technology Center in Ukraine staffer 4, October 27, 2005.
Science and Technology Center in Ukraine staffer 5, October 27, 2005.
Science and Technology Center in Ukraine staffer 6, October 27, 2005.
Science and Technology Center in Ukraine staffer 7, October 27, 2005.
Science and Technology Center in Ukraine staffer 8, October 27, 2005.
Science and Technology Center in Ukraine staffer 9, October 28, 2005.
Science and Technology Center in Ukraine staffer 10, October 28, 2005.
Science and Technology Center in Ukraine staffer 11, October 28, 2005.
Science and Technology Center in Ukraine staffer 12, October 28, 2005.
Science and Technology Center in Ukraine staffer 13, October 31, 2005.
Science and Technology Center in Ukraine staffer 14, October 26, 2005.

Interviews — United Kingdom
British government official 1, April 28, 2003.
British government official 2, December 12, 2002.
British government official 3, December 12, 2002.

Interviews — U.S. Congress
Congressional source 1, August 8, 2003.
Congressional source 2, August 4, 2003.
Congressional source 3, August 12, 2003.

Interviews — U.S. Department of Energy
Department of Energy official 1, May 21, 2002.
Department of Energy official 2, May 20, 2002.
Department of Energy official 3, June 3, 2003.
Department of Energy official 4, May 29, 2002.
Department of Energy official 5, August 12, 2003.
Department of Energy official 6, May 21, 2002.
Department of Energy official 6, June 3, 2002.
Department of Energy official 6, August 14, 2005.

Interviews—U.S. Department of State
State Department official 1, May 1, 2007.
State Department official 2, May 1, 2007.
State Department official 3, May 1, 2007.
State Department official 4, May 1, 2007.
Former State Department staffer 1, July 16, 2003.
Former State Department staffer 2, July 9, 2007.
Former State Department staffer 3, February 20, 2003.
Former State Department staffer 4, May 5, 2007.

Interviews—U.S. Government Officials
U.S. government official 1, April 9, 2007.
U.S. government official 2, April 10, 2007.
U.S. government official 3, February 22, 2007.
U.S. government official 4, February 22, 2007.
U.S. government official 5, January 29, 2007.
U.S. government official 6, May 28, 2002.
U.S. government official 7, May 28, 2002.
U.S. government official 8, February 22, 2007.
U.S. government official 9, May 30, 2002.
U.S. government official 10, July 15, 2002.
Former U.S. government official 1, April 4, 2003.
Former U.S. government official 2, April 4, 2003.
Former U.S. government official 3, December 8, 1999.
Former U.S. government official 4, June 2, 2003.
Former U.S. government official 4, October 2, 2007.
Former U.S. government official 5, October 2, 2007.
Former U.S. government official 6, April 12, 2001.
Former U.S. government official 7, October 10, 2003.
Former U.S. government official 7, February 14, 2007.
Former Clinton administration official 1, September 17, 2003.
Former Clinton administration official 2, May 21, 2002.
Former Clinton administration official 3, March 31, 2003.

About the Author

Sharon K. Weiner is Associate Professor in the School of International Service at American University in Washington, D.C. Her research focuses on understanding the impact of organizational interests, institutional processes, and domestic politics on U.S. defense, foreign, and national security policies. She holds a Ph.D. in Political Science from the Massachusetts Institute of Technology.

Index

Belfer Center Studies in International Security

Published by The MIT Press

Sean M. Lynn-Jones and Steven E. Miller, series editors
Karen Motley, executive editor
Belfer Center for Science and International Affairs
Harvard Kennedy School, Harvard University

Acharya, Amitav, and Evelyn Goh, eds., *Reassessing Security Cooperation in the Asia-Pacific* (2007)

Agha, Hussein, Shai Feldman, Ahmad Khalidi, and Zeev Schiff, *Track-II Diplomacy: Lessons from the Middle East* (2003)

Allison, Graham T., Owen R. Coté, Jr., Richard A. Falkenrath, and Steven E. Miller, *Avoiding Nuclear Anarchy: Containing the Threat of Loose Russian Nuclear Weapons and Fissile Material* (1996)

Allison, Graham T., and Kalypso Nicolaïdis, eds., *The Greek Paradox: Promise vs. Performance* (1996)

Arbatov, Alexei, Abram Chayes, Antonia Handler Chayes, and Lara Olson, eds., *Managing Conflict in the Former Soviet Union: Russian and American Perspectives* (1997)

Bennett, Andrew, *Condemned to Repetition? The Rise, Fall, and Reprise of Soviet-Russian Military Interventionism, 1973–1996* (1999)

Blackwill, Robert D., and Michael Stürmer, eds., *Allies Divided: Transatlantic Policies for the Greater Middle East* (1997)

Blackwill, Robert D., and Paul Dibb, eds., *America's Asian Alliances* (2000)

Blum, Gabriella, and Philip B. Heymann, *Laws, Outlaws, and Terrorists: Lessons from the War on Terrorism* (2010)

Brom, Shlomo, and Yiftah Shapir, eds., *The Middle East Military Balance 1999–2000* (1999)

Brom, Shlomo, and Yiftah Shapir, eds., *The Middle East Military Balance 2001–2002* (2002)

Brown, Michael E., ed., *The International Dimensions of Internal Conflict* (1996)

Brown, Michael E., and Šumit Ganguly, eds., *Fighting Words: Language Policy and Ethnic Relations in Asia* (2003)

Brown, Michael E., and Šumit Ganguly, eds., *Government Policies and Ethnic Relations in Asia and the Pacific* (1997)

Carter, Ashton B., and John P. White, eds., *Keeping the Edge: Managing Defense for the Future* (2001)

Chenoweth, Erica, and Adria Lawrence, eds., *Rethinking Violence: State and Non-state Actors in Conflict* (2010)

de Nevers, Renée, *Comrades No More: The Seeds of Political Change in Eastern Europe* (2003)

Elman, Colin, and Miriam Fendius Elman, eds., *Bridges and Boundaries: Historians, Political Scientists, and the Study of International Relations* (2001)

Elman, Colin, and Miriam Fendius Elman, eds., *Progress in International Relations Theory: Appraising the Field* (2003)

Elman, Miriam Fendius, ed., *Paths to Peace: Is Democracy the Answer?* (1997)

Falkenrath, Richard A., *Shaping Europe's Military Order: The Origins and Consequences of the CFE Treaty* (1994)

Falkenrath, Richard A., Robert D. Newman, and Bradley A. Thayer, *America's Achilles' Heel: Nuclear, Biological, and Chemical Terrorism and Covert Attack* (1998)

Feaver, Peter D., and Richard H. Kohn, eds., *Soldiers and Civilians: The Civil-Military Gap and American National Security* (2001)

Feldman, Shai, *Nuclear Weapons and Arms Control in the Middle East* (1996)

Feldman, Shai, and Yiftah Shapir, eds., *The Middle East Military Balance 2000–2001* (2001)

Forsberg, Randall, ed., *The Arms Production Dilemma: Contraction and Restraint in the World Combat Aircraft Industry* (1994)

George, Alexander L., and Andrew Bennett, *Case Studies and Theory Development in the Social Sciences* (2005)

Gilroy, Curtis, and Cindy Williams, eds., *Service to Country: Personnel Policy and the Transformation of Western Militaries* (2007)

Hagerty, Devin T., *The Consequences of Nuclear Proliferation: Lessons from South Asia* (1998)

Heymann, Philip B., *Terrorism and America: A Commonsense Strategy for a Democratic Society* (1998)

Heymann, Philip B., *Terrorism, Freedom, and Security: Winning without War* (2003)

Heymann, Philip B., and Juliette N. Kayyem, *Protecting Liberty in an Age of Terror* (2005)

Howitt, Arnold M., and Robyn L. Pangi, eds., *Countering Terrorism: Dimensions of Preparedness* (2003)

Hudson, Valerie M., and Andrea M. den Boer, *Bare Branches: The Security Implications of Asia's Surplus Male Population* (2004)

Kayyem, Juliette N., and Robyn L. Pangi, eds., *First to Arrive: State and Local Responses to Terrorism* (2003)

Kokoshin, Andrei A., *Soviet Strategic Thought, 1917–91* (1998)

Lederberg, Joshua, ed., *Biological Weapons: Limiting the Threat* (1999)

Mansfield, Edward D., and Jack Snyder, *Electing to Fight: Why Emerging Democracies Go to War* (2005)

Martin, Lenore G., and Dimitris Keridis, eds., *The Future of Turkish Foreign Policy* (2004)

May, Ernest R., and Philip D. Zelikow, eds., *Dealing with Dictators: Dilemmas of U.S. Diplomacy and Intelligence Analysis, 1945–1990* (2007)

Shaffer, Brenda, *Borders and Brethren: Iran and the Challenge of Azerbaijani Identity* (2002)

Shaffer, Brenda, ed., *The Limits of Culture: Islam and Foreign Policy* (2006)

Shields, John M., and William C. Potter, eds., *Dismantling the Cold War: U.S. and NIS Perspectives on the Nunn-Lugar Cooperative Threat Reduction Program* (1997)

Tucker, Jonathan B., ed., *Toxic Terror: Assessing Terrorist Use of Chemical and Biological Weapons* (2000)

Utgoff, Victor A., ed., *The Coming Crisis: Nuclear Proliferation, U.S. Interests, and World Order* (2000)

Weiner, Sharon K., *Our Own Worst Enemy? Institutional Interests and the Proliferation of Nuclear Weapons Expertise* (2011)

Williams, Cindy, ed., *Filling the Ranks: Transforming the U.S. Military Personnel System* (2004)

Williams, Cindy, ed., *Holding the Line: U.S. Defense Alternatives for the Early 21st Century* (2001)

Belfer Center for Science and International Affairs

Graham Allison, Director
Harvard Kennedy School
Harvard University
79 JFK Street, Cambridge, MA 02138
Tel: (617) 495-1400; Fax: (617) 495-8963
http://belfercenter.ksg.harvard.edu belfer_center@hks.harvard.edu

The Belfer Center is the hub of the Harvard Kennedy School's research, teaching, and training in international security affairs, environmental and resource issues, and science and technology policy.

The Center has a dual mission: (1) to provide leadership in advancing policy-relevant knowledge about the most important challenges of international security and other critical issues where science, technology, environmental policy, and international affairs intersect; and (2) to prepare future generations of leaders for these arenas. Center researchers not only conduct scholarly research, but also develop prescriptions for policy reform. Faculty and fellows analyze global challenges from nuclear proliferation and terrorism to climate change and energy policy.

The Belfer Center's leadership begins with the recognition of science and technology as driving forces constantly transforming both the challenges we face and the opportunities for problem solving. Building on the vision of founder Paul Doty, the Center addresses serious global concerns by integrating insights and research of social scientists, natural scientists, technologists, and practitioners in government, diplomacy, the military, and business.

The heart of the Belfer Center is its resident research community of more than 150 scholars, including Harvard faculty, researchers, practitioners, and each year a new, international, interdisciplinary group of research fellows. Through publications and policy discussions, workshops, seminars, and conferences, the Center promotes innovative solutions to significant national and international challenges.

The Center's International Security Program, directed by Steven E. Miller, publishes the Belfer Center Studies in International Security, and sponsors and edits the quarterly journal *International Security*.

The Center is supported by an endowment established with funds from Robert and Renée Belfer, the Ford Foundation, and Harvard University, by foundation grants, by individual gifts, and by occasional government contracts.